Thomas A. Fudge is Professor of Medieval History at the University of New England in New South Wales, Australia. He is author of *The Magnificent Ride: The First Reformation in Hussite Bohemia* and *The Crusade Against Heretics in Bohemia, 1418–1437*. He has worked as Senior Lecturer in European History at the University of Canterbury in Christchurch, New Zealand. More recently he taught in the Texas prison system and served as Director of the Hewitt Research Foundation in Washington.

JAN HUS

Religious Reform and Social Revolution in Bohemia

THOMAS A. FUDGE

I.B. TAURIS
LONDON · NEW YORK

New paperback edition published in 2017 by
I.B.Tauris & Co. Ltd
London · New York
www.ibtauris.com

First published in hardback in 2010 by I.B.Tauris & Co. Ltd

Copyright © 2010 Thomas A. Fudge

The right of Thomas A. Fudge to be identified as the author of this work has been asserted by him in accordance with the Copyright, Designs and Patents Act 1988.

All rights reserved. Except for brief quotations in a review, this book, or any part thereof, may not be reproduced, stored in or introduced into a retrieval system, or transmitted, in any form or by any means, electronic, mechanical, photocopying, recording or otherwise, without the prior written permission of the publisher.

Every attempt has been made to gain permission for the use of the images in this book. Any omissions will be rectified in future editions.

References to websites were correct at the time of writing.

ISBN: 978 1 78453 684 8
eISBN: 978 1 78672 984 2
ePDF: 978 0 85771 855 6

A full CIP record for this book is available from the British Library

A full CIP record is available from the Library of Congress

Library of Congress Catalog Card Number: available

Meminerim tui; intellegam te; diligam te.
Augustine, *De trinitate* 15.28.51

For Melissa Frizzell, O.S.B.
an unexpected gift

Thousands are still asleep . . .
They continue their dreams,
And shall wake soon and long for letters,
And none will hear the postman's knock
Without a quickening of the heart,
For who can bear to feel himself forgotten?

– W.H. Auden

CONTENTS

List of Maps and Illustrations   ix
Abbreviations   xi
Acknowledgments   xv

	Introduction	1
1	Biography	9
2	Prague	19
3	Theology	27
4	Proclamation	57
5	Spirituality	75
6	Politics	95
7	Trial	117
8	Revolution	147
9	Commemoration	175
10	Iconography	189
11	Historiography	209
12	Rehabilitation	227
	Epilogue	241

Notes   247
Select Bibliography   323
Index   351

MAPS AND ILLUSTRATIONS

Maps
1 Bohemia in the fifteenth century   xvii
2 Prague around the time of Hus   xviii
3 The Kingdom of Bohemia during the reign of King Václav IV   xx

Illustrations
1 Hus as martyr, heretic and saint. Smíškovsky Gradual, Vienna, ÖNB suppl. mus. sam. MS 15492, fol. 285ʳ   192
2 The heretical deacon. Retable for the Vlněves altarpiece (now at Nelahozeves Castle)   194
3 The prophesying Hus. Wickiana Collection, in Zürich, Zentralbibliothek PAS II 13/20   196
4 Dream of Elector Frederick the Wise. Berlin, Staatsbibliothek, Handschriftenabteilung, YA 91a   198
5 Hus and Luther. Title page of Samuel Martin Horzov, *Hussus et Lutherus, id est: Collatio Historica duorum fortissimorum Jesu Christi militum*, Prague, Sessii, 1618   201
6 Hus among the reformers. Amsterdam, Rijksmuseum RP-P-OB-78.421   202
7 Martyrdom of Jan Hus. Ulrich Richental, *Chronik des Constanzer Concils*, Prague, NK MS XVI A 17, fol. 123ᵛ   205
8 The burning of Jan Hus. John Foxe, *The Acts and Monuments*, London, 1583, p. 624   206

ABBREVIATIONS

AČ	František Palacký, ed., *Archiv český čili staré písemné památky české i moravské*, 6 vols
Betlemské texty	Bohumil Ryba, *Betlemské texty*
Bílková	Milena Bílková, *Ikonografie v utrakvistické teologii*
BRRP	*The Bohemian Reformation and Religious Practice*, 7 vols., eds., David R. Holeton and Zdeněk V. David. Prague, 1996–2009
Castle Archive	Prague Cathedral Chapter Library
CCL	*Corpus Christianorum, Series Latina*
CECE	Paweł Kras, ed., *Christianity in East Central Europe*
Cochlaeus	Johannes Cochlaeus, *Historia Hussitarum libri duodecim*
Collecta	Anežka Schmidtová, ed., *Sermones de tempore qui Collecta dicuntur*
ČSAV	Československá akademie věd
CSEL	*Corpus Scriptorum Ecclesiasticorum Latina*
CV	*Communio viatorum*
Dcerka	Jan Hus, *Dcerka: O poznání česty pravé k spasení*, in *Opera omnia*
De ecclesia	Jan Hus, *De ecclesia*, ed., S. Harrison Thomson
De Vooght	*L'Hérésie de Jean Huss*
Documenta	František Palacký, ed., *Documenta Mag. Joannis Hus vitam, doctrinam, causam in constantiensi concilio actam et controversias de religione in Bohemia annis 1403–1418 motas illustrantia*
Flajšhans	Václav Flajšhans, *Mistr Jan řečený Hus z Husince*
FRA	*Fontes rerum austriacarum*
FRB	*Fontes rerum bohemicarum*
Friedberg	Emil Friedberg, ed., *Corpus iuris canonici*, 2 vols
Fudge	Thomas A. Fudge, *The Magnificent Ride: The First Reformation in Hussite Bohemia*
Graham	Barry Frederic Hunter Graham, *Bohemian and Moravian Graduals 1420–1620*
Hardt	Hermann von der Hardt, ed., *Magnum oecumenicum constantiense concilium*, 7 vols

Hefele/Leclercq	Karl Joseph von Hefele and Henri Leclercq, *Histoire de Conciles*, 11 vols
Hilsch	Peter Hilsch, *Johannes Hus (um 1370–1415): Prediger Gottes und Ketzer*
Historia bohemica	Aeneas Sylvius Piccolomini, *Historia bohemica*
Höfler	Konstantin von Höfler, ed., *Geschichtschreiber der Husitischen Bewegung in Böhmen*, 3 vols
Holeton, La Communion	David R. Holeton, *La communion des tout-petits enfants: Étude du mouvement eucharistique en Bohême vers la fin du Moyen-Âge*
HT	*Husitský tábor*
JSH	*Jihočeský sborník historický*
Kaminsky	Howard Kaminsky, *A History of the Hussite Revolution*
Kejř, Husův process	Jiří Kejř, *Husův proces*
Kejř, Počátků	Jiří Kejř, *Z počátků české reformace*
Klicman	Ladislav Klicman, ed., *Processus iudiciarius contra Jeronimum de Praga habitus Viennae a. 1410–1412*
Lášek	Jan B. Lášek, ed., *Jan Hus mezi epochami, národy a konfesemi*
Loomis	Louise R. Loomis, ed., *The Council of Constance*
Machovec	Milan Machovec, *Husovo učení význam v tradici českého národa*
Mansi	Giovanni Domenico Mansi, ed., *Sacrorum conciliorum nova, et amplissima collecto . . .*, 53 vols
Marin	Olivier Marin, *L'archevêque, le maître et le dévot: Genèses du mouvement réformateur pragois années 1360–1419*
MC	František Palacký, ed., *Monumenta conciliorum generalium seculi Decimi Quinti*, 2 vols
Nejedlý	Zdeněk Nejedlý, *Dějiny husitského zpěvu*, 6 vols
NK	National Library, Prague
NKM	National Museum Library, Prague
Novotný/Kybal	Václav Novotný and Vlastimil Kybal, *M. Jan Hus: Život a učení*, 5 parts.
Novotný, Correspondence	Václav Novotný, ed., *M. Jana Husi Korespondence a dokumenty*
ÖNB	Österreichische Nationalbibliothek, Vienna
Opera omnia	František Ryšánek, et al., eds., *Magistri Iohannis Hus, Opera omnia*, 25 vols
Pez	Bernard Pez, ed., *Thesaurus anecdotorum novissimus seu veterum monumentorum*, 6 vols
PL	Jacques Paul Migne, ed., *Patrologia Latina*, 221 vols
Positiones	Anežka Schmidtová, ed., *Iohannes Hus, Positiones Recommendationes, Sermones*
Protocollum	Ivan Hlaváček and Zdeňka Hledíková, eds, *Protocollum visitationis archidiaconatus Pragensis annis 1379–1382 per Paulum de Janowicz archidiaconum Pragensem, factae*

Regulae	Matěj of Janov, *Regulae veteris et novi testamenti*, 6 vols
Relatio	Petr Mladoňovice, *Relatio de Mag. Joannis Hus causa*
Richental	Ulrich Richental, *Chronik des Constanzer Concils*
Royt	Jan Royt, 'Ikonografie Mistra Jana Husa v 15. až 18. století'
Seibt	Ferdinand Seibt, ed., *Jan Hus: Zwischen Zeiten, Völkern, Konfessionen*
Sermones in Capella Bethlehem	Václav Flajšhans, ed., *Mag. Io. Hus Sermones in Capella Bethlehem, 1410–1411*, 6 vols
Šimek, sermons	František Šimek, ed., *Mistr Jan Hus: Česká kázání sváteční*
Šmahel	František Šmahel, *Husitská revoluce*, 4 vols
Šmahel, HR	František Šmahel, *Die Hussitische Revolution*, 3 vols
Spinka	Matthew Spinka, *John Hus: A Biography*
SRB	František Palacký, ed., *Staři letopisové češti od r. 1378 do 1527* in *Scriptores rerum bohemicarum*
Strauss	Walter L. Strauss, ed., *The German Single-Leaf Woodcut*, 3 vols
Super IV Sententiarum	Jan Hus, Commentary on the Sentences of Peter Lombard, in Václav Flajšhans, ed., *Mag. Jo. Hus Opera omnia*
UB	František Palacký, ed., *Urkundliche Beiträge zur Geschichte des Hussitenkrieges*, 2 vols
WA	*D. Martin Luthers Werke. Kritische Gesamtausgabe* (Weimar Ausgabe), 127 vols
Werner	Ernst Werner, *Jan Hus: Welt und Umwelt eines Prager Frühreformators*

ACKNOWLEDGMENTS

Paying lip service to multitudes without whom a book could otherwise not have been written has become fashionable. I would like to say that my academic and professional colleagues were indispensable. That would be untrue. Research and writing is often a lonely undertaking. Working on arcane subjects only exacerbates the isolation. From time to time one does accumulate massive indebtedness in the course of producing a scholarly monograph. This is not the case with this book. Only my colleague Lubomír Mlčoch in Christchurch with his skill and generosity in terms of fifteenth-century Czech might be said to have been essential. His patience is a virtue. There are others who made the way easier though it ought to be said that acknowledging help from different quarters does not imply commensurate endorsement by those same sources. Cole Dawson, now Vice-President and Dean of the Faculty at Warner Pacific College, helped facilitate my need for inter-library loan materials. April Purtell ranted and raved with me over some atrocious sixteenth-century German texts and in the end improved my understanding. I am grateful to Chris Bachmann for a profitable winter morning spent discussing Paul De Vooght's work on Hus' *Dcerka*. Craig Atwood very generously sent draft chapters of his book on the Unity of Brethren months before publication. Milena Bílková made her doctoral dissertation available, answered numerous questions about iconography and shared her collection of Hus images. František Šmahel, David Holeton, Zdeněk David and Barry Graham replied to questions, many of which were technical and obscure. Jiří Kejř sent useful offprints and I owe him considerably for two decades of stimulating conversation about Hus and Hussite history. To my former Canterbury colleague Professor Vincent Orange I owe much especially for discussions on the philosophy of history. I am grateful to Gregory Clark for directions in the world of Netherlandish art; to Dorothe Schneider at the Zentralbibliothek in Zürich for the necessary identification of some elusive images of Hus; to Kees van Schooten at the Museum Catharijneconvent in Utrecht for answering queries about particular images and for providing access to one previously unknown; to Constanze Itzel for illuminating conversation while I was in Belgium which revealed her expertise as an art historian, and, finally, to Professor Norman Housley at the University of Leicester and Dr. Helen Nicholson at Cardiff University for suggestions on improving the text.

I have derived considerable pleasure over the years while working at repositories and archives. In Prague, especially in the reading rooms at the National Library, the National Museum Library, and the Prague Castle Archive (Cathedral Chapter Library), in Vienna at the Austrian National Library, in Rome at the Vatican Library, in the Rare Books and Manuscripts Reading Rooms at Cambridge University Library, in Seattle at the University of Washington Library, in Vancouver at the University of British Columbia Library and in the silence of the Patristics and Latin Christian Literature Collection Room at the Benedictine Abbey Library in Mount Angel, Oregon. I have fond memories of Blanka Šmídlová my friend in Prague whom I have known since Cambridge days. I benefitted from audience responses to lectures I gave on the iconography of Hus at Texas A&M University and on the Hus trial at the Center for Christian Studies in Portland. In what now seems to me like another life there is good reason to recall my eager graduate students between 1996 and 2003 at the University of Canterbury in Christchurch, New Zealand who participated with keen interest in my seminars on medieval Bohemia, especially Jack Fergusson who went on to write an MA thesis on Hussite history. I learned more from them all than they are aware. In writing this book I am reminded once again of my intellectual debt to the late Bob Scribner. Two years at Cambridge with him shaped my scholarship considerably.

In less academic ways I am grateful to my father, Reverend James G. Fudge for his abiding interest, to my son Jakoub Luther who has tolerated mutterings about Jan Hus his entire life!, and to the community of St. Anne's Episcopal Church (Washougal, WA), many of whom often inquired about the book and its progress. In numerous and quite essential ways, my longsuffering colleagues Brent Anderson and April Purtell saved me from several computer-related catastrophes, some real, others only imagined in my Luddite mind and they consistently and with considerable patience presented workable solutions to a myriad of problems I was altogether helpless to overcome on my own. Their invisible imprint is all over this book. My editor at I.B.Tauris (London), Liz Friend-Smith, originally commissioned the work and enthusiastically supported its production, along with her successor in that position Joanna Godfrey together with her colleagues Jayne Ansell and Matthew Brown, the latter expertly overseeing and managing the transition of the typescript to publication. It would be an understatement to say that Matthew was indispensable.

Just as this book literally was being sent off to press, I discovered among my papers a long-lost card from my former colleague Louis G. Foltz given on the occasion of my exile to the South Pacific. The card read, 'we are looking forward to the first edition of the Maori Huss' and was accompanied by a wonderful pencil drawing of the 'Māori Hus' as conceived by Lou Foltz. Four other books, and several large research projects, prevented me from producing my intended book on Hus whilst living in the antipodes on Aotearoa. Despite Lou's suggestive drawing, I regret that my research failed to turn up any evidence whatsoever which might have allowed me to present Jan Hus wearing a moko, carrying a pouwhenua, a tewhatewha, or a taiaha (the drawing was admittedly somewhat ambiguous!), nor yet performing a haka. Nevertheless, at long last, Hus has finally appeared.

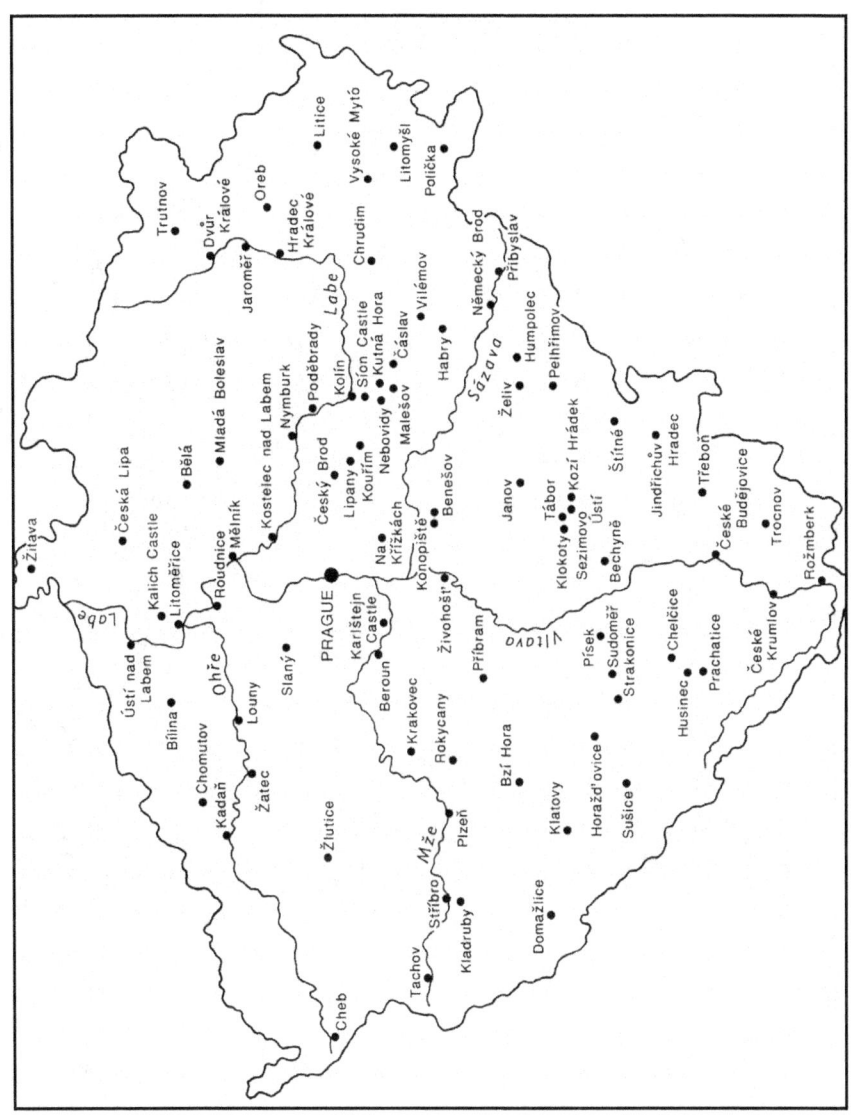

Map 1 Bohemia in the fifteenth century

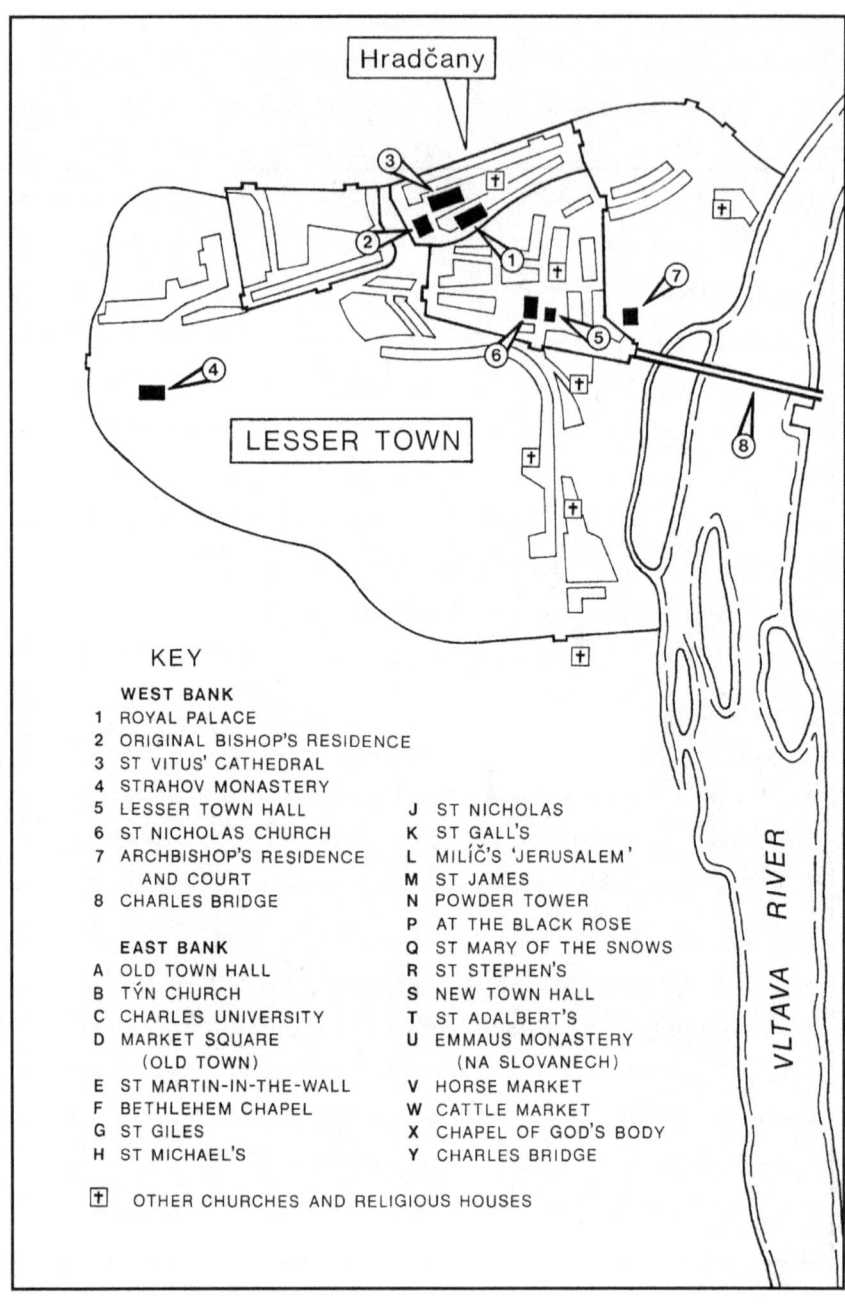

Map 2 Prague around the time of Hus: west side and (facing) the main city

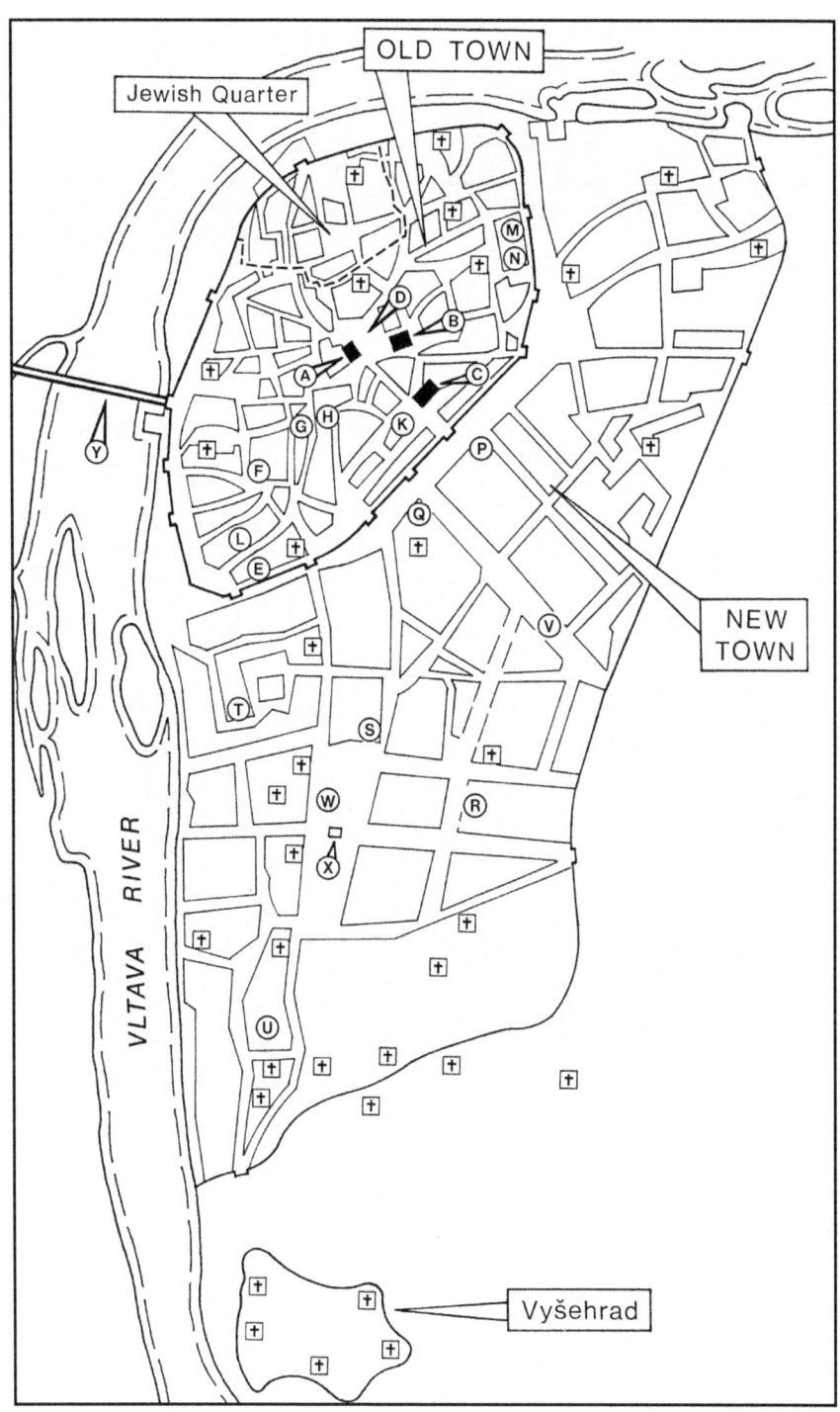

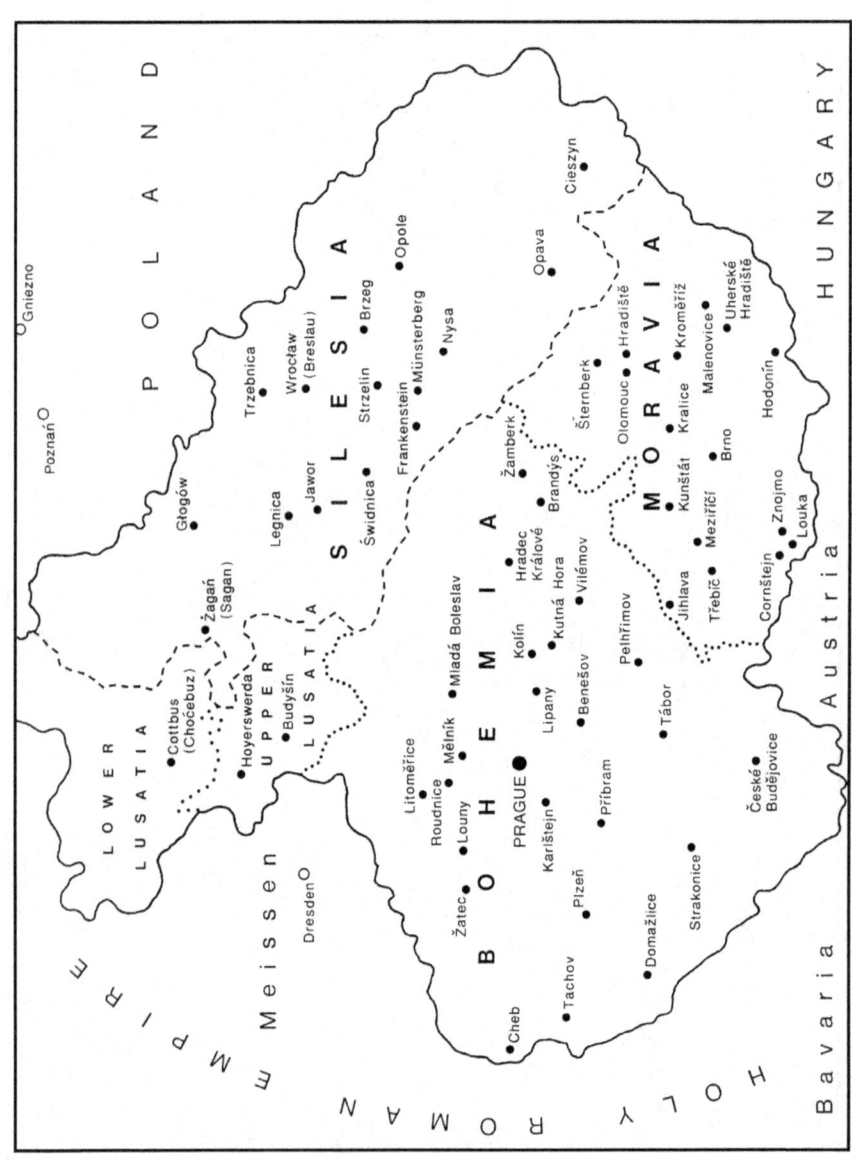

Map 3 The Kingdom of Bohemia during the reign of King Václav IV

INTRODUCTION

In 1938 on the eve of World War Two, British prime minister Neville Chamberlain famously described the troubles in the former Czechoslovakia as 'a quarrel in a faraway country between people of whom we know nothing'.[1] Many people know Jan Hus was burned alive as the result of a quarrel in a distant land between opposing factions but the details are often blurred. Anglo scholars and students are quite aware generally of Hus and his place in history but the subject is more often mentioned as something ancillary than formally studied. The burning of Hus electrified a nation. As the centuries passed the fires of a revolution which once commanded European-wide attention slowly went out. There are two reasons for this. First, Jan Hus is part of the problem of the 'Middle Ages'.[2] Invented by the Italians the term provided a means of disassociating the rebirth, or 'renaissance' of classical Greek and Roman culture from the millennium separating that classical age from its resurgence. These 'Middle Ages' were viewed as motionless history between towering eras of human achievement.[3] The nineteenth-century French historian Jules Michelet contemptuously described the Middle Ages as a 'thousand years without a bath'; a time of unspeakable ignorance, superstition and all manner of uncleanness.[4] After the glory that was Greece and the grandeur that was Rome these 'Middle Ages' were somewhat of a letdown at least according to the Italians who proudly claimed to have ended that historical disaster. Classical civilization and its revival in Italy seemed proof enough to some historians that the intervening time had been practically useless. 'I know nothing of those ages which knew nothing' trumpeted one perspective.[5] If the Middle Ages constituted a protracted period of abysmal ignorance in western Europe one could only imagine the darkness pervading areas east of the Elbe in even more distant lands inhabited by peoples speaking unknown tongues and steeped in strange cultures. The Kingdom of Bohemia where Hus lived was part of the Slavic land between the eastern Orthodox Christian world and the mainstream of western European civilization. It was terra incognita. Coupled with these geographical and linguistic disadvantages was the timing of the age of the Hussites. The fifteenth century by almost every reckoning is an historical no man's land. If one speaks of the fifteenth century in Italy than it is renaissance. If the reference is continentally elsewhere then it is medieval. Unfortunately many medievalists regard the Middle Ages as pretty well over by the fourteenth century.⁶ This leaves Hus among the orphans of the vanishing Middle Ages. Happily the resurgence of the study of medieval history in the last two generations has undermined these artificial assumptions about those 'dark' or 'Middle Ages'. There are now encouraging trends aimed at including these lesser known places and important personalities in the histories being written.

Second, the challenge of Jan Hus is further revealed in context by the riposte to A.J.P. Taylor's question 'what happened next'?⁷ Within a hundred years of Hus' fiery death the force of Martin Luther's ideas and personality acted like a high-powered drill on the multiple worlds of European culture. Add to Luther the astonishing developments in religion, technology, politics and economics and what came next overshadowed much of the Middle Ages especially religious and social quarrels in the faraway land of Bohemia between people with unpronounceable names of whom most of sixteenth-century Europe knew nothing. By the year 1400 it was the end of the road – the 'autumn of the Middle Ages' – and in terms of intellectual stimulation these dreary times had degenerated into sad and powerless confusion.⁸ What happened after Hus tended either to overlook him entirely or absorb him completely into an emerging Protestant potpourri. Neither scenario is helpful.

From a religious perspective, the German Reformation arguably has been made the cornerstone of European history at the end of the Middle Ages. Hus and his followers were relegated to the role of forerunners, ultimate failures, while Martin Luther boldly strode the pathways of revolutionary success. This gloomy picture has been compounded by altogether hasty research which rushed headlong to the conclusion that Hus was an unoriginal thinker and little more than a plagiarizer of that Oxford man John Wyclif.⁹ A careful investigation into the sources of late medieval Czech history reveals quite the opposite. The acts of Hus and his colleagues were a small step toward freedom of individual conscience. From a political point of view events in Bohemia constituted an early manifestation of national or state identity and a nascent movement toward democracy by means of a definite and particular social revolution. Seen in this light, Jan Hus cannot be considered episodic or a minor stage in the evolution of European history and civilization. Since the dramatic and sweeping changes in Central and Eastern Europe since 1989 the field of Hussite studies has broadened enabling students and scholars alike to better understand that 'quarrel in a faraway country between people of whom we know nothing.'

There is no academic writing without a point of view, opinion or particular interest.¹⁰ In this study I have made no conscious effort to distill a narrative of events from the 1370s to 1415. Instead, I have attempted to place emphasis on Hus' ideas, their implementation in Prague and elsewhere, and particularly on his reputation and legacy. I am especially interested in theology, the history of doctrine and its social function. This is a result of my conviction that the long arm of theology and ethics pervades all of Hus' public life and thought. In this sense I regard Hus as a vehicle for analyzing theological history. I have explored in some detail his religious convictions and theological commitments for these reveal the foundations of his conduct and career. It should be noted that the study of theology in this context is applied theology, meaning the social dimensions and implications of religious practice and doctrine are also considered. However, the importance of Hus as a social thinker should not be ignored.[11] This book recognizes and hopefully contributes in some sense to the history of religion revival which is discernable from the last quarter of the twentieth century. This approach underscores the value of the study of religious practice and accepts that religion plays a role in the explanatory matrix of history. Autobiography is the most direct expression of reflections on life.[12] Unfortunately, like many people of his time, Hus did not write an autobiography. But in his literary work, both Latin and Czech, Hus is best discovered as a person, priest, professor, polemicist, and perhaps prophet. These are the vital sources for understanding the meaning of his life. They reveal the widest available contours of his strengths and weaknesses, his courage and conviction. Having said this, I do not subscribe to the assumption that texts – any text – contain an inner logic even if that coherence is not readily apparent to the reader. The history of ideas simply does not possess within itself an independent principle of congruity. There is the possibility that Hus was confused, mistaken or simply wrong. That caveat does not render his works suspect. Nevertheless, a careful analysis of Hus' writings alone cannot account for his condemnation. His refusal to disavow Wyclif, his persistent withering attack on wicked priests, and his willingness to alienate whomever he considered a detriment to the gospel are important aspects in understanding his dramatic downfall. The protracted crisis of authority and the strain of the papal schism placed a high responsibility on the Council of Constance. Hus' refusal to submit to conciliar authority and synodal judgment doomed him. However, the final verdict was also fueled by the collision of stubbornness and intractable natures, both on the part of some Council members as well as Hus himself.

The book proceeds on the premise of two basic but essential assumptions. That Hus was a medieval man and that he must not be removed from the fifteenth-century fabric which formed his life. Jan Hus is a figure who clarifies important aspects of the religious world of the late Middle Ages. This clarification also has social application. Hus presented a fundamental challenge to the Latin Church and his legacy confronted and challenged the old and entrenched social order. This conviction pervaded the consciousness of fifteenth-century Europe. Scholarship on both sides of the Atlantic in the past fifty years or so has done considerable to make that clear. The significance of Jan Hus cannot be limited to Constance nor to his book *De ecclesia* nor to his work at Bethlehem Chapel nor yet to his extraordinary appeal to Christ at the height of his legal ordeal. Rather, his place in history must be understood as commencing in the fourteenth-century reform impulses and continuing apace in aspects of the Hussite Revolution. His life was both intense and dramatic filled with passion and tragedy. The turbulent world in which Hus lived guaranteed he would not be forgotten. Among the useful services provided by historiography is the explication of the fervor and conviction with which prior generations pursued goals and outcomes which today we might find disgraceful and objectionable. Our standards must be applied with humility for in time the judgment of history will render a verdict on us. In my consideration of Hus I have shown little interest in the 'Catholic', 'Protestant', 'Marxist', 'Moravian' or 'modern' Hus. These are unavoidable but of chief concern is Jan Hus the medieval man standing against an omnipotent church, the might of secular power represented by the emperor, and a cogent world view a thousand years deep. Avoiding fashionable theoretical approaches I have sought to place Hus within the context of his times. History is made up of people, stories, and stories about people. Hus' story is part of a larger tale. The tales which make up medieval historiography are often, by modern critical reckoning, 'inauthentic, unscientific, unreliable, ahistorical, irrational, borderline illiterate, and worse yet, unprofessional'.[13] What a predicament! The challenges are severe. Perhaps what is needed most are historians of medieval historiography capable of coming to terms with the historians and writers of history in the Middle Ages.[14] The source difficulties noted, I am convinced that the available materials do allow for a useable portrait of Hus to emerge. To that end the labors of this book have been directed.

In the course of research I have come to the conclusion that there is no such thing as a mainstream interpretation of Jan Hus. The idea is nothing more than a subjective construct reflecting the preference of the individual scholar or a particular community of thinkers. There is no value projecting onto the past modern answers to medieval questions. Reflecting on that principle I have become convinced that some scholars have misread Hus and misappropriated him precisely because they have been focused on contemporary situations and concerns. After twenty years I have arrived at four new perspectives on Hus. First, he actively contributed to his own death. Second, he cultivated a martyr's complex. Third, the men of the Council of Constance did much in their power in an effort to spare his life. Fourth, Hus can be regarded both as reformer and heretic. The apparent inconsistency cannot be sustained. Neither conclusion negates the other. Historical interpretation need not assign Hus exclusively either to the medieval Catholic reformers or the proto-Protestants. In explicating Hus' thought I have not attempted to place him in any specific category. I share particular systems of interpretation with a number of scholars in the history of Hussite studies. To large measure I find myself sharing common views on theological matters with the late Paul De Vooght, on liturgy and eucharistic thought with David Holeton, on the Prague context with Olivier Marin, on law and legal matters with Jiří Kejř, on art with Jan Royt and Milena Bílková, and on historical interpretation generally with the late František M. Bartoš, Howard Kaminsky and František Šmahel. I differ with all of them in the treatment of certain issues and particular evaluations. Nevertheless I have learned much from each one of them. I have carried on a dialogue with Jan Hus in an effort to understand a world which no longer exists and which can only be partially reconstructed. These conversations with a dead priest have continually brought me back to his writings.

The limitations of this study are not well hidden. The book exemplifies a comment from antiquity. 'When one comes to the end . . . one is still at the beginning and when one is finished, one will still be incomplete'.[15] The study of Jan Hus is in large measure a consideration of theology itself; the intersection of reason and Christian mystery which seeks its own understanding. Theologians such as the important fourth-century

Hilary of Poitiers and the influential thirteenth-century Thomas Aquinas understood this intersection with striking clarity: 'haec credendo, incipe, procurre, persiste . . . intellige incomprehensibilia esse'. Paraphrasing Hilary, one might apply his ruminations to the task of theology generally and to Hus specifically. To wit, it is important to pursue understanding with perseverance. Progress is to be commended even if one knows it is quite impossible to reach the fullness of knowledge. Complete understanding is impossible, but the inevitable progress which comes by pressing ahead has its own rewards. One must not presume to know too much or profess solutions to all mysteries but rather accept that certain matters are beyond comprehension. Put simply, the scholar must set forth his or her findings and opinions with humility.[16] The truly erudite need no instruction on the obscurity of truth and the difficulty of extracting it from beneath the layers of sediment which accumulate unavoidably over time. Careful work is required to come to a proper understanding and even this process cannot ever be more than inchoate. Whatever the subject, it emerges slowly in bits and pieces. Discoveries and conclusions are never final. There is always more to be known.[17] The study of Hus is no different.

Many a furrowed brow has accompanied a variety of queries all reducible to 'why are you writing a book on Hus'? The advantage to writing about dead people is that they cannot answer. In setting forth my specific understanding of Jan Hus I have given attention to three main considerations. First, the world in which Hus lived and worked. The priority of context cannot possibly be exaggerated. Second, I have focused specifically on his work and ideas. Here I have endeavored to develop a significant discussion of Hus' theology and spirituality with the conviction that religious thought and belief is indispensable for understanding Hus. Situating Hus in terms of wider medieval thinking remained the goal in treating Hus' theology and mission. Third, I have given much attention to Hus' fate, reputation and legacy by considering his posthumous commemoration, the iconography which accompanied that recognition and the subsequent historiography which shaped and facilitated a culture of remembrance. Sharing common ground with few medieval personalities, Jan Hus made headlines at the end of the twentieth century. The book deals with the recent debate on where Hus stands today in Christian polemics. I have taken a clear minority position on the matter for two reasons. First, the other side has been vigorously defended already. Second, there has been a general tendency to give political and ecumenical correctness the pride of place in the debates on this topic. Believing this approach to be fatal I have set forth an alternative view in the conviction that it is my task to understand the past not judge it. Happily, my conclusions will be controversial. This should underscore the vitality of the study of Hus and refocus the value of his life and ideas in the wider consideration of late medieval thought and the influence of religious thinkers on society. As Peter Abelard once noted, the same thing over and over again is the mother of all weariness.[18] Moreover, the book has been written to fill a gap in scholarship. The last scholarly monograph on Hus in English is now more than four decades old.[19]

Twenty-five years have elapsed since I first read the *Relatio de Mag. Joannis Hus causa* written by Petr Mladoňovice about Hus' tragic end.[20] I felt an immediate attraction to this man who had been willing to die for principle. In the intervening years I made Hus and his followers my research focus and announced a dozen years ago my intention to write a book on Hus.[21] In a sense this book comes as the culmination of a quarter century of reflection. Some will say I have waited too long to write it, others may suggest it ought not to have been written at all. I am impervious to the force of those arguments. Forty two years have passed since Matthew Spinka committed to print his biography of Hus, the last major study in English. I have not attempted to write a conventional biography preferring instead to focus on ideas and identity in Hus' life and legacy. Geoffrey Elton pointed out that biography is not a good way of writing history anyway and I tend to agree.[22] The limits of a human life no matter how formidable rarely has the weight to determine the interpretation of history. In the case of Hus it is not possible at all to write a proper history with a singular focus on him. Attempts to do so run the risk either of distorting context or failing to deal properly with it. Nevertheless, his personality was powerful enough to impact his world. In defense of his ideas he could be truculent and determined. When ordered by his superiors to stand down Hus insouciantly went further and became defiant. The efforts of men like Michael de Causis to discredit Hus were fatuous. Like innovators and reformers in all disciplines Jan Hus became convinced that he alone understood truth. The conviction made him intransigent and immune to reason. The results were martyrdom, reform and revolution. Without wrenching him from his context, Hus has relevance and applicability for a twenty-first century postmodern world.

The pages of this book will reveal my own interpretation and understanding of Jan Hus but my view of Hus is not limited to this study. My years of thinking about Hus have convinced me that he is best described as a late medieval Catholic reformer. He is closer to that milieu than he is to Luther or any of the later Protestant movements. He was driven neither by land-nationalism nor by a sense of Czech national spirit. There is little direct or unimpeachable evidence of anti-German motivation. He strove for church reform, not its destruction. His work at Bethlehem Chapel and theology are what were most important to him. He was influenced by a Czech tradition, associated with Jan Milíč of Kroměříž and Matěj of Janov, as well as by John Wyclif. He used native Czech religious reform ideas but couched them deliberately in the conceptual language of Wyclif. He is not rightly characterized as a Wyclifite. By the standards of the fifteenth century Hus was a heretic. He died heroically. He was a good man, ethically upright, morally sound, committed to principle, honor and integrity. Idealistic, he could be stubborn and his naïveté is a matter of historical record. Intellectually he was not of the first order and from 1409 onwards became more radical (perhaps even to a reckless extent) while proving himself an effective popular leader and successful speaker. He is a man worthy of admiration and rightly acknowledged as a person of historic importance. He should be numbered among the martyrs of the Christian faith and the fathers of the Czech nation. I agree completely with both Robert Kalivoda and

František M. Bartoš in the opinion that in terms of his thinking Jan Hus was ahead of his time.[23]

Though I touch on the matter in chapter eight, a word should be said here about certain nomenclature adopted in this study specifically and in my work generally. In this book, the term 'Hussite' refers either to something directly connected to Hus, for example his thought might be called 'Hussite theology', or to the perception of an alternative form and practice of Christianity in fifteenth-century Bohemia. Jan Hus and his colleagues, followers, and disciples, regarded themselves as standing within the historic progression of the faith. The official church of the later Middle Ages saw them as dissenters, separatists and heretics who had deviated from the sacred truths of the 'one, holy, catholic and apostolic church'. The ecclesiastical and legal definition of Hus and his associates was negative and intentionally derogatory. Whether Hus and his colleagues, especially in the first half of the fifteenth century, are called 'Hussite', 'Utraquist' or something else, cannot alter the fact that Jan Hus did emerge historically as the figurehead of a movement which no longer could be considered synonymous with the mainstream of western Christianity. The Latin Church – as defined by popes, Curial officials, the episcopate and Councils – unambiguously considered itself the legitimate heir and continuation of the apostles and fathers. That same identification was claimed by Hus and defended by the adherents of reformed religious practice in fifteenth-century Bohemia. Could both be right? It seems most unlikely in that world. To refer to the movement associated with Hus as 'Hussite' both illumines the nature of an alternative form of the faith within late medieval Christianity while acknowledging the symbolic importance of Jan Hus as an inspiration from 1415 on. In the Czech lands the fifteenth century was *aetas hussiana*, the age of Hus. The term further provides an umbrella identification for those alternative beliefs and faith practices in Bohemia even though these admittedly and undeniably were not uniform. Táborite Christians and the specific practices of religious faith among much more conservative and traditional communities in Prague were quite clearly dissimilar. By comparison, in the contemporary Christian world, theological reflection and faith practices are quite diverse, for example, in Roman Catholic, Baptist, Pentecostal and Methodist churches. Significant differences notwithstanding, all of these are still Christian.

Heresy is the second issue. This book concludes that Jan Hus was a heretic. The specificity and complexity of the medieval understanding of heresy demands this conclusion. By the ecclesiastical and legal standards of the later Middle Ages, Hus placed himself, and therefore was correctly adjudicated, outside the official church. To conclude otherwise is to apply something other than a fifteenth-century standard. The history and textual evidence of medieval canon law, heresy trials, theology in the Latin west, and the prevailing religious ethos, cannot be summarily ignored and set aside. As chapter seven points out, the world in which Hus lived determined he was heretical and that finding was neither arbitrary nor indefensible. Legal procedure was neither the issue at Constance nor can it be made so today. Procedure is not what convicted Hus. Whether or not he departed from traditional Christian theology, and to what extent, is arguable but that important consideration is not the sole determinant in establishing dissent and heresy. Those who continue to find themselves offended by the grating classification of Hus as heretical might like to consider that the term need not, in our time and culture, be thought of as opprobrious. St. Paul said, there must be heresies (*oportet esse haereses*) and St. Augustine commented that only great men have been the authors of heresy. Jan Hus was a great man. Some of his ideas were salutary. As stated above, he was a heretic and at the same time remains a great Christian. The late medieval church surely disagreed but as a martyr, religious thinker, faithful priest, and a man for all ages, Hus' significance and stature suggests much more. Heresy is essential. Heretics ought to be embraced. The medieval church and the Council of Constance notwithstanding, dissent, difference and diversity enhance, not destroy, the Christian faith. John Milton once rhetorically asked, 'whoever knew truth to be put to the worst in a free and open encounter'? The life and ideas of Jan Hus are sufficient testimony to the fact that truth prevails. There are other perspectives on these particular matters, but I am unpersuaded by the force of argument which presumes that 'heresy' and 'Hussite' nomenclatures are somehow unscholarly, pejorative and offensive. It may be politically correct and ecumenically expedient to ban 'heresy' and 'Hussite', and their cognates, from public discourse but I have written with neither of these impulses as motivations. In this book I use both of these taxonomies consciously and deliberately.

I have resisted the urge to Anglicize or Germanize the spelling of Czech proper names. These have been given in their native form. The two main exceptions are Prague rather than Praha and Charles IV instead of Karel. King Václav IV is usually rendered Wenceslas in English but in this book the Czech form is used to avoid confusion with the better known 'good king' Wenceslas of John Mason Neale's widely known nineteenth-century Christmas carol. The latter lived in the tenth century while the former's forty one year reign covered most of Hus' life. In general the names of churches and religious houses have also been given in English. In the case of a few obscure individuals whose ethnicity is uncertain or unknown to me I have elected to render those names in an English form. The book has been written to honor the memory and significance of an individual whose life could inspire us all.

Cistercian Abbey
Lafayette, Oregon

1

BIOGRAPHY

On a Saturday morning, 6 July 1415, a group of seven bishops gathered around a kneeling man dressed in clerical vestments in the cathedral in the south German city of Constance. They denounced him as a 'cursed Judas' and removed his clothes. After an argument they disfigured his hair with a pair of scissors. In solemn tones they collectively committed his soul to hell. Shortly thereafter the condemned man was led out of the city and burned alive before several thousand onlookers. The man chained to the stake on a woodpile, wearing a miter-shaped crown featuring demons, was a native Czech, the Bohemian priest Jan Hus from Prague. The events of that Saturday morning brought to an end a meteoric career and secured Hus' place in history. The Hus of history can be divided into four general categories with obvious overlap: Hus the scholar (1390–1402), Hus the pastor (1402–1412), Hus the exile (1412–1414) and Hus the accused heretic (1414–15).

Little is known of his early life. In the absence of parish registers, we can only surmise his birth around 1372. This estimation is based upon his probable age at the time of ordination in 1401. The biographical details of Hus' life have been told sufficiently and in detail elsewhere.[1] Only a brief overview is necessary here in order to provide a basic outline of his life. Jan Hus came from the small village of Husinec in southern Bohemia. His father's name was Michael and we know nothing of his life. Hus' mother's name has not survived. Hus had one brother who died before he did and we know that Hus took responsibility for his young nephews for whom he expressed concern while incarcerated awaiting death at Constance.[2] The ruler of the country, King Charles IV, died in 1378. His death opened the door for significant changes on practically every level in Bohemia. Those changes included the career of Jan Hus. Around 1385 Hus ostensibly left Husinec to attend school in Prachatice, a town five kilometers south.[3] Since there is no evidence of a school in Prachatice before the sixteenth century it is necessary to question the validity of the claim. Almost nothing is known for certain about Hus' life or activities before he came to Prague. The stories which have come down to us are of later origin and are almost certainly hagiography rather than history. As such they are useless for understanding the historical Hus. Only rarely do we find comments or clues in the corpus of Hus' writings which shed any light on his early years. He referred to his mother once or twice and revealed that she taught him how to pray.[4] He spoke with regret of his youthful participation in the popular but sometimes scandalous Feast of the Ass.

> What manifest outrage they perpetrate in the church by wearing masks. In my youthfulness I also was once to my shame a masquerader! Who could possibly depict everything that transpired in Prague? Having designated a cleric, dressed in monstrous attire, as bishop, they cause him to sit backwards on an ass with his face turned towards the tail. Then they take him into the church to Mass. They carry a plate of broth in front of him, and a jug or can of beer, and he eats in the church. I saw how the ass incenses the altars and, raising one leg, calls out in a loud voice Boo and the priests carry before him large torches instead of candles. He rides from one altar to another altar, incensing as he goes. And I observed how the priests turned their fur-lined vestments inside out and danced in the church. All the people watch this and laugh, thinking that all of this is holy and proper, since it appears in their rubric and in their statutes. Nice statutes alright! What undisciplined abomination! . . . When I was still young both in years and in reason I also adhered to this crazy rubric. But when the Lord God helped me understand the Scriptures I eliminated such notions and the statutes of delusion from my weak intellect.[5]

For a long time the Latin Church unsuccessfully tried to eradicate the observance of such traditions and feasts but as late as 1435 we find the Council of Basel condemning these practices.[6] Archbishop Jan of Jenštejn had forbidden the Feast of the Ass as early as 1386 in Prague but clearly the practice continued.

Around 1390 Hus left south Bohemia and went to Prague to study at the university. He later wrote of his proclivity for playing chess and how badly he felt over the amount of time wasted on the game and the quarrels it caused. Hus also bemoaned his early and inordinate devotion to entertainment and frivolity.[7] These reflections of self-condemnation reveal a man of considerable austerity. The absence of any charges against his character even by his most vociferous enemies associated with Michael de Causis leads to the conclusion that Hus's greatest moral failing consisted in playing chess to excess and taking occasional delight in aspects of the medieval carnival. He wrote dismissively of the courtly and popular culture of singing, music, dancing and games.[8] In this severity of personal deportment, Hus was not unlike others in Prague before him, namely Konrad Waldhauser and especially Jan Milíč of Kroměříž. Hus' personal life might be considered compatible with the tradition of Christian asceticism which characterized aspects of Latin Christendom throughout the Middle Ages. In a statement made late in life, Hus lamented his service to God had been characterized by numerous shortcomings.[9]

We know little of the details of Hus' student days in Prague save that he, like many medieval university students, suffered the ravages of poverty. Hus wrote of how he made a spoon out of bread in order to eat his peas and once he consumed the peas he ate the spoon too.[10] It is quite impossible to say with any degree of certainty just when the young Jan Hus decided for a career in the church. That decision was not extraordinary. After all, the medieval Latin Church was a major employer by the end of the Middle Ages and opportunities for advancement, power, prestige and the assurance of eternal salvation were not unattractive enticements for many. That Hus did not elect to pursue the priesthood from purely pious motives can be determined from his own words. 'Whoever wishes to live well should enter the monk's cell.' Hus admitted he decided on the religious life for unspiritual reasons. He chose the priesthood and desired to advance as quickly as possible in order to secure a reasonable standard of living, be able to dress well and thereby earn the respect of others.[11] Later, Hus repudiated such motivations and castigated relentlessly wicked priests who put carnal desires ahead of the cure of souls. By 1393 Hus managed to secure a Bachelor's degree. He was placed sixth out of twenty-two graduands presented that year. This is the first confirmed date in the life of Hus. On the occasion Hus heard the customary speech from his promoter Jan of Mýto who based his address on the comment made by Aristotle that through hardship one comes to a sense of well-being. The formal address commended Hus for his hard work which enabled him to gain knowledge and understanding but apparently at the expense of his health. Jan of Mýto alluded to an unspecified illness brought on by the intensity of constant study. We also find an early reference to the various puns on Hus' name which even Hus himself later employed. Hus, meaning goose in Czech, possessed wings that Jan of Mýto claimed would lift Hus to higher places.[12] In 1393 neither man could possibly see twenty years into the future.

In the same year he attained his university qualification, Hus came into contact with a practice which later served to propel him into revolt against the church and into conflict with religious authority. During the jubilee of 1393 Hus heard the Cistercian preacher Jan Štěkna expound forcefully on the subject of indulgences at Vyšehrad, the castle-fortress situated on the right bank of the Vltava River just south of Prague's New Town. Inasmuch as indulgences represented the remission of all or part of the debt of temporal punishment owned to God due to sin after the guilt has been forgiven, the practice of buying a certificate of indulgence had become a normal religious practice. Since the indulgence generally extended only for a particular time period it became necessary to buy another once the previous one expired. Part of the economic stability of the later medieval Church depended upon the preaching and sale of indulgences. Hus was so taken by the persuasive rhetoric of the proclamations of Jan Štěkna that he spent all of his last coins to purchase an indulgence at Vyšehrad.[13] A few years later, the sale of indulgences turned violent in Prague. Blood ran in the streets. Jan Hus found himself caught up in the disturbances. On that occasion he took a staunch position against the practice. That posture had not always been his preferred stance. But in 1393 he remained a firm believer in the merits of the indulgence. He seemed prepared to be penniless and live a life of utter poverty so long as he possessed the assurance of the forgiveness of sins.

Three years later Hus proceeded to the M.A. having been examined on this occasion by the important university master Stanislav of Znojmo. This man later played an important role in religious affairs in Prague, first as a supporter of Hus and later in opposition. By 1398 Hus became a full-fledged faculty member of the university. He taught full time from 1396 and the two year period was consistent with university rules before a scholar could be considered a regular faculty member. Curiously and regrettably none of his lectures in the arts faculty are extant. During his tenure as an academic, Hus presided over the elevations of twenty-three students.[14] The requirements and rigor for one achieving a doctorate in the later Middle Ages were onerous. Hus did not obtain that ultimate academic qualification mainly because his career took a significant and permanent detour early in 1402.

Hus had determined to seek a place within the medieval church. On a date which has not been recorded, but likely in 1401, Hus received ordination and took up holy orders. His early preaching occurred at St. Michael's in the Old Town but also in other parish churches around the city. On 14 March 1402, Hus was appointed preacher in Bethlehem Chapel in the Old Town, a private chapel established in 1391. Thereafter he styled himself as the 'rector and preacher in the Chapel of the Holy Innocents of Bethlehem in the old and great city of Prague.'[15] Indeed, apart from his fiery death at Constance more than thirteen years later, Jan Hus remained indissolubly linked forever with Bethlehem Chapel. Here his career reached a city-wide reputation, later transcended local significance, and came to a place of prominence on a European platform. Hus achieved his goal of ordination to the priesthood, with an acceptable standard of living and the respect of his peers and the people of Prague. He admitted he was initially reluctant to speak out against evil and irregularities which he observed tolerated and unchecked among the religious of his day.[16] Soon, however, he became the vigorous correcter of the religious. The world of Hus can only be appreciated with an understanding of his career as a committed preacher in Bethlehem Chapel and with his principal identification as a priest. The life of Hus reveals a number of functions or categories into which he may be placed. All of these must be subordinated to his main work which had to do with the proclamation of the gospel and the cure of souls.[17]

Even though he became preacher at Bethlehem Chapel, Hus continued with academic affairs. From 1404 to 1406 he lectured and wrote commentaries on several of the smaller epistles in the New Testament, namely James, I and II Peter, I, II, and III John and Jude. Likewise he devoted considerable attention to Psalms 109–118.[18] A careful consideration of these works leads to an unavoidable conclusion that Hus followed in the native Czech preaching and reform tradition established a generation before he arrived in Prague. This charismatic spirituality can neither be accurately described as a preparation for Hus nor in any meaningful sense as 'pre-Hussite'. That said, it is difficult to avoid the conclusion that in these commentaries Hus was familiar with the religious and spiritual impulses already established in Prague. It is not misleading in that sense to see Hus as a disciple of Milíč and Matěj of Janov. After all it is impossible to assign a *tabula rase* – blank mind – to Hus. Between 1407 and 1409

Hus delivered an important series of lectures on the Sentences of Peter Lombard, the standard medieval theological textbook. The significance of Hus' theological acumen can best be gauged from this commentary.

The fourteen and fifteenth centuries cannot be regarded as a time of intellectual stagnation and from a religious history standpoint there is much of value and vibrancy in the history of ideas. One of the more contentious intellectual developments was that connected to the thought of the Oxford professor, John Wyclif. From 1403 Wyclif's ideas gained currency and controversy in Prague. Hus became embroiled in a long-standing dispute over Wyclif; a debate which proved fatal for him at the Council of Constance in 1415. The political, theological, social and economic implications of Wyclif's thought garnered considerable attention. It is clear that no where else in Europe did Wyclif make as strong an impact as in Bohemia. Rightly or wrongly, Hus came to be styled as a disciple of Wyclif and up until 1420 his followers were frequently labeled 'Wyclifites'. In addition to the influence of Wyclif, it is clear that Waldensian heresy penetrated Bohemia by the early fourteenth century. Hus denied any dependence upon Waldensian thought. However, the Waldensian world cannot be excluded from the foundations of religious belief and practice in Bohemia after 1360.

Crucial to Hus' career and also for the religious life of early fifteenth-century Prague was the election of a new archbishop in 1402, eight months after Hus' appointment as preacher in Bethlehem Chapel. Consistent with the medieval practice of simony, Archbishop Zbyněk bought the appointment for the sum of 2,800 gulden and had the backing of royalists loyal to King Václav IV. This man Zbyněk has been unfairly pilloried by the Hussite tradition to the extent of suggesting he knew nothing of theology and could not even read. There is no basis for these accusations. He had been prior of a religious house in Mělník which included a canonry in Prague, though the degree of absenteeism among clerics in late medieval Europe meant he may have done absolutely nothing as the holder of these appointments. Moreover, his career to date had been largely military. Whatever his merits, Zbyněk was unsuited for the archbishopric of Prague. Initially, Zbyněk favored Jan Hus and the direction of religious reform and practice in the capital. Later he developed an animus against Hus and actively interfered in religious affairs. Much of this had to do with the infusion and popularity of Wyclif, the debate over indulgences, and the politics of the papal schism. Nevertheless, Zbyněk clearly sided with the reform-motivated caucus in Prague up until 1408.

In addition to his academic work, preaching in Bethlehem Chapel, prominence within the Prague synod, and reform activities, we catch glimpses of Hus' pastoral work. During the spring of 1403 the episcopal warrior Zbyněk was commissioned by the king to help bring to justice a robber bandit named Jan Zúl of Ostředek. The archbishop succeeded in capturing the fugitive who was hanged together with his men. At the gallows Hus accompanied the condemned man to his execution and evidently succeeded in bringing the criminal to repentance. A contemporary chronicle recorded Zúl asking the people gathered to pray to God for his soul.[19] This incident shows Hus the pastor actively engaged in the work of ministry. A few years later Hus set down a brief exposition of the duties of a priest. He included five in number: preaching the gospel, prayer, the ministry of the sacraments, study of the scriptures, and setting the example of good works.[20] His career admirably reflected all five.

By the fifteenth century, popular piety and religious devotion in Central Europe had embraced the power of pilgrimage and a cultural appropriation of the eucharist came to dominate popular imagination. A veritable cult of the sacrament emerged. The emphasis shifted to the body of Christ. This was evident in the striking social observance of the feast of Corpus Christi manifested in various places throughout Europe. The host carried publicly in a monstrance, bleeding hosts, holy blood, and the popular perception that the body and blood of Christ could effect social change, informed religious practice and suggested a new sense of religious devotion. Shrines devoted to the holy blood and bleeding hosts began to capture popular imagination in the later fourteenth century. When Archbishop Zbyněk decided to look into the cult at Wilsnack in Brandenburg in 1405 he appointed Hus to act on the investigating committee. Clearly, at that time Hus was a favorite of the archbishop. This assumption can further be strengthened with the appointment of Hus as synodal preacher in 1405 and 1407.

Somewhere in the period between 1406 and 1412 Hus undertook a significant revision of the Czech language. *De orthographia bohemica* is an anonymous undated Latin manuscript setting forth a simplification of the Czech language and introducing a pronunciation key using a system of diacritics. The work has been attributed to Hus though this assumption cannot be maintained with complete assurance.[21] At this time Hus worked on the Czech New Testament and later on the entire Czech Bible. It was during this period also that Hus became involved in what some claimed then and later as nationalistic interests. By 1409 the university in Prague witnessed the mass exodus of German students and masters in the aftermath of the 'decree of Kutná Hora' issued by the king which placed control of the university into the hands of the native Czechs. This reversed a previous German domination. The 'decree of Kutná Hora' had two immediate effects. First, it paved the way for increased radical reforms generated out of the native impulses rooted in the fourteenth century but, second, it reduced the university from an international place of inquiry to a provincial institution. On 17 October 1409 Hus was elected rector of the university, giving him a place of prominence and priority in academic affairs and decision-making. This marked the apex of Hus' public career in Prague before he became openly controversial and the road to Constance became inevitable.

Hus' reluctance to swear off Wyclif, his increasing attacks upon clerical irregularities, his commitment to reform, his opposition to indulgences, and the politics of the protracted papal schism led to a souring of relations between Hus and the archbishop. Soon Hus became flagrantly defiant to archiepiscopal orders and went so far as to defy a papal directive to cease preaching. Once Hus appealed against Zbyněk and the papal order, he set in motion a legal process which wound its way inexorably to the greatest gathering of western Christendom in the later Middle Ages; the Council of Constance which convened on the shores of the Bodensee in 1414 and sat for four years. These events and issues created increasing isolation for Hus especially with the unfortunate defection of Archbishop Zbyněk, Stanislav of Znojmo and Štěpán Páleč from the ranks of the reformers. More than simple defection, all three actively opposed Hus both on theological and personal grounds. The vitriolic Michael de Causis introduced virulent opposition to Hus. Only his colleagues Jerome of Prague and Jakoubek of Stříbro could be counted upon to defend or support Hus openly. Hus remained steadfast and even defiant. His detractors promulgated a grievance against Hus over the matter of indulgences charging him with declaring the pope was Antichrist and that the manifestation of wickedness had now entered the world.[22] The Antichrist attribution was a deliberate falsehood on the part of the authors of the grievance. In an effort to rouse the king against Hus, his enemies charged he had wilfully defied the king's orders. A malignancy began to characterize the ideas and theologies underlying religious practice and spirituality in Prague. Hus remained unmoved and made a short but direct rejoinder that should the king wish to enforce his royal will over religious matters, perhaps he ought to open an academic prison.[23] The consequences of the deepening rift led Hus to Constance.

By autumn 1412, after the violence over indulgences had claimed the lives of three young men – followers of Hus – protesting the illicit sale, all of Prague came under the serious ecclesiastical censure of interdict. The penalty was imposed because of Hus' continued presence in the city and his refusal to obey his ordinary. Zbyněk died suddenly at age thirty-four, possibly poisoned, but this did not alter Hus' precarious position with respect to Church authority. Interdict had been used as early as the fifth century and gained wide currency in the period after 1100. It was a fairly successful means of forcing obedience on the recalcitrant. While punishment in this case aimed at Hus it extended over the entire city of Prague, affecting everyone equally. In practice, interdict amounted to spiritual or religious starvation. All ecclesiastical activities were suspended for the duration of the interdict. Though a religious matter, the imposition of interdict could not be separated from the political and economic turmoil which inevitably surrounded it. Not only were church services suspended – no marrying, burying, or formal religion whatever – all of the industries which depended upon the operation of official religion, from wine merchants to candle makers, were also affected. In order to spare Prague the severity of this censure, Hus left the city and went into exile. One of his vitriolic opponents regarded Hus' exit from Prague as a consequence of the righteous judgment of God.[24]

Despite being out of the capital with no connection to the university or Bethlehem Chapel, Hus did not remain idle. He preached in various places in south Bohemia and did not cease to inveigh against the need for reformed religious practice.[25] Visible signs of open revolt began to emerge. A German tract discovered in a Cistercian monastery in south Bohemia at Vyšší Brod, dating to 1412, suggested the dawn of eschatological time when religion and the sword were melded. Hus was transformed into a military captain behind whom the faithful were marshaled. All those intending to be Christian were obliged to take up the sword and prepare to wash their hands in the blood of

God's enemies. Jan Hus was no longer a timid goose but a ferocious lion prepared to confront the papal Antichrist and all wickedness.[26] There is no unimpeachable evidence Hus endorsed this kind of approach but his inability or unwillingness to separate himself sufficiently from these sentiments produced a conviction in the minds of others which later proved unshakeable. Based on what had transpired in Prague up to 1412 the fathers at Constance believed they were dealing with a 'turbulent, seditious and subversive heretic'.[27] Nothing Hus could say or do altered that perception. His teaching and writings did contain elements of subversive doctrine. This placed him in opposition to the authority of the Latin Church and its appointed representatives. His position implied the fathers at Constance were in error. After all he had refused to distance himself from Wyclif. He persisted in overt provocation against members of the priesthood he considered wicked. He alienated many powerful people. Intractable in nature, Hus was stubborn and disinclined to submit to authorities he felt were inconsistent with the law of God. These were among the factors which brought Hus to trial at Constance.[28] The impulses in Bohemia which coalesced around Hus validate the observation that in times of revolution the leaders are often overtaken by their troops.[29] Hus planted the seeds which his disciples watered and the Hussites reaped the harvest. Religious reform and social revolution were unavoidable. By the time of his death, various radical groups in Bohemia were looking to Hus for inspiration. Important aspects of the Hussite movement were certainly anchored in popular sources but the perceived initiative can be traced to Jan Hus.[30]

Hus stayed at the small castle of Kozí Hrádek, near Tábor, from autumn 1412 until the spring of 1414. He then went to Sezimovo Ústí for a short period of time before taking up residence at Krakovec Castle, west of Prague, from mid July until October 1414. During these two years in exile, Hus wrote no fewer than fifteen books, some of them among his most important and influential. Shortly after his departure from Prague, Hus completed his 'Expositions' on the faith. These were commentaries on the Apostles' Creed, the Ten Commandments, as well as the Lord's Prayer.[31] These commentaries reflected the perspective of pastoral care and a desire for the education of people in basic Christian teachings. Hus employed a fairly simple but nevertheless effective pedagogical approach to an understanding of the faith. By early 1413 he completed an important book on the problem of simony, or the buying of spiritual power.[32] It amounted to a relentless and scathing attack upon a widespread practice in the later medieval church. In an entirely different vein, Hus produced a classic of spirituality aimed at providing instruction on how to find and follow the path to salvation.[33] The most important of his works from exile was his large book *De ecclesia*, an exposition on the nature of the church. This was completed by May 1413. The pace of his writing was almost frenetic but much of what Hus put on paper during those two years had been developed in his thought and practice over the previous ten years. He translated and expanded his treatment on the errors of the Mass not long after he completed *De ecclesia*.[34] On account of the attacks leveled against him by his former teacher and colleague, Stanislav of Znojmo, Hus felt obliged to make a formal reply to aspects of Stanislav's charges. Hus opposed the idea that all of the condemned articles from the works of Wyclif were erroneous. He set forth a contrary understanding of the church and challenged Stanislav to prove that the ecclesiastical magisterium was truly the essence of the church. Given the corruption which attended the pontificate of John XXIII, that challenge proved formidable. Even more daring was Hus' denial that the papacy possessed the fullness of power and that the power possessed by the church was spiritual rather than temporal or political. Popes could only claim to be the true vicar of Christ to the extent their lives mirrored that of Jesus.[35] This became a theme in Hus' preaching and writing. He denounced the fleecing of the faithful for every priestly function. His tone was unmistakably caustic. 'Something for confession, something else for Mass, this for an indulgence, that for a blessing. This for sprinkling, that for prayer, and something else for burial'.[36] His letters from this period were likewise peppered with similar disdain for the state of religious practice and piety in the Czech Church.[37]

By autumn 1413 Hus completed an important revision of his Latin Postil in Czech. This was a series of sermons for an entire year. The expansions sometimes provided valuable autobiographical comment as well as references to the controversies he had been part of. In one sense it is possible to regard the Postil as a mature expression of reform.[38] Hus produced a short catechetical instruction by spring 1414 which set out in summary form an explanation of the Christian religion.[39] This was followed up by a curiously titled polemical work which endeavored to answer charges advanced by a former priest who had denounced Hus as a dangerous presence.[40] The attack by this anonymous 'priest-cookmaster' was not an anomaly. Stanislav of Znojmo ostensibly called Hus and his disciples a group of 'infidels, perfidious, insane and cursed clerics'.[41]

While in exile, Hus did return occasionally to Prague. Interdict seemed to have been ignored so long as he did not preach. Technically his presence in the city was sufficient cause for the censure to be applied. It is apparent the authorities knew of his presence. On one occasion when he did enter a pulpit there was immediate intervention and he was prevented from delivering a sermon and forced to withdraw.[42] Just before Hus left Prague, the king ordered an episcopal intervention in an effort to resolve the theological conflict. Archbishop Konrad of Prague and Bishop Jan 'the Iron' of Litomyšl were ordered to convene a synodal convocation of the clergy on 3 January 1413.[43] The effort proved unsuccessful. There could be no meeting of the minds. Instead, eight members of the theology faculty drew up a document on 6 February 1413, known as the *Concilium*, purporting to set forth the issues behind the controversy while recommending a remedy.[44] The prevailing difficulties were blamed on Hus who refused to accept what the rest of the Prague priests were represented as holding as immutable truth. Hus's ostensible intractability had influenced others and the practice of religion in Prague had been regrettably polarized. The premise was defective. The document went on to enumerate a traditional expression of faith in terms of the sacraments, the power of the keys, the authority of the Church, and the general practice of late medieval religion including comments on relics, indulgences, various rites and customs. The *Concilium* stressed papal primacy and authority and defined the church as an organism made up of the pope and cardinals. The Prague theologians declared that absolute submission to the pope and complete obedience in all matters of faith and conduct were essential. Clearly Hus could neither support this tenet nor pledge unequivocal submission. The document attempted to impugn Hus on the by-now old charge of Wyclifite heresy stating that any person holding to any article of Wyclif should be exiled from the country as a heretic. The battle lines were clearly drawn. Hus' reformist impulse confronted a traditional, pro-papacy, non-negotiable posture of ecclesiastical obedience. Moreover, the *Concilium* exhibited intolerance towards dissenters. At the time of this attack, Hus was defended by the rector of the university Šimon of Tišnov and Jakoubek of Stříbro.[45] In exile, Hus wrote against the document and it was likewise refuted by Hus' legal advisor Jan of Jesenice.[46] The matter could not be resolved and created even more friction. The increased hostility and an inability to reach a compromise forced the authors of the *Concilium* out of Prague and into exile with Hus. It appeared as though the authorities had managed to solve the dilemma by simply getting rid of all the participants. King Václav ordered the banishment of Stanislav of Znojmo, Peter of Znojmo, Štěpán Páleč and Jan Eliášův. He went on to deprive them of their ecclesiastical appointments and university positions. The unpopular theologians did not return to Prague so long as the king remained alive.[47]

Jan Hus never again set foot in Prague. His destiny lay elsewhere. After two years of exile, mainly in south Bohemia, Hus went to Constance, never to return. His life in Bohemia and his death in Germany contributed in significant ways to religious reform and social revolution. In his living but especially in his dying, Jan Hus became the most famous Czech. His influence permeated the Czech national consciousness and lingered long after his death.

2

PRAGUE

The immediate context for coming to terms with the life of Jan Hus is the city of Prague. A basic understanding of that world is fundamental.[1] The religious and political environment is essential for coming to terms with Hus as an historical figure and also with what he taught. At the end of the Middle Ages, Prague ranked among the top cities of Europe. It featured the oldest university in Central Europe and was the seat of an archbishopric; both foundations had been established in the 1340s. During the third quarter of the fourteenth century, Prague became a center of relics and religious practice. The extent of this visual religious culture suggests a conscious sacralizing of a late medieval city. The city likewise served as the residence of Charles IV, Holy Roman Emperor. There was every reason to regard Prague as a center of political and religious authority. The city's virtues had been praised since the tenth century and that reputation remained intact extending to the fifteenth century. The earliest written reference to Prague appeared in an Arabic text from 965 composed by the Spanish merchant-traveler Ibrāhīm ibn Yaʿqūb who personally visited the city.[2] An anonymous text at the dawn of the fifteenth century placed Prague among the most illustrious of European cities noted for its many astute university masters, beautiful women and beneficent citizens; features which ranked it with Paris and Rome in fame.[3] The accolades were sometimes exaggerated especially when the Czech capital achieved an on-par evaluation commensurate with the historic traditions and prestige of cities such as Rome and Constantinople.[4] In the course of the fourteenth century Prague city was made up of four separate civic entities each with independent municipal authority: Old Town, New Town founded in 1348, the Lesser Town or Small Side situated on the left bank of the Vltava River, and the rather small Hradčany perched on the hill above the Lesser Town. Vyšehrad constituted part of the New Town, becoming separate only much later.

Three important factors defined fourteenth-century Prague: political identity, social structure, and its religious world. There have been numerous studies of Prague. The unsurpassed magisterial study is over one hundred years old but is still useable.[5] The transformation of the city after the mid 1340s resulted in its elevation on every level so far that a social and cultural renaissance occurred. The context of this development was important for the life and career of Jan Hus.[6] Prague occupied a place within the configuration of the Holy Roman Empire of the Middle Ages yet is it often regarded as a separate historiographical consideration. This is all the more curious when it is remembered that Emperor Charles IV made Prague the political center of the empire between 1346 and 1378. It has been estimated that the population of Bohemia in the fourteenth century was about two million. Population figures for Prague are rather inexact, as calculations of this nature are for practically all medieval cities. The estimates range from 30,000 up to 100,000 but the figure most defensible for Prague city at the end of the fourteenth century is in the vicinity of 40,000. One hundred years later the population had diminished by 35 per cent to around 25,000.[7] Looking ahead to Hus, an argument cannot be sustained for regarding the fifteenth century as an independent historical era. The crises of the fourteenth century and the religious upheavals of the sixteenth century are evident in the fifteenth century and both must be related rather than regarded as separate considerations. In general, I have found little evidence to support Huizinga's thesis of a general decline over against the progress in Prague. In a word, fourteenth-century Prague flourished in many ways and the 'autumn of the Middle Ages' so evident elsewhere seems conspicuously absent in Prague.[8]

Caroline Prague constituted a magnificent edifice but its foundations crumbled within a generation of the emperor's death. The collapse cannot be ignored. Clearly, what Charles IV was able to hold together during his lifetime and imperial administration could not be sustained into the fifteenth century. While general social or cultural malaise may have been absent there existed a growing crisis of authority. The Hussite Revolution provided sufficient proof.

It is perilous to reads history backwards. The fourteenth century must be evaluated on its own merits, not through the prism of the calamitous events which followed. Politically, the Luxemburg dynasty shaped fourteenth-century Prague. John of Luxemburg ruled for more than three decades and while he seemed to be absent from his kingdom almost as often as he was there, Bohemia was relatively stable. Charles IV reigned from 1346 until 1378 and the administration of the 'glorious prince' was crucial.[9] It was a 'golden age' wherein the expansion and glorification of Prague reached an apex. It was Charles who founded the university and presided as emperor. He promulgated the 'Golden Bull' through the Reichstag at Nürnberg in 1356 which became the foundational legal code of the empire for centuries. His autobiography was one of the few medieval examples.[10] Charles managed to subdue all of his enemies without bloodshed and death intervened before serious turmoil engulfed Prague. The role played by Charles in the elevation of Prague to a place of European prominence cannot be overstated. Upon his death he was succeeded by Václav IV who ruled until 1419. Václav was shrewd but unstable. He seemed unable to avoid the conflicts which his father eluded. Not only did he become enmeshed in political intrigue he likewise exacerbated a deepening controversy with his archbishop, Jan of Jenštejn. In March 1393, Václav threatened the prelate. He called for his castles to be turned over to the crown and for the archbishop to stay out of Bohemia. The king warned Jan of Jenštejn that should he lift a hand against the royal house the king would end all disputes by simply drowning the archbishop. Contradicting his previous order, Václav summoned the church leader to Prague.[11] The debacle climaxed with violence, torture, murder and more difficulty. The archbishop stood down, tendering his resignation in 1396. A political conspiracy formed against the king. From May through August 1394, Jošt, the Margrave of Moravia, held the king captive. By 1399 Václav encountered renewed opposition from the Czech nobility. Ultimately in 1400, Václav was deprived of his imperial authority on the grounds that he was functionally *inutilis* - useless. The assumption was politically fatal. Václav never fully recovered politically. Twice incarcerated by his enemies, the king became marginalized and eventually presided over the disintegration of the Kingdom of Bohemia. There is some possibility he was mentally incompetent.[12] The last Luxemburg to sit on the Czech throne was Sigismund. His Czech career belongs rather to the Hussite period than to the fourteenth century even though he had been unofficially involved in Bohemian affairs more than twenty years before his coronation.[13]

Prague consisted of an ethnic diversity chiefly comprised of Czechs and Germans, though there was a substantial Jewish population.[14] There was a relatively peaceful coexistence among the various groups in Prague. This changed after the death of Charles IV. At Easter 1389 up to 3,000 Jews were killed following allegations that a eucharistic host and a Christian priest had been abused by Jews.[15] As much as half of the population of fourteenth-century Prague lived in or on the cusp of poverty.[16] The economic foundations of the city rested upon regular payments, known as rents, which existed mostly as a permanent feature established by virtue of their own terms in perpetuity. Rents were often subject to religious foundations and when these payments were not made promptly, penalties were applied.[17] Rents theoretically could be paid in several ways: cash, by goods, or with labor. An episcopal visitation conducted in the years between 1379 and 1382 revealed complaints concerning the numerous rents owed to parish churches.[18] Bitterness over this situation and the levying of fees for religious services led to violence in city streets as early as the 1330s. Lay people sometimes were caught up in the fractious public confrontations between Prague Mendicants and parish priests.[19] Royal taxation could also be applied at numerous times in any given year. Wages fluctuated and this was affected by considerable immigration into Bohemian towns, including Prague, in the fourteenth century. Prague escaped the ravages of the Black Death which decimated Europe between 1348 and 1350. The plague was not a significant factor until an outbreak in 1380 but even then the results were nowhere near as devastating as other areas of the continent suffered. It is possible to argue that the 1380 epidemic disrupted the relative tranquillity of relations between the various ethnic communities, may have contributed to increased social tension, and thereby may have became a factor in the upheaval which began to manifest itself in the years thereafter during the time of Jan Hus and the later Hussite Revolution.[20] Definite conclusions or corollaries on this point are suspect.

Under the initiative of Charles IV, Prague became a late medieval city of imposing religious importance. Turning to religion, it is possible to describe the Bohemian Church as a colossus with clay feet.[21] This was the world into which the young Jan

Hus stepped when he came to Prague as a student. Depending on the criteria of reckoning, there were between forty-four and fifty-one parishes within the Prague city deanery. By the end of the fourteenth century there were 151 religious houses in Bohemia and 2,084 parish churches in the Prague diocese. This computes into one priest for every 200 citizens, an extraordinarily high number. After Rome, Avignon and Florence, Prague was quite possibly the largest ecclesiastical center in medieval Europe.[22] An examination of the visitation protocol conducted by Archdeacon Pavel between 1379 and 1382 reveals, at best, an elementary acquaintance with doctrine. That did not seem to preclude rather high numbers of elevations into the church. Between 1395 and 1416 at least 20, 496 candidates were ordained in a variety of capacities.[23] By 1380 all of the major religious orders had a house in Prague. This translated into twenty-six houses in the city or in the immediate environs, including the Cistercian house at Zbraslav and the Benedictine foundation of Břevnov. However, the fourteenth century only saw irregular synodal meetings. Archbishop Jan of Jenštejn encouraged annual meetings but Václav Králík of Buřenice, former Dean of the Vyšehrad Chapter and Bishop of Olomouc, noted at the synod in Vyškov in 1413 that no meeting had been convened in the previous thirty years.[24] The papal schism from 1378 exacerbated the increasing radical nature of religious reform in Bohemia and may well have been a factor in the urgency which underlay the eucharistic program which also commenced in Prague just before the schism.

The problem of periodization in late medieval Bohemia presents a challenge. The term 'pre-Hussite' is too imprecise, extravagantly general, and ultimately misleading, to characterize the second half of the fourteenth century.[25] It cannot be gainsaid that both Wyclifite and Waldensian influence had penetrated Prague during the fourteenth century. Konrad Waldhauser, Jan Milíč of Kroměříž, Matěj of Janov, Vojtěch Raňkův, Tomáš Štítný, Jan Štěkna, Jan of Jenštejn and Štěpán of Kolín are among those often considered precursors to Jan Hus or labeled 'pre-Hussite' reformers in traditional historiography. The forerunner motif is understandable and even unavoidable when reading the fourteenth century from a fifteenth-century point of view. However, these men should not be regarded principally as tributaries leading to the Hussite river. The nomenclature of 'pre-Hussite' or 'precursors of Hus' is worn-out and no longer viable. It unnecessarily simplifies the complexities of the multiple religious and social worlds of medieval Prague in a misleading fashion. It is accurate and permissible to see some of these figures as reformers or religious personalities in their own right quite apart from Hus and the Hussite movement yet to come. Referring to himself as the 'simple preacher of the gospel of Christ' Konrad Waldhauser seemed to have been the first in Prague to distinguish himself in this manner. There were others.

Konrad came to Prague in 1363 having been attached to the Augustinian house in northern Austria at Waldhausen. Ostensibly he possessed a remarkable preaching facility. In addition to popular homilies he attacked the practice of simony, church wealth and never ceased to agitate against the Mendicant Orders. He went to Žatec in the spring of 1365 where he inveighed against the Mendicants but his efforts were not successful. His extant sermons reveal a concern for the eternal fate of human souls and he desired to acquit himself of responsibility by pointing the path to salvation. For all of this, Konrad was essentially an absentee priest from his parish of All Saints in Litoměřice. Later he abandoned that living altogether and was named to the Týn Church in Prague which, should be noted, at the time was under construction. His death notice identified him as a reformer of sterling importance whose preaching alone was sufficient to cause men and women to turn from their wickedness virtually on the spot. The accolade is astonishing. Konrad was lauded as a man of 'perfect love' who endured the vituperation of his enemies with enormous fortitude.[26] The epitaph is quite untrue as any careful examination of his life reveals. His bellicosity was first rate. However, the Austrian canon's career in Prague highlighted a climate of religious agitation and reform tendencies, both of which must be regarded as essential to the social fabric of the city.

From Konrad to Hus there was also considerable evidence of concern with morality which not only came to bear upon religion in fourteenth-century Prague but was a pillar upon which Jan Hus and the Hussites later established a platform featuring a wide variety of reformed religious practices in Prague and throughout Bohemia. A clear preoccupation with moral behavior appeared in Czech religious reform. One example will suffice. Between 1379 and 1382 Archdeacon Pavel of Janovic visited about 300 parishes throughout the archdiocese of Prague. The surviving visitation protocol contains a fairly significant dossier of irregularities among the priesthood. In opposition to prevailing canonical legislation, some of the priests married. Others devoted more time to entertainment than the cure of souls. Concubinage was rife. In the deanery of Podbrdy, the priest Václav drank to excess and made a nuisance of himself. Priests in Všeradice constituted a fair percentage of the known town drunks. Other clerics misbehaved and one presbyter operated a brothel which catered to other priests. Gambling, fighting, absenteeism, unlawful disposal of ecclesiastical property, violence among priests, are only some of the irregularities which Archdeacon Pavel underscored in his report.[27] The visitation protocol presented evidence that up to forty percent of Prague parishes had issues with prostitution.[28] The notorious brothel called 'Venice' had been a long-standing foundation.[29] It had been closed and shuttered before Archdeacon Pavel undertook his visitation. Another brothel in the Old Town also had an unsavory reputation. The priest of St. Valentine told the archdeacon that in and around this house of ill repute a vibrant sex trade persisted accompanied by considerable violence including homicide.[30] The problem was not local but extended into the New Town. In Krakow Street a considerable number of sex workers plied their trade.[31] The protocol likewise revealed a concentration of illicit sexual activity in the Lesser Town on the left bank of the Vltava.[32] Some priests admitted consorting with whores and engaging in sex.[33] The canon of St. Apollinaris in Prague, a man named Peter, kept a concubine known as Clara who was also rumored to be engaged in prostitution.[34] In the Old Town, Priest Prokop accused a number of his colleagues, whom he specifically identified to Archdeacon Pavel, of enjoying the company of loose women in a parish rectory.[35] In the New Town, the priest Ludwig Kojata was frequently caught red handed as it were with sexually available women. Archdeacon

Pavel's report revealed that on more than one occasion Priest Ludwig fled naked from the company of a whore as the authorities closed in on him.[36] Outside the city proper, the problem persisted. In Třebotov, a few miles south of Prague, the vicar Beneš, had a girlfriend named Dorothy who was reputed to be a hooker.[37] Archdeacon Pavel's protocol has been used to good effect to illuminate the regular and irregular lives of Prague priests.[38] With brothel closures in 1372, ostensibly the women working therein were expelled. Where did they go? No one knows. It may be presumed they sought employment in one of the other brothels of Prague or worked the streets. Brothels may have undermined morality but they also contributed to the Prague economy. Corruption was rife and endemic. Financial loans were sometimes made to brothel owners by civic officials in order to maintain a solvent business.[39] With knowledge of all this, Jan Hus later wrote about clerical depravity noting how unbelievable it was that many did not wish to be referred to simply as a priest but desired the appellations 'lord priest', 'lord canon' or 'lord prelate'.[40]

The perceived problem of prostitution was appropriated as a basis for social and religious reform. Jan Milíč of Kroměříž took his reform message literally to the streets and brothels of Prague. Emperor Charles IV allowed the aformentioned brothel called 'Venice' to be turned over to Milíč. It is rumored that he converted and looked after up to 200 former prostitutes.[41] The figure seems somewhat unlikely. It is possible that Milíč's biographer, Matěj of Janov, exaggerated the scope of success. Notwithstanding, it was clear that Milíč believed Antichrist had already entered the world. Enemies rose up against him in force. Milíč was accused of sodomy because he condemned fellow priests who consorted with loose women and who did not hesitate to go to extraordinary lengths to conceal their activities. Ostensibly one cleric installed a secret door in his residence in order to allow prostitutes to come and go undetected.[42] Incensed at his campaign, angry detractors brought a number of charges against Milíč in an effort to demonstrate just how subversive and unsavory a character he was. Among these charges were accusations that all rents received by priests were illegal and ought to be regarded as usury; that the eucharist should be received by the faithful laity on a daily basis or at the very least twice weekly, and that priests should not on any account hold private property.[43] Whatever impact Milíč made upon the prostitution industry in Prague did not eliminate the problem. Five years after Milíč died, Archdeacon Pavel commenced his visitation. While Milíč cannot be extracted from his historical context without serious damage, it is possible to agree with the observation that he exerted a substantial indirect influence on Hus.[44] Milíč's community took the name 'Jerusalem' and indeed Prague later was compared to the city of Jerusalem. Popular songs and sermons well into the 1420s continued to use this metaphorical equation. The immorality of the earthly Prague stood in stark contrast to the ethical moorings of the kingdom of God which Konrad and Milíč preached. The theme of moral reform and religious renewal began to sound a consistent note as the fourteenth century wore on. In time, Jan Hus joined the chorus finding the basis for many of his central ideas in these native Czech sources.[45]

The relative peace which had been established and preserved in Prague under Charles IV began to unravel in the latter years of the emperor's life. Milíč found himself at the short end of heresy suspicions. The 'Jerusalem' community was closed and he went off to Avignon to defend himself but died before his process concluded. Matěj of Janov drew on the work of Milíč and made a distinction between the visible church of Caroline Prague and the true invisible community of the faithful. Matěj argued the two had no necessary correlation going so far as to declare the visible church, so prominent in Prague, might have no part in the mystical body of Christ.[46] The unity of Caroline Prague came to an abrupt division in 1389 when Matěj was forced by a Prague synod to recant his views and stand down. Matěj admitted imprudence in his sermons and withdrew some of his more strident conclusions.[47] The future of religion in Prague did not bode well thereafter. Despite the efforts of the reformers, moral issues persisted, prostitution did not dissipate, and even religious initiatives begat ill will. The 1393 jubilee, announced by Pope Boniface IX, proclaimed widely and enthusiastically was reported in some sectors as taking plenty of money from the poor but failing to produce any measurable holiness or piety in the people.[48] Jan Hus wrote of his own witness to this perspective. Moreover, the gilded prosperity and piety which seemed to have characterized the golden age of Caroline Prague was harder to detect by the end of the century. Indulgences played a significant role in religious life in Prague by 1400 and despite numerous efforts to curb abuses, simony and simoniacal practices persisted. Some sources reported the greed of the priests reached extortionist proportions.[49] The matter was neither a Hussite one nor a 'pre-Hussite' problem. There were quite important and independent figures, ideas and movements in fourteenth-century Prague, each of them with specific religious motivation, reform agendas, and approaches to the practice of the faith. Perhaps the idea of charismatic spirituality might be an appropriate designation for the various impulses of religious reform between Konrad Waldhauser and Jan Hus.[50]

The civic union achieved by Charles IV in the fourteenth century was soon disrupted. Gates and walls and even a moat signified divisions between the Old and New Towns which flared into open conflict and violence in the generation after Charles died. The Old Town and Lesser Town had a diminishing but still majority German population while the New Town was largely Czech.[51] The general direction which post-Caroline Prague took in terms of politics, ideas, and social structure did not succeed. The reasons are legion.[52] Early fifteenth-century sources contrasted the golden Prague of 1378 and the honor afforded Charles with the dishonor which befell his sons. Václav did not get a proper funeral befitting a king and was later disinterred and his corpse abused. Sigismund was barred from his lawful right to the throne and kept out of Prague for nearly two decades by the inheritors and appropriators of religious and social reform.[53] By 1419 much had changed for Prague. Preaching in that year the university master Šimon of Tišnov drew attention to the golden age of Caroline Prague asserting that the city now had come to a quite different end.[54] How came this to pass? According to an anonymous Latin poem the downfall of Prague can be linked to the abrupt rise and spread of heresy which seemed to the poet to have poured unchecked into the land once Charles died.[55] The explanation was both superficial and simplistic. Yet a measure of truth resided in the throwaway remark. Religious upheaval did split Prague and brought Bohemia to civil war and exposed the country to the threat of crusade by foreign powers. Caroline Prague was a temporary success. Beneath the calm surface of stability and continuity an intense pressure had begun to build. This pressure can be seen in the charismatic spirituality which characterized the lives and work of men like Konrad Waldhauser, Milíč and Matěj of Janov. The aftermath of the life of Charles and the growing time of troubles associated with the beleaguered reign of Václav IV demanded political, social and religious resolution. After the relative tranquility which characterized the burgeoning 'golden age' of Caroline Prague, the atmosphere noticeably darkened and became charged with unavoidable approaching storms. Prague had to have its Hus.[56]

3

THEOLOGY

Jan Hus belongs to the religious history of medieval Europe. His life cannot be understood apart from that world. Aspects of popular religious practice provide a point of entry. Relics and pilgrimage remained significant features of religious life at the end of the Middle Ages. These phenomena are an opportunity for raising questions of authority and theology. In August 1383 the northern German village of Wilsnack in the archdiocese of Magdeburg was torched. The parish church burned down. Several days later the local priest, Johannes Kabuz, had a dream revealing a miraculously preserved eucharistic host amid the ruins of the stone altar. Going to the site Priest Kabuz discovered three hosts, undamaged either by fire or rain, perfectly preserved, each marked with a single drop of blood. Almost immediately miracles began. Knights making vows to the holy blood were successful in duels. A robber named Peter locked up in prison for his crimes committed his fortune to the Wilsnack miracle. His chains miraculously fell from his limbs and he escaped captivity. Healings were reported, the dead came to life, candles mysteriously were lit or could not be extinguished, one of the hosts began bleeding. Soon pilgrims flocked to Wilsnack.[1] The events were not without detractors and Zbyněk, archbishop of Prague, ordered an investigation. He appointed a three member commission consisting of Stanislav of Znojmo, an unnamed university master, and Jan Hus. Similar occurrences had been reported in Bohemia – at Kutná Hora, Chrudim and Litomyšl – and elsewhere in Europe. The Prague commission concluded the miracles at Wilsnack were fraudulent. At a synod on 15 June 1405 Zbyněk issued a ban on pilgrimages from Bohemia and required Czech priests to preach against Wilsnack once a month.[2] Hus went further. His work on the Wilsnack commission completed, he spoke out against the alleged miraculous blood. With reference to the Litomyšl miracle, Hus claimed it was simple fraud perpetrated by dishonest priests.[3] Just prior to this, he prepared a treatise dealing specifically with the Wilsnack deception.[4] From a strictly theological perspective, Hus argued that when the resurrected Christ ascended to heaven he glorified his blood so that none remained literally on earth. Only sacramental blood existed. It was implausible for the faithful to truly venerate the literal blood of Christ on earth even if it was declared locally or visibly apparent. Relics such as breast milk from the Virgin

Mary shown in Prague were indisputably false. The crucial issue was faith, not tangible evidence. Hus asserted honest Christians should not attempt to locate proof for their faith but instead be contented with the witness of faith in scripture. Those requiring miracles were individuals of little faith.[5] Moreover, alleged miracles from the holy blood were proven decisively under oath not to have occurred. Some of the claims were extravagant. A citizen of Prague named Petr of Čechy had a withered hand. He went to Wilsnack hoping to be cured. He took a duplicate silver hand along which he placed on the altar. There was no miracle. This did not deter the priest who later, holding up the silver hand, announced to the congregation that the healing did occur on account of the miraculous blood! Raising his clearly withered arm, Petr of Čechy rebuffed the claim: 'priest, you are a liar! Look, my hand is still withered just as it was before'.[6] According to Hus, two women whose eyesight had been restored swore before a notary they had never been blind in the first place. He waxed polemical denouncing the priestly practitioners of the Wilsnack miracles as worshipers of the Devil who manufacture 'bleeding hosts' out of greed. Hus alleged that corrupt priests paid people to go round claiming they had been to Wilsnack and miraculously delivered from various afflictions.[7] Following Zbyněk's injunction, Hus urged his fellow priests to teach their hearers not to seek after alleged miracles.[8] He called into question the focus of devotion at Wilsnack declaring that in Prague 'we adore the body and blood of Christ which exists at the right hand of God and is present in the blessed sacrament'. Hus concluded that the reported blood at Wilsnack did not effect miracles.[9] There is nothing theologically suspect in Hus' position, but it does underscore independence of thought and regard for truth.

Nature of theology

The point of departure for an examination of Hus' theology is his devotion to truth. The idea is slippery. Truth claims within religious traditions, Christianity included, are subjective, determined by temporal authorities, and culturally mediated. The task of medieval Christian theology was pursuit of truth. By the late Middle Ages there were skeptics. 'As the shameful acts of humans increase so does the hatred of truth and the kingdom is given over to flattery and falsehood'.[10] Hus does not seem party to that trend. For him 'God's truth' was the centering ideal, although nowhere in his work does Hus develop a theoretical argument or definition of truth.[11] It seemed infinitely better to die for truth and the law of Christ than to live in the rewards of flattery and falsehood.[12]

> Therefore faithful Christian, seek the truth, listen to the truth, learn the truth, love the truth, speak the truth, adhere to truth and defend truth to the death. For truth will set you free from sin, the Devil and the destruction of the soul, and ultimately from eternal death which is eternal separation from God's grace and the joy of salvation.[13]

His life and career indicates that for Hus truth consisted of a moral and ethical position based upon his own belief system.

Hus gave slight attention to particular medieval theological speculations. He neither hypothesized on how many angels could perch on the head of a needle nor did he essay an opinion on whether the heavens were shaped like a sphere or a barrel and he seemed not to wonder what humanity might have been like had Adam not sinned. Such theological trivia were useless and vain. Hus wondered about the advantage of such debates. Theological dialogue must have regard for three concerns: the glory of God, the elimination of fraud and intellectual arrogance, and the advancement of truth. Anything else was quite unworthy.[14] Accordingly, Hus regarded the minutiae of scholastic theology as 'useless questions'.[15] Theology teaches one to respect and honor God's majesty, love and goodness, to develop piety, explore faith, obey the requirements of love and ultimately to come to a knowledge of the truth.[16] Hus took care to distinguish truth in scripture, truth arrived at through deductive reasoning, and truth perceived by the senses and experience.[17] Hus began his lectures on the Sentences of Peter Lombard in the autumn of 1407. The scholastic Hus can be seen in this work and especially in the philosophical commentaries on various topics.[18] This work is a major source for understanding the theological Hus. The main idea in his commentary seems to be that theology (which Hus often calls 'sacra scriptura') is wisdom originating in God which can penetrate the human heart. This stream of divine wisdom seems to have two loci in Hus, namely the law of Christ and the church. The former is rooted in scripture while the latter is comprised of the totality of the elect. Both ideas shall be taken up below.

It is difficult to put Hus into a theological category. He is both traditional and innovative. The former proclivity limited his reforming initiative while the latter brought him to censure and condemnation. In his *De Trinitate* Hus established his approach to theology. 'From the very beginning of my studies I made it a rule that whenever I encounter a sounder opinion to happily and humbly surrender the one previously embraced. For I am quite certain, just as Themistius says, that what we know is considerably less than what we do not know.'[19]

From where did Hus derive his sense of religious authority which undergirded his theology? Certainly Hus' moderate position on medieval realism forms a bedrock to his theological ideas. The premises underlying Hus' realism are five in number.[20] Mediation of divine authority is subject to the faith and character of the one exercising authority, to the extent that either the authority of Christ or human authority prevails. Ecclesiastical authority does not exist isolated from scripture, tradition and conscience but all exist in a symbiotic relationship. Divine communication utilizes direct and indirect channels. Direct appeal to divine authority is superior to mediation. Transcendent authority can never be completely identified with human understanding. These positions thrust Hus into conflict with the conciliar fathers at Constance. There is an irony, indeed puzzling contradiction, in Hus' philosophy. Realism held that ideas such as a stone had objective existence and reality, existing outside human conception and expression. Nominalism asserted that ideas such as a stone or tree had no reality corresponding to them and no existence apart from concepts or words. Applied to theology, realism regarded the absolute truth of church doctrines as binding and not open for question. '*Roma locuta, causa finita est*': Rome has spoken, the case is closed.[21] Nominalism subjected dogma to critical investigation and defended the right of inquiry. In theory, Hus was definitely a realist but in practice he was a nominalist. Thus he could argue that everything existing in the material world had an 'ideal' existence in the mind of God, everything good which humans strove for was a result of the goodness of God.[22] Such expressions were unmistakable positions taken in medieval realist philosophy but Hus clearly had no compunction about assailing church doctrine and subverting its authority. In his commentary on the Sentences of Peter Lombard, Hus assumed a consistent realist perspective. He relied to large measure on Augustine and Thomas Aquinas. Anselm was quoted quite often. Predictably, Ockham was not favored and Duns Scotus was only cited three times. In fact, while explicating a position on the transmission of original sin, Hus explicitly said Scotus was of no particular advantage.[23]

A comprehensive survey of the extant writings of Jan Hus reveals the nature of his indebtedness to particular streams of thought in the history of Christianity. It is easy to give too much credit to John Wyclif in this regard though the connections between Wyclif's theology and the realist philosophical climate resident in some medieval intellectual traditions cannot be denied. Those connections were not lost on Hus who repudiated the new learning associated with nominalism which in his day was gaining ground in many theological faculties in Europe.[24] Hus clung to a realist conviction rooted deeply in Augustinian thought and frequently drew upon the bishop of Hippo. In his *De ecclesia*, Hus quoted Augustine at least 100 times though the presumption of Augustinian dependence is not always certain and at times quite wrong.[25] The Platonic world view of Augustine is apparent in Hus but it is specious to imagine Hus read Plato or the Platonists. Notional Augustinian constructs can be found throughout Hus.[26] There is no gainsaying that Hus regarded himself as a faithful disciple of Augustine and conceived that the African father would in no sense have rejected him. His ultimate fate at the stake was in part because Hus believed that in following the authentic teachings of one of the greatest theologians in the western church he was serving the catholic faith. It is possible to measure the extent to which Hus relied upon Augustine for ideas such as the church, predestination and clerical wickedness. It is reasonable to conclude that in his final rejection of the proposed recantation formula offered at Constance, Hus feared that accepting that option would imply going against Augustine.[27] Hus regarded Augustine as the greatest of theologians, an excellent interpreter of Scripture, and the most important of the doctors. But to what extent did Hus have access to the works of Augustine? It seems likely he accessed much of what he knew of Augustine from quotations in the Sentences of Peter Lombard. Paul de Vooght has shown that Hus almost certainly did not have direct access to Augustine's original work.[28] Derivative scholarship in the Middle Ages, however, was not unusual.

His enemies accused Hus of adopting a *sola scriptura* position but the charge is easily refuted. Hus stood unambiguously within the *regula fidei* of the historic church.

Certainly, as we shall examine below, Hus adhered to a principle of biblical authority but never to the exclusion of tradition. He acknowledged the summary of Christian faith located in the Apostles', Nicene and Athanasian Creeds. There is nothing in his work to suggest he ignored the rulings and canons of the ecumenical councils of Nicaea, Constantinople, Ephesus and Chalcedon. Hus likewise cited frequently from numerous patristic authorities namely Augustine, Jerome, Origen, Cyprian, John Chrysostom, Ambrose, Athanasius, the Cappadocians – Basil of Caesarea, Gregory of Nyssa, and Gregory of Nazianzus – and of medieval authorities he quoted Gregory the Great, John of Damascus, Bede, Anselm, Bernard of Clairvaux, Bonaventura, Hugh of St. Victor, Thomas Aquinas, canon law, among others. All of this led some scholars to recognize that Hus' matrix of authority was scripture, apostolic tradition, the historic creeds, the writings of the doctors, together with canon law and the councils.[29] John Wyclif was frequently cited though this fact must be taken up separately below. It will suffice to say that claims that Hus read only Wyclif, apart from scripture and a few fathers, cannot be sustained.[30] In his important commentary on the Sentences of Peter Lombard, Hus often borrowed from Bonaventura and Aquinas, but relied to large measure on Augustine and Wyclif's *Trialogus*. There is likewise evidence of Anselm, Scotus, Ockham and the fourteenth-century Archbishop of Canterbury, Thomas Bradwardine. A careful analysis of Hus reveals that much of his extra-biblical material and ideas come from Augustine, Hilary, Bede and other authorities with whom Hus was familiar. Hus was never reluctant to confirm his sources and set forth his basis of authority. He respected Lombard and at the conclusion of his commentary on the Sentences honored him as a man worthy of remembrance who had been approved by God to benefit the church.[31] From his own writings on the matter of authority, we learn that Hus held to the supremacy of the holy doctors of the Christian faith. He deferred his own intellect to the headship of Christ. He denied being influenced by heretics, claiming instead the arguments of the holy apostles and revered theologians of the faith. He rejected the tenets of the 'Waldensian heresy' and held to the truth of Christ. Hus dismissed the teachings of the 'Armenian sect' in preference to the doctrines of the apostles.[32] Of course few heretics admitted to heretical tendencies and citing traditional sources was no guarantee of orthodox theology. The matter of Hus' alleged heresy will be examined below. Despite the condemnation of Wyclif, Hus openly confessed to being drawn to the Oxford don because he perceived in Wyclif a genuine effort to convert souls to the law of Christ, a fidelity to that principle and a love for Christ.[33] Four major influences emerge from an examination of Hus' writings and career: scripture, Augustine, the native Czech reform tradition, and John Wyclif. The evidentiary claim for three of these are easily extrapolated from the Hus corpus. The fourth is more subtle.

In excavating Hus' approach to theology and his understanding of religion and spirituality, the value of his commentary on the Sentences of Peter Lombard cannot be overemphasized. Even Hus' most ardent modern critic had to admit that any consideration of Hus' commentary would offset opinions of his dependance on others or lack of original thought and that in many respects the value of Hus' work would have to be esteemed considerably higher.[34] It has been noted that Hus' work on the nature of theology, evidenced in his commentary, is not traditional.[35] The claim is ambitious but it can be admitted that within a relatively standard treatment of the preeminent medieval theological text there is departure from routine and a demonstration of originality. Indeed, this major work reveals wide reading and independence of thought, pointed out a century ago by Flajšhans and others.[36] Hus sometimes used the term *sacra scriptura*, a generic term for theology popular in the late twelfth and early thirteenth centuries. He regarded theology as a science. Arguing in his commentary on the Sentences, Hus postulated this was so because its study led the student to truth and every discipline which concludes in an unassailable confrontation with truth is a science. According to Hus, the major premise can be demonstrated by the fact that any assent to a truth evinced by reason or supernatural revelation is a science. The minor premise consists in the fact that theology is derived from evident principles. Therefore, the discipline of theology, in similar fashion to every other discipline of study, exists to reveal the essential basis of an assumption since scientific inquiry exists for the purpose of gaining knowledge.[37] Thus, theology is not void of reason and first principles.

The task of theology must distinguish very clearly between the truth conveyed and the means by which that truth is communicated. Hus postulated three kinds of faith. These were belief itself, the faith which is believed, and the faith by which one believes.[38] For Hus, as pastor, priest and prophet in late medieval Prague, theology was a means but not an end. The words of religion functioned as a conveyance to the essential Word of God. Religious practices, though important, likewise pointed to a transcendent spirituality beyond religion. Faith was not confined to intellectual concerns or ecclesiastical doctrines but motivated application and social implication. In these convictions, Hus the priest became a prophet and the pastor functioned likewise as a reformer. In terms of *sacra scriptura* Hus set forth three understandings of theology. First, it was the revelation of Christ. Second, it encompassed the knowledge of Christ and the teachings about Christ as accepted by Christians. Third, it constituted the written, spoken and visual signs which functioned as indicators pointing beyond themselves to revealed Truth.[39] Scripture, preaching, and iconography were instruments in the service of divine revelation. Essential for an understanding of Hus' approach to theology is the notion in his thinking that ultimately truth did not exist in the instrument itself but rather beyond the indicator in a realm accessed by faith.

Religious authority for Hus resided in a complex structure. It is specious to reduce Hus either to a blind adherent of *sola scriptura* or a wide-eyed radical intent upon a reform program of his own devising. The fathers at Constance required strict obedience to the authority of the conciliar gathering. Hus was prepared to accept that emphasis only if it remained consistent with scripture, tradition and conscience. All of these factors were operative and necessary. None could be excluded, and none could function with validity in isolation. It is incontrovertible that Hus rejected the idea of absolute obedience to ecclesiastical authority. One ought to adhere to the law of Christ even if that meant actively disobeying one's superior.[40] Hus' philosophical commitments allowed for a combining of both 'transcendent and immanent authorities'.[41] That dynamic posture must be kept in mind in order to properly understand Jan Hus and his career. The exercise and understanding of theology in Hus allows for access to the divine mysteries to all those who are humble, open, maintain an attitude of godliness, and are prepared to submit to those truths. That posture threatened to subvert the method and exclusivity of prevailing medieval scholasticism. Practitioners of the scholastic method appeared to function as though theology – *sacra scriptura* – having been disclosed to humankind by God was now the provenance of the theologians who could deal with it according to intellect and reason irrespective of the heart of the theologian. Hus refused to acquiesce and asserted both in word and deed that a transformed heart, living a life of active obedience, *meritum*, could receive the riches of the divine inheritance ahead of the doctors of the church.[42] The position struck theological Europe as preposterous.

In terms of religious authority, scripture, tradition and conscience in the thought of Jan Hus sought one common denominator and that was the law of Christ. Writing in 1414 shortly before his trial Hus addressed the question of this principle defining it succinctly and generally as the gospel articulated and modeled by Christ and the apostles and arguing that all law had to be subservient to this law.[43] Apostolic traditions advanced nothing beyond what Christ taught or authorized.[44] Hus declared the law of Christ sufficient as the guiding motif for the church. Nothing could be added or subtracted to that rule. Moreover, Hus adamantly argued he would sooner be killed than defend an error contrary to the truth of the law of Christ. Indeed, 'I have defended, do defend, and resolutely intend to continue defending' the truth of Christ's law. That guiding principle, imbedded in law, enables one to behave properly.[45] Hus' clear intent aimed at the subordination of all human authority, including papal and conciliar, to the law of Christ. It was an exceptionally noble but dangerous posture in the conflict-riven world of late medieval Europe.

In his important 1411 *Quodlibet* address in the university at Prague, Hus defended the proposition that God who was absolutely perfect created a world in the most admirable and positive manner.[46] His academic treatment of the question amounted to a quite conservative theological approach defending traditional ideas in very traditional ways. To a certain extent this is an accurate characterization of Hus as a late medieval Catholic reformer. Coupled with the activities of Jakoubek of Stříbro, and the disciples of Hus, together with their reforming antecedents, the Hussite era represents one of the more interesting chapters in the history of the western church. Because the theology of Jan Hus is important for the history of Christian doctrine, as well as for understanding his life, we now turn our attention to some of his specific teachings.

Church

When he appeared before the Council of Constance late in life, Hus' concept of the church came under sharp assault. Dietrich of Niem already had melodramatically declared that Hus' views on the church posed as great a threat to papal power as did the Muslim Qu'ran to Christianity.[47] Of the final thirty charges lodged against Hus, two-thirds of them were related directly to his concept of the church. This was no misapprehension on the part of the conciliar fathers for indeed Hus' ecclesiology went to the core of the medieval doctrine of the church. His theology logically led to revolution. The potentially catastrophic consequences were noted by Jean Gerson and others. Shortly before his journey to Constance, Hus had written a big book on the subject which summed up his mature thinking crystallizing his views on the matter. *De ecclesia*, completed in 1413, is perhaps the best of all Hus' works which passionately and eloquently laid out his reforming ideas arguing for the cessation of simony and a return to apostolic purity. Still, it is fair to conclude that Hus' doctrine of the church even in its most strident call for reform remains an internal criticism. Hus does not reject the sacramental function of the church or the place of the priesthood and certainly does not advocate the dissolution of ecclesiastical hierarchy. Critiquing abuses did not prompt Hus to abandon the institution. It can be argued that Hus' ecclesiology is mainly spiritual and his reforms within the church limited because he failed to develop his theology of the church sufficiently. The criticism is not without merit. However, Hus died in his early 40s and it is quite unfair to judge such a short life too harshly.

The medieval doctrine of the church had already attained robust articulation by the time of Hus. His contemporary Štěpán Páleč understood the communities of the predestinate, militant and Roman churches as comprising the spiritual church. These were subsumed within the idea of the one holy church and each component was also holy. Páleč did not distinguish to any degree the differences within these ecclesial communities.[48] By contrast Hus formulated a doctrine of the church which articulated the militant, dormient, and predestined communities. Kybal has aptly illustrated this concept as three concentric circles with the communion of the predestined at the center.[49] Medieval ecclesiology conceived of the church as a visible entity including all of the faithful confirmed by the sacrament of baptism. This earthly kingdom was ruled by the pope – as the vicar of Christ – and the priestly hierarchy. The government of this kingdom was a spiritual aristocracy claiming power directly from God. Popes and higher churchmen were rightly regarded as the administrators of God and not the representatives of the Christian community. The distinction is critical. The presence and function of the bishop as a defining characteristic of the church is as old as second-century Ignatius of Antioch. By the later Middle Ages it had become the defining attribute. By this time Boniface VIII could declare in his 1302 bull *Unam Sanctam* that obedience to the Roman bishop was essential for salvation. Hus demurred on this point. The church need not be defined by the pontiff but rather understood as the totality of the elect, past, present and future. 'The church is the body of the elect and the faithful who have been justified'.[50] Hus used the same language in preaching.[51] One can be connected to the church *aliud est de ecclesia* but not necessarily of the church *aliud in ecclesia*.[52] That distinction likewise featured prominently in Hus. Therefore it is impossible to know who is truly of the elect apart from revelation. Hus explained the church was like a field in which both wheat and weeds grew together. The elect and the reprobate coexist. There is good and evil. But only the wheat, the elect and the good, may be said to belong to the church. Since the true nature of the righteous and the wicked cannot be absolute, one ought to submit to the dictates of the clergy unless those directives are contrary to the law of Christ. For it is possible that the church as an visible entity may be in fact a spiritual whore.[53] The mixed membership within the church included the reprobates whom Hus denounced as '*ecclesia malignantium*'.[54] That malignant church was not of the elect. Chiefly there was nothing too alarming about this but Hus went farther and willingly trespassed upon the prerogatives of the institutional body. Hus did not discourage the laity from seizing the revenue of wicked clerics. He ignored the imposition of interdict and encouraged the kings of Bohemia and Poland to actively put an end to the practice of simony with the aid of secular force if necessary. By implication this meant that lay men and women had the right and the duty to reform ecclesiastical practices. Fifteenth-century theologians were suitably distressed and condemned Hus' initiative as an insufferable 'pernicious error' which incited 'scandal' and 'sacrilege' and impinged upon the liberty and rights of the church.[55] Hus remained unmoved and related a story wherein a cook withstood a bishop when the latter reproved him for reading scripture in the vernacular. The cook infuriated the bishop by quoting scripture declaring no bishop was greater than Christ and since the cook did not regard himself as less than the Devil there was justification for speaking. After all, Christ listened to Satan during the temptation, therefore a bishop being unequal to Christ should not be annoyed at the words of a layman.[56] So far as Hus was concerned, no superior should be above correction.[57] Additionally, Hus left little room for speculation on the matter that secular rulers had authority over all property in his or her realm including church land.[58] Prelates and princes endowed with the force of secular and spiritual power possessed the authority and had the obligation to prevent the growth and spread of evil and to protect the good.[59]

Inasmuch as the constituency of the true church cannot be determined absolutely, it is sometimes permissible to disobey established authority. The church can only be relied upon to the extent that it does not violate scripture, tradition and conscience. Up to that point the church is important. In a sermon for Trinity Sunday Hus elaborated on the theme that the faithful are nurtured in the spiritual womb of the church. Even if one of the faithful should later stray and become estranged from God and holy mother church, repentance allows the wayward to return to the womb of the church and be reborn.[60] In Hus' theology the church is a 'dear mother' and it is certain that Hus endorsed Cyprian's adage 'one cannot have God for one's father if one does not have the church as one's mother'.[61] Moreover, Hus' ecclesiological premise that the church is composed only of the predestined, which he enumerated in some detail in his *De ecclesia*, can be found without argument in the Augustinian corpus.[62] In June 1410 Hus preached on Matthew 16:16 enunciating the perspective of the church as the totality of the elect and further that the rock upon which the church found anchor was not Peter but Christ.[63] It is demonstrable that Hus drew upon Bernard of Clairvaux and Robert Grosseteste for his critique of the church.[64] It is even more apparent that Hus based his ecclesiology upon Augustinian concepts. A careful comparison of the church in Hus and Augustine reveal significant similarities and divergences. Hus did utilize the language and principles of Augustinian theology in framing his own idea of the church. But the duplication of language and concepts alone do not necessarily produce identical doctrines. It may be argued that Hus began in Augustine but deviated from his master in developing his rather negative views of the militant church on earth. It is a matter of scholarly debate to what extent Hus devalued the church militant in preference for the church of the elect. The emphasis of the latter at the expense of the former resulted in a serious questioning of the value and authority of the papacy and overall ecclesiastical hierarchy. Without doubt, Augustine recognized shortcomings in the fourth and fifth-century north African church as did Hus in the fifteenth-century Czech church. Yet Augustine seems not to have allowed for the same latitude of obedience as did Hus. The invisible pure church was elevated by Augustine as the ideal for the visible impure church to emulate while Hus seems to have declared the perfect church was the only true body of believers existing in the here and now and not confined to an eschatological period in a future 'not yet'. The subversive seeds latent in his ideas were not lost on those examining his doctrines at the end of the Middle Ages. Given the rise of eschatological themes in Bohemia after 1410, there is every reason to give close attention to the possibility that the key to understanding Hus' doctrine of the church may be found within a theoretical eschatology.[65]

Hus' doctrine of the church could not avoid dealing with the papacy and here Hus found himself in deep troubled waters. Against the stream of medieval thought Hus argued that Christ alone was the absolute head of the church. The pope could not be preeminent.[66] 'What is a pope? A man! The son of a man, clay from clay, a sinner who is likely also to sin. Two days prior he was just the son of a poor peasant now he is made pope. Is he no longer in need of confession, penance and contrition? Or has he become as an angel and incapable of sin? The pope is human and can sin just as a man may err'.[67] Jan Hus did not write those words but he might well have. The words come from his older contemporary Dietrich of Niem. Dietrich attended the Council of Constance throwing his weight behind the conciliar efforts aimed at ending the protracted papal schism. This ecclesiastical crisis only confounded the doctrine of the church as maintained by theologians in the Middle Ages. Hus described the schism as a contest in which three beasts fought each other in arrogance and greed for a position of dignity.[68] In such situation the church had no necessary dependence on the papacy. The church exists wherever believers are assembled anywhere on earth. Whether there be one pope or several popes has no bearing upon the true church. The church is one in Christ, one in love, hope and faith.[69] It is not essential that a pope govern the church.[70] Nevertheless, in his *De indulgentiis* Hus stressed the need for a 'just pope' and it is quite wrong to conclude that Hus considered a reformed church without a pope.[71]

In 1412 Hus wrote a treatise in which he attacked the sale and underlying doctrines concerning indulgences.[72] In that work Hus stated unambiguously that the pope could err, that papal power was limited. When a pope erred, as Hus insisted with respect to the 1411 crusade bull of John XXIII, resistance was required. Hus considered any doctrine of papal infallibility to be nonsense. Scripture did not provide justification for the use of the sword as Pope John XXIII mandated. Hus submitted the 1411 bull constituted little more than a crude attempt to legalize violence and murder for political gain. That a pope ratified such measure made it not one wit more righteous or godly. Hus denounced the theologians who refused to stand against the bull, accusing them of fear or opportunism. Hus declared such men were betrayers of the truth. The offer of the forgiveness of sins, implicit in any indulgence document, was improper because no human could forgive sins and to assume that payment could effect pardon was unconscionable. If forgiveness was within the scope and power of a man, Hus wondered why the pope did not forgive the sins of all the world instead of only those who purchased the certificate. Bulls published by popes need only be obeyed if they were consistent with scripture and conscience. 'No one is required to believe anything which he or she is not moved by God to believe and God does not cause an individual to believe something which is untrue'.[73] Clearly the 1411 crusade bull fell outside these criteria for it did not even qualify as a 'just war'.[74] More damning was Hus' comment in his academic treatment of the Sentences where he stated the pope may even err in matters of faith and discipline.[75] To safeguard against this contingency Hus argued the Holy Spirit, not the pope, was the teacher of the church and a most secure refuge.[76] Papal rulings need only be observed when they conformed to the law of Christ. To rebel against an erring pope was to obey Christ.[77] The theme became redundant in his writings but this only underscored the centrality of the conviction. Especially dangerous and unacceptable to Hus were papal claims that whatever was absolved on earth was likewise absolved in heaven.[78] Hus asserted he dared to maintain that popes could err and if all cardinals and popes were to be destroyed, the true church would remain.[79] Since the true church, but not necessarily the Roman Church, is founded upon the rock, which is Christ, the true church cannot be overthrown.[80] Poison entered the system of the church in the days of Constantine and the effects of that poisoning continued through the entire body. 'Today poison is poured into the church'. Little wonder calls were escalating for reform for the whole church *in capite et in membris*: in head and in members. It stood to reason that no reprobate pontiff ought rightly to be called a holy father.[81] Hus believed as did all others in his day that the 'donation of Constantine' literally occurred in the fourth century. Wickedness having settled into certain occupants of the See of Peter caused that venerable office to be contaminated by Antichrist, the abominations of the apocalyptic beast, and vain glorying.[82] In the case of John XXIII, the Council of Constance had been convened by John who was acknowledged by the conciliar fathers as the Lord Pope but later deposed as a 'heretic, simoniac, perjurer, murderer and sodomite'.[83] Hus asserted that many popes had been heretical. Boniface VIII, Clement VII, Boniface IX and John XXIII clearly were deviant according to Hus and he knew very well that the Council of Pisa had declared heretical both Gregory XII and Benedict XIII.[84] Hus understood immorality as disqualification from the legitimate exercise of the priestly office.[85]

John Wyclif dismissed the papacy as Antichrist and Hus' colleague Jakoubek of Stříbro perceived the incarnation of Antichrist as manifested in the popes. Hus remained unpersuaded and did not subscribe to this idea. However, he did affirm that if a pope lived contrary to the law of Christ in terms of pride, greed, personal vengeance, or sensuality, then such an individual had gained that ecclesiastical position in a manner other than through Christ and was therefore not of Christ but of Antichrist.[86] For Hus, Antichrist is one who acted contrary to Christ. The distinction was lost on his detractors. According to Hus, two sets of clerics existed within the church, those of Christ and those of Antichrist. The former adhered to Christ and to the law of Christ while the latter held to human law. Those of Christ exemplified holiness, piety, humility and sanctity while those of Antichrist were cruel, vindictive, proud and wicked.[87] Either way, the verdicts of Jakoubek and Hus on the papacy denied that popes were infallible. In arguing that obedience to a pope was not related to salvation, Hus stepped outside the boundaries of medieval orthodoxy into the realm of heresy. Paul De Vooght is right about this and Matthew Spinka wrong.[88] The former's interpretation is technically correct though rigidly applied while the latter is unable to appreciate fully the complexity of heresy in the later Middle Ages and ends up employing Protestant methodology to absolve his hero. Ultimately, for Hus inasmuch as the papacy as an institution deviated from the law of Christ it became heretical and Antichrist. In a valid sense, Hus saw himself as engaged in the final battle against Antichrist. Hus' obsessive nemesis, Michael de Causis, accused him of adhering to the ancient heresy of Donatism. The charge appears valid on the surface but any close inspection of the Hus corpus reveals otherwise. Hus did argue that a bishop or priest living in sin did not worthily occupy an ecclesiastical office. Those persisting in that situation cannot rightly be called a bishop or a priest. Sin destroyed character and not all who called themselves Christian were in fact of Christ. Priests and higher clerics who lived in this fashion were not worthy holders of their offices for God did not approve of their rule, dignity or position. However, this did not mean that baptisms performed by such churchmen were invalid, or their preaching worthless, or indeed the absolutions they pronounced ineffective. They were not performing worthy and clean acts of ministry but God honored the faithful who came under the authority of an unworthy cleric. Hus had the temerity to say that 'no one can be a prelate or a bishop so long as that one existed in mortal sin'.[89] The idea can be traced to Richard FitzRalph. Hus later was excoriated for holding this view but it is clear that no where did he deny the validity of the liturgical or sacramental ministrations of unworthy priests. Therefore it cannot be said that Hus was a Donatist. Still he would come right to the brink of that charge by asserting the power of the keys was contingent upon obedience to the law of Christ.[90] In fact, Hus argued the power of the keys had been invested in the true church, the body of the elect, not in particular offices within the institutional church.[91] No priest had any inherent sacerdotal right to the arbitrary exercise of the keys. Those who attempted to do so from an unworthy or improper motivation performed an empty exercise.[92] It is noteworthy that Hus' first mention of John Wyclif came in a discussion on the question of the power of the keys. In his exposition of the Apostles' Creed, Hus affirmed his conviction that God was not bound by the judgments or actions of a priest because clerics were prone to treachery and ignorance whereas God always acted according to truth. Here Hus referred to Wyclif whom he called *mistr hlubokých smyslóv* - 'the master of deep thoughts'.[93] In the theology of Jan Hus, the church was catholic but not Roman, and the faith was first and foremost emphatically about Christ, not Christendom.

The main points of Hus' doctrine of the church appear in *De ecclesia* and are five in number. The true church consisted of the elect. There was one head which was Christ. Authority could not reside in one person because original apostolic authority was shared equally among the disciples of Jesus. The pope was not infallible. All prelates were obliged to obey holy scripture without exception. Without neglecting Hus' authority paradigm it is important to note that *De ecclesia* cited biblical texts well over 400 times. David Schaff comments that *De ecclesia* is the best known work on the subject between Augustine and the Reformations.[94] However, a textual and theological investigation makes apparent that *De ecclesia* does not occupy the front rank in terms of importance or originality. Because Hus died on account of his theology embedded in the book, *De ecclesia* has profound historical significance. His martyrdom ensured his writings would never be forgotten. His detractors on the theology faculty of the university in Prague called upon Hus to 'yield and obey'.[95] Hus did neither. Instead, he relied upon the apostolic injunction (Acts 5:29) that it was preferable to obey God rather than humans. So he wrote it is better to be bound not by custom but by the example of Christ and his truth.[96] For Hus, this was Christian duty. For his judges at Constance, it constituted contumacy.

Salvation

As the hour of death drew near Jan Hus testified that his life's work had been to turn men and women from sin to eternal salvation. His status as a reformer and martyr must not obscure the fact that Hus was foremost a priest. 'Behold, there are three things set before our eyes. Horrible death, fearful judgment, and a burning hell. Death will come, judgment approaches and hell is prepared'.[97] There cannot be any doubt that Hus, along with most medieval theologians, conceived of a literal 'last judgment' and a very real hell, a place of torment and appalling eternal punishment.

> The Savior frequently reminded his apostles of Judgment Day and how terrible it would be. The horrible judge sits above humankind angry with the wicked. The Day of Judgment is terrifying. On the right, the sins accuse, on the left a multitude of devils pull the [damned] into hell. Behind is the burning world while in front angels push [the wicked] into hell. Within is the terrible gnawing of conscience. This horrible verdict of the court has seven parts. The first is a terrible chasing away . . . . the second is separation from God . . . . the third malediction . . . . the fourth sulphurous torture . . . . the fifth, despair of being liberated, because [the judge] declares 'it is eternal'. The sixth relates to torture . . . . the seventh is eternal fellowship with devils . . . . Oh, what a terrible

verdict! There is no end to it! Even if the entire world from the earth to the sky was filled with poppy-seeds, and each grain signified thousands of years, even at the time the last grain was laid, the damned ones hoping to be delivered from torture at that time, would still have to wait . . . . The eternal fire will burn the soul and the body . . . .[98]

According to Hus there were four hells. The first held the truly damned who existed beyond all hope or divine mercy. The second held non-baptized babies in a place of no suffering. Third, the traditional medieval concept of purgatory, and fourth, a realm where divine mercy does extend. Christ descended into this hell and led the captives out.[99] Hus remained convinced that at the day of judgment the full extent of God's power would be revealed.[100]

The main focus of Hus' ministry converged on the cure of souls. The disease Hus undertook to combat was sin. Original sin was one consideration and personal sin another. The former disenfranchised all of humankind collectively, without imputing actual individual guilt, while the latter stemmed directly and causally from the former. Therefore, all were lost (in a theological sense) and subjected to hopeless depravity.[101] Any act, action, or attitude impeding an ideal relationship between God and humankind constituted sin. There were minor or venial sins (*minuta peccata*) such as sleeping too much, excessive talking, or being annoyed. There were also mortal or deadly sins. In the Middle Ages there were seven 'deadly sins', namely lust, greed, anger, pride, gluttony, envy, and sloth. Hus held this view. Interestingly, Hus attached particular demons or demonic entities to specific sins. For example, Mammon was associated with greed, Bel with gluttony, Asmodeus with lechery, Lucifer with pride, Satan with opposition to Christ and so on.[102] Though, he does not deal with intention as did Abelard and Héloïse, Hus does underscore that consent is a necessary element for actions to be classified as sin. One may sin if he or she defended a sinful deed, assisted in its commission, advised the sinner, approved of the sin, did nothing to prevent it, or failed to punish it. Therefore, consenting to a misdeed, even if carried out by another, became a deadly sin.[103] It is submission to desire that constituted sin. The process is clear in Hus: desire leads to action which resulted in unrestrained sinful activity. Such activities led to habit and confirmation of that pattern and on to a state of unrepentance. That produced death and eternal condemnation.[104] By the fifteenth century a well-developed theological understanding of a cycle of sin, absolution and penance had emerged. Baptism dealt with the initial sin question. But humans had a fairly predictable tendency to continue sinning even after the regeneration of baptism. Sinners confessed their transgressions, received absolution by the church, did works of penance to demonstrate godly sorrow for their shortcomings and reentered a state of grace. If insufficient penance had been accomplished at the point of death, the pilgrim went to purgatory until sufficient works of satisfaction had been made. The pilgrim might finally be elevated to heaven. In order to avoid the calamity of hell, conceived by Hus, the problem of sin had to be addressed. The weight of sin, however, was massive. Had it not pulled Satan down from the place of exaltation to the lowest pit of hell? Hus argued to that conclusion, describing sin as a heavy burden which always pulled the bearer down as far as possible. Sin takes the soul to the deepest realm of existence. It remained the pastor's brief to alert the sinner to his or her impending fate. 'A dog in a boat with a large stone tied round its neck cannot discern the weight unless he is thrown from the boat and drowned. Likewise the soul does not feel the weight [of sin] as long as it remains in the body. However, once it leaves the body, then one can sense it, just as it falls into the depths of hell'.[105] Humankind cannot resist the weight of inherited sin which has plagued them from the beginning. According to Hus, fallen humans are bound by seven chains: hunger, thirst, coldness, excessive warmth, work, weariness, and death. These chains lead to increasing susceptibility to sensual desires.[106] Sin is rooted in pride and disobedience.[107] The darkness of sin causes both maladies because the fallen are unable to appreciate the nature of sin and the extent of that consequence upon humanity. This dilemma, according to Hus, occured as a result of the original fall of humankind. Among the results of this human tragedy emerged a division of mind and soul. By extension, Hus did not think prayers for the dead were of any avail.[108]

In his early Commentary on James, Hus argued that one part of human nature (soul) continued to yearn for God but the other part (mind) continually sought the satisfaction of sensual pleasure.[109] One may recall Augustine's famous prayer in his *Confessions*, 'Lord, give me chastity, but not yet'.[110] Satan was the first to fall into this existential dichotomy and that cosmic event eventually caused all humankind to follow suit.[111] On account of sin, one loses completely the divine grace of creation. The light of authentic living is extinguished, and the darkness of alienation from God descends.[112] Sin is a catastrophe. Hus adamantly affirmed that salvation was not within the purview of humankind. Good works alone, while important, do not avail, and even deathbed repentance cannot be relied upon as a guarantor of redemption.[113] The sole hope for salvation lies within the divine will.[114] Hus took a consistent and firm stand against the doctrine of indulgences which were preached in Prague prompting public dissension which came to a head in 1412. Hus maintained a priest should only issue an indulgence for a specific period of time which had been declared and communicated by divine revelation. Otherwise it constituted a purely arbitrary exercise of human will availing nothing.[115] Hus did not go so far as to declare that indulgences were deceptions of Antichrist and specifically stated he did not hold that position. However, he actively refuted the abuses associated with the trade without remorse.[116] A careful analysis of Hus' position on indulgences reveals he maintained only God could forgive sins and in this posture Hus remained completely orthodox. Some sins were regarded as more heinous than others. Hus thundered against priestly pride, greed and the neglect of the cure of souls concluding that such offenses were worse than flagrant sexual misconduct.[117] The only unpardonable sin is not one of commission but of omission. 'It is evident that a good God never condemns anyone unless that person remains impenitent to the end and thereby blasphemes the Holy Spirit'. The only utterly damning transgression is final impenitence. Those elected by

God, should they be in sin, are nevertheless part of the body of Christ. Divine grace can restore the elect even if they are in mortal sin.[118]

Reading through Hus' sermons and writings confirm that he perceived humankind as totally depraved. Sin had blinded men and women, left them powerless, filled with error and made destitute of all righteousness. The sinner cannot recognize God and cannot assist in any manner to facilitate salvation. The unrighteous are incapable of following the law of Christ and on that account become ever more profoundly lost and alienated from God. In keeping with medieval theological tradition, Hus did not hold God accountable for sin and unrighteousness as did the eternally provocative Héloïse in twelfth-century France in her discourse with Abelard.[119] Salvation can only be accessible to humankind on divine initiative and with an understanding of election to redemption. Curiously the word 'predestination' does not appear, to my knowledge, in the Hus corpus. The Czech word *predvedeny* does appear but it carries the connotation of being foreknown which, theologically, is somewhat different. However, there is every reason not to apply Calvinist categories to the fifteenth century. Hus discussed sin and asserted that while it was impossible to determine the identity of the elect, evident sinfulness is not the final determination. Children of Satan and children of God may both sin but the latter, being elected by God from eternity, ultimately turn from wickedness while the former persist in mortal sin for all time. Grace for salvation is extended only to the children of God chosen by 'eternal election'.[120] Even if one appeared righteous and performed all good works that person could not be part of the church unless he or she had been previously elected. Theologians like Jean Gerson found the suggestion subversive and dangerous.[121] There does not appear to be an understanding of irresistible grace in Hus. Divine grace enabled one to respond to the call of God, Hus suggested, but that same grace did not remove the human ability to reject divine favor. Therefore Hus maintained that final damnation was a result of human choice so that an eternal sentence to hell became the fault of the individual.[122] The argument is both tendentious and flawed. Hus appears to ascribe salvation to God but simultaneously attributes damnation to humans. In a sense he may have been attempting to closely follow Augustine who maintained a commitment to single predestination. If so, Hus was not consistent for we read in his commentary on the Apostles' Creed of the congregation of humankind divided into two groups by God. This separation, determined from eternity, consisted of the chosen 'universal community of saints' and the rejected 'universal community of the damned'.[123] Hus did admit the difficulty in balancing divine sovereignty and human responsibility.[124] In terms of salvation the idea of obedience remained a crucial point of Hus' teaching and a critical aspect of his theology. The proper response to grace was confession and repentance which Hus declared sufficient for salvation.[125]

In a Christmas Eve sermon Hus announced that repentance secured forgiveness of sin and at that stage the penitent became filled with the Holy Spirit. Hus did hasten to point out that only God, and not the priest, could grant the forgiveness of sin. Regardless of what they preached or how they behaved, Hus declared clerics were not the wardens of heaven and hell.[126] If sin was the cause for separation from God then divine grace through Christ became the basis for salvation and both scripture and sacrament functioned as channels of that grace.[127] Divine grace was the means by which God caused one to be pleasing to God for the benefit of the individual. Such grace was nothing other than the good will of God through which God extended care for creation. The soul dead in sin and alienated from God came to life through Christ and this process was predicated only upon divine grace.[128] The grace of election bound the Christian to Christ in such a manner that nothing could separate the elect from the favor of God.[129] Such grace was the gift of God given without regard to merit in order that humanity might be redeemed from sin. This infusion of grace worked in several ways. First, it inaugurated the work of God for salvation in humankind and this led to good works which produced merit. Superior merit gained meant the greater infusion of grace occurred so that the cycle continued. Prevenient grace became a form of cooperating grace wherein God enjoined the elect to acquiesce with God in the work of salvation. Ultimately, divine grace brought the Christian pilgrim to final perfection and eternal salvation.[130] Hus denied certainty in the matter of salvation maintaining that while one may rely upon divine grace the assurance of salvation was an eschatological gift which could not be apprehended in historical time. Therefore, predestination, grace, faith and works remained symbiotically in tension. Elsewhere Hus articulated four kinds of forgiveness: that which came from God alone, that which was applied through Christ, that which was mediated through a priest, and a mutual pardon between people.[131]

If divine grace was the basis for salvation, then faith became the foundation for the Christian life and as such was the result of prevenient grace.[132] The cause was the word of God from which faith came and this made children of God.[133] But faith had to be formed by love or good deeds: *fides caritate formata*. This, accompanied by divine grace, was sufficient for salvation. Hus argued that without faith none could be pleasing to God. Therefore faith was a result of grace infused into humankind. But faith was different from hope inasmuch as it was anchored in the past, particularly in what God had done in Christ, yet looked ahead to the consummation of history in which God rewarded the faithful who persevered in grace. Faith implicitly meant that the true Christian must hold to everything which the Holy Spirit endorsed, namely the truths of sacred scripture. The focus of faith was Christ upon whom the church had been built.[134] In Hus' theology, faith had an intellectual component.[135] However, his concept of faith was not only intellectual assent to a religious truth or principle. It was first of all more than 'correct belief', it was complete trust in God, but such confidence came only from God. Specifically, 'faith is a habit of the heart through which eternal life takes root creating mental assent in things unseen, rather than things apparent, which scripture through divine inspiration makes clear'.[136] He followed St. James, Augustine and Aquinas in developing a doctrine of active faith. His doctrine of faith is *tout court* quite different than Luther's.[137] The term *fides caritate formata* and the implied idea frequently appeared in the Hus corpus. Good works were stimulated by grace.[138] Hus held with St. James that faith without evidence was useless and no true faith. Hus likewise appealed to Augustine who apparently said one should do what they believed and then it was faith. In his commentary on the Sentences Hus urged the faithful to 'live like Christ and you will know Christ well.'[139] In consistent medieval fashion Hus stressed the value of works, claiming good works aided in securing divine approval. This meant works were part of the process of salvation.[140] Elsewhere, Hus announced his conviction that God would be rather unfair if there was not a corresponding reward for good works.[141] The doctrine *fides caritate formata* propounded by Hus enumerated several benefits or effects of good works. In his commentary on James, Hus listed seven: good works aided in purging sin, they reduced the punishment of transgression, they provided a form of protection against further iniquity, good works merited reward, they provided God cause to be merciful, they tempered divine judgment, and ultimately led the pilgrim to heaven. However, Hus emphasized that only God could provide the ability to live in righteousness, otherwise it might be assumed that humans could perform sufficiently so as to merit salvation on their own terms, an idea Hus deplored.[142] In every human action, Hus cautioned that sinners should take responsibility for whatever is imperfect but anything good done by humans should be ascribed to God so as not to think too highly of one's own ability.[143] Here it is useful to keep in mind his theology of resistible election noted earlier. Given Hus' theology of salvation it seems probable he would subscribe to the idea *simul iustus et peccator* that one existed simultaneously as righteous and sinner. However, Hus denied this as a contradiction in terms arguing that one being righteous and unrighteous, faithful and faithless was not consistent with the truth.[144] His objection noted, in theory this was precisely Hus' position, but in practice he does seem to allow for dynamic tension though as we shall see below Hus deplored the permissive attitude which tolerated deliberate sin. Musing upon the concept of the dead in Christ rising, Hus acknowledged such resurrection in an eschatological sense but also suggested it might mean spiritual life given to people by means of grace, in the here and now, in history.[145]

Theology – *sacra scriptura* – should be read, heard and proclaimed for the sake of eternal life. It is clear that human mediation is essential in order for the eternal word of God and divine grace to come alive in the here and now. Of that, Hus seemed never in doubt.[146] So he set himself the task of preaching and writing in hope of offering himself as a facilitation of divine grace for human salvation. Whoever would be saved must fulfil the law of God and believe.

> Because I am a priest, commissioned by God for the purpose of teaching people to believe, to fulfil the commands of God, and to pray properly to God, I wish to explain these three things to simple people. For a person wishing to draw nearer to God the first essential thing is faith, the main foundation in God. The second is keeping the commandments, and the third is useful prayer. Therefore I desire first of all to make known the great king to his servants . . . Whoever wishes to know the greatest of kings should know him with the heart, that is to believe, and also with the mouth, so if necessary to confess him before all people unto death.[147]

Hus regarded salvation as the union of humans with God through *visio dei* and obedient love. Faith formed by love and good works remained critical. Preaching and the sacraments were means of grace necessary for salvation. Hus never wavered from these principles.

Christ

Following Augustine's exegesis of Matthew 16:18, Hus articulated the rock upon which the church had been built as Christ, not Peter. He likewise discovered a critique against malicious excommunications. The focus, the center, the truth, for Hus was Christ. Everything else had to acknowledge the centrality of Christ. Christ should be regarded as the mirror for all Christians to emulate.[148] In his theological work, Hus regarded the gift of *sacra scriptura* not only as an act of grace but a means given to people by God for salvation. The center of all Christian theology must be Christ and Hus' theology is profoundly Christocentric.[149] Hus was entirely orthodox in accepting the Nicaean and Chalcedonian definitions that Christ was fully human and fully divine.[150] Throughout his career, Hus could often be found explicating the life and ministry of Christ.[151] The person of Christ remained central for Hus because he believed the human knowledge of God was limited to the revelation of God which Hus understood in the incarnation.[152] That historical event had a single purpose and that purpose was both historical and eschatological. Christ came to humankind to offer his life as the means for the redemption of many.[153] Just as Satan conquered humankind via a serpent in a tree, so Satan had been vanquished by another tree, the cross of Christ.[154] The crucified Christ was the means of salvation and the water which came from the side of Christ a source for the remission of sin.[155] Hus postulated that Christ came for the benefit of humanity and not out of personal ambition nor yet to secure divine satisfaction. Like Peter Abelard two centuries earlier, Hus maintained the sole motivation for the incarnation was love.[156] The Christ event was foundational for Hus' theology and he proclaimed that all human merit came from Christ and directly from his redemptive work. Without Christ there was no possibility of human merit and by implication there was no salvation.[157] Following St. Paul and the main stream of medieval theology, Hus argued that Christ did not die without purpose. The example of Christ enabled the pilgrim to live well and thereby receive the grace of God.[158] The process of salvation and Hus' emphasis on Christ are tightly woven together.

Committed to the centrality of Christ, the notional construct of the Trinity was Hus' point of departure in order to come to Christ who is the center.[159] Divine perfection was apparent and reached its highest form in the incarnation. 'Everything God could do, can do, or will be able to do in the future, God knew from eternity. In the same manner God knew everything from eternity and knows the same in the present. Whatever God willed, God willed from eternity and God's will is unchanging'.[160] God's ultimate will, according to Hus, had been human salvation and redemption and this will was realized and accomplished in Christ. Faced with trial for his life Hus committed himself to God. 'The Father and the Son and the Holy Spirit, the one God, in whom I believe and trust, will grant me the help of all the saints and holy people the spirit of wisdom and courage to enable me to escape the traps set by the Devil, and in the end come to rest in God's mercy'.[161] We have already seen that for Hus there was no possibility of justification through law or works. Salvation was a result of faith in Christ and this remained feasible for Hus because it was Christ who removes the way of sin through the law of grace. This *lex christi* was sufficient for all aspects of human life.[162] Defending the law of Christ became Hus' preoccupation, one might even say obsession, a task which led him to appear before all the sage men of Christendom at Constance. He wrote there was no greater cause for martyrdom than undertaking a steadfast defense of the law of Christ.[163] Whoever put on Christ likewise took on the ethics and morals of Jesus and it was quite impossible for one truly to be in Christ, *imitatio christi*, without imitating his ethics. 'Live Christ', Hus taught, 'and you will come to know Christ very well. If you live wickedly you will not know Christ and may perish for all eternity'.[164] What Hus seemed to be advocating was that the practice of love and truth was essential for understanding. One must believe the faith and practice the faith in order to understand the faith. Throughout his preaching the law of Christ occurs as a key principle. This must be grasped and appreciated in order to understand Hus' thought and motivation.[165]

Christ is truth and for Hus truth was the bedrock of theology and religious practice. Criticized for his use of Wyclif, Hus had this rejoinder.'Whatever truth Wyclif taught I receive not because it is the truth of Wyclif but because it is the truth of Christ'.[166] For Hus, Christ redeemed sinful humanity, extended divine mercy, and suffered death to make the election of God an absolute certainty.[167] Truth was simultaneously the law of Christ and promise. Throughout the Hus corpus one finds terms like *lex christi*, *veritas*, and *promissio dei* (law of Christ, truth, and promises of God) frequently.[168] In 1405, while commenting upon I Esdras 4:35–8, Hus underscored one of the central motifs of his thought.

> 'But truth is great and stronger than all things. The whole earth calls upon truth and heaven blesses her. All God's works quake and tremble, and with him there is nothing unrighteous. Wine is unrighteous, the king is unrighteous, all the sons of men are unrighteous, all their works are unrighteous, and all such things. There is no truth in them, and in their unrighteousness they will perish. But truth endures and is strong for ever, and lives and prevails, for ever and ever. With her there is no partiality or preference, but she does what is righteous, instead of anything that is unrighteous or wicked. All men approve her deeds, and there is nothing unrighteous in her judgment. To her belongs the strength and the kingship and the majesty of all the ages. Blessed be the God of truth!' He ceased speaking: then all the people shouted and said: 'Great is truth, and strongest of all.'[169]

Jan Hus defended two compelling reasons to speak the truth: fear of God and love of Christ.[170] When it came to choosing between the material realm and the ultimate

Hus did not hesitate. Referring to his former colleague turned opponent Štěpán Páleč, Hus made this declaration. 'Páleč is my friend. Truth is my friend. Of the two it is better to prefer the truth'.[171] Páleč will pass away but truth is not susceptible to decay or destruction. Raging against the burning of Wyclif's books by order of Archbishop Zbyněk in 1410 Hus made clear that fire could not suppress truth. Fire had no control of truth. Hus took the view that only small-minded people burned books. The Prague bonfire depreciated the nation.[172] As noted previously, Hus discriminated among different kinds of truth. There is divine truth codified in scripture. There is also the truth which can be apprehended by reason and the human mind. Further, there is the truth gained by experience. Keeping in mind Hus' concept of authority the common denominator is truth. For him, there remained an important relation between truth and reason. Reason was required when dealing with divine truths in scripture. Truth was not subject to reason but divine truth, in Hus, does not repel reason and demand blind adherence. The integrity of faith required the presence of reason. In an odd sense Hus endorsed both Anselm and Peter Abelard. Anselm of Canterbury argued 'unless you believe you will not understand' while Abelard asserted 'by doubting we come to inquiry and by inquiry we perceive the truth'. Perhaps Hus' 'both-and' position is less surprising when it is recalled that his master Augustine once promoted both approaches. Abelard wrote books on theology to give students rational explanations for doctrine and declared in his *Historia Calamitatum* 'nothing can be believed unless it is first understood'.[173] Hus' unflinching reluctance to submit his reason, and his truth to the non-negotiable authority of Constance proved fatal. His focus remained truth above the Council, not truth invested in the Council. He defended a dichotomy between Christ and the fathers. '[Christ] is the way, leading to salvation. He is the truth, illuminating the thinking of the faithful. He is everlasting life, which the elect shall happily live in forever. That life, that way and that truth, I wish to follow, and to it I desire to bring others'.[174]

Scripture

Because scripture is a witness to the truth, Hus affirmed that scripture was also truth. This was apparent in his conviction that within the sacred literature of scripture everything necessary for salvation could be found.[175] That said, it is also obvious that Hus' definition of scripture was wider than the canon.[176] While Hus' exegetical methods still await a comprehensive analysis and explication one principle seems clear. Interpretation should follow a balanced pattern of established authority. For Hus that meant tradition and conscience. Biblical interpretation should be reined in and guided by tradition and not permitted to be unduly influenced by personal preference or appeals to the unsubstantiated leading of the Holy Spirit. However conservative Hus' views on scripture were, he cannot be boxed into a *sola scriptura* stance nor made to be the narrow biblicist the conciliar fathers accused him of being. Hus clearly regarded the Sentences of Peter Lombard as an alternative form of scripture in terms of authority.[177] His theological confession was that he desired nothing other than to proclaim whatever was essential to salvation. Hus maintained that the basis for determining whether something was of salvific importance lay in the explicit and implicit declarations of the scriptures which all faithful Christians were obligated to adhere to. In that conviction Hus declared his fidelity to scripture 'wishing to maintain, believe and proclaim whatever is contained in them' so long as he lived.[178]

The focus of scripture for Hus was the story of Christ. Christ is the head of the church and in Christ all useful truth for the church and for salvation can be found.[179] Without Christ, scripture remained only literature and without scripture there would be no historical record of the Christ event. Both were necessary for the faith. Hus did not allow for arbitrary judgment of scripture. He rebuked those who engaged in useless debates reducing scripture to a lifeless body of 'words, vowels and written letters.' Hus demanded to know 'what is the purpose of all this cackling' if one is unprepared to come to terms with the significance of a living text.[180]

Practically speaking, Hus desired the scriptures be available to the laity and in the vernacular. He accused the 'disciples of antichrist' of trying to keep the scriptures away from lay people. In 1406 Hus published the St. Mikulovský Czech Bible.[181] The argument that the common language was susceptible to heresy was specious. Latin was equally susceptible.[182] Such prelates and priests do not wish for the laity to have the ability to query them. Hus noted those who attempted to challenge the priesthood were denounced as 'Wyclifites' and dismissed as not part of the church.[183] The Hus corpus abounds with quotations from and references to scripture. In a sense, scripture functioned both as the final court of appeal and truth for Hus. But once more reference to his concept of authority is essential. *Scriptura numquam sola*! Scripture is never alone and there is never a time in which the naked text of scripture functions apart from all other considerations. Certainly Hus made every effort to find traditional moorings for his exegesis and understanding of scripture. But in the end, it was Hus' interpretation of scripture, not scripture itself, that functioned as the basis for his final appeal. Thus, at Constance he demanded to be instructed according to scripture. There is no evidence the Council attempted to persuade Hus by this methodology. Regardless of what the fathers thought theologically about scripture, in practice they were committed to a theory of conciliar authority as practically more relevant than any text. Therefore, there was no confrontation between judges and the accused over exegetical principles or authoritative interpretations to be decided. In his reply to his former colleague Štěpán Páleč, Hus declared his hope that when he appeared before the judgment bar of God he might be acquitted of having erred or deviated on even a single point of scripture.[184] Ambitious to be sure, but Hus' fidelity to scripture is unimpeachable. That said, it is not an easily defensible thesis to insist Hus suffered condemnation and execution on account of his allegiance to scripture. He could have insisted on being instructed by the works of Augustine, or Origen, or the Decretum of Gratian for that matter. The issue for the Council was not scripture but Hus' persistent noncompliance. His sin in their eyes was contumacy. That was an offense they could not abide. It is not surprising that in several of his final letters from Constance Hus exhorted his readers to study and proclaim the word of God.[185] It remains to be said that Hus did not manufacture his allegiance to scripture late in life in order to thwart the agenda of the Council. Indeed, his commitment to the authority of the Bible was a lifelong one and he had already fully and formally articulated his views on the matter.[186]

Eucharist

Arguably, the sacrament of the altar became the doctrine of specific controversy during the Hussite Revolution with the chalice emerging quite dramatically as its central symbol. It cannot be maintained that Jan Hus brought anything special or innovative to a discussion of the sacrament. Wyclif definitely lapsed into eucharistic heresy, rejected the Lateran doctrine of transubstantiation, but made no appeal for the lay chalice. Prior to this in the High Middle Ages the eucharist had become a flashpoint of controversy as ninth-century theologians, like the Carolingian monks of Corbie Abbey Paschasius Radbertus and Ratramnus, argued over the identity of the eucharistic body of Christ while the eleventh-century Berengar of Tours created an even greater stir by suggesting there was no change in the sacramental elements. The fourth Lateran Council of 1215 formulated the doctrine of transubstantiation.[187] Hus remained a son of Lateran acknowledging the sacraments as the most powerful medicine for humankind. The eucharist functioned religiously as a means of grace and strength, while the spiritual power of the sacrament was communicated to the faithful via the ordained priesthood.[188] In the spirit of Ignatius of Antioch who once declared the eucharist as the 'medicine of immortality', Hus described the sacrament as 'the most delicious food' and the 'most noble drink'.[189] Christ became human for the sole purpose of bringing salvation to all people. Hus preached that the body and blood of Christ was offered so the faithful might come to the feast. 'Come in faith, hope and love, doing good deeds'.[190] Salvation was the eternal medicinal remedy found in the eucharist and the blood of Christ was able to cure all people for all time.[191]

Early in his career Hus set forth the benefits of the eucharist. These included fulfilling the scriptural mandate of remembering Christ and concluded with a means of accessing eternal life. Additionally, Hus considered eucharistic benefits included a cleansing from sin, a strengthening in Christian virtue, a cessation of sensual desire, the comfort of the Holy Spirit, nourishment of the soul, a sense of peace, and a quickening of the spirit. Even prior to the excitement at Wilsnack, Hus had warned the spectacle-seekers against the idea that the miraculous mysteries of the altar could be visibly apprehended in the sacrament.[192] As he did in his report on Wilsnack so likewise he developed his idea that the body of Christ crucified was different than the body of Christ which appeared in the sacrament of the altar.[193] There are no grounds for assuming other than that Hus followed traditional authorities, especially Peter Lombard, in his theology of the eucharist. There are no apparent reservations expressed in his work and he appears to accept uncritically the broad thrust of orthodox medieval eucharistic thought.[194] He knew indubitably what Wyclif taught and firmly rejected it.[195] He did regard the communion as a social leveling. All Christians are clothed with the same garment, which is love, reside in the same house, the church, and share the one holy food and drink in common. Distinctions of hierarchy were subordinated and the communion of the saints remained.[196] His disciples radicalized this understanding even more.

In 1411 Hus wrote to Pope John XXIII asserting his belief in the doctrine of the eucharist as maintained by the church, protesting that his teaching had been subjected to false accusations.[197] It is true that some of his more vitriolic detractors accused him of remanentism, meaning he denied the doctrine of transubstantiation. A throwaway comment Hus made in a social setting with Bernard, priest of St. Michael's in the Old Town of Prague, later became the subject in a charge of eucharistic irregularity more than ten years later at Constance.[198] Cambridge University master John Stokes testified that in 1411 he had been in Prague and personally seen a treatise authored by Hus defending remanentism. Hus said it was a lie.[199] Michael de Causis leveled a similar charge at Constance.[200] In that formula of transubstantiation, the bread and wine underwent a change in substance so that the literal flesh of Christ replaced physical bread and the literal blood of Christ replaced material wine. However, while the substance was radically altered, the bread and wine (accidents) continued to appear, feel and taste as ordinary bread and wine. John Wyclif denied this could be the case, constrained by a commitment to realism. That philosophical perspective could not allow for the destruction or annihilation of any real thing. Universals (abstract concepts) have an existence apart from the particulars (accidents) in which they exist and are perceived. It was untenable to the realists that a universal might be altered or annihilated while the particulars remained unchanged.[201] Had he been consistent, admittedly Hus should have rejected the doctrine of transubstantiation along with Wyclif for the same reasons. But what he may have been expected to do and what he actually did are separate considerations. Michael de Causis insisted Hus was deviant on the eucharist. Testimony had been submitted in 1410 at the trial of Jerome of Prague in Vienna that Hus had specifically been excommunicated for teaching that the eucharistic bread in the sacrament was not the body of Christ. Both claims were specious. There is no evidence Hus ever held to a remanence doctrine at any stage of his life. All of his writings on the topic mitigate against such opinion. Among western scholars, the one to investigate this matter most thoroughly has been Paul De Vooght. His conclusions are compelling. Hus rejected most emphatically any and all semblance of remanentism.[202] I have been unable to find any evidence anywhere in the Hus corpus to suggest he did not hold to the traditional doctrine of the sacrament. Hus' orthodoxy in all of his eucharistic writings, teachings and comments is apparent.[203] At first glance it is difficult to sustain an accusation of heresy against Hus when his position on weighty matters like the eucharist, the office of the bishop, the validity of the sacraments, and scripture are unimpeachable in terms of orthodoxy.[204] In 1406 Jan Hus wrote a significant book on the eucharist, *De corpore Christi*, in which he asserted unambiguously a definite pro-transubstantiation position emphasizing real presence.[205] Likewise the same posture can be seen in his commentary on the Sentences. The priest created the body of Christ. This occurred at the moment of consecration. The accidents remained but the substance was changed into the body of Christ.[206] In his *Postil*, Hus stated that bread and wine were definitely transubstantiated into the body and blood of Jesus Christ. It is difficult to state the official theology any clearer. This is the traditional doctrine of transubstantiation. There is neither heresy nor hint of alternative views.

For nearly thirty years before Hus came to prominence in Prague there had been a developing practice of frequent communion among Bohemian reformers. Before controversy engulfed him, Hus took an entirely neutral position on the question of daily or frequent communion.[207] Several years later, when he came to set forth aspects of his theology while exiled from Prague he encouraged his hearers to commune frequently as one feels led, even the option of daily communion.[208] Reading the Lord's Prayer, Hus interpreted the phrase 'give us this day our daily bread' in a eucharistic sense.[209] Hus neither made it a liturgical requirement nor a religious demand that the laity exceed the stipulations set forth by the official church. Clearly, there had been an evolution in his thinking on the matter. Hus' followers from Jakoubek on down, championed the cause of the lay chalice *communio sub utraque specie*; both bread and wine for all baptized believers. Early on, Hus did not think the laity ought to receive the cup.[210] The western church had concluded the entire body and blood of Christ was truly and completely present in both eucharistic elements and therefore it was not essential to partake of both. Thomas Aquinas put it succinctly following Anselm of Canterbury and Alexander of Hales. Hus agreed with the doctrine of concomitance. It was not that he regarded the chalice as unimportant. It was simply redundant. Unlike the eastern communion, the historic utraquist practice fell into general disuse in the Latin Church in the course of the twelfth and thirteenth centuries. Once Hus went off to Germany to defend himself against charges of doctrinal deviance and contumacy, his colleague Jakoubek of Stříbro inaugurated the practice of the lay chalice in Prague at several locations. This was the commencement of a eucharistic rapprochement in Bohemia. Ostensibly, Jakoubek shared his plans with Hus who initially assumed a conservative point of view counseling Jakoubek not to move too quickly with his eucharistic innovations. 'Go slow Kubo' he cautioned.[211] The fact that Jakoubek regarded utraquism as essential to salvation does not mean Hus concurred. In fact there is no evidence to support the suggestion Hus ever entertained the idea. The origins of the utraquist initiative in Bohemia is an important chapter in the history of the western church and there has been some very solid scholarship devoted to the question.[212] Our concern here is limited to Hus' view of the lay chalice. As we have seen he displayed little enthusiasm for it. Once out of Bohemia, a eucharistic revolution erupted. Factions formed on both sides of the issue. Jakoubek pulled none of his punches on the matter. Anyone who opposed the lay chalice should be cursed and thrown out of the fellowship of the godly.[213] Hus never went along with such strident demands.

It was inevitable Hus would be forced to revisit his earlier opinions and thereby drawn into the Prague debates. Shortly after arrival in Constance Hus wrote a letter to an unknown priest in Bohemia and encouraged communion in both kinds.[214] During this same period, Hus wrote a short essay on the subject.[215] The title reveals its contents and Hus attempted to deal with the question whether the laity ought to receive the blood of Christ under the form of wine. It is interesting that Hus cited the fifth-century Gelasius who had argued the two elements ought not be separated in the sacrament for fear of committing sacrilege. He also appeared to deviate from the idea that there was no greater benefit in communing *sub utraque specie* than communing *sub uno*. Hus quoted Ambrose to the effect that the body of Christ strengthened the physical while the blood of Christ strengthened the soul. The comment is subtle. Hus concluded his short tract by affirming that lay people should partake of both elements at the same frequency as priests. It is possible Hus read his colleague Jakoubek of Stříbro's *Pius Ihesus* inasmuch as the same authorities are cited.[216] Early in January 1415 Jan of Chlum wrote to Hus asking the imprisoned theologian to provide an opinion on the question of the lay chalice. Despite the tensions in Prague over the matter (which Hus could certainly not have been unaware of) his reply is once more curiously measured. He referred to his recently composed treatise on the subject, noting scripture did not forbid it, admitting the practice had been observed throughout Church history, but urging that if possible to secure formal ecclesiastical sanction for the idea.[217] There is no evidence Jakoubek or his colleagues made any particular effort to secure official approval for their eucharistic practices. By spring the bishop of Litomyšl in eastern Bohemia, Jan Železný, informed the conciliar fathers that utraquism was being widely practiced in Bohemia and people were being catechized that it was necessary for salvation.[218] On 15 June 1415, in its thirteenth session, the Council of Constance formally condemned the practice of utraquism calling its practitioners heretics, ordering their confinement, and threatening priests who persisted in the practice with major excommunication.[219] Writing from the Franciscan prison a few days after the announcement, Hus called the decision madness and erroneous. Jakoubek posted Hus' words on the wall of Bethlehem Chapel.[220] Hus then wrote to his successor at Bethlehem Chapel, the incumbent Havlík, and begged him not to oppose the lay chalice which Hus pointed out was instituted by Christ and was opposed by no scriptural text. He told Havlík the withdrawal of the cup must be a human custom developing out of negligence but faithful Christians should follow the truth of Christ, not human traditions. Alluding to the turmoil in Prague over the chalice, Hus implored Havlík to cease attacking Jakoubek because the schism which was forming over the eucharist was nothing more than a tool of the Devil aimed at destroying the church. Finally, Hus advised Havlík that the faithful ought to prepare for suffering on account of utraquism.[221] It is doubtful Hus had any idea what would transpire in the western church as a result of Jakoubek's *revelatio* and initiative.

Following his doctrines set forth on the church, it is clear that Hus accepted the validity of sacramental function even at the hands of bad priests though he was consistently clear that such ministrations were unworthy and in need of immediate reform.[222] He remained equally convinced that those who endeavored to change the administration of the sacraments were indeed wicked for the sacraments belonged to the one true church of the entire elect and were neither the provenance of the priesthood nor the ecclesiastical hierarchy.[223]

No one today reading Hus' writings on the eucharist can maintain any inkling that he followed Wyclif in renouncing the doctrine of transubstantiation. None of Hus' works read in context provide even the flimsiest support for the notion. It is likewise without merit to assume that in his latter days when he began to advocate frequent communion and muster lukewarm support for the lay chalice that likewise in his heart he began to question core eucharistic doctrine. These points are unassailable. It is true that Jerome of Prague apparently thought Hus' eucharistic theology to somehow be unorthodox and akin to Wyclif.[224] The statement has either been garbled by the respective recorders or Jerome is flat wrong. Nevertheless, it is possible to detect hints of where Hus' allegiance to official church theology began to become suspect and it seems useful to address those instances in order to understand Hus' posture with respect to the sacrament of the altar. While Hus clearly taught the real presence and the sacramental character of the elements in his *De corpore Christi*, he sidestepped some of the more extravagant assertions made by other medieval theologians. He refuted the claim advanced by some of his colleagues that priests could in fact make the body of Christ upon demand or at will calling the idea heresy and blasphemy.[225] Inasmuch as Christ had existed from eternity it seemed senseless and theologically ignorant to Hus for anyone to claim they had created Christ in time. The statement cannot be read to imply that Hus held reservations about transubstantiation. His point is concerned with arrogance and shoddy theology. He made the same point even clearer when he expounded the Apostles' Creed. Hus castigated foolish priests, as he perceived them, who boasted of creating God or the body of Christ at will. Hus dismissed the idea as nonsense commenting that the creature cannot create the Creator and that all the priests combined could not create even a fly let alone God or the son of God! He mocked those who thought otherwise. Such heretical priests are 'lunatics' who 'howl like wolves wishing to make themselves more important then lay people' asserting they can do something even greater than accomplished by the mother of God. Hus accused his colleagues of claiming that while Mary created Christ once, they were capable of creating Christ numerous times.[226] Once again, there is no denial of ecclesiastical doctrine. Correcting abusive claims was quite different than proposing an alternative theology. Only by extracting a sentence here or there from context can Hus be made to appear antithetical to official church doctrine. Once he remonstrated with such illegitimate boasting Hus immediately qualified his critique by pointing out that the power which enabled bread to become flesh on the altar comes not from the consecrating priest but instead from God.[227] The faithful who partake are united with Christ and eat to their salvation.[228] But there is no doubt that in the sacrament 'the real body and the real blood of Christ are truly eaten and drunk'.[229] Hus likewise wrote a Latin treatise on the errors of the Mass – *De sex erroribus* – which he later expanded into a Czech version – *O šesti bludiech* – which advanced the same crucial point. Of the six errors enumerated by Hus, the first dealt with the idea that a priest could of his own volition create the body of Christ.[230] Those admitting as much he called 'crazy' and 'mistaken'.[231] Hus had these 'errors' posted on the walls at Bethlehem Chapel. As early as *De corpore Christi* Hus distinguished between the literal physical body of Christ and transubstantiated bread. The unworthy partake only of material bread while the faithful commune with Christ.[232]

While incarcerated in Constance in the final months of his life, Hus wrote a tract at the request of his jailer Robert. In that short work 'Concerning the body and blood of the Lord' Hus reiterated a well-established doctrinal theme. The consecrating priest 'transubstantiates . . . the real body of Christ . . . and the real blood of Christ' according to the power and word of God and what occurs is truly 'transubstantiating the bread into his body and the wine into his blood'.[233] Full transubstantiation occurs, God performs the miracle irrespective of the merits of the celebrant, and body and blood are fully present in each element. If Hus entertained any doubts on the doctrine it seems highly unlikely he willingly would have defended it while awaiting death in prison. Only by the grossest misreading can Hus be made to deny transubstantiation. He clearly used the language of sacrifice, even as he discussed the 'errors' of the Mass perpetrated in his own time. Statements like those made by Hus against the extravagant claims of certain arrogant Bohemian priests have led some, quite erroneously, to imagine that Hus harbored doubts about official eucharistic theology. For all of his efforts to demonstrate his orthodoxy, the accusation of eucharistic heresy remained one of the final thirty charges against Hus at Constance. It should be noted that on the day he died, Hus once more declared publicly to the Council that he had never 'held, taught or preached that in the sacrament of the altar the physical bread remains [unchanged] following the consecration'.[234]

Theologically, Jan Hus remained quite conservative in doctrine. He esteemed the communion of the saints, taught that all people should avoid mortal sin, and thereby participate in the goodness of all creation. True religion finds its center in faith, hope and love. Sin impeded one's ability to join in the communion of all the saints. Hus urged moral reform and moral vigilance.[235] He did not subscribe to the anti-monastic views of the Cathars, Waldensians and Wyclif. Hus regarded the religious life as an ideal in which the Christian life of poverty, chastity and humble obedience might be practiced and exemplified. He denounced monastic abuses without abolishing the religious life. And in a deep irony in the history of ideas, Hus rejected the death penalty as punishment, arguing at some length against the idea before concluding that those who killed heretics were among the most evil assistants of Antichrist and Satan.[236] Institutionalized murder, even if sanctioned by law was a dangerous practice, Hus argued, and while there were exceptions to the rule, the executioners usurp divine prerogative.[237]

Much of Hus' academic writing on doctrine is reflected in his sermons. From a theological perspective, it may be said that Jan Hus was devoted to Jesus Christ. He remained resolute on truth at all costs, consistently submitting to the principles of scripture, tradition and conscience at every turn. His work as a theologian was marked by a refusal to compromise and a commitment to theology as liberation and foundation for applied Christianity, rather than doctrine as duty. Though conservative, almost without exception, Hus demonstrated a willingness to take the occasional theological risk. His life and work exemplified the heart of a pastor, the devotion of a priest, and the vision of a prophet. It is certain he would not be remembered for theological brilliance were that a criterion. But in the history of Christianity he remains significant for integrity and the melding of theology, faith and life. In medieval thought, teaching, providing counsel, correcting the wayward, consolation, forgiveness, bearing the burdens of others, and prayer are the seven spiritual gifts of mercy. The seven material works of mercy include visiting the sick, giving drink to the thirsty, feeding the hungry, freeing the prisoner, clothing the naked, caring for strangers, and burying the dead.[238] According to Hus, such acts and attitudes functioned at the heart of proper theology and informed ideas which motivated him as a priest to become a late medieval Catholic reformer. His own words are rather apropos. 'May our way be directed by faith and reason. May we take heed to what is good and avoid whatever would impede salvation. Let us never be ashamed to speak the truth. May we never oppose God's truth'.[239]

4

PROCLAMATION

Hus' mature reason for becoming a priest had to do with the fact that even though Christ knew he would be killed he determined to be a priest to all humankind.[1] Initially Hus had been motivated to secure a good living and attain a good reputation. Later he desired to practice the imitation of Christ. Since death was imminent, the proclamation of hope became urgent.[2] Preaching on Palm Sunday 1406 Jan Hus encouraged his congregation neither simply to hear nor know, but to feel the message. 'He [Christ] puts death to flight, and restores us to life: Feel this! He was killed that he might make whole, he died that he might live: Feel this! He is spotted that he might cleanse: Feel this!'[3] The repeated Czech equivalent of the Latin *Hoc sentite* brought preacher, gospel and congregation together in a dynamic liturgical and spiritual relationship.

Whatever conclusions historians may draw about him, Jan Hus was first and foremost a preacher. Popular songs sung by his followers provided that testimony: 'If you want to know the Bible, you must go to Bethlehem and learn it on the walls as Master Jan of Husinec preached it'.[4] On the walls of his preaching center, Bethlehem Chapel, Hus had inscribed several texts in Latin and in the common tongue. Later he counseled his followers to learn the truth on the walls of Bethlehem Chapel.[5] Other popular songs lauded Hus as an honest preacher.[6] Even later detractors acknowledged his exceptional presence as a preacher. Aeneas Sylvius Piccolomini, later Pope Pius II, referred to Hus as a powerful speaker.[7] Modern scholars describe Hus' sermons as the chief event of the times.[8] Pulpits in fifteenth-century Prague were rather like the modern daily newspapers and quite naturally became a customary vehicle for reformist ideas.[9] Some suggest Hus controlled Prague from his pulpit.[10] The hyperbole is obvious but a kernel of truth is implied. One of the primary sources for an indication of Hus as a reformer can be accessed through his homiletical activity and his commitment to the art of preaching (*ars praedicandi*).[11]

Preaching specifically, and the sermon in general, played an essential role in later medieval European society. There is a fundamental distinction between sermons and homilies in medieval preaching. The homily was effectively a commentary on a specific text (normally one of the liturgical passages nominated for the day in question) while a sermon usually took a single verse or quotation from the liturgy and was then developed. Preaching took on the importance of instruction, the communication of ideas and therefore functioned as an unrivaled social force. By the fifteenth century popular preaching increasingly came to function in the life of the community. Jan Hus preached *ad cleros* [to the clergy] and also *ad populum* [to the people]. Understood in this manner, his sermons became both a lamp and a mirror on life in late medieval Bohemia. It was his sermons to popular audiences which galvanized a reform movement in Prague. The repetition of sermons, frequent preaching, increased the effects of reform and potentially expanded the range of advocates for the reforms demanded. In this attention to popular preaching Hus was no innovator. Indeed, he occupied a place in a popular preaching tradition in late medieval Bohemia following Konrad of Waldhauser, Jan Milíč of Kroměříž, Matěj of Janov, Jan Protiva, Štěpán of Kolín, Jan of Štěkna, Petr of Stupna and others.[12] Such traditions were not unusual. Popular preaching had been widespread in Europe from at least the twelfth century and there is legislation in the capitularies of Charlemagne dating to the ninth century calling for vernacular preaching. Sermons in the common language remained central in religious practice in Bohemia. Sermons preached in the vernacular both to clerical and lay audiences were fairly widespread throughout western Europe by the fifteenth century.

Jan Hus inherited this medieval preaching tradition. What makes Hus worthy of attention is his persuasive and successful preaching. Bethlehem Chapel stood as an example of unusual religious communities in Prague.[13] According to the foundation charter of 1391 the chapel was established because while there were many churches in Prague, preaching in the vernacular was not a priority. Bethlehem Chapel existed for this purpose. The appointed preacher received an annual stipend of not more than 1200 groschen and was obligated to reside near the chapel to avoid the pervasive scandal of absentee priests.[14] By comparison, an unskilled day laborer in Prague might earn 300–400 groschen per year, a skilled laborer 900, while the holder of a desired benefice might be paid 1800 groschen.[15] A recognition of his qualities as a preacher precipitated Hus' appointment to the pulpit of Bethlehem Chapel in 1402.[16] His preaching primarily centered on issues of moral and social reform. Hus used the pulpit of Bethlehem Chapel as a venue for addressing pressing needs in Czech society, including issues concerning ecclesiastical renewal. In this Hus attracted the condemnation of those not so inclined. While Hus' sermons included many references to social conditions in Prague and Bohemia, his comments must not in every instance be taken as factual without independent corroboration. Religious reformers like Tomáš Štítný (†1401) and Hus frequently complained of the unfair taxation of peasants and attempted to make this a source for widespread social ills. This may have been the case in certain times and particular places but extant records do not always support such claims. Nonetheless, vernacular preaching seemed attractive to many citizens in Prague. Petr of Stupna preached Czech sermons in St. Vitus' Cathedral but otherwise only Hus' chapel featured regular vernacular preaching. His audiences consisted of a revealing cross-section of Prague: women, children, servants, magistrates, university masters, tradesmen, artisans, merchants, Queen Žofie, the archbishop's sister, and other political and military figures including Jan Žižka. Contemporary sources suggest

Bethlehem Chapel was nearly always full with one claiming audiences numbering 3,000.[17] This non-parochial chapel functioned as an essential venue for the spoken word in the late medieval world of Bohemian religion. Though it produces a certain repetitiveness, an investigation of Hus' sermons clarifies the public aspects of the theology contained in his writings.

It is estimated Hus preached between 3,000 and 3,500 sermons during his career as rector of Bethlehem Chapel, or nearly one per day for ten years.[18] There are at least nine collections of Hus' Latin sermons extant in addition to his Czech homilies.[19] His early sermons of 1401–1403 survive in manuscripts in the Praemonstratensian Strahov Monastery in Prague.[20] These sermons preached in the Church of St. Michael in Prague's Old Town and in Bethlehem Chapel are quite orthodox in their call for moral reform, while they reflect the influence of the Czech reform tradition. There are seventy-seven sermons on the church festivals wherein one finds discourses on New Testament personalities such as SS. Matthew, John Baptist, Mary Magdalene and others. There are also sermons dealing with the holy men and women of Bohemian history: SS. Vojtěch, Ludmila, and Václav. The doctrinal content is consistent with the topics and interpretation of medieval preaching in the official Catholic tradition.[21] Even modern scholars who tend to see doctrinal irregularities in Hus at every corner admit the essential orthodoxy of Hus' early sermons wherein there is present the exposition of church doctrine without polemic, argument or contest.[22]

Hus' *Sermones de tempore qui Collecta dicuntur* consist of ninety-nine sermons and date from 30 November 1404 to 22 November 1405.[23] These sermons, together with those preserved from 1408, continue the conservative reformist trends, and are also devoid of any discernable Wyclifite influence.[24] His later sermons in Bethlehem Chapel from 1410–1411 begin increasingly to critique the institutional church and its practices and may be related to parallel political and ecclesiastical developments. Hus' consistent orthodox sermons did create controversy as early as 1405 by denouncing popular religious superstitions at Litomyšl in eastern Bohemia and, as we have see, especially at the aforementioned Wilsnack in Brandenburg. In these sermons Hus spared none of those responsible for leading the people of God astray.[25] In 1408 Hus defended preaching without official approbation and drew criticism from his clerical colleagues and especially from the higher clergy. The exacerbation of the papal schism in 1409 as a result of the election of a third pope by the Council of Pisa thrust Hus into opposition with Archbishop Zbyněk who in turn fell from favor with King Václav IV. Religious conflicts precipitated the public burning of heretical books in 1410 by order of Zbyněk despite great outcry. There is good reason for associating these events with the radicalizing of Hus' preaching. Indeed, he had proclaimed that all bulls against the books of John Wyclif were the same as sowing weeds among the wheat. By limiting the freedom of the word of God, the result paralleled the acts of executioners who killed Christians and the betrayers of Christ.[26]

As early as 1404 in his sermon 'throwing aside the works of darkness', Hus condemned the practice of charging fees for divine ministry. This custom was contrary to the law of God.[27] Grace was free and to extort payment for what had been proffered without charge was, for Hus, entirely reprehensible.[28] Hus' last important collection of sermons is his Czech Postil which was completed at Kozí Hrádek on 27 October 1413. The Postil contains sermons on the gospel for each Sunday of the year and the most important holy days. In the introduction to this collection Hus stated that he wished to place the gospel text first, followed by the exposition so that the word of God might speak first and louder than the word of Hus.[29]

Consistent with his theological writings the sermons of Master Jan Hus abound in references to scripture, the fathers, and canon law. Among the fathers Hus referred most often to Augustine, Gregory, Cyril, Jerome, and John Chrysostom. Frequently Hus quoted extensively from Augustine, Gregory, Bernard, Thomas Aquinas as well as other patristic and medieval luminaries. He did not eschew classical sources. One finds references to the life of Alexander the Great and Virgil in his sermons.[30] There is also a clear doctrinal element present with emphasis upon morality and spiritual edification. Hus castigated faithless priests relentlessly.

Given the radicalism of the later Hussite movement one is somewhat surprised to find a lack of revolutionary material in the corpus of Hus' sermons. This is not to suggest that his preaching was entirely jejune. Indeed not. His sermons produced a significant and lasting effect. But the polemical notions of Hus shouting heresies from the pulpit of Bethlehem Chapel are clearly unwarranted. Instead, Hus' sermons are genuinely orthodox and were delivered with pastoral concerns. An analysis of his important 1411 sermon *Dixit Martha ad Iesum* reveals unimpeachable orthodoxy.[31] As we have already seen, in the introduction to his commentary on the Apostles' Creed Hus wrote that because he was a priest who had been sent by God he desired to explain the gospel to common people.[32] This approach is reflected in the admonitions of later Hussite preachers. Mikuláš of Pelhřimov proposed a homiletical 'Ockham's razor'. He agreed with Hus saying it was preferable to clarify matters of importance by simplicity rather than cloud the issues by excessive philosophizing.[33] Hus' sermons are more like commentaries on texts rather than expositions based on a pericope, and as such, are lacking in illustrative material. The preaching of reform had disadvantages. Sermons generally were not repeated, they were singular events. This meant the impact was by necessity limited. Furthermore, what Hus said and what people heard were two separate questions. Verbal texts, like written ones, have a life of their own. Resulting interpretations are not susceptible to control.

To underscore the conservative, orthodox nature of Hus' preaching it may be noted that in 1403 Hus preached twenty-five times on the Virgin Mary and her festivals. In these sermons he accepted uncritically the medieval doctrines of her virginity, annunciation, assumption and intercession on behalf of sinners. His preaching revealed thorough orthodoxy on topics such as baptism and penance.[34] Hus' christology is likewise consistent with later medieval theology *vis-à-vis* the dual nature of Christ and his sinlessness. There are repeated exhortations to follow Christ and a call for transformation, both moral and spiritual. In his exposition of morality Hus exhibited strong ascetic preference: he denounced sexual misconduct, greed, gluttony, drunkenness, ostentatious clothing, pride, games, dancing, hunting, and simony. His message of moral renewal was one of discipline, humility, poverty and a consistent rejection of the world.[35] In this world-negating context, Hus offered the alternative of Christ who came in human form specifically to rectify the follies and foibles of humankind. Human restoration could only be accomplished by the promise of eternal life extended in the shedding of blood.[36] Hus' doctrine of salvation is not misrepresented as a theology of the cross. In his Postil the water of baptism symbolized by the flow of water from the side of Christ on the cross indicates 'an abundant spring for the cleansing of sin'.[37] This theology of the cross constituted the heart of Hus' preaching. '[Christ] came to call sinners to repentance in order to compel carnal people away from the vices of carnality. He came to draw those stricken with cold to the fires of love. To those blinded by ignorance he has come to shine upon them. This all-powerful lord came not to kill the living but to call to life those already dead, in body and in soul'.[38] This was the remedy for those who followed Satan, the first to fall, into the ways of unrighteousness.[39] According to the preacher in Bethlehem Chapel, Christ came to give his own single life in exchange for the lives of many. '[Christ] came to humankind, came on account of humankind, came as a human'.[40] Rather than human works, Christ became the foundation for redemption and the power of God for salvation. Humans, spiritually dead in sin, find new life through God's action in Christ. On this Hus was thoroughly Augustinian. Salvation was based squarely on a predestination determined by God. Neither popes nor peasants were different in this regard. Both were recipients of divine grace, neither one nor the other could penetrate the mysteries of God.[41] The soteriological principle was entirely the prerogative of God. Humankind were the recipients, the beneficiaries, but never the cause or the reason. Even the human longing for God was a result of God. In a series of sermons Hus dispatched the ghost of Pelagius and proclaimed Christ as the gift of divine grace.[42] For Hus it was a matter of acceptance. 'Feel this sensation within yourselves . . . .' It was incumbent for the faithful to practice their faith and to come to terms with an experience of the crucified.[43] Preaching in Hus' Prague became a matter of knowledge, acceptance and experience. But even in this overwhelming Augustinian sense Hus did not admit that divine grace was irresistible. There are those, the preacher asserted, who spurn the grace offered.[44] Humans were not merely pawns in a cosmic game. Hus did allow for choice in the offering and accepting of divine grace. Humankind have been given the gift of free will by God and no one can be compelled to forsake evil and do good. The dignity of humankind consisted, for Hus, in the matter of free will.[45] Here he seemed to swerve toward the Pelagian option, but in the context of his corpus of sermons that option consistently paled in the light of divine initiative.[46]

Just as he had in his theological writings, so too in many sermons Jan Hus stridently decried the sale and acquisition of indulgences as developed by the fifteenth century. The preaching of indulgences for the forgiveness of sins was nothing other than deception, theological error and ecclesiastical abuse. His sermon for 10 December 1410 put a fine point on the abuses of the practice. The priests declare, 'give nothing but money and your sins shall be forgiven, free from punishment and guilt'. Hus affirmed that Prague indulgence sellers would spread wide their hands and announce to their hearers that whoever placed money in their out-stretched hands would immediately have their sins remitted. Even if the one who bought an indulgence were wicked and should die, their soul would go to heaven. By contrast a morally upright person, failing to procure an indulgence, would be consigned to eternal damnation in the absence of the formal certificate.[47] The entire enterprise lacked all merit, according to Hus, indeed no biblical justification could be found. St. Paul taught nothing of the practice, but rather expended his energy on preaching the gospel of Christ.[48] Hus declared the proffering of indulgences to be pompous and an arrogant affront to Christ. In a sermon Hus inferred that such priests actually preached to their congregations in this manner: 'You knaves! We can give you the Holy Ghost or send you to hell'.[49] Hus' preaching divested clerics of that assumed power and declared that God alone possessed the authority of salvation and damnation. As Christ in the Apocalypse of S. John asserts: 'I have the keys of death and hell' (1:18). A contemporary chronicler claimed that Hus convinced many faithful people not to buy indulgences.[50]

The theology of Jan Hus expressed in his sermons centered around the tripartite advent of Christ. In his sermon for the first Sunday in Advent Hus explained the three-fold coming of Christ. The first visit was as a child through the Virgin Mary. The second visitation was spiritual through divine grace. The third coming of Christ lay in the future in the day of judgment. Knowing these things, Hus preached, 'we ought to be diligent in the practice of right living. [Christ] came in his incarnation to secure salvation, by grace he comes to us and for the third time he will appear in judgment to provide for us a kingdom which shall have no end'.[51] Final judgment is a theme in his sermons. In his preaching, Hus becomes 'an eschatological figure and his preaching is an eschatological act'.[52] Thus far Hus' preaching was entirely consistent with the teachings of the official church.

Hus' sermons are less orthodox on the subjects of authority and the nature of the church but this is consistent with his theology. He stood firmly upon the medieval and social theories regarding authority. Unlike Wyclif, Hus did not reject canon law outrightly until late in life. However in a sermon on 22 June 1410 Hus rejected the authority of the local hierarchy but in the same year made it clear that authority was legitimate insofar as it adhered to the law of Christ. In 1410 after Archbishop Zbyněk carried out the destruction of more than 200 volumes of the works of John Wyclif, despite the protests of many including Hus, the rector of Bethlehem Chapel preached to overflowing crowds appealing to the word of God as the principle rule in what was interpreted as a challenge both to temporal and ecclesiastical authorities. His extant *Sermo de ecclesia* from 19 January 1410 dealt with the scriptural and doctrinal foundations of the church wherein Hus contended the church was comprised not of popes and cardinals but of the predestinate.[53] As in *De ecclesia*, the early sermons preached by Hus consistently identified Christ, not Peter, as the rock upon which the church had been built.[54] In support of his proposition Hus called upon St. Augustine's *Retractations* and appealed also to the Pauline conclusion of the first Corinthian letter (3:11): 'For no other foundation can any one lay than that which is laid, which is Jesus Christ'. His later sermons continued to define the church in this manner. Hence, Christ remained the head of the holy, universal church. The community of the faithful constituted his body, the predestined were part of this body and as such belonged to the church. Hus based his theology on the grounds of divine wisdom and purpose. Once again an Augustinian influence is evident.

Throughout his tenure as preacher at Bethlehem Chapel Hus raised the ire of the clergy by consistently denouncing clerical misconduct. His earliest sermons contain denunciations of the scandals of clerics.[55] His later sermons condemned priests for lack of concern for their specific ministries. Bishops, priests and canons came under the censure of the preacher in Bethlehem Chapel. Hus deplored the commonplace of hurrying through the order of divine service and then rushing out to secular duties, dances and other forms of debauchery. Jan Železný, Bishop of Litomyšl, was notorious for hurrying from a celebration of the Mass, laying aside his vestments, putting on armor, mounting a stallion and heading off to battle. The bishop became the general within minutes. Hus castigated such clerics as unfaithful and devilish in the manner of Judas of old.[56] In St. Vitus' Cathedral in the Prague Castle there is a full figure sandstone corbel on the north portal of the St. Wenceslas Chapel dating from the 1370s. A wild-eyed demon seizes Judas from behind and takes his soul, depicted by the demon tearing Judas' tongue from his mouth. The image may have influenced Hus. Moreover, in his *Quaestio de Indulgentiis* Hus argued that priests ought not to engage in warfare under any circumstance.[57] But he reserved his most severe and cutting invectives for those who filled ecclesiastical offices and abused the privilege entrusted to them.

> Priests are now sent but rather than preach they fill their bags [28 October 1411]. . . . They deserve hanging in hell [26 April 1411]. . . . They wander like bulls in heat, they are not worthy of anything other than sitting in the kitchen and filling their bellies [24 June 1411]. . . . The voice of some of the spiritual ones is like the Devil and they congratulate themselves for it, being immoral and opposed to preaching in the chapel. Egotistical preachers cry in high voices like wolves [2 June 1411]. These priests are parasites, whose work amounts to nothing in the Church. They are not true spiritual fathers [7 June 1411]. . . . They serve mass for the sake of money, and then gamble for this money. They are money misers. . . . and have become fat pigs [5 July 1411]. We resemble the swine who are in the mud, as long as husks fall for us, we roll in the dirt and eat them but when the husks stop coming we raise our heads from the mud and look for more. . . . If a common man admonishes a priest who is immoral, he receives this answer from the priest: "What are you trying to proclaim to me? Did I tend the plow with you"? [3 May 1411] . . . . "I am to serve in my office for the glory of God, serve Mass so that I can accumulate a large offering" - those who say this and do so are corrupt. They are drunks, whose stomachs

growl with great drinking. They are gluttons whose stomachs are so engorged, their double chins hang down [3 December 1410].[58]

His opponents condemned Bethlehem Chapel as a vociferous den of heresy, where heretics hide.[59] His frequent use of the term 'we' in describing the clergy may suggest that Hus did not assume a posture of self-righteousness but instead included himself among the preachers in need of consistent accountability and reform. Clerics committing fornication were sons of Satan and without correction, repentance and a change in lifestyle ought to be excommunicated and expelled from their office. The practice of simony, rooted as it was in avarice, led to a spiritual divesting of the church. Simoniacs, or 'the Lord's fat ones', came under special and continual censure in Hus' sermons.

In 1405 Hus was appointed synodal preacher in Prague. At the convocations of the Synod of Prague Hus remonstrated with his fellow priests encouraging reform. His synodal sermons of 1405 and 1407 particularly called the clergy to accountability.[60] In his 1405 sermon Hus invoked the authority of Bernard of Clairvaux in contrasting the lives of fifteenth-century clerics with that of Christ. He placed these words in the mouth of Christ: 'Everyone who passes by, pause and consider if there has been any sorrow like mine. Clothed in these rags I weep while my priests go about in scarlet. I suffer great agony in a sweat of blood while they take delight in luxurious bathing. All through the night I am mocked and spat upon while they enjoy feasting and drunkenness. I groan upon the cross as they repose upon the softest beds'.[61] Hus appealed to his colleagues to abandon the pursuit of material wealth, ecclesiastical ambition and the acquisition of temporal property. He demanded *imitatio Christi* and a pursuit of godly virtue. Hus accused many of his colleagues of having taken holy orders with the singular desire of feeding themselves and gaining wealth by appropriating money from the poor in the manner of Judas Iscariot.[62] Such clerics do not feed the sheep. Instead Hus declared that in their hands the keys were used to gain worldly power rather than opening the doors to the kingdom of God.[63] Priests were obligated to live up to their calling. Those who failed to do so were Antichrist. Referring to the armor motif in Ephesians 6, Hus argued either the armor of Christ is worn or the armor of the Devil.[64] Hus' consistent, strident calls for a reform of the church in head and in members attracted resistance from several quarters. Spies appeared in Bethlehem Chapel and made regular reports on the content of the sermons.[65] In 1408 members of the Prague clergy accused Hus of preaching scandalous sermons before great congregations. Some of his peers alleged these sermons caused the common people to hate the priesthood.[66]

The city of Christ stood opposed to the city of Antichrist in Hussite iconography and Hus used the distinction to drive home his emphases on moral reform. The house of God built on the foundations of faith and virtue had four corners: courage, modesty, justice and prudence.[67] The gods of the world were identified by Hus as avarice, gluttony, lechery, pride and the hatred of Christ.[68] Hus sought to uphold the house of God and destroy the gods of the world. The distinction can also be found in Hus' preaching on the nature of the church.[69]

Following the imposition of interdict upon Prague in 1412 Hus retired to south Bohemia where he continued his sermons. He began preaching in towns and marketplaces, in rural villages, in the forest, in fields, in barns and outside castles.[70] His preaching became increasingly recalcitrant and began to exhibit ideas now in the shadows of orthodoxy. In his Postil Hus condemned the pride of the papacy and denounced the veneration of the office as blasphemous and offensive to Christ.[71] Hus identified Rome as the pinnacle of Antichrist wherein the evils of pride, sexual immorality, hypocrisy and simoniacal greed were most evident.[72] In this identification Hus essentially divorced the official church from the aforementioned house of God and seemed to place her among the gods of the world. According to Hus, the only reliable means for ascertaining whether a pope was the vicar of Christ or the minister of Antichrist was contingent on whether that pope conformed to the law of God both in lifestyle and administration. 'The one who acts contrary to Christ' in these matters is a member of Antichrist. Among his early sermons we find the suggestion that a pope persisting in conduct unbecoming to holiness and godliness might in fact be deprived of office by the clergy.[73] Referring to Matthew 18:6, Hus deplored the several offences perpetrated by the clergy. 'Dear Christ! Should all who offend others by pernicious behavior be drowned, there would be left very few lawyers and priests. From the pope on down there were only a few not guilty of greed, pride and fornication, to say nothing of monks and priests living in concubinage'.[74] A critical assessment of the papacy can be determined from comments and arguments found in his sermons.[75]

Hussite iconography from around 1412 throughout the fifteenth-century regularly portrayed Christ and the pope in contrasting ways. One example featured Christ washing the feet of his disciples while the pope had his feet kissed by monks. Another portrayed Christ and the pope passing through town. This motif can be found in the sermons of Hus. While Christ rode on a small donkey, the pope sat upon a large white horse or war horse. The pope's stallion had a golden bridle, the harnessing was decorated with precious stones and colored tassels hung down to the ground. So opulent did the pope appear that the people barely noticed and paid no heed to the lowly Christ passing by on his humble donkey. Instead they knelt before the pope, adored him, declared his holiness as he rode beneath a richly embroidered canopy. According to Hus, the pope enjoyed the scene as multitudes pressed together attempting to get near and took great pleasure in the praise being lavished upon him. All the while, Hus preached, Christ passed by on a small donkey weeping, ignored and humiliated. The preacher in Bethlehem Chapel declared that such a scene accurately reflected the state of affairs in the official church in later medieval Europe and constituted blasphemy against Christ and the Word of God. Moreover, it patently bore the marks of Antichrist.[76] This was not an isolated example of Hus' attitude in his preaching. His sermons and writings are regularly peppered with denunciations against the spirit of Antichrist which Hus felt pervaded the Latin church during his lifetime.

Yet even in these strong words we find Hus referring to the Curia as the ministers of Christ.[77] This may suggest Jan Hus continued to be reticent about equating completely the official church with the gods of the world. In this posture he reveals himself less of a radical preacher and reformer than Wyclif, Jakoubek of Stříbro and, later, Jan Želivský.

One of the critical elements in the eventual downfall of Jan Hus was his presumed intellectual and spiritual alliance with the English archheretic John Wyclif. That question is considered in chapter six. Sufficient to say, Wyclif severed all ties with the official church in 1380 when he published his *De eucharistia*. That treatise constituted a full-scale attack upon the doctrine of the sacrament. A commission at Oxford declared it heretical. With this verdict Wyclif lost the support of his protector John of Gaunt and suffered subsequent banishment from Oxford University. He retired to his parish in Lutterworth, defiantly breathing out further fulminations against the papacy and the official church. It was his heresy with respect to the eucharist which gave him such notoriety. In essence, Wyclif's acceptance of the philosophical position of realism consequently led to his public denial of transubstantiation. In its place Wyclif advanced the theory of remanence. Jan Hus was charged with following the Englishman into this error. While Hus steadfastly denied the charge – and these denials can quite easily be buttressed by an examination of his writings as enumerated in chapter three – it persisted as an issue throughout his legal ordeal culminating at Constance in 1415.[78] It is manifestly clear that Hus did not teach the Wyclifite doctrine of the sacrament of the altar.[79] The closest Hus appears to come to Wyclif was in his ninth sermon for Holy Trinity, 1413. While expounding on Luke 9:1–8 Hus declared it blasphemy to consider or teach that in the words of consecration a priest actually created the body of God in the Mass.[80] This assertion was repeated by Hus at least once thereafter in print and inscribed upon the wall at Bethlehem Chapel. Notwithstanding this, only by the greatest stretch of the imagination, as previously noted, can these comments in Hus' Postil be construed as an attack upon the dogma of transubstantiation. Instead of challenging tradition Hus was decrying ecclesiastical abuses. Refraining comment entirely on the nature of the communion elements the Prague preacher was reserving for God the ability to create while declaring emphatically that humans, priests or otherwise, have not the power to create. Yet again the theology of Augustine is evident. This is substantially different from the themes developed by Wyclif in his works. Even during the early days of reform in Prague when the works of Wyclif were being publicly debated and defended it was not Hus but rather the erstwhile reformers Štěpán Páleč and Stanislav of Znojmo who defended vigorously Wyclif's eucharistic propositions. Following these debates and the defection of both masters to the anti-reform side, Hus reminded them of their outspoken enthusiasm for heresy. Writing in 1412 Hus suggested what may have been a painful recollection for Štěpán Páleč. 'Can you not recall the arguments of your colleague Stanislav, who, before the assembly of the university withstood calls for the condemnation of those articles [of Wyclif on the eucharist]. Can you not recall how you approved those articles'?[81] That Wyclif was one of Hus' sources, even in preaching, cannot be denied. His sermon,

'Vos estis sal terre' in 1410 quite clearly is dependent on Wyclif especially in the early stages.[82] But even overt and acknowledged influence does not necessarily inculpate one in heresy, a fact Hus' judges appear not to have considered.

His theology was very clear in his sermons. On the matter of the sacrament, Hus appeared to have always maintained the traditional doctrine. His early sermons reflect his position. Moreover, his Postil, written in exile contains clear articulation of Hus' position that in the sacrament the elements of bread and wine are changed into the body and blood of Christ.[83] This is entirely consistent with the medieval dogma of transubstantiation and completely at odds with the theory of Wyclif concerning the eucharist. Distinguishing between spiritual and sacramental communing, Hus asserted the one partaking without mortal sin received the body of Christ both spiritually and sacramentally, while those who communed unworthily received a sacramental condemnation. According to Hus the sacrament of the altar symbolized the death of Christ, remitted sins, provided the Christian with an effective defense against temptation and sin, communicated divine grace and in the end was the means for receiving eternal life.[84]

It was not Wyclif, however, who played the principle role of influence in Hus' sermons. In his book *De ecclesia* Hus made reference by citation or otherwise to Augustine more than one hundred times.[85] The Hus sermons reveal a similar dependence. Early sermons indicate that concepts and language had been borrowed from the church father.[86] While all of this is true it is possible that the Augustinian influence upon Master Hus was not always that of Augustine. Frequently, Hus misquoted or mis-attributed quotations. Hence, there are times when Hus cited Augustine but in reality was confusing Augustine with Gregory or some other ecclesiastical luminary, yet even in light of the evidence demonstrating numerous citation errors Augustine remained a fundamental influence upon Hus in the latter's preaching of reform.

Most of Hus' extant sermons were prepared in Latin thus the majority of the sermon texts are in Latin, though Hus delivered them in Czech. This assumption is supported by the fact that the bulk of his sermons were delivered in Bethlehem Chapel which had been founded specifically for preaching in the vernacular. Having prepared the sermon in Latin, Hus then preached his message in the common language, probably in a freer, extemporaneous manner. The same could be said for many of the later Hussite preachers such as Priest Jan Želivský (†1422) who would prove to be the most popular preacher in Prague after the death of Jan Hus. There is a considerable gap between the records of a sermon and the performance of preaching. The extant outlines of Hus' sermons are fairly extensive with an abundance of Biblical and patristic quotations, a point underscored by scholars who have studied Hus' sermons.[87] His preaching style was direct and personable. Frequently, Hus addressed his audience in Bethlehem Chapel according to their occupations, referring to them as his beloved in Christ, 'tailors, clerks, shoemakers and cobblers'. Hus' quotation of biblical texts in his sermons avoided the use of technical, archaic Czech and utilized language close to colloquial speech.[88] This was an integral aspect of preaching in Bohemia. Hus endeavored to speak on the level of his audience and thus we find him making constant reference to the practical experiences of daily life in Prague. Though the language used in the sermons was often blunt and concise Hus personalized the sermonic delivery by using personal pronouns to emphasize the relevant nature of his discourse. In preaching Hus identified himself with sinners referred to in Biblical pericopes. Occasionally he noted specifically with personal reference '. . . the sinner himself, such as Hus . . . .' In his later career when his preaching became more radicalized the persistent use of 'we' instead of 'they' served intentionally to motivate the people to see themselves in the context of the sermon as the direct recipients of the implications of the gospel and the intended audience for the message of the Biblical mandates.

On Christmas Day, 1413, Hus prepared a Christmas sermon in the form of a letter for his former congregation at Bethlehem Chapel. It underscored the simplicity of his sermons, his straightforward approach and his general avoidance of theological abstraction.

> Dearly beloved! Today, as it were, an angel is saying to the shepherds: 'I bring to you glad tidings of great joy for all people. . . .' As you remember these things, dear friends, be joyful for today God has been born in flesh in order that there may be glory to God in the highest and on earth, peace and good will among humankind. Be joyful that today the infinitely great one has been born a child. . . . Be joyful that today a reconciler has been born in order to reconcile humans with God. . . . Be joyful that today one has been born in order to cleanse sinners from sin. . . in order that there may be glory to God in the highest. . . . Be joyful with exceeding great joy that today a king has been born and has come to distribute the fullness of the kingdom of heaven . . . . Be joyful that today God has become bread for the hungry and refreshment for the weary that there may be peace on earth. Be joyful that as the eternal God has been born, we mortals may live forever. Be joyful that the rich lord of the universe lies in a manger as a poor person in order that he may make all needy people rich. . . . that there may be glory to God in the highest. . . . Be joyful that today is born one who can free us from all misery. . . . there is born this day one to comfort the sorrowful that there may be glory to God in the highest and peace on earth for all people. May it please the God born this day to grant to us that good will, peace and joy.[89]

This Christmas meditation is representative of Hus' sermons in terms of style, tone, language and message. Even in exile the pastor continued as shepherd. Protected by the nobles Ctibor and Jan of Kozí in south Bohemia, Hus remained a preacher. 'Previously I preached in towns and in the markets but now I preach among the hedges, in villages, castles, fields, in the forests as well as beneath a linden tree at Kozí Castle. If it were possible I would preach at the seashore and from a boat just as the Savior'. Hus went on to say that while Christ went on foot to preach, priests in his day rode in carriages which Hus admitted he did also from time to time in order to reach remote areas more quickly.[90] Hus claimed he was in demand as a preacher in south Bohemia.[91]

In preaching, Hus emphatically called his parishioners to an intimate understanding of their faith and a personal experience of the reality of Christ. 'Feel this'! His Palm Sunday sermon for 1406 noted earlier is a classic witness of this motivation. The sermon functioned in the reform program of Hus as a vehicle for bringing together the spiritual and the worldly and in that union an opportunity for grace, revival and reform.

Hus' preaching consistently removed the gospel from its biblical context and appropriated it to a fifteenth-century Czech context. For example, Hus' sermon on the Feast day of St. Stephen (26 December 1410) likened Prague to the biblical Jerusalem. Where Jesus once said, 'O Jerusalem, Jerusalem, who murders the prophets', so now Christ called in Hus' voice, 'O Prague, Prague, who murders my prophets, Milíč, Konrad and Matěj, and stones them'![92] He went further, 'if Prague will not receive the gospel, then she shall suffer as did Bethsaida, Capernaum and Sodom....'[93] The form of Hus' sermons is generally consistent with the style of preaching in the later Middle Ages, especially in its allegorical, anagogic and tropological dimensions.[94] His preaching was particularly pedagogical and exhortatory, always with the goal of moral transformation and spiritual awakening. The form of many sermons was distinctively aesthetic in their use of prose writing, declensions, the old Czech rhyme and poetic forms. Hus' sermons also employed the vehicles of sarcasm, irony, warning, instruction, admonition, and encouragement. Many of the extant sermons of Hus were of course taken down in shorthand by hearers and thus the problem of accuracy becomes a concern in any scholarly investigation of them. Apart from the Postil the texts of Hus' sermons are not reliable inasmuch as in the copying process they were possibly altered by others. The printed sermons reflect one response to the disadvantages of preaching noted earlier. Preachers like Jan Milíč of Kroměříž made available the texts of his sermons to be copied by scribes in order that what was preached one day theoretically might be circulated the next.[95] While the printed sermon texts certainly reached a potentially wider audience there remains the problem of literacy and the reality that printed texts almost without exception lack the fiery emotion and appeal which must have accompanied the oral delivery of the sermon. These printed versions of verbal texts provide more evidence of Jan Hus as a teacher, scholar and writer than they do of Hus the preacher.[96]

For Jan Hus, preaching was the chief task of the pastor. This is clear from his *De quinque officiis sacerdotis* wherein Hus listed the duties of a priest and made preaching the primary item.[97] 'God has instructed we priests to preach and give witness. This is the mandate of all preachers, none are excluded. There is no other command even from the common people than to preach the word of God'.[98] Yet all around, Hus declared, priests failed to fulfil the duty of their office which was to preach the gospel.[99] In his sermon *Vos estis sal terre*, Hus applied the metaphor of salt principally to the priesthood. Through preaching, this salt provided seasoning which brought hearers to Christ.[100] If preaching was the chief task of the priest, Hus was able also to enumerate the several benefits preaching held for those who faithfully attended the sermon. Those benefits included stimulating reason, aid in eliminating sin, comfort in controlling evil desire, destroying the propensity toward carnality and sin, keeping the enemies of salvation at bay, and finally a channel of divine grace.[101] Thus, when ordered to desist from his regular preaching, Hus refused to comply.[102] In defiance to the order Hus appealed and introduced his appeal in a sermon.[103] In a letter to the supreme court of Bohemia Hus admitted '. . . I am not willing to obey either the pope or the archbishop in their prohibition of my preaching, for it is contrary to God and to my salvation'.[104] He later remarked he did not care if 1000 bishops condemned him, he had an obligation to obey God and preach.[105] Hus' refusal to comply with the authorities on this matter was something he consistently drew public attention to. In his sermon for Palm Sunday 1411 Hus insinuated that the use of the vernacular in Bethlehem Chapel was a key motivation in the campaign to curtail his preaching activities.

> The Devil has taken notice of this and now he attempts to persuade masters, priests even lawyers to denounce those who sing praises to God . . . . They insist that those who do so should be silent. . . . In the name of God they say, 'we curse in Jesus' name everyone who goes to Bethlehem [Chapel] and also all those who sing [in the vernacular] *God has arisen from the dead, Christ Jesus, bountiful priest.* . . .' But Jesus the Lord responds to those who raise such objections: 'Indeed, I say to you, if these people are silent, then rocks will speak up'. Know this that the meek, ignorant ones will sing regardless of your complaints. The humble people shall sing with great joy to the savior of mercy, Christ Jesus.[106]

Hus claimed to be amused by the volleys of slander, vilification and condemnation he seemed to attract, asserting he lost no sleep over it and rejoiced in being hereticated and excommunicate.[107] There is other evidence he bristled at the charges.[108] In his fourth sermon for Pentecost 1411, while preaching on John 6:1–14, Hus digressed into the prohibition against preaching and dismissed it as an 'unworthy' and 'evil scheme'.[109] In his fourth Trinity sermon, preaching on Luke 14:16–24 Hus again condemned the prohibition.[110] In his Trinity V homily on Luke 5:1–11 yet again the defiant preacher underscored his refusal to obey the decree.[111] According to Hus, a good priest was a true servant of Christ and in his spiritual office was therefore of greater dignity than the secular king. Thus the commands of Christ, in this instance to preach, superseded all commands to the contrary. The king, however, was also ordained of God and was thus, in his secular office of greater importance than the priest.[112] Yet Jan Hus claimed that obedience to God was of greater significance than obedience to temporal authority. On 20 December 1410 he defended his preaching prerogative in a sermon on obedience. Not only did Hus withstand the order of the authorities, he suggested he would do all he could to impede those same authorities in their execution of that which he considered contrary to the law of God.

But someone will say, 'Nevertheless you, Hus, do not want to be submissive to your prelates, do not hear your elders, not even the archbishop. I respond: 'I wish to be like Balaam's ass. Because indeed the prelates of Balaam are seated upon me and desire to compel me to go against the commands of the Lord and not preach. I will impair the feet of their desire and will not listen to them; but in freedom and honesty will be in subjection to God in all things, because the angel of the Lord stands before me. . . .'[113]

Hus likewise proclaimed from his pulpit that should ecclesiastical leaders set forth ideas and commands contrary to the law of God, people were under obligation neither to adhere to them nor obey. If fact, disobedience in such circumstances was entirely appropriate.[114] As one who stood squarely on the medieval ground of political and social theory respecting order, Hus did regard civil and ecclesiastical authority as ordained by God. The prelate and the prince had been given power to protect the good and hold in check the evil.[115] One should neither hinder nor impair the operation of the other. Hus' opposition to the preaching of the cross in the crusading context is well known and indeed the point at which King Václav IV and Hus began to go separate ways. Preaching by Hus included a firm critique of the offer to forgive sins to those aiding the holy war declared by crusading bulls.[116]

As we concluded earlier in examining Hus' more formal theology, the charges of Donatism leveled against the Prague preacher are generally illegitimate though not without some basis. In sermons, especially, Hus condemned unworthy ministrations of the divine service and clearly stated that priests in mortal sin were unworthy ministers. Yet, the sacraments and proclamation of the gospel by such individuals still had benefit for the hearers and those receiving the sacraments, even if it produced damnation in the unworthy priest. A sinful priest saying Mass might bring condemnation on himself, but for the faithful it remained an untainted channel of grace in the sense *ex opere operato*.[117]

On 23 April 1411, preaching on Hebrews 13:17 Hus related his divine calling to preach the Word of God to the whole world and to withstand commands to the contrary even until death. Just before his death at the stake in 1415 Hus again, for the last time, gave witness to his own sense of mission as a preacher: 'the main point of my preaching. . . was. . . to turn people from sin. . . . In the truth of the Gospel that I. . . proclaimed. . . I am willing gladly to die today.'[118]

There are two misconceptions about the preaching of Jan Hus. First, he is too often cast as a proto-Protestant and made to bear the ideology of certain sixteenth-century reformers. While Hus did speak much of grace, faith, and the authority of Scripture *a fortiori* he knew nothing of *sola fide* or *sola scriptura*. Throughout the works and sermons of Jan Hus we can locate emphases upon the theological principle *fides caritate formata*, that salvation is apprehended when faith is formed or completed in love or good works.[119] The preaching of reform in the later Middle Ages should not be required to conform to the emphases of the European movements associated with Luther and Calvin. Second, Hus did not follow other Czech preachers or Wyclif in their emphasis of preaching at the expense of liturgy.[120] The claim that Hus was more concerned with preaching than liturgy is tenuous.[121] Arguments that Bethlehem Chapel was anti-liturgical, anti-Catholic and thereby anti-Roman are not persuasive.[122] Hus introduced a sung mass at Bethlehem Chapel every morning before the sermon. A balanced, proportional blending of preaching and liturgical celebration marked Hus' tenure at Bethlehem. While he was the first to introduce biblical exegesis into Czech preaching he contributed modestly to the developing liturgical reforms which the Bohemian Reformation was later to yield up to the evolution of ecclesiastical history.

On 23 May 1416 the university in Prague published a testimony that Jan Hus as a minister and preacher was an unequaled master.

> O incomparable man shining greater than all by the example of magnificent holiness. O humble man gleaming with the light of great piety, who scorned wealth and ministered to those in poverty. He opened his heart and did not refuse to kneel at the bedside of the sick. With tears he drew the hardened to repentance. By his matchless sweetness he calmed fierce minds. He raged against the vices of humankind particularly the rich and arrogant clergy. He founded his appeals on the ancient and neglected scriptural remedies. Formed in great love, this new motive caused him to follow in the footsteps of the apostles and through pastoral care he revived in both clergy and laity the righteousness of life as in the primitive church. Through courage and wisdom in speech he surpassed all others, demonstrating in all things the works of love, pure faith, and consistent truth. . . . in everything he became a master of life without compare.[123]

The repetition and duplication of ideas found both in Hus' formal theological writings and in his sermons underscores the nature of Hus' approach to his work. He did not normally theologize abstractly in his academic treatises and then enter the pulpit only to deal with utterly different concerns and topics. His scholarly ruminations reflected the realties of the religious world of his time and his sermons drew heavily upon the ideas he developed in his books. The consistency is important and in the construction of his memory after his death his preoccupation with preaching forms an essential component in his legacy. Here he is presented as a second Elijah, a faithful preacher, a Christ-like figure, and a holy man who spoke on behalf of God. These themes are reflected in the medieval "lives" of Jan Hus and can found in the narrative texts of sermons and literature throughout the fifteenth century.

His presence, passion and prowess as a preacher was later acknowledged by the prince of sixteenth-century preachers, Martin Luther who read Hus' sermons in an Erfurt monastery library. Luther found the sermons so moving he could not understand why so great a man had been condemned and executed.[124] Jan Hus was a university professor, academic administrator, priest, author, eventual saint to many, national hero, and religious martyr. He was all of these things, but to himself he was pastor and preacher to the faithful church of God in Prague. His own words are perhaps the best summary of his motivation and career: 'By the help of God I have preached, still am preaching, and if His grace will allow, shall continue to preach; if perchance I may be able to lead some poor, tired, blind, or halting soul into the house of Christ to the King's supper'.[125]

5

SPIRITUALITY

Aspects of the inheritance of late medieval religion centered on the spiritual life, which is not the same thing as formal religion itself. Augustine wrote, 'human voices must be still, human thoughts must rest. For they attempt to come to things which cannot be comprehended, not with the idea they can be grasped, but rather to share in them. And we can share in them'.[1] Mysticism may be described as the experience of unmediated, direct or immediate consciousness or awareness of the presence of God. In other words, mysticism is a form of religious knowledge derived directly from God. Its goals are three: union with the divine, inner peace, and the experience of the nature of God. From the late antique period Augustine is once more instructive. 'Do not go without, but turn within. Inside the inner person is where truth abides'.[2] Mysticism was an outgrowth of the medieval church wherein religion had become institutionalized and some Christians desired a more personal, spiritual faith relationship. Jan Hus is not generally thought of as a mystic but he shared some of the same concerns as the medieval mystics did. The outward form of religion without inner depth had no meaning and prayer which did not come from the heart was useless.[3] Hus did not advocate spirituality to the disparagement of the church but he admitted that at times organized church religion was unprofitable. He condemned the emphasis on the sensual at the expense of substance. He wrote that many people take delight in the visual culture of pictures and liturgical ornamentation. They preferred the aural pleasure of the bells, organs and songs which Hus dismissed as sometimes indecent, serving to stimulate a craving to dance rather than spiritual reflection. Instead of spiritual contemplation, the attention of the faithful too often became diverted to the appearance and actions of the priests. This included glamorous vestments, and the sometimes irreverent deportment which Hus described as talking, laughing and walking about within the sacred precincts. When these things were part of the context of divine worship, Hus opined that people waste their time at church. In the same reflection, Hus wrote of how the spiritual and wise man and woman take no note of such distractions but, mastering his or her senses, meditated on God and the eternal things of the faith.[4]

One of the great themes of the medieval mystical tradition was love. Mystical religion encouraged union and wholeness with God as the focus. This emphasis on love found inspiration and nurture in the Hebrew Bible *Song of Songs*, Bernard of Clairvaux, a succession of Cistercian writers, and John of the Cross at the end of the Middle Ages developed a series of commentaries on the text. Love comes to fullness when the lovers are so alike that each is mirrored in the other. When that occurs, love is complete.[5] This is the unity and union between God and the Christian pilgrim envisioned and sought for by the mystics.

Beatrice of Nazareth (1200–1268), a Beguine-trained Cistercian nun in what is today Belgium, wrote a vernacular work called *The Seven Manners of Loving*. It admirably summarizes aspects of mystic spirituality. There is no evidence Hus read Beatrice but both share common spiritual goals. The first manner constituted an active longing which motivated the soul. The second manner is the totally disinterested nature of true love. The third manner described the torture of love in which the soul cannot be satisfied because of the limitations of creation. The fourth manner involved great pleasure and great sorrow. In terms of the former, the idea of the 'abyss of love' is developed; a kind of rapture involving the loss of consciousness. It may be useful to keep in mind that the word 'abyss', from its Greek root, means 'without ground.' The fifth manner emphasized the 'madness and violence of love'. To quote Beatrice, 'it seems to the soul that the veins are bursting, the blood spilling, the marrow withering, the bones softening, the heart burning, the throat parching, so that the face and all the members perceive the inward heat, and this is the madness of love. At this time, one feels an arrow piercing through the heart all the way to the throat and beyond to the brain, as if one would lose their mind'. The sixth manner subdued all conflict and the mystic became the Lord's bride. The soul nears oneness with God. The seventh manner described how the soul is drawn upwards into the eternity of love, into the deep abyss of God.[6]

It is important to note that ordinarily mystics did not leave the church but sought a more inclusive spirituality within the church. Similarly, nowhere did Hus advocate religious practice apart from the church. Female mystics figured prominently in northeast Germany in the early thirteenth century and among them Gertrud the Great, Mechthild of Hackeborn, Mechthild of Magdeburg, Jutta of Sangershausen and Elisabeth of Thuringia. Angela of Foligno, Margaretha of Cortona, and Claire of Assisi in northern Italy represent another major center. More relevant for the world of Hus is the Beguine movement. Beguine communities existed everywhere in the Low Countries in the fourteenth and fifteenth centuries. Both sexes, but especially women in central Europe, took up the religious life. They did not live in convents or adhere to a particular rule. But they took private vows of continence and simplicity of life. These were sisterhoods founded in the Netherlands in the twelfth century featuring no common rule or hierarchy. The members were free to hold private property or even marry. They did not take formal vows and there was an emphasis upon manual labor. These were unofficial, unenclosed convents. The idea spread throughout western and central Europe during the later Middle Ages and we know that Beguines reached Prague. On 16 December 1273 Bishop Bruno of Olomouc reported to Pope Gregory X that Beguines were in Bohemia and he referred to them as women living in an unauthorized order without a rule.⁷ In the life of one of the early Beguines, we find 'she stayed at home and while living in the world she did not live in a worldly manner'.⁸ While the *Devotio moderna* and its influence seems limited in Bohemia, it cannot be ruled out as a stimulus for reform. The work of Hus reveals an affinity for the spiritual life.

From the twelfth century, mystics like Bernard of Clairvaux stressed the necessity for full human experience in the path to union with God. Hus drew considerably on Bernard. Shortly before Hus was born, the fourteenth-century Dominican nun Margaret Ebner described her encounter with Christ. 'As I went into the choir a sweet fragrance surrounded me and penetrated through to my heart and into all my limbs and the name *Jesus Christus* was given to me so powerfully that I could pay attention to nothing else. And it seemed to me that I was really in His presence. I experienced such great grace that I could not pull myself away'.⁹ This was the experience of God in the here and now; the mystical desire of the ages. The desire for God can be linked also to an important consciousness prevailing from the High Middle Ages. This too finds expression in Jan Hus.

In 1189 Lotario de' Conti di Segni wrote a book with the title *De contemptu mundi, sive de miseria conditionis humanæ libri III*.¹⁰ Within a decade its author became Pope Innocent III, perhaps the most noted of medieval pontiffs. The book proved influential, surviving today in more than 500 manuscripts. The argument of the book predated the late twelfth century by hundreds of years and persisted in literature until the sixteenth century. *Contemptus mundi* is more a mentality than merely a pessimistic outlook on human existence. There are several themes in this literature. The 'contempt of the world' is linked to the fact that human life ultimately is unsatisfying because it is temporary and subject to change. The natural order itself is undermined by irreversible decay. Everything in life and within the human condition is empty and worthless. All human structures are evil, devoid of ultimate value. Temporal life should be scorned with a view to the more important consequences of punishment or reward in the world to come. As we shall see below, one of Hus' more significant works on spirituality embraced these same themes. Innocent's very popular book appeared after more than a century of remarkable treatments of the theme. Among those noted are the *Apologeticum de contemptu mundi* of Peter Damian from the third quarter of the eleventh century which deplored lack of discipline in the monastic world.¹¹ Anselm wrote a short work addressing the theme of scorning the material world in deference to the eternal realm.¹² Hugh of St. Victor continued the theme underscoring the vanity of the world and counseled an alternative to the transitoriness of earthly life.¹³ The 'pious meditations on the knowledge of human life', falsely attributed to Bernard of Clairvaux, is perhaps the best of the theme's articulation by the twelfth century.¹⁴ Finally, it may be mentioned that the early part of *The Imitation of Christ* by Thomas à Kempis is very much in the *contemptus mundi* tradition.

It is evident Jan Hus attempted to come to terms with the realities of *de contemptu mundi* and his remedy for the 'misery of the human condition', following Innocent and especially Bernard of Clairvaux, is for the pilgrim to know himself or herself and to take account of one's sinfulness. In his short treatise 'The mirror of a sinful person' Hus counseled against worldliness and sin. By this means the Christian pilgrim may come to know God. This knowing oneself implied a renunciation of the world and all that is in the world, 'the lust of the flesh and the lust of the eyes and the pride of life' (I John 2:16) for these things are not of God but of the world. Only in this sense can the pilgrim begin truly to love God. Hus cautioned his hearers that those who loved the world would certainly perish but those who loved God would live and reign with Christ and the saints forever. God desired that pilgrims seek spiritual realities in God with the whole heart.[15] It was wise to separate from the world in order to avoid and resist the temptation of sensual pleasures.[16] Spirituality in Hus transcended the mind just as it did for medieval mystics. Humans were required to surrender faulty intellects to the guidance of the Holy Spirit in order to grasp and participate in the divine mysteries.[17] This did not mean spirituality lacked a rational component. The pilgrim was engaged in spiritual warfare and the enemies of the inner life were many. Hus took the view that one ought to love the soul of one's enemy more than one's own body. Therefore, the specter of martyrdom should not loom as terrifying to the faithful. Banishing the fear of death and embracing suffering is the pathway to obtaining the crown of the martyr. When Hus wrote these sentiments in his *Exposition of the Ten Commandments* he could not have known that his life would follow this particular pathway. However, Hus continued to press the point that he was obligated to set a good example for others, to do all in his power to confirm others in the same goodness, by example, even if that meant enduring suffering. Laying down one's life in humility and suffering not only brings the pilgrim to eternal salvation but remained as a witness to others as a 'glorious martyr to the entire church'.[18]

Central to the life of spirituality, and evident everywhere in the study of medieval mysticism, was prayer. So far as Hus was concerned, prayer was valuable because it established connection with the divine.[19] However, effective prayer cannot simply be a ritual act. Love for God was essential. Penitential acceptance of one's own sinfulness and reliance upon divine mercy were also vital aspects. If those elements were absent from the one praying the prayer becomes a stench before God. In his *Exposition on the Lord's Prayer*, Hus rather vividly described benefits of proper prayer and the dangers of improper supplication. 'Prayer is the fire of love which enables one to rise in strength to God. It has two wings, namely a recognition of our own sinfulness and of God's mercy. These two agreeable wings enable prayer to ascend to God. However, if holy thoughts, which facilitate prayer and piety, are not present then such prayers only create a foul unpleasant smoke. With this in mind, dear brother, if you do have love and holy thoughts, and piety, then [do not] smoke and stink'. Hus concluded his thought on prayer by wondering how often, as a sinful man, he created a stench and disagreeable smoke against the holy love of God.[20] Prayer functioned not as a solitary devotion or exercise in personal piety alone but Hus underscored a social dimension in prayer which brought the community of believers under the lordship of God as a heavenly parent. Proper prayer therefore was both humble and social. Hus developed the idea that God does not accept the pilgrim as an individual in isolation from others.

Thus, he instructed his hearers to pray not 'my father', but 'our father'. Social rank does not ultimately spare anyone from the vicissitudes or ultimate fate of human existence and by the same token does not allow anyone special access to the grace of God. Hus warned that those who assumed so were by the same calibration of their pride demoted and made all the more unworthy and therefore rejected by God who remained judge over all. Hus was keeping in mind the deadly sin of pride. Prayers which were not humble, even by great individuals, became liabilities before God. Since all have sinned and all are sinners and all desperately in need of divine grace, Hus cannot imagine why anyone should think of themselves more highly than another. The spiritual life was betrayed by arrogance. 'The unpretentious children of God pray with love and humility keeping in remembrance their Lord's instruction: "our father who dwells in heaven! Our father, who is almighty, who is our creator! Our father, who is pure in love! Our father, who is rich in heritage! Our father, who is merciful in redemption! Our father, who is capable of providing protection! Our father, who is ever prepared to listen! Take note of the kind of father we have who dwells in heaven"'.[21] Praying properly produced spiritual benefit. 'The one who desires to be heard must take heed to prayer . . . . whoever follows Christ in patience, humility and other virtues is his disciple'. Prayer should be addressed only to God. Hus condemned the excessive practice of directing prayer to saints more than to God to the extent where it seemed that some Christians appeared to give no thought to God at all. 'God wishes to teach us patient perseverance in prayer. Christ invites us to pray in all humility. Every Christian is obligated to pray, but not for temporal advantage, for honor or for revenge'.[22] Hus also considered it nonsense for people to pray in a language they can not understand.[23] Colleagues like Jakoubek agreed.

At the root of Hus' spirituality is a living and active faith which Hus argued illuminated the mind and caused excitement in the heart.[24] Whoever loved God, irrespective of their place of origin, Hus claimed to love most of all, even more than one's kin.[25] Sin oppresses, the *contemptu mundi* deadens the pilgrim as he or she contemplates the spiritual life, and Hus recognized that the way was quite difficult. 'Do whatever you have to do in order to find out whatever is wrong with you and then take comfort in God's unlimited mercy'.[26] The spiritual life was both inner and outward. The mitigating factor was the human propensity to sin. According to Hus, one sin can easily encompass several transgressions. For example, a violation of the sixth commandment on a holy day can involve seven sins. Fornication on a holy day implied disobedience to God. It was further a manifestation of greed by indulging in what was inappropriate, in this case women. Fornication was the sin of lust in and of itself. The act was often predicated upon envy. Such behavior produced anger towards one's own soul. It was an example of slothfulness because instead of sexual misconduct the perpetrator should have been attending divine liturgy. Finally, assuming one has committed but one sin, more enjoyable than gluttony, was really a violation of seven.[27] The logic seems extraordinary. Commenting on sin, Hus' younger contemporary Petr Chelčický observed that the prevalence of sin and moral infractions were so rife in society that the threat of severe punishment like the death penalty would result in a very sparse population in Bohemia.[28] Hus had already said as much.

Writing to a group of female religious, Hus noted he included a song which they should sing together at Vespers. He instructed them to sing with their lips, savor the words as they sang, and cultivate joy in their hearts.[29] Interestingly, Hus warned the women not to allow any men to overhear their singing lest they, overcome with indecent desires, cause the pious women to fall into scandal. An emphasis on the mystical experience of pity was apparent in the works of Hus. This is connected in a significant way to his devotion to the work of a priest which clearly underlay his career from 1402. Even at Constance while in prison Hus devoted himself to writing works of pastoral care (seven in all) which he either dedicated to his jailors Robert and Gregory or composed for them. These include *De mandatis dei et oracione dominica* which consisted of a discussion of faith and the commandments of God in light of the last judgment. *De peccato mortali* dealt with ethics. *De cognicione et dilectione dei* treated the subject of love as a basis for the Christian life. *De tribus hostibus hominis* warned against the dangers of the world, the flesh and the Devil. *De penitencia* underscored the need for penance. Hus wrote *De matrimonio* for Robert who had confided to Hus that he planned to marry. The other prison writing was the *De sacramento corporis et sanguinis domini* which has been discussed above.[30]

The service of God and the pursuit of the spiritual life is not an undertaking which necessarily removes one from the world, though one is clearly not of the world once the pilgrim joins the pathway to God. In his preface to his Postil, Hus enunciated the purpose of the incarnation as a bearing witness to the truth, a proclamation of the kingdom of God, a rescue of erring humanity, and an example of the true path to eternal happiness. The pattern is the same for the pilgrim seeking that mystical union with Christ and authentic spirituality. Humility, silence, poverty and love were the hallmarks of Hus' understanding of spirituality. Hus lamented that the world was filled with priests but few were intent upon the labor of salvation and spirituality in the Lord's fields of harvest, distracted as they were from fulfilling the priestly calling. Hus delineated his purpose in compiling his Postil as for the salvation of faithful Czechs who read and hear his words. Those desiring to know truth, to fulfil the will of God and ultimately of salvation, must seek God. Hus explained specifically how that might best be accomplished: avoiding sin, loving God above anything else, cultivating love for each other, and fostering a life of virtue. Such people were implored to pray to God on behalf of Hus who described himself as a sinner. Hus wrote that he proposed to 'loudly sound forth the word of the Savior so that it might be heard and known by the faithful for their salvation. . . . We should with diligence, love and resolve joyfully take heed to the words of our merciful Savior in order to proclaim and preach to others, to guide them into an understanding'.[31] Preaching on the first Sunday of Advent Hus enumerated the three-fold visitation of Christ as occurring in the flesh, in the spirit, and in the eschaton. The first of course had to do with the historical incarnation. The second was entirely a visitation of grace. The one who loved God may find the Christ of grace standing at his or her door prepared to draw that one by grace. If the pilgrim at that stage turned away from sin – the world, the flesh and the Devil – divine grace took hold and Christ entered. Hus used the imagery of a meal illustrating the reality as when two eat together. For the pilgrim on spiritual journey the meal was taken at table with Christ and the communing was attended with eternal joy.[32] This coming of Christ in grace was the immediate benefit of the spiritual life, the goal of the medieval mystics.

Consistent with his theological principle *fides caritate formata*, Hus argued that all people should seek to improve themselves by practicing virtue ever more diligently keeping in mind that Christ came for the purpose of redeeming humankind from sin. That was the first visitation. Daily visitations of grace strengthen the pilgrim for that third visitation which will come in judgment and for the faithful results in an everlasting kingdom.[33] Looking ahead to that oneness with God, Hus developed a number of principles to guide the pilgrim along the spiritual pathway. One should conduct themselves reverently and make preparations. Hus conceived of a house guest coming to visit and employed that analogy to make his point. The preparations are three. These include cleaning the house. In spiritual terms Hus implied cleansing from sin. The second preparation was for the host to dress in an appropriate fashion. The spiritual application suggested a glorious garment of virtue which symbolized sinlessness. Hus drew upon the biblical metaphor in Isaiah 52 of Jerusalem putting on a beautiful garment. The ancient city functioned as a metaphor for the congregation of the faithful, a holy place, where Christ would come to live and reign as king forever. The third preparation was to have a scrumptious meal in place. The theological implication here Hus tells us is fulfilling the will of God. The faithful pilgrim provided nourishment for Christ when the Christian observed his commandments. Hus alluded to Matthew 24 to make the point and drew upon Augustine in declaring that the visitations of Christ for the faithful are life but to the wicked they signify only the rule of the Devil and ruin.[34] The themes of preparation, advent, and reward dominate Hus' view of the spiritual life and these were consistent with the aims and objectives of the mystical approach in the later Middle Ages.

Setting aside sin, viewing the world with contempt, and embracing divine virtues became motivating factors for Hus. 'If we live in this manner we rightly remember the threefold visitation of Christ. We shall be acceptable subjects when Christ comes with grace in the here and now, and also at the hour of death and ultimately at the day of judgment'.[35] The witness of God is clear, Hus asserted, Christ came not to judge but to save, not to destroy but to redeem. But the pilgrim must prepare. 'Dearly beloved, may this be sufficient. Make preparations for his second and third visitations. Express regret for your sins. Make progress in virtue, be penitent, and await his visitations with wholehearted longing'.[36] The way of spiritual pilgrimage is one of penitence, with expressions of pain and sorrow for past transgressions and 'careful avoidance of all sins in the future'.[37] The inner life of the spirit involved the 'patient endurance of all manner of self-denial such as fasting, prayer, vigilance, and the several works of mercy which holy scripture calls the proof of repentance'.[38] A faithful Christian was a penitent sinner who had embarked upon the pathway to spirituality and God. Such a one possessed the assurance of the forgiveness of all sins if the pilgrim demonstrated penitent sorrow for those transgressions and made adequate satisfaction to God. Keeping the commands of God, doing righteousness, correcting all sins and excesses, and doing good to one's neighbor was more important to godliness than donating riches to the church.[39]

During his trial, Hus took the extraordinary step of appealing directly to God. This unusual move bypassed all mediation and effectively declared that the most relevant and effective seat of judgment was not in human courts but with God alone. Implicitly, Hus was dismissing law, judicial procedure, and legal custom completely. He did remove his case from the temporal jurisdiction of human judgment by invoking God directly even though, somewhat inexplicitly, he went to Constance. This position assumed by Hus at the Council mirrors, from a judicial point of view, the attitude of the late medieval mystic. It was possible to come directly to God and Hus stood on the principle that there existed no mediator between humankind and God save for Jesus Christ. Hus' surprising appeal may be regarded as the social application of his spiritual convictions. Hus would never have declared that purity of life was evidence of spiritual status or indicative of salvation. The thought consistently remained abhorrent to him. However, it is noteworthy that not a single accusation of moral failing or ethical impropriety was ever brought against Hus even by his most virulent enemies. After his death, Hus featured in a sermon preached by Jakoubek of Stříbro in 1417 or 1418 in Bethlehem Chapel. The sermon was based on Matthew 5:10, 'blessed are those who are persecuted for righteousness' sake, for theirs is the kingdom of heaven'. The purity of Hus' life was emphasized as a model of Christian behavior and worthy of the faithful Christian on pilgrimage. The sermon is worth quoting in extenso.

> First, let us give an account of the magnanimous Master Jan Hus, a preacher whose life is known to many of you. I therefore call you to witness that he was truthful and glorious in his deeds and preaching. The Lord gave him the capability to speak wisely, so he knew when to speak. He loved all people with compassion and affection and did not exclude his enemies and persecutors. Just as the second Elijah, he attacked with great zeal the rampant wrongdoing of the Antichrist and his simoniacal priesthood.[40] Tormenting his own body with such endurance he worked for the salvation of the people and everyone who saw him was convinced that his effort exceeded the scope of human and physical capability. He did not allow himself to rest but heard confessions, converted sinners, brought joy to the sad, preached and wrote. He was pure, chaste, pious, did not indulge and from the very beginning there was no arrogance, grudging, envy or hypocrisy in him. He sacrificed everything, even himself, for the salvation of souls.[41]

> His faithful teaching and interpretation of the gospel is still alive not only all over Bohemia and Moravia, but almost throughout the entire church. He was like the clear sound of a trumpet, a tireless preacher of the truth and the gospel,

an enemy of simoniacs, and a speaker on behalf of God. This equitable man left all of us who live in this contemptible, scorn deserving world, and joined Christ, his God and master.

Through the wisdom of his sayings and through the privileges he received from the heavens he served both locals and foreigners. Whom did he ever allow to leave empty-handed? If a rich man visited him he received advice, a poor person received support. He did not care at all about profit, he worked more than anyone else, took less than others did, yet hate was his reward.

How sad, he was taken away from us, and losing him we lost all the delights we have mentioned above. No sooner had he departed from us, than worries rush at us, troubles are knocking at the gate, only distress is left to us everywhere. I do not betray the eulogy of the holy man, I do not complain about the decision by which everyone receives what he or she deserves: he the crown that he deserved, we, who stayed here, endless misery and suffering which we deserve. I wish we do not miss him, he just went before us! I hope we might follow him one day, even from afar, to life in the company of angels! Let us lament for ourselves then; to lament for him is against reason. I think that if he could he would say to us 'do not weep for me but weep for yourselves' (Luke 23:28). How dishonored was this man who was as Christ! How despised he was by many wicked people. How perversely and how falsely he was suspected! He endured with patience unjustified accusations, excommunication, injustice, and Antichrist's anathemas imposed upon him by the simoniacal clergy only because he preached faithfully with such enthusiasm! He was exposed to many dangers both at home and on the streets of Prague! He was in danger when travelling and wherever he arrived he was in danger from those of the false brethren, that is from vicars and prelates, as well as from dukes and other secular rulers. But he endured all of this patiently for the gospel of our Lord Jesus Christ.[42]

Previously we noted that Hus regarded songs and singing as conducive to the spiritual life. Apparently he introduced congregational singing at Bethlehem Chapel.[43] He took the same view of books and preaching and the full scope of the religious and liturgical life of the later medieval church. This included the use of visual images. Hus regarded these as good for teaching the unlettered and for appealing to those for whom sermons proved ineffective. Moreover, the use of a positive visual culture served as a reminder to the forgetful and a call to remembrance for all the faithful.[44] Some scholars have argued for a prominent role of religious art in Hus' theology and spirituality.[45] The claim is ambitious. It can only be affirmed that Hus did not forbid the visual religious culture and authorized its use in churches. It is known that both Hus and Jakoubek after him placed upon the walls of Bethlehem Chapel visual aids for the faithful. It would be too ambitious to argue for too much in terms of Hus' understanding of the spiritual value of pictures based only upon the fact that he placed texts on the wall of his church. It cannot be determined precisely when visual images appeared in the chapel or what part Hus played in their introduction. Certainly, visual images played a significant role in the history of Hus' disciples but that constitutes a separate consideration and it may well be anachronistic to include Hus to any significant degree in the history of that phenomenon. Hus did regard books and images as important in the sense they represented something greater than themselves. Pictures were signifiers or signposts.[46] Regardless of the importance once should or should not attach to Hus' use of visual sources of piety, what remains clear is that purity of conduct, ethical behavior and fidelity to imitating the life of Christ remained at the core of Hus' understanding of spirituality. Pictures and books were secondary.

A fully-orbed study of Hus' ethics also awaits a thorough scholarly treatment.[47] If Jakoubek is to be believed, Hus' life is the best study for his ethics and indeed at Constance his refusal to acquiesce in an inducement to perjure himself is a significant testimony. The posture Hus assumed emerged from his understanding of spirituality. Hus declined to confess culpability for the articles brought against him at Constance. The conciliar fathers judged his reticence as another example of his contumacious nature. For Hus, it had nothing to do with being stubborn or proud. He wrote from the Franciscan prison three weeks before his death explaining his position. 'To abjure means to confess that I have held errors' but since Hus had never adhered to the articles presented, to submit the required retraction would be in effect to lie.[48] One of the extant trial records has Hus addressing the Council on this point. 'If I were to abjure all of the articles laid against me . . . I would, by lying, set myself up for damnation. To "abjure" . . . is to renounce a previously held error. But inasmuch as many of these articles attributed to me have never been held or even been in my heart, it seems to me therefore that to abjure them would be against conscience and to lie'.[49] Several prison letters underscore Hus' concern that in recanting he would be lying and committing perjury. 'Having preached for so many years about patience and faithfulness, how can I now fall into falsehood and perjury'?[50] Efforts to persuade Hus to reconsider failed. Further letters, personal appeals, and a visit *in camera* to his prison cell by an anonymous member of the Council, argued that even if Hus had not held the propositions lodged against him, he should nevertheless say that he did hold them, even if technically that meant committing perjury. If he did perjure himself, the blame would lie with the Council, not Hus. The point revolved around issues of authority. Effectively the prisoner was told that if the Council determined something was black when in truth it was white Hus ought to confess it was black in concert with conciliar authority. Alternatively, if a superior authority told Hus that he had but one eye when in fact he had two he ought to believe and say that he had only one eye.[51] During the evening before he was executed Hus received his friends Jan of Chlum and Václav of Dubá in his cell. The former counseled Hus to follow the dictates of his conscience and under no circumstance deviate from that commitment. Do nothing against conscience.[52] To the end Hus remained resolute. He did not confess, recant or perjure himself. There would be no one-eyed Hus in Constance.

Hus' spirituality and religious orientation found roots in ethical behavior. His firmness on this point did not arise when faced with crisis at Constance. Instead, Hus had long made the same point. In his exposition on the ten commandments Hus deplored the voluminous slander in society and the sheer numbers of what he described as 'backbiting dogs'. Hus had in mind especially the religious who ought to have known better and who should have been prepared to set a proper example. Claiming the practice had become so widespread it was no longer regarded as sin, Hus submitted that priests in the vestry preparing to celebrate Mass engaged in slanderous conversation. Once the liturgy ended these same priests went off to table and before they consumed the cooked flesh they devoured the living. The lack of compassion and malicious statements was appalling. Such behavior, Hus thundered, served the Devil. The slandering extended to the monks and nuns under holy orders as well as to the laity.[53] Spirituality and the Christian faith had definite social implications for Hus. It is not difficult to think that Hus in his enthusiasm for scripture might well have followed Matěj of Janov in his conception of theology. But in fact Hus did not. There is little to suggest that he followed the direction of the *Regulae*. While his theology remained conservative, Hus' spirituality was quite strictly biblical both in nature and orientation.

'How shall I act'? For Jan Hus, this question had only one possible answer. That answer lay squarely within Hus' understanding of the gospel, the example and ethics of Jesus, and spiritual identity. Guided by conscience, which Hus attempted to have informed by scripture and religious tradition, he determined that ethical conduct, fidelity to the truth, and concern for the welfare of his parishioners must take priority. Faced with the ban of interdict and the decision to comply or ignore its stipulations, Hus turned to conscience, scripture and tradition. He went to some length to explain his decision making. His struggle, enumerated in his own words, underscored the spiritual depth and dimension he cultivated while laboring in Prague.[54]

Hus' daughter

Any meaningful discussion of Hus' understanding of spirituality or mystical union with God must take account of his most profoundly spiritual text. In 1413 or 1414, while in exile in south Bohemia and living in the forest at Kozí Hrádek, Jan Hus wrote a devotional treatise titled *Dcerka: O poznání cěsty pravé k spasení* (The Daughter, or how to know the correct way to salvation).[55] It was written for a community of women living together in a house near Bethlehem Chapel in Prague. This was not the first time Hus had provided women with literature. The vitriolic Abbot Štěpán of Dolany complained that Hus had even supplied ladies with written heresies.[56] The community seems to have been essentially Beguine though there is opinion suggesting the women were rehabilitated prostitutes in the tradition of Jan Milíč's Jerusalem community.[57] I find no compelling support for this view. Contemporary sources allege that Beguines were followers of Hus, hyperbolically reported as 'women without number'.[58] Among this group of women was the noble woman Petra Říčany and the highly educated Anežka Štítný. The latter was the daughter of the university–educated vernacular writer Tomáš Štítný, and she had been a leader of this community since 1401. From the correspondence of Jan Hus and the extant records of the Old Town of Prague dealing with the purchase of property we have the names of fifteen women and an indeterminate number of female servants associated with Hus living in the immediate vicinity of Bethlehem Chapel. These women occupied at least six houses though the precise number is impossible to determine. In addition to the 'saintly' Petra Říčany and Anežka Štítný we know the names of Kunka of Vartemberk, Střezka of Čejkovice, a young woman named Ofka, the four sisters Bětka, Anežka, Zdena and Ofka, Důra of Bethlehem, Markéta of Peruc, Kateřina Bohdal (whom Hus called Ješkova), Markéta of Ostrý, and the sisters Ludmila and Kateřina of Pasovaře. Flajšhans thinks the latter might be the woman Hus called Kateřina Hus, 'a holy virgin'.[59] Some of Hus' female supporters drew considerable fire. Anežka of Mochov was specifically named in an anonymous anti-Hussite verse around 1417. She was denounced as a disciple of Hus, a 'raging Jezebel', an 'inglorious female' and a 'cruel witch', who persecuted righteous priests and whose faithlessness would be punishment with demons in the tortures of hell.[60] It is noteworthy that Hus regarded women as sometimes more zealous in defending truth than theologians.[61] Like Peter Abelard, Hus recognized it was a woman who became an apostle to the apostles (*apostola apostolorum*).[62] Mary Magdalene was honored by Christ since he appeared first to her.[63] Women were the first to be chosen to share in the resurrection of Christ. The glorious announcement came to women first and thereafter through women to the apostles. Therefore, all should take heed to the faithful counsel of women, especially faithless priests. Hus asserted many priests refused to be instructed in any way by a woman but he considered that attitude unhelpful. Women were fine examples, Hus declared, of responsiveness which God honored with special gifts of revelation.[64] Overall, there has been too little research done on women in late medieval Bohemia.[65]

The themes of this treatise enjoined the readers to know themselves and to take into full account the factors and forces present in this life which served to detract the faithful from finding salvation. This was Hus' central contribution to the tradition of *contemptus mundi*. The struggle, which Hus enumerated, concerned the three principal ancient foes: the world, the flesh and the Devil. Hus encouraged the female readers of his book to consider the act and value of repentance, the coming final judgment and the love of God. As a devotional writing, concerned with spiritual formation and union with God, *Dcerka* may be compared to the works of Thomas à Kempis, *On the Imitation of Christ* and Gerard Groote, *Following of Christ*. The Czech vernacular of the later Middle Ages ensured the book remained in limited circulation and therefore never came to a European-wide audience as did Kempis and others. Indeed, even scholars of Hussitica sometimes ignore this book.[66] It remains to be seen if the daughter of Jan Hus is simply a construct for making a theological point or a tool through which Hus communicated the values of his culture.[67] For his arguments, Hus drew upon the influence of several authorities but especially on that of John Wyclif in chapter four only, and Pseudo-Bernard throughout. It has been suggested that Hus had a Latin model in mind as he wrote but I have found no evidence for this.[68] Because of its importance and relative obscurity it has been selected to exemplify aspects of Hus' concern for spiritual formation and mystical inclination in the religious world of late medieval Prague. Unlike Hus' commentary on the Sentences of Peter

Lombard, *Dcerka* is not an exercise in academic writing. The daughter of Jan Hus is a classic within the literature of Christian spirituality.[69]

The Daughter, or how to know the correct way to salvation is a formal treatise of about 13,000 words. Consisting of ten chapters, Hus began each chapter with the declaration '*slyš, dcerko*', 'hear , O daughter'. It has been suggested that *Dcerka* was meant to be heard, not read.[70] In the prologue he carefully articulated the themes of the chapters to follow. Each one was devoted to an aspect of spiritual understanding aimed at facilitating a life of piety and devotion.

> Hear, O daughter, and listen carefully, for I want you to learn about yourself, to know in whose image you have been created. Second, so that you can learn about your conscience. Third, so that you can learn about the misery of this life. Fourth, so that you can learn about the temptations of this world. Fifth, so that you can learn about the three enemies. Sixth, so that you can do penance properly. Seventh, so that you can respect the dignity of the soul. Eighth, so that you can realize that there will be a day of judgment. Ninth, so that you can respect eternal life. Tenth, so that you can love the Lord God more than anything.[71]

It is clear that Hus' aims were not unlike those writing earlier in the *contemptus mundi* tradition.

Seeking to alert his females readers to the unsatisfying nature of life and the temporal order, and the coming day of judgment, Hus pressed the importance of self-knowledge with a view towards eternity. It is clear Hus adopted the position that while knowledge abounded, inner contemplation was lacking in late medieval society.[72] It is a judgment call on Hus' part and ostensibly he stresses spirituality and mystical union with God in ways that ordinary society did not. The beginning of the spiritual path is the interior way. There, Hus encouraged the women in the Bethlehem Chapel neighborhood to start with themselves. It was pointless to attempt to contemplate the mysteries of the divine while ignoring one's own condition. 'Begin with yourself . . . learn about yourself, because the more you learn about yourself, the more you will learn about God. The closer you are to God the more you will love God. The more you love God, the more God will love you'.[73] This was consistent with the medieval mystics. Earlier we noted where Hus postulated the bifurcation of human nature which then strove for competing values, God versus sensuality.[74] That same basic division appears in *Dcerka*. According to Hus the human being was both soul and flesh. The flesh was external, the soul internal. The body had a tendency to sin while the soul was predisposed to virtue. The soul was made up of three components: memory, reason and will. These components comprised the human ability to think about God, to know God and to desire God.[75] Hus argued that if his community of women understood the nature of soul they would realize their superiority in the created order. The tripartite nature of the human soul paralleled the triune nature of God. Hus went to some length to draw this comparison, articulating a Trinitarian understanding of the divine nature preserving the unity of the Godhead wherein God existed as three persons but as one being. The Trinitarian nature of God is co-equal, co-eternal, one in essence, nature, power, action, and will. The three persons exist in God as one unity. There is nothing in Hus to suggest anything other than an orthodox Trinitarian understanding of God.[76] Applied to humanity, Hus declared the soul as one spirit or substance but made up of three things: memory, reason and will. When these three aspects were combined in the soul they reflected and contained the image and likeness of the Holy Trinity.[77] Applied theologically, the Father provided the human soul with power in order to successfully oppose sin. The Son provided wisdom in order to avoid evil while the Holy Spirit contributed free will to enable humans the ability to not choose evil. When these three things were observed and known, Hus argued, then that person possessed the image and likeness of the Holy Trinity to the extent that nothing else in all creation was more similar. By means of memory, reason and will, the pilgrim may be inclined to God. However, memory, reason and will cannot bring one to the knowledge of God alone. Knowing oneself had considerable spiritual benefit, Hus tells the Prague women, for 'you will find God in yourself. . . . whoever knows God . . . and loves God, is loved by God'.[78] With the knowledge that one has been created by God in the image of God (*imago dei*) it was incumbent to avoid mortal and venial sin to the best of one's ability. Here we see a subtle allusion to the doctrine *fides caritate formata* with the result that God resided in the faithful pilgrim. Hus urged his readers to 'reflect every day on how similar you are to God so that you will not ruin this similarity through mortal sin'. The women whom Hus addressed in this treatise were reminded they were creations of God, beautiful in their souls, moving towards God and eternal joy, but cautioned against damaging the image of God within by means of sin. The faithful pilgrim finds God as their beloved spouse. So 'learn about yourself', Hus urged, in order to know God and to become one with God.[79]

Knowing oneself means also learning about conscience. Hus submitted that everything one does, sees, wherever one goes, all is stored in the soul and remains within so long as one lives. Once the pilgrim dies all of it comes back. This is a harbinger of final judgment which Hus turned to eventually in his discussion of the spiritual life. The role of conscience takes on an important aspect of avoiding sin and moving closer to God. 'The conscience is the prosecutor, memory the witness, and reason the judge'.[80] Conscience functions as a 'personal teacher' in revealing sin and alerting the pilgrim to various pitfalls which might terminate his or her spiritual pathway. Hus identified at least five impediments to the proper operation of conscience. These included ignorance, carelessness, pride, lust and fear.[81] True to his commitment to the biblical witness, Hus advised that scripture ought always to be consulted with respect to all 'past, present and future acts'. Moreover the example of Christ should be regarded as paramount to all else. In this emphasis, Hus was consistent in applying his theology to the question of spirituality. He warned his readers to avoid a conscience which may be either too broad or too narrow. The former might allow for practically any thought, word or deed, while the latter led the pilgrim to desperation and despair.[82]

One of the abiding central themes of the *contemptus mundi* literary tradition was the preoccupation with how unsatisfactory human life was on account of the tendency to decay, the inherent evil in social structures and the result that all of life ultimately was worthless. For Hus these were incentives to the pursuit of the spiritual life. Therefore, the pious women living near Bethlehem Chapel were encouraged to learn about the misery of human life. Hus pointed out that misery was a condition of both body and soul. Misery of the soul resulted from sin and absence of divine grace. It was far more serious than misery of the body. The latter was caused by the needs of the flesh, to wit, hunger, thirst, heat, cold, nakedness, lack of adequate shelter and so on. The misery of the human condition is such that there is never enough of everything. The healthy may be poor. The rich are weighed down by having to manage their vast holdings. The sick are miserable from pain. Those in authority must administer their responsibility. Those who have property are miserable because they might lose their belongings. The young are susceptible to lust and impulses of the flesh and may be 'driven to fornication, pride and debauchery. If one does not have it, they are troubled, if they do have it they are defeated'.[83] Then life moves on inexorably and the challenges of old age only intensify the misery of the human condition.

> Then old age comes and one's heart becomes sad, their heads shake, their soul is mournful, the spirit sinks, the face becomes wrinkled, one becomes smaller, their eyes are runny, the nose is drippy, the mouth drools, they lose their teeth, the lips are rotten, their hair falls out, they become deaf, the voice grows hoarse, the heart is faint, the lungs are rattling and the throat sounds as though there were musicians inside. And many more imperfections are in the body. And what is the sickness of the soul of old people? I found it to be like this: an old man, who became old while angry, does not get better easily, just as an old crooked tree can hardly be straightened by anyone. An old man gets angry very easily and it is very difficult to make him happy, he believes in bad things easily and it is very difficult for him to abandon this belief. An old man is greedy, sad, and always complaining, he likes to speak, but does not listen properly, he is always ready to be angry: if he has money he hides it, he is afraid to indulge in anything, he does not like to give it away, and if he gives, he likes to receive; he praises old people and those deceased, he harshly criticizes the living ones, he longs for the past, he takes pride in his past deeds, he sighs for them, he shakes his head, he rattles his teeth complaining that he can not sin. His heart shakes, his lungs can hardly breathe, he stoops, his back bends, his body shakes; he pisses on his own feet and death waits outside the door, but the old woman still shouts: 'Hey, John let me hop over the garden fence'. Oh, what craving! Even such misery will not tame an individual![84]

Even joy in life, the pleasures of the flesh, were filled with sadness. Sexual indulgence rated highly on the pleasure scale, Hus wrote, but scripture confirmed there was only happiness in sin for a short time. Moreover, he cited secular sources which asserted that sexual pleasure drains the soul. In this pleasure there is sadness, injury, shame and death. 'There is as much pain in pleasure as flowers in the field'.[85] The misery of worldly existence may be reduced to the fact that 'the longer we live the more sin we accumulate and the more punishment await us'.[86] Therefore Hus concluded chapter three with the admonition the pilgrim ought to take heed that life is filled with misery, one should not enjoy it or seek long life. It is better to hurry onward to God and eternal joy. Elsewhere we find Hus encouraging a group of young women to the spiritual life and sexual abstinence.[87] Implicitly, Hus suggested the earlier one commits to the life of spirituality the better. He suggests that up to age fourteen each person existed in the morning of life. From fourteen to twenty eight was the beginning of sorrow. From twenty eight to forty eight strength starts to fail, social disadvantage sets in and there was a tendency for more sin. Between forty eight and seventy life slows and there is little to do. From seventy to the end of life old age takes hold and everything is increasing loss.[88]

Chapter four was a lengthy treatment concerning the temptations of the world.[89] Hus argued that the body would not experience temptation were it not for the soul's existence. That was the focus of all temptation. The Devil was no more interested in the flesh than in animals or inanimate objects. Hus forcefully stressed that temptation in itself did not constitute sin. Temptation only had power and sinful value if the will consented with the temptation. He called upon the traditional authority of Augustine and Gregory to support his assumption. According to Augustine, if one did not choose to yield to the temptation evil did not exist and one could not be harmed by temptation if one did not allow it.[90] Similarly, Gregory asserted that regardless of how impure a thought may be, it could not tarnish the soul unless the human will allowed it.[91] Hus argued that if St. Peter saw a beautiful girl and felt carnal desire for her but resisted the urge to act on that desire he had not sinned.[92] The Devil was the main source of temptation and these diversions were administered where they were thought most effective. So the Devil focused on holy people especially because they were the ones who interfered most with the kingdom of darkness.[93] Above all the Devil wished that people would not repent of sin and thereby forfeit spiritual progress. Hus suggested the Devil could best be refuted if those devoted to the spiritual path carefully observed three principles.[94] First, one should not focus too much attention on emotion or the cares of life. This caused potential vulnerability. Second, the pilgrim ought to strive for enlightenment by faith, hope and love and all three may be strengthened by scripture. Third, the best antidote was to constantly observe devotion through prayer, writing (if one were able), singing, communicating with godly people, and by avoiding isolation. Hus engaged in a lengthy admonition on how to practically refute the Devil and render useless all advice against following the pilgrims' path to God.[95] The source of eternal truth resided in Christ. This is the only chapter in *Dcerka* where it is possible to detect any allusion to Wyclif.[96]

Consistent with the spirituality of the later Middle Ages, the concerns of the mystics, and the themes of the *contemptus mundi* tradition, Hus turned the attention of his female readership to the three enemies of all people: the world, the flesh and the Devil. Citing the Psalter Hus declared those enemies surrounded the soul and attacked the soul through five gates. These gates were the five senses – vision, hearing, taste, smell and touch – and through these portals the world and death entered. For example, 'touch encourages fornicating and if it is not rejected soon it burns the body immediately. It encourages the mind to accept these pleasures and the will to agree with it. In this manner the sin is accomplished'.[97] So the Devil sets traps and with the traps used the added danger of glue. This glue was desire for riches, an inclination to friendship, the pleasure of glory, and physical debauchery. The glue sticks to the soul and prevented flight to God. A military scenario unfolded. The Devil's arrows were anger, envy, pride and fornication. Humans were exposed to these assaults everywhere and nowhere can one be assured of being safe. The struggle was constant and ongoing. Temptation, traps, snares and open assault perpetrated by the Devil, nevertheless require the assistance of the flesh for success. So Hus encouraged the women of Prague to take heed to bringing the flesh into subjection. The grace of God was the infallible remedy and Hus referred to the autobiographical lament of St. Paul in Romans chapter seven to encourage the pilgrim.[98] The best defense against temptation and sin was through the word of God. The joys of the soul were superior to the joys of the body; the pleasures of the flesh were temporary while the pleasures of the spirit are everlasting.[99] There is a commonplace medieval distinction between literal and spiritual meanings in a text. There is evidence that Hus sometimes approached texts with a mystical reading aimed at getting to the spiritual meaning.[100]

Through all of the tests, trials and temptations which the faithful pilgrim can expect to encounter, one must learn about the value of repentance. This learning, Hus suggested, came about by careful listening with the physical ear and the inner ear. The true penitent does not care about the pleasures of the world and takes all steps to avoid sin following repentance. Hus approvingly referred to Augustine who taught the benefits of repentance were nullified by further sin.[101] And Hus added that subsequent sin made a mockery of penance and the penitential system.[102] Hus placed a very firm point on the value of repentance. 'Just as ultimate repentance, which is full and proper, will save one no matter how much they have sinned, so ultimate non-repentance, no matter how good that person is, will damn that individual'.[103] Alone, the pilgrim is not able to withstand the schemes of the Devil and the challenges of the pilgrimage. Only the grace of God can help. Hus advised the faithful to prevail upon the cult of the saints for assistance. But equally as important was a regular exercise of self-reflection. Evaluate all personal actions. Control all impulses which lead to thought, word and deed. Then, very much in the trajectory of the church reforming climate in Bohemia, Hus placed emphasis on the eucharist. The pilgrim can be strengthened by the 'living bread, the body of Christ'.[104] Questions of sin or temptation were addressed through the sacrament of the altar. 'Approach the holy body in remembrance of the Lord Jesus Christ and for your benefit. I will not set any standard for you . . . [but] eat that bread either every day or every other day, or once a week, or only on Sundays, or once a month, or as God prompts'.[105]

Along with the eucharist, Hus underscored those on spiritual pilgrimage must love God with all one's heart, remain in God's grace and practice the penitential life. This consisted of sorrow, confession and atonement. The latter was accomplished through prayer, fasting, and spiritual works such as wisdom, advice and discipline. It was also facilitated by works of mercy which included feeding the hungry, clothing the naked, visiting the sick or those confined in prisons. But the primacy of repentance remained. While elsewhere in the Hus corpus he expressed some doubt, here he declared that 'no one will be deprived of the heavenly kingdom if they repent at the time of death'. For indeed, Hus admonished his readers that there was power in the penitential path, the dead are brought to life, the blind see, the servants of the Devil become the servants of Christ, and those who previously did not know themselves come to know themselves through repentance.[106]

The value of the soul was the counterbalance to the transitoriness of human life, the decay of the natural world, and the evil of worldly structures. The soul, according to Hus was more valuable to God than either heaven or earth. Accordingly the soul is the dwelling place of God, the context of prayer, and a venue of sacrifice to God. On this third point Hus enumerated this interior altar as 'living faith' and love for God as the fire which one ought never allow to be extinguished. God resided in the soul through grace and God takes greater delight in this sanctuary than in all of the churches, monasteries and chapels in Christendom. Such physical sanctuaries exist only for the salvation of souls which will live forever while the material buildings will be destroyed at the day of judgment.[107] Turning to a theology of the cross, Hus declared the death of Christ liberated the soul for God and released the shackles that otherwise confined the soul eternally to hell. Hus encouraged the devout women in the Bethlehem Chapel neighborhood to not fear suffering. The terrors of suffering have been absorbed by Christ. The value of the soul was measured by the fact that God desired to become human for the purpose of redemption in order that humankind could become God. This allusion to humankind becoming divine remained a significant idea both in Latin and Greek churches especially during the Patristic era. Churchmen like Ignatius, Irenaeus, Clement of Alexandria, Gregory of Nazianzus, Gregory of Nyssa, Maximus, John of Damascus, Tertullian, Cyprian, Origen, Hippolytus, Methodius, Athanasius and Augustine were all exponents. Hus was therefore reflecting a well-established theological tradition.[108] Therefore, 'hear O daughter', respect the dignity of the soul, keep it pure for the reward is great. Following the example of the saints, Hus elsewhere wrote the faithful need not fear death. One should adhere to the law of God even to death. Hus painted a portrait of the pilgrim in this temporal world as a sailor on a sinking ship, a traveler in a foreign country, a resident in a disintegrating house, an inmate in a cruel prison. The Christian should know that his or her pilgrimage is truly on the high seas, on a journey, in a strange land, in a crumbling world, and held captive in a body which was a difficult prison.[109] The soul was so much more valuable than the changing, unreliable structures of human life.

Hus then turned the attention of his female audience to the prospect of judgment and the life to come. Everyone would be judged and the coming judgment horrible. 'Hear, O daughter'! All of God's enemies will be destroyed by fire. Part of chapter eight reads very much like book three of Innocent III's *contemptus mundi* treatise on the misery of the human condition. The emphasis in Hus was on fire either for purification (purgatory), utter destruction (the physical earth), or everlasting punishment (hell). The judgment of sinners would be horrific, Hus warned, the judge would be terrible, demons would pull sinners into hell, and their transgressions announced so all would hear and know. The sentence was dreadful. The fire was eternal, body and soul would burn forever in darkness in the company of demons and there would be no hope for deliverance. Hus used the appalling portrait to caution the women of Prague to avoid all sin so as not to sacrifice eternal joy for the temporary pleasures of lechery.[110] Elsewhere Hus marveled that men and women could be so blind as to live lives devoted to the world, the flesh and the Devil, resulting in exclusion from eternal joy, damnation in fire with demons, in total darkness, anguish and everlasting pain.[111] He wondered aloud how the wicked could possibly give account for lifetimes of negligence.[112]

Innocent III's treatment of the misery of the human condition concluded with weeping, wailing, gnashing of teeth, the torment of the damned in fire and brimstone which never ended. Hus did not leave his audience with such a hopeless scenario. Rather, he turned his female readers to the joys of the kingdom of heaven which awaited the faithful pilgrim and those who set aside useless desires and persevered on the path to God. Eternal life for the pilgrim consisted in knowing God – Father, Son and Holy Spirit – and enjoying a fullness that knew no need of anything.[113] Citing Origen, Hus declared that Christ was the means of this fullness.[114] Referring to the last judgment scenario in Matthew 25, Hus incorporated the social implications of authentic spirituality into his instructions to the pious women of Prague. When the kingdom of God comes to fullness, the suffering Christ, having been ministered to by the faithful, reaches wholeness. When the holy saints of all the ages come to eternal life then the suffering body of Christ would be completely glorified.[115] In contrast to the utter loss of hell the eternal kingdom of God had no sad memory, reason would grasp everything, and the transformed will would experience all good things. Sin, pain, sadness, fear, death, temptation, hunger, thirst and anything else not conducive to the joy of the soul will have been banished. In their place there would be absolute freedom, immense pleasure, everlasting fulfillment and eternal light.[116] The enemies of the inner spiritual life, the world, the flesh and the Devil, are defeated by the Father. Christ protects the faithful from sin, and the Holy Spirit shields the righteous from the terrors of hell. If the human heart could experience even briefly what eternal life in the presence of God would be like, it would instantly recognize how trivial supposed earthly things of value really were.[117] But Hus declined to say much about this heavenly realm on the grounds that he did not know very much about it. However, he was confident that the better choice was Jesus whom he portrayed as the best lover for young women and for married women the husband who never dies.[118]

Coming to the last chapter of his instructions on the spiritual life, Hus returned to the theme of love. Loving God is the highest aim of the spiritual life. One ought to love God above all else. Hus anticipated his female readers posing the question of how they could be assured they had kept the commandments of God. 'My answer is that if a person is determined in their heart to die rather than violate God's commandments and adheres to this determination, then it is a sign they are observing God's commandments and that they love God more than their own body.' Hus then went on to name several holy women – SS Catherine, Margaret, Dorothy, Lucy and Barbara – who seem to have loved unconditionally thereby setting an example.[119] Loving God was the heart of the mystical way and the ground of the spiritual life. If the faithful pilgrim loved God they would find the correct way to salvation. Loving God enabled one to recognize they were like God and that a divine sense of conscience lay within. They could recognize the misery and temptations of the world. They would be aware of the three enemies. With these understandings, they would know how to repent correctly, would value the dignity of their soul, would look ahead towards the day of judgment, and value eternal life.[120] Love of God was the essence of spirituality, the antidote for the impoverished human condition, and an appropriate response to *contemptus mundi*. 'Hear, O daughter, see and listen carefully. Listen with your ears, see with your reason, incline your attention to understand, to remember and fulfil . . . . be diligent to read, to understand, to learn about yourself, love God, fight and overcome the world, the flesh, and the Devil. Convert your labor into rest, your sorrow into joy, in order to see, after the darkness of this world, the sun of righteousness, Jesus Christ with his mother and all saints and being glorified have joy together with them'.[121]

These were the spiritual admonitions to the women in the neighborhood of Prague's Bethlehem Chapel. Beyond this, Hus suggested that those who followed Christ must carry one's own cross. The pilgrim must remain on his or her cross just as Christ did right up to the end until the pilgrim was summoned by the Spirit to put an end to earthly labor. Hus urged his hearers to take no note of those who suggested coming down from the cross. The pilgrim should ignore the demands of the flesh when the body protested. Hus insisted the faithful Christian must pay no heed to the body, the mind, the Devil or any other influence. 'Let us remain on the cross, let us die at the cross, let others take us from the cross'.[122]

6

POLITICS

Late in 1408 a printed notice, in Latin and Czech, appeared on church doors in Prague calling Jan Hus a 'disobedient son of the holy mother church' and advising he was forbidden to perform priestly duties.[1] From about this time on Hus' life became increasingly engulfed in political matters. Some of these were social, others ecclesiastical but often the two could not be separated. The religious ideas espoused by Hus had social implications and applied theology took the priest from his pulpit to society and politics.[2] Hus condemned the seizure of goods belonging to the poor. He denounced social oppression and favorably quoted Augustine who concluded those who did not share would go to hell. Hus urged the well off to be merciful to the less fortunate.[3] It should be noted that while some of Hus' writings like the *Expositio decalogi* contains a strong critique of the moral turpitude of the wealthy who oppress the poor, there is no real argument against poverty itself as a social evil. Arguments have been advanced suggesting Hus was more a '*homo politicus*' whose life and work sought reform in social structures and secular society than a proper religious figure or theologian.[4] The claim is not convincing. Although Hus may be regarded as a critic of social abuses, a caveat is essential. It can be argued that even in his most strident social reform comments, Hus was only repeating common medieval ideas. Nowhere did Hus claim originality. It appears his ideas were advanced to address current social issues whether these concerns sprang up in the church or in society at large. It is true that from the middle of the fourteenth-century the clergy ceased to function as the only voice of the nation.[5] Nevertheless, they continued to maintain a crucial role. It is quite certain Hus was a patriot but it is equally certain he did not live for a Czech identity nor did he fight for Bohemia nor yet was his life forfeit on account of nationalism.[6] Still, Hus definitely stressed the honor of the Christian realm of Bohemia.[7] In an early sermon, perhaps delivered at the Church of St. Michael in the Old Town, Hus referred to events in 1401 wherein Bohemia suffered foreign invasion by the troops of the margrave of Meißen.

> The Czechs are more pathetic than dogs or snakes. A dog will defend the couch he is lying upon and should another dog attempt to chase him off, he will fight with him. A snake does the same thing. But we are oppressed by the Germans.

They seize all of the state offices and we do not say a word. According to every law, including the law of God, and the natural order of things, Czechs in the kingdom of Bohemia should be preferred in the offices of the Czech kingdom. This is the way it is for the French in the French kingdom and for the Germans in the German lands. Therefore a Czech should have authority over his own subordinates as should a German. What would be the point of a Czech who knew no German becoming a priest or a bishop in Germany? He would be about as useful to a herd as a dog who cannot bark. And just as useless to we Czechs is a German. Knowing that this is contrary to the law of God and the regulations, I declare it to be illegal.[8]

Accusations were not slow to follow and Hus fell under the bane of suspicion on a number of levels. Some of these were legitimate while others lacked sense and purpose. His old foe, Štěpán, the Carthusian abbot of Dolany, charged Hus with being insufficiently respectful to the saints.[9] Ecclesiastical authorities in Prague stood against the first wave of accusations. On 17 July 1407 Archbishop Zbyněk declared to the synod of Prague that he could find no heretics anywhere in Bohemia.[10] Later, Zbyněk retreated from that optimistic stance becoming one of Hus' definite detractors. Under duress he later composed a letter to Pope Alexander V in which he absolved Hus of all heresy or suspicion of any irregularity. The letter was never received by the pope. Several years later, in 1414, formal testimony was submitted that Konrad of Vechta, Archbishop of Prague, had no knowledge of heresy espoused by Hus nor any doctrinal deviations which concerned the archiepiscopal see. That statement should be qualified inasmuch as Konrad took the view that the Hus matter was a papal concern and not his responsibility.[11]

Decision at Kutná Hora

From a constitutional law perspective, German identity in Bohemia was not historically clear at the time of Hus.[12] Animosity between Germans and Slavs has been traced into the thirteenth century and has been the subject of considerable inquiry.[13] This social conflict became one of the factors in the Hussite Revolution. Hus was accused of being prejudiced against Germans. The accusation is politically motivated and specious. In fact it is only possible to attribute one clearly direct anti-German statement to Hus.[14] Other statements may be adduced from the Hus corpus but the interpretation is ambiguous such as the well-known gloss 'ha, ha, Germans, ha, ha, out, out'![15] The matter came to a head in the cleavage between European level church politics and the social struggles in Bohemia. Power in the Czech land was held both by the monarch and the nobility.[16] On an international platform, Europe was convulsed by the protracted papal schism. Suspicions of heresy in Prague likewise served to put the Czechs on the defensive. At the center of these struggles was the university. In 1403 German masters succeeded in having the university condemn forty-five articles ostensibly extracted from the works of John Wyclif. The political motivation caused the Czech masters to be identified with the condemned articles and by extension with heresy. In the spring of 1408 the leader of the Prague reform party, Stanislav of Znojmo, was cited to appear at the papal court of Gregory XII to answer charges of heresy concerning the eucharist. He was given two months to comply. There can be little doubt that this summons had been instigated by Germans in Prague at the behest of the Saxon Ludolf Meistermann who was attached to the Theology faculty.[17] The Wyclifite doctrine of the eucharist was thereby made heretical and placed the Prague reformers in danger. But the matter had deep, concomitant, social implications. While this was going on, a church council began preparations to convene in Italy to solve the papal schism. The Council of Pisa deposed both Gregory XII and Benedict XIII and forbade any obedience to either. King Václav IV assumed a neutral position but Archbishop Zbyněk continued to support Gregory. Papal allegiance and suspicion of heresy became effective political tools. The Czech master Matěj Knín was arrested on charges of heresy and made to stand trial before the archbishop on 14 May 1408. Refusing to demonstrate his guilt according to legal procedure, the examiner Jan Kbel demanded unqualified recantation. Zbyněk backed Kbel up and Knín was forced to accept the humiliation and withdraw heresies he claimed not to hold.[18] Meanwhile Stanislav of Znojmo and Štěpán Páleč set out from Prague to appear before the Curia as ordered. The king, for purely political reasons, wished to have his realm declared free from heresy and ordered Zbyněk to issue a statement to that effect. The archbishop initially demurred but when Václav's rage reached boiling point a hasty declaration was issued on 17 July 1408 stating he had diligently convened a careful examination throughout the diocese of Prague and had been unable to detect any trace whatsoever of any error or clear heresy.[19] No investigation took place. The statement constituted coerced submission.

When Stanislav went off to the papal court Jan Hus assumed leadership of the reform party. Working with Jerome of Prague and Jan of Jesenice, Hus now became clearly involved not only in matters of doctrinal evaluation but also directly in political issues. Cardinals loyal to Gregory XII and Benedict XIII abandoned the feuding pontiffs in a conscious effort to end the papal schism. To facilitate their initiative they attempted to persuade leaders of European nations to side with them. Václav was tempted. He was able to perceive two salutary outcomes. The crisis of Christendom could be solved and he might be in position to be reinstated as Holy Roman Emperor. There is almost no possibility that Václav had any particular theological inclinations which may have motivated his decisions in 1408 and 1409. Ruprecht of the Palatinate, his chief enemy, held firmly with the Roman obedience. Václav saw an opportunity. He began formulating a policy of political unity. However, the university in Prague remained divided. The Germans masters more or less maintained Roman obedience as well inasmuch as the German princes did. There were political considerations in that choice as well. The king regarded as disloyal the stance of the German university masters. The *Quodlibet* of January 1409 became a political agenda.[20] The leader for 1409 was to be the aforementioned Matěj Knín. The Germans threatened a boycott claiming reluctance to sit under the direction of one suspected of heresy. King Václav ordered the Germans to participate and forbade further resistance. The university

Quodlibet in Prague occurred annually on 3 January and normally lasted several days. The process was subject to very strict regulations. The leader of the debate was chosen six months prior to the event to allow for careful and comprehensive preparation. All participants were notified of the specific questions several days in advance. All masters were obligated to attend under penalty of sanction and fine. The proceedings were divided into several parts. The leader of the debate opened with a speech and then presented his solution to the principal question (*questio*). The opening *questio* was always divided into three parts. A debate followed and the leader had the last word usually defending his thesis. The second part of the *Quodlibet* allowed all participating masters opportunity to solve the *questio* originally set. The leader of the debate had to be prepared to deal with all of the submissions. Handbooks are extant containing a list of arguments on each *questio* and providing positive and negative answers. Depending on how a specific master answered the question the leader took up the other option. There are four of these handbooks known. These belonged to Matěj Knín (1409), Jan Hus (1411), Šimon of Tišnov (1416) and Prokop of Kladruby (1417). In addition to the *questio* each master was obliged to deal with a *probleum*, meaning he had to find a suitable answer to the question at hand with a humorous character. Once all participants had spoken the leader closed the *Quodlibet* debate with a speech. In 1409, the Prague *Quodlibet* featured the general question of whether or not God, as the immutable highest good in all creation, was the creator of the sum parts of the universe. The clear underpinnings of realist thought were evident. Both Jerome of Prague and Jan of Jesenice weighed in.

Jerome used the occasion to invite the visiting French embassy, Jacob of Nouvion of Paris University and others, commissioned by the king, Charles VI, and a delegation from Brabant, including the bishop of Chalons-sur-Saône, who were in Prague hoping to persuade Václav to help end the papal schism. He also seemed to have been instrumental in having the city councilors of Prague's Old Town attend. Prior to the *Quodlibet*, Nouvion had been engaged by Jakoubek of Stříbro on the question of clerical poverty. Jerome used the university debate setting to deliver an impassioned speech defending Wyclif, openly criticizing the Germans, railing on the wickedness of simoniacal clerics, and promoting the Czechs. He went so far as to assert that whoever denied the basic premises of realism ought to be considered a 'devilish heretic'.[21] Jesenice's *questio* for the 1409 *Quodlibet* queried if a judge should condemn a defendant knowing false witnesses had been brought against that person. The suggested answer was negative. This subverted one of the main principles codified in the medieval ecclesiastical system of law. Hus agreed with Jesenice's conclusion. The emphasis fell on the law of God. When applied to theology, the thesis implied that a writ of excommunication or determination of heresy may be quite worthless.

These elements of intrigue, ideas, and influence form the backdrop to social change in Bohemia. The details are scanty but it appears that Hus and Jerome convinced King Václav to change the constituency of power on the city council of Prague to a Czech majority. We do not have evidence of this from Hus himself. However, the heresy trial against Jerome in Vienna in 1410 provides some evidence and Jerome testified to this effect at his final trial in 1416.²² If this be true, and there is no reason to dismiss Jerome's statements, then it seems evident that ideas of reform in Prague were beginning to coalesce in a political sense under the leadership of Hus. The real prize lay in the university and by 1408 Jan Hus, together with his colleagues Jerome of Prague and Jan of Jesenice had set their sights on the rise of Czech ascendancy in their own university. In fact, Jerome had publicly implored the city councilors at the 1409 *Quodlibet* to defend the cause of the university. There can be little secret to his allusion. The king now seemed prepared to formally abandon all allegiance to Gregory XII. His support for the reformers of Hus' party seemed politically expedient to the king and he acted quite dramatically. The French and Brabantine delegations delivered their message to Václav that if he suspended all relations with Gregory XII the cardinals would support his restitution as emperor of the Holy Roman world. Václav agreed. Apparently he did not foresee opposition from Zbyněk and the university. We have noted his policy and procedure towards the archbishop above. He took another tact with the university. Summoning representatives of the four nations comprising the university to his residence in Kutná Hora he demanded statements of allegiance. The Czech nation was represented by Jan Eliášův, canon of the Cathedral Chapter, and Ondřej of Brod. Hus was not among that delegation.²³ The confrontation took place on 18 January 1409. The Czechs supported the king. The other nations declined. Outraged, Václav swore drastic measures and punishment if they persisted in defying his will. But the king had a trump card tucked away. This was a plan advanced privately by Jan Hus, Jerome and Jan of Jesenice and more publicly driven by Mikuláš Bohaty of Lobkovice. Mikuláš was a royal councilor and manager of the royal mines at Kutná Hora.²⁴ That same day the king issued the 'decree of Kutná Hora'. Reduced to its simplest form it declared that in all university functions from henceforth the Czechs would have the power of three votes, while the others would be reduced collectively – as the 'German nation' – to a single vote.²⁵ The formulation of the decree was not an afterthought. The 'decree of Kutná Hora' had been part of Václav's plan all along. With a stroke of the pen, King Václav IV secured the support of the university for his Pisan policy and delivered the university into the hands of the Czechs. In one moment the constitution of the university was altered. On that date Hus lay seriously ill in Prague. Mikuláš Bohaty of Lobkovice sent Hus a copy of the decree of Kutná Hora. Hus was overjoyed and when Jan Eliášův and Ondřej of Brod came to visit him he showed it to them begging that should he die they were to defend the rights and freedom of the nation and university.²⁶ Many years later Ondřej of Brod accused Hus of being the impetus behind the decree of Kutná Hora. Hus did not disagree. At the *Quodlibet* he had spoken that God would be praised and the famous Kingdom of Bohemia should rejoice. The 'magnificent university' was now set for distinguishment.²⁷ The king's fiat made clear that continued opposition to the preferred church policy of the royal house in Prague would no longer be tolerated.

The surprised Germans would not yield. University rector Henning of Baltenhagen presented a formal protest to the king on 6 February. Václav summoned the Czech masters to an audience. Hus and Jerome were among that number. According to the sole surviving source the king had decided to repeal the 'decree of Kutná Hora' but was persuaded by Hus to maintain the decree.[28] The king held firm though his resolve found unexpected support. Elector Ruprecht called the German masters and students to his own University of Heidelberg and the margrave of Meißen undertook to establish a new university at Leipzig. Moreover, Pope Gregory XII placed Prague University under a ban and ordered faithful Germans to depart. By May the German dean Albrecht Varentrapp and rector Henning of Baltenhagen were deposed, the university insignia forcibly removed from their hands by police and were replaced by Czechs. Zdeněk of Labouň was appointed rector for the summer session and Šimon of Tišnov became dean. In the autumn of that year Hus was elected rector of the university and we know he preached at Bethlehem Chapel referring to the decree of Kutná Hora calling it a great victory and urging his hearers to be thankful to Mikuláš for the triumph.[29] Hus was now head of the university and the leader of a religious reform movement.

Firing a volley of salvos, the disenfranchised Germans left for Leipzig and other points abroad. Hus and Jan of Jesenice were made the focus of vilification by the incensed Germans. A so-called 'Wyclifite Mass' soon appeared implicating Wyclif, Hus, Jerome, and Jan of Jesenice in frightful apostasy, heresy, and the ruination of the university in Prague.

> I believe in Wyclif, the lord of hell and patron of Bohemia, and in Hus, his only begotten son, our nothing, who was conceived by the spirit of Lucifer, born of his mother, and made incarnate and equal to Wyclif according to the evil will . . . ruling at the time of the desolation of the University of Prague at the time when Bohemia apostatized from the faith. Who for us heretics descended into hell and will not rise again from the dead nor have everlasting life. Amen. . . . The book of the generations of all the accursed sons of the heretics: Wyclif, the son of the Devil. . . Stanislav of Znojmo begat Jan Hus, Hus begat Marek of Hradec, Marek begat Zdeněk of Labouň, Zdeněk begat Šimon of Tišnov, Šimon begat Petr of Koněprusy. . . Knín begat Jerome, the athlete of Antichrist, Jerome begat Jan of Jesenice before the migration of the three nations and after the migration Jesenice begat Zdislav the Leper. . . .[30]

Perhaps more than 1,000 students and masters left Prague for Leipzig and other destinations.[31]

After 1409 the victors in the struggle over the decree had more enemies than before the momentous declaration at Kutná Hora.[32] Even before tensions began to settle Jan of Jesenice composed a legal defense of the decree of Kutná Hora in a treatise titled *Defensio mandati* in which he offered Mikuláš Bohatý of Lobkovice and the Crown specific guidance.[33] The text has been attributed to Hus but this seems quite unlikely and there can now be little doubt as to its proper authorship.[34] Combining Wyclifite theory, ideas on medieval royal power and Czech legal and social realities, Jesenice argued for the necessity of the decree of Kutná Hora. For his authorities he drew upon canon and civil law, scripture and the fathers. Preference was given to the king in terms of priority of power. The king's first prerogative was his own native Czech people. This was based on a notional application of the law of God and the king was entitled to act as he pleased. Jesenice also referred to the foundation decree of Charles IV which seemed to indicate the university had been established with a pro-Czech mandate. The *Defensio mandati* has been called a remarkable example of Hussite political theory.[35] It seems clear after looking at the surviving sources that Hus, Jerome and Jan of Jesenice worked quite ardently before and after 18 January 1409 to secure a prominent place for the decree of Kutná Hora in Czech society, law and university affairs.[36]

After the Council of Pisa sat the Bohemian ecclesiastical province shifted almost completely in obedience to the new pope Alexander V. There were two notable exceptions: Archbishop Zbyněk of Prague and Jan Železný, 'the iron', bishop of Litomyšl. Eventually, the former did capitulate but not before being threatened with legal action by the papal auditor at Pisa. Zbyněk was ordered to root out heresy in his province by implementing a three-pronged attack. First, he was to examine the books of the 'damned heresiarch' John Wyclif. Second, if heresy was discovered therein the books were to be destroyed by fire. Third, preaching was to be stopped save in cathedral, parochial and monastic churches.[37] There can be little doubt the third directive was aimed at Hus though he was not named specifically. Dated 20 December 1409 the bull did not reach Prague until 9 March 1410. Hus knew very well what the intention was and having no mind to obey appealed 'from a poorly informed pope to a better-informed pope'. The appeal is not extant but Hus referred to it elsewhere.[38] Meanwhile the seeds of rebellion began to sprout an early crop. The harvest turned out to be somewhat different than the reformers expected. Zbyněk organized a bookburning. In the meanwhile the order to cease and desist from preaching in Bethlehem Chapel reached Hus. The indefatigable preacher addressed both concerns head on. His bottom line quite predictably lay in the query about where the law of Christ confined or restricted preaching to parish churches or monasteries.[39]

Zbyněk wasted no time acting on this mandate despite the fact that Alexander V died on 3 May 1410. University masters protested. Zbyněk ordered all owners of Wyclif books to surrender the offensive volumes within six days. Those failing to comply faced excommunication. Hus thought it preposterous. In late June he wrote *De libris hereticorum legendis* against Zbyněk's proposed action.[40] 'One must read the books of heretics and not burn them, for little other than truth is found there. This thesis is supported by the authority of the saints – Augustine, Jerome, Ambrose, Bede, Theodore, Liberatus, Cyril, Pope Gelasius – as well as by the canons and reason'.[41] Hus argued 'the faithful ought to read heretical books' in order to know what was written therein. It was indefensible to simply destroy them. Hus argued only a fool would condemn something before determining the truth therein.[42] In order to combat true heresy or be able to refute real heretics, the nature of their ideas must be known. It is important, Hus argued, to debate about the faith not to cause dissension but in order to correct error and bring light on the truth of the Christian faith.[43] As the faggots were being gathered for the bonfire, Hus took the papal bull into his pulpit and told his hearers he had no plans to cease from preaching. How did they feel about it? The support was near unanimous. Hus told his congregation it remained his duty to preach, and preach he would until he was driven from the earth or died in prison.[44] In anger Zbyněk ordered immediate destruction of the collected Wyclif corpus, some 200 volumes, on 16 July 1410 and had Canon Zdeněk of Chrast light the fire behind the closed and locked gates of the archiepiscopal courtyard. Apparently a number of priests attended the book-burning and chanted the *Te Deum* loudly 'while the bells were tolled as though it were a funeral'. Enormous conflict erupted amongst the people on account of the unpopular act. On 22 July a mob entered St. Vitus' Cathedral and forcibly removed forty priests from the altars. At St. Stephen's in the New Town six armed men with swords drawn attempted to murder a 'blaspheming preacher'.[45] Hus' followers were defiant and according to some hostile sources taunted Zbyněk claiming he had failed to confiscate all the books and would he like to try again. They were already collecting more copies and stoutly announced continued disobedience.[46] By September even the king complained about the book-burning going so far as to bring the matter to the attention of the new Pope John XXIII: 'how can the vineyard flourish if the vines are cut down by the root?'[47] Hus later found out that a curial commission of theologians convened at Bologna to investigate the book-burning concluded Zbyněk erred.[48] The ideas being debated or assailed did not go unnoticed by the people of Prague. Three points can be made. Supporters of Hus and his colleagues began to engage in iconoclasm and acts of violent protest. Houses of priests were pillaged and burned down. Wicked priests and their girlfriends were sometimes clamped naked in pillories, thrown into rivers or run out of the locale.[49] As early as 1411 Hus began attacking the misuse of indulgences and certain of the Prague priests began to mobilize against him. A controversy over the sale of indulgences in Prague turned violent. Riots broke out and three young men were executed despite Hus' efforts at intervention. The martyrs were buried in Hus' Bethlehem Chapel.[50] Abbot Štěpán of Dolany claimed Hus orchestrated the funeral.[51] The assertion cannot be proven. Finally, an attempt was made to destroy Bethlehem Chapel. During a worship service a group of men armed with swords and crossbows attacked the building. Hus devoted considerable space in a later sermon commenting on the incident. 'Note the gall of the Germans! They would not dare attack a neighbor's kitchen or stable without having the consent of the king. But they are sufficiently brazen to undertake an attempt on the house of God'!'[52] Songs circulated about the incident circulated throughout Prague noting how 'Germans charged recklessly against Bethlehem'.[53]

Men like Štěpán Páleč and Michael de Causis hounded Hus from the time of the decree of Kutná Hora to his death. Hus claimed Páleč was a backslider who crept away from the truth walking backwards like a crab.[54] It is difficult to overemphasize the importance of the decision made at Kutná Hora in the winter of 1409. Both the urging of Jan Hus and the signature of King Václav were prompted by the politics of ecclesiastical authority, the papal schism, and the politics of culture which had come to a point of contention between the Germans and the Czechs. The decree of Kutná

Hora set the tone for the political aspects of Hus' reform efforts and those of his colleagues from 1409 onwards. There could be no retreat now. The effort to make God more accessible to the laity had taken on a further dimension.[55] A visible downside could be detected. Not only had the university lost its international luster and became a provincial institution, Kutná Hora marked the beginning of the end for the law university which continued for awhile but by 1419 had been shuttered.[56] The circumstances surrounding the formation of the decree also reveal the dimensions of the social implications of the reform effort; implications which led to social revolution. A crucial element was John Wyclif.

Wyclif's influence

While living, John Wyclif was viewed as a spider lurking at the center of a web of intrigue and unrest. In death, the spider's true identity came to light as the 'angel of Satan and the forerunner of Antichrist'. He appeared as the consummate heresiarch. 'The mouthpiece of the Devil, enemy of the church, confuser of common people, idol of heretics, model of hypocrisy, inciter of schism, sower of hatred, the inventor of lies'. He was struck down by the judgment of God and despairing like Cain released his wicked soul to Satan.[57] Indeed, the preacher at St. Giles Church in Prague, John Peklo, claimed to have had a vision of Wyclif in hell.[58] Anti-Hus polemicists concluded books against the Prague reformer by invoking a curse that Wyclif the 'sack of filth' would be damned.[59] To some Wyclif symbolized pestilence, gross heresy, a source of vice, the incarnate devil, a bucket of shit ('vas stercoris') and those who took heed to his ideas the descendants of a heresiarch of 'damnable memory'. To others, however, Wyclif seems to be the 'fifth evangelist', or the 'evangelical doctor above all doctors'.[60] The question is less how Wyclif was perceived in early fifteenth-century Bohemia and more his influence on Jan Hus. At issue is a single query. Were Wyclif's theological and doctrinal heresies a direct result of his realist philosophy? There are persuasive arguments with polar views.[61]

No serious study of Hus in the past 125 years has avoided the question of Wyclif. Conclusions have been entrenched. There has been a tendency to deal with Hus' thought and ideas in a case by case comparison with Wyclif. This is both tedious and unnecessary. I do not propose undertaking a similar exercise for ultimately it is misleading. However, it is impossible to avoid qualifying the relation between these two late medieval theologians. It has been argued that there is no ground for speaking of a Hussite system of doctrine. More to the point Hus has been charged with being a plagiarizer of Wyclif who possibly read nothing other than the Bible and a few of the fathers.[62] Johann Loserth undertook a massive textual comparison and published columns of material from the works of Hus and Wyclif to make his point. Loserth concluded that Hus simply copied Wyclif. However, a careful analysis of the Hus corpus reveals that some of the material or ideas allegedly extracted from Wyclif can also be located in Augustine, Hilary, Bede and other authorities with whom Hus was familiar.[63] It should not be surprising that at numerous turns both Hus and Wyclif were drawing on the Sentences of Peter Lombard. Others assert that Hus' debt to

Gratian was equal to his reliance on Wyclif and both rely on Augustine.[64] Hus did refer to Wyclif by name but even that practice was not customary at the end of the Middle Ages. For example, Jakoubek of Stříbro never once cited Wyclif, Matěj of Janov, or Milíč of Kroměříž by name.[65] Yet we can be quite certain he used all three. It is clear that Hus used Wyclif. It is equally clear that Loserth's parallel columns suggests more than may be warranted. A close examination of those columns does not confirm *prima facie* evidence when the fathers, canon law or scripture take up a fair amount of space. Hus' practices cannot be regarded as unethical or uncommon. Thomas Aquinas and Alexander of Hales used the same technique.[66] In his book against Hus, Štěpán Páleč borrowed entire passages from Jan of Jenštejn. Even Wyclif was known to have copied large portions from Augustine, Grosseteste and other medieval authorities. Among his accusers at Constance we know that Jean Gerson appropriated Henry of Langenstein taking over several chapters almost verbatim while Pierre d'Ailly copied William of Ockham's *Dialogus*.[67] Clearly, Hus did not blindly follow Wyclif. In his sermon *Vos estis sal terre* in 1410 Hus clearly used Wyclif in the beginning, sometimes verbatim. Then he abandoned Wyclif and used scripture and the fathers to support his views.[68]

Most assessments of Hus conclude he was far more orthodox than Wyclif. The movement Wyclif engendered, if it can be called a movement, was largely political. Hus' movement was chiefly religious and theological. It is not necessary to refer to Wyclif in order to explain the theology of Hus or his activities as a reformer. There are front rank scholars however who continue to regard Hus' doctrine as essentially mature Wyclifite teaching.[69] John Wyclif was the only first-rate philosopher at Oxford in the fourteenth century. Hus was chiefly a reformer and neither interested in nor able to engage in the more wide-ranging originality of a Wyclif.[70] Jan Hus predicted the negative response Wyclif's philosophical works would produce in Prague but he likewise saw in Wyclif a theoretical framework which might be critically applied to the Czech context.[71] It was not necessary but it was available and it worked. It is fair to say that Hus was not as original as Wyclif, but he was more effective.[72] In assessing the place of Wyclif in Hus' work and ideas it is important to note the essential differences in the social and intellectual contexts the two men emerge from. David Holeton makes the important observation that 'Hus was the inheritor, rather than the architect, of an already widespread reform movement'.[73] The same might not be said of Wyclif. To what extent Hus can be regarded as independent of Wyclif on doctrine remains a contentious point in Hussite scholarship. There are in fact distinctions between Hus and Wyclif. The single necessary point has been made by De Vooght which is that Hus used Wyclif selectively. In terms of content, he was neither a disciple nor a plagiarist and in terms of form, Hus extracted from Wyclif according to his own convictions and opinions.[74] Moreover, Hus corrected Wyclif at various times. It is doubtful that scholarly unanimity will ever be achieved on this question. At times one reads Hus and one cannot help but see and hear Wyclif. At other times it is patently unlike Wyclif. In certain Hus texts, Wyclif is verbally or ideologically present while in others he is conspicuously absent.

With notable exceptions, German scholars in the late nineteenth and early twentieth centuries followed Loserth's thesis. Czech historians mainly attempted to debunk the idea. Some have been stridently opposed to a Wyclifite dependence. Others argued for Hus as a natural continuation of the religious and charismatic spiritual traditions of fourteenth-century Prague. Others strive for a via media suggesting Hus fused the social program of Milíč with the ideas of Wyclif to produce a 'potent political synthesis'.[75] It is misleading to place the emphasis on the Czech origins of reform as a response to Loserth. Palacký advanced that argument as early as the 1840s. More importantly the Lutheran church historian Johann August Wilhelm Neander (1789–1850) devoted over sixty pages to Milíč and Matěj concluding their work constituted the roots of Bohemian reform.[76] Careful analysis of the alleged Wyclifite material in Hus suggests only a small percentage of material can actually be attributed to Wyclif.[77] These figures are reduced even further if the quoted material from Wyclif is stripped of the references Wyclif borrows from elsewhere. Other views suggest Hus relied on Wyclif more than scholars like Novotný, Kybal and Bartoš admit.[78] Loserth's position is firmly rebutted by other perspectives. 'The view that Hussitism is simply an artificially constructed Wyclifism seems to me logically and historically as nonsense'.[79] Paul De Vooght's view has gained considerable currency in the west promoting the view that Loserth was mistaken. It might also be noted that Loserth did not deal with any of Hus' Czech works, a serious omission which unfairly left a general view of his Latin works inapplicably attached to the vernacular studies. Even so, the evidence of the parallel columns does not convince that Hus depended on Wyclif for his ideas. Equating Wyclif and Hus or forms of Lollardy with Hussitism is a 'mortal fault' which obfuscates more than anything else.[80] It must be admitted that it is difficult to add anything new to the question of Hus and Wyclif. The extent of Wyclif's influence in Czech reform remains an open question.[81]

Regardless of Wyclif's theological positions, it was in the area of politics broadly speaking where his influence proved critical in Bohemia. This is especially apparent in the application of his ideas on lordship and dominion. Beyond this, the adoption of Wyclif's concepts of the relation between church and state proved useful to Hus, his colleague Jan of Jesenice, as well as to the king. Taking the overall view, the lapsed Wyclifite Štěpán Páleč declared that together Hus and Wyclif constituted the most potent danger to the Christian faith ever to assail the church.[82] Preaching in the Church of St. Gall, Páleč frequently issued warnings about Wyclif. Hus sarcastically claimed Stanislav of Znojmo and Páleč discarded their prior realism in the toilet ('*ad cloacas*').[83] Hus followed Wyclif's political theory but as in practically every other sense he cannot be considered an uncritical disciple of Wyclif. Hus admitted he admired Wyclif for several reasons including that he enjoyed excellent rapport with good priests at Oxford and was admired by the people. Hus found his works attractive because it seemed to him that Wyclif shared his desire to lead all people to the law of Christ, especially erring priests. 'I am drawn by the love he has for the law of Christ in defending his truth which cannot be wrong in any way. In the end he also wrote a book concerning the veracity of holy scripture in which he proves right to the end the truth of the law of the Lord'.[84] It may have been politically incorrect in his ecclesiastical world to speak well of Wyclif but this seemed not to deter Hus from marveling at how Wyclif continued to command attention.[85] And it is surely correct to admit that the Czech reformers 'began to play with fire when they endorsed and borrowed the rhetoric of John Wyclif' in their own work.[86] Before the main conflagration of protest and controversy convulsed Prague Hus expressed his view that it was by no means certain that Wyclif had gone to hell as a damned sinner. Hus hoped Wyclif was saved and said so.[87] He then qualified his alleged Wycliffite identity. 'I admit I adhere to the true opinions taught by that professor of sacred theology, Master John Wyclif. Not because he taught them but on account of the fact that scripture or sound reason declares its veracity. If he has taught something in error I have no intention of following that in any sense'.[88] Hus challenged John Stokes to a debate in Prague but Stokes declined. Hus defended Wyclif and the substance of his treatise on reading the books of heretics has Wyclif largely in mind.[89] Later at the Council of Constance, Stokes accused Hus of following in the footsteps of Wyclif.[90] The first condemnation of Wycliffite articles in Prague dates to 1403 when Jan Kbel and Václav of Bechin, canons of the Prague cathedral chapter, brought twenty-four articles condemned by a synod in London. These, combined with twenty-one additional articles extracted from Wyclif's works by Johannes Hübner, were presented to the masters of the university in Prague on 28 May 1403. The rector, Walter Harasser, having recorded the votes of the masters announced that no one ought henceforth 'dogmatize, preach or promote' any of the forty-five articles.[91] It might be useful to note that Hübner's list included the attribution to Wyclif that God was obligated to be obedient to the Devil. At the *Quodlibet* in 1404, Hübner asserted that Wyclif was a heretic and anyone reading his books heretical. Hus considered the charge foolish and defended against it.[92]

It is without merit and quite misleading to cull expressions like 'lex evangelica' and 'sola scriptura', which are quite plentiful in Bohemia in the decades before Hus, and see therein the witness and influence of John Wyclif. These phrases do not indicate anything remotely Wycliffite whose ideas on such matters seem to have been imported to Prague much later. While the question remains unsettled I am not convinced of certain references to Wyclif's work until the mid 1380s and even these are not theological. I acknowledge the work and conclusions of František Šmahel, Damascus Trapp and Włodzimierz Zega especially, but there remains too many unanswered important queries to conclude too much on too little.[93] Though manuscript evidence seems to suggest otherwise, I regard the source are too unreliable with respect to dating, and possible textual emendations.[94] In the late 1390s Wyclif's philosophical works appeared but the theological treatises do not make any appearance or impact until the turn of the century. That chronology is quite significant, otherwise Wyclif gets credit he does not deserve.[95] That must not detract from the fact that Wyclif does figure prominently in the Bohemian political struggles in the early fifteenth century.

Once Wyclif went out of favor, Hus' enemies immediately used the English heretic as a weapon against Hus. Tales of the ghost of Wyclif appearing and his posthumous murder were seized upon by the credulous.[96] Hus' old colleague Ondřej of Brod raised the alarm with Archbishop Zbyněk who was then at Roudnice. He warned the archbishop that many unsuspecting lambs were in danger of being seized by a vicious wolf. The intimation is clear. Ondřej claimed it was the duty of all priests to watch vigilantly against those who would trap and poison the helpless lambs. He suggested the erring ought to be returned to the sheepfold of truth with force if necessary. Then Ondřej told Zbyněk he feared the effect of Wyclif's books which were multiplying in Prague and which, according to Ondřej, were filled with serious errors. He specifically mentioned the *Dialogus*, the *Trialogus*, and Wyclif's controversial work on the eucharist. The 'poisonous doctrines' therein were sufficient to endanger the entire flock. Accordingly the archbishop was urged to take action. The venom of Wyclif, flowing into Bohemia by the 'multiplication of these pestilential books' should the faithful 'imbibe that infidel poison it will destroy their souls'. Ondřej opined that neither disease, nor famine, nor war, can inflict greater harm on the faithful then the depraved doctrines of such heretics.[97] Compounding this was the conviction that Hus had inspired heretics which were turning up everywhere from the royal house to the university to the cloistered cells of the religious.[98] As we have seen previously, Zbyněk took steps to eradicate the heresy from his province.[99] That act and the subsequent excommunication of Hus two days later had consequences outside ecclesiastical confines.[100] These acts produced considerable hostility in Prague aimed at the church. Violence erupted. A mob entered the cathedral and chased the priest from the sanctuary. In another church six armed men threatened to kill the presiding priest.[101] Popular songs were sung in the streets accusing the archbishop and his cronies of acting badly and thereby bringing shame upon the Czechs.[102] The issue was Wyclif. Štěpán of Dolany claimed Hus had been infected by Wyclif.[103] Ondřej of Brod hurled accusations against Hus. 'You paint the ten commandments on your walls. It is a pity you did not keep them in your heart'. The problem remained Wyclif. 'Was Wyclif crucified for us? Were we baptized in his name'?[104] Wyclif was both bane and blessing for Hus. It accompanied him to death.

It seemed odd Hus would balk at the Wyclifite doctrine of the Mass since it seems in some interpretations of Hus that he was prepared to side with Wyclif at every turn. Hus was almost entirely more conservative than Wyclif on practically every doctrinal or ideological point of comparison. On his textual borrowing it does not seem out of line with late medieval practice. Both De Vooght and Loserth make claims on this but the validity of both can only be critically sustained with a much wider range of comparison among other medieval thinkers, something neither of them did and something which has not been attempted in this study. It is fascinating to see that Thomas Aquinas cited patristic authorities almost 23,000 times; Augustine alone more than 8,700.[105] To what extent are Thomas, Peter Lombard and others cited by theologians during and after their times? For the fathers at Constance it was beneficial to find Wyclif lurking beneath or behind every word Hus uttered or committed to paper. But on many points, especially predestination, the church consisting of the elect, the importance of scripture, *fides caritate formata*, and the need to emulate a primitive Christian ethos, we find clear evidence already in Hus' own Czech tradition before the advent of Wyclif. Hus and the Hussite religious traditions could have existed without Wyclif essentially in the same form. The notable exception may have been the political dimensions. In other words, there was no need to import Wyclif coming as he did thirty to forty years after the rise of charismatic spirituality and renewed religious practice in Bohemia. It seems rather disingenuous to claim Hus as a Wyclifite who balked at the eucharistic doctrine out of fear. It is difficult to detect fear in Hus at virtually any stage and quite impossible to attribute to him a lack of character, aversion to integrity, or ethical lapses in the interests of political expediency. A monogenesis explanation for the meteoric rise of Jan Hus and the revolution bearing his name thereafter is neither tenable nor convincing.

Morality

The politics of ethics and morals seem accentuated in Hus. His ongoing activities in this respect might be characterized as a consistent razor of vice. His corpus is peppered with condemnations of the absence of morals and ethics especially among the clergy. This is not an unusual feature and may be considered a commonplace among fourteenth-century reform minded preachers in Bohemia. Milíč underscored the moral failings of clerics and urged reform of the priesthood.[106] There were few good priests devoted to preaching truth.[107] Ondřej of Brod, Hus' former colleague and later opponent, wrote in 1426 at Leipzig about the heresies of Hus and his followers making a remarkable observation. 'Among the clergy there was no discipline whatever. In the papal curia there was public simony. In the monastic state, if I may use the term, there was endless greed. In the end there was no vice among the laity which the clergy had not practiced first and more notoriously. There is nothing else to say except that what the holy church reads and sings: "everything you have done to us, Lord, you have done in righteous judgment because we have sinned against you and have not obeyed your commandments"'.[108] As discussed earlier, Hus' language at times comes very close to a Donatist position but he makes clear that a mass sung by a corrupt or sinful priest remains a true channel of grace for the faithful but the priest is indicted by it.[109] 'Every good Christian is a priest, but not every priest is a good Christian'.[110] Elsewhere Hus preached entire strident sermons on the abuses within the church.[111] Hus fell back on St. Jerome cited in canon law by noting 'a priest stained by sin should not celebrate' and to the *Decretum* of Gratian where Jerome once more was heard to say that not all bishops are bishops and the rank or office does not automatically make its holder a Christian.[112] How can a wicked priest show another his or her faults?[113] Hus left nothing to question in posing rhetorical questions. What was the point if a man is called holy when God has damned him? Or what does it matter if Antichrist assumed a position higher than God, when Christ will hurl him into hell?[114] The holy church was the bride of Christ but those ignorant of the true nature of the church fall into many errors.[115] Hus defined heresy in a strictly Augustinian manner to denote contumacious adherence to anything contrary to scripture.[116] Once again we see Hus' devotion to biblical authority. Hus commented he wished all priests would live properly and preach the word of God. He complained they fornicated, were greedy and negligent and practiced simony.[117] This aspect of Hus' reform program gained him significant animosity from the Prague priests.[118] Later sources suggested Hus struggled against the very kingdom of Satan.[119] He went so far as to write an indigent letter to Archbishop Zbyněk in the summer of 1408 over the case of the priest Mikuláš of Velešovice, known as Abraham, who was disciplined for preaching without official approbation and subsequently banished.[120] Hus considered it frivolous to enforce arcane rules when more serious matters were ignored.

There are several prominent issues which come under withering critique from Hus which he deemed erroneous, contrary to scripture, thereby heretical, and inconsistent with Christian faith. These included indulgences, crusade, clerical wickedness and priestly irregularity, simony, and sexual immorality. Each of these contained social and political implications. The buying and selling of indulgences – a certificate guaranteeing the holder the remission of all or part of the debt of temporal punishment owned to God due to sin after the guilt has been forgiven – constituted part of the simoniacal trade.[121] Owing to what Hus regarded as the intransigence of aspects of late medieval Christianity, he submitted it seemed easier for many to buy with money what could be obtained by purity of heart.[122] Because of Hus' firm stand on the matter, the theology faculty met at a conference, convened by King Václav in the parish priest's house in Žebrák on 10 July 1412, and advanced a number of articles against Hus declaring them heretical.[123] Hus apparently challenged his opponents to a daring test. He announced his willingness to suffer death by fire in defending the veracity of his views on condition that his detractors bind themselves over to the same standard. The audacious challenge was not satisfactorily answered.[124] The next day Prague received its first martyrs in the clandestine execution of three men, moved by Hus' sermons, protesting the sale of indulgences.[125] The furore over indulgences drove a permanent wedge between Hus and Archbishop Zbyněk. Likewise Hus attacked the idea of crusading.[126] Noting that bishops and priests in his time were accustomed to wage war, Hus posed the question of whether it was proper for clerics to kill people. Hus inferred it was not, referring to the mirror of Christ, despite arguments raised to support the practice. He urged his warring colleagues to give up warfare which was a rather uncertain path to salvation and instead be prepared to die for Christ.[127] Bishops wearing armor, bearing arms, and riding war horses were contrasted with the wounded, crucified Christ. The latter endured death for the salvation of humanity while the former killed people in order to possess the world. Even in political considerations Hus consistently called for comparison between bishops and Christ. That remained the prime criterion. Some of his sermons presented a cutting evaluation of the pomp and circumstance of papal appearances over against the humble Christ.[128]

Turning to clerical wickedness Hus denounced slothful priests.[129] This served to raise the ire of many Prague priests and the incumbents of more than forty parish churches in Prague took umbrage at Hus' reform activities. Soon, Hus and his supporters discovered themselves maligned as 'diabolical clerics'.[130] Hus remained unmoved declaring wicked priests unworthy of their calling.[131] Christ takes away the sin of the world, priests cannot. The power of the keys was contingent upon the prerogatives of God.[132] Hus deplored the arbitrary and inappropriate use of ecclesiastical power. This extended to the abusive practices of excommunication and the anathema which Hus regarded as tools of wicked priests to oppress the laity and secure material gain.[133] Preaching on the second Sunday of Easter, Hus excoriated the practices of priests. If a priest felt wronged while gambling or cavorting with prostitutes the offender was taken before a spiritual tribunal and summarily excommunicated. Interdict might be declared to placate the cleric and his adversary sent on pilgrimage as far away as Rome. If however the priest was at fault there were no consequences. Those who protested at such political machinations were declared heretical, slanderers, and banned from further public comment. Such actions were the work of Antichrist.[134] On the sixth Sunday of Easter, Hus declared that priests committed more harm when drunk and carousing than anyone else. It must have been a sobering claim. Hus went on to charge such clerics with oppressing the faithful. In another declaration, which in hindsight seems all the more poignant, Hus spoke of the reaction of these wicked priests when they found themselves criticized. 'They curse him, bring him to trial, imprison him, and declare loudly that according to their rules such a man must die and by no means an easy death but instead he should be consumed by fire'.[135] Hus accused his clerical colleagues of misplaced values. Acts of mercy were sometimes condemned as sinful, in violation of some obscure ecclesiastical ordinance, while deeds emanating from greed were passed over in silence.[136] Priests, prelates and monks eat at table in view of images of beautiful women displaying voluptuous breasts.[137] Hus was scandalized. Loving God ought to mean obeying the divine commandments.[138] The houses of priests in Prague were denounced as places of gambling, dancing and immorality run by manifest sinners. Such acts allowed by a lay person were venial sins but for a priest they constituted mortal sins and Hus appealed to Bernard as his authority.[139] It comes as no surprise to find Hus defending clerical celibacy.[140] Clearly the priests who felt they were being targeted did not abide the volley of condemnation coming from Bethlehem Chapel and the writings of Jan Hus. So long as he preached against the foibles of the common people Hus was commended. But when he turned his sights on sinful priests he found himself in trouble.[141] Hostile reports claimed Hus roused the common people to hatred of the priesthood.[142] Detractors said he was worse than any devil.[143] Spies appeared at Hus' sermons, taking notes, and posters appeared on church doors barring Hus and his supporters from performing priestly functions therein.[144] Hus remained adamant. He noted his enemies actually cursed in the name of Jesus those who went to Bethlehem Chapel to hear sermons.[145] Moral worthiness formed the chief prerequisite for the priesthood.[146] Standards apparently sank so low in Prague that Hus went so far as to say that few of the clergy would actually be saved since they seemed devoted to fulfilling the works of the flesh.[147] These were incendiary words. Still, Hus could not retreat from his conviction that everything was useless if one's life was not properly conducted.[148] By this standard which Hus extrapolated from scripture many of the clerics were corrupt, they failed to exhibit Christ in their lives, and their conduct suggested they were more aptly ministers of Antichrist than representatives of Jesus

Christ.¹⁴⁹ Instead of such practices, Hus urged the priesthood collectively to admonish the sinful to turn from sin and repent.¹⁵⁰ Ostensibly, little had changed as a result of Milíč's preaching or the findings of Archdeacon Pavel thirty years earlier. When his uncompromising critique forced him into exile he simply took his message with him. We read that in 1412 Hus was denounced and expelled from the capitol. He celebrated Mass and preached in a barn at Kozí Hrádek. Many people from the town of Sezimovo Ústí came to hear him ostensibly because he preached against the pope, the bishops, and the canons and because he continually censured the spiritual order.¹⁵¹

One of the persistent difficulties facing the western church at the end of the Middle Ages was rampant simony. The intention in some of Hus' writings seems to be aimed at equipping students and priests alike to avoid simony.¹⁵² In his history of the Council of Constance, contemporary observer Dietrich Vrie noted sarcastically that popes ascended to their holy office by means of simony and if Simon Magus himself were alive he might be able to purchase the Father, the Son, and the Holy Ghost.¹⁵³ Hus regarded the practice as turning the priesthood into hirelings who cared more about animals, material possessions and money than the cure of souls.¹⁵⁴ Such clerics resembled Judas Iscariot who bought and sold the truth.¹⁵⁵ In like manner, wicked priests in Hus' day charged fees for the administration of grace.¹⁵⁶ Hus castigated them relentlessly. In his exposition of the ten commandments, Hus told a story of a sermon he heard in Prague, underscoring the manipulation tactics of some priests eager to increase wealth. 'I once heard in a sermon, God is my witness, spoken during a sermon at St. Henry's in the New Town of Prague, "hear my children that three devils have come to this festival. One to close the heart so that people will not be sorry for their sins . . . a second to close their mouths in order that they might not pray or praise God. The third, my children, is the worst of all, to close purses. O dear children, do not permit this terrible devil to close your purses. Come near to the relic and open your purse and pocket"'.¹⁵⁷ Hus condemned such tactics as greed and simony. The older notion of simony as heresy was revived in Hus. In 1413 Hus completed his important and major treatise on the subject of simony. Hus defined simony as the buying and selling of holy things – spiritual power (*svatokupectví* is the technical word in Czech) – or exchanging spiritual things for the non-spiritual.¹⁵⁸ Hus traced the origins of the practice to Gehazi in the Hebrew Bible (2 Kings 5:19–27) and to Simon Magus in the Acts of the Apostles (8:9–24). Both offered or accepted material goods in exchange for spiritual power. Hus considered the practice a highly contagious 'spiritual leprosy'. In attacking the practice, Hus called upon the fathers, Gregory, Ambrose, Gregory of Nazianzus, Popes Paschal I, Gelasius I, Innocent II, Innocent III, and Leo I, canon law, medieval authorities such as Peter Lombard, Remigius of Auxerre, and Peter Damian, major councils like Nicaea, other obscure synods, and John Wyclif. The main contours of Hus' book can be reduced as follows. The will of Antichrist was the impetus, and the progenitor of the practice was the Devil. Consent was essential and may be discovered in six different forms: abetting, defense, counsel, approval, neglect of duty, and failure to correct.¹⁵⁹ The idea of consent or will was essential for understanding Hus' unyielding attack. The practice was rampant. Hus claimed that when Zbyněk died in 1411 there were no fewer than twenty-four candidates bidding for the archbishopric, including Jan Železný, bishop of Litomyšl. Hus says he recorded the names commenting tersely that it seemed more likely the bridge over the Vltava River would collapse than for the Prague archbishopric to be filled via a holy process. If Hus considered the business as unholy, there were others who did not. Štěpán of Dolany claimed that while Hus and his followers regarded the early and unexpected death of Zbyněk as divine retribution the late archbishop was more a martyr who died in the midst of the struggle and in so doing received the crown of victory.[160] The trade and trafficking in holy affairs had become big business. Dietrich of Niem, horrified by the simoniacal practices of the early fifteenth-century papacy, noted that it was done openly without shame and curial officials said it was legitimate since the pope could not sin in such matters.[161] Hus found the stance preposterous.

His detractors appealed to longstanding tradition and practice. Hus dismissed this argument by sarcastically saying it would be like defending illicit sex on the grounds that 'it is an ancient custom to fornicate'. Truth must always prevail over custom and tradition. Other arguments advanced the claim that if one did not buy the office someone else would. Hus replied 'if others sin openly that is no reason for another to sin'.[162] Polar opinions deadlocked. Hus related stories of confronting those engaged in simoniacal practice only to have them storm off in anger. The sins of Gehazi and Simon Magus were commonly committed with impunity by popes, cardinals, higher and lower clergy, ordinary parish priests, along with those in religious orders. Simony was a sin and Hus held accountable not only those who committed it actively but also those aware of it who remained silent. God repudiated all sinners, Hus claimed.[163] Offenders were Judases selling truth and Christ. Apostolic poverty remained an ideal for Hus and the example to emulate.[164] Hus lamented that only a few priests were not implicated in simony. Wicked bishops and priests guard an empty tomb but only devout Christians are comforted.[165] Right about the time Hus was writing his big book on simony, Konrad of Vechta bought the archbishopric of Prague while he was the incumbent bishop of Olomouc.

The propensity toward sensuality and sexual misbehavior among Prague clerics concerned Hus. He felt that true piety suffered as a result. It seemed insufferable to hurry through the divine liturgy in order to more quickly get to the pub, to dances, or to lewdness.[166] Hus did not shrink from denouncing drunkenness among clerics in his first sermon to the synod coupling that with a reproach for poor preaching, and demanding a better example be set.[167] But the severity of clerical malfeasance went farther declaring that such priests had perverted the gospel. In his Advent II sermon Hus preached that faithful servants of God were in dire straits in Bohemia, Moravia, England, the German lands and elsewhere. 'Faithful priests are killed, tortured, cursed' without remedy. It was pointless to appeal to the papacy inasmuch as that office was beset by the wickedness of Antichrist, sexual misconduct, pride, greed and simony which now flowed like a rushing tide into Bohemia. Bishoprics cost more than a baronial estate. Fear prevented many from complaining and the faithful were confused.[168] Anticlericalism abounded.[169] Hus became a target of the outraged clerics and complaints were brought against him because of his criticism of the moral laxity of the priesthood.[170] The broad thrust of the complaint seems to have been that Hus made certain clerics look bad. They asserted he claimed that charging fees for priestly functions constituted simony. He had apparently defamed holders of numerous benefices and condemned priestly vices. It was altogether insufferable. Hus defended himself quite easily on all charges even commenting that the notorious pluralist Petr Všeruby, whom he had mentioned whilst preaching, might be saved though Hus doubted it.[171] Preaching on the dominical words of how better it would be for the wicked to be thrown into the sea before offending even the youngest of the faithful, Hus dryly commented if this were to come to pass there would scarcely be a priest left. From popes on down they were guilty of sexual immorality and other sins. Further, there was not enough sea in all the world to contain the number of priests and monks existing in concubinage.[172]

The severity of moral standards held by Hus must be noted. He thought that anyone committing fornication after baptism could not ascend to the priesthood. Any priest committing such an act should be defrocked. That remained an ideal. The reality of the situation was that priests lived openly in fornication and concubinage and often kept women in their houses claiming they were sisters. Hus fumed that many sexually immoral priests spent their parishioners' money on whores.[173] It is fair to note that unlike Wyclif and other late medieval reformers, Hus did not call for the dissolution of the monasteries and cloisters. Cleansed of abuses and immorality, the religious life retained a valuable expression of the Christian life and faith. After all his fulminations, Hus knew the only plausible condition for ecclesiastical reform lay in the hands of the faithful laity. To these he encouraged reform of life, change of habits, aversion to temptations and penitential tears which he asserted aided in washing away all former sins.[174] If this example did not prevail upon irregular priests to amend their ways then Hus advised no one ought to obey wicked priests.[175] It is significant that even in his earliest works there were reforming tendencies and moral comment. These features followed Hus all the way to Constance. There remains one other important dimension to Hus' involvement in political issues.

Around the time of the Council of Constance the Augustinian hermit from Osnabrück Dietrich Vrie wrote a Latin poem which summed up a particular point of view concerning the late medieval church.

> The pope, once the wonder of the world, has fallen. With him fell my members the heavenly temples. Now is the time of the reign of Simon Magus. The wealth of the world impedes right judgment. The papal court fosters every sort of scandal and converts the houses of God into markets. The sacraments are despicably sold. The wealthy are preferred and the poor despised. Whoever can afford the most is better received. Golden was the first age of the papal court. Then came the more inferior age of silver followed by the iron age which placed a yoke upon the stubborn neck. Then came the time of clay. Could anything be

worse? Yes, shit and in shit the papal court sits. Everything is degenerate. The papal court is rotten. The pope himself is the head of all wickedness. He plots every sort of disgraceful scheme. He absolves others while he himself hastens to death.[176]

Hus would not have disavowed the portrait. His life and work revolved around ecclesiastical reform, social concerns, truth, and a God-consciousness. With the caveat in mind that the unity of the church and state was indissoluble in the Middle Ages, it is clear Hus desired to create a change in the social structures of Prague society so that justice might be achieved in conformity with the law of God. Hus preferred royal power over episcopal authority when it came to such matters. Preaching on the text *Exi in vias* (Luke 14:23/Matthew 22:9) in 1411 Hus made that perfectly clear. He noted that when King Václav seized the revenues of wicked priests he exercised a God-given right and duty.[177] Indeed, the state had the power to rule and discipline the clergy. This was all the more needful because once the body of Christ suffered injury, infection could set in. Evil should be punished regardless of where it occurred. Priests should be subject to royal authority because these powers had been ordained by God.[178] Royal authority ordained by God extended all the way to the curia with the implication that a pope living contrary to God might be dispossessed.[179] There was no such thing as unlimited papal power for indeed popes and the authority they wield was subject to the law of God.[180] Hus took the polemic one step farther in declaring it was blasphemous to maintain a pope could not err and went on to point out, as we have seen previously, that many popes had been heretical.[181] Such perspective placed Hus in opposition to prevailing views in Prague and elsewhere in Europe.

Given the frequency with which Hus addressed this issue it seems quite clear it constituted a major plank in his house of social and political ideas. The crusade indulgence preached in 1410 led Hus to declare unequivocally that secular rulers might seize ecclesiastical land and remove temporal goods from priests who failed to exercise the duties of their commission properly. The very fact that individual priests and the church as an institution owned property, placed them within the jurisdiction of the secular authority. Instances of habitual delinquency were justification for the state to act. The irregularities of the priesthood had clear social and political effects and therefore a conscientious ruler ought to root out such abuses before more dire consequences arose. The removal of property might work, Hus argued, as a warning against sin in much the same way as the ecclesiastical measures of interdict and excommunication did. Since many priests were sinful, the king must intercede to correct those clerics by removing their worldly goods. Hus claimed it was just as legitimate for a secular power to act in these instances as a king would if treason or assassination conspiracies were uncovered.[182] It is little wonder Hus drew condemnation from his priestly colleagues as he did. Reform was essential. If wayward clerics refused to be corrected by the word of God and the example of faithful Christians then the secular power should intervene. Those opposing the law of God anywhere in the Kingdom of Bohemia should be subdued by all means possible. Those resisting the king were in effect in opposition to God. The secular authorities had been endowed with material wealth, temporal power, and respect by God. This latter right extended even to the pope.[183] Hus did not maintain a consistent position on the matter of temporal authority for he also advocated that one had an obligation to obey one's superiors in all things.[184] It is difficult not to conclude that Hus argued one way when it pleased him and another when it suited him. This is not to suggest that Hus was capricious and manipulated ideas arbitrarily. It does suggest it was his interpretation of any given issue or situation where ultimately the question of authority lay.

Hus may have occasionally advocated obedience to superiors but his own career is a record of noncompliance. On 20 December 1409 Pope Alexander V, recently allied with Zbyněk, declared the common enemy of humankind had promoted errors in Prague and elsewhere detrimental to the faith. The reference implied Wyclif. The pope ordered measures taken to contain the problem.[185] In response to the order, by papal bull, for preaching to cease and desist in Bethlehem Chapel, Hus filed an appeal which he read from his pulpit. He then preached what might be regarded as an inflammatory sermon in which, judging from the surviving fragments, he asserted there were no Czech heretics of the stripe the papacy suspected and suggested the authors of the order to cease preaching were persecutors of the gospel and the faith of Christ. He urged his hearers to pay no heed to the threat of excommunication.[186] Hus later explained his refusal to obey noting the bull was contrary to the words and deeds of Christ, lacked an apostolic mandate, was harmful to the church, placed unnecessary restrictions on the word of God, and was itself heretical.[187] Hus' explanation for disobedience cannot be judged consistent with canonical rules. Whether Hus' arguments have theological validity the point remained: he disobeyed and had no difficulty justifying his behavior going so far as appearing to boast to his enemies that he covered the walls of Bethlehem Chapel with his views on the papal directive.[188] This hardly resembles submission to authority which Hus sometimes advocated. For Hus, Christ was the ultimate authority and if an order failed to conform with Hus' understanding of the law of Christ he simply ignored it, despite his own counsel.

Of particular importance is the thesis that Hus ultimately advanced in which he declared that no one existing in a state of mortal sin can rightly be considered a legitimate secular lord, bishop or prelate. If a ruler persisted in mortal sin that one was neither justly nor properly to be regarded as an authority.[189] It is little wonder Emperor-elect Sigismund had this rebuttal at Constance: 'Jan Hus, no one lives without sin'.[190] The emperor was correct and surely Hus knew it. He may well have written that sinful men and women were corrupt in nature so that everything they did was unjust inasmuch as one cannot do anything else in any sphere which was fundamentally different from one's own nature.[191] The subversive nature of this doctrine of dominion is unmistakable. Hus did not derive this idea from Wyclif as sometimes assumed. It can be found explicitly in Tomáš Štítný. One must wonder where Hus regarded the line of demarcation between theology and politics or how he conceived of reformed social order. At times Hus does not seem to appreciate the implicit dangers in his political ideas. If sinners had no right to administer the sacraments, or law that provided no room for negotiation, Hus was left on the brink of social and religious anarchy should his ideas have been implemented. Questions of what constituted the state and the church would have to be seriously rethought. Sigismund grasped the issue cogently. Perhaps the most incisive analysis of Hus on this point came from Jean Gerson. On 24 September 1414 he wrote to Konrad, Archbishop of Prague. Hus' thinking on this issue, according to the chancellor of Paris University, was faulty. The principal error lay with assuming that a person in sin has by consequence no jurisdictional authority over others. The idea had to be exterminated either by reason, fire or sword. The concept was that pernicious. Those holding the view of dominion as Hus did were judged deficient in common sense. Even scripture enjoined obedience even to questionable leaders. Gerson judged that only the arrogant and seditious would disagree. Political dominion therefore was not a matter of predestination. Instead it had been established according to ecclesiastical and civil law.[192] Modern defenders of Hus claim Gerson misunderstood his statements.[193] Gerson scholars admit ambiguity in Hus and his lack of clarity difficult.[194] Frankly, I think Hus said what he meant and meant what he said. It was neither the first nor the last time he failed to consider the wider picture.

7

TRIAL

In the fall of 1414 Jan Hus left Bohemia and went to Constance to stand trial. Whether he went voluntarily or upon the orders of the king is unclear.[1] Ultimately, the charge was heresy. Hus had long been suspected of disseminating errors.[2] While some may argue the medieval category of 'heresy' itself is useless to the modern scholar there is no good reason to manufacture another construct.[3] Hus was a dissenter who placed himself outside the realm of obedience to medieval authority. For Hus, appearance at Constance was not the beginning of a legal process. It was the final chapter in a judicial procedure that had been put in motion several years earlier. The imposition of interdict drove Hus from Prague into a period of exile. The case of the church versus Hus continued apace. With the deepening crisis in the western church and more strident anti-heresy measures being threatened, the legal problems facing Hus intensified. Once Hus left for the Council, King Václav did not actively do anything to protect his subject. Silence from the royal house persisted. Hus was left to the vagaries of imperial and ecclesiastical politics. There may been collusion between Václav and Sigismund respecting Hus.[4] The king earlier had expressed his own frustration with Hus, going so far as to threaten to burn the reformer personally if he continued to cause problems.[5] There is no doubt that the king, queen, and other officials of the Czech kingdom initially tried to intercede on behalf of Hus but these efforts dwindled once he went to Constance. It should be noted, however, that while these letters of appeal were dispatched they are no longer extant as once believed. The texts which do exist have been proven to be exemplars prepared by university students.[6] Though forbidden by the fathers at Constance to attend public services, presumably for fear his presence might be disruptive, it does seem that Hus celebrated private masses. And it is possible he worked in local libraries in composing his short tract on the question of lay utraquism.[7]

The specter of John Wyclif continued to hover over Hus and the opponents of the Englishman continued to press the case. On 10 February 1413 Wyclif's books were burned in Rome. This action came at the end of an inquiry appointed by Pope John XXIII which concluded Wyclif's books contained many heresies and false doctrines and the teachings deemed so perverse the books simply had to be destroyed before the faithful were hopelessly infected.[8] Hus' legal advisor Jan of Jesenice essayed a strident critique of the commission and its conclusions. He pointed out that the papal bull condemning Wyclif failed to cite a single scriptural proof and he called into question the competency of the commission members to pass judgment on the voluminous writings of Wyclif. It seemed preposterous that a group of cardinals, bishops, monks and other people, even law professors, might in four days read, examine and draw up a verdict on all of the books of John Wyclif. Jesenice could hardly suppress his feigned astonishment at such a feat. Indeed, 'even a hundred of the shrewdest demons, experts in all wickedness could not do it'.[9] The force of argument favored Jesenice. This critique had no positive effect on the case against Hus. In fact the condemnation of Wyclif now had papal sanction. Conciliar approval was achieved on 4 May 1415 when Constance formally condemned Wyclif as a 'false Christian', authorized the destruction of his books, and ordered his remains disinterred from consecrated ground and burned.[10] The process was problematic for the posthumous condemnation of Wyclif as a heretic contravened canon law.[11]

Process I

By appealing against Zbyněk's decision with respect to Wyclif on 25 June 1410, Hus set in motion a legal process which took five years to reach conclusion. The Council of Constance, so far as Hus was concerned, convened as a continuation of the trial initiated four years earlier. One might say the case against Jan Hus had been largely conducted *in camera* but at Constance the final hearings were public and the process constituted a show trial. The case for the prosecution was admirably summarized by the papal notary Jacob Cerretano in the terse comment 'Jan Hus, the Wyclifite, who had been teaching the wicked doctrine of Wyclif'.[12] That was the prevailing assumption. This accusation had deep roots. Preaching in Bethlehem Chapel Hus noted, 'now they are shouting throughout the entire world that the Czechs are heretics. Above all else they call Hus a heretic asking, "is that heretic still alive"'? As noted earlier Hus made a decision not to appear in 1411 when summoned to the papal curia. That decision proved decisive. The complications put in place then led to the verdict at Constance. The 1411 summons placed Hus in a predicament. He either had to appear and face condemnation or decline to appear and be denounced as disobedient.[13] The latter transpired and Hus' disobedience remained a crucial factor earning him the dubious distinction of multiple ecclesiastical sanctions. On 18 July 1410 Archbishop Zbyněk excommunicated Hus as a corrupter of the faith.[14] On 24 September 1410 he was placed under the censure of aggravated excommunication.[15] His third writ of excommunication was for contumacy connected with his refusal to appear as demanded.[16] The ban on Hus was proclaimed in Prague in all churches. Only Křišťan of Prachatice at St. Michael's and, surprisingly, the priest at St. Benedict's (Teutonic Knights) refused.[17] According to canonical rules failure to appear within twelve months meant the verdict of guilt might be applied without any legal requirement of evidentiary proof. If one remained excommunicate longer than one year there was cause to regard the defendant guilty of heresy.[18] By the fall of 1412 Hus received his fourth excommunication but this time he was classified as a major excommunicate by

Peter degli Stephaneschi, the cardinal of St. Angelo.[19] A bishop could excommunicate any one who refused canonical obedience. Hus fell into this category. The essential element in excommunication was separation from the faithful. The offender was regarded as outlaw. It is important to draw attention to the difference between minor and major excommunication as articulated in canon law. The former prohibited one from receiving the sacraments while the latter called for the offender to be removed from the community of the faithful altogether.[20] In practical terms, major excommunication implied no religious rites, exclusion from entry into a church, a prohibition against keeping company with faithful Christians in good standing, and extended to aspects of secular life including pleading in court. In the event of death there could be no canonically sanctioned burial. The sentence of this excommunication was announced in Prague at the annual meeting of the synod convened on 18 October. Cardinal John of Lisbon had been dispatched to Bohemia to pronounce the solemn verdict. The heretic Jan Hus was declared cut off from 'food, drink, buying, selling, conversation, hospitality, the giving of shelter and all acts of kindness'. If he fled elsewhere that locale would be subject to ecclesiastical sanctions. All church services would be suspended for three days after his departure. If he died he could not be buried. If he had already died and been buried his remains would have to be exhumed. Hus had twenty-three days to comply with the order or he would be officially excommunicated from all 'churches, monasteries, and chapels'. This was accompanied by the customary drama of bell, book and candle – the ringing of a bell, closing of a book, and the extinguishing of a candle – symbolic aspects of the formal ritual of excommunication. This was followed by the throwing of three stones at the excommunicate's house as a sign of perpetual damnation. On the same day Hus responded by appealing to Jesus Christ.

A second bull of condemnation against Hus owed something to the persistence of Michael de Causis. Hus was to be arrested and turned over either to Archbishop Albík of Prague or Jan the 'Iron' bishop of Litomyšl. Once condemned he was to be burned. Bethlehem Chapel, characterized as a 'nest of heretics', was ordered torn down. Followers of Hus were subject to excommunication should they refuse to abjure the errors of Hus. They had thirty days in which to comply otherwise they should expect formal citations to the Roman Curia. Those who did submit should be examined by Michael de Causis.[21]

When the nominated twenty-three days passed and Hus failed to reply to the writ of major excommunication in the proper, canonically required fashion, Cardinal Peter degli Stephaneschi reaffirmed the sentence of aggravated excommunication initially assigned by Odo Colonna in 1411. Simultaneously Prague was placed under interdict. This punishment extended over the entire province affecting everyone for it involved the suspension of all ecclesiastical activities. With Hus in exile, Jan of Jesenice wasted little time attempting to mitigate the damage. On 18 December he argued at a university disputation that the condemnation was invalid.[22] His argument amounted to a shrewd legal brief which can be reduced to three main points. First, from a canon law perspective, excommunication can only be applied for cause. In the case of Jan

Hus, Jesenice argued there was no legitimate cause. The basis for the censure against Hus related to his failure or unwillingness to answer the initial citation two and a half years earlier. Jesenice considered that charge a manifest falsehood. He pointed out that Hus' legal representatives (including himself) made every reasonable effort to act. Moreover King Václav, Queen Žofie, and members of the ranks of Czech barons, all submitted evidence to the Curia. The claim then was specious. Second, the authority of Peter degli Stephaneschi, the cardinal of St. Angelo, in the Hus case being delegated had particular legal limitations. The exercise of that authority had clearly breached the limits of application. Since the cardinal overstepped his authority, his procedural faux pas invalidated the ultimate verdict pronounced. Jesenice also pointed out other elements in the writ of excommunication which caused the sanction, from a legal perspective, to be rendered null and void. Third, Jesenice argued that Hus' legal rights had consistently been ignored throughout the process because he had not been permitted to have his case presented and argued at the Curia. This was unacceptable since that basic legal right could not be abrogated by any authority whether secular or ecclesiastical. Jan of Jesenice's arguments were unimpeachable. Ultimately, they made not one wit of difference in the trial of Jan Hus.

The year prior to his departure for the Council at Constance, Hus laid down in some detail his rationale for choosing to disobey ecclesiastical authority in 1411.[23] The decision made by Hus turned out to be so pivotal his explanation deserves an extended summary. Hus compared himself to Jesus who elected not to attend a feast at Jerusalem. Hus noted that he sent his representatives who had been refused a hearing for three years. Instead, these men were arrested and imprisoned when they demanded justice. Hus also claimed the distance from Prague to Rome, some 800 miles, was somewhat prohibitive. More to the point, Hus declared there was no injunction in the law of God which might be applicable in demanding his appearance in Rome at the behest of papal authorities. This point gets at the heart of Hus' refusal. He goes farther. Judging there to be little divine truth at the Curia, Hus expressed his conviction he had little confidence in any judgment proceeding from an appearance in Rome which might be consistent with the law of God. Going to Rome would remove Hus from his pulpit for an indeterminate period of time and this amounted to depriving the people of the word of God. The cost of such a trip likewise mitigated against obeying the summons. Hus refused to go because his brief was at odds with the exercise of papal power which he determined had been invented by the Devil and had no divine origin or basis. Alexander V issued a bull which called for the cessation of preaching everywhere in the archdiocese of Prague save for parish churches and monastic chapels. This order, Hus concluded, constituted an egregious affront to the gospel. After all, places like Bethlehem Chapel had been established expressly for the preaching of the gospel and official approbation had been secured at the time of the foundation. Why should that approval now be revoked? The bull promulgated by Alexander V had been received and acted upon by Zbyněk and other prelates especially Jaroslav, a monk and titular bishop. Hus objected to the declaration latent in the bull that many people throughout the Kingdom of Bohemia and the Margraviate of Moravia were already infected with heresy and on that account required immediate correction and spiritual oversight. The cure of their souls under Hus had failed. Hus went on to argue that both Alexander V and Zbyněk had acted in violation of the law. The bull was illegal in its proclamation by Alexander and equally illegal in application by Zbyněk. The bull's intention and application violated the freedom of preaching which Hus clearly esteemed. Moreover, it was contrary to the gospel and inconsistent with the command of Christ who instructed his followers to go throughout the world proclaiming the gospel. Hus poised a blunt question: does the bull conform to scripture and the intention of Christ? 'Definitely not'! This being true, Hus pointed out that for these reasons he appealed against the bull.

Hus then ruminated on the possible advantage there might be in calling for a cessation of preaching. He concluded the bull was conceived because of jealousy, greed and specifically to put an end to reform at Bethlehem Chapel. Noting that other archbishops established similar foundations for the same purpose, Hus called to remembrance former Archbishop Jan of Jenštejn who sanctioned Bethlehem Chapel. Unfortunately, Hus suggested, Zbyněk had been manipulated by canons and monks and certain priests who had agreed on a plot to disadvantage Bethlehem Chapel and its ministry. Hus claimed the offensive was personal. He suggested that had he followed the requirements of the bull, no one in Prague among the clerics or monastic orders would have granted him another pulpit in any of the approved churches. This was the strategy designed to expel Hus from the pulpits of Prague. The bull therefore had a prime motivation to silence Hus. Perceiving this, Hus took a stand against what he called the unrighteousness and wickedness of the bull.

Finally, Hus claimed he did not travel to Rome for he suspected he might be summarily executed and his death would be pointless. He asserted his enemies lurked everywhere and all of them desired his death. Both pope and cardinals were enemies. Hus seemed especially affronted and took umbrage at being called a heretic without so much as having been seen or heard by his accusers in Rome. Hus suggested the Curia felt targeted by his sermons against pride, greed and simony among other irregularities Hus condemned in his sermons. He underscored the bane of false witnesses and statements made in Prague and forwarded to Rome. He mentioned the charge of eucharistic heresy – a clear reference to remanentism – which remained a perennial suspicion. He enumerated other specious allegations and expressed dismay that such gossip might be accepted uncritically by the officials in Rome. He alluded to the published opinion of his initial judge – Odo Colonna – who had denounced him as the inventor of errors and an unreliable priest. Hus mentioned Michael de Causis by name referring to the latter's claim that all faithful Christians in Bohemia ostensibly regarded Hus as a heretic and that gross errors were proclaimed daily in Bethlehem Chapel by Hus who had been nominated as an heresiarch. Hus asserted that the charges did not disturb him and they could not harm him. He claimed to feel no resentment because this was what happened to Christ who had also been falsely accused, tortured and killed. Hus firmly asserted his obligation was not to popes or judges but to Christ even if that meant censure and death. The focus remained on the truth of Christ. This constituted Hus' fullest statement on why he refused to obey the summons to Rome.

Elsewhere Hus provided other details on the Roman process.[24] Once Alexander V died and was succeeded by John XXIIII the case against Hus continued. Hus' understanding of the case at this stage once again requires summary. Evidently John XXIII did not consider the Hus matter significant enough to warrant direct papal attention and despite entreaties from Hus' representatives declined to look into the case personally. Hus revealed that his delegates attempted to prevail upon Pope John on the necessity of a hearing which custom allowed even to 'pagans, Jews, heretics or even the Devil' should they demand a hearing. John remained unpersuaded and delegated the case to his cardinals. Hus suggested the cardinals in question were bought off by his enemies through the offer of extravagant gifts to delay passing judgment thereby disadvantaging Hus all the more. After these initial delays John referred the case to others but Hus once more opined a similar development occurred. Still no formal decision. Whereupon Pope John decided that he would, after all, take up the case personally. Having withdrawn the brief from the auditor Johannes de Tomariis and Odo Colonna, John assumed personal responsibility. Hus sarcastically alleged the pontiff did so with the motivation that everyone else had benefitted from the matter save him. Hus' representatives once again requested a hearing but were denied when Hus declined to buy a favorable verdict from the pope. Unhappy, John imprisoned Hus' delegates but all three managed to escape in one fashion or another and eventually returned to Prague. After Zbyněk died his enemies hatched another plot and succeeded in obtaining the writ of major excommunication against Hus. Convinced that his appeal to the Curia would not be effective since the pope had no concern for truth, Hus appealed to God. He justified this step on the grounds that appealing thus meant to ask for help from a higher judge. Because the Lord God was the greatest judge and the counsel most concerned with justice and incapable of error, Hus asserted he had entrusted the cause to God. Since the pope had refused to deal with truth Hus refused to appear in Rome. On top of this the pope had revealed he was not a man of probity. He unjustly imprisoned Hus' representatives and robbed Stanislav of Znojmo and Štěpán Páleč of '207 gulden and horses'. More to the point, Hus admitted he did not appear because he was conducting his cause against the pope and knew the pope would not condemn himself. Hus boasted that he withstood the pope's dishonest henchmen who came to Prague with papal directives aimed, according to Hus, at defrauding the faithful people. 'And so, giving preference to the cause of God and not wishing to squander life and deprive the people of the word of God' Hus refused to obey. These two accounts from Hus are important in understanding his thinking and his perception of the legal issues before he journeyed to Constance. His detractors remained unpersuaded. Štěpán of Dolany argued Hus ought to have gone to Rome as required. If he trusted in God, as he claimed, the Carthusian abbot wondered what Hus had to fear. If he truly relied upon the grace of God Hus should have been prepared to face any judge, even an unjust one. After all Christ himself appeared before Pontius Pilate, should Hus do any less? He had a point and it also goes to show that Hus was not devoid of pragmatism. Abbot Štěpán concluded Hus was a coward.[25] Others were equally dismissive. Dietrich of Niem said the appeal should not even be considered at the Curia. Suspicion of heresy was sufficient for action and he urged an immediate crusade against the heretics of Prague in order to 'imprison, degrade and hand over to the secular arm' with the aim of putting an end to the Hus problem.[26]

Earlier, it was noted that political pressure had been brought to bear upon the increasingly ineffective Zbyněk who was pressured to appeal to the pope on Hus' behalf. In a personal letter to John XXIII, Zbyněk asked the pontiff to consider dismissing and canceling the writs of censure and excommunication which had been issued against Hus and also absolving him from any obligation to appear personally in Rome. The letter was never sent.[27] It is not possible to conclude what effect it may have had on the case against Hus had the missive come to John's hand. Jiří Kejř has undertaken the most thorough and revealing analysis of the Hus trial from a procedural and legal history perspective.[28] Kejř's work is of seminal importance replacing all previous studies and certainly going well beyond every study in English. In examining the several facets of the Hus case it becomes immediately apparent that the court records from the Hus trial are not all extant and this presents a serious drawback.[29] One of the indispensable source collections for the Council of Constance is Hermann von der Hardt's great work but its usefulness is vitiated by its appalling confusion.[30] The *Chronicle of the Prague University* has some unique material relating to the Hus case which can be drawn upon to some advantage.[31] The sources of the Hus trial at Constance are discussed in more detail below. I use both Hardt and Mansi. The latter is not merely an inferior reproduction of the former. Hardt is preferred but Mansi's value should not be eschewed.

Process II

The decree *Haec Sancta* may have theorized that the Council of Constance had been assembled in the Holy Spirit but the practice and its proceedings were somewhat less lofty. 'The theologian may indulge the pleasing task of describing Religion as she descended from Heaven, arrayed in her native purity. A more melancholy duty is imposed on the historian. He must discover the inevitable mixture of error and corruption which she contracted in a long residence upon the earth, among a weak and degenerate race of beings'.[32] Did the Council of Constance deliberately manipulate evidence and material in the case against Jan Hus? This has been an historiographical debate from 1415 down into the recent past. Matthew Spinka is among modern scholars arguing that Hus was a victim of political machinations at Constance and systemic malfeasance at the hands of the conciliar fathers. Spinka advances four arguments to support his theory. First, the Council refused to hear Hus, preferring to rely upon the testimony of his accusers especially Michael de Causis, Štěpán Páleč, Jean Gerson and others.[33] Second, the Council unsuccessfully tried to coerce Hus into committing perjury because they did not wish to know the truth of his teachings. Third, the trial proceedings were conducted by canon lawyers committed to scholastic principles and nominalist theology. By contrast Hus rested his defense on scripture and patristic authorities, especially Augustine. Spinka's implication is that the men of Constance preferred law over truth. Fourth, the Council itself may not have been a legitimate body despite the decrees *Sacrosancta* (1415) and *Inter cunctus* (22 February 1418). One must avow conciliar theory otherwise the proceedings ultimately are invalid. Spinka appealed to Martin V who forbade further appeals from pope to council, which Spinka regarded as an implicit repudiation of conciliarism, to Eugenius IV who dismissed *Sacrosancta* as 'impious and scandalous', all the way to Pius IX in 1870 who declared that only the pope can define matters of faith and morals, and can do so apart from cardinals and bishops. For Spinka, the Council committed judicial murder following a wholesale manipulation of evidence.[34] Conversely, there may be a legitimate claim lodged that Hus was sufficiently ambiguous so as to disadvantage himself.[35]

Procedurally the Council of Constance was a mess. The synod had been called by Pope John XXIII but he was deposed by the Council as a false pontiff. The eighty-nine year old Gregory XII offered to voluntarily resign as a gesture at solving the papal schism. He had already been deposed by the previous Council of Pisa in 1409 which made his offer curious. There was a string attached to Gregory's overture. He wanted the official records amended to say that he had called the Council. Somewhat astonishingly the fathers at Constance agreed and two days before the Hus case ended, Gregory stood down having been recognized as the legitimate pope in the protracted papal schism. Inasmuch as Gregory did not recognize the earlier convocation of the Council by John XXIII, the Council agreed with him and the synod received official sanction on 4 July 1415. This political reality must be considered when making any assessment of the Council of Constance though it must be noted Constance offered Benedict XIII the same right of convocation as Gregory. In these gestures the Council was not seeking to address a legitimacy question. Instead the Council was pursuing a strategy of unity in order to solve its greatest challenges: heresy and schism. Philosophical differences also played a role in the Hus case.[36] As noted earlier, realism seems to have been a foundation for the Prague reformers while nominalism prevailed at Constance among the fathers. The collision of ideas should not be minimized.

In the early days of the conciliar proceedings Pope John XXIII and Emperor-elect Sigismund played crucial roles. John later suffered deposition, imprisonment and humiliation. He had few defenders. Sigismund, on the other hand, was vilified by the Czechs and ever after regarded as a traitor. Hungarian scholars describe his character as riven by compromise and manipulation.[37] Scholars of Hussitica traditionally have regarded the two negatively. 'Sigismund was cruel and sensual, dishonest and vain, greedy and lecherous, loud and cowardly. He was dismissed as an object of horror to the Czechs. He was hated and vilified by Germans and became a warning to all rulers. His companion John XXIII was lewd and murderous, faithless and a simoniac. He was a good friend to Sigismund in every wicked deed and he serves as a warning to all future popes'.[38] This assessment is clearly biased but into the hands of these two men the Hus case passed in the autumn of 1414.

Hus requested and eventually obtained a letter of safe conduct from Sigismund dated 18 October 1414. The *salvus conductus* was addressed to all ecclesiastical and secular officials and to all of the subjects within the Holy Roman Empire. Sigismund stated that the honorable master Jan Hus was traveling to Constance under the personal protection of the emperor and the empire. The safe conduct appealed to all to receive Hus with kindness and generosity and to facilitate his safe passage and all those with him in every way applicable. All gates, roads and cities were to be open to him for free movement as he determined to 'pass through, to stop, to stay and to return'.[39] There has been considerable debate over whether or not Sigismund intended to provide Hus with a round trip pass to Constance. The text of the document given to Hus does seem to imply Hus had the protection of Sigismund to return from the Council to Bohemia. It is possible that in the beginning, before Hus left Bohemia, Sigismund thought Hus could defend himself against the charges of heresy and thereby lift that bane from the Kingdom of Bohemia. This would have considerable political advantage for Sigismund who had his eye on the Czech throne. Hus clearly believed he had protection to go to Constance and also to return and stated that Sigismund gave these assurances to him. However, Hus was not so benighted to suspect circumstances could change or that Sigismund might be capable of treachery.[40] What seems likely is that Hus got a safe conduct upon demand and that he had asked specifically for round trip protection. This probably was the case though clearly the second leg of the trip was never permitted. It has been argued that Sigismund simply changed his mind or from the outset had no intention of allowing Hus to return to Prague.[41] Alternatively, it is possible the emperor never intended, never stated, or never gave any thought to a safe conduct implying a round trip pass. Moreover, whatever Sigismund's intentions may have been it is possible that the round trip guarantee was less implied in the actual text of the safe conduct and more in the verbal assurances Sigismund offered to Hus through Jindřich Lefl and Mileš Divoký.[42] Of course the technical matter of heresy should have been a mitigating factor in any safe conduct or guarantee of passage. It is possible to argue that no one, including an emperor, could assure a suspected or convicted heretic the right of safe passage. At issue is the extent of Sigismund's knowledge of canon law and heresy trials. If the emperor was sufficiently versed in legal procedure he should have understood his limitations. It seems likely the emperor was as much out of his depth on such matters as Hus clearly was.

It was obvious that Hus' safe conduct included no limitations or noted any special conditions affecting the viability of the provisions therein. Even the unsympathetic author of the *Chronicle of the Council of Constance*, Ulrich Richental, stated firmly the safe conduct was issued to 'ensure his coming and return'.[43] The promise of round trip protection was considered serious and binding in the later Middle Ages.[44] The problem however was that inquisitorial law and practice allowed for no concessions. Clearly Bohemia had experience with inquisitorial procedures in the fourteenth century.[45] An inquisitorial office had been established in Prague with papal inquisitors appointed as early as 1318. Perhaps the strict application of canon law in the matter of heresy was not widely known or remembered. If so this underscores a particular naïveté which helps explain why the level of outrage over the alleged violation of the Hus safe conduct reached such levels in Bohemia. For several years before he went to Constance Hus had been widely condemned as an heresiarch. That formed the basis for why the Council desired his presence in Constance. Legal precedent in the matter of heresy was very well established by the fifteenth century. Unless Hus successfully defended himself on the charges against him, which was unlikely given how well entrenched they were, or received absolution, which was even less likely, his fate was clear. No safe conduct or intervention by secular authority could save him. Bluntly put, in such circumstances suspected heretics had no legal rights. Kejř submits that Sigismund could not possibly have intended what Hus assumed in the safe conduct.[46] That assumption is not as firm as Kejř suggests. Sigismund's reaction to the lack of authority his safe conduct carried in Constance revealed that he was not closely acquainted with the particulars of canon law with respect to heresy. Either that, or he put on an admirable political performance. When informed that Hus had been arrested, Sigismund blustered threatening to break down the prison doors if the matter was not rectified immediately. When he arrived at Constance he exuded great indignation and threatened to leave immediately and suspend imperial protection over the Council. There can be little doubt that the emperor did consider his promise to Hus as constituting a safe conduct and he had defenders.[47] Of more immediate consequence, though completely lacking in effect, was the action of Jan of Chlum, one of the knights Sigismund assigned to accompany Hus to Constance. On Christmas Eve he posted in various public places, including church doors as well as the cathedral doors, in Constance a formal protest written in Latin and German bearing his baronial seal. Initially, John XXIII denied he ordered Hus's arrest but later admitted he had but did not move against him canonically on account of Sigismund's protests.[48] Meanwhile Sigismund received letters complaining of the delay in bringing Hus to judgment and expressing hope the accused would not be shielded by the safe conduct.[49]

Sigismund's complaints of dishonor over the breach of the safe conduct met with a rejoinder from the canon lawyers present in Constance. The emperor was told that no law or secular sanction could shield a suspected heretic or protect such a one by means of a safe conduct.[50] Sigismund allowed himself to be placated by that advice and later when personally addressing Hus at the hearing on 7 June repeated that admonition.[51] It is noteworthy to see that the emperor persisted in using the language of safe conduct even at that late date. Sigismund refuted the claims circulating around Constance that his safe conduct had been retroactively issued more than two weeks after Hus was incarcerated. Though he erred in details, Sigismund established that the document had been determined before Hus left Bohemia. The emperor advised Hus that he had taken counsel and been told he could neither provide safe conduct to a heretic nor to one under suspicion of heresy. In this the emperor was correct. He could not claim power or authority to protect Hus. While he did issue a comprehensive safe conduct it was manifestly evident that placed against the might of the Council that document was impotent and not worth the paper it was written on. If Hus were condemned the emperor could do nothing safely to enforce or guarantee the provisions of the safe conduct. In some ways the notice gave witness to the enormous courage and integrity of Jan of Chlum, one of the unsung heros of the Hus case.

It is possible to compare letters of safe conduct from the later Middle Ages with that issued to Hus. The results are pedestrian and prove nothing of value.[52] Of more practical and applicable value might be to compare the safe conducts issued by Sigismund and the Council to John XXIII on 2 May 1415 and the one given to Jerome of Prague on 17 April. All three contained definite limitations and restrictions.[53] It is likely the furore over the Hus safe conduct caused the emperor and the Council to be quite specific thereafter. Ultimately on 8 April 1415 Sigismund revoked all safe conducts issued to anyone in Constance.[54] At his final appearance before the Council Hus referred to his safe conduct and looking at the emperor told the fathers he had come to Constance with a promise of protection. It is said Sigismund blushed at the words.[55] One hundred years later, other emperors commented on the embarrassment of that moment. On 23 September 1415 the Council passed a decree formally stating that no secular authority could intervene in any way, including issuing a safe conduct, to interfere with the process of dealing with heresy even to the extent that had a safe conduct not existed the accused would not have appeared at the trial venue. While there was no direct allusion this stance echoed Innocent III who famously noted in 1208 while battling Cathar heretics, 'there is no obligation to keep faith with someone who does not keep faith with God'.[56]

It may be argued that Hus committed two serious tactical errors. The first was departing from Bohemia on 11 October 1414 without waiting for delivery of the letter of safe conduct. Hus arrived in Constance on 3 November without it. Technically and from a canon law perspective it may not have mattered. However, it indicated a certain recklessness or naïveté on the part of Hus. The letter of safe conduct was issued on 18 October but not brought to Hus' hand until 5 November. The second error was not joining the emperor's entourage. The original rendezvous at Nürnberg was missed since Sigismund had predictably been detained elsewhere. Hus proceeded on with imperial escort to Constance arriving there fifty three days ahead of the emperor. In the intervening weeks Hus was arrested on 28 November. How different would the Hus case have turned out had he waited in Nürnberg for the emperor? It is impossible to say. Sigismund later attached great significance to this blunder and on 21 March 1416 advised the Czech nobility that things may have turned out quite differently had Hus not gone ahead.[57] Claiming the death of Hus disturbed him quite profoundly while saying he had never been more grieved in his life amounted to little more than political grandstanding. The violation of the safe conduct was often commented upon in the documents of the later Hussite Revolution.[58] By the time Sigismund arrived in Constance the case against Jan Hus was poised for its final chapter.

On Christmas day, at two o'clock in the morning, Sigismund entered Constance and shortly thereafter went directly to the cathedral before dawn. John XXIII sang the Mass and the emperor, dressed as a deacon and wearing a crown, read the gospel for the day from the text about the decree from Caesar Augustus that all the world should be taxed. The service went on interminably between nine and eleven hours.[59] The proceedings of the Council had already gotten underway several weeks earlier and once the pageantry of the emperor's arrival faded the business at hand continued. It is noteworthy that neither the archbishop of Prague, Konrad of Vechta, nor the bishop of Olomouc, Jan 'the iron', attended the proceedings. During the first session of the Council which sat on 16 November the Mass was said by Cardinal Giordano Orsini. Cardinal Francesco Zabarella warned the synod that any laughter or noise during the sermon could result in a canonical penalty of three days excommunication. Pope John XXIII then delivered a discourse based on Zechariah 8:16–17 enjoining his hearers to speak the truth, to render judgments based on truth, to seek peace and avoid devising evil, noting that God hated such things.[60] The proceedings of the Hus trial suggest that neither the counsel of Cardinal Zabarella nor the injunctions of Pope John were followed.

It is quite clear from the extant documents that the Hus case was not considered important. Indeed, almost all of the evidence shows the trial of Jan Hus constituted a minor element in the proceedings. Council chronicles and diaries kept during the Council confirm that observation. Since the case was not regarded as important only later did it take up a significant portion of the Council's attention. What remained unprecedented were the three sessions before the entire Council devoted to the matter of Hus and his alleged heresies. It has been pointed out that not even this detail of attention was devoted in the case of John XXIII's deposition.[61] Even at the climax of the trial the papal notary Jacob Cerretano and the cardinal priest of St. Mark's, Guillaume Fillastre, made only bland references in their respective records.[62] It is certain that a commission was appointed to consider the case against Jan Hus. The notary Cerretano says that on 1 December 1414 a twelve member commission was appointed to try Hus.[63] Six names were recorded: Pierre d'Ailly, Francesco Zabarella, Guillaume Fillastre, Rainald Brancacci, Anthony of Pereto, Master-General of the Franciscans, and Leonard of Florence, Prior-General of the Dominicans. Petr Mladoňovice says the Hus commission consisted of three members: Jean Rupescissa, titular patriarch of Constantinople, John of Borsnitz, bishop of Lebus, and Bishop Bernard of Città di Castello.[64] The apparent contradiction may be resolved by understanding that much of the preliminary work may have been delegated to the latter three. We know that the smaller Hus commission visited Hus in prison on several occasions with notaries and witnesses. In any event, Cardinals d'Ailly, Zabarella and Fillastre headed up the Hus process.

The Council had convened with the expressed desire to put an end to the papal schism. The conflict had persisted for more than thirty-five years with no end in sight. The Englishman Jore Dorre put forth a prescription aimed at solving once and for all the intransigence of the squabble which seemed to paralyze the western church. 'Recipe for the stomach of St. Peter and its total reform, given at the Council of Constance. Take twenty-four cardinals, a hundred archbishops and prelates, the same number from each nation, and as many priests as it is possible to get. Immerse in Rhine water and keep submerged for three days. It will be good for the stomach of St.

Peter and for the removal of all of his afflictions'.[65] It is likely Hus might have agreed with the strategy. Likewise he must have been appalled at the carnivalesque atmosphere which chroniclers record in the city. Hus had come to defend the truth and the conciliar fathers ostensibly had gathered to reform the church 'in head and in members'. Over 1,700 musical instrumentalists entertained in the streets. Seven hundred prostitutes were counted working out of rented houses but those who worked the streets were not counted. Other sources claim quite specifically '718 public whores' while others claim upwards of 1,500 'loose women' in Constance in the days of the Council.[66] The poet Oswald von Wolkenstein has provided us with further first hand information on the corruption of the women of Constance but also wrote of how 'pretty' and 'angelic' they were with 'auburn hair', 'rose-red lips' and 'beautiful blushing cheeks'.[67] All things Wyclifite and Czech seemed anathema. After all, the Council had convened not only to deal with the schism but to check the advance of heretical thought. Hus' colleague Křišťan of Prachatice arrived in Constance in mid-February 1415. But when he professed utraquism on the basis of John 6:53–4, Michael de Causis protested and Křišťan was promptly arrested. After an examination he was set free on condition that he return for sentencing. He left Constance around 19 March never to return.[68]

Before Hus went to the Council, Jan of Jesenice prepared a detailed chronological summary of events concerning Hus' previous trials and legal process. In the absence of official records this so-called *Ordo procedendi* is essential for determining the various stages.[69] It has been the subject of a recent study.[70] The unsatisfactory progress of the trial proceedings from 1410 onwards left Hus frustrated and he announced his intention to appeal to a better informed pope or to a future council. He did neither. Instead, on 18 October 1412 he appealed to Jesus Christ.[71] The appeal away from public and human authority to the competence of Christ was an unprecedented step. It has been argued that Hus appealed to Christ only after he had exhausted all channels of law and ecclesiastical judicial options known to him. That assumption is not altogether convincing. In the end Hus regarded all human authority as subservient to Christ and the court of highest appeal lay within the law of Christ. The salient question must be, does Hus' appeal amount to a repudiation of ecclesiastical authority? The answer must be affirmative. The extraordinary step of appeal to Christ constituted a fateful moment for Hus in his legal affairs. No matter how it is explained or analyzed it implies an ultimate rejection of canon law and all forms of ecclesiastical authority including papal and conciliar.[72] That possibility was not lost on the members of the Council of Constance.

The appeal to Christ is such an important aspect of the trial of Hus that it cannot be passed over without further comment. Was it a spontaneous, impulsive act, or had Hus contemplated this step all along as a contingency plan? Can his appeal be put down to an emotive display of bitterness and a sense of injustice? The thought is compelling. It does not seem likely that Hus set out with a strategy of ultimately appealing to a spiritual authority higher than the available ecclesiastical legal channels. From a canonical point of view, Jesus Christ was a non-existing judicial authority.

Even Jan of Jesenice avoiding making any reference to the appeal.[73] The appeal to Christ from the papal court certainly may be regarded as a response by Hus to what he regarded as mounting grievance over continuing injustice. It is unlikely the appeal was premeditated. It is more sensible to see it as a spontaneous response to the growing pressure of his increasingly untenable situation. Falling back on one of his basic theological principles Hus resigned himself to the will of Christ. It is possible to locate throughout the Hus corpus allusions to divine justice and the conviction that God ultimately will judge everyone fairly. During exile Hus made this point that God being the greatest judge of all and the one unsullied by injustice could not err and therefore Hus appealed to that judge.[74] The legal conundrum caused by Hus' appeal to Jesus can be explicated by drawing attention to the manner in which Hus seemed to understand law.[75] The main contradiction between the standard view of law and its usual application and Hus' appeal seems that Hus relies on law not so much in terms of legal argument but on its morally binding nature. Often medieval canonical collections contained moral or ethical comment. These were always regarded as secondary. Hus relied on the theological or moral authority sometimes in opposition to the legal thrust by asserting his principle *lex Christi* which he considered more authoritative. Here he allowed himself that legal option of appealing to Christ. It was theologically justified and a legitimate position to assume. Human law, both secular and ecclesiastical, was temporary while the law of God was eternal. Hus' views on law have been dealt with elsewhere.[76] There is no question that Hus knew the law theoretically but it is equally apparent he was out of his depth when it came to the application of law in a concrete social or ecclesiastical context. This raises the obvious question about Jan of Jesenice. He was a legal expert and Hus' lawyer. Unfortunately, had Jesenice been able to advise Hus directly, at every turn in the legal process, Hus would have fared much better. But Jesenice left Prague in late 1410 and went to Rome as Hus' representative. He became embroiled with the vitriolic Michael de Causis who accused him of heresy and filed a complaint. By March 1412 Jesenice had been remanded to an Italian prison. Details are scanty but he managed to escape his captors and fled to Bologna. Here he applied himself to the formal study of law and earned a degree. In the meanwhile he too was excommunicated on 29 July 1412. In the autumn of that year Jesenice made his way north and reappeared in Prague. We have seen already that he immediately threw himself into a legal defense of Hus though by this time Hus had already lodged his appeal to Christ. It is extremely doubtful Jesenice would have advised such strategy. He did give Hus instruction and drew up the useful *Ordo procedendi*. Being an excommunicate himself, Jesenice was not permitted to travel to Constance in any formal or official capacity and certainly not as Hus' lawyer. This left Hus on his own, bereft of the one man who could have steered him safely between the dangerous legal straits he had to navigate.[77] As it became painfully apparent at Constance the appeal to Christ became a liability and the posture of appealing to conscience legally incomprehensible. On 7 June 1415 Pierre d'Ailly summed it up rather succinctly. 'We are unable to judge matters according to your conscience. We can only proceed in terms of what has been proven and concluded against you and on what you have confessed'.[78] It is doubtful Hus understood that reasoning.

It is not possible to absolve Hus from all culpability in the ultimate sentence handed down by the Council of Constance.[79] The legal process lasted five years and led to conviction on charges of heresy. The punishment was execution. It is impossible to read the various accounts of the trial at Constance or letters and documents Hus wrote between 1412 and 1415 and not conclude that Hus lacked tact or the ability to assess the impact of his bluntly stated opinions. He had come to the Council under the protection of Sigismund yet he alienated the emperor with comments on how sin turned legitimate authority into an illegitimate charade and not even a king in mortal sin remained a king and was thereby excluded from any meaningful application of dominion. Understandably Sigismund took umbrage at the gross impertinence. To make the point in the presence of his protector surely suggests at the very least a lack of wisdom. Under the circumstances Hus' assertions constituted folly. The same suggestion might be applied to Hus' continued insistence upon his appeal to Christ. Refusal to concede even in the slightest to the ponderous ecclesiastical authority at Constance supposed either a total repudiation of the church or an inability to assess the benefit of compromise. Continuing to press his views on authority only exacerbated the Hus case and made resolution short of capital punishment impossible. Jean Gerson made the point clear enough to Archbishop Konrad of Prague in the fall of 1414. By the time he arrived at Constance Gerson was even more certain of the danger Hus posed to the church. The only appropriate response could be legal condemnation. Reason could not avail since men like Hus already held the a priori assumption that secular and religious authority might be invalid if these powers existed in conflict with what Hus considered principles of the law of God. Gerson argued such a position contravened divine law. Earlier he had warned Archbishop Konrad. The secular powers must root out the heretics with their heresies and burn them. Otherwise their pestiferous influence like an infection will destroy everything it comes in contact with. Gerson argued it was impossible to debate those holding such views for they could not concede a suitable basis for discussion save their own platform which precluded dialogue. People were only confused by such procedures anyway, Gerson wrote, and truth suffered. Therefore, the axe must be laid at the root and the powers that be must not hesitate to wield the axe. The salvation of souls depended upon it.[80] The Council fought to establish and control the administration of authority. To concede to Hus would have weakened the moral authority of the church. Debating Hus meant losing control of the Council's agenda. So much of the anxiety over Hus centered on his doctrine of the church. Nineteen of the final thirty charges against him were concerned with this idea. The implications were severe. Vienna theologian Nicholas of Dinkelsbühl preached a sermon before Sigismund on 19 February 1415 touching on the horrors of heresy and telling the emperor the fate of Christendom lay in his imperial hands.[81]

Hus could not retreat from his principles or ideas. Judicially, it was an unwise posture to assume inasmuch as it could be understood that he was admitting the possibility of theological deviance but remained unwilling to stand down. The main problem with an appeal to Jesus Christ and insistence upon the law of God as the moderating doctrine meant that individual judgment or conscience ultimately had to prevail. It boiled down to personal interpretation. The Council cognitively was incapable of allowing this to happen. The very possibility did not exist. Hus outwitted himself. Štěpán of Dolany, his old foe ensconced as abbot of a Carthusian house in Moravia, demanded to know who accepted the appeal to Christ. 'From whom did you get release from the jurisdiction of the lower authorities? You could not say either from the laity or from your daughters the Beguines'.[82] There is little doubt that Štěpán rightly perceived the subjectiveness of Hus' appeal.

Jan Hus naïvely went to Constance, naïvely argued with the Council, naïvely attempted to extricate himself from the quagmire of heresy. Wrongly he appealed to an imaginary exoneration by Archbishop Zbyněk which Hus seemed convinced had freed him from accusations of heresy. Nothing could be further from the truth. We have already clearly seen that the letter Zbyněk did write had been extorted from him presumably under threat of grievous bodily harm. In any event it was never sent to Rome. Hus' argument had no validity, no force and no legal meaning.[83] It seems astonishing he did not realize this.

Why had Hus come to Constance in the first instance if he steadfastly would not consider the authority of the Council? The answer lies in a fundamental error Hus made. Hus appeared to have had no realistic idea of what he faced at the Council. This can be measured initially by the preparation of a sermon – *De pace* – he expected to preach to the delegates. The assumption he would be permitted to do this is without any foundation. Clearly Hus did not appreciate that he was voluntarily going to an ecumenical Council as an accused heresiarch to stand trial on charges of heresy and disobedience. Hus was doomed from the moment he rode into Constance on his horse Rabštýn.[84] Once in the city Hus assumed, once again incorrectly, that the context for his hearing was something quite different from what it truly was. His hearing was a court trial. He seemed to have thought it might be an academic debate. Hus simply did not understand his situation as an accused heretic. He was convinced he was somehow guaranteed a free scholarly disputation rather like the annual Prague *Quodlibet*. There would be no debate. There would be no formal scholarly exchange. This was a heresy trial. At this point it might have been personally advantageous for Hus to have left Constance and gone back to Bohemia. There is an account of an attempted escape but the story is unreliable.[85] Hus then requested a lawyer.[86] In medieval heresy trials the accused normally were not permitted legal counsel. Apparently the full gravity of his situation had not yet settled on Hus. These misunderstandings, the lack of appreciation for the nature of the forum at Constance, and his inability to be tactful must be numbered among the contributing factors in the final verdict. More importantly than any of these factors, however, was the unsolvable conflict between the law of God and civil laws. An impasse loomed and persisted over ideals and norms. Hus' commitment to the ideal law of Christ prevented him from evaluating reality and thus he remained constrained by his ideal to the bitter end.

Presumably, once the reality and the force of his situation and impending fate came to bear upon his thinking, though he still hoped for deliverance, Hus set his face towards a resolute stand. Certainly he must have been aware that a recantation on his part would seriously injure the Prague reform movement which continued to advance even in his absence.[87] In terms of the Hus trial at Constance, it must be conceded that he was treated much better than other accused heretics in late medieval Europe. He was granted opportunities others did not have and among these were some rather unprecedented concessions. For example, early on John XXIII sent two bishops and a doctor to Hus proposing the matter should be quietly taken care of. Hus declined. Evidently he desired public triumph and vindication.[88] Hus was granted three public hearings which has no equal in the history of medieval heresy trials. It is possible this was a conciliar concession to Sigismund who had granted a safe conduct to Hus. The Council later pointed out that procedural exceptions had been made in the Hus case. The law provided for heretics to be questioned from their cells. Hus was allowed three personal appearances before the synod.[89] Previously Hus' concern with perjury was noted. This had been on Hus' mind since autumn 1412.[90] The Council eventually did take into account Hus' fear that he might fall into this error.[91] Repeated efforts to secure a retraction from Hus failed. Ordinarily accused heretics who did not recant were summarily burned. The fathers at Constance watered down earlier demands for recantation and shortly before the end Hus was presented with a revised and considerably milder formula. This surprising effort seems to indicate the Council as a whole, excepting men like Michael de Causis, was not determined to burn Hus. Shortly before his departure for Constance, Hus prepared a discourse intending to deliver it to the Council. In it he proposed giving an account of his faith. He wrote that he had placed the Apostles' Creed on the wall of Bethlehem Chapel. He asserted an unwillingness to teach anything contrary to the decisions of the councils and the authority of the theologians so long as these were consistent with the law of God.[92] It is clear that Hus found the Council of Constance in opposition to his idea of that principle. The final statement essentially calls upon Hus to submit to the wisdom and authority of the Council which would endeavor to adjudicate for the salvation of Hus' soul.[93] By this point Hus' intractability was absolute. In the final rejection of the submission formula Hus declared that he feared accepting it on the grounds that it would be to go against Augustine.[94] Kybal has noted Hus' psychological dependence on Augustine.[95] More accurately Hus feared violating his own understanding of the law of Christ. With that refusal Hus severed all possible routes to saving his life.[96] Further, on the efforts of the Council it appears that while Michael de Causis and his particular associates were intent on securing Hus' death, others like Cardinal Francesco Zabarella tried to see to it that Hus had a modicum of due process.[97] It is not correct to attribute to Zabarella a great onus for Hus' fate.[98] I regard Zabarella as the best identifiable candidate for the individual Hus described in his letters as 'pater'.[99]

Any discussion of the trial of Jan Hus must consider carefully the extent to which Hus embraced the idea of martyrdom evident from as early as 1410. Certainly considerable legend and hagiography have accumulated on the matter. But even a casual read through the Hus corpus reveals some arresting commentary on the subject. Reflecting on the ten commandments Hus wrote that the true believer ought to engage in spiritual warfare and should humbly and with gratitude surrender to death in that cause. By loving suffering for the cause of Christ Hus argued he might obtain for his body the martyr's crown. It was essential to set a good example and Hus speculated that death in that sense ought to be welcomed for the testimony it made to Christ. It was possible then to become a 'glorious martyr to the entire church'.[100] Legend places the martyr complex in the mind of the young Hus. Walking with his mother to Prachatice the two witnessed lightning striking a bush whereupon Hus is made to exclaim to his mother that one day he would depart from this life in flames.[101] The incident is unreliable yet Jan Hus did wish to be a martyr. Another unverifiable tale has Hus as a young man reading of the sufferings of the third-century St. Laurence and impulsively thrusting his hand into the flames.[102] At the beginning of his journey from Bohemia to Constance he wrote a short letter to his parishioners at Bethlehem Chapel referring to his possible suffering and death a dozen times.[103] Elsewhere he expressed his willingness to endure martyrdom. Writing to Pope John XXIII on 1 September 1411 Hus declared his willingness to be burned.[104] So far as Hus was concerned compromise was not an option. He voiced his preference to be led to the fire before acting against conscience. Hus asserted he was prepared to oppose the enemies of God until he was consumed by fire if need be. 'It is better to die well than to live badly'.[105] Then reflecting on his life to 1413 Hus regretted that to date he had been unable to suffer martyrdom for Christ. He vowed never to turn his back on the law of God even if the fire to destroy his body were to be kindled before his eyes.[106] These repeated statements of willingness to die suggest a lack of wisdom on Hus' part prompting suspicion in the minds of others that he may have been aware of theological guilt.[107] At the very least, Hus' cheerful attitude at the prospect of death raised even more questions. Štěpán Páleč accused Hus of pride and being willing to be burned on principle rather than retreat and submit to proper authority.[108] Abbot Štěpán of Dolany said much the same thing.[109] Hus saw the situation much differently and refused to concede, repetitively saying, even if the fire meant to consume him was kindled before his eyes.[110] Surely Hus regarded martyrdom as *gloriosa mors* - the glorious death. His ruminations on death can be contrasted with those of Luther in the next century. In older age the latter was fed up with life and longed for the deliverance of death. Luther often remarked that he was 'like a prime piece of shit' and the world a 'big asshole' and each increasingly anxious to let go of the other.[111] Luther died in bed. Hus embraced martyrdom at the stake.

'Hus' surviving letters superbly illustrate martyrological sensibility in late medieval Christianity'.[112] His works resonate with the willingness to suffer death before any denial of the faith or acceptance of any tenet which might contradict the truth.[113] The same sense can be found in Hus' public declarations in sermons. Death was the initial step towards the birth of glory. Death was a release from prison, the end of exile, the completion of a pilgrimage, and the final surrender of a heavy load.[114] There are numerous references to martyrological conscience in Hus from 1410 on and explicit statements about being prepared to suffer death for the faith.[115] It is too ambitious, however, to draw too close a parallel between the passion of Christ and the sufferings of Hus in terms of trial and death.[116] The common elements are all there – accusation, interrogation, condemnation and execution – but those components might easily be extracted from virtually any medieval heresy trial. The crucial issue facing Hus and the Council was heresy. Hus failed to appreciate the gravity of the situation and the conciliar delegates considered heresy too significant an issue to be taken lightly. Hus had many enemies at Constance but none more vitriolic and persistent than his countrymen Štěpán Páleč and Michael de Causis. The malignant presence of these two with fabricated accusations were held by some as responsible for Hus' condemnation and death.[117] They were aided by Petr of Uničov, a Dominican friar from St. Clement's in Prague, who announced in front of the prison in Constance that he was Hus' greatest enemy.[118] The personal hostility towards Hus exhibited by certain Council participants clearly exceeds *odium theologicum* and explaining that motivation is a crucial component in understanding the Hus trial.[119] There is also a mentality frequently adopted with respect to dissenters. 'When the church perceives a threat, the principles of morality are suspended. With unity as the goal, everything to that end becomes sanctified: simony, duplicity, betrayal, brutality, imprisonment and death. Since order serves the community the individual must be sacrificed for the common good'.[120] This observation has clear application in the case of Jan Hus.

Páleč routinely attacked Hus from the pulpit of the Týn Church after the former converted from the reform party to the official church. He delivered homilies in Latin and Czech and these sermons were particularly negative about Hus. The two became bitter enemies right up to the proceedings at Constance. Hus preferred truth over his friendship with Páleč and the latter agreed. 'Hus is a friend and truth is a friend. Because Hus and truth are completely disagreeable, truth must be preferred over Hus'.[121] It went well beyond that for Páleč. He took up a campaign to discredit Hus absolutely. His efforts pale, however, in contrast to those of Michael de Causis. The latter seemed determined not only to discredit Hus but to break him and, more than that, to see him dead. Years before Constance, de Causis accused Hus of eucharistic heresy, to wit remanentism, and Donatist tendencies. His unceasing opposition and boundless energy made him the single greatest liability to Jan Hus in the legal process. Hus regarded Páleč as his more formidable opponent but a case can be made for Michael de Causis.

His real name was Michael Smradař, of German ancestry, and before coming to prominence lived in Německý Brod.[122] He was appointed parochial priest at St. Adalbert's in the New Town of Prague in 1399 and remained there until around 1408 when he absconded. Ostensibly he was an absentee priest more interested in personal gain than the cure of souls.[123] His disappearance from Prague has been linked to an embezzlement scheme connected to a mining project in Jílové wherein Michael possibly misappropriated royal funds indicating his greater interest in the reform of mines than reform of the church. The evidence is not firm but there are two witnesses.[124] He surfaced in Rome and is likely the author of a complaint against Hus on behalf of the Prague clergy which was delivered to Pope John XXIII. Therein Hus stood accused of spreading pestiferous opinions throughout the Kingdom of Bohemia, Poland, Hungary and the Margraviate of Moravia.[125] This charge became his signature in the campaign against Hus. For his efforts he was appointed by John XXIII to the nebulous position of 'procurator de causis fidei', or a special advocate in matters of the faith. Thereafter he became known to history as Michael de Causis. He attacked Hus as the 'prince of heretics' who corrupted the faithful through sermons at Bethlehem Chapel.[126] Hus referred to him as the 'enemy' and the instigator' in his appeal to Christ and attributed his excommunication principally to the nefarious activities of Michael de Causis.[127] These efforts to discredit Hus began years before the final legal proceedings at Constance and his activities were vivid.[128] It was at Constance, however, where de Causis distinguished himself as the persecutor of Jan Hus. Ahead of his arrival Hus discovered that de Causis had posted on the cathedral doors accusations against him. These announcements maligned Hus as an excommunicate, pertinacious, contumacious and a suspected heretic.[129] We learn also that these notices were re-posted throughout the city on a regular basis by the indefatigable Michael de Causis.[130]

Numerous charges had been leveled against Hus over the years but de Causis presented a new list once he arrived in Constance. These charges contained new and additional accusations of irregularity. For example Hus was alleged to be a preacher of utraquism. Sinful priests were held to be incapable of actually consecrating the elements in the eucharist. Lay people might legitimately administer communion. Priests in sin were false clerics without divine authority and the church should be divested of all material property. Moreover he claimed Hus adhered to the errors of the Waldensians.[131] The burden of proof was unnecessary. Suspicion and accusation were sufficiently powerful weapons alone. Observers at the Council pointed out that de Causis continued to be the instigator in the case against Hus.[132] It is reported that de Causis conducted himself in the manner of a zealous persecutor of heretics to the extent he boasted he would happily testify against his own father if the latter were guilty of heresy.[133] Michael's father was not on trial but since Hus was de Causis drew up a revised list of charges against Hus for the consideration of the Council.[134] Unwilling to leave any hostages to fate, Michael de Causis and his colleagues went round on a daily basis visiting important conciliar figures among the cardinals, archbishops, bishops and prelates, and those of the religious orders, urging the arrest of Hus and attempting to persuade the fathers of the danger Hus represented.[135] One can only admire his industry. It has been suggested that de Causis incited even reform-minded men like Dietrich of Niem to persuade the pope against Hus.[136] As we have seen already Hus eventually was arrested and remanded to a prison cell in the Dominican monastery. When news of this development broke de Causis is reported to have danced with joy and cheered declaring confidently Hus could not escape now.[137] With Hus now in his clutches de Causis had only to work to ensure Hus never left Constance alive.

After languishing in prison for more than six months Hus was finally granted an appearance before the Council. At the first hearing on 5 June Michael de Causis publicly called for Hus and his heretical books to be burned. So eager was he to see his nemesis dispatched he seemed unable to contain himself and wait for the hearings to conclude and for the legal process to play out.[138] During his imprisonment de Causis frequently came to Hus' prison but evidently never entered his cell. However he did actively attempt, sometimes successfully, to interfere with Hus' mail and he lobbied to deprive Hus of all visitors. During visits to the prison de Causis openly told guards he desired to see Hus burn.[139] In addition to harassing Hus de Causis continued his efforts further afield and reported to the Council that he had cited 424 individuals from Bohemia on account of their 'Hussite beliefs'.[140] Perhaps as a testimony to his moral character Jan Hus wrote to Jan of Chlum two weeks before the end saying he had no animosity towards de Causis and more than that earnestly prayed to God for him. Hus regarded de Causis as an agent of God sent to afflict him on account of his sins.[141] It must be said, to the credit of the Council, that even they in general ultimately recognized the bile and venom in many of the charges and accusations Michael de Causis manufactured against Jan Hus. Regardless of how Hus' judges perceived him, they correctly detected the lack of probity in the de Causis campaign. This may be assessed most convincingly in the fact that the final charges lodged against Hus did not include many (or any?) that Michael de Causis had submitted. That should have had a meliorating influence on de Causis but later he would be found, still in Constance, fulminating against Hus' colleague Jerome of Prague.

The case against Jan Hus from beginning to end was a procedural and legal investigation into suspicions of heresy. Štěpán Páleč who knew Hus as well as anyone else regarded him as the second most dangerous heretic of all time. First place honors went to Wyclif.[142] The accusation was meaningless except to the extent that it does shed light on the seriousness in which the Hus matter was regarded in some quarters. As a rejoinder Hus concluded his book against Páleč by denying the heretical label and insisting he followed the gospel of Christ.[143] Moreover Hus also declared he preached openly in Bethlehem Chapel and taught nothing to seduce the faithful from the truth.[144] That claim of course could not be taken on face value. After all, few heretics ever imagined they were truly heretical and it is nearly impossible to impute error to oneself when one is convinced, as Hus clearly was, their focus is truth. John Stokes took a different view and accused Hus at Constance of following in the footsteps of John Wyclif.[145] That was a perennial charge and to some extent it was true. Nevertheless the imputation of Wyclifite heresies to Hus must be carefully qualified and the footsteps that Hus may have followed did not conform exactly to those trodden by his English predecessor. The bandying about of 'Wyclifism' had as much value as placing the label 'Hussite', twenty years later, on certain religious practices in the vicariate of Bosnia.[146] Accuracy and interpretation aside for the moment the pertinent matter was heresy. Jean Gerson characterized the religious soil in Bohemia as rife with seeds of error.[147] Sigismund declared he was just a boy when heresy began in Bohemia and now it flourished in strength.[148] Hussite heresy undermined truth, religion, justice and the church.¹⁴⁹ Hus' Bethlehem Chapel acquired the reputation as a cavern of insidious depravity.¹⁵⁰ Heresy was the screen through which Christian Europe viewed Jan Hus. Heresy was the assumption against which the later medieval church evaluated reformed religious practice in Bohemia. Heresy was the category in which those associated with Hus were identified.

Heresy and Law

The definition of heresy is a complex one and so are the medieval legal procedures for prosecuting suspected heretics. Augustine defined heresy as erroneous doctrine contrary to scripture and stubbornly defended.[151] Canon law only slightly enlarged that adding the objectionable ideas had been chosen by human will and were publicly declared. Contumacy remained the most disturbing factor.[152] The real issue was disobedience and contumacious disobedience constituted heresy (*'contumacia dicitur heresis'*). In other words, contumacy is equivalent to heresy.[153] Prevailing opinion in the Middle Ages held that apart from restoration to the church every heretic would be joined to the Devil and demonic angels in the flames of eternal fire.[154] The sentiment can be found among the decretals of Gregory IX, in Aquinas, Hostiensis, Bernard Gui, Zanghino Ugolini, Johannes Andrae, Nicholas Eymeric and other medieval authorities including canon law where it is thrice cited with attribution to Augustine.[155] As long ago as the eleventh century Gregory VII wrote in his *Dictatus papae* that anyone disagreeing with the church should not be regarded as a faithful Christian.[156] One hundred years before Hus, Boniface VIII famously declared in his *Unam sanctam* that obedience to the pope was essential for salvation. Aquinas regarded heresy as denying any article established by the church. The authority for establishing doctrine rested mainly with the pope while the canonist Hostiensis said whoever refused to accept a papal decretal qualified.[157] At issue for any determination of heresy were several factors: an authoritative body must recognize and condemn a doctrine as unacceptable. The teaching must persist and was generally done so as a matter of faith and conscience. Articles flagged for evaluation though often theological sometimes contained social or political implications. These ramifications frequently extended beyond approved teachings and toleration of the church and exceeded acceptable behavioral boundaries. Additionally, heresy had to be public. As d'Ailly told Hus his conscience could not possibly be assessed. The church cannot judge something which exhibited no manifestation. That principle laid down by Innocent II has been studied.[158] Despite the fact that in 1231 Gregory IX made belief in heresy the same thing as heresy there is no such thing as mental heresy in the Middle Ages.[159] Gregory's point is prima facie unprovable and undetectable without some form of utterance so the canonical equation is, in practical terms, useless. Asserting 'heresy is primarily a sin of thought' will not do.[160] The fourth Lateran Council mandated that heretics should be sought out and exterminated. Thirty years earlier (1184), Pope Lucius III left heretics to the punishment of secular judgment. There is sufficient ambiguity in both statements though Thomas Aquinas glossed the word with the meaning 'remove from the world by death'. In 1199 Innocent III rounded off pre-Lateran legislation.[161]

Gregory IX's essential statue of 1231 imposed the penalty of capital punishment for unrepentant heretics.[162] Important legal codes in the German territories before and after Hus, namely the Sachsenspiegel and the Schwabenspiegel and the *Constitutio Criminalis Carolina*, mandated death by fire for heretics. The influential fourteenth-century Catalan inquisitor Nicholas Eymeric wrote a book elaborating the legal and theological guidelines to support inquisitorial authority in which he cited Hostiensis who defined 'ultio debita' as being burned alive.[163] By any calibration heresy remained a serious issue in medieval Europe.

Heresy trials and executions in the German territories, including the Kingdom of Bohemia, were substantial in the century before Jan Hus. The inquisitor for Bohemia, Gallus of Neuhaus (Jindřichův Hradec) tried at least 4,400 suspected heretics and ordered more than 200 executions by conservative estimate.[164] There were dozens of executions in fourteenth-century Silesia as well as in other German territories, and over one hundred in Austria. In southern France, according to his *Liber sententiarum*, Bernard Gui tried nearly a thousand suspects, executed forty-two and exhumed a further sixty-nine.[165] In the thirteenth century, in northern France and the southern Netherlands, the Dominican Robert the Bugger burned fifty in Douai, Lille and Cambrai, or about half of the accused. On 13 May 1239 more than 180 were burned at Mont-Aimé in Champagne.[166] Heresy seemed well-entrenched in Bohemia by the fourteenth century. Significant inquisitorial activity led to thousands being denounced as heretics and tried and sometimes entire villages were hereticated. Bohemia experienced a reign of terror.[167] And in the period just before Hus came to prominence in Prague another inquisitor, Celestine prior Peter Zwicker, prosecuted at least 500 heretics between 1392 and 1394 and also conducted heresy trials in Hungarian, Austrian and Slovak territories in 1401.[168] In the 1260s the unknown author of the *Anonymous of Passau* wondered why there seemed to be so much heresy about and answered the query by asserting widespread ecclesiastical corruption.[169] As a result of this a new kind of criminal trial, inquisitorial procedure, emerged based upon the ideas of Innocent III established at Lateran IV.[170]

Applied to Hus, aspects of his doctrine had been condemned by a pope and a general council. One may wish to argue that neither John XXIII nor the Council of Constance were legitimate authorities. The claim against John might be sustained but it seems more difficult to dismiss the authority of the Council. Despite condemnation Hus continued to hold his views and proclaim them in every way possible. No one can suggest on firm evidence that Hus' doctrines were not matters of faith and conscience for him. Right or wrong, he believed steadfastly in what he preached and wrote. We have already assessed a number of these ideas and found them pregnant with religious, social and political possibilities. All of these were regarded as intolerable by the church and practically everything Hus did in Prague seemed in the public domain. By canonical definition then, Hus seems to qualify as a heretic. There are two possible mitigating factors. First, as noted above, that the nominated authoritative body lacks jurisdictional authority. Second, that the doctrines ascribed to Hus are in some sense inapplicable to him. I do not think the former has validity. John XXIII was deposed as a false pope. One might reasonably argue this discredits all of his acts and rulings. The legitimate pope emerging from the Council was Gregory XII. However, his connection to the Hus trial was somewhat distant. In 1408 Gregory, acting on intelligence from Bohemia, condemned Wyclif and cited Stanislav of Znojmo and Štěpán Páleč to Rome to show cause why they ought not be repudiated as heretics. Gregory's delegated ruling of 20 April handed down by Cardinal François of Bordeaux made clear that no one might thereafter hold the Wyclifite doctrines in question, debate them, or own books containing the said heresies.[171] King Václav went neutral on papal obedience in the same year but Archbishop Zbyněk remained loyal to Gregory. A little over a year after his ruling Gregory was deposed by the Council of Pisa. If conciliar authority superceded papal power during the schism then from 5 June 1409 when he was denounced as a notorious schismatic and heretic his acts were null and void up until 4 July 1415 when the Council of Constance declared he was the true pope after all.[172] Hus died two days later and Gregory had no role in the verdict against Hus at the Council. Once recognized by Constance the pontifical acts of Gregory were retroactively ratified. Is it possible to argue that the condemnation of 1408 might now be applied to Hus? Hus claimed it was not necessary to the catholic faith to believe that Alexander V, John XXIII or Gregory XII were true vicars of Christ.[173] Since Benedict XIII, Alexander V and John XXIII were all deposed as antipopes any rulings with respect to Hus could not be considered binding. The only other option on papal authority was even more tenuous than claims for Gregory. Martin V was not elected by the Council of Constance until 11 November 1417. However, he had presided over aspects of the Hus case as early as 1410. In those days he was known as Cardinal Odo Colonna and as such issued the censure for non-appearance in February 1411. The writ did not classify Hus as a heretic. Even if it had the censure would not have been a papal excommunication. At any rate Cardinal Francesco Zabarella later ruled Colonna's writ had been unjustified inasmuch as the action was predicated upon a legal error. That error lay in the failure to note that an appeal in the Hus matter was pending.[174] Having struck down the verdict Colonna delivered against Hus allowed a legal defense for the accused and thus a new date was calendared for a hearing. But then, as we have seen, Zabarella was taken off the case and so Hus came to Constance. Therefore, formal papal action against Hus is virtually impossible to maintain but the proceedings of the Council of Constance remain and it seems rather disingenuous to attempt to absolve Hus of heresy based upon a claim that the Council lacked the authority to try him. The matter of whether or not Hus truly held the doctrines ascribed to him is equally a thorny dilemma. Paul De Vooght has argued that the heresies ascribed to Hus by the Council have more to do with formulation rather than content or wilful error.[175] That claim has considerable merit. The agendas of men like Štěpán Páleč and Michael de Causis call into question the validity of many charges laid against Hus. Pierre d'Ailly and Jean Gerson were at philosophical loggerheads with Hus and this resulted in a basic failure of communication and understanding. But charges of heresy, and particularly in the Hus case, are more than doctrine and ideas. Contumacy is equally at issue. Dismissing that concern as an irrational banality or feeble excuse on the part of the Council, either reveals ignorance of medieval canon law or a willingness to apply post-Enlightenment constructs to the later Middle Ages. Either scenario fatally impairs an evaluation of the Hus case. On the evidence, it is difficult to argue that Jan Hus was not contumacious. Hus had also been advised by a member of the Council that without contumacy there was no heresy.[176] Nevertheless, Gerson pointed out that the Council could condemn both ideas and persons and named Hus as an example.[177]

The Council of Constance recorded that its proceedings were inquisitorial.[178] The Hus case at Constance is one of the best heresy trials in terms of extant records and preserved documents though these are by no means complete.[179] Jean Gerson had put forth four theses as guiding principles for procedure in the Hus case. The Council ought to adjudicate heresy without regard for the identity of the defendant, if the discovery process indicated error, condemnation should follow. The Council had the right to pass sentence and appeals to scripture could only be valid within the context of ecclesiastical tradition. Concern over doctrinal deviance and contumacy dominated the proceedings involving Hus. He was not unaware of the seriousness. In his commentary on the Sentences of Peter Lombard several years earlier, Hus commented on the subject and its heretical implications. He was quite clear that while beliefs may be erroneous, the one holding those views became heretical because he or she stubbornly refused to obey authority on correction.[180] There were procedural irregularities in the Hus process. These have been expertly studied elsewhere in some detail.[181] Kejř does not consider these to have invalidated the trial. Others disagree.[182] It has been suggested that a heresy court in the Middle Ages might proceed at will and was bound by no rules.[183] From a legal point of view this is quite incorrect though in practice heresy trials were anything but standard and variations may be found in the study of legal procedure and the application of law. In any event it was necessary for the defendant to be presented with formal charges and the cause for trial to be established. Accusers were not always named or identified. After the mid-thirteenth century the matter of lawyers for the defense became somewhat unclear. If found guilty the accused had the right of appeal to the pope after conviction but before the sentence was determined. Torture was permitted in cases of heresy though this was not applied consistently. The main penalties resulting in conviction from heresy procedures seem to have been imprisonment or death. Torture cannot be regarded from a legal standpoint to be applied, if it was at all, as punishment. For comparison only, nearly half of the 636 condemnations handed down by Bernard Gui between 1308 and 1322 resulted not in death but imprisonment. Prisons were sometimes used to break the suspect. The mid-thirteenth-century archbishop of Narbonne called for accused heretics to be remanded to conditions of confinement aimed at securing confession and recantation, to wit hard prison and little food. Canon law, however, ruled that in the pre-conviction stage prisons should be for custody not punishment.[184] Initially, Hus was placed into a very difficult situation in a cell in a monastic jail by the lake under very unsanitary conditions. He soon fell ill. This may have been more negligence on the part of the Dominican friars than by some malevolent order of the

Council. After 24 March 1415 the situation was remedied and he was transferred to the tower of Gottlieben Castle about two and a quarter miles outside of town and thereafter to the Franciscan convent inside the city. Apart from being chained by one hand to the wall at night for ten weeks at Gottlieben, Hus does not seem to have suffered any particular torture. Witnesses in the Hus case were hardly needed inasmuch as Hus' books were available and apparently formed the basis for the charge of heresy which had been extracted from them. By the time his legal ordeal came to a climax virtually everything Hus had ever written or said became the bedrock of the roads of his life and all of his roads led to Constance. That said, there were witnesses like John Stokes who appeared at Constance and gave testimony. Apparently fifteen witnesses were taken to Hus' cell in order for him to have opportunity to see them sworn.[185] Unlike others in similar situations during heresy proceedings Hus was not tortured even though he persisted in denial on all of the charges laid against him. Since 1252 the use of judicial torture had been an option in heresy trials and the legislation had papal approval.[186] Commensurate with that constitution we know that inquisitors regarded the use of torture as salutary. Some encouraged its application in increasing severity if confession was not forthcoming and allowed for its continuation on subsequent days. It is also noteworthy that failure to confess and recant did not automatically lead to acquittal of the preferred charges.[187] Stubbornness could be regarded as a sure sign of guilt. Impenitent heretics were executed by burning at the stake in the later Middle Ages without exception. That measure promulgated by Emperor Frederick II became incorporated into canon law.[188]

Jan Hus asked for a lawyer. This request was denied. On a technicality accused heretics were permitted legal counsel but those judicially convicted of heresy were forbidden to have legal representation.[189] There were exceptions to that rule but generally that seems to have been the practice. There appears to be some difference of scholarly opinion on this matter. Some experts suggest lawyers were sometimes unjustly and illegally prohibited thus perverting the course of due process and have nominated the Hus case as an example.[190] The preponderance of evidence suggests to me that a defendant in a medieval canonical criminal proceeding such as heresy normally does not have an advocate.[191] In terms of the Hus matter it seems the coda on the question appeared in 1418 when Pope Martin V ruled that suspected heretics could not have lawyers.[192] It is not possible to say if Martin V had the Hus trial in mind.

The language used to condemn Hus' books was insightful.[193] Declaring the Council to be a representation of the church catholic, the judges argued that a tree was identifiable by its fruit. Wyclif of 'damnable memory' had sons of perdition who taught perverse doctrines. The Council being obligated to deal with these issues by use of the 'knife of ecclesiastical authority' endeavored to uproot errors before they took further root in the life of the church and the Christian community. Noting that Wyclif had already been condemned Hus was denounced as a disciple of Wyclif and not of Christ. Therefore, by extension, he also was heretical. After examining the books of Hus and finding them infected with 'erroneous, scandalous, offensive, seditious and notorious heresies' the Council determined they must be destroyed by fire. They were burned in the church cemetery. By implication, Hus' entire system of thought was suspect and must be avoided by the faithful. In this way, the pernicious teachings of Hus could be eliminated from the church. Anyone found promoting or defending Hussite errors could be remanded to heresy trials conducted by inquisitors skilled in such matters. In one sense, Jan Hus did in fact die for Wyclif's doctrines and in his place. The definitive statement asserted by the Synod at Constance concluded Hus' teachings were blatantly dangerous.[194]

There is considerable irony in that Hus was condemned partly for a view held by the Council. That being the head of the church was not the pope. Even Gerson had preached in 1404, in opposition to *Unam sanctam*, that it was possible to be saved without a pope.[195] The charges laid against Hus in 1414 included testimony of John Peklo, rector of St. Giles in Prague, who affirmed that Hus had frequently preached that popes were of no consequence for salvation.[196] The only bodies in medieval Europe capable of deciding a case involving papal heresy was either the college of cardinals or a general council. Constance deposed two popes and accepted the resignation of a third and in its most famous declaration, *Haec Sancta*, affirmed itself the highest spiritual authority on earth which had to be acknowledged and obeyed by all including popes. In that sense *Haec Sancta* gave the last word on matters of faith and procedure to a general council. To a certain extent Hus agreed. However, the Council had authority only to the extent that it remained within the law of Christ. Twice in 1415, on 23 March and 21 July, Jean Gerson asserted that while the gates of hell had prevailed against popes they could not prevail against the church.[197] But at some point during his stay in Constance Hus became convinced that the Council, every bit as much as the popes it opposed, failed to function within that absolutely necessary paradigm of the law of Christ. Already Hus had declared himself not amenable to unqualified obedience to any authority save the law of Christ.[198] He had once argued that the function of canon law was to restrain whatever conflicted with the church and revealed truth.[199] During his own legal process, Hus was unable to see how that applied to him. Blind obedience constituted an error. Hus argued that required fidelity to the word of God in scripture and the apostles did not imply continued submission to those in apostolic succession if they spoke with a different voice.[200] Therefore Hus rejected the Council as surely as he had rejected John XXIII. By placing himself apart from and above the authority of the Council it seemed to that synod that he presented himself superior to all judgment. The dissemination of that concept allowed others to classify Hus as a criminal and master of errors. Hus pleaded that his objective was truth. As noted above, in the first session Pope John XXII urged the Council to 'speak the truth'. No one seems to have actively remembered that advice. Cardinal Zabarella had also warned of disorderly conduct at the first session. The hearings in the Hus trial were filled with shouts, laughter, and noise. Ostensibly, the same solemnity required during preaching did not apply when adjudicating whether a man should live or die. That seems rather appalling to the modern mind. Reflecting on the advice of Innocent III it occurred to some quite impossible to break faith with an individual who already had not kept faith with God.²⁰¹ Just as Páleč considered Hus an almost unparalleled danger to the faith later voices judged there was no worse fornication than the kind Hus had planned and committed with the church.²⁰² The fact that a certificate of theological orthodoxy had been issued by the inquisitor in Prague concerning Hus before his departure for Constance carried no weight with the Council and could be explained away.²⁰³

As we have learned previously, Hus did accept force in matters of faith, at least theoretically, but certainly not to the extent of death.²⁰⁴ By the time his third hearing concluded Hus must have been aware that anything short of recantation would surely cost him his life. It is facile to attribute malevolent motives to the entire Council.²⁰⁵ His judges, struggling with the crisis of authority which had engulfed the Latin Church, needed Hus to submit to conciliar authority. Failing that, those same judges were determined to find him guilty, if not of outright doctrinal deviance than certainly of contumacy. One was as good as the other; either was more than sufficient for a heresy conviction under prevailing canonical legislation and custom. That mentality drove the judges and controlled the legal process. One might go so far as to say their resulting conduct reflected very poorly on them.²⁰⁶ There is certainly no justification for their behavior, chilling inhumanity, and utter contempt for a man of principle whose own conduct throughout his grueling legal ordeal remained unimpeachable. At the bitter end, whatever patience the conciliar fathers may have once held for Jan Hus had all drained away. The final hearings degenerated into raucous affairs. If Cardinal Zabarella may be identified as that anonymous sympathetic 'pater', he too had run out of patience. Instead of kindliness he now came to his feet and angrily shouted at Hus to be silent. His colleagues joined the humiliating chorus. Nothing at this stage could halt the inexorable march to the stake. Hus was doomed. The outcome would be burning. Aware now of his inevitable fate, on 22 June, Hus asked for a confessor and received absolution.²⁰⁷

Culmination of the Process

On 6 July Hus was made to hear the customary sermon preached against heretics at the conclusion of the legal process.²⁰⁸ Taking his text from Romans 6:6, the Dominican Jacob Balardi Arrigoni, Bishop of Lodi, emphasized that the body of sin had to be destroyed. Too many heresies had appeared, he thundered, and far too many remained unpunished. Churches have been plundered, cities oppressed, pure religion ruined. Heresy held the true church in contempt. Diseased limbs had to be amputated for the good of the entire body for if they were permitted to remain attached, the whole body would become infected and die. Bishop Jacob characterized the church as a ship on treacherous high seas beset by pirates who threatened her well being. These pirates were the heretics who seemed to be springing up on all sides. The bishop deferred to Sigismund whom he acknowledged as the protector of the church and the one through whom the scourge of schism and heresy would be eliminated. Therefore generations will praise the virtues of Sigismund as the destroyer of the church's enemies and the avenger of the faith. The emperor must have been pleased with the accolade that God had given to him the most holy and noble task. It is worth noting that eleven months later the Bishop of Lodi preached at the trial of Jerome of Prague on unbelief and hardness of heart (Mark 16:14). In that sermon he referred to Hus as a faithless heretic and a contemptible man of no repute whose origins were unknown.[209]

Following the sermon Hus was degraded from the priesthood and his soul handed over to the Devil. Condemning the soul to Satan seems excessive and malicious.[210] The legal process at an end there remained only the matter of executing the sentence. The Council relaxed Hus to the secular authorities omitting the customary plea for mercy that the prisoner be neither mutilated in members nor suffer death. He was taken from the city through the Gelting Gate in the company of a large crowd. Some sources say the priest Ulrich Schorand offered to hear Hus' confession at the stake but Hus declined.[211] Hus could have saved his life even at the last moment. There are cases when convicted heretics at the stake even after the fire had been lit changed their minds and were spared.[212] In Hus' case this would certainly have translated into perpetual imprisonment. Sigismund already had declared no one ought to rely on a recantation anyway. Even if Hus did recant the emperor declared he would not believe it was sincere.[213] Three months after Hus' death Jean Gerson delivered a speech on the question of recantation in which he argued the act did nothing with respect to the guilt of having been a heretic. The offender may repent but the penitent must remain incarcerated.[214] At the stake Hus expressed gratitude to his jailors for their kindness.[215] It is doubtful anyone really expected Hus to back down but the opportunity was afforded him at the stake. He declined saying he was happy to die in the truth he had long defended. For him this was a stand on principle. For the Council it remained persistent, unrepentant contumacy. Hus' comments on the Sentences now convicted him. Since he could not and would not recognize the authority of the Council his position left no option but condemnation for heresy. Ulrich Richental recorded that Hus expired screaming while Petr Mladoňovice claimed he died singing.[216] The stake to which Hus was bound had been erected over the buried carcass of an old donkey belonging to Rainald Brancacci, Cardinal Pancratius. When the fire began to burn an awful stench arose and hung over the area.[217] Hus seems to have died quickly and the officials made certain no bodily or material remains were left to be carried away by the Czechs as relics. In a sermon of 21 July Jean Gerson justified Hus' execution affirming that heretics ought to be punished and exterminated in the fire of the stake.[218] The ironies in the case against Hus are many. His judges were conciliarists, his most ardent opponents were Czech, his ecclesiology was Augustinian, and his alleged Wyclifism generally mis-attributed.

Pierre d'Ailly represented that a general council could err in matters of fact and also in matters of law but more importantly could err in matters of faith. Few at the Council seem to have taken that admonition seriously.[219] Well before the Council of Constance convened, heresy in the Latin west had evolved to where behavior more than doctrine, though not to minimize the latter, became at issue. This broadened the scope of heresy so that anyone, theoretically, on less than good terms with ecclesiastical authority, might be denounced as heretical. The roots of this attitude are deep. Medieval heresy was neither accidental nor incidental. Among the ante-Nicene church fathers the foundations of heresy were consistently found in issues where the principle involved was important and beneficial to human life.[220] Constance reflected the nature of ecclesiastical politics which increasingly shaped Christianity from the Nicene period down through the Middle Ages. The political inheritance of Nicaea created, marginalized and often destroyed heretics. Origen may have famously celebrated diversity and openness in Christian thought but he fell victim posthumously to the Nicene urge to purge and his tolerance found little sympathy in the world of Christian Europe. More than a century after Constance, Erasmus commented Hus had been burned but not convicted.[221] That assessment implied Hus had been a victim of judicial murder and the opinion has had plenty of support over six hundred years. The conclusion carries more weight on a theological level than it does in terms of a heresy trial. Hus' refusal to recant or submit to the authority of the Council could be, and was, judged contumacious. That finding was not improper.

8

REVOLUTION

The judicial process against Jan Hus and his summary execution electrified Bohemia. There were pockets of satisfaction at his demise but widespread indignation seems to have been the general response. Alive, Hus had been moderate, even conservative, on many doctrinal and social issues. Dead, he became a martyr and his name and memory appropriated to validate doctrines and practices he clearly would not have approved of. This is sufficient cause for some historians and scholars to regard the continued use of the nomenclature 'Hussite' as inappropriate to describe social and religious developments in Bohemia following the death of Hus. As noted above, the argument is only partially persuasive. Symbolically, Hus is the fountainhead of the revolution which followed his death. Without Constance it is doubtful there would have been revolts and wars on the scale which characterized Bohemia in the 1420s and 30s. Religious reform would have continued without Hus for its antecedents were well established prior to his career. And there were important ideas which formed apart from his influence or input. The use of the term 'Hussite' cannot be understood as assuming or affirming that doctrines like utraquism were rooted in Hus any more than social experiments at places like Tábor took their point of departure from the teachings of Hus. No serious scholar can make that mistake. It would be tantamount to agreeing that Christianity is based on the teaching of Jesus or that Christian history is a natural extension of the life of Christ. Remove Calvary and its aftermath and Jesus is little more than another itinerant Jewish rabbi of the ancient near east. Had Hus survived Constance, at best he would be remembered as a minor Catholic reformer of the later Middle Ages. Martyrs make movements and their names provide identity to the myriad of followers who make multiple uses of the opportunities afforded by those who die for one cause or another. Hus was not the starting point. That is certain. Instead he was a hinge upon which part of the history of Bohemia turned. Beyond this the term is so deeply embedded in the historiography that successful extraction and replacement is doubtful. The only suitable alternative is utraquism which, while accurate, tends to reduce reformist religion in Bohemia to a single doctrine and practice. It is evident there was much more to the history of the Hussites than communion under both kinds. It is clear that when some scholars use the term 'utraquism' or 'Utraquists' they only mean a certain sector of reformed Bohemian

Christianity. Táborite religion is excluded. Exercising an illegitimate use of editorial prerogative, some of these same scholars unilaterally attempt to eradicate the objectionable nomenclature from the work of others. It is disingenuous to dismiss 'Hussite' as a term used only by the movement's enemies. Surrendering to a 'proof through etymology' conviction or principle can be a perilous path. The followers of Hus did not call themselves 'utraquists' either. 'Hussite' is not the only possible term scholars may employ but I use it intentionally both for its convenience and its accuracy. The term 'Bohemian' came to signify ecclesiastical disobedience and heretical depravity from the time of Hus on. The term 'Bohemus' more specifically signified 'hereticus' in European public opinion. And the term 'Hussitae' remained equally pejorative. Six hundred years later it need not carry the same connotation.

Jerome of Prague

As the fallout from the Hus trial continued to gather, the case against Jerome of Prague continued at Constance. That process commenced before the legal case against Hus ended. Unlike Hus, Jerome was a layman. He was considerably more flamboyant than Hus, a born agitator and rather outspoken. There are sound reasons for assuming it was Jerome, rather than Hus, providing the impetus behind the king's policy culminating in the decree of Kutná Hora in 1409.[1] Regrettably Jerome seems not to have written much but unlike Hus he traveled widely. So much of our knowledge about Jerome comes from two legal procedures against him, the first in Vienna in 1410 and the second at Constance in 1415–6.[2] Jerome seems to have moved about as far afield as Russia and Jerusalem with significant stays in Prague, Paris, Vienna, Heidelberg, Cologne, Hungary, and Poland. In England he copied some of Wyclif's books and brought them to Prague.[3] Between 1404 and 1406 he was in Paris and we learn he seemed to have been unconcerned about the possibility of falling into heresy despite warnings to that effect.[4] On the eve of being forced by Jean Gerson to renounce his errors he left the city under cover of night.[5] He went to Heidelberg but encountered more difficulty and was forced to undertake another clandestine getaway.[6] He then appeared briefly in Cologne.[7] By this time Jerome had gained something of a reputation as a renegade. He had already made an enemy of Gerson and was soon to pick up a few more formidable foes who would come back later in life to haunt him. Apparently Jerome publicly announced in Prague during the 1409 *Quodlibet* that he wished his soul to be where Wyclif's was.[8] It was this sort of declaration which brought Jerome to legal accountability. In Buda in 1410 it was alleged Jerome preached eucharistic heresies though details are slender and proof lacking.[9] His intemperate Hungarian address, in the hearing of Sigismund, infuriated that monarch to such a degree that he ordered his immediate arrest and confinement under the authority of the archbishop of Esztergom.[10] Sigismund became the second powerful man Jerome offended and as a consequence a dangerous enemy. By August 1410 Jerome went voluntarily to Vienna determined to confront his detractors who had been accusing him of heresy and doctrinal irregularities. He was arrested and imprisoned by the inquisition on the orders of the archbishop of Passau.[11] The trial at Vienna provides a useful example of heresy proceedings in the early fifteenth century. With reference to the Hus trial at Constance it is noteworthy that Jerome was permitted legal counsel. He refused it.[12] Despite a promise to remain in Vienna until the conclusion of the proceedings Jerome absconded.[13] Once it came to light that the defendant had disappeared a citation was posted on the doors of St. Stephen's Cathedral on 20 September summoning Jerome to appear within eight days to answer a charge of contumacy. Jerome did not appear and thus the Vienna trial concluded with a guilty finding on several counts including heresy and perjury and a sentence of excommunication.[14] On 12 September Jerome sent a letter to Andreas Grillenperk, canon of the Passau consistory and lead prosecutor in the Vienna case proceedings. The correspondence may be characterized as insulting.[15] Jerome's behavior at Vienna was unwise. Several of the judges there were later at Constance including Peter Pulka, Caspar Maiselstein and Nicholas of Dinkelsbühl. The latter played a crucial role at Constance. He became the third dangerous opponent Jerome succeeded in antagonizing. It is possible Jerome had an affect in Vienna long after his unauthorized flight. In 1411 an indeterminate number of people were arrested on suspicion they had been seduced into heresy by Jerome. At least one was burned and heresy remained a problem in the area for some time.[16]

Jerome seemed to have taken no note of his status as excommunicate and the ruling appeared not to have been effectively enforced in Prague. Once back in Bohemia we hear of Jerome putting up posters against Zbyněk around the city and publicly ridiculing the archbishop. According to some witnesses this behavior went on even during divine worship. On one occasion as Hus preached in Bethlehem Chapel, Jerome leaned out a window and vilified Zbyněk in the hearing of those outside.[17] There is ample evidence Jerome agitated against indulgences and relics, participated in various acts of iconoclasm, harassment of clerics, assault and the kidnaping of a friar.[18] A circulated document of 1412 against indulgences may have been prepared by Jerome or produced on account of his influence. By 1413 we find Jerome in Poland and Russia.

Less than a month before his execution Jan Hus commented that Jerome had warned him that should he go to Constance it was unlikely he would return.[19] Paying no heed to his own counsel Jerome followed Hus to Constance arriving there on 4 April 1415. At the urging of friends he withdrew outside the city and on 7 April wrote to the Council requesting a safe conduct in order to present his views. The application was denied.[20] Jerome posted placards in the city defending Hus, nailing them on gate-houses, the gates of the town, church doors, the doors of houses where the cardinals were lodged and on the houses of other distinguished prelates.[21] The Council immediately thereafter ordered the citation of Jerome to appear as an accused heretic and likewise ratified a rule 'forbidding the dissemination of libelous pamphlets against anyone at Constance on pain of excommunication'.[22] Hus' old enemy Michael de Causis promulgated the citation in several churches in Constance. Jerome withdrew from the area and headed back to Bohemia. Along the way he got into a discussion wherein he denounced the Council as a demonic 'school of Satan' and a congregation of iniquity.²³ This intemperate outburst aroused the interest of his hearers. His identity revealed, Jerome was arrested and marched back to Constance in chains. At a preliminary hearing, with Gerson present, his death by burning was demanded but Eberhard III von Neuhaus, archbishop of Salzburg intervened with the counsel that repentance and conversion was preferable to death.²⁴ Jerome was turned over to Johann von Wallenrode, archbishop of Riga who imprisoned the suspect in the tower of St. Paul's cemetery. Remanded to confinement for nearly a year, Sigismund apparently seemed determined to have done with Jerome and told the Council to deal expeditiously with the situation. The emperor was told that since Hus was the master and Jerome the disciple the matter could be disposed of in short order.²⁵ Jakoubek of Stříbro included details in a sermon preached in 1417 in Bethlehem Chapel. 'Master Jerome was imprisoned for over one year in very cruel jails in heavy chains, his legs and hands were in the stocks or fettered. On one occasion, in a tower he was hanging head down for over eleven days from a joist with holes so tight and sharp that his legs started to rot as the skin and flesh were torn. On top of this he was tortured with hunger and thirst as well as other sufferings. This hanging was so cruel and so long that he almost died because of it'.²⁶ By June Bishop Jan 'the iron' informed King Václav that the case against Jerome was bring prepared.²⁷ During this same period Hus referred to Jerome as a colleague of some regard.²⁸ By September the Council achieved with Jerome what it had failed to secure with Hus: recantation. Jerome's written retraction was announced publicly on 11 September 1415.²⁹ Jerome admitted that both Hus and Wyclif had erred, the condemnation of the Council just, and he swore off all allegiance to their ideas. It is possible he hoped to secure his freedom by submitting to the authority of the Council. That expectation had no basis in reality. The next month Jean Gerson justified Jerome's imprisonment and lectured on the limits of recantation concluding that penitent heretics could not be released but faced life in prison.³⁰

Sigismund wanted the case against Jerome made short. Gerson clearly advocated a no-release policy. Things took another turn for the worst when agitators like Michael de Causis succeeded in having the case against Jerome reopened and Nicholas of Dinkelsbühl was nominated as one of the prosecutors. The case went to trial in late April 1416 with Jerome confined to his cell. The prosecutor did not want Jerome to be permitted to speak but only to supply yes or no answers to the preferred charges. He was to be tortured and if contumacious to be treated as a heretic.³¹ Zabarella and d'Ailly resigned from the judicial commission at one stage of Jerome's trial in protest over the legal proceedings.³² If the Council saw the ghost of John Wyclif in the case against Hus then it was the ghost of Hus which pervaded the process against Jerome. Observers at the Council referred to Jerome as a devoted follower of Hus of 'cursed memory'.³³ The Council did grant Jerome a public hearing and in the end he retracted his recantation and thus faced the same consequence as Hus. On Saturday 30 May the bishop of Lodi, Jacob Balardi Arrigoni, who preached at the Hus trial mounted the pulpit. The sermon is an excellent summary and exposition of the church's attitude on the matter of heresy.³⁴ Taking Mark 16:14 as his text Bishop Jacob addressed the congregation facetiously with the comment he had no desire to stir the fires by using the sword. That said, he insisted that heinous crimes committed in the open ought not be punished in secret. The offender ought to be made an example to deter others. The issue with Jerome was contumacy, not his honest errors or faithlessness but resistance to correct and ecclesiastical authority. With direct reference to Hus, Bishop Jacob accused Jerome of inciting all of Bohemia to dissension, rebellion and damage to the church. It would have been better had Jerome never been born. Drawing on the heretics of early Christianity the preacher denounced Jerome as a worse offender than Sabellius, Arius and Nestorius and the pertinacity of his heresies had spread across Europe from England to Italy, Lithuania to France. The sermon also included the bishop's wish that Jerome had been tortured. Cardinal Guillaume Fillastre described it as 'a fine sermon'.[35] Several accounts of the execution are extant. Dietrich Vrie said the smoke and flames drew out his soul from his body and carried it down to hell to be burned forever. Poggio Bracciolini observed that Socrates did not drink the hemlock as eagerly as Jerome embraced the fire and went to his death. Richental noted Jerome sang the liturgy but expired with terrible shrieks. 'He was burned on the spot where Hus was burned, and, as with Hus, no one heard his confession. He lived much longer in the fire than Hus and shrieked terribly, for he was a stouter, stronger man, with a broad, thick, black beard. After he was burned, they threw all the ashes and everything else into the Rhine. Many learned men were grieved that he had to die, for he was a far greater scholar then Hus'.[36] The tragedy of Constance lies in the fact that Jan Hus and Jerome of Prague insisted upon dying.[37] Hussites later contended he had been destroyed because he refused to consent to the condemnation of Wyclif and Hus.[38] Still others described the torments waiting for the doctors of the Council while alluding to the pleasures in store for the Hussites.[39]

The martyrdoms of Hus and Jerome provided the emotional basis for revolution. The other motivation was theological and had everything to do with the eucharist. The central plank in the house of religious reform in medieval Bohemia was the eucharist. The fact that Jan Hus cannot be made an important part of that development does not diminish the significance. Hus' contributions to eucharistic theology are slight. He inaugurated nothing and facilitated little. The movement towards eucharistic reform predates his life and the history of that development cannot be overemphasized.

Eucharistic Reform

The eucharist has been a central component of Christian worship and liturgy from earliest times. Indeed early Christian sources reveal its prominence in divine worship. The celebration of the sacrament, not preaching, was the focus.[40] In the High Middle Ages the doctrine of concomitance prevailed. In the course of the twelfth and thirteenth centuries the Latin Church withdrew the lay chalice though not by any universal decree. Following Lateran IV which mandated a minimum standard of annual communion at Easter, theologians unsuccessfully encouraged more frequent observation. The practice can be found only as a rare exception in the medieval Latin west. For a period of 250 years between 1370 and 1620 frequent communion can be found widely observed in the Bohemian church and the subject of the eucharist a matter of unique significance. According to those who have done the main research, the frequency of lay communion throughout church history has varied.[41] In Bohemia, the Czech indigenous liturgical movement led to frequent communion, the recovery of the lay chalice, the inclusion of children in eucharistic practice, a vernacular liturgy and popular hymnody. Much has been made of the influence of John Wyclif in Bohemia. Ostensibly the problematic aspects of Wyclif's eucharistic theology had been raised in Prague as early as 1378.[42] However, Wyclif contributed nothing to the components of the Czech movement. Specific eucharistic reforms began with Jan Milíč of Kroměříž.[43] The details of his career have been glossed elsewhere. The distinctive feature of his religious community was frequent communion. The obvious social leveling effects were unmistakable and came to characterize an important aspect of the revolution. The evangelistic effort among Prague prostitutes and the increased frequency of communion found impetus in a deepening eschatological awareness.[44] In his Postil, 'Gracia dei', Milíč energetically advocated frequent communion.[45] The salvific character of the sacrament was evident in Milíč.[46] No where else in later medieval Europe can we find a community of the faithful communing frequently, perhaps even daily. What may seem as an insignificant religious practice became seed for revolution. According to Milíč, the sacrament filled the believer with the Holy Spirit to the extent that he or she was able ever more ardently to strive for truth. The eucharist remitted sin. This being a theological conviction in the Jerusalem community a case for frequent communion could be advanced. We learn for example that Milíč personally communed on a daily basis.[47] It was likely members of Jerusalem took communion daily as well or at the very least twice weekly. We cannot know for certain the precise cycle of eucharistic practice in Milíč's Jerusalem but even twice per week is extraordinary for the laity in fourteenth-century Europe. Beyond the practice it is worth noting that when one considers the advocacy of frequent communion by several well-respected academics another unique feature in the Bohemian religious world emerges.[48]

To Matěj of Janov we owe considerably for it was he in the period immediately after Milíč who wrote about the subject thus systematizing the thought of these early reformers, interpreting and theologizing the eucharistic practices at Jerusalem, thus providing a better indication of the theology behind the practice.[49] He wrote in his preface to the *Regulae* that he had written his books on the subject out of love and devotion to the sacrament of the altar. Matěj took on contemporary eucharistic doctrine and practice and challenged the prevailing orthodoxy and presented an argument for frequent communion in his *De corpore christi*.[50] If it was essential for one to eat in order to live physically then Matěj argued it was also important to receive spiritual sustenance in order to flourish spiritually. That nourishment could only be obtained through the sacrament.[51] Frequent communion remained the privilege of all the faithful not just for the celebrant.[52] Matěj made it abundantly clear that the medieval assumption, expressed in Thomas Aquinas and William Durandus, that a priest may commune on behalf of the faithful was not tenable.[53] Matěj explicitly argued there were priests who regarded themselves more important than the laity and had no desire to allow common people to be equated with them through the practice of frequent communion. Matěj claimed these clerics accused those who did commune frequently of belonging to the Beghards and Beguines and attempting to become priests themselves.[54] Matěj was dismissive of the stance and drew attention to the fact that believers were a royal priesthood. While underscoring disputes over the practice Matěj advocated for it concluding men and women should commune frequently.[55] With the Jerusalem community in mind Matěj deliberately included women in his insistence upon frequent community.[56] In this sense Matěj regarded the eucharist as a social leveler. This caused immediate problems. In 1378 a servant girl named Kačka in Šternberk came under investigation on account of frequent communing and was questioned by the vicar-general.[57] Developing his argument even further Matěj asserted that mere observation of the sacrament – adoration of the host – had no particular efficacy. Participation in the elements was essential and he argued this built respect for the body and blood of Christ.[58] A foundational principle found throughout later Hussite history was thus enumerated first in Matěj. If one was a member of the church by means of baptism then one ought also to commune with that body through the eucharist.[59] Later exponents of eucharistic devotion have convincingly suggested that frequent communion enabled the participant to experience Christ more fully. The bread facilitated union with Christ while the blood washed sins away.[60] For Matěj, frequent communion facilitated the proper worship of Christ.[61] The sacramental benefits of the eucharist, to wit universal grace, were evident in Matěj.[62] Infrequent communion, Matěj argued, was a source for social stress and anxiety to say nothing of pervasive sin. The same argument found cogent expression among the Hussites a generation later.[63]

In terms of the importance of the sacrament Matěj went so far as to suggest that the church was established chiefly for the sake of the eucharist. The statement while theologically indefensible nevertheless drove the point home. Hymnody prepared the faithful for eucharistic devotion. There was nothing else in the church more salutary than the daily eating and drinking of the body and blood of Christ. It was the common right of all believers. From this practice emerged every good thing ordained by God for humankind. In this participation happiness in the present life was obtained and the life of the world to come guaranteed. For Matěj it was a foretaste of the glory to come.[64] The burden of book four of the *Regulae* treated the question if all Christians ought to receive communion on a daily basis. The conviction of Milíč and Matěj was affirmative. It was thought better to allow all people to commune, even at the risk of damnation to those who participated unworthily, than to deprive the faithful of sacramental grace.[65]

The initiatives proposed by Milíč and Matěj met with opposition. Clerics took to their pulpits to defend traditional custom calling for an end to the practice of frequent communion which seemed to have become popular with the laity. The acts of a 1389 synod in Prague are lost and the sole source appears to be the account given by Matěj himself. Matěj summarized the arguments against frequent communion from Thomas

Aquinas, canon law and the synod.⁶⁶ At this assembly Matěj was condemned and the practice of lay communion limited to once a month. The lower clergy and the laity were not permitted to commune more frequently. All this came about, Matěj tells us, on the feast day of St. Luke (18 October). Immediately thereafter those who had been involved in the liturgical innovation had 'much to endure publicly' on account of the synodal ruling. This provincial synod forced Matěj to recant publicly from his unacceptable ideas and disciplined him with two other priests. The punishment leveled against Priest Ondřej is unknown. But Priest Jakub Matějův of Kaplice was suspended for ten years ostensibly for making an indecent gesture at an image of the Virgin and saying he'd like to use the wood to boil peas. By contrast, Matěj was forbidden to preach, hear confessions or celebrate the eucharist outside his own church for a period of six months.⁶⁷ The recantation forced upon Matěj included acknowledgment that he had preached certain things which the church regarded as incorrect resulting in error or scandal. There were five retractions, the first three dealt with images and the saints. The last two focused on the sacrament. The final article dealt specifically with the issue of frequent communion. Matěj conceded that the laity ought not to be encouraged to daily communion. Matěj undertook not to offend in like manner in the future.⁶⁸ The recantation was insincere. There is no indication Matěj truly abandoned his point of view. Eucharistic reform may have suffered a very serious blow were it not for the intervention of Jan of Jenštejn, Archbishop of Prague. Initially opposed to the sacramental reforms, Archbishop Jan went on a pilgrimage in 1390 to Rome and shortly thereafter fell seriously ill and nearly expired. He attributed his recovery to the miraculous benefits of the sacrament.⁶⁹ From that point on he supported the idea of frequent communion.⁷⁰ By 16 June 1391 another Prague synod permitted the laity to commune as often as they desired.⁷¹ On 17 June 1392 a synodal statute, at the behest of Archbishop Jan, ruled that not even a criminal prior to execution should be denied communion.⁷²

Neither Milíč nor Matěj appear to have advocated for the lay chalice. There are passages in the *Regulae* which might seem to suggest a proclivity in that direction (David Holeton says utraquism is unconsciously present in the *Regulae* and František Šmahel says advocacy of the cup is possible) but close reading reveals weak evidential value.⁷³ Scholars devoting considerable attention to the question arrived at the same conclusion.⁷⁴ The movement towards the chalice had to wait another two decades but even so the influence of Matěj remained evident.⁷⁵ That said, the final article of book five in the *Regulae* suggested frequent communion as an antidote for the ills of humanity, both moral and spiritual, which afflicted the church. It was likewise the weapon needed to defeat Antichrist and to bring the work of Christ to consummation in the last days in which Milíč and Matěj, and the Hussites yet to come, believed they were living.⁷⁶ Of further note was that Matěj even more than Milíč drew out the political and social implications of the theology of the eucharist and its frequent observation. The effects were salutary. At least Matěj thought so. 'Through the grace of Jesus Christ and thanks to the efforts of Milíč, Prague has turned back from Sodom to its old views and by the Holy Spirit, become not Babylon, but Jerusalem, filled with the word of Christ and the teachings of salvation'.[77] Taken as a whole, it might be said that Matěj confronted the entire tradition of eucharistic piety in his day.[78]

Milíč and Matěj were the key figures in the later fourteenth-century eucharistic movement. The scholarly contributions of the academics Vojtěch Raňkův of Ježov, Matthew of Cracow, and Heinrich of Bitterfeldt prevented the movement from being dismissed by assembling the essential intellectual support. Tomáš Štítný popularized the idea propounded by Milíč and Matěj and the other scholars by writing in the vernacular. Therein he asserted 'anyone can receive communion daily'. Štítný's work played a key role in the development of the eucharistic movement.[79] Following Matěj, Štítný argued communion should be practised daily just as one eats for daily nutrition.[80] The broad thrust of Milíč, Matěj and Štítný helped create a popular eucharistic piety and imagination without parallel in the medieval Latin west. The alleged hazardous social implications which some perceived required refining. Frequently practiced the eucharist may have been perceived as a threat on the grounds it suggested theological democracy among the faithful. That did constitute direct challenge to the nature of medieval Christianity.

We have seen previously how Hus retained a conservative approach on the matter of liturgical and sacramental reform. The most revolutionary doctrinal idea in Hussite Bohemia proved to be the lay chalice. Hus came rather lately to that idea. During his tenure at Bethlehem Chapel he placed no emphasis or importance upon the cup for the laity initially denying lay people needed to receive the cup. He denied that laypeople received the blood of Christ sacramentally. Hus agreed that both the body and blood of Christ were present in each sacramental element. Given that understanding of concomitance the faithful communicate does receive the blood of Christ. They participate sacramentally in the body of Christ but since they do not receive the cup the blood of Christ is not sacramentally received.[81] Hus did not perceive this as a problem. If one follows the theological history of Jan Hus there appeared to be no advance in terms of eucharistic reform until he arrived at Constance. Two things happened there in terms of his attitude. First, as we have already noted, shortly before his arrest and incarceration Hus wrote a very short tract in which he addressed the question of utraquism which was rapidly becoming the theological and liturgical issue in Prague. Apart from a few references in his prison correspondence this is the only document wherein Hus discussed utraquism.[82] Somewhat surprisingly Hus was explicit in expression that the faithful laity should partake of the bread and the wine in the sacrament. Hus argued the practice seemed sensible and salutary inasmuch as Christ when establishing the practice separately took bread and wine and gave it to those who were at table with him.[83] Admittedly the bulk of Hus' short essay consisted of a rather standard scholastic recitation of authorities with little comment from Hus. He appealed to the fifth-century Pope Gelasius who frowned upon the eucharistic *sub una* and called upon the authority of Cyprian, Ambrose, Jerome, Ambrosiaster, Augustine, Gregory the Great, Albert the Great, Bernard, Rupert of Deutz (whom he wrongly identified as Fulgentius of Ruspe), William of Mont Lauzun and Nicholas of Lyra, among others. He concluded by arguing it was salutary for the faithful laity to receive the blood of Christ via the cup. His basis seemed to be that Christ offered both elements to the faithful. The bread aroused the participant to spiritual eating while the cup drew the mind into active participation in the shed blood of Christ. It was legitimate therefore to partake sacramentally in both kinds.[84]

When questioned on it Hus regarded the practice of the early church sufficient for ratifying utraquism.[85] On 15 June 1415 the Council of Constance passed a decree forbidding the practice of utraquism and threatening with disciplinary action those who violated the statute.[86] That decision against the lay chalice forced Hus into further rebellion against ecclesiastical authority. Earlier he suggested seeking some type of sanction for utraquism but when the Council effectively cut off any possibility of that the die was cast. Hus called the policy at Constance 'great insanity' which contravened the gospel, the authority of St. Paul and other saints.[87] Once the Council's ruling had been publicized, Hus actively encouraged Prague priests to ignore Constance and not oppose the cup.[88] It is possible that Hus' restraint in his endorsement of the chalice before June 1415 can be put down to his desire not to provide his more strident enemies, like Michael de Causis, with any additional ammunition. It is more likely Hus simply did not fully appreciate the impetus behind the cup. He had been out of the mainstream of events in Prague for two years and prior to that had not shown any inclination towards utraquism. He came to Constance with considerable naïveté convinced of the veracity of his positions. He was a free man when he wrote his piece on utraquism and had no inkling he would be arrested. It seems likely he wrote his essay based on news from Prague about developments there. His restraint in supporting the practice must be attributed to his lack of commitment to it. He did not regard it as essential or of salvific import. When the fathers outlawed the practice Hus' complacent taciturnity turned to outrage and his thinking underwent drastic change. Two weeks after he condemned the ruling and urged the practice of the lay chalice Jan Hus was dead and played no further role in eucharistic reform.

The utraquist controversy from 1414 to 1417 constitutes an important chapter in the history of ideas as well as in the history of doctrines. At the end of the twelfth century we read of a Czech priest carrying the sacrament to a person near death and being instructed to practice intinction to avoid accidents but also to ensure utraquism.[89] That latter concern vanished in the western church until fifteenth-century Bohemia. Two men promoted utraquism with the explicit urgency of it being necessary for salvation. Those men were Jakoubek of Stříbro and Nicholas of Dresden. One of the early histories of the Hussite movement began a chronicle account with an event that must be regarded at least symbolically as one of the great moments in the history of doctrine and religious practice in later medieval Europe.

> In the year 1414 after the birth of the Son of God there began to be given to common faithful people the venerable and divine utraquist communion of the sacrament of the body and blood of the Lord Christ by the honest master Jakoubek of Stříbro, a scholarly bachelor of Holy Scriptures, and by some priests, his helpers, in the glorious town of Prague, first in the churches of St.

Vojtěch [Adalbert], St. Martin-in-the-Wall and in St. Michael in the New Town, and in the chapel of Bethlehem in the Old Town. This giving of communion was suppressed by various horrors, threats and imprisonments by the Roman and Czech King Václav [IV] and his clerical officials, and especially by Konrad, the Archbishop of Prague and other prelates and monks and also by masters of the glorious university in Prague and also by doctors. But it was spreading even more among religious people of both genders, so that within two years priests and masters, adhering to Master Jan [Hus], who were from the group of Wyclif, though a party resisting them that was of Mohammed, were given freedom to preach and give utraquist communion to people in two or three churches. But in all the other community churches in Prague and in monasteries the archbishop and prelates excommunicated them and issued anathema and the ban throughout Prague. But they, ignoring it, attracted large numbers of people, so that not only in Prague but also in many royal towns of the Margraviate of Moravia, in castles and in towns and villages, common people in great numbers with great religious feeling and honesty were often preparing themselves for utraquist communion. Though the adversaries and blasphemers of this truth, both clerical and profane, were angry, they could not suppress it. Because, as is written in 2 Esdras 10, the truth remains and spreads and is alive for ever, and achieves victory for ever.[90]

On 18 October a Prague synod declared that utraquism had been started in violation of a prohibition established by Archbishop Konrad.[91]

The question of the origins of utraquism has been a preoccupation of the historiography for some time. There are a variety of suggestions and two of these are particularly appealing. According to one fifteenth-century source, in Prague 'in Na Příkopě at the Black Rose lived masters and bachelors from Dresden and they had a college there. Master Peter, Master Nicholas, English [Peter Payne] and Nicholas Loripes. They had been expelled from Dresden because they were giving secretly the blood of the Lord. They began to advise Master Jičín to give the blood of the Lord and Jičín took the initiative and convinced Master Jakoubek to do the same together with many other priests to adhere to this'.[92] These men at the Black Rose stimulated theological development leading to utraquist practice in Prague.[93] The Dresden school is significant for the history of ideas.[94] The second theory is that the stimulus lies with Jakoubek.[95] I prefer to accept an explanation which combines both constructs. I cannot subscribe to the idea that somehow Matěj of Janov provided the impetus or that the Byzantine rite settled in Bohemia as a result of Jerome of Prague's peregrinations. The Hussites did appeal to the utraquist practices of the eastern church but this attempt at justification was dismissed by contemporaries.[96] The appeal was a grabbing at straws. It is worth looking a bit closer at Jakoubek.

On 7 June 1414, during the feast of Corpus Christi, Jakoubek preached noting that he had received a revelation in support of utraquism and that this had come ostensibly as a result of careful research.[97] In terms of Czech theological thinkers in the period between 1370 and 1470 Jakoubek was among a handful of the most significant which include Matěj, Hus and Jan Rokycana. He played an important and leading role in the establishment of the lay chalice, his doctrine of eucharistic presence, and his theology of the cup are significant.[98] There is no doubt in my mind whatever that Jakoubek had intercourse with the Dresden school in Prague and that a cross-fertilization of ideas transpired. He told Ondřej of Brod he came to an understanding of the lay chalice as a result of revelation.[99] That revelation, Jakoubek explained, was a kind of knowledge and understanding which resulted from a careful study of scripture and patristic authorities. Of these he named Augustine, Cyprian, John Chrysostom and others. The understanding yielded *revelatio*.[100] Elsewhere Jakoubek referred to the revelation of utraquism.[101] In his university *posicio* on 11 October 1414 Jakoubek publicly argued that utraquism was essential.[102] Christ instituted the eucharist in both kinds for all of the faithful.[103] If one form of the eucharist was necessary for the faithful then the other form must equally be obligatory.[104] Jakoubek quoted Pope Leo I from a Lenten sermon wherein the Manicheans were ridiculed because they refused the cup of redemption.[105] In 1417 Jakoubek assailed the idea that since the church had for a long time communed *sub una* innovation ought to be avoided. Questioning the Dominican master Petr of Uničov, one of Hus's accusers at the Council, Jakoubek demanded to know which church assumed such posture: the one represented by Constance, filled with the heresy of simony, or the church described in the Apocalypse sitting on a monster with many heads and horns?[106] At the Council it had been argued that if a layman allowed consecrated wine to wet his beard, he ought to be burned along with his beard.[107] Jakoubek and the Hussites were having none of that. It was clear that, unlike Hus, Jakoubek followed Wyclif into the doctrine of remenentism.[108] However, his 1420–1421 exposition on the Revelation of St. John does not reveal the same proclivities, at least overtly, and some statements therein appeared to contradict the doctrine altogether.[109] In reply to his public comments Jakoubek received a rebuttal from Ondřej of Brod.[110] That rebuttal from early 1415 argued John 6:53-4 should be understood spiritually, not sacramentally, and since there were no lay people at the last supper the words of Christ were inapplicable. In response Jakoubek submitted that the eschatological 'abomination of desolation' was manifested in the withdrawal of the lay chalice and after mounting a prolix rejoinder concluded by asserting the lay chalice would aid in bringing an end to sinfulness and the kingdom of Antichrist.[111] It has been noted that Jakoubek had the useful gift of being able to produce texts to prove his arguments even when the authorities barely related to the issue at hand.[112]

Referring to the Luke 14 parable of the man who invited everyone to a banquet only to have them make excuses and fail to appear Jakoubek identified the man as Christ. The man in the story became distressed at those who would not come to the banquet. During the octave of Corpus Christi Jakoubek argued that Christ was angry with those who did come to the table but ate only half the meal! Jakoubek insisted this was how the parable was to be understood.[113] Utraquism was not optional. In order to retain divine grace and be found obedient to Christ the faithful were obligated to come to the table and partake in both kinds. This was the thesis of Jakoubek's *Salvator noster*. He concluded his dissertation by asserting it was evident from scripture and the doctors of the early church that it was necessary to believe that faithful Christians must commune *sub utraque specie*.[114] Immediately after the public inauguration of utraquism in Prague Nicholas of Dresden preached the lay chalice was essential for salvation and the following spring once more argued his thesis while preaching on the text *quod fuit ab inicio* (I John 1:1).[115] Nicholas and Jakoubek preached convincingly that when Christ spoke in the Gospel of John (6:53) about eating and drinking those words were directed not simply to the disciples but to the people in general.[116] The teaching did not remain academic in nature and the practice spread through the Kingdom of Bohemia. We read that priests in Prague rebelled against the canons of the church in the matter of the lay chalice. Jakoubek was credited with starting it at the church of St. Michael and from there it spread to Ústí. We read further of utraquist priests going to Moravia and providing the lay chalice there. Orthodox Moravian bishops were unhappy about this development but the utraquists paid them no heed. The chronicler noted the adherents to utraquism multiplied and did much evil and the authorities began to call them heretics.[117] The main intellectual forces in the implementation of the lay chalice remained Jakoubek and Nicholas. One may see in Jakoubek the ideas of Matěj being brought to their logical conclusion. It is specious to try and find support in Hus. Hus' successor at Bethlehem Chapel, Havlík, resisting the utraquist doctrine, came under withering attack and was soon replaced.[118]

By 1417 most university masters supported utraquism and in March the university referred to the chalice as a 'memorable symbol on the road to the promised land'.[119] It was true the Hussites did not deny the complete Christ was present in both bread and wine. In this they remained faithful to the traditional doctrine of concomitance. Likewise the body of Christ was regarded (at least in the mainstream of Hussitism) as existing permanently and indissolubly linked to the divine nature and as such capable of being present in many places simultaneously.[120] Detractors of the reformers represented the utraquists as holding to a concept where only one sacramental element implied half of the grace of the sacrament.[121] The argument was unsound. Transubstantiation was not a doctrine prevailing at Tábor but elsewhere in the Hussite movements an understanding of the real presence can be found. All of the major non-Táborite theologians held to this belief and even Jakoubek cannot be excluded entirely.[122] At the end of the revolutionary period a synod convened at Kutná Hora concluded an unimpeachably orthodox position on the sacrament on 4 October 1441.[123] That did not, however, include acquiescence in the decisions of Constance. Nicholas of Dresden was only one of the utraquist ideologues who directly rebutted the ban on the lay chalice.[124] Nicholas claimed that if Christ came into the congregation at Constance and attempted to celebrate holy communion as he had in the first century he would encounter some difficulty and were he not to submit he might be hereticated and condemned.[125] On 10 March 1417 the university in Prague gave its official seal of approval to the practice of utraquism recommending its salvific character.[126]

From irregular sacramental communion in the High Middle Ages the Czechs advocated frequent communion, perhaps on a daily basis, implemented the lay chalice, and finally widened the scope of sacramental grace to include all the baptized. This meant infants and small children were now welcomed at the altar.[127] At the St. Wenceslas Day Synod, 28 September 1418, twenty-three articles of theology were passed. The first one dealt with the communion of infants. 'Following baptism, children must receive the eucharist in the proper manner which is in the form of the body and blood of the Lord. If the child is not able to receive the sacrament without spitting it out, then it will be necessary to wait before communing. If the child is able to receive, a small piece of the sacrament should be placed in his or her mouth. After the mouth has been closed for a time, place a drop of the blood of Christ in his or her mouth taken from the chalice with one's finger taking care to keep the paten under it'.[128] On 4 July 1421 the St. Prokop Synod also adopted twenty-three articles in which article six mandated the eucharist should be given to adults and children weekly and if possible daily while article twenty forbade any baptized person from being excluded. This synod had been convened in Prague under the auspices of Archbishop Konrad who had converted to the Hussite cause. Radical communities likewise called for the administration of the eucharist for all the baptized.[129] All of this only aggravated further the official church and by spring 1418 Pope Martin V demanded unconditional ecclesiastical submission and complete renunciation of the Bohemian eucharistic developments.[130] That demand fell on deaf ears. The advance of eucharistic reform from frequent communion to utraquism to inclusion of all the baptized, including infants, unfolded as a natural progression. There are three possible references to infant communion in the writings of Matěj of Janov though any careful consideration of those texts must conclude it is wishful thinking only to imagine that Matěj had this eventuality in mind.[131] The implementation of the practice in Bohemia created considerable debate and led to discord among various Hussites.[132] The question of specific origin is vexing. There is some chance that Václav Koranda of Plzeň inaugurated the practice but the suggestion has never been proven satisfactorily.[133] However, it seems evident that by the beginning of 1415 the matter of infant communion had arisen. How else can the chapter on children in Ondřej of Brod's rebuttal to Jakoubek be explained?[134] Moreover, the practice of infant communion was mentioned in the midst of a narrative about the ban of the lay cup by the Council of Constance in 1415.[135] Nevertheless, a dossier of authorities justifying the practice of infant communion began to emerge. This included biblical, patristic, and medieval sources. The most important were those extracted from Pseudo-Dionysius, Cyprian and Augustine.

The prime mover was Jakoubek who composed texts defending the practice and had these placed on the walls of Bethlehem Chapel where they were rediscovered during restoration in the mid-twentieth century.[136] Nicholas of Dresden argued for the inclusion of children in the sacrament in a sermon of 12 November 1414.[137] We find reference in Jakoubek to the Greek insistence on the communing of children.[138] But this was nothing more than indication of the continuing search for justification and legitimacy. The same strong sense of eschatological awareness we noted earlier in Milíč continued unabated in the later history of Bohemian eucharistic reform.[139] To regard infant communion as outside the mainstream of Hussite liturgy or consider it a secondary issue indicates failure to appreciate the development of the central theological issue in medieval Bohemia. Balking at infant communion destroys the universal character of the eucharistic community.[140] The anti-Hussite Moravian abbot Štěpán of Dolany complained that infant communion only proved the liturgical abuses perpetrated by the Hussites which he had warned about all along.[141] Because it was considered essential for salvation, Jakoubek petitioned King Václav IV to allow the practice inasmuch as it harmed no one.[142] In January or February 1419 Jakoubek argued that social problems facing the realm might be alleviated if irregular communion practices were curtailed and children permitted to partake of the sacrament.[143] Conflict remained and by autumn Jan Želivský noted continuing opposition.[144] Preaching on Ascension Day (25 May 1419) Želivský attacked the anti-utraquist ruling at Constance. Drawing on the long ending of Mark, Želivský took up the theme of poisonous drink. Noting the steadfastness of Master Jan Hus and others Želivský accused the fathers of Constance of offering the faithful a poisonous drink through the prohibition of the lay chalice when all along faithfulness to the gospel of Jesus implied life through the chalice for adults as well as children.[145] Even adherents of the reformed message stubbornly opposed the inclusion of children, Želivský reported, and among these he identified Jan of Jesenice and Šimon of Tišnov.[146] Between Easter and Trinity V, Želivský took up the subject of infant communion nearly a dozen times.[147] Without Želivský the cause of infant communion may have disappeared. Ultimately, the efforts of Jakoubek and Želivský prevailed and the crisis passed. The practice widened and was reflected in the hymnody of the period wherein we find lyrics confirming that children had been invited to the Lord's table and they must not be forbidden from eating and drinking the body and blood of Christ.[148]

Still the Latin Church remained unpersuaded and the practice continued to be anathema. The sacral quality of the consecrated elements remained an obstacle. The Bishop of Coutances, Philibert, witnessed Jan Rokycana communing a number of babies. One spat the wafer out and Rokycana had to replace it. The bishop was horrified.[149] By the time the Hussites were invited to appear at the Council of Basel their dossier of authorities and argument for the practice had been in evolution for two decades. On 16 January 1433 Rokycana argued the case for the Czech eucharistic program. Initially he did not specify infant communion but it is not amiss to suggest Rokycana assumed an inclusive understanding of all the baptized.[150] That assumption was consistent with a central Hussite theological idea. In a second presentation before the Council, Rokycana did address the case for infant communion on 2 March arguing for its essentiality.[151] Jan Stojković, a Croatian Dominican from Dubrovnik (Ragusa), offered a rebuttal to Rokycana.[152] He admitted that from an historical perspective utraquism was not improper. However the practice might be terminated by the church, as it had been, and it was quite improper for those lacking legitimate authority (like the Hussites) to go against ecclesiastical custom. Despite Rokycana's skillful integration of the several points of the Bohemian eucharistic reform into a single argument the two sides remained at impasse. Despite significant disagreements the Council had sufficient motivation to try and come to a compromised agreement. This reached fruition in the famous 'Compactata' of late 1433. This agreement was a ruse to enforce conformity to Rome. The archdeacon of Barcelona, Juan Palomar, asserted that since Hussites were like wild horses they needed to be captured, tamed, fitted in a halter and tied to a fence. After that they might even be thrashed.[153] The 'Compactata' guaranteed Hussites their priests would continue to be consecrated, conceded on utraquism but remained firmly against infant communion.[154] The Hussites did not acquiesce in the exclusion of infant communion. At the St. Gall's Day diet (23 October 1434) thirteen statements were produced relating mainly to the 'four articles of Prague'. The last two indicated the matter remained up in the air but the practice would continue. That posture produced formal complaints for violation of the 'Compactata' and non-compliance with the agreements brokered at Basel. Specifically the allegations accused Rokycana of communing infants.[155] The archbishop-elect remained undeterred and preached in favor of the practice in the spring of 1437.[156] One final round brought the topic to the forefront of consideration in the autumn of 1437 when Hussites once more went to Basel. Prokop of Plzeň defended the practice of infant communion presenting the fullest dossier on the matter yet unveiled.[157] On behalf of the Council, Archdeacon Juan Palomar dismissed every argument for infant communion. While ecclesiastical agreement and approbation failed completely, this did not prevent the Hussites from communing children in Bohemia right up to the 1620s. A case can be advanced concluding that Jan Stojković and Juan Palomar were not men of theological probity in their dismissive treatment of the dossier for infant communion.

Despite these struggles and failures, eucharistic reform in Bohemia continued and there does not seem to have been any commensurate decline in interest. A Czech language version of the Mass circulated and Jan Čapek wrote an instructional manual for lay people on the eucharist.[158] Nicholas of Dresden reacting to the decree by the Council of Constance took up the argument that the faithful attending a parish church where utraquism was not offered ought to be permitted to receive the sacrament from utraquist priests elsewhere.[159] Detractors persisted. In 1451 Aeneas Sylvius claimed that prior to the advent of Hus and Jerome and their erroneous teachings, communion had been properly administered in Bohemia.[160] Once made Pope Pius II he advised Kaspar, bishop of Meißen, that throughout Germany there were utraquist priests under the influence of 'damned Bohemians' destroying the vineyard of the Lord.[161] The agreements of Basel notwithstanding, the Hussites were not warmly regarded as faithful Christians. The ecclesiastical province of Olomouc remained in opposition to all things Hussite stoutly refusing even to comply with the requirements of the Basel agreements. The 'Compactata' constituted a solution prompted by an extraordinary situation posing a persistent danger to the church. Like *Haec Sancta* twenty years earlier the settlement with the Bohemians was an emergency measure. The fathers at Basel did not recognize the force of Hussite theological argument. While in Prague Philibert, Bishop of Coutances consecrated utraquist priests and celebrated the eucharist in both kinds.[162] I suggest he was an exception to the prevailing rule. After crusades and councils, debates and decrees, at least significant portions of the Hussite movement were prepared to pursue a reformist path even if that meant continued separation from Rome. Considered in the context of the history of Christianity it may be asserted that the Bohemian eucharistic movement stood alone between the patristic era and the twentieth century. Some years after the revolutionary storms of the initial Hussite period a virtually unknown Czech scholar named Prokop Ryšavý of Jindřichův Hradec presented a difference approach to faith altogether. 'Let everyone know that anyone wishing to be a Christian may do so on the basis of his or her own judgment and not through force'.[163]

For all of the strides made by the Czech reformers in the fifteenth century the social implications of the lay chalice were never fully realized. That failure had severe consequences for the future of the Hussite religious communities.[164] Even Tábor, for all of its rhetoric remained a clerical community even at the height of its social experiment and the elimination of social barriers and hierarchy, never achieved realization. Internecine conflict reduced the number of priests by half but the reality remained.[165] The eschatological dimensions of eucharistic practice clearly evident in early Christianity disappeared in the course of the Middle Ages. This returned in the Bohemian liturgical practices and can also be located in aspects of the social revolution which accompanied that development. When Jakoubek preached that the faithful ought not to lock Christ up in their hearts his reference settled upon the social consequences of an apocalyptic interpretation of eschatology.[166] Moreover it ought not be forgotten that in the minds of many Hussites the 'donation of Constantine' was the work of the Devil.[167] Taken in context the Hussite movement constituted a true theological and social revolution.

From Ideology to Insurrection

It is not possible to exclude Hus from popular religion in Bohemia after 1409.[168] Hus' ideology encouraged others to revolt and carry that revolt into revolution. Those same principles led Hus to Constance where he accepted submission and martyrdom.[169] Three weeks after his death, on 26 July 1415, the Council of Constance formally notified the Czech nobility of the execution and called upon them to assist in eradicating all of the heresies associated with Hus.[170] On 31 August, the 'iron bishop' of Litomyšl, Jan Železný, received a commission to carry out the repression.[171] Close to sixty barons assembled in Prague on 2 September 1415 in Hus' Bethlehem Chapel to discuss the situation. Here they formulated a reply which provided some proof of the consternation which motivated continued disobedience.[172] Referring to Hus as a preacher of the gospel, the nobles affirmed they could not understand why he had been condemned. They accused the Council of malignant motives in executing Hus in a cruel and ignominious fashion as a heretic which they stoutly asserted he was not. Without naming names, these barons asserted Hus was not guilty of error or heresy and had been the victim of false and sinister accusations leveled by his enemies and 'certain traitors'. Doubtless they had in mind men like Michael de Causis and Štěpán

Páleč. The death of Hus had created a perpetual scandal. Therefore the assembled nobles protested. With one heart and voice they affirmed Master Jan Hus had been a good, just and catholic man who had lived among them for many years without offense and whose conduct had been above reproach and his life pure. They extolled Hus' virtues as a teacher of scripture and of the holy doctors noting the approval of the church. Moreover the barons referred to Hus' many writings which they argued consistently avoided heresy and error and that Hus had preached that others might avoid the same. The Czech nobles accused the Council of not being content to disgrace the kingdom in condemning Hus but likewise drew attention to the plight of Jerome of Prague who even then was in prison at Constance awaiting trial. The barons decried accusations that Bohemia had been infected by heresy. The rejoinder was uncompromising. Anyone who said such things were liars, traitors, dangerous heretics themselves, and children of the Devil. With an air of defiance, the barons asserted their willingness to die on behalf of the law of God and in defense of faithful preachers who defended its veracity without concern for any laws or statutes which might be marshaled against them. This protest was then circulated throughout Bohemia and in the end 452 Czech nobles (representing about one-third of aristocratic families in the Czech lands) affixed their seals to the letter which was delivered to the Council in eight copies.[173] Not wishing to leave hostages to fate, three days after this act of defiance the barons formed a league to defend the commitments made to the Council.[174] Free preaching was permitted and any hindrances would not be tolerated. Any priest accused of error or heresy was entitled to have that charge sustained on the basis of scripture. Bishops seeking to act outside this parameter would be opposed. Improper exercise of ecclesiastical discipline or the use of force to curtail the proclamation of the word of God would be answered in kind.

The Council was not impressed. On 23 February 1416 all 452 signatories were cited to appear along with Archbishop Konrad, King Václav and Queen Žofie. None of these obeyed. The formal summons to Constance of 27 March was ignored with contempt and the barons likewise disregarded the call to assist in the repression program headed up by Bishop Jan Železný.[175] The alleged offenders were again cited in September but without result. Those faithful to the official church argued the nobles supported the reform cause chiefly motivated by greed and opportunity to seize ecclesiastical wealth. Defying the Council was unconscionable. The actions of the barons resulted in a 'devilish brotherhood' and 'monstrous league' with peasants and other elements of society.[176] Moreover there seemed to be sufficient backlash to prevent the 'iron bishop' from carrying out his conciliar commission effectively. Fearing for his safety after leaving Constance, Bishop Jan seemed to have stayed indoors.[177] His return to Litomyšl proved impossible and later he became bishop of Olomouc in Moravia. A similar fate caused Štěpán Páleč to forfeit his living in Prague. He spent the remainder of his life at Kraków.

The Latin Church indicated active willingness to exterminate the Hussite heresy. With Hus and Jerome disposed of, their adherents were targeted. It is possible to find reference to this urge to purge even before the Council of Constance convened. On

6 March 1414 Dietrich of Niem called for a liquidation policy. Czech eucharistic doctrines and practices were unacceptable and Dietrich suggested the heretics had expelled from the land those who refused to acquiesce. Arguing the futility of examining the miscreants, Dietrich simply concluded that suspicion of heresy was more than adequate for condemnation and went so far as to suggest a crusade as a means to accomplish the objective.[178] Hussite heresies had arisen with 'canine fury' and had to be stopped.[179] Two events in early 1418 raised the stakes. The papal legate Ferdinand of Lucena sent an ultimatum to King Václav and the newly elected pontiff, Martin V, published a bull calling for the followers of Hus to be tracked down and punished.[180] Four weeks later Ferdinand proclaimed a crusading bull on the authority of Pope Martin from a pulpit in Wrocław.[181] Imperial armies would be essential in order to put down the perceived Hussite threat and Sigismund expressed readiness to take command. Sigismund had used crusading language as early as March 1416 and several months before Martin acted formally Sigismund expressed a desire to eradicate all heretics from Bohemia and told his brother King Václav he anticipated killing every Hussite he could find.[182]

Many adherents of the practice of utraquism and reformed religion in the Kingdom of Bohemia came under the influence of radical preachers and an eschatological vision promoted by some of the priests. This resulted in mass meetings on mountain tops in southern Bohemia in 1419. There are numerous accounts. Fifty thousand men, plus women and children, are reported to have congregated on these hilltops within the space of three short months.[183] Because priests faithful to the official church and in obedience to the decree of Constance would not commune believers in the lay chalice, these followers of Jan Hus began regularly to go to a hilltop near Bechyně Castle.[184] Children were communed as well as adults in an utraquist sacrament and the word of God was preached without restraint.[185]

Repressive measures taken against those of the reformist party in Prague ignited a short fuse. Jan Želivský led an armed group from church on a July Sunday morning to the New Town Hall where they defenestrated the city councillors and installed a new civic order. King Václav died shortly thereafter.[186] 'There is no revolution without dictatorship and violence'.[187] In Bohemia the looming violence found men of high caliber willing and able to defy pope, council and emperor. The priest Jan Želivský referred to Sigismund as the great red dragon and his sermons helped galvanize resistance. If Želivský dominated Prague pulpits Jan Žižka commanded the field and under his strategy and orders a sort of popular army offered armed resistance to the invaders.[188] Both men took the threat seriously that reformed religious practice in Bohemia faced dire challenge. The emperor had made no bones about it. When the crusaders entered Bohemia anyone refusing to surrender and submit were ordered killed and their possessions confiscated.[189] Hussites were unmoved and motivated by Želivský published a manifesto in which they swore to defend their faith against papal, imperial and crusader mandates.[190] Accusing Sigismund of culpability in the death of Jan Hus, prominent noblemen in Bohemia sided with the Hussite group.[191] The issue at hand continued to center to some extent on Hus. In the bull *Inter cunctus* Martin V referred to Hus of 'damnable memory' and called for attention to the fact that Hus had been cast out of the house of God as a wicked man and heresiarch. Against the onslaught of approaching military might and strident admonitions to stand down, the reform group formalized and publicized their program. This had been known as the 'four articles of Prague' and may be regarded as the agenda upon which all Hussites agreed. These articles first appeared in 1420 and called for free preaching in the land, communion in both kinds for all Christians, divesting of church wealth, and punishment of all serious sins.[192] Ambushed at Sudoměř in March 1420, Žižka had to fight his way out of a difficult situation but prevailed and in May defeated a crusader contingency along the Sázava River coming away with the crusade banners.[193] In the midst of these skirmishes the university masters in Prague declared it was lawful for the laity to take up arms in defense of the faith.[194] Hussite warriors took their religious values from the Hebrew Bible and the Maccabees.[195]

Neither side showed any hint of backing down. In the summer of 1420 Prague faced a formidable crusading army. According to contemporary sources no fewer than thirty-three nations lent support to the effort against the heretics.[196] Led by Žižka the popular forces repulsed the crusaders during a dramatic encounter on a hill just east of Prague. The eucharist played a role in the imperial defeat. One of the Hussite chroniclers related that during a moment of great crisis with Žižka himself in peril a priest came out of the city carrying the sacrament. When the crusaders saw him approaching they inexplicably took fright and in their hesitation and fear were routed by the men and women fighting with Jan Žižka.[197] The equally puzzling failure of Sigismund to mount an immediate counterattack caused the battle to go to the Czechs and the superior crusading forces retreated to their camps in defeat. Vítkov Hill, upon which the battle transpired, from that day to this has been called 'Žižka's Hill' though there are sources which tell us that following the battle many referred to it as the 'mountain of the chalice'.

Beaten but not whipped the crusaders struck again in hopes of dislodging the recalcitrant heretics. An effort to take Vyšehrad, a castle and fortress on the south side of Prague, failed. Royalists loyal to Sigismund were reduced to eating their own horses to stave off starvation and in the end surrendered.[198] The strength of the reform grew with each victory. Žižka proved to be a harsh and unrelenting promoter of the cause of reform. When repressive measures were implemented against the Hussite cause we read of Žižka marching to set things straight. Once more the sacrament of the altar played a role. On the road to Prachatice in November 1420 priests carrying the sacrament marched in front of the army. Once the walls of the rebellious town had been breached the body of Christ was carried inside with singing while the warriors of God under Žižka's command slaughtered the residents of the town to the number of several hundred.[199] This was not an isolated incident and atrocities perpetrated during the long years of war and revolution were carried out by crusader and Hussite alike.

Meanwhile, a concerted effort had unfolded aimed at turning the world upside down. The year 1419 marked crucial transition from ideas of reform associated with Jan Hus, Jakoubek and others, to a clearly articulated reformation. Perhaps more importantly for Hussite history the step from revolt to revolution took place. The mass gatherings and the defenestration of Prague provided two important phases of that step. Most of the crowd which gathered for the 22 July meeting ultimately dispersed and returned home. A nucleus remained and Táborite religion and society was formed. The people who gathered on the mountain composed an eschatological community shaped by biblical symbolism. In scripture, mountains often functioned as the place where events of revelation occur. On Mt. Sinai the law was given to the Israelites through Moses. Jesus went to the mountains to pray. From the mountains he proclaimed his message and sent his followers out to preach. In the Apocalypse a mountain formed the setting on which events leading to the glory of the messiah was revealed. Here the elect gathered around the Lamb of God who ruled with power from Mt. Zion. A perusal of the visions of the prophets reveal that the final events of the age would occur on mountains. In the sacred literature of Christians mountains are eschatological places. The Hussites who decided to name the place where they congregated, Mt. Tábor, thereby caused that place as well as the entire movement to come under the rubric of both a biblical and eschatological heritage.[200] Tábor came to denote more than the mountain upon which the first community was built. In a short period of time the popular mountaintop religion and the old Mt. Tábor of 1419 evolved into a fortified city which took the name Tábor. This Táborite community assumed the abandoned fortress of Hradiště. From its inception Tábor facilitated a religious, political and social revolution. To be a Táborite meant participating in the experience of the mountains. 'Henceforth, at Hradiště and Tábor there is nothing which is mine or thine. Rather, all things in the community shall be held in common for all time and no one is permitted to hold private property. The one who does commits sins mortally. No longer shall there be a reigning king or a ruling lord; for there shall be servitude no longer. All taxes and exactions shall cease and no one shall compel another to subjection. All shall be equal as brothers and sisters'. People thronged from across Bohemia and Moravia to the priests at Tábor. They sold their possessions, placed the proceeds at the feet of the Táborite leaders, and everything was shared in common, except women, and theoretically all people were equal. This communism, or community of goods, seemed to follow the pattern of early Christians outlined in the *Acts of the Apostles*. Community chests aimed at serving the faithful were established at Písek, Tábor, and elsewhere. A new social order had dawned. In theory, social divisions had been eliminated and social hierarchy mainly dissolved. Payment for rent and services was forbidden, personal property became common goods and those wishing to join Tábor were required to forfeit material wealth before entrance to the community could be allowed.[201] Implementing the fourth of the 'four articles', four-fifths of ecclesiastical Czech property became secularized.[202] Existing civil laws were disregarded. Debtors were released from former obligations inasmuch as the old lord-peasant relations were dissolved.

These measures threatened the stability of late medieval society which perceived itself as God-ordained. Even detractors of this radical religion of the hills were forced to admit that an ideal of sorts had been achieved. But there were problems. The community chests were not bottomless. The various prophecies of the end of the world failed to materialize and soon disenchantment set in. Anticipating trouble in April 1420 the community elected four military captains, among them Jan Žižka. This step represented another transition from pacifism to militarism. There were those at this stage who ceased to identify as Táborite. A notable here is Petr Chelčický. The armies which formed became known as the 'warriors of God'. By autumn the communist principles were at an end. Taxes were collected. Politically the country had been reduced to shambles.[203] The experiments with radical social change succeeded at Tábor for a time because there was no hindering force in the country powerful enough to divert the heretics. Konrad of Vechta, Archbishop of Prague became a Hussite and when he died in 1431 the see of Prague remained vacant until 1561. Military affairs kept Sigismund weakened and unable to address the Táborite question until it was too late. Doomed by its chiliasm the more radical aspects of the community ceased. A firm belief in the parousia negated any consideration of moving from consumption communism to production communism. The driving forces at Tábor were more theological and religious than social and economic.[204]

Violence begat violence and mass killing in eastern Bohemia by forces loyal to Sigismund counted casualties in the hundreds. Retribution followed.[205] This prompted a union of German bishops to form at the annual Reichstag in April 1421.[206] At the same time as the German bishops were mobilizing support for an anti-Hussite initiative, Archbishop Konrad of Prague defected from the Roman Church and 'turned to Satan' and became a Hussite.[207] In early June a convocation of the Bohemian estates met at Čáslav and the records from that meeting indicated quite clearly the depth and breadth of opposition to Sigismund, as the heir of the Czech crown, the strength of the Hussite movement, and the resolve to preserve reform by means of a provisional government. Among the delegates were Jan of Chlum, Hus' friend from Constance, Jan Žižka and his lieutenant Jan Roháč of Dubá. The diet affirmed the 'four articles' and expressly defied Sigismund.[208] Later sources provided interesting details about Žižka's military strategy and of the misfortune which claimed his eyesight but he continued as commander of the field armies.[209] The second crusade involved a protracted siege of the town of Žatec and involved 125,000 crusaders, though such numbers cannot be relied upon. Despite now being totally blind, Žižka showed up with his warriors and the crusaders were scattered.[210] Determined to try again a third crusade was preached against the Czechs and more battles took place. An important struggle for the town of Kutná Hora took place just before Christmas 1421. That event and its immediate aftermath turned the tide decisively against the crusade effort. Jan Žižka won an improbable victory at Kutná Hora forcing Sigismund to flee for his life while the crusaders suffered much disaster and defeat in the Sázava River Valley as Žižka's warriors pursued them relentlessly, striking them down in the name of God.[211]

Distressed at the lack of success in curbing the activities of the enemies of God, Pope Martin pressed for further military intervention and there are more than 500 letters from his office relating in one sense or another to the Hussite problem. It would be impossible to say that religious affairs in Bohemia were not on the pope's agenda. According to Martin all of the faithful, the church, and even God, were at risk on account of the Czech heretics. They had to be exterminated. This particular heresy, noted as 'disgusting', undermined law and society, overturned political institutions, and disrupted all of life. It was a 'mad disease', 'irrational grossness', a 'nefarious pestilence' and a 'befouling heresy'. The holy father begged Sigismund to eradicate it.[212] On 4 September 1422 the crusade banner was raised once more. A solemn liturgy sung at St. Sebald's Church in Nürnberg blessed the living cross against the heretics for their defeat and sent the crusaders on their way once more into the lands occupied by 'the vicious enemies of the cross'.[213] Jan Žižka drew up a military ordinance in the summer of 1423, a document which occupies an important place in the history of medieval European war.[214] In a solemn session on 8 November 1423 the Council of Pavia-Siena imposed an economic blockade on Bohemia in an attempt to bring even more pressure on the Hussites.[215] It seemed clear that the social implications of the reformist movement in Bohemia played some role in the repeated crusade efforts. On New Years' day 1424 the papal legate, Branda da Castiglione, Cardinal of Piacenza, addressed King Władysław Jagiełło of Poland: 'The purpose of my mission is for the glory of God, the cause of the faith and the church as well as the salvation of human society. A significant proportion of the heretics hold that all things should be held in common and that no tribute, tax or obedience should be given to a superior. This is an idea which would destroy civilization and abolish all government. They intend to destroy all human and divine right through force and it will happen that not even kings or princes in their own kingdoms and dominions, or even people in their own houses will be safe from their insolence. This terrible heresy not only attacks the faith and the church but it also, under inspiration of the Devil, makes war upon humanity in general, attacking and destroying those rights as well'.[216] Therefore Branda thought it useful to bring to bear the full force of the law with respect to heresy against the disobedient Czechs. Drawing on legislation from the Council of Vienne (1311–12), canon law, common law, and conciliar decrees up through the Council of Pavia-Siena, Branda declared war on the Hussites as public enemies.[217] Meanwhile the crusaders gathered for a third invasion which failed and at a decisive battle fought at Malešov on 7 June 1424 the blind general Žižka won yet again.[218] There were two important outcomes of the battle. First, it ended all domestic military opposition to the Hussites and it determined the course of Bohemian domestic history for the next ten years. As it turned out Malešov was Žižka's last stand. That autumn he died while on a campaign in eastern Bohemia and in due course the armies passed under the command of the priest Prokop Holý. This is noteworthy inasmuch as priests were excluded from military involvement by the 1420 decision of the university masters as well as by Hus.

Despite three defeats the new papal nuncio for the crusade, Cardinal Giordano Orsini, a veteran of the Council of Constance, wanted nothing to do with diplomacy and urged a new military offensive against the Bohemians.[219] Three days after that ill-advised plan, anti-Hussite forces went down to crushing defeat at the northern Czech town of Ústí on the Labe River. One account of the carnage portrayed the fallen Germans as lying like sheaves of grain in the time of harvest all the way from Ústí to the mountains of Meißen. On account of the great slaughter of men and horses, reports claimed the stream flowing through Ústí turned red and the stacks of bones which remained unburied on the battlefield 'lie there to this day'.[220] The German Reichstag organized further ventures in a rather ingenious plan for a simultaneous four-pronged invasion of Bohemia.[221] By 1427 Henry Beaufort of England was appointed papal legate and nuncio for the fourth crusade. Only two of the four proposed armies materialized. The confrontation took place at Stříbro. The result was unmitigated catastrophe once again for the crusaders. Foolishly they attempted to replicate Hussite military strategy developed by Žižka. This proved unsuccessful. By the time Beaufort arrived the crusaders were in full retreat. Unable to avert their headlong flight out of Bohemia, Beaufort tore the imperial banner to pieces and threw it to the ground. Hussite warriors butchered crusaders through the Šumava (Bohemian forest) into the upper Palatinate. One chronicle placed the number of dead at the impossible figure of 100,000. Roused, Prokop Holý turned his attention to the nearby royalist stronghold of Tachov. Using siege warfare and incendiary missiles Prokop took the city in less than a week.[222] A war reporter lamenting on the tragedy proposed that perhaps if as many prostitutes as military men had been dispatched to Bohemia they would have prevailed.[223] The assumption being that the Hussites were in general lewd fellows of the baser sort. Martin V could not hold back his chagrin at the 'disgraceful flight' of the crusade armies.[224] Sigismund, who had not been involved, encouraged Beaufort to persevere in putting down the Hussites.[225] Plenty of saber-rattling could be heard, meetings convened, funding proposals advanced, petitions for continued support, and repeated warnings about the dire threat of the Czech heresy and religious practice continued to reverberate through Europe, especially at Rome and within the Holy Roman Empire. An initial attempt at diplomacy convened at Bratislava in April 1429. Sigismund attended as did the 'iron bishop' Jan Železný, who by this time had been elevated to the archbishopric of Esztergom [Gran], Philip the Good of Burgundy, along with a number of other dignitaries.[226] The former English Wyclifite-turned Hussite, Peter Payne delivered a speech which greatly annoyed Sigismund especially as Payne described Jesus Christ as the invincible Prague warrior! Payne admonished Sigismund to put aside the futility of trying to defeat divine truth. Insinuating that the emperor perhaps belonged amongst the unjust rulers who would perish, Payne suggested the emperor undergo some self-examination. He went so far as to call Sigismund 'foolish'. He finished off with the popular Hussite slogan 'truth conquers all'.[227]

The effort at diplomatic resolution failed miserably. So upset and aggravated by the impertinent comments made by Peter Payne, the emperor urged the crusaders to invade Bohemia yet again with the intent of annihilating the Hussites.[228] While the empire sought adequate backing for the renewed crusade from the French, English, Hanseatic League, and other principalities, the Hussites elected to take the war to the enemy. Under the new policies of Prokop Holý, Hussite armies expanded their military portfolio and no longer waged defensive warfare only, which had been Žižka's forté. After 1426 and the battle at Ústí when Prokop assumed the mantle of supreme commander, his policy had been to strengthen the Czech borders by waging warfare outside of Bohemia. During the winter of 1426/7 the Hussites invaded Silesia and Austria. In March 1427 a Táborite army commanded by Prokop defeated Austrian forces at Zwettl, an Austrian town halfway between České Budějovice and Vienna. Between 1428 and 1434 there were three separate Hussite invasions into the Duchy of Silesia in retaliation for previous anti-Hussite military action. The heretics burned churches, rectories, taverns and the estates of barons as well as monasteries. The author of the chronicle of St Mary's monastery on the Sand, Abbot Joss von Ziegenthal, blamed the Hussites for the famine and shortages in the Duchy of Wrocław in 1433/4. From 1429 to 1433 the Hussites fought many times outside Bohemia. The climax of these 'magnificent rides' came in late 1429 and early 1430 under Prokop's command. Saxony, Meißen, Upper and Lower Lusatia were overrun. Five armies consisting of 40,000 infantry, 4,000 cavalry and 3,000 battle wagons were involved. Grimma, Leipzig, Altenburg, Plavno, Bayreuth, the lands of the Hohenzollerns and the bishoprics of Bamberg, Kulmbach and Bayreuth seemed in danger as did Nürnberg. Friedrich of Brandenburg hastily met with Hussite leaders at Beheimstein Castle, three miles from Nürnberg, on 11 February 1430 and negotiated a temporary truce.[229] Orphan armies under the command of Prokůpek went into Moravia and Slovakia and fought against Hungarian forces at Trnava in March 1430. During the fierce battle Windecke tells us 2,000 Hussites were killed and 'nearly 6,000 Christians. May God have mercy on us'.[230] Four crusades against the heretics had accomplished little beyond inadvertently enabling the Hussites to strengthen their borders. Now the theatre of war expanded threatening the empire. It appeared crusade strategy had backfired.

On new years' day 1431, and among his last acts after fourteen years as pope, Martin V appointed Cardinal Guiliano Cesarini as papal legate to lead a fifth crusade against the Czechs. Martin died on 20 February. Less than a month later Cesarini outlined his proposal to the emperor and the Reichstag in session at Nürnberg. Eschewing diplomatic options Cesarini embarked upon a three month campaign preaching the cross.[231] He made the fatal mistake of assuming little could be expected of an illiterate peasant army.[232] On 14 August a large crusader army approached the western Bohemian town of Domažlice. Prokop and the warriors of God marched out to meet them. There are accounts which say that when the crusaders heard the approaching Hussites singing they took fright and in a panic fled losing all but thirty of their 4,000 wagons. Cesarini escaped through the forest incognito having lost his robes, gold cross, cardinal's hat, and the crusade bull naming him crusade legate. He reported to Sigismund that the only hope for peace had to be achieved through non-military options.[233] Prokop's policies continued to be followed and accounts of Hussite armies carrying out sorties into Moravia, Silesia, Lusatia, Austria and Hungary are extant.[234]

As the fifth crusade organized against the resilient Bohemians, the ecumenical Council of Basel, on the authority of Martin V convened. Just prior to death Martin appointed Cesarini to act as president of the council. In an unprecedented move the Hussites were invited to attend the Council.[235] The gesture was quite extraordinary for nowhere else in the history of the western church do we find evidence of condemned heretics being invited to an international platform as equals. The Czechs were not flattered and drove a more difficult bargain arguing for pre-conference terms upon which they would appear and by which the case would be settled. On 18 May 1432 at the western Czech town of Cheb an agreement was hammered out to which both sides agreed. This agreement is known as the 'Cheb Judge', or the basis for discussion at the Council of Basel.[236] The invitation to Basel, the 'Cheb Judge', and the actual arrival of the Hussites at the Council were events of significance in ecclesiastical history and all three can be accounted for as a result of the strength of Hussitism and the failure of the church and empire to suppress the movement.[237] The three months ended without a clear mandate and we know of plans for a sixth crusade.[238] Those plans never got off the ground though it does indicate there were still those who considered military operations a viable option.

Meanwhile, Hussite armies marched throughout Great Poland and Prussia and eventually reached the Baltic Sea.[239] That was 4 September 1433. It marked the last foray into foreign territory. Politics prevailed over military power and by the end of 1433 the first draft of a compromise aimed at ending the protracted crusade reached agreement and representatives of the Council signed off as did leaders of the major Hussite factions. The following spring longstanding bickering and factionalism revived the quarrels Jan Žižka had so adroitly quelled a decade earlier. A decisive battle between Czechs near the village of Lipany on 30 May 1434 accomplished what five imperial crusades had failed to achieve: the virtual end of the Hussite field armies.[240] A later account reported that the legendary commander Prokop Holý killed many of his enemies and nearly saved the day. However, betrayed at last and 'surrounded by a great number of horsemen he was hit by a stray arrow and fell wearied with conquering, rather than conquered himself. Like him, the other Prokop, who as mentioned previously was called "the smaller" [Prokůpek], fought bravely in the same battle and was killed. This was the end of the two most harmful and heinous monsters. Thus the previously undefeated army of criminal Táborites and Orphans were defeated and annihilated'.[241] One of those who escaped was Žižka's former lieutenant Jan Roháč of Dubá. He had no intention of submitting to Sigismund and thus a final short chapter to the revolution had to be played out. For three years Roháč opposed the emperor and refused to stand down. With a remnant of warriors from the days of Žižka and Prokop a final stand was taken at an old fortress near Kutná Hora. After a protracted siege Roháč's fortress called Sión fell and the revolution ended. Roháč and his men who survived the fighting were arrested. Roháč refused to even look upon the despised emperor even though he endured torture so terrible his intestines fell out. In a great display of imperial might Roháč and his men were hanged in the Old Town Square of Prague on a three-story gallows.[242] Three months after the execution of the Sión garrison Sigismund died attempting to get back to Hungary away from the intense hatred which fulminated against him in Bohemia by the followers of Jan Hus.

Hussitism by no means ended with the cessation of military activities. The original and important work and ideas of Petr Chelčický, a Táborite separatist, as early as the 1420s, defined the social dimensions of Hussitism as rejection of medieval society with its class divisions.[243] That idea prevailed to some extent within the communities of the Unitas Fratrum (Unity of Brethren), a Hussite group forming in the 1450s. The more theologically conservative and traditional Utraquist Church was dominated to some extent by Jan Rokycana until his death in 1471 and along the way Bohemia even had its own Hussite king in the person of Jiří of Poděbrady. The study of reformed religion after Basel and Lipany must necessarily deal with the political history of Bohemia. Hussite ideas proved persuasive enough to attract a majority of the population.[244] The legacy of Hus continued to be appropriated and underwent several transmutations. For example it is easy to overlook the influence Hus exerted on the ideas of the Unitas Fratrum. Pope Pius II repealed the Compactata of Basel on 31 March 1462 calling the agreement null and void, an act some have labeled a felony.[245] Thirteen months later Pius issued a bull repudiating conciliar theory. 'Accept Pius, reject Aeneas' while concluding 'we have recognized our mistake, we came to Rome, we have cast aside the doctrines of Basel'.[246] The 'compacts' had withdrawn the excommunication of Bohemia as an heretical nation. Few in Bohemia seem to have taken any special note of Pius. The agreements reached at Basel became part and parcel of the law of the Kingdom of Bohemia. Every ruler from Sigismund to Maximilian II (†1576) officially affirmed the binding nature of the agreements. Not until 1567 was it removed from the royal confirmation oath. Religious toleration was achieved to some extent by the 'Peace of Kutná Hora' in 1485.[247] A common religious confession was achieved in 1575 and despite the rise of the Lutheran and Calvinist reformations it is possible to argue that the Hussite tradition, broadly speaking, maintained a unique identity.[248] By 1596 the vernacular Bible of Kralice appeared and in 1609 the 'letter of majesty' was issued by Emperor Rudolf II affirming the right of the Hussite traditions to exist.[249] Meanwhile the practice of utraquism could be found not only in Bohemia, Moravia, Austria, Hungary, Silesia, Sweden, but throughout the German lands, and elsewhere. Permission for the lay chalice was gradually withdrawn country by country. Bohemia was the last.[250]

The traditions of Czech reformed religious practice encountered a fatal setback at the Battle of the White Mountain outside Prague on 8 November 1620. Defeat was total.[251] The revolutionaries were summarily executed on the same spot where Žižka's old cohort Jan Roháč had been hanged nearly 200 years earlier. Upon the authority of Pope Gregory XV the practice of utraquism was prohibited. Those disobedient were arrested and incarcerated. The provisions of the 'letter of majesty' were nullified, the document itself slashed crossways with a knife. The 'Peace of Kutná Hora' no longer had legal force. The gilded chalice which Rokycana had set within a niche on the Týn Church in Prague was removed under the cover of a winter night (17 January 1623) in an act symbolic of the suppression of the Hussite spirit and reform, and especially of Utraquist religious practice. In a definite triumph of the Counter Reformation, Roman Catholicism became the sole state religion in the Kingdom of Bohemia.[252] In an irony of religious history, Hussitism was outlawed in Bohemia while Judaism retained official recognition. The enforced re-Catholicizing of Bohemia drove the resisting Hussite remnant underground or into exile. The life and activities of Jan Amos Komenský [Comenius] and the Moravian Brethren form the final chapters.

9

COMMEMORATION

Memory and myth, history and hagiography inevitably followed the lives of the martyrs. Stories about Hus as a saint were sometimes more hagiographical than historical and the former can render the latter sterile. Jan Hus has always aroused deep sentiment. An anonymous Latin poem may have declared Hus deceived the Czechs but he remained a hero to others.[1] On one hand he was considered a heretic and martyr while on the other a reformer of theology and ethics. The two portraits must be fused. There is the Hus of history and the Hus of myth.[2] Some took the view the sentence of the Council of Constance remanding Hus to the stake to be burned to death was also condemnation to the eternal sufferings of hell for corrupting the true faith and such a fate was justified.[3] An early history of Bohemia described it thus.

> When the representatives of the great synod recognized the intractability and inflexibility of these cursed fellows [Hus and Jerome], they came to the conclusion that the rotten limbs of the Church that could not be cured must be cut off so as not to infect the whole body. In a session of the fathers a verdict was brought in saying that those who reject the teaching of the Church should be burned to death. At first Jan was burned to death. Jerome was then for a long time kept in prison, and when he would not be reasonable he received the same punishment. Both of them endured death even-minded and rushed to the stake as if they were invited to a feast, not even making a sound, which could be a sign of their anguish. When the flames took hold of them they sang hymns which the flames and crackling of fire could hardly deafen. None of the philosophers is said to have gone through death so bravely like these endured burning to death.[4]

Other reports declared Hus possessed by Satan[5] or derisively declared 'the fat goose had been fried at Constance'.[6] Inside Bohemia another portrait emerged praising Hus as a man of probity and honor.[7] From many contemporary sources we learn that the death of Hus produced an immediate response in Prague. As soon as word reached the capital concerning the execution of Hus and Jerome we are told their sympathizers gathered and agreed that an annual commemoration should be observed.[8] This plan of action found immediate implementation followed by predictable protests. In December 1416 the canons of Olomouc in Moravia filed a formal complaint with the Council of Constance alleging Hus had been elevated above the traditional saints of the church and beyond this was being celebrated liturgically in churches. According to the Olomouc canons, renegade priests convened divine worship before crowds of people honoring Hus and Jerome as though these men were faithful Christians when in fact both had been denounced, convicted and condemned as heretics. Ostensibly liturgical feasts were celebrated and songs sung lauding Hus as a martyr with direct comparisons with St. Laurence and the canons further alleged that Hus appeared more significant to these Czechs than even St. Peter.[9] Clearly the canons were scandalized and their outrage must surely have reflected a wider opinion. Writing a generation later Aeneas Sylvius repeated the same theme.[10] The Moravian priests gave the Council specific information on the liturgical aspects of the celebration of Hus by claiming that Hus and Jerome were being inserted into the *Gaudeamus*, an adaptable introit for use on saints' days.[11] The rhymed composition 'Everyone listen, adults and children' asserted that certain people would not observe holy days but honored Jan Hus as a saint.[12] We can now be assured the allegation was true. Liturgical manuscripts in Prague have been shown to have been altered from a celebration of the Common of the Virgins to a 'festive celebration of the holy martyrs Jan Hus and Jerome'.[13] The Hus commemoration was denounced by the Olomouc canons as a great and terrible horror against the catholic faith.[14]

The Council indeed considered the Hus commemoration inappropriate. In February 1418 the synod at Constance published a series of twenty-four resolutions against Hussites. Among that list number seventeen addressed in part the liturgical celebration of Hus. '. . . All of the songs introduced to the detriment of the sacred Council and of catholic men of whatever state who resisted the Wyclifites and the Hussites, or the songs which praise Jan Hus and Jerome, the condemned heretics, are forbidden under the heaviest penalty which is to be decided'.[15] By implication Pope Martin V declared that hymnody and liturgy were not to be put to use in the service of remembering Hus. The Council made its will explicit to Sigismund concerning the 'dangerous scandal', 'error' and 'heresy' confronting the faithful on account of Hus. Having been slain, Hus and Jerome now presented a perfidious problem. Their veneration simply had to stop.[16] These injunctions did nothing to stall the development of Hus evolving into a saint of the more conservative Hussite church and being featured in commemoration events and his memory coming under increased veneration. What is apparent is a gradual but steady development of the liturgical celebration of Hus from 1416 on. Much of the evidence for this development and tradition was lost during the ravages of the Counter Reformation in the seventeenth century. However there is not an insubstantial catalogue of extant texts and others continue to emerge.[17] Despite the efforts of some scholars to coax Hus into the role as a liturgical reformer it now seems clear this was not true at least in any substantial or meaningful sense. Hus' chief contribution to a liturgical renaissance in the medieval Bohemian church came about through his death.[18] Once martyred, as his followers conceived his death, he became 'Master Jan Hus of blessed memory' and a man of 'holy memory'.[19] Meanwhile reports continued to filter to the Council of the activities of the recalcitrant Hussites including the ongoing veneration of Hus and Jerome as saints. This concern can be located in judicial citations with reference to events in 1416 which in context even further corroborated the complaint filed by the canons of Olomouc.[20] In sympathetic areas within the Bohemian lands Hus became a popular saint almost immediately entering the liturgical life of the church and occupying an important place in Czech popular piety. By implication, Sigismund possessed a brief from the Latin Church to put an end to the Hus veneration. Since he had been entrusted with the power to act militarily against the Czechs, should it come to that, and since the liturgical commemoration of Hus had been identified among the errors and objectionable practices in Hussite Prague and elsewhere, that specific matter remained at issue for the church. Before he could act Hussite sympathizers involved Sigismund in their own schemes. Writing from the royal house in Buda the emperor was assigned the authorship of a satirical letter addressed to the magistrates of the Old and New Towns of Prague in 1419 sarcastically encouraging them to persevere in the heretical sacrament. Sigismund especially commended the Hussites for their veneration of Jan Hus. 'You have entered into the list of saints Jan Hus and Jerome and some lay people, murdered as you insist for the law of Christ, and you celebrate ostentatiously their day, neglecting the days of the other saints'.[21] Facetiously the emperor claimed he wished to be instructed in such faith. The letter constituted politically motivated propaganda.[22] The veneration of Hus can be documented well outside the precincts of Prague. We know of sermons in Poland wherein preachers went to some lengths to dissuade their hearers of the saintliness of Hus.[23] In 1458 Matthäus Hagen went to the stake in the German town of Stettin on charges which included claiming Hus as a saint.[24] In the same year utraquist heretics in the German territories of Pomerania and Brandenburg were found cultivating religious practices which included the veneration of Hus as a saint in heaven.[25] It is doubtful Hus would have approved of such practices given his theology of worship.[26] Among the prolific anti-Sigismund polemical literature we find Hus referred to as 'pious', 'virtuous', 'loyal to the truth', a 'preacher of truth', and described as 'one of God's valuable priests'.[27]

We know of sermons in which Hus is referred to as a saint.[28] This practice persisted despite the Council of Constance ruling that anyone preaching, teaching or defending Hus, or regarding him a saint would be considered heretical and subject to the appropriate punishment.[29] Jakoubek of Stříbro's Bethlehem Chapel sermon in 1417/8 cannot be regarded as an anomaly and surely there were numerous others like it.[30] Jan Želivský invoked the *passio* and martyrdom of Hus on many occasions from the pulpit of Our Lady of the Snows in the New Town.[31] The death of Hus was clearly observed in some instances but there was definite evidence he was celebrated also as a saint. It was this celebration which caused the greater scandal. Records of Hus' *passio* were read publicly from the first anniversary of his death with a number of contemporary attestations. These included accounts of Abbot Štěpán of Dolany and Nicholas of Tempelfeld, canon of the cathedral chapter in Breslau [Wrocław]. The latter asserted that Czechs canonized Hus and celebrated his feast on 6 July according to very strict rules. Both Štěpán and Nicholas remained robust enemies of Hus and his followers.[32] This underscored the evidence which came to the indignant attention of the canons of Olomouc. The commemoration of Hus served many purposes from the time of its inauguration throughout the course of subsequent history and the changeable historiographical depiction of Hus remained one of the topics of considerable interest in the religious history of Bohemia.[33] The fact that the medieval cult of the saints had not, and was not, repudiated by the conservative Hussites, allowed the assimilation of Hus to occur liturgically. Jan Rokycana made the case for the continued liturgical invocation of the saints and the practice prevailed.[34] The damned and defeated heretic at Constance underwent transformation from sinner to saint, from hell to heaven. During the ceremony of degradation at Constance when Hus was defrocked from the priesthood he had a paper crown depicting demons placed on his head as the bishops declared his soul forfeit to the Devil. Hus was reported to have declared that Christ wore a heavier and more terrible crown of thorns even though he was innocent. Hus admitted his own sins and accepted with gladness the crown of vilification for the name and truth of Christ.[35] The crown of thorns worn by Christ became the crown of shame worn by Hus. The apotheosis of Jan Hus as conceived in the Litoměřice Gradual (see chapter ten) depicted in graphical detail the scenario outlined by Petr Mladoňovice.[36]

In the immediate Hussite tradition none of his followers accepted that Hus' death constituted anything but gross injustice. A 1431 manifesto published, hyperbolically, on behalf of the entire Czech land, insisted Hus had not been convicted on the basis of scripture but rather had been subjected to 'wanton and unrighteous violence' and the perpetrators would eventually be called to account at the judgment seat of God.[37] The demise of Hus can be traced indubitably to his critique of wicked clerics whom he embarrassed to such extent they determined to have him destroyed.[38] The motivation of malice succeeded. Hus' enemies like Michael de Causis must have seemed confident they had seen the end of the troublesome Prague priest. As we have seen, his virtual resurrection in the liturgical life of the Bohemia church caused no small dissension. Of course the liturgical celebration of Hus would not have been found at the Hussite community of Tábor or among their allies in eastern Bohemia or later among the Unity of the Brethren. It is practically a certainty that the inclusion of Hus in liturgy can be located only among the conservatives and after 1437 those communities which are more precisely called Utraquists. Therefore the commemoration of Hus was not a factor at Tábor or among the radical brotherhoods. Moreover it is strange that an important source of Hussite history made not a single reference to the celebration of Jan Hus in the entire fifteenth century.[39]

No one has done more to illuminate the scope and significance of the liturgical commemoration of Jan Hus than David Holeton. His researches and publications on this subject span three decades and the results are as revealing as they are important. Over a 200 year period from Hus' death until the suppression of the Hussite tradition during the Thirty Years' War it is possible to discover liturgical evidence for the presence of the feast of Jan Hus for the eucharist and the office. Within this body of manuscripts Holeton has drawn attention to introits and graduals written specifically for the feast of Hus. In the introit *In bonitate* Hus became the new Phineas atoning for the sins of the people so that God established a covenantal relation through him.[40] In the book of Numbers in the Hebrew Bible, Phineas presented as the grandson of Aaron, stood up for the law of God and averted a disaster by plague. God made a covenant with Phineas declaring that among all of the sons of Israel he was the only one who exhibited the same zeal for righteousness. This narrative was picked up in the history of the Maccabean revolt and the perpetual priesthood in Israel was linked to Phineas and his zeal for God's law. In these liturgical texts the virtues of Jan Hus were praised. He was referred to as 'teacher', 'protector of truth', 'good shepherd', 'consoler of the hopeless', 'light of the Czech people', and the 'light of Bohemia'.[41] With language like this it is not surprising to find the liturgical prose *Rex regum* drawing parallels between the lives and passions of Hus and Christ. The indignation of the Council of Constance, the canons of Olomouc, and Aeneas Sylvius are quite understandable. In some cases the *passio* of Hus, either accounts of his death and/or letters written by him from the Constance prison, were added to the feast of Hus.[42] The Sobotka Gradual is one liturgical book which makes an unequivocal statement about the esteem Hus had come to enjoy in the life of the Czech people.[43] In the office for the feast of Hus, which will be considered below, this same sense of union between the martyrs and the Czech nation can be seen.[44] During divine worship the faithful can and do sing 'O happy Constance' because the Council sent to heaven those who would serve as intercessors of divine grace before God in order to lead the faithful to heaven and in the meanwhile to pray to Christ for the salvation of the people. The Alleluia *Letetur in domino* picked up the same theme while the Alleluia *O felix Bohemia* contrasted the wolves of Constance with the lamb Hus who became a friend of God reinforcing the Christian paradox that in losing one's life eternal life is gained.[45] Thus in the prose *Clericalis turma* Hus can be found among the congregation of all those who shared in the victory of Christ along with all the saints and martyrs and the faithful Czechs who fought a good fight right up to the finish, who remained resolute on behalf of the law of God, and who followed unto death the martyrs who died for truth at Constance. Hus was joined with the noble army of all Christian martyrs who shed their blood and in doing so discovered the fountain of everlasting life. Therefore all Christians should rejoice in the glory of the 'rose-colored martyrs', the victorious Bohemian faithful, who fought to the finish. These were the warriors who stood firm, zealous for the law of Christ and in the name of the suffering Christ washed their clothes in the blood of eternal life.[46] The prose *O quam per contrarium* took the unhappy events of Constance and related them to the similarly unhappy events in the trial and passion of Jesus.[47] These aspects of the liturgical celebration of Jan Hus make it abundantly clear that he belonged to the great cloud of witnesses where he was venerated as the faithful Czechs remember him. 'A Christian of heroic character whose transparent goodness attracted to him followers of all classes and degrees and whose death for the renewal of the church won him the reverent devotion of succeeding generations'.[48] That identification of Hus with Jesus is not uncommon. Early sources deliberately placed Hus in a Christ context by calling the place of execution in Constance Calvary and presenting Hus as the ultimate martyr; a virtual saint.[49] The liturgical witnesses to the veneration of Hus can be found in at least a dozen kyriale or graduale from the fifteenth and sixteenth centuries which contain the feast of Hus. The celebration of the feast of St. Jan Hus, commemorated on the day of his death, 6 July, can be found added to traditional religious texts with an amendment adding the name 'Jan Hus'.[50] Other examples reveal the Hus feast written into the calendar for 6 July and Czech translations of the propers.[51] An examination of the liturgical sources reveal significant differences in the titles for the feast in the kyriale and graduale. 'Holy Jan Hus', the 'blessed martyr Jan Hus', 'St. Jan Hus', the 'glorious martyr Jan Hus' are among the variants. It would seem evident that the feast of Hus gained considerable currency and widespread popularity based on the fact alone that the propers for the feast existed both in the traditional ecclesiastical Latin and in the vernacular Czech.[52] Of course extant songs about Hus were both liturgical and secular.[53] The celebration of Hus differed from that of other saints insofar as no miracles were attributed to him, he did not appear in visions and there were no records of pilgrimages to his place of birth.[54] Between 1490 and 1510 two utraquist liturgical books were produced each containing one sequence for the feast of Hus.[55]

It is clear that upon examination of the texts one discovers a combination of 'historical, theological, hagiographical, polemical and euchological' elements which present a commemorative representation of Master Jan Hus.[56] Aspects of the liturgical celebration of Hus sometimes provided no specific information about Hus and remained general in terms of martyrs for the faith. In the various *prosae* this is not the case. A summary, partisan though it is, comes out clearly in the *Rex regum*. Hus died at Constance but his life and ministry in Prague were then alluded to as well as the events leading him from Bethlehem Chapel to the Council. This summary provided the worshiper with an intentional biographical survey of the martyr's life. Hus appeared as a godly priest committed to Christ and his life became an example of the way of truth. Characterized as a godly lamb, Hus went to Constance but was seized by the enemies of God. Hus bravely drank the cup of suffering. The focus, however, remained the drama of the stake. Degraded from his priestly office he was made to wear a blasphemous crown. There is no doubt that deliberate parallels were drawn between the life of Hus and the life of Christ. In synopsis: both drank the cup offered to them, both were innocent but found guilty, both endured denunciation, both were mocked, both were made to wear crowns of opprobrium, and both were killed. In Christian theology, Jesus became the lamb of God who took away the sins of the world. Jan Hus became another lamb of God designed to bear the sins of the Bohemian people. Both men ultimately were vindicated by God irrespective of their judicial condemnation. The forgiveness of sin was a repeated liturgical motif and Jan Hus the 'glorious preacher and blessed martyr' was held up in hopes of the unity of all believers. At the last judgment everyone would behold Hus wearing the martyrs' crown.[57] This idea was touched upon in a Jewish account of events at the Council of

Constance wherein the *passio* and death of Hus were spoken of as a sanctifying of the divine name. Hus died for the cause of Christ and his death was holy.[58]

The canonization of Jan Hus within the liturgically conservative communities of Hussite religion contained further witnesses within fifteenth-century manuscript evidence. We find amendments changing texts from 'St. John' to 'St Jan Hus'.[59] Other texts celebrated 'holy Jan Hus' moving through the components of the liturgy to a musical setting for the *passio* of Hus followed by a collect for the feast of Hus before concluding with the 'glorious blessed martyr Jan'.[60] In some graduals, the office text for the martyrs was dedicated to 'St. Jan Hus'.[61] Utraquist kancionals [hymn books] sometimes made quite detailed references to 'St Jan Hus' including songs and repeated citations.[62] All Utraquist books made between 1510 and 1537 had proper chants for Hus. Between 1539 and 1620 there were at least sixty-six more books produced, fifty-eight of them in Czech, and almost all of these liturgical books had proper chants and one or more sequences for Hus and the Bohemian martyrs.[63]

During the Middle Ages, the divine office functioned as a means of fulfilling the biblical injunction to pray at all times. In the development of the medieval liturgy this constant praying became incorporated into a series of services observed at set times throughout the course of the day and night. In this liturgy of the hours, prayer was arranged specifically for liturgical use and that configuration became known as the divine office. The office could be utilized apart from formal liturgy and in certain circumstances might be observed privately. Ordinarily the office remained part of the liturgy with a canonical form consisting of a collection of texts which were recited or chanted at the set times of the day and most often by a community. Up until the 1980s it appeared that the office material for the liturgical commemoration of Jan Hus was no longer extant. Mutilated texts suggested the prior existence of the office.[64] The question was settled definitively and the lacuna bridged when the liturgical scholar David Holeton discovered among the manuscripts in a Hungarian library a Utraquist antiphonary containing the office for the feast of Jan Hus and the Bohemian martyrs.[65] This discovery demonstrated conclusively that an office had been composed and had existed for the liturgical celebration of the feast of Jan Hus. This consisted of First Vespers, Matins and Second Vespers. These were sung regularly by Hussites in connection with the major religious feasts. This office represents the most extensive independent collection of liturgical texts for Hus.[66] In these texts we find reference to Constance and the steadfast faith of Jan Hus which is connected to the other martyrs who suffered the torments of fire, torture, being hurled into mine shafts, and drowning in defense of the truth of the law of God. Now all of these having ascended to God interceded with Christ on behalf of the faithful still on earth. The faithful, singing the office, raised their voices in praise to God for the faithfulness of all the Bohemian martyrs. God was worshiped on account of Jan Hus who was called a 'precious martyr of Christ' who died in the faith of Christ having hope in God. The same was said of Jerome and the other martyrs. Their faith became cause for joy in the Bohemian land and Hus as the teacher of truth brought light to the world. Some of the Latin songs associated with the feast of Hus had polemical overtones and these became quite popular in vernacular renditions.[67] The popularity and enduring value of certain aspects of the Hus commemoration persisted through the Counter Reformation period where we learn that a comprehensive effort to convert this Utraquist-Hussite hymnody into an orthodox form took place.[68] Previously it was held by scholars from Novotný on, that a period of re-Latinization took place during which time liturgical texts which previously existed only in Czech were reintroduced in Latin form. That idea persisted into the 1990s but is now being abandoned with leading interpreters suggesting Novotný's observations of liturgical development are suspect inasmuch as they offer speculation without evidence and conclusions which cannot be sustained by the emerging corpus of liturgical sources.

Further examination of the liturgical sources of Hussite history make clear the Hus commemoration broadened to include Jerome of Prague as well as the numerous, nameless others who fell during the crusading period in defense of the chalice and a commitment to the memory of Jan Hus. Illustrations appeared in liturgical manuscripts showing the mass execution of Hussites in the shafts of the silver mines at Kutná Hora. Chroniclers verified that these atrocities did occur.[69] Czech chroniclers related that in 1492 the Kutná Hora silver mines were reopened and human remains were found. These included Jan Chůdek the priest of Kouřim and all of these were numbered among the faithful and came to be included in the noble army of the Bohemian martyrs.[70] It has been alleged that Jan Žižka and Michael Polák, martyred in 1480, also joined the panoply of Bohemian martyrs.[71] There is no liturgical evidence to include Žižka even though we know his image was painted on banners and carried about reverently by the armies of the radical brotherhoods.[72] Fifteenth-century sources claimed Žižka was venerated as a saint. 'The Táborites, who otherwise disliked images, painted above the town gate a picture of Žižka and an angel holding a chalice in his hand. Every year a mass is celebrated to honor Žižka'.[73] We know nothing of masses for Žižka. The sixteenth-century polemicist Johannes Cochlaeus repeated the claim that Žižka was venerated.[74] The old warrior of God did appear in heaven along with Jan Hus and the heavenly hosts but this also does not indicate liturgical commemoration.[75] Žižka does turn up iconographically in one liturgical source. I am unaware of comment on this by liturgical scholars.[76] As for Michael Polák, at one stage there did not appear to be evidence either but more recently he appears to be included in the liturgical celebration of the Czech martyrs.[77] And there were others, including Marta of Poříčí who went to the stake in 1527 along with a wooden chalice.[78] The argument has been advanced that the inclusion of the general Hussite martyrs likely did not begin prior to the 1430s.[79] That may well be the case but there are earlier texts, like the satirical letter of Sigismund noted above, which alleged that Hussites added to the list of saints the names of 'Jan Hus and Jerome and some lay people'. In evaluating the significance of the feast of Jan Hus some interpreters work from the principle enumerated formally in the fifth century by Prosper of Aquitaine that the law of prayer is the law of belief. David Holeton believes *lex orandi, lex credendi* provides a useable key for understanding the place of the Hus commemoration in the life of the Bohemian church.[80] An equally strong and valid case may also be made for inverting Prosper's dictum and arguing the 'law of belief is the law of prayer.'

It seems likely the official church feared the possibility of an influential posthumous Hus. Great care was taken to eradicate all traces of him at Constance. All items belonging to Hus were carefully burned and the ashes thrown into the Rhine River.[81] Evidently the same procedure attended the execution of Jerome. 'The ashes of those burned to death were thrown into a lake so that the Czechs could not get hold of them. Their disciples took soil from the place where the stake was and brought it as a relic with them to their homeland. Jan [Hus] and Jerome [of Prague] enjoyed reverence as martyrs and were considered no less important than Peter and Paul to the Romans'.[82] That assertion had basis in reports thirty years earlier. Ludolf of Żagan, abbot of an Augustinian house in Silesia, noted in disgust that certain people regarded Hus as a prophet and their apostle.[83] During the time he spent in the vicariate of Bosnia between 1436 and 1440, the inquisitor Giacomo della Marca [James of the Marches] filed a report in which he declared that suspected heretics in that area also venerated Hus considering him holy and believed those who condemned Hus were really false Christians and ought to be punished.[84] In Poland, there were people who admitted belonging to the 'sect' or 'heresy' of Jan Hus.[85]

The memory of Hus remained green throughout the sixteenth century reformations which engulfed much of Europe. During the 1520s more than twenty publications about Hus appeared. I have collected numerous allusions to the respect accorded Hus in the sixteenth century especially by Luther but also extending to other parts of Europe including England.[86] Luther regularly referred to Hus as a 'saint', a 'holy martyr', a 'saintly man of God', and a man of Christian probity. The language of holiness and sainthood can be found regularly and with ease among many reformation communities when speaking of Hus. Certainly there was a tendency on the part of reformers to justify their activities with reference to Christian history and in many cases uses were made of earlier figures which were historically indefensible. Luther's suggestion that he and his followers were in reality 'Hussites' had no more validity than his declaration that Augustine and St. Paul had been proleptic followers of Hus too! Not only did Luther overemphasize his commonality with Hus he was quite wrong about it.[87] Hus did not prophesy about Luther. The legend of the Bohemian goose and the Saxon swan served theological purposes and while containing considerable hagiographical significance are historically meaningless in terms of Hus.[88] Notwithstanding, Luther had visitors inquiring about the so-called Hus prophecy and wondering if Luther was the predicted swan.[89] What remained important was that Hus became a functional saint for many Protestants and an archetypal heretic in the hands of those loyal to the official church. For example Duke George of Saxony wrote an alarmed letter in 1525 in which he described Luther's reforms as a revived Hus inspired by Satan.[90] Others in the tradition of Štěpán Páleč considered Hus the most dangerous and harmful man ever to afflict the church.[91] Hus turned up in a pseudo-liturgical context in a parody of the *Te Deum* by the Danish Carmelite Povl Helgesen. In an anti-Luther 'office', complete with antiphon, verse and oration, the Johannine prologue has been appropriated to read 'in the beginning was the error'. Hus replaced John Baptist. 'There was a man sent from the Devil' whose name was Jan Hus. The heretics included Simon Magus, Wyclif, Hus and Luther. The 'Te damnamus' parodied the canonical hours suggesting Hus and the others were slated for hell unless they repented.[92] Hus as the heretical forerunner of the great Antichrist can be found elsewhere. In a 1524 song the Hus prophecy began with Hus as the goose then suggested Luther was also a goose but masquerading in the feathers of Jan Hus. The goose was the forerunner but a close inspection revealed not a goose but a 'rotten cockroach'.[93] Against these attacks Protestant polemicists wrote dramas about Hus which cast him into the role of the prophet Elijah over against the figure of Antichrist, a role assigned to Pope John XXIII.[94]

Meanwhile the celebration of Hus' memory in Prague continued and, according to one of the old Czech chroniclers, by 1517 reached significant social proportions. On the vigil of the feast the city council took responsibility for a bonfire on Kampa Island in the Vltava River near the bridge. Trumpeters and drummers joined the celebration from the bridge towers. Cannons were fired in the direction of Petřin Hill. The burgomaster and other civic leaders were in attendance and many people gathered to participate in the events.[95] Four years later the commemoration of Hus featured a procession from the Minorite monastery of St. James in the Lesser Town to St. Clement's by the Bridge, across the bridge to Our Lady of the Snows, Želivský's old church in the New Town. Along the way the celebrants, who were described as 'defenders of the truth of God', sang songs about Hus including one called 'Master Jan Hus in the hope of God'.[96] As late as 1590 evidence suggested the reading of Hus' passion continued annually in churches.[97] By 1560 altars consecrated to Hus could be found in churches in Prague, Čáslav, Kostelec, Kutná Hora, Litoměřice, Český Dub and Hradec Králové.[98] The construction of the memory of Jan Hus shaped his posthumous identity in extraordinary religious ways. There is evidence that John Wyclif was called a saint in some contexts at the end of the Middle Ages and a number of artists included a dove or a nimbus to indicate that Martin Luther was a divinely inspired saint, but neither of these figures were ever commemorated as a holy man in quite the same way as Hus.

In the course of the sixteenth century Jan Hus enjoyed renewed attention in the hands of several Protestant martyrologists who appropriated him for specific agendas. Among a myriad of texts I shall mention briefly only four: Ludwig Rabus, Matija Vlačić (Matthias Flacius Illyricus), Jean Crespin, and John Foxe. The Strasbourg Lutheran pastor Ludwig Rabus produced an exhaustive treatment of the Bohemian martyrs in his eight volume history of the martyrs which appeared first in 1552.[99] Rabus understood Hus as a reformer whose aims were crushed by a resistant church. Hus was Christlike while the fathers at Constance could only be likened to the Pharisees and jealous religious leaders who took steps to ensure the crucifixion of Jesus. Sigismund was portrayed as the betrayer of Hus while the latter was made an example and model of faithfulness for Lutherans to emulate. In 1556 Flacius produced his collection of miscellaneous documents aimed at providing evidence of the authentic church.[100] For Flacius, history was an available arsenal filled with the necessary weapons to defeat the church-pretender which then prevailed. Among his heros we find Jan Hus. Two years later Flacius anonymously published a collection of materials relating to the life and death of Hus. Flacius justified his publication on the grounds that Hus was a holy man faithful to God who opposed unto death the corruption of the medieval church. Prefatory comments reveal the importance of celebrating the memory of those who devoted themselves to truth and remained steadfast unto death. The significance of this collection is that it was the *editio princeps* of Hus and remains the most complete edition of Hus materials in existence up to the present.[101] The French Huguenot in Geneva, Jean Crespin produced a martyrology in 1554 in which the history began with Jan Hus and used excerpts from the work of Petr Mladoňovice.[102] John Foxe published his work twice in the 1550s on the continent and then finally in English in 1563. In modern times popularly called 'Foxe's Book of Martyrs', its proper and complete title is the 'Acts and Monuments of these latter and perilous days, touching matters of the church, wherein are comprehended and described the great persecutions and horrible troubles, that have been wrought and practised by the Romish Prelates, specially in this Realm of England and Scotland, from the year of our Lord a thousand, unto the time now present'. The text running to over 2,000,000 words proved to be a landmark Elizabethan work exerting enormous significance in the English speaking world. The matter of Jan Hus is treated on over 100 pages and the entire history of Bohemia extends even farther.[103]

The objective of Foxe's enormous work is reflected in the title of his book that being the 'great persecutions and horrible troubles' created by the Roman prelates. The great apocalyptic struggle against spiritual wickedness in high places and ecclesiastical reform began with Wyclif and Jan Hus. It is absolutely correct to note that these historians of the martyrs who used Hus had no objective to see a continuity between the medieval church and the emerging reformed communities of the sixteenth century. While Hus was revered as a sterling example of holiness and commitment to Christ, in the hands of Rabus, Flacius, Crespin and Foxe, his *passio* at Constance provided *prima facie* evidence of using history hagiographically to argue a conviction about history in order to advance their concept of a religious future. All three seemed to regard the martyrs as the central criterion within Christian history. Historically the church owed its identity to its stand and survival in a universal battle between good and evil. The children of the light, best exemplified by martyrs like Jan Hus, struggle unceasingly against the children of darkness, manifested for Rabus, Flacius, Crespin and Foxe as the corrupt priests, bishops and popes of the medieval church. The advent of Antichrist only accentuated this conflict. Faithful witnesses to the law of Christ only cause the forces of darkness to gather ever more profoundly around the defenders of truth. The blood of the martyr became seed. In the apocalyptic 'night of Antichrist' in Bohemia the blood of the righteous enabled the true faith to grow and flourish.[104] And thus the example of Hus in his self-sacrifice for the truth of God's law inspired faithful followers to stand up for truth and defend truth, as Hus taught, unto death. 'And the sons of this country, Bohemia, remained faithful and strong and they said unanimously that they would die or avenge their brother's blood that had been shed, for no reason, through falsehood and lies - he gave his life for the right'.[105] Commemorating Hus implied various uses of his memory. An old Czech chronicler recorded that in 1503 Prague Hussites held a vigil on the feast of Jan Hus in hopes of interceding with God to send rain upon the dry summer land but the vigil failed because Roman Church loyalists resisted the vigil and refused to participate.[106] The notion of Hus as intercessor was not new. In 1496 the administrator of the Utraquist Consistory, Václav Koranda the Younger, expressed what must have been a wider sentiment that faithful Czechs were not ashamed of the martyred Hus and regarded him as advocating before God for all those who adhered to the law of Christ.[107] Hussite history and the celebration of Hus continued to have both religious and social appeal. We learn from the memoirs of Sixt of Ottersdorf, chancellor of the Old Town, that socio-political revolutionaries passing the Týn Church in Prague in 1547 paused to doff their hats and bow.[108] When the official calendar of state holidays omitted the days reserved for Hus and Jerome in 1585 the Utraquist Consistory successfully lobbied for its restoration.[109]

In general, the commemoration of Jan Hus can be shown to embrace one essential point. He had been put to death but rather than destroying the Bohemian priest, Hus' death provided a means for his ultimate triumph. The extant liturgical texts support this and the note of triumphalism sounded in the sixteenth century only corroborated it.[110] For over 200 years the celebration of Jan Hus continued without interruption in Bohemia. The onslaught of the Counter Reformation and especially the appearance of the Society of Jesus in the Czech lands signaled a turning point in the religious culture of Bohemia and Moravia.[111] During this period of enforced recatholicizing, Utraquist books and materials in favor of Hus were systematically destroyed. On his deathbed the Jesuit censor Antonín Koniáš boasted of having personally destroyed more than 60,000 volumes of Czech literature.[112] The hyperbole nevertheless makes a point. Anti-Hussite iconoclasm prevailed. Should this be decried one must keep in mind the scale of iconoclastic fury unleashed by the Hussites themselves especially in the second and third decades of the fifteenth century. One action does not justify the other but this was an age of religious intolerance and violence and fractious attitudes can be found as easily on one side of the controversy as the other. After the battle of White Mountain fought outside Prague on 8 November 1620 Hussitism was either destroyed, exiled or driven underground. Czech resistance to Roman Catholicism and the pro-Catholic imperial forces was broken. The twenty-four year old 'winter king', Frederick V, fled to Holland. Many Czechs welcomed the restoration of Catholicism. Twenty-seven leaders of the insurrection leading to White Mountain were tried and executed the following spring in the Old Town Square of Prague near the same place where Sigismund hanged Jan Roháč of Dubá and the Sión garrison 184 years earlier. Monday, 21 June 1621 has been called 'the day of blood' and in modern Prague there are twenty-seven crosses inlayed in the cobblestones of Old Town Square commemorating the leaders of the last rebellion. For Hussites it meant the end of independence, religious freedom and the suppression of the cult of St. Jan Hus. On 6 July, 1622 with the feast of Hus prohibited people gathered outside locked church doors.[113] In the decades to come dissenters were arrested on charges of heresy, offending books burned publicly, songs sang 'burn, burn, Jan Hus' and frescos in counter-reformation churches in Prague depicted reformers being thrown into hell.[114] Of considerable anomalous interest is a sixteenth-century Roman use of Hus to promote eucharistic orthodoxy. After the rancorous condemnation at Constance on the grounds of eucharistic irregularity the use of Hus by a Catholic on such a matter was striking.[115]

Despite the considerable setbacks in the seventeenth century we still find traces of extraordinary devotion to Hus on the part of common people who retained an emotional attachment to Hussite history. These expressions of popular piety continued in public veneration of Hus even after White Mountain. For example a chair thought to belong to Hus in Bethlehem Chapel was kissed by those thinking it had healing power to cure the misery of toothache.[116] Ostensibly Hus replaced Apollonia as the preferred patron saint invoked for aid and remedy against dental problems at least in some Czech religious communities. The attribution must have been slight. Jan Hus as the healer of toothaches was never a major aspect in his commemoration.

The history of the Jan Hus commemoration experienced revival in the early twentieth century. The liturgical innovations in the Czechoslovak Hussite Church approach definite 'Husolatry'.[117] Some of the translations of the liturgy into the Czech vernacular around 1920 provided propers for the feast of Jan Hus. Further developments allowed for the reading of Hus's letters which were written in June 1415 from the Constance prison and addressed to all faithful Czechs and also portions of the *Relatio* written by Petr Mladoňovice.[118] Two of the liturgical propers are texts based on Hus' own words or extracted from the *Passio* composed by Petr Mladoňovice. At the offertory Hus' famous prayer of fidelity to truth is intoned.[119] After the communion, Hus's words about wearing the shameless cap of the heretic are spoken along with his faith in Christ and prayer for perseverance to faithfully die in the hope of Christ. As Holeton makes clear these words are a pastiche of texts drawn from Hus' *Passio*. An identification between Hus and Christ reach a peak when the clergy stand before a bust of Jan Hus and sing together, 'behold a heretic; bravely he helps Jesus to carry the saving cross'.[120] Elsewhere, the Old Catholic Church in the Czech Republic intentionally claims continuity with earlier Hussite traditions and observes the feast of Jan Hus on the historic day of 6 July. The collect appears to be the most relevant to the Hus feast. Hus and Jerome together are nominated as saints who confessed the truth of God and gave witness to their faith through martyrdom. The Orthodox Church likewise celebrates Hus on 6 July and of note in this commemoration are prayers which name Jan Milíč of Kroměříž, Tomáš Štítný, Jan Hus and Jerome of Prague with other Czech saints. On Hus specifically, his effort at ecclesiastical reform in the spirit of the early church is mentioned and in defense of this offered his life at the stake. All of the 'zealous teachers of purification of the life of the church' are named including Jan Milíč, Tomáš Štítný, Master Jan Hus, Jerome of Prague, King Jiří of Poděbrady and petition is made that they might be remembered eternally.[121] This is a modern development. Up until the nineteenth century Hus had been included on the list of heretics in the liturgy of the Orthodox Church. Thereafter Hus was de-hereticized and transformed into a martyr of Orthodoxy who sacrificed himself for his Slavic brethren.[122] The liturgical remembrance of Hus is observed outside Bohemia today especially in the Moravian Church, the Lutheran Church in America, the Evangelical Lutheran Church of Canada, as well as the Anglican Church of Canada.

The Hus commemoration is celebrated annually in Prague on 6 July with a nationally televised service from Bethlehem Chapel. These events are ecumenical. Hierarchy of the Roman Catholic Church attend. Polemics are set aside and Hus is remembered as a reformer of the church. One of the regular songs sung includes the refrain which asks the question about who is the flames and the sung response answers 'it is Master Jan Hus, the most famous Czech'. In the modern Czech Republic 6 July is a national holiday. The current presidential flag carries the motto of the Czech Republic which some suggest goes back to Jan Hus: 'Pravda vítězí' - truth conquers. The religious tradition of remembering Jan Hus for almost 600 years has been rooted intentionally in the conviction that 'the gospel we have today has been brought forth by Hus with his own blood'.[123]

10

ICONOGRAPHY

Eight hundred years before the time of Hus, Gregory the Great suggested that visual images played a crucial social role especially among those unable to read. The Gregorian principle may be reduced to the idea that pictures are the books of the illiterate.[1] The theory has been assailed and some scholars have questioned its validity.[2] Throughout medieval history Gregory's observation was repeated by men such as Bede, the anonymous artist of the St. Alban's Psalter, Peter Abelard, Albert the Great, William Durandus, Bonaventure, Thomas Aquinas and John Wyclif.[3] Iconographically, the Hussite movement is significant. The Táborites were ferocious iconoclasts and the havoc they wreaked on the artistic culture of late medieval Bohemia can only be deplored. On the other hand we find among the more moderate branches of the movement a rich tradition of visual representations. The dominant symbol of the Hussite movement became the chalice, the central motif of reformed Bohemian religion. There is very early evidence for the chalice as an iconographical topos and this can be identified from stove tiles found among the ruins of Sión Castle sacked in 1437. Here we can identify two floating angels holding up a chalice with a host on both sides.[4] Hussitism cannot be reduced to utraquism but without utraquism there is no such thing as Hussitism. Jan Hus did not attempt to interpret or expand on Gregory's dictum but he glossed the text in his academic discourse on the Sentences of Peter Lombard.[5] Elsewhere Hus explained his understanding of the function of the visual image. 'It seems to me that I adore the image of Christ not because it is a sign, not because it is an image of Christ; I adore Christ in the presence of the image of Christ because it is an image of Christ and makes me want to adore Christ.'[6] It was precisely this distinction which eluded the Táborite mentality in their urge to purge the church of idolatry and false worship. For Hus, a difference existed between the image and the signified. Venerating an image of Christ was acceptable to Hus but worship properly belonged to God alone not to representations of God. Praying, making offerings or placing candles before an image was not at issue for Hus so long as it was understood that such acts should be done in the name of Christ and not on account of the image itself.[7] The distinction was lost on the radical Hussite iconoclasts. Commenting on matters of doctrine and ecclesiastical discipline Hus wrote that those who refused to believe his instruction should learn it on the walls of Bethlehem

Chapel.[8] His reference was to inscriptions and images which adorned the walls of his chapel in Prague. In his 'lives of the Táborite priests', Jan Příbram asserted that even in the consciousness of the radical brotherhoods Hus continued to play a role. When the eschatological fullness of time arrived the Táborites fully expected to see the resurrected Jan Hus along with others chosen by God and the Hussites anticipated joining them in a great feast before the last judgment.[9] Chapter nine has shown with some evidence that the memory of Hus continued to remain active in the religious culture of Bohemia for more than 200 years after the Council of Constance. Aside from liturgical commemoration the legacy of Hus can also be found in the visual sources of late medieval and early modern Europe. As a basis for the observations in this chapter I have taken into account 143 images of Hus in the period between the 1420s and the end of the seventeenth century.

Shortly after his death we find evidence of the uses of his visual image in Bohemia. The Council of Constance complained to Emperor Sigismund that portraits of Hus and Jerome were painted in chapels and churches as though the two were saints.[10] We know that images of Hus could be found on altars and on church walls and statutes were erected in public places.[11] Hus was also present in art forms, in fresco and on canvas, on altar panels, as manuscript drawings and illuminations, in Bibles, on stove tiles and coins, medallions, bells, on banners, in woodcut and broadsheet depictions, on book covers and bindings, and of course, in liturgical materials. No medieval heretic ever achieved the place of prominence in art as did Hus. Researches carried out by historians and art specialists reveal that only a small percentage of these depictions have survived the ravages of time and the concerted efforts of the Counter Reformation to eradicate the memory of Hus from the religious landscape of western Christendom. Beyond this we can be certain that art collectors pilfered manuscripts removing images of Hus and excising his presence from various fifteenth and sixteenth century books. The iconography of Jan Hus survives especially in terms of a 'passion cycle' which may be as early as the second quarter of the fifteenth century.[12] Previously we have seen that the passion cycle of Hus followed a clearly articulated Christomorphic pattern. This consisted of his acts of life, trial at Constance, and death at the stake. Churches embracing the Hussite faith and accepting doctrinal tenets and religious practices of a reformed utraquist perspective often featured portraits of Hus and the Bohemian martyrs on the same level as the martyrs of the early church.[13] There should be no doubt that Hus occupied the pride of place in these depictions. We noted earlier that the Council of Constance took particular care to make certain that all remnants of Hus' body and belongings were destroyed at the stake.

> When the wood of those bundles and the ropes were consumed, but the remains of the body still stood in those chains, hanging by the neck, the executioners pulled the charred body along with the stake down to the ground and burned them further by adding wood from the third wagon to the fire. And walking around, they broke the bones with clubs so that they would be incinerated more quickly. And finding the head, they broke it to pieces with the

clubs and again threw it into the fire. And when they found the heart among the intestines, they sharpened a club like a spit, and, impaling it on its end, they took particular [care] to roast and consume it, piercing it with spears until finally the whole mass was turned to ashes. And at the order of the said Clem and the marshal, the executioners threw the clothing into the fire along with the shoes, saying: 'so that the Czechs would not regard it as relics; we will pay you money for it.' Which they did. So they loaded all the ashes in a cart and threw it into the river Rhine flowing nearby.[14]

This process was intentional in order to prevent the veneration of any possible relics of Jan Hus and to erase all memory of his from the consciousness of the faithful Bohemians.[15] Writing a generation later Aeneas Sylvius claimed that deprived of actual relics the Czechs took soil from the ground near the stake and carried this back to Bohemia.[16] Whether this was true is less important than the reality that Hus became venerated, made a functional saint in the Hussite communion, and that his memory was made visible for generations to come. We have already noted this rapid elevation and Abbot Štěpán of Dolany is only one witness claiming that Masses for Hus as a holy martyr were sung in Bethlehem Chapel.[17]

The life of St. Francis of Assisi has often been held up as a striking example of the imitation of Christ theme in the Middle Ages. This can be traced through commentary and art. A case can be made for a similar sense when the depictions of Hus are examined. Noteworthy are the early examples wherein Hus was placed in heaven, accorded status among the faithful saints, or otherwise began to resemble the iconographic features of Christ, a point noted more than sixty years ago by Roland Bainton.[18] As the history of Hus iconography progressed it has been argued that Hus comes to more closely resemble Christ. It is not conclusive but the depiction of the heavenly court wherein the Hussite warrior Jan Žižka plays a central role may likewise include Hus.[19] Žižka is unmistakable in the role of St. Peter holding the keys of the kingdom and brandishing a red banner displaying a chalice on a long pole. Of the other two figures in the front row the man on the far left wearing a red gown and green tunic and holding a chalice may well be intended as Jan Hus. There are no authentic likenesses of Hus as there are of Luther and many other historical figures beginning with Renaissance portraitures. Therefore there is no reason to assume that any depiction of Hus has any basis in reality when it comes to features. Arguments have been advanced for an iconographical evolution in the portrayals of Hus. In some images Hus is beardless and of a healthy girth while in others he is bearded and gaunt. The latter images tend to make him appear more closely related to the medieval and early modern Christ of art. However there is no unimpeachable basis for assuming that this reflects a conscious development for both general depictions of Hus can be found in early as well as later art. However, it is almost certain that Hus was clean shaven.[20] A woodcut from the later fifteenth century, around the same time as the Jena Codex, shows Hus in the bearded gaunt mode.[21] The depiction employed an all-purpose printing wood block which means it had no correlation to actual appearance. He may well be in a pulpit and his left hand is raised as though in the midst of a dis-

Illustration 1 Hus as martyr, heretic and saint

course. The image appeared with variations a dozen times or more in the sixteenth and seventeenth centuries. Of course Hus considered himself a preacher above all things and so it is not surprising to find him in a pulpit addressing a seated congregation.[22] The congregation included men, women and children and a tonsured Hus speaks from a text spread out before him. He appears to be wearing a white surplice with a cross visible on his upper chest. The depiction bears no meaningful reflection of the Bethlehem Chapel.

Liturgically, theologically and iconographically, the image of Hus in a codex made in 1491 for the Church of the Holy Trinity near Kutná Hora at the sponsorship of a Hussite noble is important (illustration 1).[23] Hus appeared flanked by the traditional martyrs SS. Stephen and Laurence in an historiated capital letter.[24] On the right Laurence holds a quill and a book while on the left Stephen appears to cradle the stones of his martyrdom. Both of the martyrs wear a white surplice and a green chasuble, are tonsured and have halos. The attention of both is directed to the activity in the middle. Here Jan Hus appears wearing a white surplice and a red chasuble. His head is covered with the miter of the heretic depicting two demons. Like the traditional martyrs Hus wears a halo. Pictures of Hus with a halo are not common but I know of at least six depictions and a further four wherein a dove appears above him. In his left hand Hus holds a large blue gospel book upon which he balances a gold chalice. His right hand is raised in the manner of the liturgical blessing of the chalice during Mass. Appropriately enough the folio in question comes in the 'Common of saints' and at the foot of the page there is a vivid illustration of heretical Hussites being thrown into the silver mine shafts at Kutná Hora. Armed men, some standing and others mounted, surround a group of ten Hussites all of whom are wearing white gowns and black belts. Seven of the condemned are kneeling with hands clasped penitentially and appear to be singing. The other three, two of whom are tonsured indicating their priestly status, appear to be diving (as opposed to being thrown) into a mine shaft. The clerical figures surely depict the martyrdom of Jan Chůdek, vicar of Kouřim, and the priests Jakub, Martin and Leonard all of whom were thrown into the shafts in 1420.[25] To the right one can see the walled town of Kutná Hora. In the background to the left, a group of people look on from a considerable distance while on the right a church sits on a hill. The Church of the Holy Trinity for which the gradual containing these illuminations was made is shown elsewhere in the book.[26]

At Litomyšl in 1510 an edition of Hus' book on the six errors of the mass appeared. The title page featured a beardless man with a tonsure sitting at a rather elegant desk and writing. The image was doubtless intended to depict Hus. The scholarly Hus is evident. Elsewhere we find him featured in a full page illumination debating with a group of cardinals and other religious at the Council of Constance. Hus stands at a lectern before a semi-circle of seated clerics. At least four of the nine are cardinals. Hus is wearing a luxurious red gown and a matching cap and appears to have a halo. The religious listening to Hus appear to be engaged with his presentation. To Hus' right, a bald corpulent man wearing a blue gown has his arm fully raised as though to ask a question while several others gesture in various fashions. About thirty other figures can be seen in the background most looking towards Hus.[27] In an early edition of Hus' commentaries there is a dated woodcut from 1520 showing Hus with a young man and Christ as the Man of Sorrows. There is some chance the young man is being presented by Hus for his first communion though others have made the point that the man in the woodcut is the printer of the book, Mikuláš Konáč of Hodíšt'kov, whom Hus is here commending to the Man of Sorrows.[28] Hus points to the Man of Sorrows, who is holding a chalice in his left hand to catch the flow of blood from his side. Of note in this depiction is once more the nimbus around Hus' head.

Somewhere between 1510 and 1520 the retable for the Vlněves altarpiece (now at Nelahozeves Castle) was made. Hus appeared in the lower right panel of the retable, in three quarter profile, where he assists the patron saint of Bohemia St. Vojtěch in a celebration of the Mass (illustration 2). The mitered and haloed Vojtěch faces the altar holding the chalice and the host. Behind him holding the altar book in his right hand is Hus wearing the crimson gown of the martyr and the cap of the heretic on which are clearly visible three demons. He does not have a halo in this portrayal. With his left hand he holds Vojtěch's chasuble.[29] The joining of two prominent Czech personalities

Illustration 2 The heretical deacon

implied either a Hussite challenge to the official church or a union between traditional and reformed religion. From the same time period there remains a predella of an altar which has not survived. Originally in the Church of the Holy Cross in Chrudim, four half figures are depicted. The second, third and fourth figures from the left have been identified previously as the patron saints of Bohemia, Wenceslas, Ludmila and Prokop. The identification of Ludmila is incorrect.[30] It is generally accepted that the first figure, bearded and holding a large chalice is Jan Hus.[31] All four of these saints have a nimbus about their heads while Hus is blessing the chalice in the identical manner as in the Smíškovsky Gradual. Wenceslas and pseudo-Ludmila wear head coverings while Hus and Prokop are clearly tonsured. Hus is arrayed in a plain white gown.

During the sixteenth century, the image of Hus often appeared in publications. In 1537 the Lutheran Johannes Agricola produced a five part drama on the 'tragedy of Jan Hus'. The play purported to depict the trial at Constance. Agricola cast Hus into the role of Elijah the prophet standing head to head with Pope John XXIII, the figure of Antichrist. The confrontation at the Council in Agricola's hands has Hus vilified by the synod, accused of extreme views, manufactured by his bête noire Michael de Causis and others, lacking supporting evidence while Hus was deprived of any legal right to mount a defense. On the title page a somber looking Hus can be seen, bearded and wearing a cap. In 1561 Hus appeared on the title page of the 'confession' of the Czech Brethren standing at a lectern, his hands on a book, while over his head a dove appears, ostensibly in place of the occasional halo but indicative of sanctity and the presence of the Holy Spirit. The dove appeared elsewhere in the visual depictions of Hus.[32] The 'holy martyr Jan Hus' is the subject of a broadsheet, noting the incorrect date of his death, where he is holding an opened book. On a pillar behind him there is a small depiction of a goose. The goose is an allusion to Hus' name. Iconographically, his portrait is quite similar to the Agricola version and by this point in art history Hus is almost always wearing a cap of some sort, is bearded and showing sharper, gaunt features.[33] In these depictions he is often referred to as a saint or a holy martyr. On the title page of a Hussite hymn book Hus is shown leading a large crowd of the faithful in singing. Hus and the others are using music books.[34]

Of particular interest is a colored sixteenth-century broadsheet featuring the prophesying 'Johannes Hus' (illustration 3). Here a large full-length figure of the Czech martyr is shown wearing a brown cap and gown. In his right hand Hus holds an open book on which there are words referring to the demise of a goose and the prediction of a swan coming one hundred years hence. Behind this main figure, in the lower third of the broadsheet and partially concealed by a low wall, it is possible to see Hus at the stake. He is wearing the miter of the heretic adorned with demons. One man is stoking the flames. Armed men in blue, some on horseback, and ecclesiastical dignitaries, observe the passio of Hus which the text has dated incorrectly to 8 July 1415. The burning is accompanied by the prophecy of Hus symbolized by a very clear utterance which manifests itself visually above the heads of two bishops and a cardinal in the form of a dove, as the Holy Spirit, encased in a nimbus. It is interesting that the presence of the dove and the brilliance of the halo appears to have knocked one of the

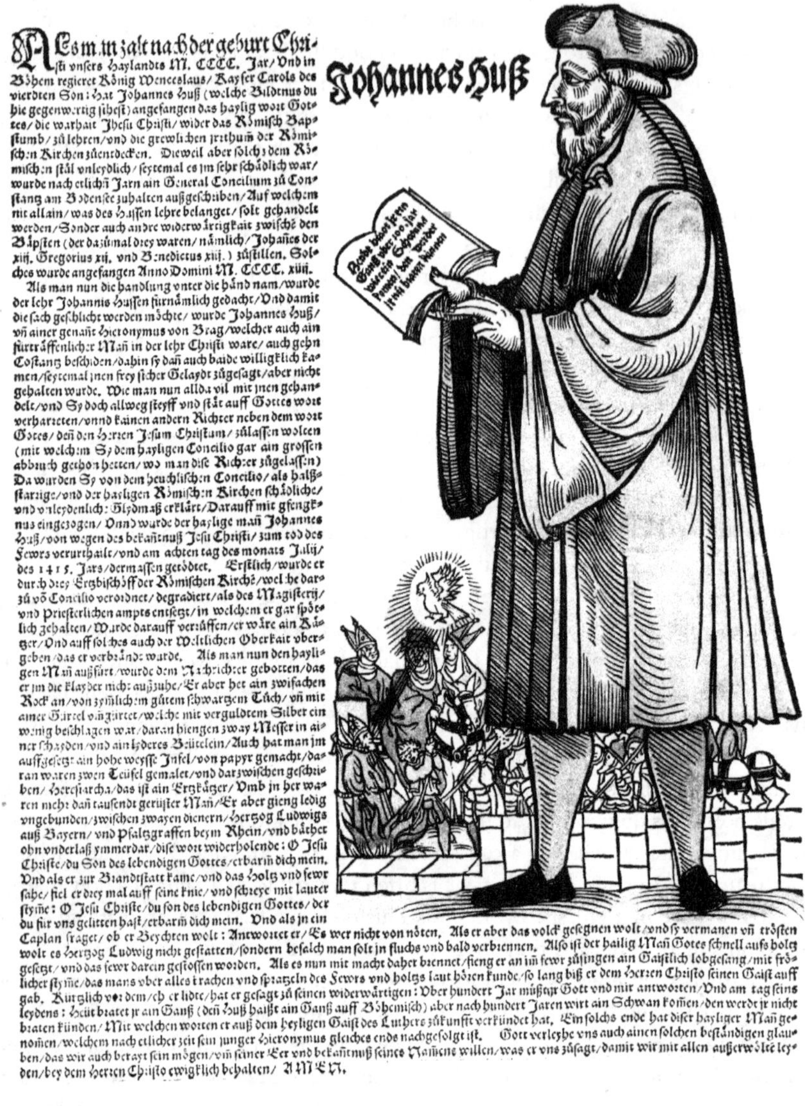

Johannes Huß

Als man zalt nach der geburt Christi vnsers haylandts M. CCCC. Jar/ Vnd in Böhem regieret König Wenceslaus/ Kayser Carols des vierdten Son: hat Johannes Huß (welche Bildtnus du hie gegenwertig sihest) angefangen das haylig wort Gottes/ die warhait Jhesu Christi/ wider das Römisch Bapstumb/ zů lehren/ vnd die grewlichen jrthum der Römischen Kirchen zůentdecken. Dieweil aber solchs dem Römischen stůl vnleydlich/ seytemal es jm sehr schädlich war/ wurde nach etlichen Jarn ain General Concilium zů Constantz am Bodensee zuhalten außgeschriben/ Auf welchem nit allain/ was des Hussen lehre belanget/ solt gehandelt werden/ Sonder auch andre widerwärtigkait zwischē den Bäpsten (der dazůmal drey waren/ nämlich/ Johañes der xxiij. Gregorius xij. vnd Benedictus xiij.) zůstillen. Solches wurde angefangen Anno Domini M. CCCC. xiiij.

Als man nun die handlung vnter die händ nam/ wurde der lehr Johannis Hussen fürnämlich gedacht/ Vnd damit die sach geschlicht werden möchte/ wurde Johannes Huß/ vñ ainer genañt Hieronymus von Brag/ welcher auch ain fürträffenlicher Mañ in der lehr Christi ware/ auch gehn Costantz beschiden/ dahin sy dañ auch baide willigklich kamen/ seytemal jnen frey sicher Gelaydt zůgesagt/ aber nicht gehalten wurde. Wie man nun allda vil mit jnen gehandelt/ vnd Sy doch allweg steyff vnd stät auff Gottes wort verharreten/ vnnd kainen andern Richter neben dem wort Gotes/ deñ den Herren Jesum Christum/ zůlassen wolten (mit welchem Sy dem hayligen Concilio gar ain grossen abbruch gethon hetten/ wo man dise Richter zůgelassen) Da wurden Sy von dem heuchlischen Concilio/ als halßstarrige/ vnd der hayligen Römischen Kirchen schädliche/ vnd vnleydenlich: Glydmaß erklärt/ Darauff mit gfengknus eingezogen/ Vnnd wurde der haylige mañ Johannes Huß/ von wegen des bekañtnuß Jesu Christi/ zum tod des Fewrs verurthailt/ vnd am achten tag des monats Julij/ des 1415. Jars/ dermassen getödtet. Erstlich/ wurde er durch drey Ertzbischöff der Römischen Kirchē/ welche darzů vō Concilio verordnet/ degradiert/ als des Magisterij/ vnd Priesterlichen ampts entsetzt/ in welchem er gar spötlich gehalten/ Wurde darauff verrůffen/ er wäre ain Kätzer/ Vnd auff solches auch der Weltlichen Oberkait vbergeben/ das er verbrändt wurde. Als man nun den hayligen Mañ außfürt/ wurde dem Nachrichter gebotten/ das er jm die klayder nicht außzuhe/ Er aber het ain zwifachen Rock an/ von zymlichem gůtem schwartzem Tůch/ vñ mit ainer Gürtel vmgürtet/ welche mit verguldtem Silber ein wenig beschlagen war/ daran hiengen zway Messer in ainer schayden/ vnd ain lederes Beütelein/ Auch hat man jm auffgesetzt ain hohe weysse Jnfel/ von papyr gemacht/ daran waren zwen Teüfel gemalet/ vnd darzwischen geschriben/ Heresiarcha/ das ist ain Ertzkätzer/ Vmb jn her waren nicht dañ tausendt gerüster Mañ/ Er aber gieng ledig vngebunden/ zwischen zwayen dienern/ Hertzog Ludwigs auß Bayern/ vnd Pfaltzgraffen beym Rhein/ vnd bäthet ohn vnderlaß ymmerdar/ dise wort widerholende: O Jesu Christe/ du Son des lebendigen Gottes/ erbarm dich mein. Vnd als er zur Brandtstatt kame/ vnd das Holtz vnd fewr sahe/ fiel er drey mal auff seine knie/ vnd schreye mit lauter stymē: O Jesu Christe/ du son des lebendigen Gottes/ der du für vns gelitten hast/ erbarm dich mein. Vnd als jn ein Caplan fraget/ ob er Beychten wolt: Antwortet er/ Es wer nicht von nöten. Als er aber das volck gesegnen wolt/ vnd sy vermanen vñ tröstē wolt es Hertzog Ludwig nicht gestatten/ sondern befalch man solt jn fluchs vnd bald verbrennen. Also ist der hailig Mañ Gotes schnell aufs holtz gesetzt/ vnd das fewr darein gestossen worden. Als es nun mit macht daher brennet/ fieng er an im fewr zůsingen ain Gaistlich lobgesang/ mit frölicher stymē/ das mans vber alles krachen vnd spratzeln des Fewrs vnd holtzs laut hören kunde/ so lang biß er dem Herren Christo seinen Gaist auffgab. Kurtzlich vor dem/ ch er lidte/ hat er gesagt zů seinen widerwärtigen: Vber hundert Jar müßtjr Gott vnd mir antworten/ Vnd am tag seins leydens: Heüt bratet jr ain Ganß (deñ Huß haißt ain Ganß auff Böhemisch) aber nach hundert Jaren wirt ain Schwan komen/ den werdt jr nicht braten künden/ Mit welchen worten er auß dem heyligen Gaist des Luthers zůkunfft verkündet hat. Ein solchs ende hat diser hayliger Mañ genomen/ welchem nach etlicher zeit sein junger Hieronymus gleiches ends nachgefolgt ist. Gott verleyhe vns auch ainen solchen beständigen glauben/ das wir auch berayt sein mögen/ vm̄ seiner Er vnd bekañtnuß seines Namens willen/ was er vns zůsagt/ damit wir mit allen außerwölten leyden/ bey dem Herren Christo ewigklich behalten/ AMEN.

Illustration 3 The prophesying Hus

episcopal miters askew. The accompanying text refers four times to Hus as a 'holy man.'[35] The broadsheet depicts Hus as a divinely inspired martyr who is foretelling a legendary event at the pyre which became part of sixteenth-century religious lore. That legend, often repeated, reflected in the text of the broadsheet has Hus declaring at the stake that in one hundred years his accusers would have to answer to God. Today a lean goose would be roasted (punning on his own name) but in a hundred years hence a swan would appear and sing and the swan could not be burned. The reference specified the 'coming holy spirit of Luther' and the latter appropriated it to himself.[36] It has been suggested that the alleged prophecy was not simply an enthusiastic invention but may have been a result of a conflation of statements made by Hus and Jerome.[37] In 1414 Hus referred to other birds more capable than the weak goose. Jerome remarked to his judges at Constance that while they might very well condemn him to death within a hundred years they would all have to answer for their deeds. A German engraving pictures the figure of Jan Hus between two trees. Under the tree on the left a swan appears while on the right side one can see a goose in flames tied to a post. The accompanying text says the goose will rise again, as a phoenix, in the form of the swan. The goose will be cooked but in one hundred years a swan will emerge from the ashes containing the unburned strength of the goose.[38] An extant colored engraving by Hans Guldenmund shows Hus holding a book in which the swan is mentioned. Behind Hus the passio is shown and represents a variation of the broadsheet discussed above.[39] Johannes Agricola used the prophecy in his drama 'the tragedy of Jan Hus'.[40] Johannes Bugenhagen cited the so-called Hus prophecy during his funeral oration for Luther in 1546. Twenty years later a group of seventeen preachers published a book on the life of Luther and the prophecy plays a part therein. Even Luther's closest colleague and successor Philip Melanchthon made use of the Hus prophecy.[41] References to the prophecy are also evident in the Hussite tradition. Hus was called 'our martyr' by Jan Komenský [Comenius] who also endorsed the goose and swan motif.[42]

The prophecy of Jan Hus concerning the goose that was roasted at Constance and the singing swan to come enjoyed an extraordinary life in the sixteenth and early seventeenth centuries and the iconography of that idea included Hus. The alleged connection between Hus and Luther was nowhere better articulated than in the famous dream of Frederick the Wise. Now Frederick was prince of Electoral Saxony and Luther's protector. His role was not inconsequential in the German Reformation. But for our purposes here he is relevant only to the extent that in 1517 the elector ostensibly dreamt about Luther but in that dream Jan Hus played a crucial role part. The dream, or more accurately a series of three dreams, was featured in an anonymous broadsheet woodcut titled 'a godly and extraordinary dream' (illustration 4).[43] On the left Luther can be seen holding an enormous quill and writing against indulgences on the door of the Castle Church in Wittenberg. This is evident from the words already written on the door *Vom Ablaß* (concerning indulgences). The quill is extraordinary in every sense. First, smaller quills fall from the larger one and these are picked up by other reformers. The length of Luther's quill stretches almost *ad infinitum* and certainly all the way from central Europe to Rome where it passed through the head of a lion, labeled 'Pope Leo X', and toppled the papal tiara from the head of a surprised and annoyed Leo X who presides amidst a group of cardinals and secular lords. Leo tries in vain to keep his crown on his head. On the right side of the broadsheet a group of saints approach Frederick the Wise. Luther is omnipresent in the image. To the right he appears as a monk kneeling with an opened Bible. Situated close to the same place he is depicted as the recipient of divine inspiration and the holy Trinity – Father, Son

Illustration 4 Dream of Elector Frederick the Wise

and Holy Ghost – are shown on the clouds. The Castle of Schweinitz, where Frederick was alleged to have had this dream, is shown to the right of the main scene. In the background to the left the pope and his supporters having produced a sizable pen of their own, appear to have carved the word 'no' on a tree while an indulgence seller preaches to a gathered multitude. Efforts to break Luther's quill fail and in the accompanying text Luther was asked where such a remarkable quill came from. Luther replied that he got it from a one hundred year old Bohemian goose. In the forefront of the overall picture one can see a goose being burned on a fiery pyre while clerics pluck feathers from its wings. The broadsheet appeared in 1617 even though the chronogram erroneously reads 1587. The dreams were alleged to have occurred on the night of 30–31 October 1517. What the broadsheet communicated in effect was the power of Hus' memory and legacy which stretched from Prague to Constance through Wittenberg to Rome. The story of the dream can be found in a variety of forms, including sermons and plays from 1591 on, but it was only produced in visual form in 1617. There are several other depictions of the dream. One is a painting which showed in more simplified fashion the complexity of the broadsheet version. On the right, Elector Frederick reclines on his bed in the royal Castle of Schweinitz while Luther holds up a book to several dignitaries at the foot of the bed. Luther writes on the church door and the white quill extended all the way to Rome where once more it disrupted the tiara of Pope Leo X. Luther's colleagues pull smaller quills from the larger one while a large goose stands, wings spread, between the quill and the castle. In the near background Luther sits reading under the inspiration of the Holy Spirit, symbolized by a Hebrew sign in the sky, while farther away in the background a huge fire can be seen, apparently the burning of the papal bull.[44] A panel oil painting by Jan Barentsz Muyckens in 1643 presented yet another variation.[45]

The iconography of Jan Hus was utilized by various factions across the religious divides of sixteenth-century Europe. Certainly one might expect to find Hus made in the image of various Protestants and put to use in the propaganda of Lutheran or Calvinist doctrine. Images of Hus can be found in the books of Ludwig Rabus, Theodore Beza, John Foxe, Flacius, Robert Boissard and others. One is not surprised to find Hus numbered with the vanquished heretics Donatus and Wyclif, and made to follow the chariot of the triumphant church on foot.[46] It is unusual to come across Hus being used by the Roman Church in a positive manner. Václav Brosius, a graduate of the Jesuit Clementinum in Prague, spent his career as a parish priest in Litomyšl and Sobotka and then later as dean in Jindřichův Hradec. In 1589 he published a treatise against the Unity of Brethren wherein he took that branch of the Hussite tradition to task for their rejection of the eucharistic doctrine of transubstantiation. The lengthy title – 'Caution to all faithful Czechs and other true lovers of religion, so they can know the difference between the teaching of Master Jan Hus and the teaching of the Boleslav Brethren' – rather gives the focus of the argument away.[47] Clearly there was nothing unusual in a Catholic priest remonstrating with dissenters over the proper understanding of the Mass. What is unusual was the use of Jan Hus to compel adherence to the teaching of the official church and Brosius correctly held Hus up as an example of eucharistic orthodoxy. This 'Jesuit' use of Hus as a means of religious instruction included a woodcut depicting Hus adoring the sacrament. A bareheaded Hus knees before a large chalice and host, clasping his hands together in reverent devotion. The counter-balance was the Jednota theologian Jan Augusta (1500–72), whom Brosius called a Pikart, who waves his right hand in a dismissive manner while pouring the chalice out on the ground with his left hand as he crushes the host underfoot.[48]

The religious uses of Hus can be translated into political uses in the same period. Among the Sutherland Collection of historical prints and drawings in the Bodleian Library in Oxford are a series of caricatures of the 'winter king' Frederick V, Elector Palatine who became the Czech ruler in 1618. The copper plate engravings are anonymous but may be dated around 1620 having originated in south Germany. The one relevant here is of the coronation of Frederick and his consort Elizabeth.[49] The monarch and his wife appear in royal regalia attended by four lions symbolizing the Palatinate, Bohemia, England and Holland. At the top of the engraving Psalm 118:3 was cited to the effect that the coronation was the Lord's doing and it was wonderful in the eyes of all those witnessing the event. In the background to the left Martin Luther, John Calvin and Jan Hus appear holding a Bible. On the right the Catholics flee before the collapsing Roman Church while over this catastrophe are flying demons. The truth of God's word symbolized by the major reformers and the heritage of Jan Hus have put to flight the wicked Catholics. Below the engraving are four columns of text in German. In the third column there is reference to the teaching of Hus which opposed the errors of the papacy. In the fourth column Jan Žižka is called the 'brave man of God' who protected the truth of Christ while the Hussite king Jiří of Poděbrady accomplished much good for Bohemia by practicing evangelical truth. Ironically the triumphal tone of this engraving did not survive the year. By November the forces of the 'winter king' had been defeated at White Mountain and the beginning of the end of the Hussite tradition had begun. The political uses of the Hussite tradition and Hus himself are evident elsewhere. In 1619 a single sheet broadsheet was printed at Augsburg under the title 'the Bohemian mirror of disorder'. The engraver divided the portrayal into eleven numbered acts.[50] The central act is number six depicting Jesuit atrocities. Jan Hus and Jerome are shown standing off to the left watching the events and both make important speeches recorded on the broadsheet. While the theme cannot be dealt with in any detail in this context, it is important to note that Jan Hus became a vital component in the political propaganda of the seventeenth century. In this literary tradition Hus rose from the dead and made his way to Bohemia to assist the faithful. Using his own passio as an example he urged the Czechs to remain resolute. The resurrected Hus appeared without warning at the Jesuit College in Prague where he rang a Hussite bell frightening the godless therein and proceeded to upbraid them for their wickedness. He called them to repentance. To the faithful Czechs Hus promised that he and Žižka would support them. He urged them to adhere to the doctrines he proclaimed more than 200 years earlier. The Hus prophecy was alluded to and Hus predicted the assent of the 'winter king'.[51] A 1679 Dutch broadsheet summarizing religious tyranny between the fifteenth and the late seventeenth centuries in Europe made iconographical use of Hus' death. Two large central boxes underscore the corruption of the papacy and the religious orders. The broadsheet is then divided into ten smaller parts each with its own particular story in visual form. The top left of the broadsheet shows Hus at the stake. He is wearing a miter but appears naked from the waist up.[52] In this case he dies as a victim of religious and political tyranny.

The pictorial broadsheet depicting the 'baptism of Christ before Nürnberg', from around 1562, included a number of Reformation personalities present at this event which took place outside the walls of the German city.[53] To the right of the central scene Hus takes first place ahead of Luther and Melanchthon. A bearded Hus knees with the others, hands together in reverence. A colored woodcut from the 1520s depicted Hus and Luther as exemplars of the good shepherd.[54] The woodcut survives only as a fragment. Inside the sheepfold Luther stands with the sheep before the crucified Christ but outside Hus can be seen holding a book. Leaving Hus outside the sheepfold indicated his perceived role as the forerunner of Luther; the vanquished goose and the triumphant swan. Elsewhere, Hus and Luther join forces to announce the gospel of Jesus. An etching in a German Bible from 1736 shows Hus and Luther standing beside a large lectern. Behind the lectern the crucified Christ appears beneath the Agnus Dei who stands on an altar-shaped mountain holding a staff and triumphal banner. On the lectern the words from the Gospel of John appear referring to the scriptures which some maintain contain the path to eternal life and these words bear witness to Christ. Hus points upward to the lamb and says, 'behold the Lamb of God'. Behind Hus one can see a goose. Luther points to the gospel words and completes

Hus' statement from John 1:29 noting this lamb takes away the sin of the world. Behind Luther there is a swan.[55] A rather famous and often published broadsheet from the Cranach school shows Luther and Hus celebrating an utraquist Mass for the dukes of Saxony.[56] The Cranach broadsheet was adapted in 1617 as part of a large painting occupying the north wall of the choir in St. George's Church in Eisenach.[57] The assumed connection between Hus and the reformers of the sixteenth century is a motif taken for granted and from an art history point of view has yielded some impressive depictions. Often the generations from Wyclif to Luther are related. The Gradual of the Lesser Town of Prague shows Wyclif rubbing two stones together to create a spark followed by Hus with a small candle and then finally Luther with a flaming torch.[58] The idea was expressed even more succinctly in a Czech broadsheet wherein the three men are joined by Philip Melanchthon who takes his cue from Luther and has an even larger torch.[59] All of this takes place under the oversight of the Holy Spirit symbolized by the dove overhead. In a simplified variation on the theme, from an anonymous woodcut, Hus passes a torch to Luther (illustration 5).[60] The notion has textual basis as well though Wyclif is excluded and Erasmus has joined the triumvirate. 'Master Jan Hus stroked the fire in such a manner that a spark caught flame. . . Erasmus of Rotterdam took a candle and lit it. Martin Luther received the lighted candle in his hands

Illustration 5 Hus and Luther

and used it to bring light to the entire world . . . the crowd of priests could not abide the voice of the goose and so they roasted the goose. And the holy man's spirit prophesied to them saying you will roast me as a goose but there is one coming after me, a swan, whom you shall not be able to roast.'[61]

The Protestant uses of Hus in sixteenth-century propaganda were prolific. When Luther confronted Leo X and the weight of the medieval church he was buttressed by the word of God, which he holds up, the pen of Philip Melanchthon and a bevy of reformers including Jan Hus who stands next to Melanchthon.[62] Elsewhere Hus could be found with Luther and others bearing witness as the wicked ecclesiastical hierarchy are sent to hell.[63] There are too many extant portrayals of Hus with Reformation figures to note here but one other deserves mention. There are two slightly different seventeenth-century Dutch engravings featuring a candlestick symbolizing the light of the gospel (illustration 6).[64] The 'light of the gospel [has been] rekindled by reformers'. Seated around the table are sixteen reformers including Wyclif, Jerome of Prague, Zwingli, Luther, Oecolampadius, Bucer, Calvin, Melanchthon, Peter Martyr, Knox, Flacius, Bullinger, Zanchius, Beza, Perkins and Jan Hus. The latter is sitting at the left (indicated by the letter B), wearing a cap and holding a book to his chest. On the near side of the depiction a pope, cardinal, monk and demon attempt to blow the candle out. On the wall behind the table are portraits of George of Anhalt, Jan Łaski, William Farel, Johann Sleidan, Philips van Marnix and Franciscus Junius.

In Hussite iconography we find depictions of the goose appearing before 1419.[65] Perhaps the oldest evidence of the goose as a symbol for Hus himself can be located in the rough drawing with the inscription 'Husska' in the margin of a manuscript copy of Hus' work on the question of lay communion in both kinds.[66] The motif is not rare.

Illustration 6 Hus among the reformers

Sometime after 1546 a broadsheet appeared showing Luther holding a crucifix while at his feet one can see a goose reading in a book. There is also a woodcut of Luther in his study with a goose and a later variant.[67] The overleaf of a fifteenth-century Latin Bible shows a 'Táborite brother' with a chalice on his shoulder and a goose tucked in his belt.[68] The goose can be found on copper engravings from the 1420s.[69] There are somewhat oblique allusions to Hus in the art of late medieval Bohemia. A drollery appearing on the title page of a Latin exegesis of the Pauline epistles by Jan Rokycana shows a goose threatened by a nobleman armed with a crossbow.[70] Elsewhere a caricature of a crusader bearing a sword and shield threatens a defenseless goose.[71] The symbol of the goose appeared several times in depictions of war during the Hussite era. The most extensive collection of pictures for the Hussite wars can be found in Vienna.[72] The meaning of the goose on Hussite banners has been disputed but I hold to the opinion that the goose indicated Hus and functioned not as an alternative to the chalice but rather as a complimentary symbol.[73] In the Vienna collection a goose on a banner can be found in several depictions.[74] Among the more interesting and controversial is a double page illustration of a war scene between Hussite armies and imperial forces.[75] On the left, crusaders and Hussites face off from behind the protection of huge moveable shields. There are about fifteen warriors behind each shield. The crusaders fly a white banner bearing a red cross while the Hussites feature a goose drinking from a golden chalice on the front of their shield. The goose has been struck by an arrow. The feature is open to interpretation. On the right the Hussite wagon fortress is shown. On the tent one can see the symbol of a chalice while prominently flying above the entire scene is a red banner on which there is a goose. Depictions like this one reinforced the deliberate juxtaposition of the two symbols. More subtle is the small goose on the chest of a Hussite messenger who is delivering a document to Sigismund in 1431.[76]

In the 1520s an illustrated work appeared in Strasbourg featuring a number of woodcuts depicting various aspects of Hus' life and death.[77] Of note were pictures of Hus preaching in Bethlehem Chapel, being brought before the court at Constance, his tonsure being defaced, being handed over to the secular authorities, and burning at the stake. Unique among visual images is that Hus is rendered bald after his defrocking and appears as such in three subsequent woodcuts.[78] One of the most lavishly illustrated sources for the latter stages of Hus' life are the illustrated manuscripts of Ulrich Richental's chronicle of the Council of Constance. I have referred to this source earlier for aspects of the Hus trial. But the illustrations are now of interest. In the early twentieth century nine manuscript copies of the chronicle were extant.[79] Three early modern editions were published.[80] The oldest copy is the Aulendorf manuscript which may be dated as early as the first years of the third decade of the fifteenth century. This codex is illustrated with numerous colored pen drawings. Up until the twentieth century it was held by the counts of Königsegg-Aulendorf in their library near Constance. In 1935 it was acquired by the New York Public Library.[81] According to Richental and other sources, once convicted of heresy Hus was made to wear headgear resembling a dunce cap. Richental described it as a white miter on which two demons were painted and the word 'heresiarch'. Petr Mladoňovice recorded the crown was round and about eighteen inches high featuring three demons and the inscription 'this is a heresiarch'.[82] This opprobrious headpiece became the mark of a saint in Hussite art and St. Jan Hus was frequently shown wearing this miter which had been transformed into a crown of sanctity. From a canonical point of view the history, intention and meaning of placing such a cap on a heretic is unknown so commentary remains conjecture.[83] The heretical headpiece on Hus appears to be the first such depiction in European art.[84] The Aulendorf manuscript of Richental's chronicle has five pages wherein the trial and passio of Hus are vividly depicted.[85] He is presented at Constance by the archbishops of Pisa and Milan and is shown being led away by two bishops.[86] There are variations of detail. In one instance he is taken away by a large group of armed men wearing a large miter featuring two demons. Two other demons fly overhead on either side of the miter.[87] Elsewhere the accompanying group has been greatly reduced. There are no flying demons and there is only one demon on Hus' miter.[88] As a portent of his impending damnation, some of the illustrations show Hus walking to his death, bare-headed, but with a horned demon hovering on his head.[89]

The central motif in the iconography of Hus has to do with his death. The earliest definite portrayal of Hus at the stake occurred in a Bible from around 1430. The miniature appears at the base of the capital letter 'I' in the sentence 'in the beginning God created the heavens and the earth' from the Book of Genesis.[90] The clean-shaven Hus is bound to the stake by ropes around his upper and lower body and by a chain around his neck. He wears a plain white gown and on his head the miter of the heretic featuring three demons. Hus is lashed to an enormous stake and surrounded by flaming bundles of wood. A man wearing a dark gown and matching hat (perhaps the garb of a university master) and holding a small red book is thought to be Petr Mladoňovice. This image of Hus at the stake wearing this peculiar miter is a 'standard iconographic topos' in the depictions of Hus' death.[91] The burning of Hus was elsewhere depicted in the margins of manuscripts.[92] Occasionally an undamaged miniature of Hus has survived.[93] In other portrayals Hus is bearded but the miter is the same as in the Martinice Bible though Hus is often burning before a larger audience.[94] In one miniature Hus is tied to the stake at the feet, waist and neck. He wears the usual plain white gown and the demonic headpiece while the wood is piled about him.[95] There are examples of Hus being burned wearing a heavy looking gown.[96] Elsewhere the scenes are rather dramatic with large crowds, blazing infernos, attended by cardinals, bishops, monks and secular princes. The demon-adorned cap is present and at times Hus is bearded but not always.[97] A five-part gradual from the Church of St. Michael Opatovice in Prague dating to 1578 shows Hus wearing his miter, adorned with three demons, at the stake amid a billowing holocaust. In the background a cardinal and bishop are engaged in an energetic exchange.[98] Sometimes the burning of Hus was connected to an illustration of the dirt being dug up around the stake which we know was committed to the Rhine.[99] Occasionally the depictions are rather unrealistic. At times the bundles of burning faggots are placed almost too far away from Hus to have much effect while in other portrayals Hus was completely engulfed

Illustration 7 Martyrdom of Jan Hus

in the flames.[100] Some of the depictions are idealistic wherein Hus appeared peaceful as he is martyred and rose to the angels or to God in the heavens above.[101] At other times a more realistic effort was made to portray the anguish Hus must have suffered (illustration 7).[102] In one portrait Hus appears to protest as two men tending the fire brandish their pitchforks at him.[103] There are a number of impressive full page illustrations in Bohemian manuscripts of Hus' passio.[104] These do not necessarily add anything new to the iconography in question but they remain important for the art history of the period.

In an early liturgical composition Hus was compared to St. Laurence where the two martyrs were tested by fire but emerged in righteousness.[105] Altar panels dating to the mid-1480s from the Church of St. Václav in Roudníky, a village near Chabařovice in the district of Ústí-nad-Labem, featured Hus as a colleague of the early Christian martyrs James, Sebastian and Laurence. Hus appeared at the stake, clean-shaven, wearing a miter adorned by three demons and chained about the neck and waist.[106] Somewhat more rarely Hus is shown being burned with a number of large books, presumably his own writings. In one such depiction of Swiss provenance the onlookers are evenly divided into two groups. On the left, among a forest of military arms, are the seculars while on the right the clergy appear below numerous croziers and episcopal miters.[107] A variation of the theme is extant but the books are missing.[108] In both cases the onlookers are removed some distance from the event whereas in the woodcut used by John Foxe spectators are within arms reach of Hus (illustration 8).[109]

Recently (in 2001) a fresco has been uncovered on the south wall of the Church of St. Václav in Písek thought to date from the 1560s. The eye-level fresco on the south wall, though badly damaged, reveals a white-robed Hus bound to the stake. He is clean-shaven and wearing a miter on which at least two demons can be detected. A great crowd form a semi-circle around the stake. In the foreground men appear to be stoking the flames. The presence of such emotive frescos on the walls of churches is indicative of the important role they must have played in the religious consciousness of pious worshipers and presumably fulfilled a similar function as illustrations within the pages of a liturgical book. Another example are the stucco reliefs in the Chapel of

Illustration 8 The burning of Jan Hus

St. Romedius in the seventeenth-century Baroque chateau in Choltice. Here Hus is numbered with the heretics Mani, Jerome of Prague, Luther and Calvin.[110]

The examples of the visual sources of the passio of Jan Hus can be multiplied. Several of particular uniqueness should be noted. In rare cases laymen observe the soul of Hus being received and carried into heaven.[111] From a liturgical point of view it is entirely expected that visual illustrations of Hus should appear in texts commemorating his passio. Unfortunately many of these have gone missing over the centuries. There are several noteworthy survivals. In one case Hus goes from condemned heretic, wearing a penitential gown, to heavenly saint, with priestly vestments and renewed tonsure, in one dramatic picture. While a large crowd gathers to watch the burning, Hus' miter falls from his head as he expires in the flames. He is then received into glory by the angels into the presence of God where he is clothed with the garments of immortality and a crown of righteousness. His ecclesiastical defrocking is negated and Hus is restored to the priesthood.[112] This is a complete iconographical apotheosis. Elsewhere a white-gowned Hus is held to a stake with a double chain. Several men tend the fire before a large crowd including numerous religious figures. High above Hus, Jesus can be seen on the clouds and below him an angel with green wings and wearing a pink robe descends to the dying Hus. The angel holds the wreath of the martyrs to place as a crown upon Hus' head.[113] This is the only uncontested portrayal of Hus at the stake which does not feature the headgear of opprobrium.[114] Another example is also a full page illumination from a sixteenth-century gradual.[115] The page bears the heading for a musical piece with the title 'concerning the holy Master Jan Hus'. The historiated capital bears a customary illumination of John Baptist kneeling before the executioner. The right margin shows the reforming triad of Wyclif, Hus and Luther, while the foot of the page reveals in striking detail the passio of Hus. A poorly preserved portrayal can also be found in an initial where the suffering Christ appeared above the stake as Hus suffered the torments of death at the hands of two executioners. One of them has pinned Hus to the stake by means of an implement on a long pole.[116]

In 1423 the wool merchants guild in Siena commissioned a new triptych altarpiece. The artist selected for the painting was Stefano di Giovanni, better known today as Sassetta. The theme of the altar seems to have been the sacrament. Three of the scenes on the predella were devoted to eucharistic themes. One is a last supper, the second focused on the miracle of the holy sacrament while the third, which is of interest here, featured the burning of a heretic while the consecration of the Mass was celebrated. The condemned man is bearded, wearing a black gown and is bareheaded. A large crowd has gathered, a man tends the fire, while a winged demon swoops down from the sky, ostensibly to capture the damned soul.[117] The identity of the heretic is not certain but suggestions have been advanced that it is Jan Hus. The strongest evidence for that claim must be linked to the Council of Siena in 1423/4 which reiterated the condemnation of Hus.[118] The proclamation may have been fresh in Sassetta's mind as he painted the death of his heretic. The attribution is not too far afield inasmuch as the eucharist and Hussitism remained intimately related on a European-wide scale and it was widely, though erroneously maintained, that Hus' doctrine of the sacrament was deviant. If Sassetta's heretic is Hus, this would be the earliest depiction of him at the stake. The other unusual depiction of Hus comes from early sixteenth-century Tábor. This is among a series of ornamental sculptures dating to 1515 which included Hus, Jerome, Jan Žižka and Prokop Holý and originally formed part of the Tábor city coat of arms. This was the work of Wendel Roskopf (1480–1549), a Franconian stonemason.

As late as the eighteenth century, books appeared featuring dramatic portrayals of Hus at the stake. A copperplate engraving by Hans Daucher is one example.[119] With the skyline of Constance in the right background and an enormous crowd congregated we find Hus standing serenely at the stake on a huge woodpile. Three men tend the fire which send a billowing cloud of smoke up and over the lake. Hus has longer hair than usual and is bearded, but he is not wearing the customary miter of the heretic. As in the Litoměřice Gradual, the miter has fallen from his head and can be seen just to the left of center at the base of the woodpile. Two demons can be detected. Oval portraits of Hus and Jerome of Prague appeared on the upper sides of the sheet bracketing a German inscription which noted their deaths.

It lies beyond the scope of this study to take into account the varieties of coins, bells, stove tiles and book decorations which featured Hus. A brief comment on each must suffice. In terms of coins these almost invariably showed a bust of Hus on one side while the obverse revealed his martyrdom at the stake. Of interest in the dozen coins considered is that in all but one case of these numismatic depictions of the passio, Hus is naked save for a loincloth.[120] The obverse of a commemorative medallion from Regensburg in 1617 showed Luther as the swan attacking the apocalyptic whore of Babylon while Hus held a Bible proclaiming the triumph of truth. Behind Hus a goose can be seen in the flames. In 2001 a commemorative medallion was struck in honor of the 600th anniversary of Hus' ordination.[121] Several bells bearing images of Hus survive from Roudnice, Okrouhlice, Hradec Králové, and Veclov dated between 1544 and 1609. Stove tiles featuring Hus are preserved in museums in Prague and Tábor.[122] In 1539 at least two volumes were bound for use by the city council in Regensburg. Among several reformers we find an image of 'Ioannes Hvs 1415'.[123] The iconographical Hus must be handled with care. History is contested and challenged by hagiography. One must be cautious in identifying which Hus is at issue. Nevertheless, the iconography of Jan Hus constitutes a rich historical tradition.

11

HISTORIOGRAPHY

In the 1930s it was suggested that on the whole Jan Hus was not acceptable to the vast majority of the Czech nation. To pick and choose aspects of Hus' legacy or to make Hus in one's own image was simply dishonest.[1] For 600 years Hus has endured that historical fate. His place in history has served to exacerbate the evaluation of his life. In life and in death Hus has remained controversial. From an historiographical point of view he is suspended in the terra incognita of the fifteenth century, between the medieval world and the age of reformations. Medievalists and Reformation scholars have differed in their assessments. Hus has not infrequently been a pawn used and abused – frequently misused – by Catholic and Protestant perspectives. His memory has suffered the vagaries and vicissitudes of the protracted German-Slavic conflict, Czech nationalism, politically motivated Marxist analysis and various forms of political censorship. Often these conflicting interpretations are ignored by those for whom Bohemian issues have always been 'a quarrel in a faraway country between people of whom we know nothing'.[2] Who is the Hus of history? In the fifteenth century Hus was a heresiarch to some and a Christ-like martyr to others. He was a reformer with honorable motives in certain views, while other perspectives regarded him as a liability to Christian unity. The sixteenth-century hardened these polar assumptions. An entire tradition claimed him as a forerunner, a proto-Protestant, indeed among the earliest Protestants. To others he remained Catholic, medieval, even heretical in the worst stereotypical sense. As time passed into centuries Hus became a hero with a dozen faces to the Czechs. In turn he became a nationalist, a Communist, a social revolutionary, a man more mythic than human, Christian martyr, Catholic, Protestant, reformer, priest and pastor, scholar, and in each of these images a hollow man whose name is remembered but whose meaning is either unknown or manipulated to suit an agenda. Wherever the truth lies in these positions it seems irrefutable that any proper understanding of Hus and his life must begin with religion and take into account the multiple religious worlds of the later Middle Ages.[3] Whatever else Hus may have been he considered himself first of all a man of God, a preacher, and a shepherd of souls.

Any historiographical evaluation of Hus must take into account the corpus of his writings. It is scandalous that 600 years have elapsed since his death and no complete or critical edition of his works have appeared. There have been four unsatisfactory efforts thus far. The *editio princeps* of Hus' works appeared in Nürnberg in 1558 edited by the Croatian Lutheran theologian Matthias Flacius Illyricus (1520–1575). The two volumes were reprinted in 1583 and 1715 without any textual changes and for 300 years remained the sole edition.[4] Flacius thought it scandalous that the Czechs whom he characterized as lazy had produced no edition of Hus.[5] In the nineteenth century a Czech edition of Hus' works appeared in Prague.[6] The Erben edition supplanted Flacius in many respects. At the turn of the century Václav Flajšhans began an ambitious project to publish Hus texts in an even better edition.[7] Flajšhans did not complete his undertaking. In the 1950s a definitive critical edition of the works of Hus in twenty five volumes was announced.[8] Disgracefully, by the year 2000 less than half of the volumes had appeared. Recently an agreement was reached with Brepols, the Belgian publishing house, and two further volumes have appeared with at least five others in progress. A number of editions of the acts of the Council of Constance appeared between the late seventeenth and twentieth centuries. The most complete with respect to Hus remain those by Hardt and Mansi.[9] A definitive edition incorporating most of the known sources on Hus, numbering twenty-six items, is essential.[10] Contemporary polemical literature dealing with Hus is voluminous but one important collection are the series of tracts written by the Moravian Carthusian abbot Štěpán of Dolany (†1421) between 1408 and 1417 and published in 1723 by Fr. Bernard Pez (1683–1735), librarian of the Benedictine house at Melk.[11] The valuable correspondence of Hus is available in several editions. By far the best collection is the one edited by Novotný.[12] There are three English versions of Hus' letters but the most recent one by Spinka is clearly the more desirable.[13] There are a variety of single text editions of Hus in a variety of languages. In English his *De ecclesia* and his work on simony are available in reliable translations.[14] Any careful study of Hus reveals an absence of logic and exceptional intellectual form. Hus was not the first rate philosopher Wyclif was nor a thinker of the caliber of Jakoubek of Stříbro who later applied that rigor to some of Hus' ideas. This neither denigrates Hus nor diminishes his significance. His historiographical evaluation centers partly on the extent to which Hus can be accused of flagrant defiance of lawful authorities and in which parts he actually deviated from the teachings of the western church. This study has shown that unwittingly or otherwise Hus did blur the line between official church doctrine and the forbidden territories of heterodoxy and heresy as defined and understood by the Latin Church at the end of the Middle Ages. Twenty years ago I was told by an established figure in the field of Hussitica that Hus had been done as a topic of scholarly inquiry. That assessment was as misguided as it was inaccurate. Scholarly inquiry continues to refine our understanding of Hus in important ways.[15]

Historiography as a discipline applied to Jan Hus began rather intentionally with the account of the Hus trial at Constance by Petr Mladoňovice.[16] That account shaped the immediate Czech understanding of Hus. Its function in the history of Hussitism has already been referenced. The account is clearly tendentious though this cannot be essayed as an argument against Petr's reliability. That claim has been widely accepted. The legal process described in the *Relatio* should be received as a narrative of unusual probity. The Latin text was translated into Czech in the period between 1417 and 1420 probably by its author or by another individual familiar with the proceedings and events at Constance and almost certainly an eyewitness. There are differences between the two versions. In places, additions to the original text appear while in certain instances abridgements have been undertaken. One can find information in the Czech text absent in the Latin and this may be evidence the translator had been at Constance.[17] The depiction of the legal process at Constance is nowhere more fully recorded than in Petr's *Relatio*. That narrative has likewise shaped historiographical opinion. Not a few scholars believe the portrayal of the men of the Council as bitter, hateful and unconcerned with truth is an accurate assessment. From the time of Hus' execution he entered the annals of history and events and ideas thereafter concerning the religious history of Bohemia often used Hus as a frame of reference. For example the death of Jan Hus became an historiographical launching pad for the religious wars and social revolution which convulsed the Czech Kingdom in the fifteenth century. His followers rioted in Prague and elsewhere. They drove priests from their livings, burned down churches, destroyed religious houses, and committed murder.[18] According to sources in the early historiography of Hus the people called Hussites were defined in two ways: adherents to the preaching of Master Hus and practitioners of utraquism.[19] Not one without the other, but both components. There are no Hussites without Hus and utraquist practice without meaningful reference to Hus may be religious and liturgical reform but it cannot be called Hussite. All too often early Hussite history is one of the cup without meaningful connection to the reform initiatives of Hus and early traditions associated with Jan Milíč and Matěj of Janov.

There are myriads of sources in the fifteenth century which mention Hus and these cannot be noted nor indeed is that exercise necessary.[20] Few of them may be said to have shaped the interpretation of Hus for successive generations. The Hussite tradition from Petr Mladoňovice onwards defended Hus as a stalwart martyr for Christ. The Dominican Johannes Nider who attended the Council of Basel and had a number of official dealings with Hussites argued at some length that Hus had been justly condemned and burned at the Council of Constance.[21] That perspective passed into a central component of the early histories of the Hussite movement and became a definitive assessment. Two deeply flawed histories of the Hussite period exerted a profound influence on the historiography of Hus right up until the nineteenth century. These were the works of Aeneas Sylvius Piccolomini (1405–1464) and Václav Hájek of Libočany (†1553).

In 1458 two important events occurred in the life of Aeneas Sylvius. He completed his 'history of Bohemia' and was elected to the papacy taking the name Pius II.[22] The first of these events is germane here. It is important to note that most historical treatments of Hus are in some sense connected to treatments of the Hussite period and vice versa. The *Historia bohemica* chronicled Czech history from its origins to the time of King Jiří of Poděbrady (1420–1471). The book consisted of seventy two chapters. Hussite matters were covered in the foreword and in chapters 35–52. It is clear that Hussitism provided Aeneas with his reason to write on Bohemian history.

In his writings Aeneas Sylvius presented Hus as an heresiarch.[23] He was sentenced to death by the Council of Constance and because he tarnished the true faith, Aeneas concluded, Hus would suffer forever in hell.[24] Chapters thirty five and thirty six summarized the view of Hus as portrayed by Aeneas. The 'perfidious Hussite lunacy' began with Hus who imbibed the ideas of Wyclif and used Wyclif's ideas to befuddle the university masters, especially the Germans, in a strategy to take over the university. This failed so Hus interceded with the king to have the university purged. Once Hus gained control of the university and emerged as the leader of the movement he started to publicly declare the heresies he had suppressed. Slandering church leadership and continuing to promote deviant ideas Hus galvantized a popular movement. Along with Jerome, Hus was considered scholarly, a leader of the people in Bohemia and a promoter of heresy. Since Hus proved intractable when brought before the Council he was deemed a 'cursed fellow' and a 'rotten limb' which had to be cut off in order to save the body.[25] Later Aeneas affirmed his conviction that filled with pride, Hus wanted to appear more divine than human.[26] Hussitism constituted a subtraction from the faith. The Bohemians were faithless heretics who disrupted true religion. Aeneas erroneously equated the reformed faith of the Czechs with the brand exemplified at Tábor.[27] It is manifestly evident that Aeneas was more interested in Táborite history than he was with Hus but the conclusions he drew concerning the radical Hussites were rooted in assumptions made about Hus. Put together, in all the earth there was no other group of people 'more monstrous' than those affiliated with Hus. Their minds were depraved and they existed in the lowest depths of hell.[28] Hussite religion was not Christian.[29] For a long time Aeneas exerted profound influence and his history survived in numerous manuscripts, printed editions, and vernacular translations.

The second source is Václav Hájek of Libočany who published a Czech history in 1541.[30] Hájek was a Czech priest and later provost of the cathedral chapter of Stará Boleslav and like Aeneas Sylvius clearly anti-Hussite. To some extent Hájek relied on Aeneas but he also used other sources and a close reading of his history reveals numerous fabrications and unreliable narrative. It is not too severe to say that Hájek was unscrupulous in ways that even Aeneas was not. Like his predecessor, Hájek was more interested in the Hussite tradition than in Hus himself. But he affirmed that Wyclif corrupted Hus and that the heresies which flourished in Bohemian soil were of foreign extraction. Hus was a pious and good man but proved himself weak and unequal to the task of rebutting heresy. The more popular he became the more he embraced the heresies he had previously suppressed or refuted. He was more objective on Hus' trial at Constance except he erred in advancing a claim that Hus opposed utraquism. Hájek portrayed Hus as a decent though misguided man who strayed from the path of truth and orthodoxy and wound up tragically at Constance. He did not regard Hus as an intentional wicked deceiver.[31] Hájek was even more opposed to Táborite religion than Aeneas and went so far as to say that everyone hated the Hussites so much they even cursed Hus.[32] The works of Aeneas Sylvius and Hájek were enduringly influential, regarded as standard historical treatments from the sixteenth through the eighteenth centuries. It might be said with some justification that no one wrote on Czech history until the nineteenth century who did not come under the influence of one or both of these histories.

Borrowing both from Aeneas and Hájek, Jan Doubravský (1486–1553), bishop of Olomouc from 1542, produced another Czech history which even further denigrated the memory of Jan Hus.[33] Devoted to his faith Doubravský was incapable of seeing Hus other than as a threat and a strident enemy of official religion. Hus was anti-German. Irritated at not securing a prebend this increased his animosity for Germans (apparently he lost out to a German candidate) and the church in general. On heresy specifically he was seduced by Wyclif. His attacks on the priesthood were indiscriminate. In the hands of Doubravský, Hus was not interested in meaningful religious reform, his aims appeared selfish, motivated by anger and revenge. This translated into an almost purely social revolution in the days of the Hussites. As we have seen previously Protestant writers of the sixteenth century saw Hus quite differently but their propagandist methodology made Hus in their own image just as surely as his enemies twisted his memory for other purposes. Even though the edition of Hus' works published by Flacius appeared during this time it does not seem to have had the same influence as the hostile interpretations. The work of the Catholic polemicist Johannes Cochlaeus (1479–1552), however, has infinitely more value than Aeneas, Hájek and Doubravský. However, his portrait of Hus was equally gloomy. Hus was a great disadvantage to Bohemia and an evil man. He caused greater grief and destruction than any one ever did to one's own country. Moreover he was afflicted with the sins of pride and hypocrisy and became the 'unhappy Hus'.[34] In the hands of Cochlaeus, he was a larger than life rebellious heretic and enemy of the church.[35]

The Protestant martyrologists mentioned in chapter nine presented Hus quite differently. Essentially the death of Hus amounted to a theological event. To Jean Crespin (1520–1572) Hus was a hero, a steadfast example of Christian piety, whose death was precious in the sight of the godly. He perished as a reformer crushed by an institution more concerned with tradition than truth. This treatment of Hus presented him as a forerunner who shone the first light of the great revivals which characterized the Protestant movements.[36] Much of the same perspective can be found in the works of John Foxe (1516–1587), Ludwig Rabus (1523–1592), Matthias Flacius (1520–1575) and others. Unfortunately there are no examples in early Protestant historiography which succeeded in presenting Hus in an objective and original sense. Even ambitious assessments of the Hussite epoch were rather unsuccessful. The Lutheran Zacharias Theobald (1584–1627) regarded Hus as a reformer somewhat independent of Wyclif. His Protestant allegiance led Theobald to refer to 'our Hus' but his treatment was facile. His focus was limited by the influence of Hájek whom he found unable to resist.[37] The limited tendencies in the historiography noted thus far continued and were revealed even in the capable work of the Jesuit Bohuslav Balbín (1621–88). Balbín was perhaps the most important figure in the Czech Baroque period when speaking of historiography. There are several works which bear noting. Balbín wrote a narrative history of Bohemia but relied heavily on Aeneas, Hájek, Doubravský and Theobald and was for that specific reason derivative, repetitive and limited.[38] In 1672 he wrote a defense of Slavic languages, especially Czech, but this remained unpublished for over a century and when it did appear there were severe repercussions.[39] Most important was his massively conceived encyclopedia of Bohemian topics.[40] Conceived as twenty volumes only ten were completed at the time of his death. Regrettably Balbín utilized Hájek without critical judgment or questioning the veracity of Hájek's sources or interpretation. His treatment of the Hussite period reflected the inadequate influence of Hájek. In two paragraphs devoted to Hussite themes the majority of source references are to Hájek and Theobald.[41] Hus remained trapped in the manufactured world of the historians. Though by no means an example of sound scholarship it is refreshing to come upon the observation that both Catholic and Protestant history erred in the presentations of Hus. The French Protestant of the Calvinist persuasion Jacques Lenfant (1661–1728) pointed out that Catholics tended to apply to Hus ideas which cannot be sustained while Protestants imputed to him their own preconceived concepts which have no meaning in the medieval world. In doing so both traditions avoided the historical Hus.[42] Lenfant maintained the Council of Constance erred in subjecting Hus to violence for he was a pious man whose life was worthy of the apostles. The executions of Hus and Jerome led to more violence in the 'streets of Prague and the highways of Bohemia' with one faction shouting 'Hus forever' while the other cried 'long live the pope'.[43] A careful consideration of the trial of Hus led Lenfant to the conclusion that Hus' reluctance to acquiesce in the condemnation of Wyclif led to his own death.[44] A more substantial assessment of Hus appeared in the work of the Czech František M. Pelcl (1734–1801).[45] This was an altogether sympathetic treatment, all the more intriguing because Pelcl was Catholic. In Pelcl's hands, Hus comes across as a national leader and a Catholic. Pelcl does not impute to Hus either a Wyclifite identity nor Protestant proclivities and he went to some lengths to minimize Hus' doctrinal deviance from the mainstream of the fifteenth-century church.[46] In his later work it must be said that Pelcl articulates a fairly balanced understanding of Hus' historical significance. Pelcl's aligning Hus closely with a nationalistic agenda proved to be a precursor for events to come.[47]

The revolutions of 1848 brought significant changes for Hussite historiography in the Czech lands. The Habsburg authorities censored every book and publication printed in the empire and everything had to be approved by the censor in Vienna. This restricted the ability of historians to deal with many issues. Prominent historians claimed the imperial censor hindered historical research and the government did nothing to promote historical study and did everything to suppress it.[48] After the revolutions of 1848 Czechs began increasingly to refer to Jan Hus. He was regarded as an important personality in a general European-wide progression towards an ethically based, individual, form of religion. In historiographical writing, in drama and sermons, one sees the memory of Hus more and more perceived as a means of both sanctifying and revitalizing the Czech nation. German and Catholic opposition to this idea only made it more popular.[49] The preeminent figure to emerge in historical writing about the Hussite era was František Palacký (1798–1876). Combining a land-patriotism with national spirit Palacký synthesized a constitutionally understood version of historical events to support the glory and grandeur of Bohemian history. Palacký regarded Czech history as consisting of two monumental clashes: a national conflict with the Germans and a religious struggle against Rome. The Hussite period featured both prominently. Therefore the days of Hus and his followers functioned as a suitable era in which Palacký could explore his historiographical convictions. Hussite history became the pinnacle of national understanding and Hus performed crucial service in the struggle for the liberation of a Czech identity from under the yoke of German oppression. Palacký's powerful influence caused the historiographical image of Hus to shift quite dramatically so that the nineteenth-century Hus appeared predominantly as a man chiefly concerned with national identity. His support for the Czech Bible, in the hands of Palacký, came to be viewed as a defense of Czech culture. Palacký seemed to have given little consideration to other more religious motivations for Hus' stance on the matter. Palacký did not emphasize, indeed one might say he minimized, the religious and theological ideas which motivated Hus.[50] He wrote little on religious subjects even though his principle interest clearly lay in the Hussite period. Neither the doctrinal ideas Hus espoused nor his role as a theologian were of particular interest to Palacký. The emphasis lay elsewhere. Palacký was very critical of his predecessors and their approach to Hus and Hussite history. By means of his writing and through the editions of Hussite source material which he produced, Palacký destroyed forever the influence of Hájek.[51] In consideration of Hus, Palacký ranked him ahead of Luther and Calvin in terms of significance in the religious development of Europe.[52] The meaning of Czech history can be found in the acts of the Hussites from Hus himself on down. From a religious point of view Palacký considered the followers of Hus to be the first Protestants. Therefore Hus was the founder of the Protestant movements.[53] For Palacký, a new period of religious history began with Jan Hus. Palacký retained some affinity for the Czech Brethren and he posited Hus as the first teacher of that movement.[54] Among the important editions of primary sources which appeared under his editorship the most relevant for the study of Hus appeared in 1869.[55] The Palacký edition included all known letters of Hus, documents relating to the case against him from 1408 to Constance, an edition of the *Relatio* of Petr Mladoňovice, letters and documents illuminating the religious history of Bohemia between 1403 and 1418, and extracts from the writings of Hus. The collection is still of value 140 years later. The importance of Palacký in Hussite historiography is difficult to exaggerate and his influence persists to the present.[56] Nevertheless he did virtually deprive Hus (and the Hussites) of medieval identity and dressed him in the garments of nationalism. Hus stood as a sentinel figure encouraging and inspiring the Czech people in their struggle for political and national independence. Palacký's magnum opus remains his great history of the Czech nation. His critics referred to it as a history of the Hussites with a long introduction. The presumption is not fallacious.

Palacký's bête noire in Hussite historiography was the German Catholic professor of history at Prague, Konstantin von Höfler (1811–1898). Höfler argued that Hus was anti-German in orientation and less concerned with ecclesiastical reform than in promoting Czech interests. For Höfler, Hus was the destroyer of the university in Prague, by means of the 1409 'decree of Kutná Hora', and the leader of a destructive social revolution. Hus was a heretic in the worst stereotypical sense of the term, effectively a common criminal, who got what he deserved at Constance.[57] Hus was to be blamed for the subsequent conflicts in Bohemia after 1409. In the hands of Höfler, Hus was both an implacable enemy of the church and an unflinching opponent of the German people. Accordingly, Höfler published a slashing hostile study of Hus arguing that one cannot admire Hus for everything he did was aimed at Slavic interest to elevate the Czechs and subjugate the Germans.[58] Moreover, nationalism was of more importance to Hus than religion or ethics.[59] Ironically as implacable enemies, Höfler and Palacký could agree on this single point: Hus was motivated by largely nationalistic interests. The views propounded by Höfler and others continued apace and reached a water shed in the work of Johann Loserth (1846–1936) noted in chapter six and this continued well into the twentieth century in various forms.[60] However, there were important exceptions within German scholarship. Johann August Wilhelm Neander (1789–1850) took a different perspective, as we have seen in chapter six, and Gotthard Lechler's (1811–1888) posthumous study of Hus treated the subject with surprising balance and unexpected insight but with the impression that Hus' death amounted to judicial murder.[61] One of the trends which began in the nineteenth century was a reconsideration of the trial of Hus with a major conclusion that Hus belonged to all people as a significant historical figure who could not be claimed exclusively by any church or tradition.[62] During the second half of the nineteenth century the memory of Hus was not infrequently a source of contention in Czech newspapers. In 1889 a protest was made over plans to erect a major public monument to Hus in Prague.[63]

The twentieth century retained the best of the school of Palacký but under the influence of Jaroslav Goll (1846–1929) inaugurated a new approach within Czech historiography.[64] Theoretically historians now worked with more objectivity and dealt with Hus as an historical figure of the later Middle Ages and not as a suprahistorical idea with significance for intellectual concepts such as the meaning of Czech history or a national identity removed from the later Middle Ages by centuries. The focus now centered more properly on the Hus of history rather than on the Hus of ideological claims.[65] Josef Kalousek (1838–1915) had already warned against politicizing Hus and making him into a symbol of nationalism even though at the time that seemed to make Hus less relevant.[66] The advent of the Goll school did not mean the end of using history as a tool to manipulate the present (within Czech historiography) but it did signal a deliberate attempt to study Jan Hus and the past more objectively, independent of the motivating agendas of religion, politics and nationalism.

Though not a proper historian at all and by consequence often overlooked in historiographical essays, the liberal Catholic literary critic and philologist Václav Flajšhans (1866–1950) wrote a lengthy biography of Hus and elsewhere referred to him as the greatest and most famous theologian of his time.[67] Though his professional ambitions were permanently thwarted, as noted above, Flajšhans likewise brought out an edition of Hus' works and edited the sermons Hus preached in Bethlehem

Chapel.⁶⁸ He felt a reassessment of Hus might be beneficial. In terms of the Hus trial he had reservations about the equity of the process but rather than focusing on the charges formally laid against Hus, Flajšhans took particular note of the twenty-eight false accusations to underscore the questionable and troubling aspects of the legal proceedings. His work encountered considerable resistance within ecclesiastical circles. Scholars such as Jan Gebaur (1838–1907), Karel Novák, Václav Novotný and Josef Truhlář (1840–1914) were highly critical of Flajšhans. But Flajšhans and his predecessors Kalousek and Palacký defended the necessity of the academic study of Hus. Those efforts likewise may be found in Václav Novotný (1868–1932) and Vlastimil Kybal (1880–1958). Both were products of Goll's school of scientific positivism. Novotný is rightly seen as the real successor of Goll. His historical method relied on critical analysis and his work was not driven by ideological motivation. However he tended to reveal consistent prejudice towards Hus' opponents. Novotný maintained the perspective that Hus was greatly influenced by ideas extracted from his native Czech environment and traditions. Novotný argued that Hus chose to express those ideas using Wyclif's language and constructs. Novotný adopted a biographical approach to the study of Hus and his great work with Kybal took theology into significant account, though this is more on account of Kybal.⁶⁹ Both men, but especially Kybal, criticized the tendentious nature of religious and nationalist interpretations of Hus. Kybal had in mind the work of Lechler, Loserth, Jan Sedlák and especially the Catholic priest and theologian Antonín Lenz (1829–1901).⁷⁰ Understandably Kybal's work was assailed by those within the Catholic tradition, among them the Jesuit Bohumil Spáčil on the grounds that it was anti-Catholic.⁷¹ Kybal took immense delight in the idea of Hus as a reformer. Novotný was also responsible for enduringly useful editions of Hus' letters and the *Relatio* of Petr Mladoňovice.

Jan Sedlák (1871–1924) took up the challenge presented by Loserth and extended the textual dependency of Hus on Wyclif to the former's Czech writing. However Sedlák also argued for Hus' intellectual independence from Wyclif and made a case for academic malfeasance and anachronism on the part of Loserth.⁷² In distinction to Flajšhans, Sedlák argued for the lawful conduct of the Council of Constance especially in the setting aside of clearly unfounded accusations. In dealing with Hus, Josef Pekař (1870–1937) emphasized the medieval theological parameters of Hus' thought. The premise assumed by Pekař, however, was sensible. That said, he may be criticized for failing to take up any meaningful note of the reforming aspects latent in Hus' program.⁷³ Elsewhere Pekař minimized Hussite history in terms of significant social progression and concluded it contributed little or nothing to the evolution of European culture.⁷⁴ For Pekař it was a serious mistake to see in the Czech national impulse a religious foundation. As a reformer Hus wished to establish a new church away from the official Roman communion.⁷⁵ Sedlák, Rudolf Holinka (1899–1953) and Augustin Neumann (1891–1948), all of whom were Catholic, argued to the conclusion that Hus was a minor figure in the religious history of medieval Europe. His death made him greater than his life ever did. That view countered the claims of Palacký and others. But Palacký had his twentieth-century defenders. In a speech delivered at Kozí Hrádek on 17 July 1910 Tomáš G. Masaryk (1850–1937), later the first president of Czechoslovakia, took the opposite view. Hus as a moral reformer sought a form of religion which improved upon that practiced in medieval Christianity which was modeled on Rome. Masaryk argued that Hus called for a faith built upon conscience and conviction not politics.[76] Masaryk's memoirs clearly showed the pervasive notion that Hus had political, social and especially nationalistic significance. Doctrine and theology were important in Masaryk's Hus but only in a secondary sense.[77] Josef Pekař opposed the Masaryk model of Hus as the cornerstone of Czech history which led to an unfolding of a Protestant religious ideal. Pekař suggested that such a concept of Hus served no objective scholarly purpose but only advanced an ahistorical, political agenda. He argued that Hus owed his existence as a reformer to the weakness and ineptitude of King Václav IV.[78] The suggestion has merit. His own perspective was also nationalist but guided by a quite conservative Catholic political perspective. With this methodological principle, Pekař saw the Hus-Hussite event as a tragedy and a deplorable mistake. Unsurprisingly Pekař preferred not to see the 'anti-Catholic' Hus among his national heros. That stance made him a lightning rod generating many detractors. One example was Kamil Krofta (1876–1945) who maintained much of Palacký's perspective and was on that account frequently in dispute with Pekař.[79]

These nationalist battles for the memory of Hus and his political uses reached a pinnacle in a public furore in 1925. The Hus celebrations that year were attended by the president and prime minister of Czechoslovakia, Tomáš G. Masaryk and Antonín Švehla. The Vatican regarded the participation of these statesmen as offensive. The papal nuncio Francesco Marmaggi filed a protest and the incident led to a suspension of diplomatic relations between Vatican City and Czechoslovakia.[80]

In February 1948, the Communist takeover of government in Czechoslovakia precipitated a profound rupture in Czech historiography. There were two serious consequences. Independence in the writing and interpretation of history was forfeit and a period of enforced isolation from international developments was imposed. Numerous historical topics were nominated as controversial. The list included Jan Hus. A number of scholars were prevented from continuing with their work. Kybal spent the last ten years of his life in exile and died in Washington. Things improved briefly but the defeat of the Prague Spring in 1968 ushered in a second period of repression called 'normalization'. Many scholars lost their jobs. František Šmahel became a tram driver in Prague for five years and Milan Machovec spent those years of academic exile as a church organist. Following World War II it is accurate to say that Czech historiography, especially on the Hus question, became largely a servant of the state. The dead hand of communist Czechoslovakia stifled academic freedom and a number of potential scholars of Jan Hus did not materialize and were lost to other endeavors. An example is George Holmes (1927–2009) who learned Czech with the intention of studying Hus. The political repression he experienced in Prague early in his career caused him to turn his formidable talents elsewhere. He went on to become the Chichele Professor of Medieval History at Oxford and a renowned expert on the

Renaissance. He left behind but one essay on Hussite history.[81] There were other casualties as well. While it is true that the Hussite movement which followed Hus became more a matter of interest to politically motivated historiography, Hus also came to be seen as a proto-Communist who waged a struggle on behalf of common people against the elite culture of his times. Thus his efforts in the fifteenth century were brought to fruition in the twentieth century. Marxist thought, which dominated the mainstream of Czech history in the second half of the twentieth century, perceived Hus as a nationalist, a social revolutionary, and a political figure, while his religious identity and concerns were severely minimized and if mentioned at all were made to function as a foil for deeper and more important social and political aspirations. This is true to a greater and lesser degree in the works of Josef Macek (1922–1991), Robert Kalivoda (1923–1989) and many others.[82] Milan Machovec (1925–2003) claimed to be concerned with an interpretation of Hus' works and regarded the roots of authentic Czech history in the ideas of Hus. Rather than a reform of religious practice or clarification of doctrine, or renewal of spirituality, the career of Hus was essentially interpreted as socio-political event committed to a power struggle with the Latin Church and its powerful leaders.[83] The Marxist Hus emerged as a social critic, posing a revolutionary challenge, while at the same time bringing together a counter tradition which effectively attacked the medieval feudal system.[84] In this interpretive scheme Hus' meteoric career can be understood as a result of the splintering crisis of medieval feudalism and has nothing therefore to do with theology or religious inquiry.[85] Notwithstanding this, Hus emerged as a sort of renaissance man, a political figure, and a revolutionary.[86]

Both Kalivoda and Macek in their books published in 1961 paid attention to Hus as a religious figure and focused to some extent on his theology but the analysis in both cases seemed driven by an agenda. Macek's Hus was a rather pedestrian study which broke no new ground. It falls in the popular biography genre but was noteworthy for the absence of the shrill political Marxism which characterized his earlier work on Hussitism.[87] In the relevant parts of his work when Hus was under investigation, Kalivoda was preoccupied with Hus' doctrine in an effort to establish that Hussitism was a social revolution and therefore Hus must be located in an intentional social locus. Hus' ideas were centered in social reform. When he took sides with common people and their plight Kalivoda assumed medieval structures were not legitimate and no longer viable.[88] The continued stress on a nationalistic Hus continued and his career was part of the late medieval crisis of feudalism. Political donatism marked Hus. His reform called for moral worthiness and stress upon ethical conduct, moral worth, toleration and a form of inclusive Christianity were features marking certain portraits of Hus. Macek played down nationalism as a motivating factor, finding religious ideas such as the law of God to be more important for Hus.[89] From Zdeněk Nejedlý (1878–1962), Marxist scholars began to move away from specific nationalistic assumptions. Stressing mainly the social elements in Hus' teaching, Nejedlý helped to create an image wherein Hus became a social critic and social innovator and ultimately a social revolutionary who broke from medieval concepts and constructs heralding a new social order.[90] The cleavage between social and national interests and theology continued to be a fertile ground in the interpretation of Jan Hus throughout much of the twentieth century. Regardless of the nature of Hus' comments on social issues there is no formal social philosophy evident in his works.[91] Masaryk, Pekař, Sedlák, Holinka, Eduard Winter (1896–1982) and Ferdinand Seibt tended to focus on religious or nationalistic motivations. On other hand, Kalivoda, Macek, Frederick G. Heymann (1900–1983), František Graus (1921–1989), Howard Kaminsky and many others tended to see social action as vital and how this emerged from theological controversy. Graus, for example, almost completely ignored Hus' martyrdom because the demise of Hus tended to eclipse entirely his life.[92] Nevertheless he correctly saw Hus' main goal as a reform of the Church not of society.[93] Macek was comfortable linking Hus with popular heresies in south Bohemia. Others demurred.[94] An exception to the Marxist historiography which dominated Prague was the work of Protestant scholars František M. Bartoš (1890–1972) and Amedeo Molnár (1923–1990). A product of the liberal branch of the Goll school Bartoš conducted widespread research on virtually every aspect of Hussite history. It is a great pity he did little by way of synthesizing the results of his many scattered articles and sometimes detailed heuristic essays. Bartoš considered Hussite history and Jan Hus positive and progressive in virtually every respect. He did not produce a detailed or definitive study of Hus.[95] While some of his conclusions are no longer regarded as valid much of the work he conducted has lasting value. Like Palacký before him, Bartoš regarded the genesis of the European Reformations in the life and work of Hus.[96] He critiqued relentlessly the perspective represented by Josef Pekař, consistently sided with Masaryk against Pekař, offering thoughtful essays which undermined the latter's theses. Amedeo Molnár's major discussion of Hus was published in Italian.[97] Unfortunately it consisted of little more than an introductory survey. Molnár agreed with Bartoš in the assumption that Hus stood at the inauguration of a new European religious order. Other interpretations of Hus tended to socialize him and the true church, or authentic community of faith, emerged as a context in which the word of God was proclaimed. This was emphatically developed in several of Hus' works.[98]

The 1960s proved to be a significant decade for international Hussite studies and a reconsideration of Jan Hus. The largest and perhaps most significant undertaking on the interpretation of Hus came through the efforts of the Belgian Benedictine Paul De Vooght (1900–1983). His assessment of Hus may be judged a thorough theological analysis. Ignoring almost completely the school of Marxist interpretation, De Vooght extended and corrected the shriller aspects of Hus as set forth in Sedlák. He also criticized the nationalist bias of German historians like Loserth and Höfler who tried to discredit Hus. However, he completely ignored the work of Novotný and Kybal which is astonishing that such a remarkable and major work could be so thoroughly ignored. Of significance in De Vooght's assessment of Hus was an exoneration of Wyclifite influence and De Vooght's Hus was essentially independent of Wyclif on most doctrinal points. This is not to suggest that De Vooght did not acknowledge the place of Wyclif in Hus' thought, but it was indicative that he had no sympathy with the Loserth thesis. The detailed analysis which Hus was subjected to in the hands of De Vooght yielded a somewhat surprising conclusion. De Vooght claimed for Hus a greater sense of doctrinal orthodoxy on a number of theological matters than had hitherto been acknowledged. That said, the title of De Vooght's study – *The Heresy of Jan Hus* – was a conclusion, not a question. De Vooght found the root of Hus' eventual heresy in 1413 when Hus adopted Wyclif's understanding of the church as the community of the predestined.[99] The concept was developed in Hus' *De ecclesia*. According to De Vooght, this idea introduced a serious contradiction into Hus' ecclesiology when he melded traditional Augustinian terminology with Wyclifite constructs. De Vooght questioned the nature of the trial and the judicial proceedings against Hus. He queried the sentence of the synod and wondered if the conviction and sentence were just. And beneath these questions lay an even more important one: was Hus truly a heretic? De Vooght's ruminations led him to conclude that Hus was heretical even if that heresy was chiefly modified from its fifteenth-century definition. No where does De Vooght acquit Hus of all blame and no where do we find a call for a reconsideration of the trial itself. What De Vooght seemed not to appreciate was that the appearance of Hus at Constance was a continuation of a legal process. The hearings at the Council were simply another stage in the Hus trial. As a matter of fact Hus also failed to appreciate the gravity of his situation and did not consider the legal implications of a process he had helped start several years earlier. The proceedings at Constance did not imply a conversation but rather an examination. In that sense De Vooght was quite wrong to argue the Council should have treated Hus differently.[100] Somewhat more puzzling was De Vooght's claim that in February 1418 Martin V issued a bull in which he accepted only thirty articles taken from the writings of Hus noting that some were heretical, the rest perhaps rash, erroneous, scandalous or offensive to pious ears, but not heretical. De Vooght concluded that Martin V left Hus to the judgment of history. The position is untenable. Martin V, after all, was the same Cardinal Odo Colonna who eight years earlier had confirmed a writ of excommunication against Hus and had also been present in the earlier stages of the Council of Constance and acquiesced in the verdict against the accused. There is no evidence Martin ever had second thoughts about the case of Jan Hus. Of course, Paul De Vooght's findings and arguments have been challenged.[101] However, his work was an important testament to the kind of responsible scholarship which took Hus as an objective subject in the west in the twentieth century. De Vooght's work appeared later with only a few changes but most importantly taking note of the more significant Czech historiographical contributions especially of the philosopher Robert Kalivoda and the historian Josef Macek.[102]

No one has done more to bring Hus to the English speaking world than the Czech-American church historian Matthew Spinka (1890–1972). Influenced by Protestantism and especially the work of Bartoš, Spinka emerged as a zealous defender of Jan Hus. He published an indignant defense of Hus against the charges of Loserth.[103] This was followed by a study of Hus' ecclesiology in which Spinka argued against De Vooght's thesis. Adopting an historical rather than a systematic approach to the topic Spinka concluded there was neither reason nor compelling evidence to show a radical development or point of departure in 1412–13.[104] Thereafter he published a very warm and sympathetic biography of Hus.[105] As we have noted above Spinka also brought to the English language editions of the trial account by Petr Mladoňovice as well as Hus' letters. Together, Spinka's oeuvre may be characterized as consistently pro-Hus, exhibiting an almost complete opposition to the Loserth-Höfler school of thought. Spinka did not accept the idea that Hus was largely a Wyclifite. He seemed to adopt the stance of Palacký, without the overt sense of nationalism. Moreover, he had little sympathy with Marxist analysis or the contributions made by the historiography produced during those years in the former Czechoslovakia. Spinka may be criticized for appearing to be willing to defend Hus at virtually every turn and adopting a favorable opinion of him at almost any cost. Spinka did not abide detractors of Hus gladly. There seemed to be an inherent bias in Spinka against any critique of Hus. In this posture he followed the example of Novotný. Spinka's Hus seems almost too perfect and heroic to be true. His books reveal a near total lack of concern with the social implications of Hus' thought. There was utter hostility towards Sigismund and the Council of Constance to the point of surrendering all semblance of historical distance and scholarly objectivity.[106] Spinka was incapable of perceiving the pressures the Council may have been under and he followed De Vooght in failing to appreciate the legal consequences of the continuing Hus trial which shifted its venue from the Curia to Constance. Spinka's defense of Hus was as much emotional as intellectual. But for these criticisms Spinka's work was rooted in primary sources and in a sound acquaintance with Czech scholarship. It provided a reasonable foundation for further work. Two other Czech émigrés who spent their careers in North America contributed more broadly to Hussite studies. Enrico C.S. Molnar (1913–1999) published seven articles in the *Anglican Theological Review* between 1953 and 1965 and other essays elsewhere. Jarold Zeman (1926–2000) compiled a bibliography of Hussite materials which became foundational for non-Czech scholars.[107]

Two of the most important scholars of Hussite history in the second half of the twentieth century have been the Czech historian František Šmahel (1934–) and the American Howard Kaminsky (1924–). Neither can be regarded as a specialist on Jan Hus though both have included him in their larger interests of Hussite history. Neither have written monographs on Hus specifically and their importance in the historiography of Hus has more to do with the application of Hus to their understandings of Hussite history, a topic which lies outside the scope of this study. A brief comment on each must suffice. Šmahel sees Hus as a contender for the reorganization of social constructs in conformity with the law of Christ.[108] Of related significance is Šmahel's observation that Hus' exile in southern Bohemia prepared the way for the coming of the Táborites. He does see a significant Wyclif influence on Hus and has referred to Jerome of Prague as a Wyclifite.[109] The scope of Šmahel's contribution can be gauged principally from his magnum opus on the Hussite Revolution.[110] Since 1992 Šmahel has collaborated actively with Alexander Patschovsky (1940–), medieval historian at the University of Constance, in compiling the 'Repertorium fontium Hussiticarum', a database of all known manuscripts containing 'Hussite' texts from the 1360s to the 1470s.[111] Most of Kaminsky's comment on Hus comes in his history of the revolution. He acknowledged that Hus was subversive and, unlike Spinka, was able to say that at times Hus very well may have been 'insincere, undiscriminating, opportunistic, and demagogic.'[112] With De Vooght, Kaminsky perceived an increased radicalism in Hus both in terms of statements and actions from 1409. Moreover he accepted in slightly modified form the argument that Hus was a disciple of Wyclif. Still, Kaminsky recognized what Spinka did not and that was the possibility that the true figure of the historical Hus had yet to emerge from the dimness of the past and that he remained shrouded in uncertainty and complexity. Kaminsky's history, though truncated by failing to go beyond 1424, retains considerable scholarly value more than forty years after publication. Unlike Šmahel, by the 1970s Kaminsky had essentially abandoned the field and moved on to other interests. That decision was unfortunate.

Writers on heresy often deal with Hus and the Hussites but not in a specialist manner. Gordon Leff and Malcolm Lambert are examples here. Lambert's work is almost entirely derivative. Leff paid more specific attention to Hus and dealt with some of his writings though both tended to see Hus in relation to Wyclif.[113] German scholarship since the 1960s has taken a more balanced view of Hus than that exhibited in the nineteenth century. This is apparent is the work of Ferdinand Seibt (1927–2003) and the more recent approach of Peter Hilsch (1938–).[114] The latter sees Hus as a forerunner of Luther, which is debatable. The other notable German writer on Hus was Ernst Werner (1920–1993). He adopted the position that the time of Hus witnessed a transition of intellectual reform into popular manifestations and efforts at religious renewal produced social transformation. Werner made a serious effort to locate Hus within his late medieval setting and anchored his life in the ideology of the reform tendencies which preceded him in Bohemia. He asserted that Hus paid more attention to spirituality than abstract theology but Werner then suggested Hus' theological reflection had no meaningful relation to a social critique. Werner argued convincingly that the clue to understanding Hus could be located within the nexus of tradition and innovation, a place where Hus seemed to have dwelt.[115] In a very real sense it appeared that Werner's Hus must be heretical, a hero who typified the struggle against authority structures. That component of Werner's interpretation was consistent with his Marxist philosophy. Werner's last consideration of Jan Hus has much to commend it as an important historiographical contribution but for a number of reasons it fails to satisfy as a definitive study.[116]

While not to be regarded as serious contributions to Jan Hus historiography it may be useful to point out the political uses of the historical Hus in the interest of modern agendas. A completely fraudulent book masquerading as an eyewitness account of the Hus trial at Constance appearing first in 1846 in German, then in 1868 in a Czech translation, later in English in 1909 and then again in 1930, has been recently reissued and has even turned up as a reference source in otherwise respectable publications.[117] The book is a nineteenth-century creation and is worthless. Another equally interesting use of Hus came in 1913 when Benito Mussolini wrote a book about Hus in which he used the fifteenth-century martyr as a means of attacking Roman Catholicism in the twentieth century.[118] The book may be dismissed as the creation of Italian socialist journalists. More recently Hus was used as a means of attack in contemporary Czech politics.[119]

In terms of serious contributions to the age of Hus, the recent work of Olivier Marin recreates perhaps better than earlier efforts a useful context for the religious and spiritual worlds of medieval Europe.[120] Marin is interested more in the intellectual and social aspects of the history surrounding Hus and this results in an almost unavoidable less than thorough treatment of certain fundamental issues surrounding Hus. Two definite examples are the doctrine of the eucharist and aspects of Hus's ecclesiology. Unlike earlier interpretations Marin rightly sees Hus as part of the priestly intelligentsia, and not simply a marginal cleric or an unimportant religious figure in the late medieval period. The book is conservative in approach, extremely cautious, but nonetheless makes an important ancillary addition to studies of Jan Hus. Important contributions to the study of Hus have also been made in the areas of law and legal procedure by Jiří Kejř, liturgy by David Holeton, on liturgical manuscripts by Barry Graham, and in art by Jan Royt, Milena Bílková and other art historians but these matters are noted in previous chapters. North American scholars working out of the spiritual heritage of Hus have produced works worth noting. C. Daniel Crew's examination of Hus' soteriology and Craig Atwood's theological history of the Unity of Brethren are examples.[121] Moreover useful interpretations of Hus for a popular audience have likewise been produced.[122]

Two important conferences devoted to a consideration of Jan Hus took place in the 1990s and the proceedings from those fora are important for understanding the state of Jan Hus studies for the twenty-first century. The first convened at Bayreuth in 1993 and the second in Rome in 1999. In many respects the former is more significant. At Bayreuth scholars took into account the crisis of the later Middle Ages, the work and reform of Hus, his contributions to the church and theology, his relation to law and the Council of Constance, the possible and potential connections to the later Hussite movement, correlations with the reformations still to come and a variety of other issues.[123] At Rome the focus was much narrower and the agenda driven in part by the question of how the Vatican and Pope John Paul II would answer the latter day reconsideration of Jan Hus. In terms of Hus, the twenty-seven academic contributions ranged from the very relevant to the arcane and irrelevant. In the published papers from the symposium two important ones by Stanislav Sousedík, on the question of Hus and remanentism, and Walter Brandmüller on Hus at Constance were left out. Eight new papers, not on the program, were added.[124] These inexplicably included actual papers published elsewhere, issues unrelated to Hus, and one taking up nearly 100 pages on a discussion of whether or not a fifteenth-century mug was authentic or a clever fake. The broad thrust of the Rome symposium is part of the subject of chapter twelve.

In 1992 two contributions were made on Hussite history during the sixteenth world congress of the Czech and Slovak Society of Arts and Sciences in Prague. That same year David Holeton and Thomas Fudge began the organization of a seminar under the auspicious of that conference. Fudge gave it the name 'The Bohemian Reformation and Religious Practice'. The first meeting took place in Prague in 1994 chaired by the co-organizers. A regular series was established to publish the selected papers of the proceedings of what became a biennial event. From 1996 the sessions were organized by Holeton and Zdeněk David. By 2000 the event had grown sufficiently to become an independent conference. It retained its original name and to date seven volumes of essays have appeared under the title of the conference.[125] The conference sessions and the published proceedings are one of the main sources for academic discussion on Hus and the Hussites outside the Czech language. Contributions to the conference in Czech are routinely published in English in the series. Specific interpretive essays on Hus dealing with the rehabilitation issue (František Holeček), on matters of authority and eschatology (Ivana Dolejšová), the eucharist (Olivier Marin), preaching (Marin and Fudge), iconographical subjects (Milena Kubíková and Šmahel), exegesis (Pavel Soukup), and the later historical and philosophical uses of Hus (Pavel Helan and Peter Morée) have appeared thus far. A host of related issues have also been examined.

In the last century many of Hus' interpreters have been intent on presenting him as somehow relevant or modern. This predisposition has inclined them to sideline his medieval identity, namely his profound religious devotion or his heretical proclivities. The non-religious Hus and the sanitized Hus are not historical. Two things seem historiographically incontestable. First, as the work of Josef Hromádka (1889–1969) indicated, Hus did not die for an abstract notion of freedom of conscience. Instead he gave his life in defense of the freedom of a true church and for the freedom of the word of God. Second, many of the images of Jan Hus constructed and modified throughout history are unhelpful, misleading, and even fictitious.[126] These contribute nothing to the task of discovering and understanding the Hus of history. It is doubtful that a comprehensive, accurate portrait will ever fully appear.[127] It is also unlikely Jan Hus would be any more acceptable to the Czech Republic today than he was eighty years ago.

12

REHABILITATION

Disciples often pervert the masters. There is an unavoidable human and historical tendency to understand the past through the filters of the present. Part of the legacy of Master Jan Hus has been a desire to see Hus absolved of the legal condemnation assigned at Constance. The call for a reconsideration of Jan Hus is not new. The history of this impulse can be traced back more than two centuries to the work of the Slovenian Catholic theologian Kašpar Royko (1744–1819).[1] This seems to be the first effort to rehabilitate Hus. The matter was raised again by a Jesuit though not with the same fervor or intent as Royko.[2] At the same time yet another Catholic scholar made Hus the center of a major and influential study.[3] Considering Hus a 'faithful son of the Roman Church' and a 'martyr of the gospel', Paul De Vooght advanced a case specifically for an annulment of Hus' excommunication.[4] It is noteworthy these appeals all originated in the work of Catholic scholars. The Protestant Matthew Spinka did not regard rehabilitation as a possibility.[5] De Vooght concluded Hus had been heretical on one point alone, that being the necessity of a pope and therefore his case might reasonably be reconsidered. That conclusion was not been shared by a number of scholars.[6] The 1960s proved to be a fertile ground for a gathering movement towards a rehabilitation of Jan Hus. Polish bishop Marian Rachowicz (1910–1983) noted opinions within his constituency concerning the Hus case with voices calling for a review of the trial and exoneration from the heresy conviction.[7] During Vatican II, Cardinal Josef Beran (1888–1969) made reference to the case of Jan Hus. Late in 1965 at the final sessions of the Council and specifically in the context of a discussion of religious freedom, Beran argued that the Roman Church in Czechoslovakia continued to suffer on account of the judgment made against Hus 550 years earlier. Beran called for a vindication of Hus making an impassioned appeal for a reconsideration of the trial and condemnation of Hus. There are several salient factors at issue to consider. First, the cardinal's comments came in the context of the conciliar session dealing with religious freedom. Second, the example of Hus was apropos for the Czech Beran. Third, the Communist regime in the former Czechoslovakia, while avowedly anti-ecclesiastical, had taken over the Hussite tradition and the figure of Hus for purely political propagandist purposes.[8] For the official church to issue a formal recognition of Hus may well have struck a fatal blow against the armor of an historiographical approach which needed an heretical Hus as a subversive hero symbolizing the struggle against hierarchy. That case has been made. The argument is not persuasive. Indeed there were aspects of the Marxist agenda in the former Czechoslovakia which tended to interest itself more in particular ideologies of history than in history itself. The comments remain ambiguous. Beran seemed to be suggesting that the difficulties facing the church in the 1960s were in some sense linked to the sins committed by the church throughout history in terms of religious liberty and nominated Hus as an example. Beran provided no expansion of this view and upon his death nothing further emerged from his papers. It is possible to argue that the appeal made by Beran came from a concern for justice in an ecumenical spirit. That he raised the idea in a session on religious freedom is significant especially when the repression of religion in the former Czechoslovakia at the time is considered. Beran himself spent fourteen years in prison upon the sentence of the ruling government. Nothing came of this proposal and the matter rested for twenty years. The short-lived battle for Hus was waged and won by the Marxists. Elsewhere in 1965 the city archivist in Constance, Otto Fegher, suggested to Pope Paul VI the possibility of rehabilitation and eventual canonization of Jan Hus.[9] The Vatican did not act.

After Karol Wojtyła was elected to the see of Peter in October 1978 as the first Slavic pope in history, a concerted effort began to secure a reconsideration of Hus. The impetus came from Professor Stefan Świeżawski (1907–2004), a Polish historian of philosophy at the Catholic University in Lublin and friend of Pope John Paul II. Świeżawski stated that his important article on Hus came at the direction of the pope.[10] The groundbreaking essay appeared in an independent Catholic weekly newspaper in Kraków.[11] Świeżawski called on the Vatican to undertake a review of the Hus case. Świeżawski maintained Hus was innocent of heresy charges but offered no evidence to support the claim. Instead he relied upon an emotive appeal charging the later medieval church and the Council of Constance with exercising a political agenda against Hus thereby victimizing him with the 'hatchery of heresy'. Świeżawski asked the pope to look at the case once more and exonerate Jan Hus from the accusations and condemnations which unjustly remained attached to his memory. There were indications and high hopes that John Paul II would declare the case against Master Hus officially reopened. That did not occur. However, Świeżawski was not the only one placing the issue of rehabilitation before the public. Others argued that a reevaluation would strengthen the religious life of Central Europe and have significant ecumenical significance while weakening the Communist regime in Czechoslovakia which quite successfully had appropriated Hus for political purposes.[12] Father Alfons Skowronek chaired a session in Warsaw in 1988 which formulated a series of questions concerning the Hus case. These queries were sent to the Episcopate of the Ecumenical Committee. Answers to the questions were never published.[13] Other groups and conferences also convened after 1986 in Prague and elsewhere to discuss the question of Jan Hus. Prominent Catholic theologians continued to think about Hus. For example Hans Küng regarded Hus' ecclesiology as relevant for the late twentieth century and expressed interest in a scholar developing a comparative analysis between Hus' theology and his own.[14] By 1989 Polish newspapers once more called for the rehabilitation of Hus suggesting that such a move on the part of the Vatican would come as a counter balance in a time of tyranny.[15] The preponderance of Catholic commentary on the Hus case was striking. Yet it was a Catholic priest and professor of fundamental theology at the Pontifical Lateran University in Rome who suggested it was only Catholics who were uncertain of which position to take on Jan Hus.[16]

At the end of the twentieth century the Christian Church began publicly admitting to a guilty conscience. While more of a Roman Catholic issue Protestants were not exempt.[17] The Hus case has always been viewed contentiously chiefly on account of the revolution which followed in Bohemia. Had the Hussites not risen up in strength, after the execution of Jan Hus, and held the official church and empire at bay for more than two decades and then forged a compromise settlement which lasted two centuries the matter might well have been relegated to the crowded historical shelves where heretics and heresy cases were normally consigned. After all hundreds of men and women, many nameless and faceless, suffered the ignominious heretic's death in the later Middle Ages. But Hus gave his name to a surprisingly vibrant movement of dissent which successfully transformed heresy into an institutionalized movement for reformation.[18] The modern world has witnessed positive appraisals of Hus, albeit in qualified forms, for the last two hundred years.[19] There have been several splendid studies of Hus in the twentieth century but none of them have suggested a formal review of the Hus case with a view towards exoneration, rehabilitation, eventual beatification and possibly even sainthood. The latter two steps were always considered unlikely but there were numerous voices suggesting the feasibility and indeed strong possibility for rehabilitation.

Pope John Paul II, in a speech at Prague Castle on 21 April 1990, addressed the Hus matter. The comments were widely reported in numerous venues.[20]

> I recall that during the Second Vatican Council Cardinal Beran, the Czech Archbishop, spoke in defense of the basic principles of religious freedom and tolerance. He spoke with great sorrow about the fate of Jan Hus, the Czech priest who was saddened by the enormous abuses rampant in his day and even later. I well remember what the Archbishop of Prague said about this priest who played such an important role in the religious and cultural history of the Czech nation. It is now up to the scholars, above all, up to the Czech theologians to define more precisely the place which Jan Hus will occupy among the reformers of the Church and among other famous reformers, such as Tomáš of Štítný and Jan Milíč of Kroměříž. Apart from the theological ideas he defended, it is impossible to deny Jan Hus' personal integrity and his well-known efforts with regard to the moral uplifting and education of his nation.[21]

This was a remarkable volte-face from the umbrage taken by the Vatican in 1925 during the pontificate of Pius XI when diplomatic relations were suspended because leaders of the Czech nation participated in the Jan Hus celebrations on 6 July. The pope's comments indicated two things. Initially that the legacy of Hus ought to be reevaluated but also that there were reservations about Hus' theology. That second point has too often been overlooked or downplayed.[22] On the other side it appeared that Świeżawski's agenda had been elevated and energized by papal authority. As a result of this renewed attention Archbishop Miloslav Vlk of Prague convened in June 1993 'the commission for the study of the problems connected to the person, life and work of Master Jan Hus'. This twenty-six member commission met regularly over a six and-a-half year period undertaking a comprehensive investigation of Hus' life and work together with his trial and condemnation.[23] Formed within the Czech Catholic Bishops Conference, the commission convened to investigate the Hus case and organize a platform for discussion between the bishops and the Vatican. There were a number of conferences which included reports on the ongoing work of the commission.

The most important convened at Bayreuth, Germany in September 1993. Cardinal Edward Cassidy, president for promoting Christian unity at the Vatican, and Johannes Hanselmann, bishop of the Evangelical Lutheran Church in Germany, presided. The ecumenical nature of the convocation was highlighted in a speech by Cassidy. 'The discussions on the life and times of Jan Hus cannot help but touch on issues that were very controversial in the past and which continue to challenge us today. That should not worry us provided that we seek the truth. It is the truth that makes us free. [Hopefully this symposium] . . . will provide a major contribution to the reconciliation of Christians that has become an urgent task of all churches and ecclesial communities at this time here in Europe and elsewhere throughout the world'. The proceedings of the conference were published.[24] Substantial media coverage followed in the Czech Republic. Some reports characterized the symposium as an effort to bring to light the truth and significance of Hus. Others suggested the convocation signaled a change in the Vatican's position with respect to Hus. Media commentary constructed the memory of Hus as a monumental figure of Czech history and a thinker of European importance.[25] Others regarded Bayreuth as a new direction in ecumenical progress while still other sources went so far as to declare that the conference itself indicated the first step on the road to legal rehabilitation.[26] The discussions went on for several months. Just as the Hus of history precipitated a contest for his memory and interpretation so likewise it appeared that in the 1990s Hus went from being a discussion among various Christian communities to a dispute within the Roman Church. One author suggested that Catholics needed to claim that Hus was theirs as well.[27] In 1996 the secretary of the commission, František Holeček addressed the Bohemian Reformation and Religious Practice conference in Brno on the nature of the work of the commission.[28] Four important aspects of the work of the commission were enumerated: a search for truth, facilitating dialogue across social, political and religious divides, acknowledging mitigating factors in past decisions, and expressing remorse or regret for decisions or events in history if need be. On 6 July 1995 a memorial service on the 580th anniversary of Hus' death was held in Prague and was attended by Cardinal Miloslav Vlk, Archbishop of Prague. On the occasion Vlk ostensibly said his presence indicated the Roman Catholic Church was rethinking its position on Hus.[29] The following year Vlk noted it was necessary to express regret for the death of Jan Hus.[30] Even politicians made statements about the usefulness of a rehabilitation of Hus.[31] Other popular media outlets advanced even more strident claims. The consideration of Hus was now a possible move towards canonization. Girolamo Savonarola (1452-1498), Bartolomé de las Casas (1484-1566) and Jan Hus were named as possible candidates.[32] Holeček then went on record as opining that within five years Hus would be cleared of the charges attached to him at Constance.[33] In 1996 other international colloquia discussed the questions surrounding the Hus re-evaluation. One example was the 'international commission for comparative church history' congress which met at the Catholic University in Lublin, Poland. A number of scholars active in research on Jan Hus and Hussite history participated including Walter Brandmüller, Thomas Fudge, František Holeček, David Holeton and František Šmahel.

Apart from the handful of academic congresses most of the public discussion of Jan Hus tended to be carried on in non-scholarly venues. Almost all of the publicity surrounding the Hus case reflected a favorable view on the question of rehabilitation. There were academics opposed to the idea but few said so openly or published views to that effect.[34] Other efforts to publish dissenting views on the proposed rehabilitation of Hus were rebuffed.[35] Prior to his death in 1990 Amedeo Molnár apparently had raised a voice of caution in the wake of the enthusiasm created by Świeżawski's seminal article. As though to counter the rising tide of disinformation circulating in Prague and elsewhere, Miloslav Fiala, spokesperson for the Czech Bishops' Conference issued a statement on behalf of the commission appearing to contradict the unofficial comments made by Holeček. While confirming that a review of the case of Jan Hus was in progress, Fiala clarified the nature of that review. The focus was neither to rehabilitate nor canonize Hus. The goal of the commission's work was considerably more modest consisting as it did in attempting to objectively assess the life and work of Hus.[36] This explication did not prevent the work of the commission from continuing to be referred to as a process of possible rehabilitation both among some scholars as well as the popular media, both religious and secular.

Throughout the 1990s the public presses continued to comment on the work of the commission and went so far as to opine the rumor the commission would suggest rehabilitation.[37] There were always two problems. First, the commission did not have the power to clear anyone, past or present, of heresy. That remained a matter for the papacy. Second, the commission itself had been fairly secretive about its findings and conclusions and in many news stories had been reported as having declined to make any definitive statement about the outcome of its years of work. Therefore predictions about rehabilitation could only be regarded as unwarranted editorial speculation. On the other hand there were unofficial comments from those on the commission or those in contact with commission members stating the general feeling tended rather directly toward exoneration. What became fairly definite were two issues. After nearly seven years of investigation the results were scheduled to be revealed at an international religious symposium in December 1999 convened at the Pontifical Lateran University in Rome.[38] This was in keeping with a papal commitment made to the president of the Czech Republic, Václav Havel, on 7 March 1994 that a proper evaluation of Jan Hus would be produced by the end of the century.[39] Second, the secretary of the commission, František Holeček, backtracking to some extent on his early predictions, insisted that the commission would in fact make no recommendation to Pope John Paul II. Instead the years of work undertaken by the commission would be summarized and presented to the pope at the Lateran Symposium which could then be utilized by the pontiff in reviewing the Hus case and in arriving at a decision.[40] The problem with Holeček's second point lay in the assumption that John Paul II was going to make a formal decision on Hus. Nowhere can it be shown that the pontiff ever intended to do so. Papal intentions aside, Holeček's summary proved inaccurate. The question of rehabilitation could have included either a legal annulment of the conviction or a moral affirmation of Hus or both. The medieval canon law specialist Jiří Kejř was of the opinion that a legal rehabilitation was impossible and later published his views.[41] The main task of the Council of Constance had been to solve the protracted papal schism. Hus' position on issues of the papacy, the nature of the church, and authority in general, were received by the conciliar gathering as subversive and rebellious, constituting a threat to ecclesiastical unity and authority. The assessment was not amiss.[42] There was never a realistic possibility that the Council would not solve the schism by electing a new pope. As Kejř made abundantly clear, it was difficult to reconstruct the entire legal process against Hus and this would be essential in order to reevaluate his trial and the legal aspects which informed and supported the verdict. As an example we do not know how the interrogations in the prison were conducted and with what results. There are no extant records either in the normally fulsome and useful *Relatio* of Petr Mladoňovice nor yet any hints in the correspondence of Hus.[43] In order to overturn a legal verdict the process must be assessed in a manner which simply is no longer possible. Even if an evaluation could be carried out on those aspects of the trial which do exist, there would still be insufficient evidence to declare a mistrial. The legal rehabilitation of Jan Hus is not possible.[44]

The commission constituted a very successful ecumenical experiment. Regardless of possible papal conclusions its endeavors had been a model example of ecumenicity. One literary example was the publication by a Protestant medieval canon law specialist with a forward by Cardinal Miloslav Vlk, Archbishop of Prague.[45] The work of the commission, ecumenical cooperation and a grappling with historic problems, however, was not the primary issue. The issue was rather, what many people expected to be, the result of the findings set forth in Rome in 1999. It seemed manifestly clear that Pope John Paul II desired to address certain aspects of conscience and guilt relating to ecclesiastical history. Whether this reflected a general ethos within western Catholic Christendom or was simply the personal projection of the pope was never altogether clear. A papal statement prepared for Ash Wednesday 2000 aimed to apologize for the church's involvement in various activities including the inquisitions of the later Middle Ages and early modern Europe, the medieval Crusades and various other chapters of ecclesiastical history including the way in which heretics were dealt with. All of this seemed rather noble. Without doubt the posture secured John Paul's place in papal history specifically and in religious world history generally. The underlying motivation was an attempt to re-right history. The stance should be commended even if its effects were minimal and regarded as insufficient and too late by skeptics. Conversely, rehabilitating real medieval heretics is perhaps less a re-righting of the past and more an example of re-writing history. One scholar took the unusual step of writing directly to John Paul II pointing this out and setting forth an argument against the proposed rehabilitation.[46] The case has been made that Hus, despite his obvious merits and clear aspects of orthodoxy, must be numbered with the medieval heretics. It is not accurate to claim that non-Roman Catholics have always denied Hus was a heretic.[47] The Belgian Benedictine Paul De Vooght though greatly sympathetic to Hus could not avoid the same conclusion. Hus' spirit may have been Catholic but his heart lay with reform impulses.[48] Some of those inclinations were heretical according to the standards of the times. It is rather specious to claim De Vooght virtually exonerated Hus from heresy charges when the title of his major study, 'the heresy of Jan Hus' was a statement, not a question. Virtual exoneration has no meaningful value. De Vooght did find in Hus heterodox, even heretical, ideas.[49] De Vooght's researches and conclusions represented his opinion and can neither be considered a reflection of Catholic sentiment nor an official view. The Catholic historian/theologian Walter Brandmüller went considerably farther than De Vooght in seeing Hus as heretical.[50] Moreover, some Catholic reviewers have vilified De Vooght.[51] It cannot be maintained that De Vooght's moderate and ameliorating views have prevailed within modern Catholic thought.

At the end of the twentieth century a preoccupation with political correctness arose sharply in many parts of the western world. That predilection for political correctness did not bypass the church. It may be argued that efforts to see Hus rehabilitated were largely examples of ecumenical correctness driven by the prevailing social climate. Many were unpersuaded by the arguments set forth for Hus' heresy.[52] In a postmodern world heresy was an unacceptable category. Quibbles persisted about Hus' views of the papacy and ecclesiology and possible adoption of Wyclifite ideas and there was still the matter of medieval canon law which could not be set aside capriciously in good conscience. The issue remained heresy, rightly or wrongly ascribed, and the contours of heresy had been laid down rather explicitly in medieval canonical legislation. Even if Hus were not a heretic dogmatically there was little room for maneuvering when Hus came to the judgment bar on the matter of contumacy. Medieval canon law was quite clear that stubborn resistance to correction and persistent disobedience to ecclesiastical authority resulted in heresy on the grounds of contumacy.[53] As chapter seven has shown, his judicial and technical conviction rested on a sustained charge of contumacy. And there is still the problem of John Wyclif. Inasmuch as Hus was convicted of 'Wyclifite' errors, a rehabilitation of the former would imply a reconsideration of the latter. If Wyclif might be considered eligible for reconsideration what about the Waldensians and Cathars? Or Luther and other reformers similarly judged heretical? John Paul II clearly saw the thin edge of the wedge.

Did Jan Hus preach and teach in opposition to the doctrines of the official church? The Council of Constance insisted he was guilty of having taught numerous errors and heresies to people in Prague's Bethlehem Chapel.[54] Popular publications suggested Hus held four key beliefs which directly contravened late medieval ecclesiastical dogma: clerical poverty, defense of Wyclif, invalidity of indulgences and refusal to recognize the pope as head of the church.[55] The first and third are problematic insofar as Hus mainly attacked abuses associated with them. The second article has always been contentious and at the very least requires close and careful qualification. For example, Hus never followed Wyclif on the latter's views of the eucharist, a fact the Council of Constance failed to appreciate.[56] As for the fourth point, Hus' own books and sermons suggest he was in fact guilty as charged. Doctrinally, the condemnation of Jan Hus culminating at Constance rested principally in two areas: ecclesiology and authority. Hus' doctrine of the church as noted above contained within itself subversive elements.[57] While it was spectacularly false for Dietrich of Niem to claim that Hus' challenge to the church equaled the threat posed by the Islamic Qu'ran, the defenders of medieval ecclesiology had reason for concern. The concept of the church as advanced by Jan Hus threatened Latin Christendom in the later Middle Ages. Based on Thomist categories, it is possible to judge Hus' concept of the church, the *universitas praedestinatorum*, heretical even though its affinities with Augustinian thought cannot be denied.[58] In terms of authority, and this is where the Council saw clearly the subversive elements in Hus even if he did not, Hus did not accept the ultimate authority of the church whether papal or conciliar. This is evident in his work on the sufficiency of the law of Christ which he prepared purposely for his appearance at Constance.[59] This work demonstrated without doubt Hus' commitment to the law of God as the normative authority, subject to neither pope nor council nor human institution. His *De sufficientia legis Christi* proved beyond reasonable doubt that his appeal to Christ contested the legal supremacy of the church and provided prima facie evidence that his understanding of the law of God superceded all human authority. This implied a theoretical rejection of the legal power of the church. The fathers at Constance were neither so benighted nor biased as to overlook this critical fact.[60] It is impossible to overlook these features of Hus' theology and argue that the Council had no right to condemn him when he refused to acknowledge their authority. Much is made of the false accusations concerning the eucharist lodged against Hus before and during the Council. Every one of those allegations were patently untrue. The malignancy of men like Michael de Causis may be credited with keeping such issues before the Council. It is noteworthy that the accusation of remanentism was absent from the final charges against Hus. From a technical and legal point of view those thirty charges form the foundation for the conviction of heresy even though much more may have been on the minds of his judges informing and influencing their decision.

The holy character of Hus' life has been fairly represented and none have argued either in the fifteenth or the twenty–first century against his character.[61] The irregular lives of men like Pope John XXIII and Sigismund could offer no challenge and even men like the conciliarist Dietrich of Niem kept concubines. Hus' record appears to be without blemish. The words of Augustine are instructive: insignificant souls do not produce heresies. Only great men have been heretics.[62] Pope John Paul II clearly underscored his conviction of Hus' personal integrity.[63] Most acquiesce in this view though it is possible to find occasional assessments which continue to regard Hus as a religious fanatic of questionable character.[64]

Beginning in the 1960s a case was advanced for seeing in Vatican II a type of affirmation for Jan Hus. Stefan Świeżawski suggested Hus was truly a forerunner of the last ecumenical council. Others took the view that Hus' protest as well as his theological positions were within the scope of orthodox Catholic teaching. The moral revolution that Hus called for in the church had now been achieved and was reflected in *Lumen gentium*, one of the principle documents emerging from the second Vatican Council.[65] It is problematic, untenable and ultimately historically meaningless to posit a connection between fifteenth-century views of Hus and the decisions of a modern council 550 years removed.[66] Even if the formulations of Vatican II mirrored those of Jan Hus, the world views, historical circumstances, and cultural contexts prohibit a de facto legitimizing of Hus. Eschewing that difficulty, reference was elsewhere drawn to the encyclical *Pacem in terris* issued by John XXIII on 11 April 1963. That papal pronouncement promoted the view that it was improper for anyone to be condemned on the basis of personal faith or conviction.[67] Asserting on the basis of this encyclical that John XXIII thereby effectively condemned the judges at Constance and by extension exonerated Hus from the charges of heresy would be indefensible. Likewise *Lumen gentium* has nothing to do with Jan Hus. Arguments for such connections are not historical inasmuch as they fail to acknowledge a basic property of history itself which is that differential change across time inevitably occurs.

Certainly the commission which studied the case of Jan Hus took into account, as far as possible, the complete trial of Hus as well as the problematic issues of heresy and contumacy. As noted elsewhere by the standards and mores of the fifteenth century Hus was a heretic.[68] It would be purely arbitrary to ignore the fifteenth-century context, the content of canon law as well as ecclesiastical and legal precedent and posthumously excuse Hus' opposition to the official church. It might have been ecumenically correct to affirm such a position at the end of the twentieth century but doing so would have constituted a serious anachronism. Such a process does not seem prudent to be the provenance of scholars and is questionable business for academic historians. Rehabilitation is technically impossible and in this case mitigated by the problem of heresy. For guilty consciences at the end of the millennium the option seemed like a good one but it underscored another equally serious dilemma. There has always been a school of thought wishing to assign arbitrariness to the later medieval papacy and the several councils which condemned heretics. That is a debatable posture. What seems less debatable is encouraging a modern pope to exercise a similar type of arbitrariness in declaring the past can be made right, wrongs can be set straight and the judgments of history reversed. John Paul II seemed resolute on apologizing for the past. Could the pope have rehabilitated Hus? The answer is yes. But in doing so he would have violated the past, overthrown the heritage and tradition he had been entrusted with overseeing and protecting, and more importantly made himself and his own historical moment normative for all times. John Paul II also ran the risk of making himself appear inconsistent. How could Jan Hus, a condemned heretic, be rehabilitated by a pontiff who in the previous twenty years saw fit to ratify the judgment that Hans Küng was no longer suitable for teaching Catholic theology at Tübingen and ordered the Brazilian Franciscan liberation theologian Leonardo Boff silenced?[69] What do Hus, Küng and Boff have in common? On the face of it not much. Perhaps their only connection has been their willingness to follow their own conscience in the execution of their work. All three found themselves outside the parameters of prevailing orthodoxy as defined by the church. Küng ceased teaching in the Catholic Faculty of Theology at Tübingen. Boff accepted the imposition of silence. Hus refused censure and persisted along his chosen path. Authorities at all levels would do well to acknowledge their limitations. Ecclesiastical decrees of the past frequently passed resolutions with the injunction that such it should be for all time. With the passage of centuries the obvious shortsightedness becomes ever more apparent. To begin to rehabilitate medieval heretics would be in effect to do the same thing in reverse. Such initiatives are attempts to change history, to explain deeds done long ago and to somehow presume to be able to control both the past as well as the future. Those who attempt such feats only inherit the wind.

Christianity has changed over time and the forces of civilization and human evolution means that the church today, even the Roman Catholic Church, is not the same in every respect as its medieval form. The post-Vatican II mentality perhaps charts a new path through the ecclesiastical future but it cannot be used as a means for determining the past. The past has already been determined, we can chose to learn from it, to appropriate it responsibly or to remain within its grip and influence. To attempt to wrest the ethos of the Second Vatican Council from its historical moorings in the 1960s and force it against the stream of time into the later Middle Ages is not only anachronistic but amounts to a hegemonic imposition of modern values onto a medieval context. Placing new wine in old bottles has always been disastrous. There is little doubt the church should exert influence and provide direction to the world. The church should embrace wholeheartedly the dictum and the reality of *semper ecclesia reformanda*. However, the church always being reformed is not about the past. It is not even about the future. It is something which can only be appropriated in the present. Reform and justice are responsibilities which each age must discover and utilize for that time leaving the past to that which was and the future to that which is to come. The legacy of Vatican II, codified in part in its decrees on ecumenism and religious liberty, is an aspect of twentieth-century Christendom perhaps worthy of utilization by subsequent generations.[70]

Some of the members of the Hus commission believed that Cardinal Beran, had he still been alive, would have been an active supporter of their efforts and indeed of a rehabilitation of Jan Hus. There is another school of thought. Beran apparently did not leave any writings about this issue and there are conflicting oral traditions about what he had in mind when he urged the church in the 1960s to reconsider the case of Hus. Unless there is further evidence forthcoming Beran cannot be used as an instrument either for or against the rehabilitation of Hus. Furthermore, there were those associated with the commission who remained quite uncertain about the meaning and outcomes of the proposed rehabilitation.[71] There appeared to be little critical awareness or appreciation of its historical implications. There were others who might be described as ecumenical enthusiasts prepared to support virtually any idea which appeared to be politically correct in a religious sense. For the historian the problem of history, heresy and Hus cannot so easily be solved. Juxtaposing Hus with other historical figures such as Savonarola, Galileo, Joan of Arc or Bartolomé de Las Casas is popular but perhaps injudicious. While heresy was ascribed in all of these cases the issue is whether or not heresy was *the* issue in each of those cases. There are those who argue that Hus was not a heretic but rather the victim of heresy-hunting and politically motivated agendas.[72] There is certainly a measure of truth in the latter portion of such assertion. Perhaps a positive and constructive outcome of the work of the commission might have been to state exactly, for the layperson, what Hus' real heresy was (in its proper historical context) and dismiss the spurious charges attached to his work and memory. Clearly the malice of men like Michael de Causis guaranteed there were plenty of trumped-up charges brought against him in the course of his protracted trial but was the entire Council so benighted as to err so greatly in calling Jan Hus a heretic?[73] One of the oft-repeated themes undergirding the call for a reevaluation of Hus with a view towards rehabilitation has been the statement that the Hus trial was illegal inasmuch as it failed to follow the legal norms of the time. This is an important consideration but it is far more complicated than at first blush. One recent support for this argument actually referenced Jiří Kejř.[74] Such claims are easily made but hard evidence is rarely advanced to support such statements. Kejř has undertaken the most recent and most thorough examination of the Hus trial. No where, in context, does he conclude that procedurally the Hus process was illegal or conducted outside the legal norms of the later Middle Ages. Irregularities do not necessarily mean a process is therefore illegal or invalid. The whole of Kejř's work on the Hus trial bears this out and he concluded it did not appear that procedural rules were violated and therefore no procedural error on the part of the court is known to Kejř.[75] That conclusion may not please postmodern ears but it is a valid assessment of the medieval European world.

John Paul II was determined to see that the church came to terms with the 'sinfulness of her children' where they had 'departed from the spirit of Christ' and in such instances where the church became involved in 'counter-witness and scandal'.

Acknowledging these shortcomings must lead to 'repentance'.[76] The question of the rehabilitation of Jan Hus became part of the collective effort to cleanse the memory and conscience of the church. 'The church feels responsibility for the actions of its members from a long time ago'.[77] In the 1990s there existed a conviction that rehabilitating Jan Hus was one of those pieces in the process of helping the church come into the new millennium with a clear conscience. In ecumenically correct terms that was entirely feasible but from an historical perspective was both ill-advised and quite impossible. To have pursued the proposed route would have been to run the risk of failing to take seriously history itself. To actually rehabilitate Hus was not only difficult, it proved impossible.[78] Ecumenical correctness seems to be a continuation of ingrained metahistorical assumptions which postulate that only Czechs can really understand Hus or that the Hus question is a subconscious aspect of the Czech people, an issue relegated not to history but part of the contemporary world.[79] These are interesting ideas but hardly principles worthy of embracing when dealing with the problems encountered on the varied terrain of history.

Meanwhile the buildup to the end of the millennium continued. The international convocation at the Lateran University in Rome was attended by scholars, ecclesiastical representatives and statesmen.[80] The commission ostensibly reported its findings over a four day academic conference, though it should be noted that many of the presentations were made by persons not associated with the commission. On 17 December 1999 Pope John Paul II addressed the congress. He began by noting that the aim of the commission had been to 'identify more precisely the place that Jan Hus occupies among those who sought a reform of the Church', the same point the pope had made nine-and-a-half years earlier in his speech at Prague Castle. Commending Hus' moral courage the pontiff acknowledged his towering historical significance and then expressed remorse for the events at Constance. 'I feel the need to express deep regret for the cruel death inflicted upon Jan Hus, and for the consequent wound of conflict and division which was thus imposed upon the minds and hearts of the Bohemian people'.[81] In that same speech it was significant that John Paul warned that the writing of history can often be unduly slanted so that the truth becomes obscured and history itself made a prisoner to particular interests. That observation may be applied to the Hus of history and to the motivations of some scholars who hoped the pope would create a new Jan Hus. A variety of rumors had speculated that the pope would make a formal decision on Hus by March 2000. That expectation had no basis. Throughout his long pontificate John Paul II had been concerned with issues of forgiveness and reconciliation. Several documents chart that course. On 2 December 1984 the papal exhortation *Reconciliatio et paenitentia* created a background for the apostolic letter *Tertio millennio adveniente* (10 November 1994) which led on to the Bull of Indiction of the great Jubilee of the year 2000 which was released on 29 November 1998. These documents frame the context for John Paul's address to the Hus symposium. There was nothing further to be added. Pope John Paul II had gone as far on the Jan Hus case as could reasonably be expected. The papal address on 17 December reflected the official position of the Roman Church on the Hus question.[82]

John Paul's remarks at Prague Castle in 1990 and again in Rome in 1999 provided unequivocal evidence of the Roman Church's moral recognition of Hus. *Cui bono*? To whom does it benefit for Hus to have been rehabilitated? The query seemed muddled at Rome. The end of the matter was this: Jan Hus was evaluated in the Vatican, not rehabilitated.[83]

On new years' day 2000 a joint declaration was issued in Prague by Miloslav Vlk, Archbishop of Prague, Pavel Smetana, Senior of the Evangelical Church of the Bohemian Brethren, and Josef Špak, Patriarch of the Czechoslovak Hussite Church. The statement implied that no church could claim Hus entirely since his ideas anticipated both the reformations of the sixteenth century and evolving Catholic ideas which came to fruition at Vatican II.[84] On 7 March 2000 the Vatican released a document titled 'Memory and Reconciliation: The Church and the Faults of the Past'. This lengthy statement formed the immediate context for the pope's homily for the first Sunday in Lent on 12 March in the course of which John Paul made a general reference to the need for the forgiveness of the sins of all believers.[85] The argument has been made that in the December 1999 Lateran speech John Paul II confirmed that Hus was a reformer for the entire church. Therefore this effectively removed the condemnation of heresy from Hus on the grounds that heretics cannot reform the church since they are by definition excluded from the community of the faithful. David Holeton says this aspect of the papal statement ran afoul of Vatican politics and was later removed from the official version of John Paul's address. The claim cannot be supported.[86] While technically Holeton is quite right that a heretic cannot properly be regarded as a reformer for the entire church, it must be said that the influence of a heretic can lead to reform. But to build a case upon a single phrase, even a phrase ostensibly spoken by a pope, seems rather ambitious. It also raises the question of the censorship of a sitting pope. Some disappointed with the Vatican's position on Hus officially expressed at the end of 1999 took the view that the church preferred the letter over the spirit, doctrine in preference to mercy, and the rule of law rather than the rule of faith.[87] It was not quite that simple.

An expression of regret or remorse cannot include the impossible task of actually reversing a decision made in a context which not only justified but legitimated that decision. Unlike the use of medical technology in modern criminal investigations there is no theological DNA analysis which can exonerate Jan Hus from his heresy conviction. Rehabilitation implies re-invention; it suggests a wilful distortion of history. John Paul II understood that predicament and wisely avoided compounding that historical Gordian knot. It should be admitted that the Council of Constance acted against Hus both from a standpoint of faith and a posture of fear. In one sense the Council believed it was removing a dangerous influence and pruning the vine of faith. On the other hand the Council acted with malice and fear and was defensive towards Hus' proposed reforms.[88] Feeling threatened, the late medieval church sacrificed Hus on the altar of what it regarded as the greater good. Removing Hus from his heresy conviction required two monumental steps. The first necessitated declaring that all of his views which came under censure were in fact correct after all.

The second step would be to demand the commensurate conclusion that the views of fifteenth-century Latin Christendom on these same points were erroneous. For a myriad of reasons both steps are impossible.[89] Rehabilitation implies the Roman Church admitting dogmatic error. That seemed unlikely in 1999. Jan Hus will never officially be proclaimed a saint. That seems fair. On the other hand one must come to terms with the fact that the Hussite tradition of late medieval and early modern Europe venerated Hus as a saint from 1416 until the practice was suppressed more than two hundred years later. That legacy is not without significance and holds within itself more meaning than formal ecclesiastical rehabilitation after six hundred years. 'To call him a saint [today] would not be objective'.[90] For Pope John Paul II to have rehabilitated Hus and declared him free from heresy would not have been objective. In the end the whims of every age are always lost in the tempests of the next. History is a mystery we must seek to know and understand while at the same time resisting the urge to manipulate the past in order to satisfy the present. Only in this way can one be faithful to the memory of Hus who preferred truth over political correctness[91] and who encouraged his hearers everywhere, regardless of cost, to practice the courage of conviction. Fidelity to truth in every sense right up to death was his maxim.[92] The legacy of Jan Hus – heretical though it turned out to be – can only be honored through emulation not re-invention.

The assessment of Hus as a medieval heretic is not to be understood in the ironic sense but instead in the sense of paradox. In the Middle Ages the word 'heretic' was emotive, derisive, implying opprobrium, scorn and dishonor. Characterizing Hus in the twenty-first century as a heretic need not carry any of these dismissive connotations. Heretics and heresies are not necessarily to be feared nor should they be perceived as a threat or a negative aspect of a social or religious culture. It is not only possible, but in the case of Jan Hus definite, that one might be a preacher of the gospel, a 'reformer' of the church and a heretic.[93] Too often heretics are created unnecessarily when the prophetic voice is silenced. Hus legitimately can neither be separated from the prevailing influences of his life nor his historical context. It has been said that a text without a context is a pretext for a proof text. One cannot 'un-hereticate' Jan Hus without doing violence to history. Rehabilitation is not about justice and even if there were expected adequate ecumenical outcomes it would still be an insufficient and illegitimate motivation. One must beware the enormous condescension of posterity. It is without merit to judge the past by contemporary standards or force our ancestors to fight our battles. According to the ethos of the medieval world, Jan Hus was a heretic. There is no shame in that.

EPILOGUE

In 1404 King Sigismund of Hungary and Duke Albrecht of Austria were poisoned during a siege at the Moravian town of Znojmo. Albrecht died. Upon medical advice Sigismund was hanged upside down by his heels for twenty four hours in hopes of staving off the ravages of the toxin. The emergency measure worked. He survived.[1] Ten years later, as Holy Roman Emperor elect, Sigismund came to Constance during the Hus trial. From that time until his own death in 1437 many Bohemians regarded him as a shameful enemy of the Czechs, an evil man, a rogue king, the betrayer of Jan Hus, ultimately abandoned by God.[2] As a matter of fact Sigismund's machinations and political intrigue had little to do with the fate of Hus. Six hundred years after his death we must ask ourselves what was the achievement of Jan Hus? In simple form it can be said that in his living and in his dying he crystallized a climate of reform in Bohemia providing it with a definitive statement and identity.

From the time he was burned alive at Constance in 1415 the story of Jan Hus has been told either in the conviction that he was a hero or on the assumption he was a villain. Hus did not start reform per se but he expanded the course of a pre-existing movement, one which finds root in the work of men like Konrad Waldhauser and Jan Milíč of Kroměříž. While there had been previous martyrs in Bohemia none were of the stature of Hus. There is altogether good reason for his name to have been attached to movements of Czech reform.[3] For more than twenty years after his death all of the principal players in religious reform in Bohemia had known Hus personally or had been involved in the orbit which he helped create in Prague. Without his martyrdom at Constance this evolving movement would have been quite different. That his name came to symbolize revolution and reform does not mean one should assume this justified everything which emerged theologically or socially in the time of the Hussite heretics. The abbot of an Augustinian house in Silesia identified the enemies of the church in Bohemia as 'Wyclifites, Hussites, Táborites, Czechs and other unbelievers'.[4] He meant the varieties of those groups commonly associated with Hus. In a sense Hus belonged to all of them and to none. His name, rightly or wrongly, came to be associated with dissent, disobedience and heresy. Sigismund's contemporary biographer referred to three deviant factions in Bohemia, namely the Táborites, Orphans and

Hussites.⁵ In the popular mind these all warmed their hands before the fire of Hus' influence. In 1418 Pope Martin V linked Hus with Jerome of Prague and John Wyclif as three foxes whose tails were tied together.⁶ The expressions of religious reform and social revolution thereafter only intensified in Bohemia. An argument might be made for the Táborites being more the inheritor of Hus than the Utraquists. The eucharistic cup for the laity was important to both schools of thought but social reform and bringing all things directly and immediately under the jurisdiction of the law of God became more an acute undertaking for the Táborite tradition – which included the Orebites and Orphans of eastern Bohemia, Petr Chelčický, the Chelčice Brethren, and later the Unity of Brethren – than the conservative movement of the Utraquists. This is neither to suggest that Hus would have approved of these radical measures nor that the Táborite conception of the law of God is the correct or preferred understanding.⁷ Nevertheless, Bishop Mikuláš of Tábor argued that his community was a direct result of Jan Hus and there have been modern scholars who have concurred.⁸ Of course the same thesis has been considered and summarily dismissed by others as impractical and impossible.⁹

To see the world through the eyes of Jan Hus is to survey a particularly bellicose and tumultuous landscape – intellectual and social – one equally dynamic and decadent seething with religious tension and nascent revolution. A careful reading of his literary corpus assembles the stage. Though many of his intellectual peers considered his views misguided Hus was utterly sincere in believing he was the bearer of an authentic apostolic tradition faithful to the gospel of Jesus Christ and consistent with the fathers of the Christian faith. In that conviction Hus seems not to have wavered. That assurance found no resonance with the theologians of many university faculties. Men like Jean Gerson harbored grave anxiety over heresy and this fact goes some distance in explaining the particular attention Gerson devoted to the Hus case at Constance. In the wider scheme of things, Gerson considered books and their production a means of preserving and communicating orthodox ideas. The writings of Hus represented a visible and tangible threat to that enterprise and therefore the books and their author had to be suppressed.¹⁰ Maintaining proper doctrine and a pure society meant ridding it of outsiders and heretics. Gerson's argument went straight to the point of defending ecclesiastical authority.

> A general council can and must damn many propositions or assertions of this type even though they cannot be corrected merely from the bare text of Holy Scripture alone leaving out the explanations of the doctors or the common usage of the church and so on. This was done during this Council concerning numerous assertions of Wyclif and Hus particularly on the subject of the laity taking communion under the elements of bread and wine. The point of law allows for the extermination of heresies and heretics since the heretics which we saw submitted at the very most to its defense since they have no wish to recant their heresies absolutely. They will do so only conditionally, namely if they might be convicted of erring from the rigid text of scripture. They claim that the

expositions of the doctors, canons, and decretals are apocryphal and that one should take no note of them. There is no one who does not understand clearly how this presumption leads to error.[11]

The errors in Hus' Bohemia which worried Gerson and his colleagues so profoundly were soon realized and replicated elsewhere. Ostensibly the ghost of Jan Hus could neither be contained nor banished.[12] The largely successful hegemonic single authority which had governed religion throughout the medieval centuries was now permanently undermined. The years of Hus' life were lived in a world of inquisitorial questions and authoritative pronouncements. There was little toleration of theological diversity and the questioning tended to discourage listening.

For all the flourish of his international reputation, together with his appearance at the greatest convocation convened in his times, Hus was provincial in nearly every respect. Unlike many of the leading thinkers of his age Hus never studied outside Bohemia. Apart from his trip to Constance in the last year of his life only once had he traveled abroad. That was ostensibly with a royal entourage in 1398 to Rheims though the evidence for Hus' inclusion on the journey is thin.[13] While both his context and formation were narrow, unlike many academic controversies and scandals in the later Middle Ages, the turbulence surrounding Hus did not soon die away. He remained a charismatic figure who inspired emotional commitment and loyalty and whose life seems to have encouraged others to live lives of examined faith. The quality of his oratory cannot be doubted and this, combined with his personal charisma, ensured success at Bethlehem Chapel. He may not have been a saint in the traditional sense but he possessed a reputation for sanctity. Moreover there were rumors of extraordinary powers. He was unreliably reported to have been a mind-reader.[14] The notion of clairvoyance amounted to contrived propaganda aimed at demonizing Hus but it does reflect aspects of his reputation. Elsewhere we read of heretics in south Bohemia who revered Hus higher than SS. Peter and Paul and regarded him capable of performing more miracles than other saints.[15] His consistent and unmistakable appeal to the masses and his perceived threat to the establishment endeared him to Queen Žofie early on, but made him contemptible to others like the Cardinal of Cambrai, Pierre d'Ailly, who told him rather heatedly, in a moment of petulance, that he was no match for the superior minds of the sage men of Christendom.[16] The suggestion seems rather disingenuous.

Given the chaos created by religious dissent and the popes in his lifetime, it is unsurprising that Hus sought spiritual focus elsewhere. In surveying his life and work, especially his books, it seems clear that Hus can neither be regarded as a monastic thinker nor a scholastic, the two main scholarly taxonomies of literary expression in medieval Europe, at least in any thoroughgoing sense. But he did carve out for himself a place in the religious and intellectual world of his time, a space which of course ultimately carried with it serious consequence. Hus was a real person who experienced success, triumph and heroism. But these were achieved in adversity, anxiety, weakness and failure. Jan Hus was a complex and fallible human marked by humility and heroism but hobbled by intemperate combativeness and injudicious choices. These are observations more than criticisms and it is doubtful Hus would have judged himself too harshly on either. Nowhere in his writings can we find any hint of moral guilt, real sustained religious doubt, or sexual desire. Hus seems remarkably impervious to such distractions and there does not seem to be evidence or propensity towards any form of vice. Unlike the inner personal details we know of in the lives of other medieval ecclesiastical luminaries such as Augustine, Peter Abelard, Héloïse or Martin Luther, Hus seems somewhat prosaic. Was Jan Hus an unusual man or representative of the Central European experience at the end of the Middle Ages? Apart from the manner of his dying, all things considered, we do not know. It is practically without dispute that John Bale and John Foxe set out to create a hero of John Wyclif.[17] By comparison Hus needed no such literary invention. His inexorable march from reforming preacher before the local Prague synods to his last stand at Constance underscored both his significance and secured his place in the history of the Latin west. The currents of commemoration and iconography shaped Hus' memory but his life had been fuller and more compellingly human than Wyclif's. Wyclifite England may well have been a premature episode but Hussite Bohemia was neither.[18] While historical vacuums are either dangerous or fabricated Jan Hus should be understood from within his context rather than in reference to a larger narrative for all such generalizations ultimately are misleading.

Condemnation came with ease and predictability in the late Middle Ages whereas understanding of difference was an almost impossible hurdle. Hus lived in a world quite different from ours where toleration was not a virtue but a vice. Medieval heresy by nature and legal definition implied aspects of reform and revolt.[19] Brute force was sometimes legitimated to control it.[20] In the aftermath of Constance all efforts by the Latin Church and empire to repress Hus' legacy proved ineffective. The methodology of Hus' judges had been flawed inasmuch as they failed to adequately separate history from fiction. The popes, bishops, inquisitors and conciliar delegates were in one sense spiritual policemen and conscientious administrators of ecclesiastical policy. Their duty required them to deal with Hus in terms of an heretical encounter as well as his beliefs as a suspect in the fight to preserve an imagined theological unity against the encroachment of diversity and dissent. This abiding suspicion tended to corrode the faith and confirm the worst fears harbored by the authorities and this produced wild fabrications of subversive heresy. The maladroit motivations of men like Michael de Causis provide evidence of the malignancy which could and did accompany more noble and honorable efforts at preserving the faith. Hus was not the scoundrel the Church assumed him to be. That mantle was worn ever more fittingly by Michael de Causis and some of his colleagues like Štěpán Páleč and Petr of Uničov. In their zeal to preserve religious unity and eliminate the climate of disquiet in western Christendom ecclesiastical authority misjudged Jan Hus taking him for what was sometimes patently untrue and overlooking his virtues as a devoted priest and faithful Christian. His heresy remained but there has never been reform without the risk of dissent and disagreement. That risk is not the disease or threat the Church often claimed in its late medieval campaign to establish and maintain control.[21] The twelfth-century Bernard of Chartres is reported to have claimed that truth was the daughter of time. It is not certain Hus could possibly have appreciated the nuance. But he clearly did agree with Augustine who once remarked that even though the times changed the faith did not.[22] In the end, Jan Hus was not so inflexible that he could not conceive of the Christian faith appearing in more than one guise. He pursued that path so resolutely and relentlessly that the guardians of the faith once delivered to the saints drove him from their midst and metaphorically delivered him to Satan as a 'damnable Judas' who could not possibly be permitted to have any part whatever in the cup of redemption. That position was unnecessary and tragic both for Hus as well as the Church.

What can we learn from Hus? There seems to be three main lessons implicit in his living and especially in his manner of dying. The first is the important difference between principle and pragmatism. Eschewing the latter, Hus clung tenaciously to the former right up to the end. The second is the living example of truth and justice versus political correctness. Hus was so fundamentally committed to the ideals of truth and justice that ultimately he was blind to all other factors. The third lesson underscores the courage and cost of conviction. History remembers Jan Hus as a man who took a stand and remained steadfast against all influences and stood firm in that persuasion without fear or wavering. His final recorded words at the stake indicate his glad willingness to surrender his life for the cause of truth and conviction. That brave testimony in the face of death requires no commentary.

The lamps of Hus' life and work surely seemed snuffed out by the great gust of rebuke delivered at Constance. The fathers of Latin Christendom, however, had grossly underestimated the depth and quality of the oil in those lamps. In the days and years which followed, the light of reformed religious practice in Bohemia glowed brightly. In the case of Jan Hus, martyrdom made the man. No one can convincingly argue that Jan Hus stands among the greatest of medieval figures. His ideas did not change the world and his stature is dwarfed by many others. But the spectacle of a grown man wearing a dunce cap chained to a thick post with wood piled to his chin and set on fire compels our attention. It not only marked the end of Hus' life it also signaled the beginning of something new. Repressive measures against Hus and his followers not only failed, but failed spectacularly. Others would die violent deaths, reform initiatives would still meet with resistance, and dissenters would continue to be banished. But no longer would kings stand barefoot in the snow and yield to the unbending and non-negotiable will of popes as Henry IV did before Gregory VII at Canossa in the brutal winter of 1077.[23] Religious and social dissent could no longer be deterred absolutely. Jan Hus and the revolution bearing his name helped to change the way power and authority were understood and administered, both in the Church and in political structures. Bold ideas quite capable of revolutionizing the human mind and by extension the Latin Church and western civilization followed in Hus' wake. These ideas had been nurtured and born in the womb of his bellicose 'world of multiple and contradictory options'.[24] Jan Hus was not the creator of this paradigm shift but his living and his dying contributed to it.

NOTES

Introduction

1. Radio broadcast of 27 September 1938 and reported in 'Prime Minister on the Issues', *The Times*, (28 September 1938), p. 10.
2. In general see Timothy Reuter, 'Medieval: Another Tyrannous Construct', *Medieval History Journal*, 1, (1998), pp. 24–45 and Otto Gerhard Oexle, 'The Middle Ages through Modern Eyes: A Historical Problem', *Transactions of the Royal Historical Society*, sixth series, 9, (1999), pp. 121–142.
3. John van Engen, 'Multiple Options: The World of the Fifteenth-Century Church', *Church History*, 77, (June 2008), pp. 257–284, but especially pp. 257–258.
4. The quote 'nul bain pendant mille ans!' is from Michelet, *La sorcière*, Paris, Collection Hetzel E. Dentu Libraire-Éditeur, 1862, p. 110.
5. Anonymous epigram printed in S.R. Maitland, *The Dark Ages: A Series of Essays intended to Illustrate the State of Religion and Literature in the Ninth, Tenth, Eleventh, and Twelfth Centuries*, London, Rivington, 1844, p. 1. Maitland notes the logical fallacy.
6. For example Étienne Gilson, *History of Christian Philosophy in the Middle Ages*, New York, Random House, 1955. This 800 page tome limited the fifteenth century to less than twenty pages under the heading 'Journey's End'.
7. A.J.P. Taylor, 'Accident Prone, or What Happened Next', *Journal of Modern History*, 49, (March 1977), pp. 1–18.
8. The classic study is Johan Huizinga, *The Autumn of the Middle Ages*, trans., Rodney J. Payton and Ulrich Mammitzsch, Chicago, University of Chicago Press, 1996. Originally published in 1924.
9. An influential book in this respect is Johann Loserth, *Hus und Wiclif: Zur Genesis der hussitischen Lehre*, Prague and Leipzig, Tempsky, 1884.
10. Thomas L. Haskell, *Objectivity is not Neutrality: Explanatory Schemes in History*, Baltimore, Johns Hopkins University Press, 1998.
11. On this matter with important comment see Robert Kalivoda, *Revolution und Ideologie: Der Hussitismus*, trans., Heide Thorwart and Monika Gletter, Cologne and Vienna, Böhlau Verlag, 1976, pp. 1–44.

12 Wilhelm Dilthey, 'The Construction of the Historical World in the Human Studies', in H.P. Rickman (ed.), *Selected Writings*, Cambridge, Cambridge University Press, 1976, p. 212.
13 Gabrielle M. Spiegel, 'Genealogy: Form and Function in Medieval Narrative', *History and Theory*, 22, (1983), pp. 43–44.
14 Bernard Guenée, 'Y a-t-il une historiographie médiévale?', *Revue historique*, 258, (1977), p. 255.
15 Ecclesiasticus 18:7
16 Hilary, *De trinitate*, II, 10, ii, in PL, vol. 10, cols. 58–59.
17 As argued by Andrew of St. Victor, *Prologue to Isaiah*, Paris, Bibliothèque Mazarine MS 175, fol. 40^v. This sage advice, in context, has been transcribed in Beryl Smalley, *The Study of the Bible in the Middle Ages*, 3rd edition, Notre Dame, University of Notre Dame Press, 1978, pp. 377–380.
18 *Sic et Non*, prologue. In Blanche B. Boyer and Richard McKeon (eds.), *Peter Abailard Sic et Non: A Critical Edition*, Chicago, The University of Chicago Press, 1977, p. 89 where Abelard is actually citing Cicero.
19 Matthew Spinka, *John Hus: A Biography*, Princeton, Princeton University Press, 1968.
20 FRB, vol. 8, pp. 25–120.
21 Fudge, *The Magnificent Ride: The First Reformation in Hussite Bohemia*, p. 4.
22 G.R. Elton, *The Practice of History*, New York, Thomas Y. Crowell, 1967, pp. 134–135.
23 Broadly expressed in Bartoš, *Čechy v době husově 1378–1415*, Prague, Laichter, 1947 and Kalivoda, *Revolution und Ideologie: Der Hussitismus*.

Chapter One

1 The standard and mainly reliable Czech and English biographies are Novotný/Kybal and Spinka, *John Hus*.
2 Novotný, *Correspondence*, p. 278.
3 František M. Bartoš, 'Hus jako student a profesor Karlovy university', *Acta universitatis carolinae - philosophica et historica*, 2, (1958), pp. 9–10.
4 *Menší výklad na páteř*, in *Opera omnia*, vol. 1, p. 392.
5 *Výklad na Páteř*, in *Opera omnia*, vol. 1, p. 342.
6 Session 21 on 9 June condemned such activities. Mansi, vol. 29, col. 108.
7 Novotný, *Correspondence*, pp. 204–5.
8 *Výklad desatera*, in *Opera omnia*, vol. 1, p. 183.
9 *Výklad na Páteř*, in *Opera omnia*, vol. 1, p. 351.
10 *Výklad desatera*, in *Opera omnia*, vol. 1, p. 320.
11 *O svatokupectví*, in *Opera omnia*, vol. 4, p. 228.
12 Text in Bohuslav Havránek (ed.), *Výbor z české literatury doby husitské*, 2 vols., Prague, ČSAV, 1963–4, vol. 1, pp. 75–79.
13 The incident is noted in the *Chronicon universitatis pragensis*, in FRB, vol. 5, p. 568 and Bartoš, 'Husův učitel Dr Jan Štěkna a kaple Betlemská', *Vestník České Akademie věd a umění*, 58, (1949), pp. 5–13.

14 *Positiones*, p. 221 and František Šmahel, *Die Prager Universität im Mittelalter*, Leiden, Brill, 2007, p. 257.
15 *Documenta*, pp. 387, 466, et al.
16 *Výklad desatera*, in *Opera omnia*, vol. 1, p. 291.
17 Fudge, '"Feel this!": Jan Hus and the Preaching of Reformation', in BRRP, vol. 4, pp. 107–126 and Hilsch, pp. 58–75.
18 *Historia et monumenta*, vol. 2, pp. 165–511.
19 Reference in František Šimek (ed.), *Staré letopisy české z vratislavského rukopisu novočeským pravopisem*, Prague, Historické spolku a společnosti Husova Musea, 1937, p. 5.
20 *De quinque officiis sacerdotis*, in *Historia et monumenta*, vol. 1, p. 191.
21 There is a modern edition in Johann Schröpfer, *Hussens traktat 'Orthographia Bohemica' - Die Herkunft des diakritischen Systems in der Schreibung slavischer Sprachen und die Älteste zusammenhängende Beschreibung slavischer Laute*, Wiesbaden, Harrassowitz, 1968. A useful study on the matter is Anežka Vidmanová, 'Ke spisku Orthographia bohemica', *Listy filologické*, 105, (1982), pp. 75–89.
22 *Documenta*, pp. 448–450.
23 *Documenta*, pp. 450–1.
24 Štěpán of Dolany, *Antihussus*, in Pez, vol. 4, pt. 2, cols. 362–430 at col. 373. The treatise dates from 1412.
25 Of special note is his *Knížky proti knězi kuchmistrovi*, in *Opera omnia*, vol. 4, p. 312 and SRB, vol. 3, pp. 471–472.
26 The manuscript text is in Bartoš, 'Hus a jeho strana v osvětlení nepřátelského pamfletu', *Reformační sborník*, 4, (1931), pp. 3–8.
27 A.N.E.D. Schofield, 'The Case of Jan Hus', *The Irish Ecclesiastical Record*, 109, 5th series (June, 1968), p. 406, relying on Kaminsky and De Vooght.
28 The conclusions of Ernst Werner, 'Jan Hus im Spiegel Moderner Historiographie', *Heresis: Revue d'histoire des dissidences européennes*, 16, (1991), p. 39.
29 Shrewdly pointed out by Paul de Vooght, *Jacobellus de Stříbro (†1429), premier théologien du hussitisme*, Louvain, Publications Universitaires de Louvain, 1972, p. 157.
30 Amedeo Molnár, 'K otázce reformační iniciativy lidu: Svědectví husitského kázání', in Amedeo Molnár (ed.), *Acta reformationem bohemicam illustrantia*, vol. 1, Prague, Kalich, 1978, pp. 5–44 at p. 9.
31 The most recent critical texts are in *Opera omnia*, vol. 1.
32 *O svatokupectví*, in *Opera omnia*, vol. 4, pp. 187–270.
33 *Dcerka: O poznání cěsty pravé k spasení*, in *Opera omnia*, vol. 4, pp. 163–186.
34 *O šesti bludiech*, in *Opera omnia*, vol. 4, pp. 271–296.
35 *Contra Stanislaum*, in *Opera omnia*, vol. 22, pp. 271–367.
36 *Výklad desatera*, in *Opera omnia*, vol. 1, p. 267.
37 Novotný, *Correspondence*, pp. 153–156, et al.
38 *Česká nedělní postila*, in *Opera omnia*, vol. 2.
39 *Jádro učení křesťanského*, in *Opera omnia*, vol. 4, pp. 330–333.
40 *Knížky proti knězi kuchmistrovi*, in *Opera omnia*, vol. 4, pp. 312–323.
41 Novotný, *Correspondence*, p. 170.

42 *Postil*, in *Opera omnia*, vol. 2, pp. 252–253.
43 *Documenta*, pp. 472–474.
44 *Concilium doctorum facultatis theologicae studii Pragensis*, in *Documenta*, pp. 475–480.
45 *Documenta*, pp. 493–494.
46 *Contra falsa concilia doctorum*, in *Documenta*, pp. 499–501 and Jesenice's refutation *Replicatio magistrorum Pragensium contra conditionis concordiae*, in *Ibid.*, pp. 495–499.
47 These events and subsequent developments are covered in the 'Chronicle of Prague University' in FRB, vol. 5, pp. 576–577.

Chapter Two

1 A recent important study is the work of David C. Mengel, 'Bones, Stones, and Brothels: Religion and Topography in Prague under Emperor Charles IV (1346–78)'. PhD dissertation, University of Notre Dame, 2003 which pays careful attention to the sources.
2 The description appears in full in P.M. Barford, *The Early Slavs: Culture and Society in Early Medieval Eastern Europe*, Ithaca, Cornell University Press, 2001, p. 255.
3 'Ammonitio baccalaureandi', in Höfler, vol. 2, p. 111.
4 See for example the comments by Heinrich von Dießenhofen (1359) in Johann Friedrich Boehmer (ed.), *Fontes rerum Germanicarum*, Stuttgart, Cotta, 1868, p. 116.
5 Václav Vladivoy Tomek, *Dějepis města Prahy*, 12 vols., 2nd edition, Prague, Řivnáč, 1892–1906 covers the period up to 1608.
6 Important for its survey of the context of Hus' life is Ferdinand Seibt, 'Die Zeit der Luxemburger und der hussitischen Revolution', in Karl Bosl (ed.), *Handbuch der Geschichte der böhmischen Länder*, 4 vols., Stuttgart, Anton Hiersemann,1966–74, vol. 1, pp. 349–580.
7 Zdeněk Boháč, 'Postup osídlení a demograficky vývoj Českých zemi do 15. století', *Historická demografie*, 12, (1987), p. 78 and Šmahel, vol. 1, pp. 352–370.
8 Huizinga's thesis has been attacked by Howard Kaminsky, 'From Lateness to Waning to Crisis: The Burden of the Later Middle Ages', *Journal of Early Modern History*, 4, (No. 1, 2000), pp. 85–125 and Kaminsky, 'Europe in the Time of Sigismund', in Michel Pauly and François Reinert (eds.), *Sigismund von Luxemburg: Ein Kaiser in Europa*, Mainz, Philipp von Zabern Verlag, 2006, pp. 7–15.
9 Ludolf of Żagań, 'De longevo schismate', in Johann Loserth (ed.), *Archiv für österreichische geschichte*, 60, (1880), p. 408. Ludolf was abbot of an Augustinian house in Żagań in Silesia. He wrote his chronicle in 1421.
10 Balázs Nagy and Frank Schaer (eds.), *Autobiography of Emperor Charles IV and his Legend of Saint Wenceslas*, Budapest, Central European University Press, 2001.
11 The letter appears in article 26 of the 'Acts of the Roman Curia' concerning Jan of Jenštejn and printed in De Vooght, *Hussiana*, p. 432.
12 The definitive study is Jiří Spěváček, *Václav IV. 1361–1419 k předpokadům husitské revoluce*, Prague, Svoboda, 1986.
13 There are voluminous, substantial, and important studies of Emperor Sigismund. A major international colloquium convened at Luxembourg in 2005 has added to our knowledge of the life and context of the great nemesis of the Hussites. Imre Takács (ed.), *Sigismundus Rex et Imperator: Kunst und Kultur zur Zeit Sigismunds von Luxemburg (1387–1437)*,

Mainz, Philipp von Zabern, 2006. See also Michel Pauly and François Reinert (eds.), *Sigismund von Luxemburg: Ein Kaiser in Europa*, Mainz, Philipp von Zabern Verlag, 2006. To these important recent volumes one might usefully consult Jörg K. Hoensch, *Kaiser Sigismund: Herrscher an der Schwelle zue Neuzeit, 1368–1437*, Munich, Beck, 1996, Hoensch, *Itinerar König Kaiser Sigismunds von Luxemburg 1368–1437*, Warendorf, Fahlbusch, 1995, Josef Macek, Ernő Marosi and Ferdinand Seibt (eds.), *Sigismund von Luxemburg: Kaiser und König in Mitteleuropa 1387–1437: Beiträge zur Herrschaft Kaiser Sigismunds und der europäischen Geschichte um 1400*, Warendorf, Fahlbusch, 1994, Elemér Mályusz, *Kaiser Sigismund in Ungarn, 1387–1437*, trans., Anikó Szmodits, Budapest, Akadémiai Kiadó, 1990, and of lesser significance Thomas A. Fudge, 'An Ass with a Crown: Heresy, Nationalism and Emperor Sigismund', in Jan P. Skalny and Miloslav Rechcígl, Jr. (eds.), *The Transformation of Czech and Slovak Societies on the Threshold of the New Millennium and their Role in the Global World*, Plzeň, Aleš Čeněk, 2004, pp. 199–217.

14   For a survey of the ethnic constituency before the Hussite period see Šmahel, vol. 1, pp. 337–352.

15   There are two narrative accounts of the incidents. See Pavel Trost, 'A Mock Report on the Prague Pogrom in 1389', *Slavica Hierosolymitana*, 7, (1985), pp. 239–40 and now more recently Miri Rubin, *Gentile Tales: The Narrative Assault on Late Medieval Jews*, Philadelphia, University of Pennsylvania Press, 1999, pp. 135–140.

16   František Graus, *Chudina městská v době předhusitské*, Prague, Melantrich, 1949, pp. 33, 70–2 and 132–134.

17   Bedřich Mendl, 'Z hospodářských dějin středověké Prahy', *Sborník příspěvků k dějinám hlavního města Prahy*, 5, (1932), pp. 161–389, a study of fourteenth and fifteenth-century rents especially valuable for its wide base of sources.

18   See Bartoš, 'Milíč a jeho škola v boji proti sociální metle velkoměsta', *JSH*, 21 (1952), pp. 121–132.

19   Peter of Zittau, *Chronicon Aulae Regiae*, in FRB, vol. 4, pp. 320–321.

20   See especially Jaroslav Čechura, 'Mor, krize a husitská revoluce', *Časopis český historický*, 92, (1994), pp. 286–303 and Jaroslav Mezník, 'Mor z roku 1380 a příčiny husitské', *Časopis český historický*, 93, (1995), pp. 702–710.

21   Šmahel, 'The Hussite Movement: an anomaly of European history?', in Mikuláš Teich (ed.), *Bohemia in History*, Cambridge, Cambridge University Press, 1998, p. 83.

22   Šmahel, *'Causa non grata*: Premature Reformation in Hussite Bohemia', in CECE, p. 225.

23   Šmahel, *La révolution hussite, une anomalie historique*, Paris, Presses universitaires de France, 1985, p. 23 and Antonín Podlaha (ed.), *Liber ordinationum cleri 1395–1416*, 2 vols, Prague, Pražská kapitula, 1910–1920, vol. 2, p. x.

24   See the statutes in Pavel Krafl, *Synody a statuta Olomoucké diecéze období středověku*, Prague, Historický ústav, 2003, pp. 175–204.

25   Marin, pp. 11–24 and to some extent Armando Comi, *Verità e Anticristo: L'eresia de Jan Hus*, Bologna, Pendragon, 2007, pp. 13–23.

26   Beneš of Veitmil, *Cronica ecclesie Pragensis*, in FRB, vol. 4, p. 540.

27   *Protocollum*, pp. 45–46, 48, 49, 63, 69, 71,142, 144, 146 and 163.

28 On the subject there are now two important studies. Wojciech Iwańczak, 'Prostytucja w późnośredniowiecznej Pradze', in Maurice Aymand (ed.), *Biedni i Bogaci: studia z dziejów społeczeństwa i Kultury ofiarowane Bronisławowi Geremkowi w sześćdziesiątą rocznicę urodzin*, Warsaw, PWN, 1992, pp. 95–104 and more recently see David C. Mengel, 'From Venice to Jerusalem and Beyond: Milíč of Kroměříž and the Topography of Prostitution in Fourteenth-Century Prague', *Speculum*, 79, (April 2004), pp. 407–442.
29 Beneš of Veitmil, *Cronica ecclesie Pragensis*, in FRB, vol. 4, p. 546.
30 *Protocollum*, pp. 82, 96.
31 *Protocollum*, pp. 62–64.
32 *Protocollum*, p. 118.
33 *Protocollum*, pp. 219, 255, 321.
34 *Protocollum*, p. 116
35 *Protocollum*, p. 90.
36 There are numerous references to Ludwig. *Protocollum*, pp. 48–9, 80–2, and 114–117.
37 *Protocollum*, pp. 390–391.
38 For example, Tomek, *Dějepis města Prahy*, vol. 3, pp. 242–247.
39 Magistrate's register, 1388–1399 in Prague City Archives MS 2073 fol. 168^r–168^v.
40 *Defensio articulorum Wyclif* in Opera omnia, vol. 22, p. 183.
41 The anonymous *Vita venerabilis presbyteri Milici*, in FRB, vol. 1, p. 420 and *Regulae*, vol. 3, p. 360.
42 *Vita venerabilis presbyteri Milici*, in FRB, vol. 1, p. 424.
43 The list appears in František Palacký, *Über Formelbücher zunächst in Bezug auf böhmische Geschichte*, in *Abhandlungen der Königlichen Böhmischen Gesellschaft der Wissenschaften*, 5, (1847), pp. 182–186.
44 Amedeo Molnár, 'L'évolution de la théologie hussite', *Revue d'histoire et de Philosophie Réligieuses*, 43, (1963), p. 136.
45 Novotný/Kybal, vol. 2, p. 17 and elsewhere in that discussion.
46 The *Regulae* bears this out and there is a concise summary in Vlastimil Kybal, *M. Matěj z Janova: Jeho život, spisy a učení*, Prague, L. Marek, 2000, p. 318. Originally published in 1905.
47 *Documenta*, pp. 699–700.
48 *Chronicon universitatis Pragensis*, in FRB, vol. 5, p. 568 and Šmahel, HR, vol. 1, pp. 198–199.
49 Adalbert Horčičke (ed.), *Chronicon breve regni Bohemiae saec. XV 1310–1421*, in *Mitteilungen des Vereins für Geschichte der Deutschen in Böhmen*, 37, (1899), pp. 454–467. The source is riddled with errors.
50 Jana Nechutová, 'Die charismatische spiritualität Böhmen in der vorreformatorischen Zeit', *Österreichische Osthefte*, 39, (1997), pp. 411–419.
51 Šmahel, vol 1, p. 342.
52 František Graus, 'Prag als Mitte Böhmens 1346–1421', in Emil Meynen (ed.), *Zentralität als Problem der mittelalterlichen Stadtgeschichtsforschung*, Vienna, Böhlau, 1979, pp. 22–47.
53 The anonymous 'Litera de civitate Pragensi', in Höfler, vol. 2, pp. 311–319.
54 See particularly Otakar Odložilík, 'Z počátků husitství na Moravě: Šimon z Tišnova a Jan Vavřincův z Račic', *Časopis Matice Moravské*, 49, (1925), pp. 3–170 but especially pp.127–145.

NOTES

55   Höfler, vol. 1, p. 563.
56   Václav Novotný, *M. Jan Hus*, Prague, Otto, n.d. [*c*.1905], pp. 20–1.

Chapter Three

1. The story is told in Matthaeus Ludecus, *Historia von der erfindung, Wunderwercken und der zerstörung des vermeinten heiligen Bluts zu Wilssnagk*,Wittenberg, Clemens Schleich, 1586. A splendid study of Wilsnack in its European context is Caroline Bynum Walker, *Wonderful Blood: Theology and Practice in Late Medieval Northern Germany and Beyond*, Philadelphia, University of Pennsylvania Press, 2007, especially pp. 23–46 and the fine recommended essay collection found in Felix Escher and Hartmut Kühne (eds.), *Die Wilsnackfahrt: Ein Wallfahrts – und Kommunikationszentrum Nord – und Mitteleuropas im Spätmittelalter*, Frankfurt, Peter Lang, 2006.
2. Text in Jaroslav Kadlec, 'Synods of Prague and their Statutes 1396–1414', *Apollinaris*, 54, (1991), pp. 251–253.
3. *Postil*, in *Opera omnia*, vol. 2, p. 232.
4. *De sanguine Christi*, in Václav Flajšhans (ed.), *Mag. Jo. Hus Opera omnia: Nach neuentdeckten Handschriften*, Osnabrück, Biblio-Verlag, 1966, vol. 1, fasc. 3, pp. 3–37.
5. *De sanguine Christi*, pp. 20–22.
6. *De sanguine Christi*, pp. 32–33.
7. Sermon for Lent 1 in *Collecta*, in *Opera omnia*, vol. 7, p. 130 and *De sanguine Christi*, pp. 26–27.
8. Sermon for Trinity 21 in *Collecta*, in *Opera omnia*, vol. 7, p. 568.
9. *De sanguine Christi*, p. 26
10. With these words the fourteenth-century humanist Petrarch opened his 'book with no name'. Rebecca Lenoir (ed.), *Pétrarque Sans titre: Liber sine nomine*, Grenoble, Jérôme Millon, 2003, p. 24.
11. Jiří Kejř, 'Husova Pravda', *Theologická revue*, 77, (2006), pp. 232–243.
12. *O svatokupectví*, in *Opera omnia*, vol. 4, p. 270 and *Knížky proti knězi kuchmistrovi*, in *Opera omnia*, vol. 4, p. 322.
13. *Výklad víry*, in *Opera omnia*, vol. 1, p. 69.
14. *Super IV Sententiarum*, p. 400.
15. Advent III in *Opera omnia*, vol. 9, p. 90.
16. *Super IV Sententiarum*, p. 5.
17. *Contra Iohannem Stokes*, in *Opera omnia*, vol. 22, p. 68 and *De decimis*, in *Historia et monumenta*, vol. 1, p. 159.
18. *Questiones*, in *Opera omnia*, vol. 21a, *passim*.
19. *Defensio libri de Trinitate*, in *Opera omnia*, vol. 22, p. 42. Themistius was a fourth-century pagan philosopher who taught at Constantinople.
20. Ivana Dolejšová, 'Nominalist and Realist approaches to the problem of Authority: Páleč and Hus', in BRRP, 2, pp. 53–54.
21. The phrase can loosely be traced to Augustine's Sermon 131, 10, in Migne, PL, vol. 38, col. 734.
22. *Super IV Sententiarum*, pp. 49 and 43.

23   *Super IV Sententiarum*, p. 320.
24   It must be noted that nominalism was not a term with currency in fourteenth-century Prague. Damascus Trapp, 'Clm 27034: Unchristened Nominalism and Wycliffite Realism at Prague in 1381', *Recherches de théologie ancienne et médiévale*, 24, (1957), pp. 320, 349.
25   For an introductory analysis of the Augustinian presence in the Hus corpus see especially C. Daniel Crews, *The Theology of John Hus with Special Reference to His Concepts of Salvation*, PhD dissertation, University of Manchester, 1975, pp. 183–201.
26   This is quite apparent in the *Super IV Sententiarum*, book 1, pp. 3–188.
27   De Vooght, pp. 445.
28   De Vooght, *Hussiana*, pp. 78–81.
29   Enrico Selly Molnár, 'Viklef, Hus a problém autority', in Lášek, pp. 110–111.
30   Johann Loserth, *Wiclif and Hus*, trans., M.J. Evans, London, Hodder & Stoughton, 1884, p. 281 and repeated in the second German edition (1925), p. 186.
31   *Super IV Sententiarum*, p. 744.
32   *Contra octo doctores*, in *Opera omnia*, vol. 22, p. 408.
33   *Contra Iohannem Stokes*, in *Opera omnia*, vol. 22, pp. 62–63.
34   Johann Loserth as reported by Franz Lützow, *The Life and Times of Master John Hus*, London, Dent, 1909, p. 20.
35   B. [Brian] Gaybba, 'John Huss' views on the nature of theology in the introduction to his commentary on the Sentences', *Studia historiae ecclesiasticae*, 20, (No. 2, 1994), pp. 79–94.
36   See particularly the astute observations of Jan Sedlák (ed.), *Studie a texty k životopisu Husovu*, 3 vols., Olomouc, Matice Cyrilometodějská,1914–1925, vol. 1, pp. 436–459.
37   *Super IV Sententiarum*, p. 18.
38   *Výklad víry*, in *Opera omnia*, vol. 1, pp. 66–67.
39   *Super IV Sententiarum*, pp. 14–16.
40   *O šesti bludiech*, in *Opera omnia*, vol. 4, pp. 279–282.
41   Dolejšová, 'Nominalist and Realist approaches to the problem of Authority', p. 55.
42   *Super IV Sententiarum*, pp. 20–21.
43   *De sufficientia legis Christi*, in *Historia et monumenta*, vol. 1, pp. 55–60 at p. 57.
44   *Výklad víry*, in *Opera omnia*, vol. 1, p. 68.
45   Kejř, *Počátků*, p. 24.
46   Prague, NMK MS V C 2 and also *Magistri Johannis Hus: Quodlibet*, Bohumil Ryba (ed.), Turnhout, Brepols, 2006.
47   *De necessitate reformacionis Ecclesiae*, in Hardt, vol. 1, cols. 277–309, see cols. 306–307. The treatise of 1414 sometimes called the *Avisamenta edita in concilio constanciensi* has often been erroneously attributed either to Jean Gerson or Pierre d'Ailly.
48   Páleč developed his ecclesiology in his 1412 *De aequivocatione nominis ecclesia* and later in his *De ecclesia*. The text of the former appears in Pavel Klener (ed.), *Miscellanea husitica Ioannis Sedlák*, Prague, Univerzita Karlova, 1996 pp. 356–366 while the latter text is summarized on pp. 142–178.
49   Novotný/Kybal, vol. 2, pt. 1, pp. 257–258.
50   *Super IV Sententiarum*, p. 616 and *Jádro učení křesťanského*, in *Opera omnia*, vol. 4, p. 331.

51 *Sermones de sanctis*, in Václav Flajšhans (ed.), *Spisy M. Jana Husi*, Prague, Vilímek, 1907, vols. 7–8, p. 242.
52 *De ecclesia*, p. 15.
53 *Documenta*, p. 55.
54 *Super IV Sententiarum*, pp. 36, 733.
55 Jean Gerson advanced this specific argument in his article against Hus at the Council of Constance. See *Documenta*, p.187.
56 *Postil*, in *Opera omnia*, vol. 2, p. 148.
57 *De ecclesia*, p. 178.
58 Part 2 of his *Defensio articulorum Wyclif* in *Polemica*, in *Opera omnia*, vol. 22, pp. 165–194.
59 *Sermones in Capella Bethlehem*, vol. 3, pp. 177–178.
60 Sermon for Trinity Sunday in *Collecta*, in *Opera omnia*, vol. 7, p. 281.
61 *Super IV Sententiarum*, p. 469, Cyprian, *De ecclesiae catholicae unitate*, 6, in CCL, vol. 3, p. 253.
62 *Postilla adumbrata* in *Opera omnia*, vol. 13, p. 294, *Super IV Sententiarum*, p. 624 and De Vooght, *Hussiana*, p. 88.
63 The text appears in Sedlák, *M. Jan Hus*, pp. 127*–135*. Pages with an asterisk indicate part two of Sedlák's work which is a collection of edited primary sources.
64 In Hus' *Sermo de pace* in Amedeo Molnár and František M. Dobiáš (eds.), *Husova výzbroj do Kostnice*, Prague, Kalich, 1965, pp. 66–68, 70–73, 79–82.
65 František J. Holeček, '"Ministri dei possunt in dampnacionem perpetuam papam male viventem detrudere . . ." (Hus a problém Antikrista)', in *HT*, supplement 1, (2001), pp. 219–44. Overview of Hus' understanding of eschatology in Novotný/Kybal, vol. 2, pt. 3, pp. 299–321.
66 *De ecclesia*, pp. 51–52.
67 Dietrich von Niem, *De modis uniendi ac reformandi ecclesiam* in Hardt, vol. 1, (5), col. 77. There is a new critical edition in Hermann Heimpel (ed.), *Dialog über Union und Reform der Kirche 1410*, Leipzig, Teubner, 1933.
68 *Contra Palecz* in *Opera omnia*, vol. 22, pp. 254–255.
69 *Contra Palecz*, in *Opera omnia*, vol. 22, p. 255.
70 *Contra Stanislaum*, in *Opera omnia*, vol. 22, p. 315.
71 Werner, p. 115.
72 *Questio de Indulgentiis, sive de Cruciata Papae Joanne XXIII*, in *Historia et monumenta*, vol. 1, pp. 215–237.
73 *De ecclesia*, pp. 56, 38.
74 *Contra octo doctores*, in *Opera omnia*, vol. 22, pp. 393–395.
75 *Super IV Sententiarum*, p. 607.
76 *Contra Stanislaum*, in *Opera omnia*, vol. 22, pp. 335–339.
77 *Contra Palecz*, in *Opera omnia*, vol. 22, p. 264 and *De ecclesia*, p. 169.
78 *Contra cruciatam*, in *Opera omnia*, vol. 22, p. 136.
79 *Documenta*, p. 59 and *De ecclesia*, pp. 172–173.
80 *De ecclesia*, p. 45.
81 *Contra Palecz*, in *Opera omnia*, vol. 22, pp. 246–247.
82 *Documenta*, pp. 55, 135, 144.

83 Thus described by Hus in a letter to his Czech friends dated 24 June 1415 in Novotný, *Correspondence*, p. 308.
84 *De ecclesia*, p. 143 and Novotný, *Correspondence*, p. 13.
85 *O svatokupectví*, in *Opera omnia*, vol. 4, pp. 205–206.
86 *Contra Palecz*, in *Opera omnia*, vol. 22, p. 249.
87 *De ecclesia*, p. 129 and also Hus' letter to Christian of Prachatice, April 1413, Novotný, *Correspondence*, p. 167.
88 De Vooght and Spinka, *passim*.
89 Full argument appears in *De decimis* in *Historia et monumenta*, vol. 1, pp. 159–167 with a very strong anti-Donatist statement arguing the objective sanctity of the sacrament cannot be compromised by the subjective character of the priest on pp. 166–167.
90 Sermon text in Sedlák, *M. Jan Hus*, pp. 127*–135*.
91 *Contra Stanislaum*, in *Opera omnia*, vol. 22, pp. 330–331
92 *Super IV Sententiarum*, pp. 606, 616.
93 *Výklad víry*, in *Opera omnia*, vol. 1, p. 91.
94 Introduction to his *The Church by John Huss*, New York, Scribner's, 1915, p. xxxi.
95 *Concilium*, 6 February 1413 in *Documenta*, p. 480.
96 Letter to Havlík, 21 June 1415 in Novotný, *Correspondence*, p. 295.
97 Sermon *Confirmate corda vestra* in *Positiones*, p. 122.
98 *Výklad víry*, in *Opera omnia*, vol. 1, pp. 82–83. Elsewhere the same imagery appears in *Dcerka* in *Opera omnia*, vol. 4, pp. 180–181 and his sermon for the sixth Sunday after Pentecost on the text I Peter 4:7–11 in his Latin Postil the *Postilla adumbrata* in *Opera omnia*, vol. 13, p. 233.
99 *Výklad víry*, in *Opera omnia*, vol. 1, pp. 78–79.
100 Sermon for Advent II, *Collecta*, in *Opera omnia*, vol. 7, pp. 35–36.
101 Commentary on I Corinthians, in *Historia et monumenta*, vol. 2, p. 148, and especially in chapter 4.
102 *Výklad na páteř*, in *Opera omnia*, vol. 1, p. 388.
103 D. E. Luscombe (ed.), *Peter Abelard's Ethics*, Oxford, Clarendon Press, 1971 and Héloïse's famous first letter. Hus, *Jádro učení křesťanského*, in *Opera omnia*, vol. 4, p. 332.
104 Sermon for the first Sunday in Lent. *Postil*, in *Opera omnia*, vol. 2, pp. 142–143.
105 *Výklad desatera*, chapter 39 in *Opera omnia*, vol. 1, p. 172.
106 Sermon for Advent III, *Collecta*, in *Opera omnia*, vol. 7, p. 39 and Sermon for Advent I, in *Ibid.*, p. 29.
107 *Super IV Sententiarum*, pp. 224, 285.
108 Sermon before the synod, 1407 in *Historia et monumenta*, vol. 2, p. 52.
109 *Historia et monumenta*, vol. 2, p. 183 and also in the sermon *Abiciamus opera tenebrarum* in *Positiones*, p. 100.
110 'Da mihi castitatem et continentiam, sed noli modo'. In *Confessionum Libri XIII*, ed., L. Verheijen, in CCL, vol. 27, Turnhout, Brepols, 1981, 8.7.17., p. 124.
111 Sermon *Abiciamus opera tenebrarum* in *Positiones*, p. 100.
112 Sermon for Advent II, *Collecta*, in *Opera omnia*, vol. 7, p. 34, and the sermon *Spiritum nolite extinguere* in *Positiones*, p. 141.

113 Sermon for Advent I, in *Collecta*, in *Opera omnia*, vol. 7, p. 30. Hus appears to contradict himself elsewhere. See his *Dcerka*, in *Opera omnia*, vol. 4, p. 178.
114 *Super IV Sententiarum*, p. 26.
115 *Contra cruciatam*, in *Opera omnia*, vol. 22, pp. 132–133.
116 Sermon *Dixit Martha ad Iesum*, in *Positiones*, p. 171 and *Questiones, De Indulgentiis*, in *Opera omnia*, vol. 19a, pp. 112–119.
117 *De ecclesia*, p. 223.
118 *Super IV Sententiarum*, p. 367, the sermon *Dixit Martha ad Iesum* in *Positiones*, pp. 164–165 and also in *Super IV Sententiarum*, pp. 317, 336, 362, 486 and 625.
119 *Super IV Sententiarum*, pp. 623 and 167. See also Jacques Monfrin (ed.), *Abélard, Historia calamitatum: Texte et commentaires*, 4th edition, Paris: J. Vrin, 1974 for Héloïse's letters.
120 *Výklad deserata*, chapter 41, in *Opera omnia*, vol. 1, p. 194.
121 *Documenta*, p. 186.
122 *Super IV Sententiarum*, pp. 167, 168, 177, 344, 623 and his sermon *Spiritum nolite extinguere*, in *Positiones*, pp. 141–143.
123 *Výklad víry*, in *Opera omnia*, vol. 1, p. 86.
124 *Super IV Sententiarum*, pp. 162, 165.
125 *Super IV Sententiarum*, pp. 598–601.
126 *Collecta*, in *Opera omnia*, vol. 7, p. 66, *Super IV Sententiarum*, pp. 592, 606 and *Výklad víry*, in *Opera omnia*, vol. 1, pp. 88–89.
127 Sermon for Easter, in *Collecta*, in *Opera omnia*, vol. 7, pp. 180–1, sermon *Dixit Martha ad Iesum* in *Positiones*, p. 171 and *Super IV Sententiarum*, p. 19.
128 *Super IV Sententiarium*, p. 17 and sermon for Advent III in *Collecta*, in *Opera omnia*, vol. 7, p. 46.
129 *Contra Palecz*, in *Opera omnia*, vol. 22, pp. 242–243.
130 Commentary on I Corinthians, in *Historia et monumenta*, vol. 2, pp. 131–132. I am indebted to Crews, *The Theology of John Hus*, pp. 326–327 for his summary.
131 *Contra octo doctores*, in *Opera omnia*, vol. 22, pp. 400–408. There is an overview of Hus' doctrines of salvation and Christ in Novotný/Kybal, vol. 2, pt. 3, pp. 158–218.
132 *Super IV Sententiarum*, pp. 452–454 and sermon for Epiphany, *Collectio*, pp. 74–75.
133 *Postil*, in *Opera omnia*, vol. 2, p. 113.
134 *De ecclesia*, pp. 53–56.
135 *Super IV Sententiarum*, pp. 10, 458–459 and also in the sermon *Dixit Martha ad Iesum*, in *Positiones*, p. 158.
136 Commentary on James, in *Historia et monumenta*, vol. 2, p. 182.
137 Fudge, 'Saints, Sinners and Stupid Asses: The Place of Faith in Luther's Doctrine of Salvation', *CV*, 50, (No. 3, 2008), pp. 231–256.
138 *Super IV Sententiarum*, pp. 54–65 and 453–455.
139 Commentary on James, in *Historia et monumenta*, vol. 2, pp. 204–205, 207–208 and *Super IV Sententiarum*, p. 6.
140 Sermon *Vos estis sal terra* in *Positiones*, p. 115 and *Super IV Sententiarum*, pp. 19–20.
141 Sermon *Dixit Martha ad Iesum* in *Positiones*, p. 164.
142 *Historia et monumenta*, vol. 2, pp. 202–203 and 194–195.

143 *Super IV Sententiarum*, p. 344.
144 Josef Smolík, 'Truth in History according to Hus' Conception', *CV*, 15, (1972), p. 102 claims *simul iustus et peccator* remained central despite clear Hus' denial in *De ecclesia*, p. 27.
145 Sermon for Advent III, *Collecta*, in *Opera omnia*, vol. 7, p. 44.
146 *Super IV Sententiarum*, pp. 19–20.
147 *Výklad víry*, in *Opera omnia*, vol. 1, p. 63.
148 *O svatokupectví*, in *Opera omnia*, vol. 4, p. 269.
149 *Super IV Sententiarum*, pp. 20, 320, 330, 356, and 533 and Daniel Didomizio, 'Jan Hus's *De ecclesia*, Precursor of Vatican II?', *Theological Studies*, 60, (No. 2, 1999), p. 257.
150 *Jádro učení křesťanského*, in *Opera omnia*, vol. 4, p. 330.
151 Sermon *Si quis indiget sapiencia* in *Positiones*, p. 199.
152 *Super IV Sententiarum*, p. 51.
153 Sermon *Confirmate corda vestra*, in *Positiones*, p. 119 and Easter sermon in *Collecta*, in *Opera omnia*, vol. 7, p. 178.
154 *Výklad na desatera*, in *Opera omnia*, vol. 1, p. 249.
155 *Postil*, *Opera omnia*, vol. 2, pp. 279–280.
156 Sermon *Confirmate corda vestra*, in *Positiones*, p. 119.
157 Sermon *Dixit Martha ad Iesum* in *Positiones*, p. 165.
158 *Super IV Sententiarum*, pp. 162, 165.
159 *Super IV Sententiarum*, pp. 374, 375 and 456.
160 *Super IV Sententiarum*, p. 49.
161 Conclusion of replies to accusations against him at Constance, 18 June 1415, in *Documenta*, p. 234.
162 Kalivoda, *Husitská ideologie*, p. 106 pointed out that Hus applied the universal principle of the law of Christ to the church as well as to the state. Elsewhere, Kybal has noted the biblical and overtly theological dimensions of the concept in Hus as well as his colleagues. Novotný/Kybal, vol. 2, pt. 1, pp. 332–370.
163 *Výklad na desatera*, in *Opera omnia*, vol. 1, p. 237.
164 Sermon *Abiciamus opera tenebrarum*, in *Positiones*, p. 107 and *Super IV Sententiarum*, p. 6.
165 Novotný/Kybal, vol. 2, pt. 2, p. 507.
166 *Documenta*, p. 184.
167 This is the main thrust of a hymn attributed to Hus in Nejedlý, vol. 3, pp. 398–399.
168 See *Historia et monumenta*, vol. 2, p. 388. Smolík, 'Truth in History according to Hus' Conception' attempted to explicate the concept.
169 Commentary on Psalm 116 in *Historia et monumenta*, vol. 2, pp. 417–418.
170 Sermon *Abiciamus opera tenebrarum*, in *Positiones*, p. 99.
171 *Contra Palecz* in *Opera omnia*, vol. 22, p. 268.
172 *Defensio libri de Trinitate*, in *Opera omnia*, vol. 22, p. 46.
173 Peter Abelard, *The Story of My Misfortunes*, trans., Henry Adams Bellows, Glencoe, Free Press, 1958, p. 36; Anselm, *Proslogium*, conclusion to chapter 1 and Augustine, sermon 43 in CCL, vol. 41, pp. 508–512.
174 *O svatokupectví*, in *Opera omnia*, vol. 4, p. 269.
175 *Super IV Sententiarum*, p. 7.

176 *Super IV Sententiarum*, p. 15.
177 *Super IV Sententiarum*, p. 9.
178 *Contra ordo doctores*, in *Opera omnia*, vol. 22, p. 380.
179 *De ecclesia*, p. 232.
180 *Contra Palecz*, in *Opera omnia*, vol. 22, p. 259.
181 John Klassen, 'Hus, the Hussites and Bohemia', in Christopher Allmand (ed.), *The New Cambridge Medieval History*, vol. 7, Cambridge, Cambridge University Press, 1998, p. 375.
182 Marin, pp. 519–520.
183 Sermon for the first Sunday in Lent. *Postil*, in *Opera omnia*, vol. 2, pp. 147–148.
184 *Contra Palecz*, in *Historia et monumenta*, vol. 1, pp. 325, 330.
185 Novotný, *Correspondence*, pp. 270–273, 277–279 and *Documenta*, pp. 147–148.
186 *De sufficientia legis christi*, in *Historia et monumenta*, vol. 1, pp. 55–60.
187 The main texts can be found in B. Paulus (ed.), *Paschasius Radbertus: De Corpore et Sanguine Domini*, Turnhout, Brepols, 1969; J.N. Bakhuizen van den Brink (ed.), *Ratramnus: De corpore et sanguine Domini: Texte original et notice bibliographique*, Amsterdam, North-Holland Publishing Co., 1974; R.B.C. Huygens (ed.), *Beringerius Turonensis, Rescriptum contra Lanfrancum*, Turnhout, Brepols, 1988; and the text from Lateran IV in Norman P. Tanner (ed.), *Decrees of the Ecumenical Councils*, vol. 1, London, Sheed & Ward, 1990, p. 230.
188 *Super IV Sententiarum*, pp. 9, 38 and 634.
189 Ignatius, Letter to the Ephesians, 20 in F.X. Funk and Karl Bihlmeyer, *Die Apostolischen Väter*, Wilhelm Schneemelcher (ed.), Tübingen, Mohr, 1970 and Hus, Sermon for Trinity Sunday, *Collecta*, in *Opera omnia*, vol. 7, p. 281.
190 Twentieth Sunday after Trinity, *Postil*, in *Opera omnia*, vol. 2, p. 416.
191 Sermon for Palm Sunday 1406, *Collecta*, in *Opera omnia*, vol. 7, p. 168.
192 These points drawn from his early sermons. Šimek, pp. 96–99.
193 *Super IV Sententiarum*, pp. 565–566.
194 *Super IV Sententiarum*, pp. 633–637.
195 Sedlák, *Mistr Jan Hus*, p. 374 quite wrongly advances the unsupportable suggestion that Hus followed Wyclif into remanentism. The assumption has been widely repeated. For example, the eminent church historian Roland H. Bainton, *The Reformation of the Sixteenth Century*, Boston, The Beacon Press, 1952, p. 20 claims that Hus was led by Wyclif into the latter's eucharistic doctrine.
196 *O svatokupectví*, in *Opera omnia*, vol. 4, p. 230.
197 Novotný, *Correspondence*, pp. 96–97.
198 *Documenta*, p. 174.
199 *Relatio*, in FRB, vol. 8, p. 76.
200 *Documenta*, p. 170.
201 See Wyclif's 1380 *De eucharistia tractatus maior*, Johann Loserth (ed.), London, Trübner, 1892 and Ockham, *Quodlibeta septem una cum tractatu de sacramento altaris*. The Latin text is in T. Bruce Birch (ed.), *The Sacramento Altaris of William of Ockham*, Burlington, Lutheran Literary Board, 1930.
202 De Vooght, pp. 68–71, 108–109, 395–397 and 506–507. See also his *Hussiana*, pp. 263–291.

203 De Vooght, *Hussiana*, pp. 263–91. Another review of the controversy concluded that Hus did not teach remanentism but did not go as far as De Vooght. Stanislav Sousedík, 'Huss et la doctrine eucharistique "remanentiste"', *Divinitas*, 21, (No. 3, 1977), pp. 383–407. Overview of Hus' eucharistic doctrine in Novotný/Kybal, vol. 2, pt. 3, pp. 235–257.

204 Hus subscribed to the traditional number of seven sacraments as part of the center of Christian faith. *Jádro učení křesťanského*, in *Opera omnia*, vol. 4, p. 332. He was likewise entirely orthodox in his views of baptismal regeneration. See his sermon for Trinity Sunday, *Collecta*, in *Opera omnia*, vol. 7, p. 280 and *Super IV Sententiarum*, pp. 588, 686. Baptism was essential but did not imply election. Baptism of the spirit which God granted to the baptized elect was the guarantor. *Sermones in Capella Bethlehem*, vol. 4, p. 36.

205 The text is in *Historia et monumenta*, vol. 1, pp. 202–207. Newer edition in Flajšhans (ed.), *Mag. Jo. Hus Opera Omnia*, vol. 1, pt. 2, pp. 3–31.

206 See the *Super IV Sententiarum*, pp. 571, 574, 576. The word 'create' should be understood according to Hus' clarification in *O šesti bludiech*, in *Opera omnia*, vol. 4, pp. 271–273.

207 *Super IV Sententiarum*, pp. 557, 581 though he did encourage a group of young women to commune often. Novotný, *Correspondence*, p. 28.

208 *Dcerka*, in *Opera omnia*, vol. 4, p. 178.

209 *Výklad na páteř*, in *Opera omnia*, vol. 1, pp. 365–369.

210 *Super IV Sententiarum*, pp. 557, 575.

211 We hear of this in Jan Rokycana's first sermon for Easter Tuesday. Text in František Šimek (ed.), *Postilla Jana Rokycany*, 2 vols., Prague, Komise pro vydávání pramenů českého hnutí náboženského,1928, vol. 1, p. 693.

212 See Jan Sedlák, 'Počátkové kalicha', *Časopis katolického duchovenstva*, 52, (1911), pp. 97–105, 244–250, 397–401, 496–501, 583–587, 703–708, 786–791; vol. 54, (1913), pp. 226–232, 275–278, 404–410, 465–470, 708–713; and vol. 55, (1914), pp. 75–84, 113–120, and 315–322; František M. Bartoš, *Husitství a cizina*, Prague, CIN, 1931, pp. 59–112; Kaminsky, pp. 127–34; Romolo Cegna, 'Początki utrakwizmu w Czechach w latach 1412–1415', *Przegląd Historyczny*, 69, (1978), pp. 103–114; and Helena Krmíčková, *Studie a texty k počátkům kalicha v Čechách*, Brno, Masarykova Univerzita, 1997.

213 Numerous comments in sermons from 1416. Bedřich Spáčila (ed.), *Mistr Jakoubek ze Stříbra: Betlemská kázání z roku 1416*, Prague, Blahoslav,1951, pp. 51, 62,104, et al.

214 Novotný, *Correspondence*, pp. 216-217.

215 *Utrum expediat laicis fidelibus sumere sanguinem Christi sub specie vini?*, in *Historia et monumenta*, vol. 1, pp. 52–54. An argument can be made for Hus' dependence on Jakoubek of Stříbro's *Quaestio quia heu in templis*. See Helena Krmíčková, 'Jakoubkova utrakvistická díla z roku 1414', in Ota Halama and Pavel Soukup (eds.), *Jakoubek ze Stříbra: Texty a jejich působení*, Prague, Filosofia, 2006, pp. 173–177.

216 De Vooght, *Jacobellus de Stříbro*, p. 125.

217 Chlum's letter and Hus' reply appear in Novotný, *Correspondence*, pp. 238–241.

218 *Relatio*, in FRB, vol. 8, p. 52.

219 Text in Tanner (ed.), *Decrees of the Ecumenical Councils*, vol. 1, pp. 418–419.

220 Novotný, *Correspondence*, p. 289. Matthew Spinka drew attention to Hus' words on the wall in *The Letters of John Hus*, Manchester, Manchester University Press, 1972, p. 179.

221 Novotný, *Correspondence*, pp. 294–295.
222 *Super IV Sententiarum*, pp. 541–542, 635–636.
223 *Super IV Sententiarum*, p. 6.
224 Fillastre, *Gesta concilii Constanciensis*, in Loomis, p. 283 and Jerome's speech at the hearing of 26 May in Hardt, vol. 4, cols. 752–762.
225 *Super IV Sententiarum*, pp. 572–573, *O svatokupectví*, in *Opera omnia*, vol. 4, pp. 194–5, *Contra predicatorem Plznensem*, in *Opera omnia*, vol. 22, p. 116 and *O šesti bludiech*, in *Opera omnia*, vol. 4, pp. 271–273.
226 *Výklad víry*, in *Opera omnia*, vol. 1, p. 75 and *O šesti bludiech*, in *Opera omnia*, vol. 4, p. 271.
227 *Výklad víry*, in *Opera omnia*, vol. 1, p. 89.
228 *Sermones in Capella Bethlehem*, vol. 4, pp. 192, 195.
229 *Sermones in Capella Bethlehem*, vol. 4, p. 190.
230 Latin text in *Betlemské texty*, pp. 41–63, the Czech in *Opera omnia*, vol. 4, pp. 271–296, but see pp. 271–273.
231 *O šesti bludiech*, pp. 271, 272 and *Výklad víry*, in *Opera omnia*, vol. 1, p. 75.
232 Flajšhans (ed.), *Mag. Io. Hus Opera Omnia*, vol. 1, pt. 2, pp. 3–5 and *passim*.
233 *De sacramento corporis et sanguinis domini*, in *Historia et monumenta*, vol. 1, pp. 47–52. This was the same as declared in *O šesti bludiech*, p. 273.
234 *Relatio*, in FRB, vol. 8, p. 114.
235 *Výklad víry*, in *Opera omnia*, vol. 1, p. 88.
236 *Responsio ad scriptum octo doctorum*, in *Historia et monumenta*, vol. 1, pp. 393–4 and *De ecclesia*, pp. 139–140 and 168–169. On 28 May 1403 Hus is reported to have called for the falsifiers of the Wyclifite articles to be executed. Noted in Lützow, *The Life and Times of Master John Hus*, p. 80.
237 *Výklad víry*, in *Opera omnia*, vol. 1, pp. 210–221.
238 *De ecclesia*, pp. 73–74, *Super IV Sententiarum*, p. 596 and *Jádro učení křesťanského*, in *Opera omnia*, vol. 4, p. 332.
239 Hus' inaugural speech in 1409 as university rector in Prague. Cited in Molnár, 'Viklef, Hus a problém autority', in Lášek, p. 109.

Chapter Four

1 *Výklad na desatera*, in *Opera omnia*, vol. 1, p. 233.
2 Sermon *Confirmate corda vestra*, in *Positiones*, p.123. Hus referred to a poem of Nicholas of Bibrach where each verse began with the phrase 'death is coming'.
3 Sermon for Palm Sunday in *Collecta*, in *Opera omnia*, vol. 7, p.168.
4 Jiří Daňhelka (ed.), *Husitské písně*, Prague, Československý Spisovatel, 1952, p.133.
5 *De ecclesia*, p. 217. See also František Šmahel, 'Literacy and Heresy in Hussite Bohemia', in Anne Hudson and Peter Biller (eds.), *Heresy and Literacy, 1000–1530*, Cambridge, Cambridge University Press, 1994, p. 238 who has underscored the problems for the laity with respect to Latin inscriptions.
6 Daňhelka (ed.), *Husitské písně*, p.143.
7 Aeneas Sylvius, *Historia bohemica*, pp. 90, 92.

8 František Palacký, *Geschichte von Böhmen*, 5 vols., Prague, Kronberger and Weber, 1836–1867, vol. 3, pt. 1, p. 214.
9 František Šmahel, *Idea národa v husitských Čechách*, Prague, Argo, 2000, p. 55.
10 František Kavka, 'The Hussite Movement and the Czech Reformation', *Cahiers d'Histoire Mondiale*, 5, (1960), p. 837.
11 Thomas A. Fudge, 'Il predicatore di Jan Hus', in Manlio Sodi and Achille M. Triacca (eds.), *Dizionario de Omiletica*, Turin: Editrice Elle Di Ci, 1998, pp. 684–688.
12 The first five are relatively well known figures often discussed in the literature of the early Hussite movement. The latter pair are rather more obscure. Jan of Štěkna (†1405) was a Cistercian and professor in the faculty of theology at the University of Kraków and served as confessor to the Polish queen, Jadwiga. He had preached in Bethlehem Chapel and had once been a colleague of the young Jan Hus. Petr of Stupna (†1407) was renowned for his musical abilities and preaching. In one of his sermons as rector of the university, on 29 November 1409, Jan Hus praised both men for their eloquent and fervent preaching. *Confirmata corda vestra* in *Positiones*, pp. 119–128. On Jan Hus as a preacher see also Anežka Vidmanová, 'Hus als Prediger', *CV*, 19, (1976), pp. 65–81.
13 On this chapel see Otakar Odložilík, 'The Bethlehem Chapel in Prague: Remarks on its Foundation Charter', *Studien zur Älteren Geschichte Osteuropas*, 2, (No.1, 1956), pp. 125–141 and Thomas A. Fudge, '"Ansellus dei"and the Bethlehem Chapel in Prague', *CV*, 35, (No. 2, 1993), pp. 127–161. Prior to its foundation the chapel of the Jerusalem experiment of Jan Milíč introduced frequent communion, moral reform and emphasized the social implications of the gospel. A second chapel known as Božieho Tela, 'Chapel of the body of God', likewise practiced lay communion and renewed religious practice which may be traced from the 1340s.
14 *Monumenta historica universitatis Carolo-Ferdinandeae Pragensis*, Prague, Spurny, 1834, vol. 2, pp. 300–308.
15 Graus, *Chudina městská v době předhusitské*, p. 180, Fudge, p. 29 and Hus, *O svatokupectví*, in *Opera omnia*, vol. 4, pp. 224–225.
16 The appointment document is in *Monumenta historica universitatis Carolo-Ferdinandeae Pragensis*, vol. 2, pp. 397–398.
17 According to the articles submitted by Michael de Causis to the Curia in 1412. *Documenta*, pp. 169–74 at p. 169.
18 Václav Flajšhans (ed.), *Mistra Jana Husi Sebrané spisy*, Prague, J.R. Vilímek, n.d., volume 6, p. iv and Vidmanová, 'Hus als prediger', pp. 65–81.
19 There is a list in Flajšhans (ed.), *Sermones de sanctis* in *Mistra Jana Husi Sebrané spisy*, vol. 7, pp. v–vii. For Czech scholarship on these sermons see Karel Červený, 'Překlad několika Husových latinských kázání', in Miloslav Kaňák (ed.), *Hus stále živý*, Prague: Blahoslav, 1965, pp. 69–86.
20 They have been edited and published in Šimek.
21 Šimek, p. xliii has pointed out that in these sermons there was neither any trace of the influence of John Wyclif nor elements which might be adjudicated dogmatically unsound or at variance with the official church.

22   For example, see Jan Sedlák, 'Husů vývoj dle jeho postil', *Studie a texty k náboženským dějinám českým*, pt. 2, pp. 397–398.
23   Hus' sermons delivered in 1404 and 1405 are in *Collecta* while the 1408 sermons are in Flajšhans, *Ibid.*, vols 7–8.
24   See also Anežka Vidmanová, 'Husova tzv. postilla De tempore (1408/9)', *Listy filologický*, 94, (1971), pp. 7–22.
25   There were a variety of denunciations against what Hus categorically dismissed as 'manufactured miracles'. *Collecta*, pp. 107, 130, 216, 568, et al.
26   *Postil*, in *Opera omnia*, vol. 2, p. 114.
27   Sermon *Abiciamus opera tenebrarum* in *Positiones*, p. 109.
28   Articulated as such in the sermon 'Abiciamus opera tenebrarum' in *Positiones*, p. 109.
29   *Postil*, in *Opera omnia*, vol. 2, p. 60. The Latin *Postil* is in *Opera omnia*, vol. 13.
30   See for example his sermon *Confirmate corda vestra* in *Positiones*, p. 123.
31   De Vooght, *Hussiana*, pp. 365–378.
32   *Výklad víry*, in *Opera omnia*, vol. 1, p. 63.
33   'The Cause of the Táborite Priests', in Höfler, vol. 2, p. 476.
34   For example his sermon for Trinity Sunday in *Collecta*, p. 280. On penance, his sermon for the first Sunday in Lent of the same year is instructive. *Ibid.*, p. 127.
35   Sedlák (ed.), *Studie a texty k životopisu Husovu*, vol. 2, pp. 394–399.
36   Sermon for Easter Sunday in *Collecta*, p. 178.
37   *Postil*, in *Opera omnia*, vol. 2, pp. 279–280.
38   This in his sermon *Confirmata corda vestra* in *Positiones*, p. 119.
39   Stated in his sermon *Abiciamus opera tenebrarum* in *Positiones*, p. 100.
40   Sermon *Confirmate corda vestra* in *Positiones*, p. 119. Hus is quoting Bernard's Advent III sermon in PL vol. 183, col. 43. Compare Hus' sermon for Palm Sunday 1406 where he again made clear that Christ assumed flesh for no other purpose than to effect salvation for all people. Salvation was offered as an eternal medicine which Hus understood as the blood of Christ designed to cure all people for all time. *Collecta*, p. 168.
41   *Postil*, in *Opera omnia*, vol. 2, p. 204.
42   Among a variety of sermon texts delivered by Hus, the following are especially cogent in their articulation of this theme: *Dixit Martha ad Iesum*, in *Positiones*, pp. 158 and 165 preached on 3 November 1411, Advent III sermon, in *Collecta*, p. 46, Christmas Eve sermon, in *Ibid.*, p. 64, Sermon for Epiphany in *Ibid.*, pp. 72, 74, Sermon for Easter, in *Ibid.*, pp. 180–181, Sermon for Epiphany, in *Ibid.*, pp. 74–75 and Sermon for Advent III, in *Ibid.*, p. 42.
43   Sermon for Palm Sunday, preaching on the text of Philippians 2:5 in *Collecta*, pp. 167–170.
44   Put forth in his sermon *Spiritum nolite extinguere* in *Positiones*, p. 141.
45   Sermon for Advent IV in *Collecta*, p. 123.
46   Sermon *Spiritum nolite extinguere* in *Positiones*, pp. 142–143. On the topic of salvation one may usefully consult Crews, 'The Theology of John Hus'.

47 Sermon for St. Wenceslas Day (28 September 1411/1412) on Matthew 16. Flajšhans has dated the sermon to 1411 though it was probably the latter year. See *Sermones in Capella Bethlehem*, vol. 5, p. 82.
48 Sermon on the feast day of St. Laurence from the text of II Corinthians 6. *Sermones in Capella Bethlehem*, vol. 4, pp. 328–332 esp. p. 330.
49 Preaching on the text of John 10 on Tuesday after Pentecost. *Sermones in Capella Bethlehem*, vol. 4, p. 171.
50 Šimek (ed.), *Staré letopisy české z vratislavského rukopisu*, p. 10.
51 *Postil*, in *Opera omnia*, vol. 2, pp. 61–63.
52 Peter C.A. Morée, *Preaching in Fourteenth-Century Bohemia: The Life and Ideas of Milicius de Chremsir (†1374) and his Significance in the Historiography of Bohemia*, Heršpice, EMAN, 1999, p. 165.
53 Sedlák, *M. Jan Hus*, p. 123 and *De ecclesia*, pp. 51–52.
54 In Flajšhans (ed.), *Sermones de sanctis*, vol. 7, pp. 80–84.
55 Sermon for Lent I in *Collecta*, p. 130.
56 Sermon for the second Sunday of the birth of Christ on the text Luke 2:42–52 in *Postil*, in *Opera omnia*, vol. 2, p. 86.
57 *Questio de Indulgentiis, sive de Cruciata Papae Joanne XXIII*, in *Historia et monumenta*, vol. 1, pp. 233–235.
58 Extracts from Hus' sermons in *Sermones in Capella Bethlehem*. SS. Simon and Jude Day on the parallel texts of Matthew 10, Luke 9 and Mark 3 in *Ibid.*, vol. 5, pp. 131–134; Second Sunday after Easter on John 10 in *Ibid.*, vol. 4, pp. 77–80 at p. 78; Feast of John Baptist on Luke 1, in *Ibid.*, vol. 4, pp. 220–224; Tuesday after Pentecost on John 10 in *Ibid.*, vol. 4, pp. 163–172; Trinity Sunday on John 3 in *Ibid.*, vol. 4, pp. 177–183; Fourth Sunday after Trinity on Luke 6 in *Ibid.*, vol. 4, pp. 258–261; Third Sunday after Easter on I Peter 2 in *Ibid.*, vol. 4, pp. 104–108 at p. 107; and *Ibid.*, vol. 2, pp. 3–6.
59 Štěpán of Dolany, *Antihussus*, in Pez, vol. 4, cols. 373–374 and 426. Štěpán was prior of the Carthusian monastery in Dolany near Olomouc in Moravia. He died in 1421.
60 Synodal sermon delivered at the archiepiscopal palace on 19 October 1405 titled 'Love the Lord your God . . .' (John 15:27) is notable for its unrelenting assault on the mischief that Prague clergy ostensibly were engaging in. His 1407 sermon constituted a classic denunciation of clerical abuses. He used the text Ephesians 6:14, 'stand therefore, having girded your loins with truth . . .' *Historia et monumenta*, vol. 2, pp. 39–47 and 47–56.
61 *Historia et Monumenta*, vol. 2, p. 44.
62 Sermon on the Feast of St. John the Evangelist. *Sermones in Capella Bethlehem*, vol. 2, pp. 154–162 at p. 157.
63 Flajšhans (ed.), *Sermones de sanctis*, vol. 6, p. 86.
64 Sermon preached before the synod in 1407. *Historia et monumenta*, vol. 2, pp. 47–56.
65 *Documenta*, p. 176.
66 *Documenta*, pp. 154–155.
67 These two motifs formed an essential component in the propaganda of the Hussite movement. Pictures positing the two cities as implacable foes appeared in the Jena Codex, Prague, NMK MS IV B 24, fols. 10ᵛ–11ʳ. Brief description in Fudge, 'Visual

	Heresy and the Communication of Ideas in the Hussite Reformation', *Kosmas: Czechoslovak and Central European Journal*, 12, (No. 1, 1996), p. 132. Hus' articulation is in his Postil. See *Postil*, in *Opera omnia*, vol. 2, pp. 455–456.
68	*Výklad na páteř*, in *Opera omnia*, vol. 1, p. 388.
69	See for example his sermon for Lent IV on the text of Galatians 4:30 wherein Hus drew a line between the church of Christ and the church of the wicked. *Collecta*, pp. 150–151.
70	*Knížky proti knězi kuchmistrovi*, in *Opera omnia*, vol. 4, p. 312 and SRB, vol. 3, pp. 471–472.
71	*Postil*, in *Opera omnia*, vol. 2, p. 179.
72	*Postil*, in *Opera omnia*, vol. 2, p. 68.
73	Sermon for Epiphany II in *Collecta*, in *Opera omnia*, vol. 7, p. 92.
74	*Postil*, in *Opera omnia*, vol. 2, p. 326.
75	See the summary in Novotný/Kybal, vol. 2, pt. 2, pp. 2–5.
76	*Postil*, in *Opera omnia*, vol. 2, pp. 178–179.
77	In his sermon *Vos estis sal terre* in *Positiones*, p. 149.
78	Several discussions during the proceedings may be located within the *Relatio*, in FRB, vol. 8, pp. 75–76, 103–104, and 114.
79	His sermon for Trinity Sunday described the sacrament in quite traditional terms. *Collecta*, p. 281.
80	*Postil*, in *Opera omnia*, vol. 2, pp. 412–413.
81	Text in *Opera omnia*, vol. 22, pp. 233–269 at p. 265.
82	*Positiones*, pp. 149–156.
83	*Postil*, in *Opera omnia*, vol. 2, pp. 130–131.
84	Šimek, pp. 96–99.
85	De Vooght, *Hussiana*, p. 66.
86	See for example Hus' sermons for Palm Sunday, Pentecost, and Trinity 1404–1405, and thereafter the sermons *Dixit Martha ad Iesum*, pp. 157–78 and *Beati oculi*, in *Positiones*, pp. 179–185.
87	For example, see Matthew Spinka, *John Hus' Concept of the Church*, Princeton, Princeton University Press, 1966, p. 56.
88	On the usage of colloquialism within the sermon texts of Hus see František Svejkovský, 'The Conception of the "Vernacular" in Czech Literature and Culture of the Fifteenth Century', in Riccardo Picchio and Harvey Goldblatt (eds.), *Aspects of the Slavic Language Question*, New Haven, Concilium on International and Area Studies, 1984, vol. 1, p. 333.
89	Novotný, *Correspondence*, pp. 182–183.
90	*Documenta*, pp. 728–729 and *Postil*, in *Opera omnia*, vol. 2, pp. 320 and 378–379.
91	*Knížky proti knězi kuchmistrovi*, in *Opera omnia*, vol. 4, p. 312.
92	*Sermones in Capella Bethlehem*, vol. 2, pp. 146–147. Hus' text was Matthew 23.
93	Sermon on the Feast of St. Matthias, 24 February 1411, from the texts of Matthew 11 and Luke 10 in *Ibid.*, vol. 2, pp. 262–266, esp. pp. 262–263.
94	Spinka, *John Hus' Concept of the Church*, p. 57.
95	Our information on this comes from the *Narracio de Milicio* in *Regulae*, vol. 3, p. 367. It is doubtful 200–300 scribes were working on the copy process at any one time as suggested.
96	Šmahel, 'Literacy and Heresy in Hussite Bohemia', p. 243.

97   *Historia et monumenta*, vol. 1, p. 191.
98   Sermon on Whit Monday 1 June 1411 on Acts 10 in *Sermones in Capella Bethlehem*, vol. 4, pp. 160–163 at p.161.
99   Sermon on the Feast of SS. Simon and Jude, 28 October 1411 on the parallel gospel pericopes of Matthew 10, Luke 9 and Mark 3 in *Sermones in Capella Bethlehem*, vol. 5, p. 133.
100 *Positiones*, p. 114.
101 *Postil*, in *Opera omnia*, vol. 2, p. 74.
102 The decree is dated 20 December 1409 in *Documenta*, pp. 374–376.
103 *Documenta*, pp. 405 and 281.
104 Novotný, *Correspondence*, pp. 157–158.
105 *Knížky proti knězi kuchmistrovi*, in *Opera omnia*, vol. 4, p. 320.
106 *Postil*, in *Opera omnia*, vol. 2, pp. 183–184.
107 *Contra Palecz*, in *Opera omnia*, vol. 22, p. 237 and Novotný, *Correspondence*, p. 90.
108 *Knížky proti knězi kuchmistrovi*, in *Opera omnia*, vol. 4, p. 317 but his indignant tone can be evidenced throughout.
109 *Postil*, in *Opera omnia*, vol. 2, pp. 165–166.
110 *Postil*, in *Opera omnia*, vol. 2, pp. 298–299.
111 *Postil*, in *Opera omnia*, vol. 2, p. 320.
112 Sermon on the Feast of the Assumption, 15 August 1411, based on Luke 10. *Sermones in Capella Bethlehem*, vol. 4, p. 334.
113 *Sermones in Capella Bethlehem*, vol. 2, p. 102.
114 Sermon 'you are the salt of the earth', in *Positiones*, p. 118.
115 Sermon on 30 March 1411, Monday after the first Sunday in Lent on Jonah 3. *Sermones in Capella Bethlehem*, vol. 3, pp. 176–178.
116 See for example his strongly-worded opposition in the *Postil*, in *Opera omnia*, vol. 2, p. 69.
117 *Positiones*, p. 165 and throughout his November 1411 sermon *Dixit Martha ad Iesum* in *Ibid.*, pp. 167 and 174–175. Hus made manifestly clear that evil priests could and did legitimately consecrate the body and blood of Christ in the Mass but they did so to their own destruction and damnation. The communicants were not affected. Sermon on the Feast of the nativity of St. John Baptist on 24 June 1411 from the text in Luke 1. *Sermones in Capella Bethlehem*, vol. 4, p. 223.
118 *Relatio*, in FRB, vol. 8, p. 119.
119 Sermon for Easter I in *Collecta*, p. 189.
120 Nejedlý, vol. 3, p. 33 has suggested some of the fourteenth-century reformers emphasized preaching to liturgical neglect.
121 On this, Ernst Werner, 'Wort und Sakrament im Identitätsbewusstsein des tschechischen Frühreformators Jan Hus (um 1370–1415)', *Sitzungsberichte der Akademie der Wissenschaften der DDR, Gesellschaftwissenschaften*, 13, (1989), pp. 3–26. It can be shown that even in preaching Hus continued to value the liturgy. See Olivier Marin, 'Les usages de la liturgie dans le prédication de Jean Hus', in BRRP, vol. 6, pp. 45–75.
122 Horst Bredekamp, *Kunst als Medium sozialer Konflikte: Bilderkämpfe von der Spätantike bis zur Hussitenrevolution*, Frankfurt am Main, Suhrkamp Verlag, 1975, p. 308.

123 *Historia et monumenta*, vol. 1, p. 103.
124 Luther's opinion appeared in the preface to the first volume of *Historia et monumenta* and is included in the introductions to the first and second English editions of Hus' letters. *Letters of John Huss*, trans., Campbell MacKenzie, Edinburgh, William Whyte & Co., 1846, p. 9 and Herbert B. Workman and R. Martin Pope (eds.), *The Letters of John Hus*, London, Hodder and Stoughton, 1904, p. 1.
125 Quoted in Workman and Pope (eds.), *The Letters of John Hus*, p. 87.

Chapter Five

1 *Exposition of the Psalms*, in *CCL*, vol. 40, p. 2130.
2 *De vera Religione*, in *CCL*, vol. 32, p. 234,
3 *Výklad na páteř*, in *Opera omnia*, vol. 1, p. 346–347 and Anna Císařová-Kolářová, *M. Jan Hus Betlemské Poselství*, Prague, Laichter, 1947, vol. 1, p. 65.
4 *Výklad desaterat*, in *Opera omnia*, vol. 1, chapter 35, pp. 134–142.
5 *The Spiritual Canticle*, 11.12, 12.7, 22.3, 38.3 et al. in Kieran Kavanaugh (ed.), *The Collected Works of St. John of the Cross*, Washington, ICS Publications, 1964, pp. 452–453, 455, 497 and 553–554.
6 Flemish text in Léonce Reypens and Jozef Van Mierlo (eds.), *Beatrijs van Nazareth: Seven Manieren van Minne*, Leuven, 1926, and the Latin text in Roger DeGanck (ed.), *The Life of Beatrice of Nazareth*, Kalamazoo, Cistercian Publications, 1991. There are differences.
7 Václav Novotný, 'Rakousko-Uhersko po stránce církevně náboženské', in Zdeněk V. Tobolka (ed.), *Česká politika*, 5 vols., Prague, Laichter, 1906, vol. 1, p. 550.
8 *Vita B. Idae Lewensis*, 1.6, R. de Buck (ed.), in *Acta Sanctorum*, Paris, 1867, pp.100–135 at p. 109. There is now an English translation. *The Life of Ida of Léau*, trans. Martinus Cawley, Lafayette OR, Our Lady of Guadalupe Abbey, 1985.
9 Leonard P. Hindsley (ed.), *Revelations* in *Margaret Ebner Major Works*, New York, Paulist Press, 1993, p. 93.
10 Migne, PL, vol. 217, cols. 701–746. Critical edition: Michele Maccarrone (ed.), *Lotharii Cardinales (Innocentii III) De misera humane conditionis*, Lugano, Thesaurus Mundi, 1955 has noted the phrase *de contemptu mundi* was added by scribes, pp. xxxii–xxxv.
11 Migne, PL, vol. 145, cols. 251–292.
12 *Exhortatio ad contemptum temporalium*, in Migne, PL, vol. 158, cols. 677–686.
13 *De vanitate mundi*, in Migne, PL, vol. 176, cols. 703–740.
14 *Meditationes piissimae do cognitione humane conditionis* in Migne, PL, vol. 184, cols. 485–508.
15 *Zrcadlo hřiešníka*, in *Opera omnia*, vol. 4, pp. 132–46. Hus depended on two works which he erroneously ascribed to Bernard of Clairvaux namely *Meditationes piisssmae de cognitione humanae conditionis* in Migne, PL, vol. 184, cols. 485–508 and *Tractatus de interiori domo* in Migne, PL, vol. 184, cols. 509–552. See also his sermon for Lent I, *Postil*, in *Opera omnia*, vol. 2, p. 143.
16 Lent I sermon, *Postil*, in *Opera omnia*, vol. 2, p. 141.
17 *Super IV Sententiarum*, p. 16.
18 *Výklad desatera*, chapter 49 in *Opera omnia*, vol. 1, pp. 236–237.
19 Sermon for the Sunday before the Ascension in *Opera omnia*, vol. 13, pp. 225–227.

20 *Výklad modlitby Páně*, chapter 81 in *Opera omnia*, vol. 1, p. 333.
21 *Výklad modlitby Páně*, chapter 87 in *Opera omnia*, vol. 1, p. 356.
22 *Postil*, in *Opera omnia*, vol. 2, pp. 239–241.
23 *Výklad na Páteř*, in *Opera omnia*, vol. 1, pp. 346–347.
24 Sermon for Epiphany, *Collecta*, p. 72.
25 *Výklad desatera*, chapter 44 in *Opera omnia*, vol. 1, p. 244.
26 *Výklad na Páteř* in *Opera omnia*, vol. 1, p. 335.
27 *Postil*, in *Opera omnia*, vol. 2, pp. 127–128.
28 Emil Smetánka (ed.), *Petra Chelčického Síť víry*, Prague, Melantrich, 1929, p. 224.
29 Novotný, *Correspondence*, pp. 27–28.
30 There is a helpful discussion of the manuscripts in Václav Flajšhans, 'Traktáty Husovy a Kronika Vavřincova', *Listy filologické*, 61, (1934), pp. 54–66.
31 *Postil*, in *Opera omnia*, vol. 2, pp. 59–60.
32 *Postil*, in *Opera omnia*, vol. 2, pp. 61–62.
33 *Postil*, in *Opera omnia*, vol. 2, p. 63.
34 *Postil*, in *Opera omnia*, vol. 2, pp. 63–64.
35 *Postil*, in *Opera omnia*, vol. 2, p. 64.
36 *Postil*, in *Opera omnia*, vol. 2, p. 65.
37 *Postil*, in *Opera omnia*, vol. 2, p. 201.
38 *Postil*, in *Opera omnia*, vol. 2, pp. 201–202.
39 *Postil*, in *Opera omnia*, vol. 2, p. 202. Hus' statement on assurance seems to contradict his conviction noted elsewhere that salvation cannot be known for certain until the advent of eschatological time.
40 Principally his great polemic against simony, which persisted as a common problem and practice in the medieval church. *O svatokupectví*, in *Opera omnia*, vol. 4, pp. 192–270.
41 Much of the opening sentences have been taken almost verbatim from Matěj of Janov's life of Jan Milíč of Kroměříž in his 'Narracio de Milicio' in *Regulae*, vol. 3, pp. 358–367.
42 The text of the sermon has been preserved in Prague, NK MSS VIII E 3 and VIII G 13 and there is an edition in FRB, vol. 8, pp. 231–243.
43 Some of the assumptions about Hus and congregational singing have been queried by Jan Kouba, 'Jan Hus und das geistliche Lied: ein Literaturbericht', *Jahrbuch für Liturgik und Hymnologie*, 14, (1969), pp. 190–196.
44 *Expositio decalogi*, in Flajšhans (ed.), *Mag. Jo Hus Opera omnia*, vol. 1, pt. 1, pp. 1–45 and Flajšhans (ed.), *Mistra Jana Husi Sebrané spisy*, vol. 1, pp. 107–134 at p. 110.
45 Enrico C.S. Molnar, 'The liturgical reforms of John Hus', *Speculum*, 41, (April 1966), pp. 297–303.
46 *Výklad deserata*, in *Opera omnia*, vol. 1, chapter 35, pp. 134–142.
47 See my forthcoming 'The One-Eyed Heretic? An Introduction to the Ethics of Jan Hus', paper delivered at the 25th SVU World Congress in Tábor, Czech Republic, 1 July 2010.
48 Novotný, *Correspondence*, pp. 292–293.
49 *Relatio*, in FRB, vol. 8, pp. 103–104.
50 Novotný, *Correspondence*, pp. 286, 282 and 296–297.
51 Novotný, *Correspondence*, pp. 283–284 and p. 313.

52 *Relatio*, in FRB, vol. 8, p. 111.
53 *Výklad desatera*, chapter 62, in *Opera omnia*, vol. 1, pp. 276–277.
54 *Postil*, in *Opera omnia*, vol. 2, pp. 220–221.
55 The text is in *Opera omnia*, vol. 4, pp. 163–186. Other scholars have asserted a specific date of composition in December 1412. De Vooght, 'Un classique de la littérature spirituelle: La "Dcerka" de Jean Huss', *Revue d'histoire de la spiritualité*, 48, (1972), p. 276.
56 *Liber epistolaris ad Hussitas*, in Pez, vol. 4, pt. 2, cols. 505–706, see col. 527. The book dates to 1417.
57 Císařová-Kolářová, *O poznání cěsty pravé k spasení, čili Dcerka*, Prague, Karel Reichel, 1927, pp. 100–101.
58 Štěpán of Dolany, *Antihussus* in Pez, vol. 4, pt. 2, cols. 381 and 390. But see also his treatise of 1411 *Dialogus volatilis inter aucam et passerem, seu Mag. Hus et Stephanum*, in Ibid., cols 434–502 at col. 492.
59 Novotný, *Correspondence*, pp. 277–279 and Anna Kolářová-Císařová, *Žena v hnutí husitském*, Prague, Sokolice, 1915, pp. 71–72.
60 *Documenta*, pp. 687–698 at p. 698.
61 *O svatokupectví*, in *Opera omnia*, vol. 4, p. 252.
62 Abelard, Sermon 13 in Migne, PL, vol. 178, col. 485.
63 Sermon for Easter Sunday, *Postil*, in *Opera omnia*, vol. 2, p. 186.
64 Easter Sunday sermon on Mark 16. *Postil*, in *Opera omnia*, vol. 2, p. 188.
65 The work of two scholars is noteworthy. Anna Kolářová-Císařová, *Žena v hnutí husitském* (though now quite dated) and John Klassen, 'Women and Religious Reform in Late Medieval Bohemia', *Renaissance and Reformation*, n.s. 5, (No.4, 1981), pp. 203–221, *Warring Maidens, Captive Wives, and Hussite Queens: Women and Men at War and Peace in Fifteenth-Century Bohemia*, Boulder, East European Monographs, 1999 and *The Letters of the Rožmberk Sisters: Noblewomen in Fifteenth-Century Bohemia*, Cambridge, D.S. Brewer, 2001.
66 There is no reference to *Dcerka* in Šmahel, only a passing comment in De Vooght, pp. 261–262 and no reference in *Hussiana*. De Vooght later devoted a substantial treatment to it including a French translation. 'Un classique de la littérature spirituelle: La "Dcerka" de Jean Huss', pp. 275–314. Kybal writes but a paragraph in Novotný/Kybal, vol. 2, pt. 2, p. 415. Lützow, *The Life and Times of Master John Hus*, p. 315 called it one of Hus' best works but said nothing of substance. David Schaff did not deal with the Czech writings at all claiming it was wholly unnecessary so his study of Hus has nothing to contribute concerning *Dcerka*. *John Huss: His Life, Teachings and Death after Five Hundred Years*, New York, Scribner's, 1915, p. vii. Matthew Spinka, in all of his several books on Hus combined, somewhat astonishingly devoted less than a half page to this text. There is an introduction by Noemi Rejchrtová to the edition *Jan Hus, Dcerka*, Prague, Kalich, 1995, pp. 5–10. The general lacuna is puzzling.
67 Klassen, *Warring Maidens*, p. 166.
68 Flajšhans, *Literární činnost mistra Jana Husi*, Prague, ČAVU, 1900, p. 29.
69 De Vooght, 'Un classique de la littérature spirituelle: La "Dcerka" de Jean Huss', p. 283.

70 Šmahel, 'The Hussite Critique of the Clergy's Civil Dominion', in Peter A. Dykema and Heiko A. Oberman (eds.), *Anticlericalism in Late Medieval and Early Modern Europe*, Leiden, Brill, 1993, p. 246.
71 *Dcerka*, p. 163.
72 Hus is most likely dependent upon the pseudo-Bernardine treatise *Meditationes piissimae do cognitione humane conditionis*. Migne, PL, vol. 184, col. 485.
73 *Dcerka*, p. 164.
74 Especially his Commentary on James in *Historia et monumenta*, vol. 2, p. 183 and his sermons for Advent I and II in *Collecta*, pp. 30 and 34.
75 *Dcerka*, p. 164. Hus appears to rely upon the same understanding of the soul as found in *Meditationes piissimae do cognitione humane conditionis*, Migne, PL, vol. 184, col. 485.
76 *Dcerka*, pp. 164–165. The persons of the Trinity 'reciprocally contain each another, in the sense that one eternally covers and is eternally contained by the other who is yet enveloped by the others.' Hilary of Poitiers, *De trinitate (I–VII)*, in *CCL*, vol. 62, 3:1, p. 73.
77 Hus made the same point in chapter seven of *Dcerka*, p. 179. This seems to parallel the narrative of St. Thomas in the 'Golden Legend' where the apostle explains wisdom in terms of 'understanding, memory, and reason'. Jacobus de Voragine, *The Golden Legend: Readings on the Saints*, 2 vols., trans., William Granger Ryan, Princeton, Princeton University Press, 1993, vol. 1, p. 33.
78 *Dcerka*, pp. 164–165.
79 *Dcerka*, p. 165.
80 *Dcerka*, p. 166.
81 Similarities may be noted with Pseudo-Bernard, *Meditationes piissimae do cognitione humane conditionis*, Migne, PL, vol. 184, col. 503.
82 *Dcerka*, p. 167.
83 *Dcerka*, p. 168.
84 *Dcerka*, p. 168.
85 *Dcerka*, p. 169. Hus referred to Hebrews 11:25 and to the Roman poet Ovid's *Remedia amoris*. The Latin text is in E.J. Kenney (ed.), *P. Ovidi Nasonis: Amores, Medicamina faciei Femineae, Ars amatoria, Remedia amoris*, Oxford, Clarendon Press, 2nd ed., 1995.
86 *Dcerka*, p. 169 with allusions to Pseudo-Bernard, *Meditationes piissimae do cognitione humane conditionis*, Migne, PL, vol. 184, col. 488.
87 Undated letter (but after 1408) in Novotný, *Correspondence*, pp. 27–28.
88 *Postil*, in *Opera omnia*, vol. 2, pp. 119–120.
89 *Dcerka*, pp. 170–175. Hus alluded to his treatment of temptation in his commentary on the Lord's Prayer, *Výklad na páteř*, chapter 94, in *Opera omnia*, vol. 1, pp. 380–389.
90 *Retractationes*, book 1, chapter 9, in CCL, vol. 57, pp. 24–26 and *Contra Iulianum Opus imperfectum*, book 4, chapter 101 in CSEL, vol. 85, pt. 2, p. 104.
91 *Moralium*, book 3, chapter 29 in Migne, PL, vol. 75, col. 627.
92 Sermon for the first Sunday in Lent, *Postil*, in *Opera omnia*, vol. 2, p. 142.
93 *Dcerka*, p. 171.
94 *Dcerka*, pp. 172–173.

95	*Dcerka*, pp. 173–175.
96	The early part of this chapter relied on Wyclif's sermon for Easter Monday based on the Gospel of Luke 24:13. See Johann Loserth (ed.), *Iohannes Wyclif Sermones*, vol. 3, London, Trübner & Co., 1889, pp. 68–69 and thereafter pp. 69–73.
97	*Dcerka*, pp. 175–176.
98	*Dcerka*, p. 176. There are significant discernable parallels in this chapter with Pseudo-Bernard, *Meditationes piissimae do cognitione humane conditionis*, Migne, PL, vol. 184, cols. 503–504.
99	Sermon for Lent I, *Postil*, in *Opera omnia*, vol. 2, p. 147.
100	*Super IV Sententiarum*, p. 35 and *Leccionarium bipartitum pars hiemalis*, in *Opera omnia*, vol. 9, p. 431.
101	Augustine, *De fide et operibus*, chapter 8.13, in *CSEL*, vol. 41, pp. 49–50.
102	*Jádro učení křesťanského*, in *Opera omnia*, vol. 4, p. 333.
103	*Dcerka*, p. 177.
104	*Dcerka*, p. 177.
105	*Dcerka*, p. 178.
106	*Dcerka*, pp. 178–179. Preaching on Advent I, in *Collecta*, p. 30, Hus appears to argue that the act of repentance does not function as a definite guarantee of salvation. The influence of Pseudo-Bernard, *Meditationes piissimae do cognitione humane conditionis*, Migne, PL, vol. 184, cols. 493–495 is once again apparent in this chapter.
107	*Dcerka*, p. 179.
108	*Dcerka*, p. 180. Pseudo-Bernard, *Ibid.*, chapter 3, col. 490. For a survey on the idea of salvation as deification see Thomas A. Fudge, 'Concepts of salvation in the western church to the sixteenth century', *CV*, 45, (2003), pp. 217–247, especially pp. 229–234.
109	*Výklad víry*, in *Opera omnia*, vol 1, p. 99. Hus expressed a very similar sentiment in his sermon text *Confirmate corda vestra* in *Positiones*, p. 127.
110	*Dcerka*, pp. 180–181.
111	*O svatokupectví*, in *Opera omnia*, vol. 4, pp. 240–241.
112	Sermon for the twenty-second Sunday after Trinity. *Postil*, in *Opera omnia*, vol. 2, p. 425.
113	*Dcerka*, pp. 181–182.
114	*Matthaeum commentariorum*, in Migne, *Patrologia Graeca*, 163 vols., Paris, 1857–1861, vol. 13, col. 1717.
115	*Dcerka*, p. 182.
116	*Dcerka*, p. 183.
117	*Dcerka*, p. 184. Hus is quoting Gregory, *Moralium*, book 7, chapter 29, in Migne, PL, vol. 75, col. 788.
118	New Years' day sermon, 1411, *Sermones in Capella Bethlehem*, vol. 2, p. 179.
119	*Dcerka*, pp. 184–185.
120	*Dcerka*, p. 186.
121	*Dcerka*, p. 186.
122	Sermon for Easter Sunday, *Postil*, in *Opera omnia*, vol. 2, pp. 189–190.

Chapter Six

1. Novotný, *Correspondence*, p. 101.
2. The foundation remains Hus' stress on good deeds for salvation. *Super IV Sententiarum*, pp. 19–20.
3. Novotný, *Correspondence*, pp. 22–25.
4. For example Machovec, p. 177.
5. Šmahel, *Idea národa v husitských Čechách*, Prague, Argo, 2000, p. 24.
6. On this see Šmahel, *Idea národa v husitských Čechách*, p. 39 and De Vooght, 'Jan Hus beim Symposium Hussianum Pragense (August 1965)', *Theologisch-praktische Quartalschrift*, 114, (1966), p. 91.
7. *Defensio libri de Trinitate*, in *Opera omnia*, vol. 22, pp. 41, 46.
8. *Documenta*, pp. 175–8.
9. Noted in Šmahel, *Idea národa v husitských Čechách*, p. 53.
10. *Documenta*, pp. 161, 392.
11. Václav Novotný, *Hus v Kostnici a česká šlechta*, Prague, Nákl. společnosti přátel starožitností českých, 1915, p. 43. The testimony was provided by the Bohemian barons Čeněk of Vartemberk and Boček of Kunštát. For Konrad's opinion on the Hus case see *Documenta*, pp. 531–532.
12. Václav Vaněček, 'Dekret Kutnohorský z hlediska dějin státu a práva', in the important collection edited by František Kavka, *Dekret kutnohorský a jeho místo v dějinách (Sborník k oslavě 550. Výročí Dekretu kutnohorského), Acta universitatis carolinae, philosophica et historia*, (No. 2, 1959), p. 60.
13. See Alfred Thomas, 'Czech-German relations as reflected in old Czech literature', in Robert Bartlett and Angus MacKay (eds.), *Medieval Frontier Societies*, Oxford, Clarendon Press, 1989, pp. 199–215.
14. *Documenta*, p. 183.
15. Šmahel suggests the gloss may not be Hus'. *Idea národa v husitských Čechách*, p. 37.
16. Bartoš, *Čechy v době Husově 1378–1415*, Prague, Laichter, 1947, pp. 113–115 and on the nobles John M. Klassen, *The Nobility and the Making of the Hussite Revolution*, New York, Columbia University Press, 1978.
17. Especially useful on these developments is Bartoš, 'V předvečer Kutnohorského dekretu', *Časopis českého musea*, 102, (1928), pp. 92–123.
18. *Documenta*, p. 338.
19. *Documenta*, p. 392.
20. For a description of the debates at Prague, see Jiří Kejř, 'Struktura a průběh disputace de quodlibet na pražské universitě', *Acta universitatis carolinae, Historia universitatis carolinae Pragensis*, 1, (1960), pp. 17–42.
21. The text of his speech is in Höfler, vol. 2, pp. 112–128. Kaminsky, p. 62 has noted it has been wrongly attributed to Hus. On Jerome see Šmahel, 'Mistr Jeroným Pražský na soudu dějin', *HT*, supplement 1, 2001, pp. 313–323, Šmahel, *Jeroným Pražský*, Prague, Svobodné slovo, 1966, and in English R.R. Betts, *Essays in Czech History*, London, Athlone Press, 1969, pp. 195–235.
22. Klicman, pp. 16, 18, 20, 23–25 and Mansi, vol. 27, col. 892.

23	As convincingly shown by Jiří Kejř, 'Sporné otázky v bádání o dekretu kutnohorském', *Acta universitatis carolinae, historia universitatis carolinae pragensis*, 3, (No. 1, 1962), pp. 95–104.
24	Bartoš attributed the decree of Kutná Hora to the influence of Mikuláš. 'Kdo vymohl Čechům dekret kutnohorský', *JSH*, 18, (1939), pp. 66–8 while Kejř submitted that Hus, Jerome and Jan of Jesenice constituted the main force behind the formation. *Husitský pravník: M. Jan z Jesenice*, Prague, ČSAV, 1965, p. 23. I agree with Kejř.
25	Somewhat surprisingly an original copy of the decree does not appear to be extant. There are editions in *Documenta*, pp. 347–348 and Novotný, *Correspondence*, pp. 199–202.
26	Flajšhans, pp. 194–195 and *Documenta*, p. 181.
27	Bohumil Ryba (ed.), *Magistri Iohannis Hus Quodlibet*, Prague, Orbis, 1948, p. 210. New edition *Iohannis Hus, Quodlibet*, in *Opera omnia*, vol. 20, Turnhout, Brepols, 2006.
28	The eyewitness official was Jan Náz who testified at the Council of Constance in June 1415. *Relatio*, in FRB, vol. 8, pp. 79–80.
29	His inaugural speech has been published in Bohuslav Havránek (ed.), *Výbor z český literatury husitské doby*, Prague, ČSAV, 1963, vol. 1, pp. 105–110.
30	Fudge, *The Magnificent Ride*, p. 194 for references to the sources. Knín is not mentioned after 1409 and we must presume he was untimely deceased by 1410.
31	See Šmahel, 'The Kuttenberg Decree and the Withdrawal of the German Students from Prague in 1409: A Discussion', *History of Universities*, 4, (1984), pp. 153–166 on the extent. More recently the number has been estimated at between 700–800. Šmahel, 'The Hussite Revolution (1419–1471)', in Jaroslav Pánek and Oldřich Tůma (eds.), *A History of the Czech Lands*, Prague, Karolinum Press, 2009, p. 151.
32	Šmahel, *Idea národa v husitských Čechách*, pp. 50–51.
33	*Documenta*, pp. 355–363.
34	Kejř, *Husitský pravník: M. Jan z Jesenice*, pp. 15–19.
35	Kaminsky, p. 67.
36	On the decree and relevant issues most of the good scholarship remains in Czech but see especially the useful collection of essays in Kavka (ed.), *Dekret Kutnohorský a jeho místo v dějinách*, along with articles by Bartoš, 'V předvečer Kunohorského dekretu', *Časopis českého musea*, 102, (1928), pp. 92–123, Kejř, 'Sporné otázky v bádání o dekretu kutnohorském', pp.83–119, and Ferdinand Seibt, 'Johannes Hus und der Abzug der deutschen Studenten aus Prag 1409', *Archiv für Kulturgeschichte*, 39, (1957), pp. 63–80.
37	*Documenta*, pp. 374–376.
38	The main instances are Hus' *De ecclesia*, p. 231, *O svatokupectví*, in *Opera omnia*, vol. 4, p. 210 and Novotný, *Correspondence*, p. 124.
39	Comment in Šmahel, *Husitské Čechý: Struktury, Procesy, Ideje*, Prague, Lidové noviny, 2001, p. 437.
40	*Opera omnia*, vol. 22, pp. 21–37.
41	*De libris hereticorum legendis*, in *Opera omnia*, vol. 22, p. 21.
42	*De libris hereticorum legendis*, in *Opera omnia*, vol. 22, p. 30 and also *De decimis*, in *Historia et monumenta*, vol. 1, p. 156.
43	*De libris hereticorum legendis*, in *Opera omnia*, vol. 22, pp. 34–35.

44 Extracts from the sermon were reported first to the archbishop and also to the Curia. *Documenta*, pp. 404–6 and Fudge, '"*Ansellus dei*" and the Bethlehem Chapel in Prague', pp. 152–153.
45 *Chronicon universitatis Pragensis*, in FRB, vol. 5, pp. 571–572.
46 Štěpán of Dolany, *Antihussus*, in Pez, vol. 4, pt. 2, col. 386.
47 *Documenta*, p. 410.
48 Relevant documents had been obtained by Jan of Jesenice and dispatched to Hus thereby incurring the indignation of Odo Colonna who was in charge of the Hus case. Novotný, *Correspondence*, p. 89, Kejř, *Husův proces*, p. 57 and *Documenta*, pp. 426–428 for a document of the public notary on the matter.
49 *Documenta*, p. 735.
50 Fudge, 'Želivský's Head: Memory and New Martyrs among the Hussites', in BRRP vol. 6, pp. 116–19 with references to the sources. Also Šmahel, *HR*, vol. 2, pp. 867–878.
51 Štěpán of Dolany, *Antihussus*, in Pez, vol. 4, pt. 2, cols. 380–381.
52 *Postil*, in *Opera omnia*, vol. 2, pp. 166–167.
53 The text appears in Havránek (ed.), *Výbor z český literatury husitské doby*, vol. 1, p. 272.
54 *Contra Palecz*, in *Opera omnia*, vol. 22, p. 269.
55 Kalivoda, *Husitská ideologie*, pp. 289–394.
56 See Kejř, *Dějiny pražské právnické university*, Prague, Karolinum, 1995.
57 These are the views of contemporary chroniclers Henry Knighton and Thomas Walsingham. See both E. Maunde Thompson (ed.), *Chronicon Angliae ab Anno Domini 1328 usque ad Annum 1388, auctore Monacho quodam Sancti Albani*, London, Rolls Series, 1974, p. 281, and Henry Thomas Riley (ed.), *Thomae Walsingham, Quodam Monachi S. Albani, Historia Anglicana*, 2 vols., London, Rolls Series, 1863, vol. 2, p. 119 along with G.H. Martin (ed.), *Knighton's Chronicle 1337–1396*, Oxford, Clarendon Press, 1995.
58 Noted by Jan Jičín in *Pro tractatu materiae et formae*, Vienna, ÖNB MS 4002, fol. 38ʳ.
59 Štěpán of Dolany, *Antihussus*, in Pez, vol. 4, pt. 2, col. 426.
60 For an overview of these two aspects of Wyclif's reputation see the succinct treatment in František Šmahel, '"Doctor evangelicus super omnes evangelistas": Wyclif's Fortune in Hussite Bohemia,' *Bulletin of the Institute of Historical Research*, 43, (May 1970), pp 24–25.
61 Robert Kalivoda definitely thinks so. See his 'Joannes Wyclifs Metaphysik des extremen Realismus und ihre Bedeutung im Endstadium dr mittelälterlichen Philosophie', *Miscellanea Mediaevalis*, 2, (1963), pp. 716–723. For a similar view see Gustav Benrath in his 'Wyclif und Hus', *Zeitschrift für Theologie und Kirche*, 62 (1965), pp. 196–216 and *Wyclifs Bibelkommentar*, Berlin, Walter de Gruyter, 1966. This was countered in a rather sharp response by Paul De Vooght in *Revue d'histoire ecclésiastique*, 62, (1967), pp. 830–834. Most recently G.R. Evans, *John Wyclif: Myth and Reality*, Downers Grove, IVP Academic, 2005 and Stephen E. Lahey, *John Wyclif*, Oxford, Oxford University Press, 2009.
62 Loserth, *Wiclif and Hus*, pp. xxx and 281 the latter point sustained and repeated in the second revised German edition of the book *Hus und Wiclif: Zur Genesis der hussitischen Lehre*, Munich, R. Oldenbourg, 1925, p. 186.
63 De Vooght, pp. 91–94 where De Vooght drew the conclusion that much of what Hus took from Wyclif was 'pure Catholic doctrine'.

64 Workman and Pope (eds.), *The Letters of John Hus*, pp viii–ix.
65 References in Matthew Spinka, *John Hus and the Czech Reform*, Hamden, Archon Books, 1966, pp. 8–9.
66 Bartoš, *Husitství a cizina*, pp. 22–23.
67 Gerson's *Declaratio compendiosa* borrows heavily from Langenstein's *Consilium pacis de unione ac reformatione ecclesiae* (1381) Louis Ellies Du Pin (ed.), *Johannes Gerson: Opera Omnia*, 5 vols., Antwerp, 1706, vol. 2, pp. 314–318 for example.
68 *Positiones*, pp. 149–156.
69 Among them should be noted particularly Kalivoda, *Husitská ideologie*, p. 100, Kaminsky, p. 37 and Šmahel, '"Doctor evangelicus super omnes evangelistas": Wyclif's Fortune in Hussite Bohemia,' p. 27.
70 Katherine Walsh, 'Wyclif's Legacy in Central Europe in the Late Fourteenth and Early Fifteenth Centuries,' *Studies in Church History Subsidia*, 5, (1987), p. 400.
71 Jiří Daňhelka, 'Das Zeugnis des Stockholmer Autographs von Hus', *Die Welt der Slaven*, 27, (1982), pp. 225–33.
72 Craig Atwood, *The Theology of the Czech Brethren from Hus to Comenius*, University Park, Pennsylvania State University Press, 2009, p. 49.
73 Holeton, 'Wyclif's Bohemian Fate', *CV*, 32, (Winter 1989), p. 214.
74 De Voogt, *Hussiana*, p. 332.
75 Atwood, *The Theology of the Czech Brethren from Hus to Comenius*, p. 49.
76 František Palacký, *Radhost: Sbírka spisův drobných*, Prague, Tempský, 1872, vol. 2, pp. 297–356, originally published in 1842 and also Neander, *A General History of the Christian Religion and Church*, trans., Joseph Torrey, Boston, Houghton, Mifflin, 1871, vol. 5, pp. 173–235.
77 According to some assessments Hus' *De ecclesia* had 12 per cent drawn from Wyclif while Hus' treatise on simony drew 10 per cent. Jan Sedlák, *Studie a texty*, Olomouc, 1914–1915, vol. 1, pp. 170–171 and 179.
78 Sedlák, *M. Jan Hus*, pp. 372–373 claimed 23 per cent of Hus' *De ecclesia* was verbatim Wyclif.
79 Kybal, *M. Matěj z Janova*, p. 318.
80 The term is Holeton's in 'The Bohemian origins of the reformation understanding of confirmation', in CECE, p. 250.
81 Vilém Herold, 'How Wyclifite was the Bohemian Reformation?' BRRP, vol. 2, p. 37.
82 *Antihus*, in Pavel Klener (ed.), *Miscellanea husitica Ioannis Sedlák*, p. 437 where he repeatedly referred to Hus as '*bone Hussko*'.
83 *Contra Palecz*, in *Opera omnia*, vol. 2, p. 252.
84 *Contra Iohannem Stokes*, in *Opera omnia*, vol. 22, pp. 62–63.
85 *Documenta*, p. 168. Apparently the comment was made in a sermon.
86 Well said by Zdeněk V. David, *Finding the Middle Way: The Utraquists' Liberal Challenge to Rome and Luther*, Washington and Baltimore, Woodrow Wilson Center Press and Johns Hopkins University Press, 2003, p. 19.
87 *Super IV Sententiarum*, p. 621 and *Contra Stokes*, in *Opera omnia*, vol. 22, p. 62.
88 *Contra Palecz*, in *Opera omnia*, vol. 22, p. 267.

89 *De libris hereticorum legendis*, in *Opera omnia*, vol. 22, pp. 21–37.
90 *Relatio*, FRB, vol. 8, p. 76.
91 *Documenta*, pp. 327–331.
92 Novotný, *Correspondence*, pp. 11–15.
93 Šmahel, '"Doctor evangelicus super omnes evangelistas"', p. 18, Trapp, 'Clm 27034: Unchristened Nominalism and Wycliffite Realism at Prague in 1381', pp. 320–360 and more recently, Zega, *Filozofia w Quaestiones sententiarum Mikołaja Bicepsa*, Warsaw, Homini, 2002, pp. 88–101.
94 Prague Castle Archive MS C XIX contains the initial parts of a commentary on the Sentences of Peter Lombard (introduction to book II) prepared by the Prague Dominican university master Mikuláš of Jevíčko Biceps. According to some interpreters there are references therein to Wyclif's eucharistic thought. I am reluctant to agree. Moreover it is unlikely Wyclif's eucharistic text was available in Prague at such an early date. Zega's *Filozofia w Quaestiones sententiarum Mikołaja Bicepsa* covers his life and work and the central ideas in his concept of God. His role in the dispute over universals is considered along with his response to the work and ideas of Wyclif.
95 František Šmahel, *Die Prager Universität im Mittelalter: Gesammelte Aufsätze*, Leiden, Brill, 2007, p. 260. Katherine Walsh has rightly called attention to the problems of chronology apparent in the assumptions of Šmahel and Jaroslav Kadlec. See her 'Wyclif's Legacy in Central Europe in the Late Fourteenth and Early Fifteenth Centuries', p. 404.
96 Štěpán of Dolany, *In Medullam Tritici*, in Pez, vol. 4, pt. 2, cols. 151–359 at cols. 246–247. The book can be dated to 1408 and it is chiefly concerned with an anti-Wyclif view of the sacraments.
97 The letter appeared in Cochlaeus, *Historiae Hussitarum libri duodecim*, pp. 16–17.
98 Štěpán of Dolany, *In Medullam Tritici*, in Pez, vol. 4, pt. 2, col. 158.
99 For details and extended narrative on the book burning see Novotný/Kybal, vol. 1, pt. 1, pp. 401–429.
100 *Documenta*, pp. 734 and 397–8.
101 *Documenta*, p. 734.
102 Nejedlý, vol. 3, pp. 344–345.
103 Štěpán of Dolany, *Liber epistolaris ad Hussitas*, in Pez, vol. 4, pt. 2, col. 596.
104 *Documenta*, p. 519.
105 The statistics are reported in Leo J. Elders, 'Thomas Aquinas and the Fathers of the Church', in Irena Backus (ed.), *The Reception of the Church Fathers in the West*, 2 vols, Leiden, Brill, 1997, vol. 1, p. 347.
106 See his sermon *Sacerdotes contempserunt* in Vilém Herold and Milan Mráz (eds.), *Iohannis Milicii de Cremsir: Tres Sermones Synodales*, Prague, Academia, 1974, pp. 50–58, 62–63.
107 *De ecclesia*, p. 190. Hus is quoting Augustine.
108 From the so-called *Tractatus de origine Hussitarum*. I cite the edition by Jaroslav Kadlec, *Traktát Mistra Ondřeje Brodu o původu husitů*, Tábor, Museum of the Hussite Revolutionary Movement, 1980, pp. 28–29.
109 See for example his sermon *Dixit Martha ad Iesum* in *Positiones*, pp. 165, 167, 174–175.

110 'Quod omnis bonus christianus est sacerdos, sed non omnis sacerdos est bonus christianus'. Sermon 66 in Flajšhans (ed.), *Spisy M. Jana Husa* (vols. 7–8), pp. 346–347.
111 *Positiones*, pp. 149–156.
112 Friedberg (ed.), *Corpus iuris canonici*, vol. 1, p. 391 and I, 2, quest. 7.
113 *De ecclesia*, p. 197.
114 *O svatokupectví*, in *Opera omnia*, vol. 4, p. 206.
115 *Výklad víry*, in *Opera omnia*, vol. 1, p. 86.
116 *O svatokupectví*, in *Opera omnia*, vol. 4, p. 192 and *Super IV Sententiarum*, pp. 586–587 relying on Augustine's *De utilitate credendi*, Migne, PL, vol. 42, fols. 64–92 *passim*.
117 *Knížky proti knězi kuchmistrovi*, in *Opera omnia*, vol. 4, p. 316.
118 *Historia Hussitica*, in FRB, vol. 5, pp. 331–332.
119 Jena Codex, Prague, NMK MS IV B 24, fols. 57^r–65^r.
120 Novotný, *Correspondence*, pp. 28–30. Novotný places the letter in the period 6–16 July.
121 *O svatokupectví*, in *Opera omnia*, vol. 4, p. 201 and *Questiones, De Indulgentiis*, in *Opera omnia*, vol. 19a, pp. 112–119.
122 Sermon for Corpus Christi, 11 June 1411, in *Sermones in Capella Bethlehem*, vol. 4, pp. 194–200.
123 *Documenta*, pp. 451–455.
124 A year later Hus recounted the matter in his *Contra octo doctores*, in *Opera omnia*, vol. 22, pp. 371–372.
125 Fudge, 'Želivský's Head: Memory and New Martyrs among the Hussites', in BRRP, vol. 6, pp. 116–119. Extensive chronicler's report in SRB, vol. 3, pp. 16–18. Hus referred to the event in his *Postil*, in *Opera omnia*, vol. 2, pp. 114–115 and *O svatokupectví*, in *Opera omnia*, vol. 4, p. 201.
126 *Postil*, in *Opera omnia*, vol. 2, pp. 68–69.
127 *Výklad deserata*, chapter 48 in *Opera omnia*, vol. 1, pp. 221–236 and *Contra octo doctores*, in *Opera omnia*, vol. 22, p. 447.
128 *Postil*, in *Opera omnia*, vol. 2, pp. 178–179.
129 *Postil*, in *Opera omnia*, vol. 2, pp. 121–122.
130 Štěpán Páleč, *Antihus*, in *Miscellanea husitica Ioannis Sedlák*, pp. 441–442.
131 *Contra Palecz*, in *Opera omnia*, vol. 22, p. 238.
132 *Contra octo doctores*, in *Opera omnia*, vol. 22, p. 406.
133 His argument on the matter at his trial is revealed in Hardt, vol. 4, col. 320.
134 *Postil*, in *Opera omnia*, vol. 2, pp. 222–224.
135 *Postil*, in *Opera omnia*, vol. 2, pp. 246–247.
136 From his sermon on Trinity 17 in *Postil*, in *Opera omnia*, vol. 2, pp. 399–400.
137 *Výklad deserata*, in *Opera omnia*, vol. 1, p. 148.
138 Sermon for Pentecost in *Opera omnia*, vol. 13, p. 55.
139 *Postil*, in *Opera omnia*, vol. 2, pp. 443–444.
140 *Super IV Sententiarum*, p. 682.
141 Chronicler's observation appears in SRB, vol. 3, p. 7 and also in Novotný, *Correspondence*, pp. 343–345.

142 An anonymous rhymed Czech chronicle in František Svejkovský (ed.), *Veršované Skladby doby Husitské*, Prague, ČSAV, 1963, p. 156.
143 *Knížky proti knězi kuchmistrovi*, in *Opera omnia*, vol. 4, pp. 313–320 wherein Hus repeatedly argued against the accusation.
144 An allusion in Hus' letter to Zbyněk at the end of 1408. Novotný, *Correspondence*, p. 42. Elsewhere we read of a monk hiding his face behind a gray cowl keeping notes as Hus preached. *Documenta*, p. 176.
145 *Postil*, in *Opera omnia*, vol. 2, p. 184.
146 *Super IV Sententiarum*, p. 637.
147 Sermon on the works of darkness (*Abicamus opera tenebrarum*), in *Positiones*, p. 103.
148 Preface to his commentaries on the several Pastoral Epistles in *Historia et monumenta*, vol. 2, pp. 172–173.
149 Commentary on I Corinthians in *Historia et monumenta*, vol. 2, pp. 139, 147 and 148–149.
150 Sermon for Pentecost, in *Collecta*, pp. 259–260.
151 Svejkovský (ed.), *Veršované Skladby doby Husitské*, p. 157.
152 *O svatokupectví*, in *Opera omnia*, vol. 4, p. 296.
153 Hardt, vol. 1, cols. 104–106.
154 *De ecclesia*, pp. 162–163, *O svatokupectví*, in *Opera omnia*, vol. 4, pp. 212–213 and his sermon for Trinity 17 in *Postil*, in *Opera omnia*, vol. 2, p. 399 where he cites Bernard as authority.
155 *Sermones in Capella Bethlehem*, vol. 2, p. 157.
156 Sermon *Abicamus opera tenebrarum* in *Positiones*, p. 109.
157 *Výklad deserata*, in *Opera omnia*, vol. 1, p. 141.
158 *O svatokupectví*, in *Opera omnia*, vol. 4, pp. 196–7.
159 Hus stressed the role of consent elsewhere. *Dcerka*, in *Opera omnia*, vol. 4, p. 65.
160 Štěpán of Dolany, *Antihussus*, in Pez, vol. 4, pt. 2, col. 418–419.
161 Georg Erler (ed.), *Theoderici de Nyem De scismate libri tres*, Leipzig, Veit, 1890, book 2, chapter 8, pp. 132–133.
162 *O svatokupectví*, in *Opera omnia*, vol. 4, pp. 233–234 and 238.
163 Novotný, *Correspondence*, p. 156.
164 *O svatokupectví*, in *Opera omnia*, vol. 4, p. 222.
165 Sermon for Easter Sunday in *Postil*, in *Opera omnia*, vol. 2, p. 189.
166 Second Sunday after the birth of Christ, in *Postil*, in *Opera omnia*, vol. 2, p. 86.
167 Hus preached on the text Romans 13:12–13 calling on priests to repudiate the works of darkness. Text in *Historia et monumenta*, vol. 2, pp. 57–62.
168 *Postil*, in *Opera omnia*, vol. 2, pp. 68–69.
169 See Hus' treatise *Contra Predicatorem Plznensem*, in *Opera omnia*, vol. 22, p. 111.
170 Novotný, *Correspondence*, pp. 343–345.
171 *Documenta*, pp. 155–63 with the comment about Petr Všeruby on p. 160.
172 Sermon for Trinity VI in *Postil*, in *Opera omnia*, vol. 2, p. 326.
173 *O svatokupectví*, in *Opera omnia*, vol. 4, pp. 203, 240–241 and 242.
174 Sermon for Advent II, in *Postil*, in *Opera omnia*, vol. 2, p. 71.
175 Noted in an early sermon *Vos estis sal terre*, in *Positiones*, p. 118.
176 Hardt, vol. 1, pt. 1, p. 11.

177 *Historia et monumenta*, vol. 2, pp. 74–75.
178 The treatise dates from 1411. Its recipient is unknown (though possibly Mařik Rvačka, a Prague inquisitor) but clearly someone favoring ecclesiastical immunity. *Contra occultum adversarium*, in *Opera omnia*, vol. 22, p. 77.
179 Sermon for Epiphany II in *Collecta*, pp. 92–93.
180 *O svatokupectví*, in *Opera omnia*, vol. 4, p. 210.
181 *O svatokupectví*, in *Opera omnia*, vol. 4, pp. 195 and 204 and Novotný, *Correspondence*, p. 13.
182 *De ablatione temporalium a clericis* in *Historia et monumenta*, vol. 1, p. 150.
183 See these points in Hus' sermon *Exi in vias* in *Historia et monumenta*, vol. 2, p. 74.
184 Hus preaching on obedience (1410). The text has been edited in Sedlák, *M. Jan Hus*, vol. 2, pp.141*–147* at 146*.
185 *Documenta*, pp. 374–6, especially p. 374.
186 Our knowledge of the sermon is restricted to excerpts Zbyněk forwarded to Rome whose editing should not be relied upon. *Documenta*, pp. 404–405.
187 *De ecclesia*, pp. 164–165 and *Knížky proti knězi kuchmistrovi*, in *Opera omnia*, vol. 4, pp. 320–321.
188 *Knížky proti knězi kuchmistrovi*, in *Opera omnia*, vol. 4, p. 322.
189 *Defensio quorundam articulorum Joannis Wicleff* in *Historia et monumenta*, vol. 1, pp. 139–140 and *De decimis* in *Ibid.*, p.162.
190 *Relatio* in FRB, vol. 8, p. 95.
191 *De decimis*, in *Historia et monumenta*, vol. 1, pp. 159–160.
192 The text is in Palémon Glorieux (ed.), *Jean Gerson Oeuvres Complètes*, 10 vols., Tournai, Desclée, 1960, vol. 1, pp. 162–166, esp. pp. 162–3.
193 Matthew Spinka, *John Hus at the Council of Constance*, New York, Columbia University Press, 1965, p. 171 correctly arguing that Gerson misunderstood Hus as a person.
194 Brian Patrick McGuire, *Jean Gerson and the Last Medieval Reformation*, University Park, Pennsylvania State University Press, 2005, p. 249.

Chapter Seven

1 An old chronicler suggests the king ordered Hus to appear before the council. Text in Svejkovský (ed.), *Veršované Skladby doby Husitské*, pp.156–163 at p. 157.
2 Štěpán of Dolany, *Liber epistolaris ad Hussitas*, in Pez, vol. 4, pt. 2, col. 528.
3 Arguing against the 'heresy' nomenclature is Howard Kaminsky, 'The Problematics of Later Medieval "Heresy"', in Jaroslav Pánek (ed.), *Husitství, Reformace, Renesance: Sborník k 60. narozeninám Františka Šmahela*, 3 vols., Prague, Historický ústav, 1994, vol. 1, pp. 133–154 and agreeing with him is Šmahel, '*Causa non grata*: Premature Reformation in Hussite Bohemia', in CECE, p. 229. A rebuttal of the thesis is offered in Thomas A. Fudge, 'Obrana "Kacířství": Teoretické pojednámí', *Medievalia Historica Bohemica*, 9, (2003), pp. 295–314 and supported by Lambert, *Medieval Heresy*, p. 8.
4 Seibt, 'Die Zeit der Luxemburger und der hussitischen Revolution', pp. 476–493.
5 According to Jan Náz at Constance. *Relatio*, in FRB, vol. 8, pp. 79–80.
6 Božena Kopičková and Anežka Vidmanová, *Listy na Husovu obranu z let 1410–1412: Konec jedné legendy?*, Prague, Karolinum, 1999, Fudge review essay in *Mediaevistik: Internationale*

Zeitschrift für Interdisziplinäre Mittelalterforschung, 14, (2001), pp. 402–405. See also Aleš Pořízka, 'Listy na obranu Husova ze 12. září až 2. října 1410: Konec druhé legendy?', *Český časopis historický*, 99, (No. 4, 2001), pp. 701–723.

7   De Vooght, pp. 378–380 and Hieromonk Patapios, '*Sub utraque specie*: The Arguments of John Hus and Jacoubek of Stříbro in Defense of Giving Communion to the Laity under both kinds', *Journal of Theological Studies*, n.s. 53, (No. 2, 2002), p. 516.

8   *Documenta*, pp. 467–469.

9   *Documenta*, pp. 470–471.

10   Hardt, vol. 4, cols. 150–157 and Mansi, vol. 27, cols. 629–636. The order was not carried out until 1428. The Mansi edition is still useful though, unfortunately, it does not include the rubrics for most of the texts.

11   Kejř, *Husův proces*, p. 141.

12   *Liber gestorum*, in Loomis, p. 469.

13   Kejř, *Husův proces*, p. 59.

14   *Documenta*, pp. 397–399.

15   *Documenta*, p. 202.

16   *Documenta*, p. 202.

17   Hilsch, p. 124.

18   Sext 5.2.7. Alexander IV, *Cum contumacia*.

19   The text has been published in Novotný, *Correspondence*, pp. 125–128 and *Documenta*, pp. 461–464.

20   The distinction is made in Gratian's *Decretum* in Friedberg, vol. 1, p. 912.

21   Described in the chronicles of Prokop the Notary in Höfler, vol. 1, p. 26.

22   The text 'Magistri Joannis Jessinetz . . . pro defensione causae Magistri Joannis Hus' is in *Historia et monumenta*, vol. 1, pp. 408–419 with useful comment in Kejř, *Husitský pravník: M. Jan z Jesenice*, pp. 68–71.

23   *Postil, Opera omnia*, vol. 2, pp. 164–166.

24   *Knížky proti knězi kuchmistrovi*, in *Opera omnia*, vol. 4, pp. 320–321.

25   Štěpán of Dolany, *Dialogus volatilis*, in Pez, vol. 4, pt. 2, cols. 464–466.

26   *Concilium Theodorici de Niem ad Wiklefistas reprimendos*, in Sedlák (ed.), *Studie a texty k životopisu Husovu*, vol. 1, pp. 45–55.

27   *Documenta*, pp. 441–442.

28   Kejř, *Husův proces* but see his brief and more recent 'K Husovu procesu v Kostnici', *Acta universitatis carolinae - historia universitatis carolinae pragensis*, 48, (No. 1, 2008), pp. 11–18.

29   Kejř, *Husův proces*, p. 12.

30   Hardt, 7 vols.

31   FRB, vol. 5, pp. 567–588 and noted also by Kejř, *Husův proces*, p. 13.

32   Edward Gibbon, *The History of the Decline and Fall of the Roman Empire*, Betty Radice (ed.), London, The Folio Society, 1984, vol. 2, chapter 15, p. 93.

33   On Gerson as a persecutor of Hus, Werner, pp. 191–200.

34   Spinka, *John Hus at the Council of Constance*, pp. 73–78.

35   De Vooght, pp. 498–499.

36   Herold, 'How Wyclifite was the Bohemian Reformation?', BRRP, vol. 2, pp. 36–37.

NOTES

37   Máyusz, *Kaiser Sigismund in Ungarn, 1387–1437, passim.*
38   Flajšhans, p. 248.
39   The text of the safe conduct appears in FRB, vol. 8, pp. 25–26.
40   Novotný, *Correspondence*, pp. 238, 275–276.
41   Bartoš, *Čechy v době Husově*, pp. 379–381.
42   Novotný, *Correspondence*, pp. 197–199.
43   Ulrich Richental, *Chronik des Constanzer Concils*, in Loomis, p. 129.
44   As pointed out by Bartoš, 'Zur Geleitsfrage im Mittelalter', *Zeitschrift für Kirchengeschichte*, 34, (1913), pp. 414–417.
45   See particularly the ground-breaking work of Alexander Patschovsky, *Die Anfänge einer Ständigen Inquisition in Böhmen ein Prager Inquisitoren-Handbuch aus der ersten Hälfte des 14. Jahrhunderts*, New York, Walter de Gruyter, 1975 and *Quellen zur Böhmischen Inquisition im 14. Jahrhundert*, Weimar, Hermann Böhlaus Nachfolger, 1979.
46   Kejř, *Počátků*, p. 23.
47   Hardt, vol. 4, pp. 12, 28, Richental, *Chronik des Constanzer Concils*, in Loomis, pp. 129, 130, *Relatio*, in FRB, vol. 8, pp. 81–82 and Prague, Strahov Monastery MS DF IV 48.
48   *Relatio*, in FRB, vol. 8, p. 40 for the denial, and Hefele/Leclercq, vol. 7, pt .1, p. 200 for the admission.
49   Ferdinand of Aragon, March/April 1415 in *Documenta*, pp. 539–540.
50   Richental, *Chronik des Constanzer Concils*, in Loomis, p. 130.
51   *Relatio*, in FRB, vol. 8, p. 81.
52   Wilhelm Berger, *Johannes Hus und König Sigismund*, Augsburg, Verlag von J. Butsch Sohn, 1871, pp. 180–208 where thirty nine similar documents are assembled and analyzed in relation to the Hus *salvus conductus*.
53   The first contains this limitation 'iustitia tamen semper salva'. Hardt, vol. 4, p. 199. The second includes the restriction 'in quantum idem dominus rex tenetur sibi dare de iure et servare alios salvos conductus sibi datos'. Hardt, vol. 4, p. 143. The third document is clearly constrained by the clause 'quantum in nobis est et fides exegit orthodoxa'. Hardt, vol. 4, p. 145.
54   *Documenta*, pp. 543–544.
55   Czech edition of Petr Mladoňovice's *Relatio*, FRB, vol. 8, p. 135. See also Hardt, vol. 4, col. 393.
56   From a circular letter in Migne, PL, vol. 215, col. 1317.
57   *Documenta*, pp. 609–611.
58   See for example the declarations of the Czech nobility on behalf of revolution, 20 April 1420 in AČ, vol. 3, pp. 210–212; the letter of the Prague city government to the Doge and Council of Venice, 10 July 1420 in UB, vol. 1, p. 40; the *c.* 1435 *Kronika velmi pěkná o Janu Žižkovi, čeledínu krále Václava*, in Bartoš, *Listy Bratra Jana a Kronika velmi pěckná a Janu Žižovi*, Prague, Blahoslav, 1949, p. 36; and the *Historia Hussitica*, in FRB, vol. 5, p. 332.
59   Richental, *Chronik des Constanzer Concils*, in Loomis, p. 96 describes the various Masses said that day.
60   Mansi, vol. 27, col. 536.
61   Kejř, *Husův proces*, pp. 14–15.

62 Fillastre, *Gesta concilii Constanciensis*, p. 256 and Cerretano, *Liber gestorum*, p. 499 both texts are in Loomis.
63 Cerretano, *Liber gestorum*, in Loomis, pp. 469–470.
64 *Relatio*, FRB, vol. 8, p. 41.
65 Hardt, vol. 1, col. 499 and Vienna, ÖNB MS 5113, fol. 1ʳ.
66 Richental, *Chronik des Constanzer Concils*, in Loomis, p. 190 for details on the musicians and prostitutes, *Historia Hussitica*, in FRB, vol. 5, p. 331 for specific numbers and Hardt, vol. 5, cols. 50–53 on the higher estimate of hookers.
67 Albrecht Classen, *The Poems of Oswald von Wolkenstein: An English Translation of the Complete Works (1376/77–1445)*, New York, Palgrave MacMillan, 2008 contains the descriptions. See pp. 74, 117, and 178.
68 According to the account of University of Vienna ambassador Peter Pulka. Friedrich Firnhaber (ed.), 'Petrus de Pulka, Abgesandter der Wiener Universität am Concilium zu Constanz', in *Archiv für Kunde österreichischer Geschichts-Quellen*, 15, (1856), p. 15. See also Kejř, *Husitský pravník: M. Jan z Jesenice*, p. 92 who claims Jan of Jesenice was with Křišťan.
69 Novotný, *Correspondence*, pp. 225–234 for the text.
70 Kejř, *Počátků*, pp. 132–145.
71 The text appears in *Documenta*, pp. 464–466. The date was established by Flajšhans, 'Husovo odvolání ke Kristu', *Český časopis historický*, 39, (1933), p. 247. The most recent study is Jiří Kejř, *Husovo odvolání od soudu papežova k soudu Kristovu*, Prague, Albis International, 1999.
72 Kejř, *Husovo odvolání, passim*. See also Flajšhans, 'Husovo odvolání ke Kristu' and Amedeo Molnár, 'Hus et son appel à Jesus-Christ', *CV*, 8, (1965), pp. 95–104.
73 My thinking has been stimulated along these lines by conversations with Jiří Kejř going back as long ago as 1991 and he suggests similar ideas in his *Počátků*, p. 35.
74 *Knížky proti knězi kuchmistrovi*, in *Opera omnia*, vol. 4, p. 321.
75 Kejř, *Husovo odvolání*, p. 52 and *Počátků*, p. 30.
76 Most recently Kejř, 'Johannes Hus als Rechtsdenker', in Seibt, pp. 213–226.
77 Kejř, *Husitský pravník: M. Jan z Jesenice, passim* for his career and p. 66 for the opinion that Jesenice would not have approved of the appeal to Christ.
78 *Relatio*, in FRB, vol. 8, p. 76.
79 Kejř, *Husův proces*, pp. 11 and 52.
80 Letter is dated 27 May 1414 in *Documenta*, pp. 523–526.
81 Hardt, vol. 2, cols. 182–187.
82 Štěpán of Dolany, *Dialogus volatilis*, in Pez, vol. 4, pt. 2, col. 492.
83 Kejř, *Počátků*, p. 33 and *Husův proces*, pp. 66–71.
84 Hus mentioned the name of his horse in a letter to friends in Bohemia the day following his arrival in Constance (4 November 1414) in Novotný, *Correspondence*, p. 219.
85 Richental, *Chronik des Constanzer Concils*, in Loomis, pp. 113–4 and a second version of the tale on p. 130. The versions differ substantially. Petr Mladoňovice makes the claim in his *Relatio* that the story circulated perhaps as an intentional pretext to justify the arrest. See FRB, vol. 8, p. 37. The curious tale is not accepted by most modern scholars including

Spinka, *John Hus*, p. 290, who sharply called into question Richental's overall reliability, as did Hefele/Leclercq, vol. 7, pt. 1, p. 173.
86 Novotný, *Correspondence*, p. 246.
87 A point argued by Ferdinand Seibt, *Hussitenstudien: Personen, Ereignisse, Ideen einer frühen Revolution*, Munich, Oldenbourg, 1987, p. 170.
88 Novotný, *Correspondence*, p. 220.
89 *Documenta*, p. 617.
90 Novotný, *Correspondence*, pp. 140–141.
91 *Documenta*, p. 560.
92 *De fidei suae elucidatione*, in *Historia et monumenta*, vol. 1, pp. 60–64.
93 Hefele/Leclercq, vol. 7, pt. 1, p. 299.
94 De Vooght, p. 445.
95 Novotný/Kybal, vol. 2, pt. 3, p. 141.
96 Suggested by Walter Brandmüller, *Das Konzil von Konstanz 1414–1418*, 2 vols., Paderborn, Ferdinand Schöningh, 1991–1997, vol. 1, p. 344. The second edition is preferred since the Hus trial is augmented in that version.
97 Hardt, vol. 4, pt. 4, cols. 326 and 329.
98 De Vooght, pp. 502, 507–508.
99 Kejř thinks 'pater' was a term used to identify both Zabarella and Paweł Włodkowicz. 'K Husovu procesu v Kostnici', p. 14. His argument is intriguing.
100 *Výklad deserata*, in *Opera omnia*, vol. 1, p. 234.
101 Lützow, *The Life and Times of Master John Hus*, p. 65.
102 'The life of Hus by George the Hermit', in FRB, vol. 8, p. 378 and dating to the 1470s.
103 Novotný, *Correspondence*, pp. 207–208.
104 Novotný, *Correspondence*, p. 98. See also pp. 93–94.
105 Novotný, *Correspondence*, pp. 169–170.
106 Novotný, *Correspondence*, p. 88 and *Contra octo doctores*, in *Opera omnia*, vol. 22, pp. 375–376.
107 Kejř, *Počátků*, p. 32.
108 *Antihus*, in Sedlák (ed.), *Miscellanea husitica Ioannis Sedlák*, p. 375.
109 Štěpán of Dolany, *Antihussus*, in Pez, vol. 4, pt. 2, col. 383.
110 *Historia et monumenta*, vol. 1, p. 367.
111 In German, 'Ich bin der reisse dreck, so ist die welt das weite arschloch; drumb sein wir wol zu scheiden.' In WA Tischreden, vol. 5 (no. 5537), p. 222.
112 Brad S. Gregory, *Salvation at Stake: Christian Martyrdom in Early Modern Europe*, Cambridge, MA, Harvard University Press 1999, p. 64. A highly recommended study.
113 *Contra Palecz*, in *Opera omnia*, vol. 22, p. 253.
114 Sermons for Trinity Sunday, *Collecta*, pp. 282–283, but see *Confirmate corda vestra* in *Positiones*, p. 127.
115 Novotný, *Correspondence*, pp. 70, 73 and 85.
116 Hubert Herkommer, 'Die Geschichte vom Leiden und Sterben des Jan Hus als Ereignis und Erzählung', in Ludger Grenzmann and Karl Stackmann (eds.), *Literatur und Laienbildung im Spätmittelalter und in der Reformationszeit*, Stuttgart, Metzler, 1981, pp. 117–118.

117 *Historia Hussitica*, in FRB, vol. 5, pp. 332 and 338.
118 *Relatio*, in FRB, vol. 8, p. 41.
119 A critical point noted by Thomas E. Morrissey, 'After Six Hundred Years: The Great Western Schism, Conciliarism, and Constance', *Theological Studies*, 40, (September 1979), p. 506.
120 Attributed to Dietrich of Niem in his 1411 treatise *De scismate*. There is an edition. Georg Erler (ed.), *Theoderici de Nyem De scismate libri tres*, Leipzig, Veit, 1890. I have not verified the attribution. Tom Izbicki tells me Edward Peters thinks the statement is possibly derived from Hostiensis.
121 *Antihus*, in Sedlák (ed.), *Miscellanea husitica Ioannis Sedlák*, p. 371.
122 *Documenta*, p. 174 and Hardt, vol. 4, col. 759.
123 Flajšhans, p. 285.
124 *Historia et monumenta*, vol. 1, preface *Relatio*, in FRB, vol. 8, p. 33.
125 *Documenta*, pp. 460–461.
126 *Postil*, in *Opera omnia*, vol. 2, p. 133.
127 *Documenta*, p. 465.
128 See De Vooght, pp. 248–249 and *Documenta*, pp. 169–174, 465 and Novotný, *Correspondence*, p. 157.
129 *Relatio*, in FRB, vol. 8, p. 33 and Novotný, *Correspondence*, p. 218.
130 Novotný, *Correspondence*, p. 220.
131 The list appears in *Documenta*, pp. 194–199.
132 *Relatio*, in FRB, vol. 8, p. 33.
133 *Relatio*, in FRB, vol. 8, p. 41.
134 *Documenta*, pp. 199–204.
135 *Relatio*, in FRB, vol. 8, p. 33.
136 Bartoš, *Čechy v době Husově*, p. 351.
137 *Relatio*, in FRB, vol. 8, p. 39.
138 Novotný, *Correspondence*, p. 261.
139 Novotný, *Correspondence*, pp. 244–245 and 300.
140 Richental, *Chronik des Constanzer Concils*, in Loomis, p. 144.
141 Novotný, *Correspondence*, pp. 300 and 218.
142 Novotný, *Correspondence*, p. 298.
143 *Contra Palecz*, in *Opera omnia*, vol. 22, p. 269.
144 *Contra octo doctores*, in *Opera omnia*, vol. 22, p. 372.
145 *Relatio*, in FRB, vol. 8, p. 76 and compare in *Documenta*, p. 519.
146 The reports of Giacomo della Marca [James of the Marches] in Rome, Vatican Library MS Vat Lat 7307, fols. 1^v–25^r are important and these have been discussed in Thomas A. Fudge, 'Image Breakers, Image Makers: The Role of Heresy in Divided Christendom', in CECE, pp. 216–217, 222.
147 Letter to Archbishop Konrad of Prague, 27 May 1414 in *Documenta*, p. 524
148 *Relatio*, in FRB, vol. 8, p. 110.
149 Ludolf of Żagań, 'De longevo schismate', Johann Loserth (ed.), in *Archiv für österreichische geschichte*, 60, (1880), p. 504.

150 Štěpán of Dolany, *Antihussus*, in Pez, vol. 4, pt. 2, col. 373.
151 *De utilitate credendi*, in Migne, PL, vol. 42, cols. 64–92.
152 Gratian, *Decretum* in Friedberg (ed.), *Corpus iuris canonici*, vol. 1, cols. 997–998.
153 Johannes Teutonicus, gloss on the *Decretum*, dist. 40, c. 6.
154 Fulgentius of Ruspe, *De fide liber ad Petrum* in *CCL*, vol. 91A, p. 756. The statement has been incorrectly attributed to Augustine in PL, vol. 40, cols. 753–780.
155 Friedberg (ed.), *Corpus iuris canonici*, vol. 1, pp. 370, 746 and 1376.
156 See the statement in Erich Caspar (ed.), *Das Register Gregors VII*, 2 vols., Berlin, Weidmann, 1920–1923, vol. 1, p. 207.
157 *Summa theologica*, 2a, 2ae, Q.Xi, article 2, ad tert.
158 As argued by Stephan Kuttner, 'Ecclesia de occultis non iudicat: Problemata ex doctrina poenali decretistarum et decretalistarum a Gratiano usque ad Gregorium PP. IX', in *Acta Congressus iuridici internationalis Romae 1934*, Rome, Pontifical Library, 1936, vol. 3, pp. 225–246.
159 X.5.7.15 in Friedberg (ed.), *Corpus iuris canonici*, vol. 2, p. 789.
160 As suggested in Henry Ansgar Kelly, 'Inquisitorial Due Process and the Status of Secret Crimes', *Monumenta iuris canonici*, series C: Subsidia, vol. 9, (1992), p. 414.
161 Third Lateran canon in *Ad abolendam*, X 5.7.9, Aquinas, and *Vergentes in senium*, X 5.7.10.
162 *Excommunicamus*, X 5.7.14.
163 Francisco Peña (ed.), *Directorium inquisitorum* (1376), Rome, Aedibus Populi Roman, 1585, p. 159.
164 Patschovsky, *Quellen zur Böhmischen Inquisition im 14. Jahrhundert*, pp. 19–23.
165 New edition in Annette Palès-Gobillard (ed.), *Le Livre des sentences de l'inquisiteur Bernard Gui (1308–1323)*, 2 vols, Paris, CNRS Éditions, 2003.
166 An older but still reliable study is Charles Homer Haskins, *Studies in Mediaeval Culture*, Boston, Frederick Ungar, 1965, pp. 193–244.
167 Patschovsky, *Quellen zur Böhmischen Inquisition im 14. Jahrhundert*, p. 23.
168 For his activity see especially Dietrich Kurze, *Quellen zur Ketzergeschichte Brandenburgs und Pommerns*, Berlin, Walter de Gruyter, 1975, Patschovsky, *Die Anfänge einer Ständigen Inquisition in Böhmen ein Prager Inquisitoren-Handbuch aus der ersten Hälfte des 14. Jahrhunderts*, pp. 90, 130–132 and, latterly, Peter Biller, 'Bernard Gui, Peter Zwicker, and the Geography of Valdesimo or Valdismi', *Bollettino della Società di Studi Valdesi*, 124, (2007), pp. 31–43.
169 The text appears in Alexander Patschovsky and Kurt-Viktor Selge (eds.), *Quellen zur Geschichte der Waldenser*, Gütersloh, Mohn, 1973, pp. 70–103.
170 Friedberg (ed.), *Corpus iuris canonici*, vol. 2, pp. 745–747.
171 František M. Bartoš, 'V předvečer Kutnohorského dekretu', *Časopis českého musea*, 102, (1928), pp. 97–113 with the critical text on pp. 107–108.
172 Mansi, vol. 27, cols. 403 and 731.
173 *Contra Stanislaum*, in *Opera omnia*, vol. 22, p. 292.
174 Kejř, *Husitský pravník: M. Jan z Jesenice*, pp. 45–9 deals with Colonna's handling of the Hus case.
175 De Vooght, pp. 498–500.

176 Novotný, *Correspondence*, p. 284.
177 Glorieux (ed.), *Jean Gerson Oeuvres complètes*, vol. 5, p. 476.
178 Explicit in the sentence against Jerome of Prague in 1416. Hardt, vol. 4, col. 766.
179 Kejř, *Husův proces*, pp. 11–12.
180 'Maior excommunicatio propter solam contumaciam est ferenda.' *Super IV Sententiarum*, p. 612.
181 Kejř, *Husův proces*, *passim* where the important question of Hus' death as an example of judicial murder is considered.
182 For example Karel Malý, 'Mistr Jan Hus a Univerzita Karlova', in *HT*, supplement 1, (2001), pp. 395–403 but lacking the critical arguments required to sustain the idea.
183 For example, Henry Charles Lea, *A History of the Inquisition of the Middle Ages*, 3 vols., New York, Harbor Press, 1955, vol. 1, p. 460.
184 Friedberg (ed.), *Corpus iuris canonici*, vol. 2, p. 1181.
185 *Relatio*, in FRB, vol. 8, p. 41.
186 *Ad extirpanda*, Innocent IV, text in Mansi, vol. 23, cols. 569–575.
187 Eymeric, *Directorium inquisitorum*, pp. 516–522.
188 Text in James M. Powell (ed.), *The Liber Augustalis*, Syracuse, Syracuse University Press, 1971, pp. 7–10.
189 *Decretals*, 5.7.11 from Innocent III's *Si adversus*, in Friedberg, vol. 2, pp. 737, 783–784.
190 Henry Ansgar Kelly, *Inquisitions and other trial procedures in the Medieval West*, Aldershot, Ashgate, 2001, p. xxi.
191 Insightful on this issue is James Brundage, *Medieval Canon Law*, London, Longman, 1995, p. 149 referencing pertinent canons.
192 *Inter cunctus*, 22 February 1418, in Hardt, vol. 4, cols. 518–531 and Mansi, vol. 27, cols. 1204–1215 with the notation in col. 1213.
193 Mansi, vol. 27, cols. 752–3 and Hardt, vol. 4, cols. 429–432.
194 FRB, vol. 8, pp. 501–503.
195 *Opera omnia*, Du Pin (ed.), vol. 2, p. 72.
196 *Documenta*, p. 178.
197 Hardt, vol. 2, col. 265.
198 *O šesti bludiech*, in *Opera omnia*, vol. 4, pp. 279–282.
199 *De decimis*, in *Historia et monumenta*, vol. 1, p. 159.
200 *Postilla adumbrata*, in *Opera omnia*, vol. 13, p. 346.
201 King Ferdinand of Aragon, letter to Sigismund, 27 March 1415 in *Documenta*, pp. 539–40.
202 Cochlaeus, *Historiae Hussitarum libri duodecim*, p. 138.
203 Nicholas, Bishop of Nezero, inquisitor of the Prague diocese. His reference text is noted in *Relatio*, FRB, vol. 8, pp. 64–65.
204 *Contra octo doctores*, in *Opera omnia*, vol. 22, pp. 464–465. Elsewhere Hus' view on the death penalty has been noted. See Jiří Kejř, 'The Death Penalty during the Bohemian Wars of Religion', in BRRP, vol. 6, pp. 145–146 but without reference to the statement in *Contra octo doctores*.

205 A more balanced view of the Constance judges avoiding the fatal temptation to impose upon them the standards of a post-Enlightenment world view is Petr Čornej, *Velké dějiny koruny české*, vol. 5, Prague, Paseka, 2000, pp. 165–169.
206 De Vooght, *Hussiana*, pp. 207–208 and Hefele/Leclercq, vol. 7, pp. 329–337.
207 Novotný, *Correspondence*, p. 298 and *Passio*, in FRB, vol. 8, pp. 142–143.
208 The sermon survives in at least 53 mss. Printed in Hardt, vol. 3, cols. 1–5, Mansi, vol. 28, cols. 546–549 and FRB, vol. 8, pp. 489–493.
209 Hardt, vol. 3, col. 59.
210 A similar thought in De Vooght, p. 507.
211 Richental, *Chronik des Constanzer Concils*, in Loomis, p. 133.
212 There was a case to this effect in Barcelona. Eymeric, *Directorium inquisitorum*, pp. 514–516.
213 *Relatio*, in FRB, vol. 8, pp. 109–110.
214 The speech of 19 October begins in Hardt, vol. 3, col. 39 and lays out Gerson's argument.
215 *Passio*, in FRB, vol. 8, pp. 143–144.
216 The relevant passages appear in Richental, *Chronik des Constanzer Concils*, in Loomis, p. 134 and *Relatio*, in FRB, vol. 8, p. 119.
217 Richental, *Chronik des Constanzer Concils*, in Loomis, p. 134.
218 Du Pin, vol. 2, pp. 273–280 at p. 277.
219 Hardt, vol. 2, col. 201 and Mansi, vol. 27, col. 547.
220 Origen, *Contra Celsum*, 3.12–13. The Greek text is in Miroslav Marcovich (ed.), *Origenes Contra Celsum libri VIII*, Leiden, Brill, 2001; translation in Henry Chadwick (ed.), *Origen: Contra Celsum*, Cambridge, Cambridge University Press, 1980, pp. 135–136.
221 See his letter of 7 May 1518 addressed to Maarten Lips, in *The Correspondence of Erasmus*, trans., R.A.B. Mynors, Toronto, University of Toronto Press, 1982, vol. 6, p.15. Erasmus called him 'Jerome Hus'. Luther repeated the opinion but it may have been misattributed. WA, vol. 50. 36, 15–16.

Chapter Eight

1 In addition to comments from the Vienna trial see Šmahel, *Idea národa v husitských Čechách*, pp. 40–49.
2 The main sources for his life may be found in Hardt, while the fifteenth-century accounts have been collected in Jaroslav Goll, *Vypsání o Mistru Jeronymovi z Prahy*, Prague, J. Otto, 1878. There are two perfectly sound secondary studies. Šmahel, *Jeroným Pražský*, and Betts, *Essays in Czech History*, pp. 195–235.
3 Hardt, vol. 4, col. 635.
4 Klicman, p. 22. This according to the testimony of Peter Pergoschl at the Vienna trial of 1410.
5 Hardt, vol. 4, col. 681, Vilém Herold, 'Der Streit zwischen Hieronymus von Prag und Johann Gerson', in *Société et Eglise: Texts et discussions dans les universités d'Europe centrale pendant le moyen âge tardif*, Turnhout, Brepols, 1995, pp. 77–89 and Zenon Kaluza, 'Le

chancelier Gerson et Jérome de Prague', *Archives d'histoire doctrinale et littéraire du Moyen Age*, 51, (1984), pp. 81–126.
6   Klicman, pp. 12 and 13 and Hardt, vol. 4, col. 681.
7   On this, Herold, 'Magister Hieronymus von Prag und die Universität Köln', in Albert Zimmermann (ed.), *Die Kölner Universität im Mittelalter*, Berlin, Walter de Gruyter, 1989, pp. 255–273.
8   Klicman, pp. 33–34.
9   Hardt, vol. 4, col. 673.
10 Klicman, p. 30.
11 Klicman, p. 2 and Hardt, vol. 4, cols. 638 and 682.
12 Klicman, p. 2.
13 Klicman, pp. 11–12.
14 Klicman, pp. 35–36. There are two very different versions of the excommunication. The first is dated 30 September in *Documenta*, pp. 417–20 and the second of 22 October in Klicman, pp. 36–39.
15 *Documenta*, p. 416 and Betts, *Essays in Czech History*, p. 213.
16 This may be gauged from the 1424 work of Nicholas of Dinkelsbühl, *Quaestio de heresibus et hereticis ac de veritatibus katholicis*, Vienna, ÖNB MS 4384, fols. 14^r–15^v.
17 Hardt, vol. 4, col. 670.
18 Hardt, vol. 4, cols. 641, 674–675 and 751 and Štěpán of Dolany, *Antihussus*, in Pez, vol. 4, pt. 2, col. 382.
19 Novotný, *Correspondence*, pp. 265–266.
20 Hardt, vol. 4, col. 103.
21 Vavřinec of Březová, 'Hussite Chronicle' in FRB, vol. 5, p. 336.
22 Hardt, vol. 4, cols. 686–687 and Fillastre, *Gesta concilii Constanciensis*, in Loomis, p. 233.
23 Richental, *Chronik des Constanzer Concils*, in Loomis, p. 131.
24 Hardt, vol. 4, cols. 215–218.
25 *Relatio*, in FRB, vol. 8, p. 110.
26 The sermon text appears in FRB, vol. 8, pp. 231–243 at p. 240.
27 *Documenta*, p. 563.
28 Novotný, *Correspondence*, p. 272.
29 Hardt, vol. 4, cols. 508–510.
30 In a sermon of 19 October 1415 in Hardt, vol. 3, col. 39.
31 The charges are summarized in Hefele/Leclercq, vol. 3, pt. 2, pp. 377–387, 394–408.
32 Hardt, vol. 4, pt. 7, cols. 766–767.
33 Fillastre, *Gesta concilii Constanciensis*, in Loomis, p. 259.
34 The sermon text is in Hardt, vol. 3, cols. 54–63 and FRB, vol. 8, pp. 494–500.
35 Fillastre, *Gesta concilii Constanciensis*, in Loomis, p. 283.
36 Vrie in Hardt, vol. 1, col. 202. For a critical edition of Poggio's letter see Tomaso de Tonellis (ed.), *Poggii Epistolae*, Florence, L. Marchini, 1832, vol. 1, pp. 11–20, Richental, *Chronik des Constanzer Concils*, in Loomis, p. 135.
37 John Hine Mundy, 'The Conciliar Movement and the Council of Constance', in Loomis, p. 43.

38 For example Mikuláš Pelhřimov at Basel according to the *Liber diurnus de gestis Bohemorum in Concilio Basileensi* in MC, vol. 1, p. 294.
39 Nicholas of Dresden, *Apologia*, in Hardt, vol. 3, cols. 653–657.
40 Justin Martyr, *First Apology*, 67 and *Didache*, 9–10, 14.
41 Peter Browe is the authority and his work is foundational. For the medieval period see his collection of previously published articles *Die Eucharistie im Mittelalter: Liturgiehistorische Forschungen in Kulturwissenschaftlicher Absicht*, Münster, LIT Verlag, 2003, and *Die häufige Kommunion in Mittelalter*, Münster, Regensbergsche Verlagsbuchhandlung, 1938. References in Holeton, 'The Bohemian Eucharistic Movement in its European Context', in BRRP, vol. 1, p. 24, n.5.
42 Zega, *Filozofia w Quaestiones sententiarum Mikołaja Bicepsa*, pp. 88–101.
43 In major languages see especially De Vooght, pp. 11–24; Morée, *Preaching in Fourteenth Century Bohemia*; David C. Mengal, 'A Monk, a Preacher, and a Jesuit: Making the Life of Milíč', in BRRP, vol. 5, pt. 1, pp. 33–55; and Marin, *passim*.
44 Expressed in a letter to Pope Urban V in 1367, a sermon 'on the last day of the Lord', and his treatise about Antichrist in particular. These texts are available in a Latin-English edition. Milan Opočenský and Jana Opočenská (eds.), *Milíč of Kroměříž, The Message for the Last Days: Three Essays from the Year 1367*, Geneva, World Alliance of Reformed Churches, 1998.
45 Höfler, vol. 2, p. 61.
46 See for example the careful study of John M. Clifton-Everest, 'The Eucharist in the Czech and German Prayers of Milič z Kroměříž,' *Bohemia*, 23, (No.1, 1982), pp. 1–15.
47 Morée, *Preaching in Fourteenth Century Bohemia*, p. 54.
48 Holeton, 'The Bohemian Eucharistic Movement in its European Context', in BRRP, vol. 1, pp. 31–32 and Marin, pp. 457–575 for an up to date analysis.
49 His treatises on the subject are contained in a larger work which has been edited and published over most of the twentieth century. *Regulae*, 6 vols.
50 Occupying the whole of *Regulae*, vol. 5.
51 *Regulae*, vol. 2, pp. 25–29, 33–37.
52 *Regulae*, vol. 1, p. 73.
53 *Regulae*, vol. 5, pp. 209–212.
54 *Regulae*, vol. 5, p. 9.
55 *Regulae*, vol. 1, pp. 51–165 *passim*.
56 *Regulae*, vol. 1, pp. 151–159, 162–164.
57 On this incident see the text in Ferdinand Tadra (ed.), *Soudní akta konsistoře pražské (Acta judiciaria consistorii Pragensis)*, Prague, Česká akademie císaře Františka Josefa, 1893, vol. 1, pp. 311–312.
58 *Regulae*, vol. 5, p. 304.
59 *Regulae*, vol. 5, p. 38.
60 Jan Rokycana, *Postilla*, vol. 2, pp. 733–735.
61 *Regulae*, vol. 5, pp. 300–301.
62 *Regulae*, vol. 5, p. 247.

63 *Regulae*, vol. 1, p. 101. Holeton, "'*Videtur quod, sicut baptismus, sic et communio sacramentalis infancium fundatur in Ewangelio quod consentire videtur*" [MS Prague, NK VIII.D.15 ff. 130ᵛ–136]: A New Text on the Communion of Infants', *Studie o rukopisech*, 30, (1993–1994), p. 25.
64 *Regulae*, vol. 5, p. 368.
65 *Regulae*, vol. 5, p. 32.
66 *Regulae*, vol. 5, pp. 13–19 but especially p.18.
67 Konstantin von Höfler (ed.), *Concilia Pragensia 1353–1413*, Vienna, Geyer, 1972, pp. 37–39 and *Documenta*, p. 702.
68 *Documenta*, pp. 699–700.
69 The archbishop relates this in his *De bono mortis*. The relevant part has been edited and published in Sedlák, *M. Jan Hus*, pp. 45*–48*.
70 See Ruben E. Weltsch, *Archbishop John of Jenstein, 1348–1400: Papalism, Humanism and Reform in Pre-Hussite Prague*, The Hague, Mouton, 1968, especially pp. 166–179.
71 Jaroslav V. Polc, 'Statues of the Synods of Prague (1386–1395)', *Apollinaris*, 53, (Nos. 3–4, 1980), p. 447.
72 Höfler, *Concilia Pragensia*, pp. 41–42.
73 *Regulae*, vol. 5, p. 165 for example. Holeton, *La communion des tout-petits enfants*, p. 63 and Šmahel, vol. 2, p. 84.
74 Josef Kalousek, *O historii kalicha v dobách předhusitských*, Prague, KČSN, 1881 and Kybal, *M. Matěj z Janova*, p. 315.
75 Kybal, 'M. Matěj z Janova a M. Jakoubek ze Stříbra', *Český časopis historický*, 11, (1905), pp. 22–37 where the connections are explored to considerable benefit.
76 *Regulae*, vol. 5, pp. 313–377.
77 Cited in the introduction to *Milíč of Kroměříž, The Message for the Last Days*, p. 14.
78 Holeton, *La communion des touts-petits enfants*, p. 61.
79 Marin, pp. 517–523.
80 Karel J. Erben (ed.), *Tomáše ze Štítného: Knížky šestery o obecných věcech křesťanských*, Prague, Pražská universita, 1852, pp. 207–69.
81 *Super IV Sententiarum*, p. 557.
82 *De sanguine Christi sub specie vini a laicis sumendo*, in *Historia et monumenta*, vol. 1, pp. 52–54.
83 *De sanguine Christi*, in *Historia et monumenta*, vol. 1, p. 52 and also Novotný, *Correspondence*, p. 215.
84 *De sanguine Christi*, in *Historia et monumenta*, vol. 1, p. 54.
85 Novotný, *Correspondence*, p. 240.
86 Hefele/Leclercq, vol. 7, pt. 1, pp. 283–286.
87 Novotný, *Correspondence*, p. 289.
88 Novotný, *Correspondence*, pp. 294–295.
89 Höfler, *Concilia Pragensia*, p. ix.
90 Vavřinec of Březová, *Historia Hussitica*, in FRB, vol. 5, pp. 329–330.
91 Based on an anonymous source in Höfler, vol. 3, p. 156.
92 Text in Svejkovský (ed.), *Veršované Skladby doby Husitské*, pp. 158–159.

NOTES

93 A principal study is Romolo Cegna, 'La Scuola della Rosa Nera e Nicolo detto da Dresda (1380?–1417?): Maestro tedesco al Collegio della Rosa Nera in Praga (1412–1415)', *Mediaevalia philosophica Polonorum*, 30, (1990), pp. 10–67.

94 A sound overview can be found in Kaminsky, et al., 'Master Nicholas of Dresden: The Old Color and the New', *Transactions of the American Philosophical Society*, n.s. 55, (Part 1, 1965), pp. 5–28 and useful comments in Šmahel, *HR*, vol. 1, pp. 568–575.

95 An important study advancing this thesis is Helena Krmíčková, *Studie a texty k počátkům v Čechách*, Brno, Masarykovy Univerzita, 1997, review by Fudge in *Kosmas: Czechoslovak and Central European Journal*, 15, (No.1, 2001), pp. 96–97.

96 William P. Hyland, 'John-Jerome of Prague (1368–1440) and the *Errores Graecorum*: Anatomy of a Polemic against Greek Christians', *Journal of Religious History*, 21, (No.3, 1997), pp. 266–267.

97 This is according to Enrico C.S. Molnar, 'Anglo-Czech Reformation Contacts', ThD dissertation, Iliff School of Theology, 1953, p. 132 and Hardt, vol. 3, col. 566.

98 The best study is De Vooght, *Jacobellus de Stříbro*, pp. 1–78 on the development towards utraquism, pp. 79–158 on eucharistic presence and pp. 159–224 on his theology of the cup.

99 Hardt, vol. 3, cols. 416–585.

100 Hardt, vol. 3, col. 566.

101 Leipzig, University Library MS 766, fol. 208^v. I have not been able to consult this text and owe the reference to the late Bob Scribner.

102 Vienna, ÖNB MS 4491, fols. 1^r–28^r.

103 The relevant texts are *Salvator noster de comunione spirituali et sacramentali integra sub duplici forma panis et vini communitatem plebium concernente* (1415), in *Betlemské texty*, pp.106–139 (Latin and Czech texts).

104 *Salvator noster*, in *Betlemské texty*, p. 108.

105 *Salvator noster*, in *Betlemské texty*, pp. 134, 136. For Leo, see Migne (ed.), PL, vol. 54, cols. 279–280.

106 *Posicio pro informatione monachi Petri*, Vienna, ÖNB, MS 4488, fol.101^r.

107 Hardt, vol. 3, col. 369.

108 See his *De remanencia panis* in De Vooght, *Jacobellus de Stříbro*, pp. 319–350.

109 Prague Castle Archive MS A 37 fols. 1^r–470^v. The printed edition of the commentary has appeared as František Šimek (ed.), *Jakoubek ze Stříbra: Výklad na zjevenie sv. Jana*, 2 vols., Prague, Nákladem Komise vydávání pramenů českého hnutí náboženského, 1932–1933.

110 *Contra communicationem plebis sub utraque specie*, in Hardt, vol. 3, cols. 392–415.

111 *De communione plebis sub utraque specie, contra Brodum*, in Hardt, vol. 3, cols. 416–585.

112 Holeton, *La communion des tout-petits enfants*, p. 123.

113 *Salvator noster*, in *Betlemské texty*, p. 116.

114 *Salvator noster*, in *Betlemské texty*, p. 138.

115 The November 1414 sermon is generally referred to by its incipit 'Nisi manducaveritis', Prague, NK MS III G 28, fols. 165^r–179^v. The text of the May 1415 sermon can be found in Kraków, Jagiellonian University Library MS 2148, fols. 34^v–39^v.

116 *Salvator noster*, in *Betlemské texty*, p. 112.

117 Svejkovský (ed.), *Veršované Skladby doby Husitské*, pp. 157–158 and 159–160.
118 Nicholas' *Contra Gallum* of the summer of 1415 is only one extant example. Prague, NK MS IV G 15, fols. 142ʳ–157ᵛ.
119 Bartoš, *Do čtyř pražských článků*, 2nd edition, Prague, Blahoslavova společnost, 1940, pp. 12–13 and AČ, vol. 3, pp. 203–205.
120 Rokycana, *Postilla*, vol. 1, pp. 722–723.
121 For example the backslidden Hussite priest Jan Papoušek of Soběslav who wrote a critical assessment after 1453. In Höfler, FRA 1, 7, pp. 158–162.
122 De Vooght, *Jacobellus de Stříbro*, pp. 95–121.
123 The text appears in Zdeněk Nejedlý, *Prameny k synodám strany pražské a táboré*, Prague, Nákladem Královské České Společnosti Náuk, 1900, pp. 33–34.
124 *Apologia*, summer 1415, in Hardt, vol. 3, cols. 591–647, where it is wrongly attributed to Jakoubek.
125 *De quadruplici missione*, in Hardt, vol. 3, cols. 624–625.
126 The text appears in AČ, vol. 3, p. 204.
127 The preeminent authority on the subject is Holeton. There are two critical studies. *La communion des tout-petits enfants* and 'The Communion of Infants: The Basel Years,' *CV*, 29, (1986), pp. 15–40.
128 *Documenta*, pp. 677–681 at p. 678.
129 See for example the important narrative of Mikuláš of Pelhřimov (bishop of Tábor) in his *Chronicon causam sacerdotum thaboritarum continens*, in Höfler, vol. 2, pp. 475–820.
130 Höfler, vol. 2, pp. 240–243.
131 Holeton, *La communion des tout-petits enfants*, p. 64.
132 A letter from Křišťan of Prachatice to Václav Koranda in 1416 highlights this. *Documenta*, pp. 633–636.
133 Kejř, '"Auctoritates contra communionem parvulorum" M. Jana z Jesenice', *Studie o rukopisech*, 19, (1980), p. 5 and Thomas A. Fudge, 'Hussite Infant Communion', *Lutheran Quarterly*, 10, (No. 2, 1996), pp. 179–194.
134 Hardt, vol. 3, cols. 406–407.
135 *Historia Hussitica*, in FRB, vol. 5, p. 334.
136 Printed in *Betlemské texty*, pp. 105–163.
137 'Nisi manducaveritis', Prague, NK MS IV G 15, fol. 148ᵛ.
138 *Salvator noster*, in *Betlemské texty*, p. 112.
139 See Holeton, 'L'Eschatologie et le mouvement eucharistique en Europe centrale pendant la fin du Moyen-Âge', in A.M. Triacca and E. Pistoia (eds.), *Eschatologie et Liturgie*, Rome, C.L.V. - Edizioni Liturgiche, 1985, pp. 115–123.
140 In my opinion Kaminsky, pp. 223–253 and De Vooght, *Jacobellus of Stříbro*, p. 280 are both wrong while Holeton, *La communion des tout-petits enfants*, p. 198 has it right.
141 *Liber epistolaris ad Hussitas*, in Pez, vol. 4, pt. 2. See cols. 520–521, 522–523, 524.
142 See the discussion in Holeton, *La communion des tout-petits enfants*, p. 141.
143 Prague, NK MS VIII D 15, fol. 135ʳ⁻ᵛ. I rely on Holeton, '*Videtur quod*', pp. 25–26.
144 In a sermon on 15 October. Prague, NK MS V G 3, fol. 149ʳ.

145 Text in Amedeo Molnár (ed.), *Dochovaná kázání Jana Želivského z roku 1419*, Prague, ČSAV, 1953, pp. 126–127.
146 Prague, NK MS V G 3, fol. 199^r.
147 Half of the texts have been edited in Molnár, *Dochovaná kázání Jana Želivského z roku 1419* while the rest remain in manuscript form in Želivský's rather atrocious hand! Prague, NK MS V G 3.
148 Nejedlý, vol. 6, pp. 203–206 and 244–245.
149 John of Tours, *Regestrum*, in MC, vol. 1, pp. 862–863.
150 Basel, University Library MS A 1 29, fols. 1–24^v. Holeton, 'The Communion of Infants: The Basel Years', p. 18.
151 Basel, University Library MS A 1 29, fols. 143^r–174^v.
152 There is an altogether accurate and fair evaluation of the reply made by Stojković in Holeton, 'The Communion of Infants: The Basel Years', pp. 23–26.
153 MC, vol. 2, p. 433.
154 MC, vol. 1, pp. 495–498 and formally accepted in 1436. See also Winfried Eberhard, *Konfessionsbildung und Stände in Böhmen 1478–1530*, Munich, R. Oldenbourg, 1981, p. 43.
155 MC, vol. 1, pp. 833 and 855.
156 MC, vol. 1, p. 863.
157 Prague, NK MS VIII F 22, fols. 384^r–399^v. I have not studied this manuscript and rely on Holeton, 'The Communion of Infants: The Basel Years', pp. 33–34.
158 Holeton, *La communion des tout-petits enfants*, p. 113. Originally linked to Jakoubek, Jan Čapek maintained radical leanings associated first with the Dresden School, later with Jan Želivský, Jan of Jičín, and still later with Tábor. Čapek may have been the author of the Czech mass though there is some doubt. See Holeton, 'The Role of Jakoubek of Stříbro in the Creation of a Czech Liturgy: Some Further Reflections', in Halama and Soukup (eds.), *Jakoubek ze Stříbra: Texty a jejich působení*, p. 79. In 1417 Čapek wrote a book on the subject of the eucharist 'Knížky o večeři Páně'; which amounted to a lay instructional manual on the significance of the sacrament. On this subject see especially Bartoš, 'Kněz Jan Čapek', *Sborník Historický*, 5, (1957), pp. 32–41.
159 From the incipit 'dominus noster Jesus Christus, lapis angularis, assit huic nostro principio . . .' Prague, NK MS XXIII F 204.
160 Letter to Juan Carvajal, 21 August 1451, in Rudolf Wolkan (ed.), *Der Briefwechsel des Eneas Silvius Piccolomini*, in *FRA* II, vol. 68, Vienna, Alfred Hölder, 1918, pp. 22–57 at p. 51.
161 Codex Dipl. Sax. Reg. II, 3, pp. 136–137. Noted in Enrico C.S. Molnar, 'The Catholicity of the Utraquist Church of Bohemia,' *Anglican Theological Review*, 41, (October 1959), p. 263.
162 There are comments about his accommodation to the Hussites in Šimek (ed.), *Staré letopisy české z rukopisu křižovnického*, p. 157 and Jaroslav Charvát (ed.), *Dílo Františka Palackého*, Prague, Mazáč, 1941, p. 109.
163 Quoted in Amedeo Molnár, 'Neznámý spis Prokopa z Jindřichova Hradce', *HT*, 6–7, (1983–1984), pp. 436.
164 Šmahel, *La révolution hussite, une anomalie historique*, p. 127.

165 Šmahel, *Dějiny Tábora*, 2 vols., České Budějovice, Jihočeské nakladatelství, 1988–90, vol. 1, pp. 314–316.
166 Werner, p. 127 ostensibly referring to his monumental commentary on the Apocalypse. *Výklad na Zjevenie sv. Jana*, vol. 1, pp. 70, 241, 267 and vol. 2, p. 105.
167 For example, Jakoubek, *Výklad na Zjevenie sv. Jana*, vol. 1, p. 329.
168 Thomas A. Fudge, 'The "Crown" and the "Red Gown": Hussite Popular Religion', in Bob Scribner and Trevor Johnson (eds.), *Popular Religion in Germany and Central Europe, 1400–1880*, London, MacMillan, 1996, pp. 38–57, 214–220.
169 Kaminsky, p. 55.
170 *Documenta*, pp. 568–569.
171 *Documenta*, pp. 574–575.
172 *Documenta*, pp. 580–584.
173 One of the copies survives in Scotland. Edinburgh University Library MS P.C. 73 where I studied it.
174 *Documenta*, pp. 590–593. It has been suggested the protest was authored by Jan of Jesenice. Kejř, *Husitský pravník: M. Jan z Jesenice*, p. 142. Among earlier authorities Bartoš and Novotný were of the same opinion.
175 *Documenta*, pp. 615–616.
176 Ondřej of Brod, *De origine hussitarum*, pp. 25–26.
177 According to Dietrich of Niem in Hardt, vol. 2, col. 425.
178 See the *Concilium Theodorici de Niem ad Wicklefistas reprimandos*, in Sedlák (ed.), *Studie a texty k životopisu Husova*, vol. 1, pp. 45–55.
179 Štěpán of Dolany, *In Medullam tritici*, in Pez, vol. 4, pt. 2, col. 158.
180 *Inter cunctus*, in Hardt, 4, cols. 518–531 and Mansi, 27, cols. 1204–1215.
181 *Omnium plasmatoris domini*, in UB, vol. 1, pp. 17–20. The bull is dated 1 March 1420.
182 UB, vol. 1, pp. 15–17, *Documenta*, pp. 609–611, and Höfler, vol. 2, pp. 252–254. For a documentary overview of the revolutionary period in Bohemia from Constance to 1437 see Fudge, *The Crusade against Heretics in Bohemia, 1418–1437: Sources and Documents for the Hussite Crusades*, Aldershot, Ashgate, 2002.
183 This according to an anonymous account in Höfler, vol. 1, pp. 528–529.
184 *Historia Hussitica*, in FRB, vol. 5, pp. 344–345.
185 Account of Jakoubek of Stříbro in January 1426 published in Bartoš, 'Sněm husitské revoluce v Betlémské kapli', *Jihočeský sborník historický*, 18, (1949), p. 99. Similar report in Mikuláš of Pelhřimov's *Chronicon causam sacerdotum thaboritarum* in Höfler, vol. 2, p. 478.
186 The best treatment of the defenestration is Kaminsky,'The Prague Insurrection of 30 July 1419', *Mediaevalia et Humanistica*, 17, (1966), pp. 106–126.
187 Šmahel, 'The Hussite movement: an anomaly of European history?', p. 89.
188 On Žižka see especially the classic work by Josef Pekař, *Žižka a jeho doba*, 4 vols., Prague, Vesmír, 1930–1935 and in English, Frederick G. Heymann, *John Žižka and the Hussite Revolution*, New York, Russell & Russell, 1969 and Fudge, 'Žižka's Drum: The Political Uses of Popular Religion', *Central European History*, 36, (No. 4, 2003), pp. 546–569. Victor Verney, *Warrior of God: Jan Žižka and the Hussite Revolution*, London, Frontline Books, 2009, is too frail to be recommended.

189   UB, vol. 1, pp. 22–23, 12 March 1420.
190   AČ, vol. 3, pp. 212–213, dated 3 April 1420.
191   For example the early stance of Čeněk of Vartenberk in AČ, vol. 3, pp. 210–212.
192   *Historia Hussitica*, in FRB, vol. 5, pp. 391–395 erroneously dated to 1421 therein.
193   For Sudoměř see SRB, vol. 3, pp. 33–35 and for the Sázava fight the *Chronicon veteris Collegiati*, in Höfler, vol. 1, p. 80.
194   The text of that decision has been published in Bartoš, 'Do čytř pražských articulů', in *Sborník příspěvků k dějinám hlavního města Prahy*, 5, (1932), pp. 577–580.
195   On this see František Holeček, 'Makkabäische Inspiration des hussitischen Chorals "Ktož jsú boží bojovníci" ("Ihr, die ihr Kämpfer Gottes und seines Gesetzes seid")', in Miloslav Polívka and František Šmahel (eds.), *In memoriam Josefa Macka*, Prague, Historický ústav, 1996, pp. 111–125 and Stanislav Segert, 'War Orders and Songs - Essenes and Hussites', *Erets Israel*, 26, (1999), pp. 176–182.
196   *Historia Hussitica*, in FRB, vol. 5, pp. 383–391 for an informative narrative of the first crusade battle.
197   *Historia Hussitica*, in FRB, vol. 5, p. 388.
198   *Historia Hussitica*, in FRB, vol. 5, pp. 435–442.
199   *Historia Hussitica*, in FRB, vol. 5, pp. 443–444.
200   Excellent overview in Amedeo Molnár, 'Eschatologická naděje české reformace', in *Od reformace k zítřku*, Prague, Kalich, 1956, pp. 28–30.
201   Fudge, '"Neither Mine Nor Thine": Communist Experiments in Hussite Bohemia', *Canadian Journal of History*, 33, (April 1998), pp. 25–47.
202   Šmahel, *La révolution hussite*, pp. 105–110.
203   Šmahel, vol. 4, pp. 54–95.
204   On Táborite identity see Kaminsky, pp. 329–336, 385–397, Fudge, '"Neither mine nor Thine": Communist experiments in Hussite Bohemia', *passim* and Šmahel, *Dějiny Tábora*, vol. 1, pp. 197–306.
205   SRB, vol. 4, p. 44 and *Historia Hussitica*, in FRB, vol. 5, pp. 476–477.
206   Dietrich Kerler (ed.), *Deutsche Reichstagsakten*, Gotha, Perthes, 1883, vol. 8, pp. 28–31.
207   Johann Loserth (ed.), Ludolf of Žagan, *Tractatus de longevo schismate*, in *Archiv für österreichische Geschichte*, 60, (1880), pt. 2, chap. 10, pp. 496–497.
208   AČ, vol. 3, pp. 226–230.
209   Fudge, *The Crusade against Heretics in Bohemia, 1418–1437*, pp. 124–126.
210   *Historia Hussitica*, in FRB, vol. 5, pp. 511–513.
211   *Historia Hussitica*, in FRB, vol. 5, pp. 528–534 which ends in mid-sentence during the battle at Kutná Hora, Eberhart Windecke, *Denkwürdigkeiten zur Geschichte des Zeitalters Kaiser Sigmunds*, Wilhelm Altmann (ed.), Berlin, R. Gaertners Verlagsbuchhandlung, 1893, p. 120, Jan Długosz, *Historia polonicae*, in Alexander Przeździecki (ed.), *Opera omnia*, vol. 13, Kraków, Kirchmayer, 1877, book 7, pp. 279–281, the *Chronicon veteris Collegiati*, in Höfler, vol. 1, pp. 85–6, and SRB, vol. 3, pp. 48–50.
212   *Deutsche Reichstagsakten*, vol. 8, pp. 119–121, composed before July 1422.
213   See Andreas von Regensburg, 'Chronica Husitarum', in Georg Leidinger (ed.), *Andreas von Regensburg Sämtliche Werke*, Aalen, Scientia Verlag, 1969, pp. 377–378.

214 Bartoš, *Listy Bratra Jana a Kronika velmi pěkná a Janu Žižkovi*, pp. 18–24.
215 Walter Brandmüller, *Das Konzil von Pavia-Siena 1423–1424*, 2 vols., Münster, Verlag Aschendorff, 1974, vol. 2, pp. 20–22.
216 UB, vol. 1, pp. 309–314.
217 UB, vol. 1, pp. 336–338.
218 There are at least seven accounts of the conflict including SRB, vol. 3, pp. 62–63.
219 *Deutsche Reichstagsakten*, vol. 8, pp. 491–492.
220 SRB, vol. 3, pp. 66–69.
221 *Deutsche Reichstagsakten*, vol. 9, pp. 41–44.
222 Chronicle of Bartošek of Drahonice, in FRB, vol. 5, pp. 596–597.
223 Poem on the fourth crusade by Hans Rosenblüt appears in Rochus von Liliencron (ed.), *Die historischen Volkslieder der Deutschen vom 13. bis 16. Jahrhundert*, 2 vols., Hildesheim, Georg Olms Verlagsbuchhandlung, 1966, vol. 1, pp. 296–299 at p. 298.
224 J.A. Twemlow (ed.), *Calendar of Entries in the Papal Registers*, London, Mackie & Co., Ltd., 1906, vol. 7, pp. 35–36.
225 *Deutsche Reichstagsakten*, vol. 9, pp. 72–74.
226 UB, vol. 2, pp. 22–26.
227 Bartoš (ed.), *Petri Payne Anglici: Positio replicca et proposition in concilio Basiliensi a. 1433 atque oratio ad Sigismundum regem a. 1429 Bratislaviae pronounciatae*, Tábor, Taboriensis ecclesia evangelica fratrum bohemorum, 1949, pp. 81–90.
228 UB, vol. 2, pp. 27–29.
229 UB, vol. 2, pp. 109–129.
230 Windecke, p. 280.
231 MC, vol. 1, pp. 73–75.
232 Bartoš, 'Manifesty nuncia Cesariniho husitům z roku 1431', in Bedřich Jenšovský and Bedřich Mendl (eds.), *K dějinám československým v období humanismu*, Prague, Tschechoslow, 1932, p. 191.
233 MC, vol. 2, pp. 27–29 and the lengthy poem by Hans Rosenblüt in Liliencron, vol. 1, pp. 334–339.
234 Chronicle of Bartošek of Drahonice, in FRB, vol. 5, pp. 604–606 and SRB, vol. 3, pp. 58–61.
235 MC, vol. 1, pp. 135–138.
236 UB, vol. 2, pp. 281–283.
237 Among the editions of the acts of the Council see Mansi, vol. 29, cols.1–227. There are many sources as well as studies. MC, vol. 1 contains valuable materials including Jan Stojković, 'Tractatus, quomodo Bohemi reducti sunt ad unitatem ecclesiae', pp. 135–286 and a journal kept by the Hussites, MC, vol. 1, pp. 287–357. An account of the Council written by Juan of Segovia appears in MC, vol. 2, pp. 299–316. On the Hussites at Basel see, most recently, Fudge, 'Prokop in the Bath: Some observations on the *Liber diurnus de gestis Bohemorum in Concilio Basileensi*', in BRRP, vol. 7, [=*Filosofický časopis, Supplementum 1*], (2009), pp. 139–155.
238 Paris, Bibliothèque Nationale MS franç. 1278, fols. 145^v–146^r.

239 Theodor Hirsch (ed.), *Scriptores rerum Prussicarum*, 6 vols., Leipzig, Hirzel, 1861–1874, vol. 3, pp. 499–503, 512–518.
240 UB, vol. 2, pp. 414–417.
241 Aeneas Sylvius, *Historia Bohemica*, chapter 51, p. 161.
242 SRB, vol. 3, pp. 103–104, Windecke, pp. 434–5, and Bartošek of Drahonice, in FRB, vol. 5, pp. 620–621.
243 The best source is English remains Murray Wagner, *Petr Chelčický: A Radical Separatist in Hussite Bohemia*, Scottdale, Herald Press, 1983.
244 Jaroslav Pánek, 'The Question of Tolerance in Bohemia and Moravia in the Age of the Reformation', in Ole Peter Grell and Bob Scribner (eds.), *Tolerance and Intolerance in the European Reformation*, Cambridge, Cambridge University Press, 1996, p. 231.
245 Pekař, *Žižka a jeho doba*, vol. 3, p. 324.
246 *In minoribus agentes*, dated 26 April 1463 in Francesco Gaude (ed.), *Bullarum diplomatum et privilegiorum sanctorum Romanum pontificum*, Turin, Franco and Dalmazzo, 1860, vol. 5, pp. 175 and 178.
247 Text in AČ, vol. 5, pp. 418–427 and see Fudge, 'The Problem of Religious Liberty in Early Modern Bohemia', *CV*, 38, (No.1, 1996), pp. 68–71.
248 The leading study is David, *Finding the Middle Way*.
249 David, *Finding the Middle Way*, pp. 302–348.
250 Barry F.H. Graham, 'The Evolution of the Utraquist Mass, 1420–1620', *The Catholic Historical Review*, 92, (No. 4, 2006), p. 557.
251 That view is challenged by David, '"The White Mountain, 1620: An Annihilation or Apotheosis of Utraquism"?, *CV*, 45, (No. 1, 2003), esp. pp. 52–59.
252 Zdeněk David deals expertly with the important question of what specifically happened to the Utraquists and the methods of obliteration, efforts at resistance, and the afterlife of the 250 year old movement while concluding that, like Jan Hus, annihilation led to apotheosis. *Finding the Middle Way*, pp. 349–377.

Chapter Nine

1 Höfler, vol. 1, p. 563.
2 Fudge, 'The "Crown" and the "Red Gown": Hussite Popular Religion', pp. 48–50.
3 Aeneas Sylvius, *Historia Bohemica*, p. 4.
4 On the heroism of the condemned it seems likely there was textual dependence on the famous letter of Poggio Bracciolini noted above. Aeneas Sylvius, *Historia Bohemica*, p. 100.
5 According to the 'Very Fine Chronicle of Jan Žižka' in Bartoš (ed.), *Listy Bratra Jana a Kronika velmi pěkná a Janu Žižkovi*, p. 36.
6 Giovanni Capistrano, *Epistola responsiva ad praefatam epistolam Johannis Borotini*, in František Wallouch (ed.), *Žiwotopis swatého Jana Kapistrána*, Brno, W Komissi u Ritsche a Grosse, 1858, p. 840.
7 According to the declaration of the Czech nobles on 11 September 1414 in FRB, vol. 8, pp. 228–230.
8 Aeneas Sylvius, *Historia Bohemica*, p. 101.

9   The text of the letter has been edited in Johann Loserth, 'Beiträge zur Geschichte der Hussitischen Bewegung', *Archiv für österreichische Geschichte*, 82, (1895), pp. 386–391 with the relevant part on pp. 386–387.
10 Aeneas Sylvius, *Historia Bohemica*, p. 100.
11 Loserth, 'Beiträge zur Geschichte der Hussitischen Bewegung', p. 387.
12 Text in Svejkovský, *Veršované Skladby doby husitské*, pp. 102–115 at p. 113.
13 This is the case in the gradual of St. Michael's Church in the Old Town of Prague preserved as NK MS XI B 1a–d and noted by David R. Holeton, '"O felix Bohemia - O felix Constantia": The Liturgical Celebration of Saint Jan Hus', in Seibt (ed.), *Jan Hus: Zwischen Zeiten, Völkern, Konfessionen*, p. 390.
14 Loserth, 'Beiträge zur Geschichte der Hussitischen Bewegung', p. 387.
15 Höfler, FRA, vol. 6, pp. 240–243 at p. 242.
16 *Documenta*, pp. 647–651.
17 Hussite content of liturgical books has been noted in FRB, vol. 8, pp. 431–444 and 458–472, Jana Fojtíková, 'Hudební doklady Husova kultu z 15. a 16. století: Příspěvek ke studiu husitské tradice v době předbělohorské', *Miscellanea Musicologica*, 29, (1981), pp. 51–142 and more recently by Holeton, 'The Celebration of Jan Hus in the Life of the Churches', *Studia Liturgica*, 35, (2005), p. 34.
18 Holeton, '"O felix Bohemia - O felix Constantia"', p. 386.
19 Terms appearing in a declaration dated 20 April 1420 signed by Čeněk of Vartenberk and Oldřich Rožmberk before their return to the royalist-Catholic side. AČ, vol. 3, p. 211 and *Historia Hussitica*, p. 351.
20 The document, prepared upon the orders of Martin V, is extant in the Prague Castle Archive and has been published in Josef Macek, 'K počátkům táborství v Písek', *JSH*, 22, (1953), pp. 119–124.
21 The letter is in UB, vol. 2, pp. 523–5, the quoted citation on p. 524.
22 Šmahel, *HR*, vol. 3, p. 1038. For a more complete overview and satisfying analysis see Jeanne E. Grant, 'Rejecting an Emperor: Hussites and Sigismund', in Christopher Ocker, et al. (eds.), *Politics and Reformations*, Leiden, Brill, 2007, pp. 460–466.
23 For example, the Polish preacher and rector of the university in Kraków, Stanisław of Skarbimierz. Bożena Chmielowska (ed.), *Stanisław ze Skarbimierza, Sermones sapientiales*, 3 vols., Warsaw, Akademia Teologii Katolickiej, 1979, vol. 3, p. 309.
24 Dietrich Kurze (ed.), *Quellen zur Ketzergeschichte Brandenburgs und Pommerns*, Berlin, Walter de Gruyter, 1975, p. 300.
25 Wilhelm Wattenbach, 'Über die Inquisition gegen die Waldenser in Pommern und der Mark Brandenburg', *Philosophische und historische Abhandlungen der königlichen Akademie der Wissenschaft zu Berlin*, 3, (1886), pp. 79–80.
26 *Výklad deserata*, in *Opera omnia*, vol. 1, chapter 35, pp. 134–142.
27 In contemporary texts edited in Jiří Daňhelka (ed.), *Husitské skladby budyšínského rukopisu*, Prague, Orbis, 1952, pp. 46 and 64.
28 FRB, vol 8, pp. 373–376.
29 Hölfer, FRA 1, vol. 6, p. 242.
30 FRB, vol. 8, pp. 231–243.

31 Among edited sermon outlines see Molnár (ed.), *Dochovaná kázání Jana Želivského z roku 1419*, pp. 56, 96, 129, 240, etc.
32 FRB, vol. 8, p. cxxviii. Štěpán's *Liber epistolaris ad Hussitas*, in Pez, vol. 4, pt. 2, cols. 520–1 and Johann Loserth (ed.), *Die Denkschrift des Breslauer Domherrn Nikolaus Tempelfeld von Brieg*, in *Archiv für österreichische Geschichte*, 61, (1880), pp. 11 and 99.
33 Ferdinand Seibt, 'Ein neuer Hus', *CV*, 35, (No. 1, 1993), pp. 62–73.
34 *De septem culpis taboritarum*, Prague Castle Archive MS D 88, fols. 223^r–233^r.
35 *Relatio*, in FRB, vol. 8, p. 140.
36 Lovosice, Regional State Archives of Litoměřice, MS IV C 1, fol. 244^v. Since I first examined the text in 1991 an edition has appeared. Barry F.H. Graham (ed.), *The Litoměřice Gradual of 1517*, Prague, L. Marek, 1999.
37 Full text of this lengthy manifesto in MC, vol. 1, pp. 153–70 with the relevant remark on pp. 154–155.
38 *Historia Hussitica*, in FRB, vol. 5, p. 351.
39 I refer to the collection traditionally known to scholars as the 'Old Czech Annalists' which constitute perhaps the most important source for the entire Hussite period. In the various recensions the manuscripts are both primary sources and reworkings of the sources. A recent and solid examination is Joel Seltzer, 'Framing Faith, Forging a Nation: Czech Vernacular Historiography and the Bohemian Reformation, 1430–1530', unpublished PhD dissertation, Yale University, 2004, pp. 162–163 for the reference about Hus.
40 Holeton, '"O felix Bohemia - O felix Constantia"', p. 394 and 'The Celebration of Jan Hus', p. 36 with references to the sources. I limit my citation of the liturgical manuscripts to those I have actually looked at. In any case Holeton should be preferred as reliable and authoritative.
41 Holeton, 'The Celebration of Jan Hus', p. 35.
42 An example of this is the Rackovský Kancional, Prague, NK MS VI C 20a, fols. 97^v–98^r.
43 According to Holeton, '"O felix Bohemia - O felix Constantia"', p. 394. For a description of the Sobokta Gradual see Graham, pp. 204–7.
44 See David R. Holeton, 'The Office of Jan Hus: An Unrecorded Antiphonary in the Metropolitical Library of Estergom', in J. Neil Alexander (ed.), *Time and Community* [Festschrift for Thomas J. Talley], Washington DC, The Pastoral Press, 1990, pp. 137–152 at p. 142.
45 FRB, vol. 8, p. 431. Holeton, '"O felix Bohemia - O felix Constantia"', pp. 394, 398–399 and 'The Celebration of Jan Hus', p. 36.
46 FRB, vol. 8, pp. 431–432.
47 FRB, vol. 8, pp. 422–424.
48 Holeton, 'The Celebration of Jan Hus', p. 57.
49 For example the so-called *Passio etc secundum Johannem Barbatum, rusticum quadratum* in FRB, vol. 8, pp.14–24, esp. p. 17.
50 Holeton, '"O felix Bohemia - O felix Constantia"', p. 389.
51 Prague, Strahov Monastery Library MS DR V 12, fol. 12^v; a printed missal from 1531.
52 Holeton, '"O felix Bohemia - O felix Constantia"', p. 392.

53 A variety of these have been collected in Fojtíková, 'Hudební doklady Husova kultu z 15. a 16. století', pp. 58–63, 100–101, 103–105, 108–110, and 112–134. See also the analysis in Fudge, *The Magnificent Ride: The First Reformation in Hussite Bohemia*, pp. 186–216.
54 Seltzer, 'Framing Faith, Forging a Nation', p. 137.
55 Smíškovský Gradual, Vienna, ÖNB MS 15.492 and Mladá Boleslav, Regional museum MS II A 1. The books are described in Graham, pp. 561–568 and 278–282.
56 Holeton, '"O felix Bohemia - O felix Constantia"', p. 394
57 FRB, vol. 8, pp. 243–246.
58 Ruth Gladstein, 'Eschatological Trends in Bohemian Jewry during the Hussite Period', in Ann Williams (ed.), *Prophecy and Millenarianism*, London, Longman, 1980, p. 246.
59 New York, St. Mark's Library, General Theological Seminary, MS BX 2043 .A3 H8, fol. 191^v. See Thomas J. Talley, 'A Hussite Latin Gradual of the XV Century', *Bulletin of the General Theological Seminary*, 48, (1962), pp. 8–13 and Graham, pp. 293–6. Graham notes the date 1532 on a colophon on fol. 25^v. Pavel Brodský does not the regard the colophon as original and Talley thinks the book was produced in the mid fifteenth century.
60 Rackovský Kancional, Prague, NK MS VI C 20a, fols. 88^r–98^v.
61 Smíškovský Gradual, Vienna, ÖNB MS 15.492, fol. 285^r.
62 Prague, NMK MS IV B 9, fols. 25r, 170^v–171^v, 172^r, et al.
63 Barry F.H. Graham, 'The Evolution of the Utraquist Mass, 1420–1620', *The Catholic Historical Review*, 92, (No. 4, 2006), pp. 565, 572.
64 I refer to Prague, NK MS IV H 12, fols. 148–149. The mutilation is described in Fudge, *The Magnificent Ride: The First Reformation in Hussite Bohemia*, pp. 128–129.
65 Esztergom, Főszékesegyházi könyvtär [Bib. Metropolitana Strigoniensis] MS I. 313, pp. 501–511 which dates from the second half of the fifteenth century. The report appeared in Holeton, 'The Office of Jan Hus'.
66 Holeton, 'The Office of Jan Hus', pp. 141–143 for a description of the texts and pp. 143–149 for the texts. Also useful, Holeton, 'The Celebration of Jan Hus', pp. 34–35.
67 Holeton, '"O felix Bohemia - O felix Constantia"', p. 397.
68 Marie-Elisabeth Ducreux, 'Hymnologia Bohemica 1588–1764: Cantionnaires tchèques de la contre-réform', doctoral dissertation, University of Paris III, 1982 deals with this effort.
69 For example, the Smíškovský Gradual, Vienna, ÖNB MS 15.492, fol. 285^r where the illumination appears on the first page of the introit for the Common of Martyrs. The full page is reproduced in Fudge, *The Magnificent Ride*, p. 97. For a narrative of events see *Historia Hussitica*, in FRB, vol. 5, p. 352. Holeton points out the theme appears in the antiphon to the Magnificat in the office texts for Jan Hus. 'The Office of Jan Hus', p. 147.
70 František Šimek and Miloslav Kaňak (eds.), *Staré letopisy české z rukopisu křižovnického*, Prague, Státní nakladatelství Krásné Literatury, Hudby a Umění, 1939, p. 304.
71 František M. Bartoš, *Husitská revoluce, vol. 2: Vláda bratrstev a její pád 1426–1437*, Prague, ČSAV, 1966, p. 229. Bartoš cites no source for his claim. On Polák see Joel Seltzer, 'Re-visioning the Saint's Life in Utraquist Historical Writing', in BRRP, vol. 5.1, pp. 158–161.
72 Bartoš (ed.), *Listy Bratra Jana a Kronika velmi pěckná a Janu Žižkovi*, p. 44.

73 Aeneas Sylvius, *Historia Bohemica*, p. 138.
74 *Historia Hussitarum libri duodecim*, p. 218.
75 Jena Codex, Prague, NMK MS IV B 24, fol. 5ᵛ.
76 Jistebnice Gradual, Prague, NMK MS XII F 14, fol. 61ʳ. I first saw this image in 1991 and it was quite faded then. Ten years later it was inexplicably obliterated. On the iconography of Žižka see Fudge, 'Žižka's Drum: The Political Uses of Popular Religion'.
77 The points made by Holeton, '"O felix Bohemia - O felix Constantia"', p. 392 and 'The Celebration of Jan Hus', p. 34.
78 Klement Borový (ed.), *Jednání a Dopisy Konsistoře Katolické i Utrakvistické*, Prague, I.L. Kuber, 1868, vol. 1, p. 32.
79 Holeton, 'The Office of Jan Hus', p. 142.
80 Migne, PL, vol. 45, col. 512 with comment in Holeton, '"O felix Bohemia - O felix Constantia"', p. 385.
81 *Relatio*, FRB, vol. 8, p. 120.
82 Aeneas Sylvius, *Historia Bohemica*, p. 100.
83 *Tractatus de longevo schismate*, p. 450.
84 Rome, Vatican Library, Codex Vat. Lat. 7307, fol. 25ʳ.
85 See Paweł Kras, *Husyci w piętnastowiecznej Polsce*, Lublin, Towarzystwo Naukowe KUL, 1998, pp. 104–5.
86 Thomas A. Fudge, '"The Shouting Hus": Heresy Appropriated as Propaganda in the Sixteenth Century', *CV*, 38, (No.3, 1996), pp. 197–231. Further examples are noted in Holeton, 'The Celebration of Jan Hus', pp. 37–43.
87 Bernhard Lohse, 'Luther und Huß', *Luther*, 36, (1965), p 118 as Lohse wrongly assumes.
88 Adolf Hauffen, 'Husz eine Gans - Luther ein Schwan,' *Prager Deutschen Studien*, 9, (1908), pp. 1–28 and Gerhard Seib (ed.), *Luther mit dem Schwan*, Wittenberg, Schelzky and Jeep, 1996.
89 Noted in Oliver K. Olson, *Matthias Flacius and the Survival of Luther's Reform*, Wiesbaden, Harrassowitz Verlag, 2002, p. 41.
90 Felician Gess (ed.), *Akten und Briefe zur Kirchenpolitik Herzog Georgs von Sachsen*, Leipzig, Teubner, 1917, vol. 2, p. 40.
91 Cochlaeus, *Historiae Hussitarum libri duodecim*, p. 114.
92 Copenhagen, Det Kongelige Bibliothek MS 1551, fols. 22–24. The focus of the piece, which should be dated to the mid 1530s, is Luther not Hus.
93 Description in Rebecca Wagner Oettinger, *Music as Propaganda in the German Reformation*, Aldershot, Ashgate, 2001, p. 318.
94 Johannes Agricola, *Tragedia Johannis Huss*, (Wittenberg, 1537). See Hans-Gert Roloff, 'Quelle-Text-Edition: Johann Agricolas Tragedia Johannis Huss', in *Internationales Jahrbuch für Editionswissenschaft*, 11, (1997), pp. 78–85 and Phillip Haberkern, '"After Me There Will Come Braver Men": Jan Hus and Reformation Polemics in the 1530s', *German History*, 27, (No. 2, 2009), pp. 179–180, 186–195.
95 Prague, NMK MS III B 12, fol. 260ᵛ.
96 Prague, NMK MS III B 12, fol. 284ʳ.

97   Prague, NMK MS 54 C 25, Daniel Adam Veleslavín, *Kalendář Hystorický*, 2nd ed, Prague, 1590, p. 369.
98   Royt, p. 410.
99   *Der Heyligen ausserwoehlten Gottes Zeugen, Bekennern vnd Martyrern... Historien...* Strasbourg, Balthasar Beck, 1552, 8 vols. Useful discussion can be found in Robert Kolb, *For all the Saints: Changing Perceptions of Martyrdom and Sainthood in the Lutheran Reformation*, Macon, Mercer University Press, 1987, *passim* but especially pp. 41–83.
100 *Catologus testium veritatis*, Basel, Oporinus, 1556. There was a second, greatly enlarged, edition published six years later. Strasbourg, Paul Messerschmidt, 1562.
101 *Historia et monumenta*, Nürnberg, 1558, 2 vols reissued in 1715. The latest work on Flacius is Olson, *Matthias Flacius and the Survival of Luther's Reform.*
102 *Le livre des martyrs depuis Jean Huss*, Geneva, 1554, with a Latin edition which followed thereafter in 1556.
103 Of the several available editions, I have consulted the one prepared by Stephen Reed Cattley (ed.), *The Acts and Monuments of John Foxe*, 8 vols., London, Seeley and Burnside, 1837–1841.
104 The term is Želivský's from his sermon for 19 April 1419 in Molnár (ed.), *Dochovaná kázání Jana Želivského z roku 1419*, p. 37 and see also Fudge, 'The Night of Antichrist: Popular Culture, Judgment and Revolution in Fifteenth-Century Bohemia', *CV*, 37, (No.1, 1995), pp. 33–45.
105 From a Hebrew source whose date is quite uncertain but likely from the period between 1449 and 1470. It was published in G.J. Polak (ed.), *Oostersche Wandelingen*, Amsterdam, Proops, 1846, pp. 79–86. I cite the translated excerpt in Gladstein, 'Eschatological Trends in Bohemian Jewry during the Hussite Period', p. 254.
106 Prague, NMK MS V E 89, fol. 253ᵛ.
107 Noted in Zikmund Winter, *Život církevní v Čechách: Kulturně-historický obraz z XV. a XVI. století*, 2 vols., Prague, Česká akademie pro vědy, slovesnost a umění, 1895–1896, vol. 1, p. 26.
108 James R. Palmitessa, 'Overlapping and Intersecting Communication Networks in Prague at the Time of the Passau Invasion of 1611', in Milena Bartlová and Michel Šronek (eds.), *Public Communication in European Reformation: Artistic and Other Media in Central Europe 1380–1620*, Prague, Artefactum, 2007, p. 273.
109 Zdeněk V. David, 'Utraquists, Lutherans, and the Bohemian Confession of 1575', *CV*, 68, (No. 2, 1999), p. 329.
110 For example see Luther's comment in WA, vol. 44, p. 744.
111 On these events see David, *Finding the Middle Way*, especially chapters 9–12.
112 A.H. Wratislaw, *The Native Literature of Bohemia in the Fourteenth Century*, London, Bell, 1878, p. 3.
113 David, 'The White Mountain, 1620: An Annihilation or Apotheosis of Utraquism"?, *CV*, 45, (No. 1, 2003), p. 40.
114 Arnošt Klíma, *Český v období temna*, Prague, Naše vojsko, 1958, p. 160 and the Church of St. Giles in the Old Town of Prague is one such example in the fresco visible above the crossing.

115 Václav Brosius, *Vejstrahu všem věrným Čechům i jiným pravého náboženství milovníkům, aby mohli znáti jakej jest rozdíl mezi učením Mistra Jana Husi a učením bratří boleslavských*, Litomyšl, 1589.
116 Noted in Bohuslav Balbín, *Epitome historica rerum bohemicarum*, Prague, Hampel, 1677, p. 414.
117 The only survey I am aware of has been prepared by Holeton in his 'The Celebration of Jan Hus', pp. 45–51 and I follow his summary.
118 Novotný, *Correspondence*, pp. 270–273 and 317–320.
119 *Výklad víry*, in *Opera omnia*, vol. 1, p. 69.
120 Holeton, 'The Celebration of Jan Hus', p. 48.
121 Holeton, 'The Celebration of Jan Hus', pp. 50–51.
122 Laura Ronchi de Michelis, 'Hus et le mouvement hussite de la condamnation de l'hérésie à sa réévaluation slave au milieu du XIXe siècle', *Cahiers du Monde russe et soviétique*, 29, (Nos. 3–4, 1988), pp. 323–336.
123 Luther, Commentary on Isaiah 9:7 in WA, vol. 25, p. 124 (7–8).

Chapter Ten

1 *CCL*, vol. 140, pp. 209, 768, 873–876.
2 See for example Lawrence G. Duggan, 'Was Art really the "Book of the Illiterate"', *Word & Image*, 5, (No. 3, 1989), pp. 227–251.
3 For example, see Blanche B. Boyer and Richard McKeon (eds.), *Peter Abailard, Sic et Non: A Critical Edition*, Chicago, University of Chicago Press, 1976, p. 209; Wyclif, *Latin Works*, vol. 2 (1888), pp. 125–126 and vol. 22 (1922), pp. 154–160, while the others are referenced in Duggan, pp. 227–234.
4 There are a number of surviving stove tiles from the Hussite era. A number of these have been reproduced in Jiří Kejř, *The Hussite Revolution*, trans., Till Gottheinerová, Prague, Orbis, 1988, pp. 18, 28, 74, 78, 98, 102.
5 *Super IV Sententiarum*, pp. 414–423.
6 Quoted in Stephen Ruby (ed.), *Roman Jakobson Selected Writings*, Berlin, Mouton, 1985, vol. 6, p. 724.
7 *Super IV Sententiarum*, pp. 421–422. For Hus' views of art see Constanze Itzel, 'Peinture et hérérodoxie: La peinture flamande à la lumière du débat sur les images', in Ludovic Nys and Dominique Vanwijnsberghe (eds.), *Campin in Context: Peinture et société dans la vallée de l'Escaut à l'époque de Robert Campin*, Valenciennes-Brussels-Tournai, Presses universitaires de Valenciennes, 2007, pp. 139–154. The same subject with wider useful application may be found in her earlier doctoral work. 'Der Stein trügt: die Imitation von Skulpturen in der niederländischen Tafelmalerei im Kontext bildtheoretischer Auseinandersetzungen des frühen 15. Jahrhunderts', PhD dissertation, University of Heidelberg, 2004.
8 *De ecclesia*, pp. 216–217.
9 I cite from the recent edition, Jaroslav Boubín (ed.), *Jan z Příbramě: Život kněží Táborských*, Příbram, Státní okresní archiv Příbram a Okresní muzeum Příbram, 2000, p. 50.
10 Jan Royt, 'The Hussite Revolution and Sacred Art', in Barbara Drake Boehm and Jiří Fajt (eds.), *Prague: The Crown of Bohemia, 1347–1437*, New Haven, Yale University Press, 2005, p. 117.

11 Zikmund Winter, *Zlatá doba měst českých*, Prague, J. Otto, 1913, pp. 145–150.
12 Suggested by Milena Bartlová, 'The Utraquist Church and the Visual Arts Before Luther', BRRP, vol. 4, p. 219.
13 Bartlová, 'The Utraquist Church and the Visual Arts Before Luther', p. 219.
14 *Relatio*, in FRB, vol. 8, pp. 119–120. I quote the translation from Spinka, *John Hus at the Council of Constance*, pp. 233–234. Richental says only that all of the ashes were thrown into the river. *Chronik des Constanzer Concils*, in Loomis, p. 134.
15 *Passio*, in FRB, vol. 8, p. 147.
16 *Historia bohemica*, p. 101.
17 Quoted in Royt, 'The Hussite Revolution and Sacred Art', p. 119.
18 Roland H. Bainton, 'Dürer and Luther as the Man of Sorrows', *The Art Bulletin*, 29, (No. 4, 1947), pp. 269–272.
19 Jena Codex, Prague, NMK MS IV B 24, fol. 5^v. Fudge, *The Magnificent Ride*, plate 4.7, p. 248. The Jena Codex dates from the end of the fifteenth century.
20 Fudge, 'Picturing the Death and Life of Jan Hus in the Iconography of Early Modern Europe', *Kosmas: Czechoslovak and Central European Journal*, 23, (No. 1, 2009), pp. 1–18.
21 See Hartmann Schedel, *Weltchronik*, Nurnberg, Koberger, 1493, fols. 240^v and 241^r which present views of Constance and the lake. Verso woodcuts include the Council, Rokycana, Jean Gerson, Hus, and others.
22 Jena Codex, Prague, NMK MS IV B 24, fol. 37^v.
23 Graham, pp. 561–568 for description.
24 Smíškovsky Gradual, Vienna, ÖNB suppl. mus. sam. MS 15492, fol. 285^r.
25 FRB, vol. 5, p. 355. Priestly remains were discovered in 1492. SRB, vol. 3, p. 249.
26 Smiškovský Gradual, Vienna, ÖNB suppl. mus. sam. MS 15492 fols. 285^r and 236^v.
27 Litoměřice Gradual, Lovosice, Regional State Archives of Litoměřice, MS IV C 1, fol. 244^r.
28 The book is *Mistra Jana Husi . . . Výkladové*. Zuzana Všetečková, 'The Man of Sorrows and Christ Blessing the Chalice: The Pre-Reformation and the Utraquist Viewpoints', BRRP, vol. 4, p. 200.
29 For helpful comment see Bartlová, 'Conflict, Tolerance, Representation, and Competition: A Confessional Profile of Bohemian Late Gothic Art', in BRRP, vol. 5, pt. 2, p. 258, Bílková, 'Depiction of the Last Supper under Utraquism', in BRRP, vol. 5, pt. 2, p. 296 and Royt, 'Utrakvistická ikonographie v Čechách 15. a první poloviny 16. století', in Dalibor Prix (ed.), *Pro Arte: Sborník k poctě Ivo Hlobila*, Prague, Artefactum, 2002, pp. 198–199.
30 Bílková, p. 87.
31 The predella is now in the Regional Museum in Chrudim, Czech Republic.
32 Bethlehem, Moravian Archives, Bd 3. The illustration is from the Ivančický Kancional (belonging to the Jednota Bratrska) dated to 1576.
33 The only reproduction of this broadsheet I am aware of appears in M.A. Kleeberg and Gerhard Lemme, *In the Footsteps of Martin Luther*, trans., Erich Hopka, St. Louis, Concordia, 1966, p. 127.

34 The kancional was prepared by Jan Roh, *Písně chval božských*, Prague, Pavel Severin, 1541. The book consists of 482 hymns on 638 pages. A sole copy survives having been discovered in 1927.
35 Wickiana Collection, in Zürich, Zentralbibliothek PAS II 13/20. The broadsheet originated in Augsburg around 1550. I am very grateful to the late Bob Scribner for bringing the print to my attention.
36 'Glosse auf das vermeinte kaiserliche Edikt', 1531, in WA, vol. 30/3, p. 387.
37 Hauffen, 'Husz eine Gans - Luther ein Schwan', pp. 1–28.
38 The depiction is from Gotha, City Museum, Schloßmuseum, inv. no. 38.8. I rely on Royt, p. 414.
39 Gotha, City Museum, Schloßmuseum, inv. no. 38.6.
40 *Tragedia Johannis Huss*, pp. Aiiiv and Fvv.
41 Hauffen, 'Husz eine Gans - Luther ein Schwan', pp. 12–18.
42 See his 'Short History of the Slavic Church', in *Vybrané spisy Jana Amose Komenského*, Prague, SPN, 1972, vol. 6, p. 341.
43 Coburg, Kunstsammlungen der Landesstiftung, Inv.-Nr. XIII, 402. There are several extant copies in archives in Nürnberg, Ulm, Wittenberg and Berlin. I have used the one in Berlin, Staatsbibliothek, Handschriftenabteilung, YA 91a. A fuller accounting of the event is Hans Volz, 'Der Traum Kurfürst Friedrichs des Weisen vom 30./31. Oktober 1517: Eine bibliographisch-ikonographische Untersuchung', *Gutenberg Jahrbuch*, 45, (1970), pp. 174–211.
44 Published in Heiko A. Oberman, *Luther: Man Between God and the Devil*, trans., Eileen Walliser-Schwarzbart, New York, Image Books, 1992, p. 56.
45 Utrecht, Museum Catharijneconvent, inv. no. RMCC s00057.
46 One example would be the Flemish painter Otto van Veen's 'Triumph of the Catholic Faith', c. 1612, Oberschleißheim, Schleissheim Palace Gallery.
47 The original has the title *Vejstrahu všem věrným Čechům i jiným pravého náboženství milovníkům, aby mohli znáti jakej jest rozdíl mezi učením Mistra Jana Husi a učením bratří boleslavských*, Litomyšl, 1589. A copy survives in the NK in Prague. The translation comes from Michal Šroněk, 'Visual Culture and the Unity of Brethren', in Bartlová and Šroněk (eds.), *Public Communication in European Reformation*, p. 360.
48 Brosius, *Vejstrahu všem věrným Čechům*, pp. 19–20 and reproduced in Šroněk, p. 361.
49 Oxford, Bodleian Library, Sutherland Collection, 169, fol. 6.
50 The broadsheet is discussed in Fudge, 'Žižka's Drum: The Political Uses of Popular Religion', pp. 564–567. It has been completely reproduced in Jana Hubková, 'Events in Bohemia as Pictured in Protestant Illustrated Single- and Multiple-Sheet Broadsheets from 1618–1620', in *Public Communication in European Reformation*, p. 254.
51 For an introduction to the idea of the resurrected Hus see Hubková, 'Events in Bohemia as Pictured in Protestant Illustrated Single- and Multiple-Sheet Broadsheets from 1618–1620', pp. 250–253.
52 The depiction is part of Jann van Aaveele, *Popish Ploys 1414–1678* (1969), London, British Museum, Department of Prints and Drawings, Satires 1075.

53 I have noted copies of this in Berlin, Staatsbibliothek, Handschriftenabteilung, YA 408, and Tábor, Hussite Museum, sig. H 545.
54 Master MS (unidentified), Berlin, Staatliche Museen Preussischer Kulturbesitz, Kupferstichkabinett 37–1889, reproduced in Strauss, vol. 3, p. 1291.
55 Seib (ed.), *Luther mit dem Schwan*, p. 62.
56 Mid sixteenth century, original wood block, Berlin, Derschau Collection, reproduced in Strauss, vol. 3, p. 1393.
57 The oil on panel work was commissioned by Prince Johann Ernst as a memorial to the Augsburg Confession. The artist is unknown. Luther had been a choirboy at St. George's and J.S. Bach was baptized there in 1685.
58 Malostanská Gradual, Prague, NK MS XVII A 3, fol. 363^r.
59 Berlin, Staatsbibliothek, Preussischer Kulturbesitz, Handschriftenabteilung, YA 872, reproduced in Fudge, *The Magnificent Ride*, plate 3.3, p. 133.
60 Title page of Samuel Martin Horzov, *Hussus et Lutherus, id est: Collatio Historica duorum fortissimorum Jesu Christi militum*, Prague, Sessii, 1618.
61 These words are in the preface to an edition of Hus' Czech works featuring his Postil published at Nürnberg, Montanus and Neuberus, 1563.
62 The woodcut, appropriately, accompanied Luther's attack on the Jesuits, *Anatomia Lutheri*, Wittenberg, *c.* 1568. It is at Coburg, Kunstsammlungen der Veste Coburg, XIII.40.1. Reproduced in Strauss, vol. 3, p. 1316.
63 This a woodcut scene which features the words 'preserve us Lord with your word'. Berlin, Staatsbibliothek, Handschriftenabteilung, YA 283.
64 Anonymous copper engraving, after 1640, Amsterdam, Rijksmuseum RP-P-OB-78.421, perhaps associated with Jan Houwens. The other version belongs to the collection at the Museum Catharijneconvent in Utrecht.
65 Šmahel, 'The War of Symbols: The Goose and the Chalice against the Cross', in BRRP, vol. 4, p. 151.
66 *De sanguine Christi sub specie vini*, Basel, University Library MS A X 66 fol. 347^r with helpful comment in Šmahel, 'The War of Symbols: The Goose and the Chalice against the Cross', pp. 151–152.
67 Wickiana Collection, Zürich, Zentralbibliothek, PAS II 13/24. The woodcut is the work of Johann Philipp Steudner. Nürnberg, Germanisches Nationalmuseum, HB. 60 and HB. 24592. Reproduced in Dorothy Alexander, *The German Single-Leaf Woodcut 1600–1700*, New York, Abaris, 1977, vol. 2, pp. 617–618.
68 Tábor, Regional Archives, MS 195, reproduced in Fudge, *The Magnificent Ride*, plate 3.6, p. 147.
69 Paris, Louvre, Rothchild Collection. I rely upon Šmahel, 'The War of Symbols: The Goose and the Chalice against the Cross', pp. 156–157.
70 Prague, NMK MS II D fol. 1^v, from 1466. Karel Stejskal and Petr Voit, *Iluminované rukopisy doby husitské*, Prague, Národní knihovna, 1990, p. 61 and Šmahel, 'The War of Symbols: The Goose and the Chalice against the Cross', p. 152.
71 This image is from the Psalter of Hanuš of Kolovrat (1438), Prague, NK MS osek 71, fol. 14^v. Reproduced in Stejskal, *Iluminované rukopisy doby husitské*, p. 152.

72 Vienna, ÖNB MS 13.975. I studied this source in the early 1990s but for a summary description see Šmahel, 'The War of Symbols: The Goose and the Chalice against the Cross', pp. 157–158.
73 See Šmahel, 'The War of Symbols: The Goose and the Chalice against the Cross', p. 156 for comment.
74 Vienna, ÖNB MS 13.975, fols. 155^r, 275^r, 298^r and 343^r.
75 Johannes Hartlieb, *Liber de arte bellica germanicus*, Vienna, ÖNB MS 3062, fols. 147^v–148^r. I am aware of the lack of specific basis for the Hartlieb attribution. Reproduced in Fudge, *The Magnificent Ride*, plate 3.1, p. 127.
76 Vienna, ÖNB MS 13.975, fol. 312^v.
77 *Processus consistorialis Martyrii Iohannis Hus*, Tábor, Regional Archives, sig. A-1809.
78 *Processus consistorialis Martyrii Iohannis Hus*, pp. 4, 30, 16, 18 and 23. The last picture appears in Fudge, *The Magnificent Ride*, plate 3.2, p. 130. All of the illustrations have been published in Šmahel, vol. 4, pp. 409–416.
79 The extant copies include Prague, NK MSS XVI A 17 and VII A 18 (the latter formerly in St. Petersburg), (Aulendorf), New York Public Library, Spencer Collection MS 32, Constance, Rosgartenmuseum, Inv. Hs.1, Vienna, ÖNB MS 3044, Karlsruhe, Badische Landesbibliothek, Codex St. Georgen 63 (Cod. Pap. Germ. LXIII), and Codex E.M. 11. There were also MSS formerly at Stuttgart, Württembergische Landesbibliothek, and St. Gall, Stifsbibliothek.
80 *Das Concilium geschehen zu Konstanz*, Augsburg, Anton Sorg, 1483, *Das Concilium: So zů Constanz gehalten ist worden*, Augsburg, Heinrich Steiner, 1536, and *Costnitzer Concilium*, Frankfurt, Paul Reffler, 1575.
81 Richental MS (Aulendorf), New York Public Library, Spencer Collection MS 32.
82 *Chronik des Constanzer Concils*, in Loomis, p. 133 and *Relatio*, in FRB, vol. 8, p. 117.
83 See the short but instructive study by Milena Kubíková, 'The Heretic's Cap of Hus', in BRRP, vol. 4, pp. 143–150.
84 Kubíková, 'The Heretic's Cap of Hus', p. 149.
85 Richental MS (Aulendorf), New York Public Library, Spencer Collection MS 32, pp. 135–139.
86 Richental, *Concilium zu Constanz*, Augsburg, Anton Sorg, 1483, fol. 33^v as well as the St. Petersburg Richental MS in Prague, NK MS VII A 18, fol. 12^r.
87 Richental MS, Prague, NK MS XVI A 17, fol. 122^v.
88 Richental MS (Aulendorf), New York Public Library, Spencer Collection MS 32, p, 135.
89 Richental, Prague, NK MS XVI A 17, fol. 123^r.
90 Martinická Bible, Prague, Library of the Academy of Sciences of the Czech Republic MS no sig, fol. 11^v. A lovely reproduction may be seen in Boehm and Fajt, *Prague, The Crown of Bohemia*, p. 296.
91 Kubíková, 'The Heretic's Cap of Hus', p. 148.
92 Sobotka Gradual, Jičín, Regional State Archives MS book 9, inv. no. 20, olim Sobotka 3, fol. 193^v, *c.* 1509–37.
93 For example, a Czech gradual, Prague, NK MS XVII B 21, fol. 441^r. Hus is at the stake wearing a miter featuring three demons.

94 Jena Codex, Prague, NMK MS IV B 24, fol. 38ʳ.
95 Smiškovský Gradual, Vienna, ÖNB suppl. mus. sam. MS 15492 fol. 400ʳ.
96 Richental manuscript, Vienna, ÖNB MS 3044, fol. 81ᵛ.
97 Examples include the important Litoměřice Gradual, Lovosice, Regional State Archives of Litoměřice, MS IV C 1, fol. 43ʳ and the Malostranská Gradual, Prague, NK MS XVII A 3 fol. 363ʳ.
98 Prague, NK MS XI B 1a, fol. 362ᵛ. Earlier variations can be found in the Jena Codex, Prague, NMK MS IV B 24, fols. 41ʳ and 48ʳ.
99 Richental MSS (St. Petersburg) in Prague, NK MS VII A 18, fol. 12v and (Aulendorf) New York Public Library, Spencer Collection MS 032, pp. 138–139.
100 For the former depiction see the picture by Master M.S. (unidentified) accompanying an early edition of Hus' *Postil* at Nürnberg in 1563, in Strauss, vol. 3, p. 1289. For the latter portrayal see especially Richental MS (Aulendorf), New York Public Library, Spencer Collection MS 32, p. 138.
101 Examples include the Litoměřice Gradual, Lovosice, Regional State Archives of Litoměřice, MS IV C 1, fol. 244ᵛ and the Kaňkovský gradual, Prague, NMK MS 1A c 109, fol. 2ᵛ.
102 Richental MS in Prague, NK MS XVI A 17, fol. 123ᵛ.
103 Richental MS in Constance, Rosgartenmuseum, Inv. Hs. 1, fol. 58ʳ.
104 For example the hymn book made for the parish of St. Michael's in the Old Town in 1587, 'Písně chval božských', Prague, NMK MS I A 15, fol. 305ᵛ.
105 *Passio Johannis Hus secundum Johannen Barbatum*, in FRB, vol. 8, p. 22. In some medieval sources, the passion of Laurence is considered exceptional among the passions of other martyrs and Laurence and Stephen occupy the front rank in terms of Christian martyrs. This is reflected in the 'Golden Legend' and therefore the iconographical association of Hus with these martyrs is noteworthy.
106 Now in the City Museum of Ústí-nad-Labem, See Bartlová, 'The Utraquist Church and the Visual Arts Before Luther', BRRP, vol. 4, p. 222 for comment. Royt, p. 408 places the date closer to 1470.
107 Diebold Schilling, *Berner Chronik*, Berne, Burgerbibliothek MS h.h.I1, p. 367.
108 Diebold Schilling the Elder, *Spiezer Bilderchronik* (1485), Berne, Burgerbibliothek MS Hist. Helv. 1.16, now the Zentralbibliothek.
109 Foxe, *The Acts and Monuments*, London, 1583, p. 624.
110 Royt, p. 417.
111 *Processus consistorialis Martyrii Iohannis Hus*, p. 23 and Wickiana Collection, in Zürich, Zentralbibliothek PAS II 13/20.
112 Litoměřice Gradual, Lovosice, Regional State Archives of Litoměřice, MS IV C 1, fol. 244ᵛ.
113 Kaňkovský gradual, Prague, NMK MS 1A c 109, fol. 2ᵛ.
114 Bílková, p. 81.
115 Malostranská Gradual, Prague, NK MS XVII A 3, fol. 363ʳ.
116 Žlutice Gradual, Prague, NMK MS TR 1 27, fol. 249ᵛ from the period 1558–1565.

117 Arte della Lana altarpiece, *c.* 1423, Melbourne, National Gallery of Victoria, E2-1976. What appears to be headgear on the heretic is part of a shield in the background.
118 On Siena see Brandmüller, *Das Konzil von Pavia-Siena 1423-1424*, 2nd edition, 2002.
119 To my knowledge, this image first appeared on the title page of Johann Heinrich Löder, *Protestatio Bohemorum*, Leipzig, Johann Ludwig Gleditsch, 1705.
120 Copies of a centenary coin can be found in Tábor, Hussite Museum, N-Me 6362 and in Washington, National Gallery of Art, Samuel H. Kress Collection. There is an excellent reproduction in Royt, p. 448 and there are thirteen exemplars in Kamil Krofta (ed.), *Mistr Jan Hus v životě a památkách českého lidu*, Prague, Žaluda, 1915, plates 74–86.
121 Both sides of the 1617 coin are shown in Seib (ed.), *Luther mit dem Schwan*, p. 63. The 2001 commemorative ordination medallion was designed and executed by Scott R. Blazek in Vancouver, Canada. It is .999 percent silver and weighs about 4.5 ounces. Only thirty five were made. The author owns number eleven in the series. One side features a profile image of Hus and Martin Luther, with the former occupying the pride of place. The obverse uses a Reformation motif and depicts Hus and Luther kneeling before the cross. Hus holds an open book while Luther has a chalice. Inscriptions draw attention to those areas of common emphases, namely the gospel, authority of scripture, utraquism, and proclamation in the common language. The goose and swan motif likewise appears. Blazek's medallion marks the seventh century of such numismatic creations featuring Jan Hus.
122 Representative bells and stove tile images may be found in Royt, pp. 446–447.
123 Master I.H. (unidentified), Regensburg, Staatliche Bibliothek, 2° Theol. syst.8. On the topic at large see Bohumil Nuska, 'Husova ikonografie ve výzdobě českých knižních vazeb 15. a 16. století', *Sborník národního Muzea v Praze*, series C, 37, (Nos. 3–4, 1992), pp. 1–38.

Chapter Eleven

1 Jiří Kotyk, *Spor o revizi Husova procesu*, Prague, Vyšehrad, 2001, pp. 87–88.
2 British prime minister Neville Chamberlain, radio broadcast, 27 September 1938 and reported in *The Times*, 28 September 1938, p. 10.
3 The same point has been made for the seventeenth century but the observation is perhaps even more important for Jan Hus. See Howard Louthan, *Converting Bohemia: Force and Persuasion in the Catholic Reformation*, Cambridge, Cambridge University Press, 2009, p. 5.
4 *Historia et Monumenta*, Nürnberg, Montanus and Neuberus, 1558, 2 vols., released again at Nürnberg, Gerlachin, 1583 followed by a third edition, again at Nürnberg in 1715. Titles of the editions vary.
5 Noted in Olson, *Matthias Flacius and the Survival of Luther's Reform*, p. 266.
6 Karel J. Erben (ed.), *Mistra Jana Husi: Sebrané spisy české*, 3 vols., Prague, Tempský, 1865–1868.
7 The Latin works were published first as Václav Flajšhans (ed.), *Opera omnia*, Prague, Vilímek, 1903–1907, 3 vols. followed by the Czech as *Mistra Jana Husi Sebrané Spisy*, Prague, Vilímek, 1904–1908, 3 vols.

8   *Opera omnia*, Prague, ČSAV, 1959–. See the overview essay by Anežka Vidmanová, 'Základní vydání spisů Jana Husa', *HT*, supplement 1, (2001), pp. 267–276.
9   Hardt, 7 vols and Mansi (ed.), vols 27–28.
10   FRB, vol. 8.
11   Pez, vol. 4, pt. 2, cols. 151–706.
12   Novotný, *Correspondence*.
13   Mackenzie, trans., *Letters of John Huss*, 1846, Workman and Pope (eds.), *The Letters of John Hus*, 1904 and Spinka (ed.), *The Letters of John Hus*, 1972. The latter is based mainly on the Novotný edition (Novotný, *Correspondence*).
14   David S. Schaff, trans., *The Church by John Huss*, New York, Charles Scribner's Sons, 1915 and later 'On Simony', in Matthew Spinka (ed.), *Advocates of Reform*, Philadelphia, The Westminster Press, 1953, pp. 196–278. The latter version prepared by Spinka is accurate but is not a complete edition/translation.
15   For example, the revisionist work of Kopičková and Vidmanová, *Listy na Husovu obrana z let 1410–1412*.
16   FRB, vol. 8, pp. 23–120. There is an excellent English translation. Spinka, *John Hus at the Council of Constance*, pp. 89–234.
17   Comments made by Novotný in the critical edition in FRB, vol. 8, p. lvi.
18   *Chronicon Universitatis Pragensis*, in FRB, vol. 5, p. 579.
19   Vavřinec of Březová, *Historia Hussitica*, in FRB, vol. 5, p. 344. The editor Jaroslav Goll seems to be the one to have attached the title 'Hussite Chronicle' to Vavřinec.
20   I would expect to publish my paper 'The Medieval "Lives" of Jan Hus in History and Hagiography' delivered at the ninth 'Bohemian Reformation and Religious Practice' conference in Prague, June 2010 in the near future.
21   *Contra heresim Hussitarum*, Basel, Universitätsbibliothek MS E I 9, fols. 386^r–453^v but especially fols. 408^r–410^v.
22   I have used the recent edition prepared by Dana Martínková, et al., *Aeneae Silvii Historia Bohemica*, Prague, Koniash Latin Press, 1998.
23   *Historia bohemica*, p. 98.
24   *Historia bohemica*, p. 4.
25   *Historia bohemica*, pp. 88–100.
26   *In minoribus*, 1463, the text can be found conveniently in Thomas M. Izbicki, Gerald Christianson and Philip Krey (eds.), *Reject Aeneas, Accept Pius: Selected Letters of Aeneas Sylvius Piccolomini (Pope Pius II)*, Washington, Catholic University of America Press, 2006, p. 394.
27   This is most apparent in his 21 August 1451 letter to Cardinal Juan Carvajal in Rudolf Wolkan (ed.), *Briefwechsel des Eneas Silvius Piccolomini*, in *FRA*, vol. 67, Vienna, Hölder, 1912, pp. 22–57.
28   Letter to Cardinal Juan Carvajal, p. 56.
29   Commented on in Thomas A. Fudge, 'Seduced by the Theologians: Aeneas Sylvius and the Hussite Heretics', in Ian Hunter, John Christian Laursen and Cary J. Nederman (eds.), *Heresy in Transition: Transforming Ideas of Heresy in Medieval and Early Modern Europe*, Aldershot, Ashgate, 2005, pp. 89–101.

30 *Česká kronika*, Prague, Jan Severýn, 1541.
31 *Česká kronika*, pp. 361–372.
32 *Česká kronika*, p. 383.
33 *Historia regni bohemiae*, Prostějov, 1552, several editions thereafter including Frankfurt, Andreas, 1687.
34 Cochlaeus, *Historia Hussitarum libri duodecim*, pp. 90–104, and 441.
35 *Commentaria de Actis et Scriptis Martini Lutheri*, (Mainz, Behem, 1549), *passim*.
36 Jean Crespin, *Le livre des martyrs depuis Jean Hus et Jerome*, Geneva, 1554 with numerous editions and translations thereafter.
37 Zacharias Theobald, *Hussitenkrieg*, Wittenberg, Lorenz Seuberich, 1609. The first edition dealt with the period between 1401 and 1436.
38 Bohuslav Balbín, *Epitome historica rerum bohemicarum*, Prague, Hampel, 1677.
39 *Dissertacio apoletica pro lingua slavonica, praecipue bohemica*. The published edition had an even more cumbersome title. F.M. Pelcl (ed.), *De regni Bohemiae felici quondam, nunc calamitoso statu ac praecipue de Bohemicae seu Slavicae linguae in Bohemia authoritate deque ejes abolendae noxiis consillis alisque rebus huc spectantibus brevis sed accurata tractatio*, Prague, Felician Mangold, 1775.
40 *Miscellanea historica regni bohemiae*, 7 vols., Prague, Georgii Czernoch, 1679–1688.
41 *Miscellanea historica regni bohemiae*, vol. 3, pp. 255–262.
42 Jacques Lenfant, *Histoire du Concile de Constance*, 2 vols, Amsterdam, Pierre Humbert, 1727. An English edition appeared shortly thereafter as *The History of the Council of Constance*, 2 vols., London, Bettesworth, Rivington, 1730. I have used the latter.
43 Lenfant, *The History of the Council of Constance*, vol. 1, p. 24 and vol. 2, p. 58.
44 Lenfant, *The History of the Council of Constance*, vol. 1, pp. 431ff.
45 F.M. Pelcl, *Geschichte der Böhmen*, 2 vols., Prague, Comptoirs, 1817. This history was originally published in 1774, expanded in 1779 with a third edition appearing in 1782. I use the fourth edition.
46 Pelcl, *Geschichte der Böhmen*, vol. 1, pp. 286–311.
47 Pelcl, *Lebensgeschichte des Römischen und Böhmischen Königs Wenceslaus . . . nebst einem Urkundenbuche*, 2 vols., Prague, Česko, 1788–1790. For a survey of Hussite historiography from the nineteenth century on see Šmahel, *HR*, vol. 1, pp. 1–84.
48 František Palacký, *Zur böhmischen Geschichtsschreibung: Aktenmässige Aufschlüsse und Worte der Abwehr*, Prague, Tempský, 1871, pp. 92–93.
49 On this see Martin Schulze Wessel, 'Die Konfessionalisierung der tschechischen Nation', in Heinz Gerhard Haupt and Dieter Langewiesche (eds.), *Nation und Religion in Europa: Mehrkonfessionelle Gesellschaften im 19. und 20. Jahrhundert*, Frankfurt, Campus Verlag, 2004, pp. 135–150.
50 Palacký, *Dějiny narodu českého v Čechách a v Moravě*, Prague, Bursik & Kohout, 1893, vol. 3, pp. 1–120.
51 Especially Palacký, *Würdigung der Alten böhmischen Geschichtsschreiber*, Prague, Borrosch, 1830, pp. 273–292.
52 Palacký, *Die Geschichte des Hussitenthums und Professor Constantin Höfler*, Prague, Tempský, 1868, p. 160.

53 Thomas A. Fudge, 'The State of Hussite Historiography', *Mediaevistik: Internationale Zeitschrift für interdisziplinäre Mittelalterforschung* 7, (1994), pp. 96–98.
54 Palacký, *Die Geschichte des Hussitenthums und Professor Constantin Höfler*, p. 66.
55 *Documenta*
56 Joseph Frederick Zacek, *Palacký: The Historian as Scholar and Nationalist*, The Hague, Mouton, 1970.
57 At least according to Palacký in his *Die Geschichte des Hussitenthums*, p. 68.
58 Höfler, *Magister Johannes Hus und der Abzug der deutschen Professoren und Studenten aus Prag, 1409*, Prague, Tempský, 1864, p. 224.
59 Höfler, vol. 3, p. 27. For an overview, see the excellent article by Peter Morée, 'Jan Hus as a Threat to the German Future in Central Europe: The Bohemian Reformer in the Controversy Between Constantin Höfler and František Palacký', in BRRP, vol. 4, pp. 295–307.
60 The work undertaken by Gerhard Graf, 'Albert Hauck über Jan Hus: Zur Selbskritik der Reformationshistoriographie', *Zeitschrift für Kirchengeschichte*, 83, (1972), pp. 34–51 shows the church historian Hauck to have imbibed fully the flawed Höfler-Loserth thesis.
61 There are two editions. Gotthard Viktor Lechler, *Johannes Hus: Ein Lebensbild aus der Vorgeschichte der Reformation*, Halle, Niemeyer, 1889. Czech edition *Jan Hus*, Pardubice, Hoblík, 1910, pp. 77–78.
62 Kotyk, *Spor o revizi Husova procesu*.
63 Michael Borovička, 'Mistr Jan Hus na českém zemském sněmu v roce 1889', *Husitský tábor*, 9, (1986–7), pp. 249–269.
64 Fudge, 'The State of Hussite Historiography', pp. 98–9.
65 Kotyk, *Spor o revizi Husova procesu*, pp. 23–90 nominates Kalousek, Flajšhans, Kybal and Pekař as representative.
66 Kalousek, *O potřebě prohloubiti vědomosti o Husovi a jeho době*, 2 vols, Prague, Nákladem a tiskem Českoslovanské akciové tiskárny, 1915, vol. 2, p. 12.
67 Flajšhans, and the introduction to *Super IV Sententiarum*, p. iv.
68 *Sermones in Capella Bethlehem*, 6 vols.
69 Novotný/Kybal.
70 Novotný/Kybal, vol. 2, pt. 1, pp. 1–7 and *passim*.
71 See especially his *Učení M. Jana Husi*, Brno, Občanská tiskárna, 1931.
72 Sedlák, *Studie a texty k životopisu Husovu*, Olomouc, Matice Cyrilometodějská, 1914–1919, 3 vols., especially vol. 2, pp. 478–527 and his *M. Jan Hus, passim*.
73 See Pekař, *Der Sinn der tschechischen Geschichte*, trans., Sofie Pommerrenig, Munich, Verlag Pressverein Volksbote, 1961. Originally published in 1937.
74 Pekař, *Žižka a jeho doba*, 4 vols.
75 Pekař, *Jan Hus*, Prague, Bursik and Kohout, 1902, p. 20.
76 Tomáš G. Masaryk, *Jan Hus: Naše obrození a naše reformace*, Prague, Bursík and Kohout, 1923, pp. 141–159.
77 T.G. Masaryk, *The Making of a State: Memories and Observations, 1914–1918*, New York, Frederick A. Stokes, 1927, pp. 58, 82, 92, 174 and 479.
78 Pekař, *Der Sinn der tschechischen Geschichte*, pp. 57–60.

79 Among numerous works Krofta wrote three important articles on fourteen and fifteenth-century Bohemia and Jan Hus for *The Cambridge Medieval History*, C.W. Previte-Orton and Z.N. Brooke (eds.), Cambridge, At the University Press, 1932–6, vol. 7, pp. 155–182 and vol. 8, pp. 45–115.
80 Kotyk, *Spor o revizi Husova procesu*, pp. 74–76.
81 G.A. Holmes, 'Cardinal Beaufort and the Crusade against the Hussites', *English Historical Review*, 8, (1973), pp. 721–750.
82 Of particular importance are Machovec, Kalivoda, *Husitská ideologie*, Macek, *Jan Hus*, Prague, Melantrich, 1961, Macek, 'Jean Hus et son époque', *Historica*, 13, (1966), pp. 51–80 and Macek, *Jean Hus et les traditions hussites (XVe - XIXe siècles)*, Paris, Plon, 1973.
83 Machovec, pp. 175–177.
84 Macek, *Tábor v husitském revolučním hnutí*, Prague, ČSAV, 1956, vol. 1, pp. 159–168 and Kalivoda, *Husitská ideologie*, pp. 151–191.
85 Machovec, p. 123.
86 Machovec, pp. 165–175, 177 and 198.
87 Macek, *Jan Hus*, *passim*.
88 Kalivoda, *Revolution und Ideologie: Der Hussitismus*, trans., Heide Thorwart, Cologne, Böhlau Verlag, 1976, pp. 37–39.
89 Macek, *Jean Hus et les traditions hussites (XVe - XIXe siècles)*, p. 70 and *passim*.
90 Nejedlý, *Hus a naše doba*, Prague, Československý spisovatel, 1952, p. 21. See also Peter Morée, 'Not Preaching from the Pulpit, but Marching in the Streets: The Communist Use of Jan Hus', in BRRP, vol. 6, pp. 283–296.
91 Werner, p. 156.
92 For example, see Graus, *Lebendige Vergangenheit: Überlieferung im Mittelalter und in den Vorstellungen vom Mittelalter*, Vienna, Böhlau, 1975, p. 311.
93 Graus, 'Krize středověku a husitství', *Československý časopis historický*, 17, (1969), p. 522.
94 Macek, *Jean Hus et les traditions hussites (XVe - XIXe siècles)*, pp. 64–65 while an objection can be found in Werner, p. 172.
95 But see his *Čechy v době Husově 1378–1415*.
96 Bartoš, *Husitství a cizina*, pp. 48, 54 and 57.
97 Molnár, *Jan Hus: Testimone della verità*, Turin, Claudiana, 1973.
98 As pointed out by Josef Smolík, 'Die Wahrheit in der Geschichte: Zur Ekklesiologie von Jan Hus', *Evangelische Theologie*, 32, (1972), pp. 268–276.
99 De Vooght, *Hussiana*, pp. 9–25.
100 De Vooght, pp. 413–415, 506–510.
101 For example Jaroslav Kadlec, 'Johannes Hus in neuem Licht?', *Theologisch-praktische Quartalschrift*, 118, (1970), pp. 163–168.
102 De Vooght, *L'Hérésie de Jean Huss*, Louvain, Publications Universitaires de Louvain, 1975, 2 vols. This combined his 1960 collection of studies *Hussiana* with the original study of Hus of the same year.
103 Spinka, *John Hus and the Czech Reform*.
104 Spinka, *John Hus' Concept of the Church*.
105 Spinka, *John Hus*.

106 Two newer studies of Emperor Sigismund, from a Czech perspective, seem to achieve more balance and objectivity. Václav Drška, *Zikmund Lucemburský: Liška na trůně*, Prague, Epocha, 1996 and František Kavka, *Poslední Lucemburk na Českém trůně: Králem uprostřed revoluce*, Prague, Mladá fontes, 2002.
107 Jarold K. Zeman, *The Hussite Movement: A Bibliographical Study Guide*, Ann Arbor, Michigan Slavic Publications, 1977, xxxvi, 390 pp.
108 Šmahel, vol. 2, pp. 61–80 and Šmahel *HR*, vol. 1, pp. 577–604.
109 Šmahel, 'The *Acta* of the Constance Trial of Master Jerome of Prague', in Helen Barr and Ann M. Hutchison (eds.), *Text and Controversy from Wyclif to Bale: Essays in Honour of Anne Hudson*, Turnhout, Brepols, 2005, p. 324.
110 For an introduction to this important and massive work see the review of the Czech edition by Paweł Kras in *English Historical Review*, 111, (February 1996), pp. 125–128 and a review of the German edition in Fudge in *Speculum*, 79, (October 2004), pp. 1142–1144.
111 This important and ongoing database project is valuable in many respects for scholars and students. It can be accessed via the University of Constance website at http://www.uni-konstanz.de/FuF/Philo/Geschichte/Patschovsky/projeckte.html
112 Kaminsky, pp. 6 and 36.
113 Malcolm Lambert, *Medieval Heresy*, 3rd ed, pp. 306–338. Gordon Leff, *Heresy in the Later Middle Ages*, 2 vols, and his essay 'Wyclif and Hus: A Doctrinal Comparison', *Bulletin of the John Rylands Library*, 50, (1967–8), pp. 387–410.
114 Seibt, *Jan Hus: Das Konstanzer Gericht im Urteil der Geschichte*, Fürth, Flacius Verlag, 1993 and *Hussitenstudien: Personen, Ereignisse, Ideen einer frühen Revolution*, Munich, Oldenbourg, 1987 and more recently Hilsch.
115 Werner, pp. 66–98.
116 For reservations on Werner see my review in *Czechoslovak and Central European Journal*, 11, (Winter 1993), pp. 131–135.
117 The text has circulated in various languages for more than 160 years. In English it appeared under the title, *The Last Days of John Hus: A Historical Romance*, trans. W.R. Morfill, London, Religious Tract Society, 1909 claiming to have been based upon historical records. The second English text was Beda von Berchem (ed.), *Hus the Heretic by Poggius the Papist*, New York, Carl Granville, 1930. This was published more recently in 1997, 2003 and 2007 by small American presses. The Morfill version was translated from the Czech edition of 1902 and the Berchem edition from a much earlier German version. There were German editions appearing in 1846, 1873, 1883 and 1892. Czech translations were published in 1868, 1875, 1890, 1900 and 1902, all under various titles. Regrettably, the work was cited by Joseph Held in his article on Hus in Hans Brisch and Ivan Volgyes (eds.), *Czechoslovakia: The Heritage of Ages Past*, New York, Columbia University Press, 1979, pp. 57–73. More recently, similar dependence can be shown for constructing an argument that Hus denied the doctrine of transubstantiation, just as Wyclif had. See Brian Moynahan, *The Faith: A History of Christianity*, New York, Doubleday, 2002, p. 313. All of Moynahan's arguments and conclusions on this matter are fatuous because he has relied upon this fraudulent source.

118 Benito Mussolini, *Giovanni Hus: Il Veridico*, Rome, Podrecca e Galantara, 1913. Two English versions appeared in 1929 and 1939. For commentary and context see Pavel Helan, 'Mussolini Looks at Jan Hus and the Bohemian Reformation', in BRRP, vol. 4, pp. 309–316.
119 Miloslav Ransdorf, *Mistr Jan Hus*, Prague, Universe, 1993.
120 Marin's range and depth is preferred to Comi's, *Verità e Anticristo: L'eresia de Jan Hus*.
121 Crews, 'The Theology of John Hus with Special Reference to his Concepts of Salvation', PhD dissertation, University of Manchester, 1975 and Atwood, *The Theology of the Czech Brethren from Hus to Comenius*, University Park, Pennsylvania State University Press, 2009, pp. 21–129. I am grateful to Atwood for his generosity in sharing those pre-publication chapters.
122 *Truth Prevails: The Undying Faith of Jan Hus*, an award-winning documentary film produced by Jerry Griffith, Cartesian Coordinates, 2007 with contributions from Šmahel, Holeček, Fudge and others.
123 A Czech edition appeared first (Lášek (ed.), *Jan Hus mezi epochami, národy a konfesemi*) but the more accessible and complete is the German/English (Seibt (ed.), *Jan Hus: Zwischen Zeiten, Völkern, Konfessionen*).
124 Miloš Drda, František Holeček, and Zdeněk Vybíral (eds.), *Jan Hus na přelomu tisíciletí*, Tábor, Hussite Museum, 2001 (= *HT*, supplement 1). Though advertized, Sousedík did not appear to deliver his paper in Rome.
125 *The Bohemian Reformation and Religious Practice*, David R. Holeton and Zdeněk V. David (eds.), Prague, Academy of Sciences of the Czech Republic, 1996–2009. Volume eight is currently being edited while the ninth biennial conference is scheduled to convene during June 2010.
126 Tomáš Halík, introduction to Kotyk, *Spor o revizi Husova procesu*, pp. 11–16.
127 Jiří Kejř, *Jan Hus známý a neznámý*, Prague, Karolinum, 2009.

Chapter Twelve

1 Principally, Kašpar Royko, *Geschichte der großen allgemeinem Kirchenversammlung zu Kostnitz*, 2 vols., originally published in 1780–1782. The work was translated into Czech as *Hystorye velikého sněmu kostického*, vol. 2 *Příběhy Husa*, Prague, Widtmann, 1796.
2 Roger Mols, 'Réhabilitation de Jean Hus?', *Nouvelle revue théologique*, 83, (1961), pp. 960–966.
3 De Vooght, *L'Hérésie de Jean Huss*.
4 Succinctly put in his 'Jan Hus: Heretic or Martyr?', trans. W.H. Zawadzki, *The Tablet*, 233, (1 February 1969), pp. 99–100.
5 Spinka, pp. 3–4.
6 Kaminsky, pp. 35–36, Bartoš, 'Apologie de M. Jean Huss contra son apologiste', *CV*, 8, (1965), pp. 65–74, Kadlec, 'Johannes Hus in neuem Licht?', *Theologisch-praktische Quartalschrift*, 118, (1970), pp. 163–168, Mols, 'Réhabilitation de Jean Hus?', Franz Machilek, 'Ergebnisse und Aufgaben moderner Hus-Forschung: Zu einer neuen Biographie des Johannes Hus', *Zeitschrift für Ostforschung*, 22, (1973), pp. 302–330, and

Machovec, *Bude katolické církev rehabilitovat Jana Hus?*, 2nd ed, Prague, Nakladatelství politické literatury, 1965, among others.

7   Marian Rechowicz, 'Jan Hus', *Tygodnik Powszechny*, 19, (No. 52, 1965), p. 833.
8   See Fudge, 'The State of Hussite Historiography', pp. 99–100 for a brief discussion.
9   Noted in Kotyk, *Spor o revizi Husova procesu*, p. 94.
10 Stefan Świeżawski, 'Jan Hus - A Heretic or a Saint?', trans. Alexandra Moravec, *Religion in Eastern Europe*, 14, (April 1994), p. 36.
11 Świeżawski, 'Jan Hus - heretik nebo předchůdce Druhégo vatikánského koncilu', *Tygodnik Powszechny*, 9, February 1986. The essay appeared in English later that year under the title 'John Huss - Heretic or Precursor of Vatican II?', trans., Richard T. Davies, *Religion in Communist Dominated Areas*, 25, (Fall, 1986), pp. 148–152, 166.
12 Blahoslav Hrubý, 'Time for another Aggiornamento - Rehabilitation of Jan Hus', *Religion in Communist Dominated Areas*, 25, (Fall, 1986), pp. 146–147.
13 There is a summary in Świeżawski, 'Jan Hus - A Heretic or a Saint?', p. 39.
14 Personal correspondence from Jan Milíč Lochman, 24 June 1989 and Hans Küng, 12 July 1989. There was a preliminary effort to take up Küng's suggestion. Thomas A. Fudge, 'The Church in the Shadow of Heresy: An Ecclesiological Analysis of Jan Hus' *De ecclesia* and Hans Küng's *Die Kirche*', unpublished paper, American Academy of Religion conference, Denver, Colorado, 1990.
15 The article appeared in English as Erazim Kohak, 'John Huss: Why Does it Matter?', trans., Richard T. Davies, *Religion in Communist Dominated Areas*, 28, (Spring 1989), pp. 56–58.
16 Karel Skalicky, 'Jan Hus, the Catholic Church and Ecumenism', trans., Alexandra Moravec, *Occasional Papers on Religion in Eastern Europe*, 10, (July 1990), p. 47.
17 Peter Smith, 'Mea Culpa: The Catholic Church revisits the past to right historical wrongs before the new millennium', *The Prague Post*, 8, (December 9–15, 1998), pp. B12–B13.
18 This is one of the conclusions in Fudge, *The Magnificent Ride*, pp. 2, 284.
19 See for example, Royko, *Hystorye velikého sněmu kostického*, vol. 2, Novotný/Kybal; De Vooght; Amedeo Molnár, 'Husovo místo v evropské reformaci', in *Pohyb teologického myšlení: Přehledné dějiny dogmatu*, Prague, Kalich, 1982, pp. 193–209, et al.
20 See for example *L'Osservatore Romano* [Weekly English Edition], 17: 1127 (23 April 1990), pp. 4–5; František J. Holeček, 'The Problems of the Person, the Life and the Work of Jan Hus: The Significance and the Task of a Commission of the Czech Bishops' Conference', in BRRP, vol. 2, pp. 39–40; Fudge, '"Infoelix Hus": The Rehabilitation of a Medieval Heretic', *Fides et Historia*, 30, (No. 1, 1998), p. 62 among others.
21 Cited in Jan Turnau, 'Jan Hus: An Examination of Conscience': Interview with Prof. Stefan Świeżawski, trans., Alexandra C. Moravec, *Religion in Communist Dominated Areas*, 31, (No. 4, 1992), p. 71.
22 An exception is Jiří Kejř, *Počátků*, p. 248.
23 Cardinal Vlk presided over the work of the commission but from late 1996 the deputy chairman was the Bishop of Plzeň František Radkovský and the secretary František Holeček. Members on the commission represented evangelical churches in the Czech Republic together with the Czechoslovak Hussite Church, the various theological

faculties of Charles University as well as specialists from the Historical and Philosophical branches of the Czech Academy of Sciences. Even eminent non-ecclesiastical historians such as František Šmahel, director of the Center for Medieval Studies in Prague, have been involved in the work of the commission.

24 Two editions, Lášek (ed.), *Jan Hus mezi epochami, národy a konfesemi* and Seibt (ed.), *Jan Hus: Zwischen Zeiten, Völkern, Konfessionen*.

25 According to reports in Prague newspapers. See for example, Miroslav Martínek, *Rudé právo*, 222, (22 September 1993), *Rudé právo*, 223, (23 September 1993) and *Svobodné slovo*, 224, (27 September 1993).

26 Zdeněk Kučera, in *Lidová demokracie*, 7 October 1993 and *Svobodné slovo*, 224, (27 September 1993).

27 Tomáš Halík, 'Not Just About Hus', trans., Morven McLean, *Religion, State and Society*, 21, (Nos. 3–4, 1993), pp. 311, 315.

28 Holeček, 'The Problems of the Person, the Life and the Work of Jan Hus: The Significance and the Task of a Commission of the Czech Bishops' Conference', in BRRP, vol. 2, pp. 39–47.

29 The comments were reported in the editorial 'Czech Reformer is Reassessed', *Christianity Today*, 39, (11 September 1995), p. 86.

30 Kotyk, *Spor o revizi Husova procesu*, p. 100.

31 Václav Havel, then-president of the Czech Republic, quoted in the editorial 'Vatican reconsidering views on Jan Hus', *The Christian Century*, 113, (3 April 1996), p. 368.

32 'Heretics may be made saints', *The Weekly Telegraph*, (London, no. 239), 21–27 February 1996.

33 The comment was made during a morning session devoted to 'Jan Hus in Contemporary Research' at the BRRP conference in Brno in 1996 convened under the aegis of the Czechoslovak Society of Arts and Sciences.

34 An exception is Fudge, '"Infoelix Hus": The Rehabilitation of a Medieval Heretic'.

35 In 1999 I submitted to *CV* an essay titled 'The State of the Question Concerning Jan Hus and Rehabilitation'. There was an inordinate delay in the review process. On 8 February 2000 the editor, Martin Wernisch, finally rejected the article for publication on four grounds: it was deemed lacking in historical neutrality, was insufficiently sympathetic with the church's handling of history, was too vague on the work of the commission, and finally the editor thought that publication in *CV* was inadvisable given its close proximity to the commission. Ostensibly an anonymous reviewer agreed with Wernisch. Once the Lateran Conference had concluded its deliberations there was no point in publishing the article. Nevertheless I replied to Wernisch on 13 April 2000 contesting each point.

36 Fiala's comments cited in the western media in the editorial 'Vatican reconsidering views on Jan Hus', p. 368.

37 For example see Elizabeth Weinstein, 'Jan Hus readies for a reprieve: After 500 years, religious commission closer to clearing Hus of heresy', *The Prague Post*, 9:27, (7–13 July 1999), pp. 1, 4.

38 The commission made this announcement on 1 July 1999 and was reported in various publications including *The Prague Post*, 9:27, (7–13 July 1999), p. 1.

39 Holeček, 'The Problems of the Person, the Life and the Work of Jan Hus: The Significance and the Task of a Commission of the Czech Bishops' Conference', p. 41.
40 Holeček was quoted to this effect in Smith, 'Mea Culpa: The Catholic Church revisits the past to right historical wrongs before the new millennium', p. B12.
41 Kejř, *Počátků*, pp. 245–61 and stated clearly on p. 247.
42 De Vooght, p. 46 incorrectly claims Hus was not revolutionary.
43 Kejř, *Počátků*, pp. 247 and 253.
44 Fudge, '"Infoelix Hus": The Rehabilitation of a Medieval Heretic', pp. 64–72 and Kejř, *Počátků*, p. 247.
45 Kejř, *Husovo odvolání od soudu papežova k soudu kristovu*.
46 Thomas A. Fudge, letter to Pope John Paul II, 24 August 1999, acknowledged by the papal office on 19 November 1999.
47 Holeton, 'The Celebration of Jan Hus', p. 59.
48 De Vooght, p. 95.
49 Kejř, *Počátků*, p. 246.
50 Brandmüller, 'Hus vor dem Konzil', in Seibt (ed.), *Jan Hus: Zwischen Zeiten, Völkern, Konfessionen*, pp. 235–242.
51 An example is Bohdan Chudoba in *The Catholic Historical Review*, 47, (October 1961), pp. 367–8 which dismissed De Vooght's work as 'puerile and uninformed'.
52 See the arguments in De Vooght and Fudge, '"Infoelix Hus": The Rehabilitation of a Medieval Heretic', *passim*.
53 Decretum, c. 31 where it reads: 'Qui in ecclesia Christi morbidum aliquid pravumque sapiunt, si correcti, ut sanum rectumque sapiant, resistunt contumaciter, suaque pestifera et mortifera dogmata emendare nolunt, sed defensare persistunt, heretici sunt.'(Augustine)
54 According to Petr Mladoňovice's *Relatio* in FRB, vol. 8, pp. 74–75 and *passim*.
55 Weinstein, 'Jan Hus readies for a reprieve', p. 1. Articles one and three cannot be found among the final thirty charges at Hus' arraignment.
56 As chapter 3 has argued at some length, there is not a shred of evidence in his extant works to show that Hus embraced the remanence doctrine advanced by Wyclif and there is no profit whatsoever in following the arguments of Walter Brandmüller who, while admitting the paucity of evidence, nonetheless persists in saying that 'in his heart Hus was a remanentist'. Brandmüller has made similar comments in private conversation and in symposia proceedings. The suggestion is idle speculation.
57 This point has been noted by virtually every scholar who has subjected Hus' doctrine of the church to a sustained critical assessment. See Patschovsky, 'Ekklesiologie bei Johannes Hus', in *Lebenslehren und Weltentwürfe im Übergang vom Mittelalter zur Neuzeit*, Abhandlungen der Akademie der Wissenschaften in Göttingen, Phil.-hist. Klasse - 3, (No. 179, 1989), especially pp. 375 and 399.
58 Brandmüller, *Das Konzil von Konstanz*, vol. 1, p. 331 where he states the conclusion 'Hus was undoubtedly a heretic'.
59 *De sufficientia legis Christi*, in *Historia et monumenta*, vol. 1, pp. 55–60.
60 Kejř, *Počátků*, p. 251.

61 Vilém Herold, 'Jan Hus - A Heretic, a Saint, or a Reformer?', *Kosmas: Czechoslovak and Central European Journal*, 15, (No. 1, 2001), p. 9.
62 Commentary on Psalm 125 in *CCL*, vol. 40, pp. 1844–1856.
63 Quoted in DiDomizio, 'Jan Hus's *De ecclesia*, Precursor of Vatican II?', p. 248.
64 For example, Wilhelm Baum, *Kaiser Sigismund: Hus, Konstanz und Türkenkriege*, Graz, Styria, 1993, pp. 126, 128.
65 DiDomizio, 'Jan Hus's *De ecclesia*, Precursor of Vatican II?', p. 247.
66 Kejř, *Počátků*, p. 248.
67 *Acta Apostolicae Sedis*, 55, (1963), pp. 257–304.
68 Fudge, '"Infoelix Hus": The Rehabilitation of a Medieval Heretic', p. 71.
69 Both were celebrated cases and commented upon widely. After a running battle with the church, the German Bishops finally withdrew Küng's *missio canonica* on 18 December 1979 with the expressed approval of Pope John Paul II. In the case of the Brazilian Franciscan theologian Boff, whose liberation theology views ran counter to the prevailing ethos of the then Roman ecclesiastical hierarchy, official notification from the Vatican demanding silence was published on 9 May 1985. See Harvey Cox, *The Silencing of Leonardo Boff*, Oak Park, Il., Meyer-Stone Books, 1988. Interestingly Küng chose to remain in the Roman Catholic Church and Boff elected to obey and retired to a cloister. Boff later left the priesthood.
70 *Unitatis redintegratio*, (21 November 1964) and *Dignitatis humanae*, (7 December 1965) can be found in Walter M. Abbott (ed.), *The Documents of Vatican II*, London and Dublin, Geoffrey Chapman, 1966, pp. 341–366 and 675–696.
71 In early July, 1999 I spoke at length with one such individual in Prague on what the definition of rehabilitation in this case meant. No clear articulation or understanding was forthcoming.
72 Świeżawski, 'Jan Hus – A Heretic or a Saint?', p. 36.
73 The final thirty charges brought against Hus at Constance are printed in *Documenta*, pp. 225–34.
74 Holeton, 'The Celebration of Jan Hus', p. 58 citing Kejř, *Husův proces*, pp. 200–218.
75 Definitive summary statements as made in Kejř, *Husův proces*, pp. 205 and 211. Kejř proposed the same essential argument in his 'Husův proces z hlediska práva kanonického', in *HT*, supplementum, 1, (2001), pp. 303–309.
76 This sentiment was enumerated in the pope's Apostolic Letter, *Tertio millennio adveniente*, (10 November 1994) cited partly in Holeček, 'The Problems of the Person, the life and the work of Jan Hus', p. 43.
77 František Holeček quoted in Smith, 'Mea Culpa: The Catholic Church revisits the past to right historical wrongs before the new millennium', p. B12.
78 This was the conclusion of Jiří Kejř in a conversation with me on 30 June 1999 in Prague; a view I endorse.
79 I remember being told by a native Czech more than twenty years ago that since I was not of Bohemian descent I could never understand Hus. The subconscious aspects of the Hus issue have been articulated by Tomáš Halík, Professor of Philosophy and Sociology of Religion at Charles University, Prague. As a contemporary question, Jan B. Lášek,

Professor of Church History at the Hussite Theological Faculty of Charles University. Both were quoted in Smith, 'Mea Culpa: The Catholic Church revisits the past to right historical wrongs before the new millennium', p. B12.

80 The commission itself appeared along with church officials who had taken an active part in the lengthy process. Scholars such as Jiří Kejř, František Šmahel and Walter Brandmüller made significant presentations. The then-president of the Czech Republic, Václav Havel, attended the December symposium.

81 The papal address is in Jaroslav Pánek and Miloslav Polívka (eds.), *Jan Hus ve Vatikánu*, Prague, Historický ústav, 2000, pp. 111–113. Versions in various languages can be accessed on the Vatican's website.

82 That view is reflected also in Pánek and Polívka (eds.), *Jan Hus ve Vatikánu*, p. 151.

83 Kotyk, *Spor o revizi Husova procesu*, p. 112.

84 Pánek and Polívka (eds.), *Jan Hus ve Vatikánu*, pp. 120–122. Špak's name does not appear on the document.

85 Each of these five documents, in full text, may be accessed directly via the official Vatican website at www.vatican.va

86 Holeton, 'The Celebration of Jan Hus', pp. 58–59 where the sentence 'Hus was a reformer for the whole church' is attributed to the pope while in David R. Holeton and Zdeněk V. David, 'Introduction', BRRP, vol. 3, p. 11 the attribution is that Hus 'was an important reformer for the life of all the churches'. Unfortunately, neither rendering of the alleged citation can be found in the printed version of the papal address. Contrary to Holeton's argument the printed text does not deviate from the speech as delivered and shows no indication of censorious redaction as suggested. It must therefore be taken as accurate. I have reviewed the video footage shot by the Vatican Television Center which captured Pope John Paul's comments in their entirety. The pope spoke for two minutes in Czech and then for a further ten minutes in Italian. It should be noted that the pontiff spoke, or rather read, from a prepared text. Nowhere in the address does he call Hus a reformer or make a statement even vaguely along the lines as noted above. I am grateful to Jerry Griffith for facilitating the video footage from Rome to me and especially to Chris Shea, Luigi Germano, and Ludmila Šafaříková O'Donnell for corroborating expert advice on the video footage.

87 Kotyk, *Spor o revizi Husova procesu*, p. 110.

88 Fudge, '"Infoelix Hus": The Rehabilitation of a Medieval Heretic', p. 73.

89 Kejř, *Počátků*, p. 247.

90 František Holeček, quoted in Weinstein, 'Jan Hus readies for a reprieve', p. 4.

91 As he commented on his adversary Štěpán Páleč: 'Páleč is a friend, truth is a friend; and both being friends it is holy to prefer the truth'. *Contra Palecz* in *Opera omnia*, vol. 22, p. 268.

92 Hus, 'Výklad viery', in *Opera omnia*, vol. 1, p. 69.

93 A recent example of this argument is Hilsch.

Epilogue

1 As recorded by the emperor's contemporary Windecke, *Denkwürdigkeiten zur Geschichte des Zeitalters Kaiser Sigmunds*, p. 98.
2 The polemical literature from the early Hussite period reveals all of this and much more. See the documentary examples in Daňhelka (ed.), *Husitské skladby budyšínského rukopisu*, pp. 23–40 and 61–79.
3 I may well have overstated this premise in the past. Fudge, 'The "Crown" and the "Red Gown"': Hussite Popular Religion', p. 39. It is not a supportable thesis to claim that all Hussites considered Hus the founder of Hussitism.
4 Johann Loserth (ed.), Ludolf of Żagan, 'Tractatus de longevo schismate', in *Archiv für österreichische Geschichte*, 60, (1880), p. 543.
5 Windecke, *Denkwürdigkeiten zur Geschichte des Zeitalters Kaiser Sigmunds*, p. 417.
6 Enumerated thus in the bull 'Inter cunctus' in Mansi, vol. 27, col. 1204.
7 On this concept see Thomas A. Fudge, 'Hussite Theology and the Law of God', in David Bagchi and David C. Steinmetz (eds.), *The Cambridge Companion to Reformation Theology*, Cambridge, Cambridge University Press, 2004, pp. 22–27 and in more detail Fudge, 'The "Law of God": Reform and Religious Practice in Late Medieval Bohemia", in BRRP, vol. 1, pp. 49–72.
8 *Chronicon causam sacerdotum thaboritarum continens*' in Höfler, vol. 2, pp. 477–478. In basic agreement, Palacký, *Dějiny narodu českého v Čechách a v Moravě*, vol. 3, pt. 1, p. 262 and Nejedlý, *Dějiny husitského zpěvu za válek husitských*, Prague, České společnosti náuk, 1913, pp. 106–25.
9 Pekař, *Žižka a jeho doba*, vol. 1, p. 210 argues it is impossible to trace a lineage from Hus to Tábor.
10 Daniel Hobbins, *Authorship and Publicity before Print: Jean Gerson and the Transformation of Late Medieval Learning*, Philadelphia, University of Pennsylvania Press, 2009, pp. 5, 13–14, and *passim*.
11 Glorieux (ed.), *Jean Gerson Oeuvres complètes*, vol. 5, p. 477.
12 See for example, the development of Hussite-inspired religious practices elsewhere in Europe noted in Fudge, 'Heresy and the Question of Hussites in the Southern Netherlands (1411–1431)', in Ludovic Nys and Dominique Vanwijnsberghe (eds.), *Campin in Context: Peinture et société dans la vallée de l'Escaut à l'époque de Robert Campin 1375–1445*, Valenciennes-Brussels-Tournai, Presses universitaires de Valenciennes, 2007, pp. 73–88.
13 Spinka, pp. 42–43.
14 John of Borsnitz, Bishop of Lebus and later Archbishop of Esztergom publicized this farfetched idea. See Novotný, *Correspondence*, p. 220.
15 The anonymous report, dating either to 1415 or 1416, comes from Třeboň, and has been printed in *Documenta*, pp. 636–638.
16 *Relatio*, in FRB, vol. 8, p. 76.
17 John Bale, *A brefe Chronycle concernynge the Examinacyon and death of the blessed martyr of Christ syr Johan Oldecastell*, Antwerp, 1544 and John Foxe, *Acts and Monuments*, book 5 in vols 2 and 3.

18 On the untimely nature of these events in England see Anne Hudson, *The Premature Reformation: Wycliffite Texts and Lollard History*, Oxford, Clarendon Press, 1988.
19 The literature is vast but see Lambert, *Medieval Heresy*, 3rd edition, and Scott L. Waugh and Peter D. Diehl (eds.), *Christendom and its Discontents: Exclusion, Persecution, and Rebellion, 1000–1500*, Cambridge, Cambridge University Press, 1996.
20 R.I. Moore, 'The war against heresy in medieval Europe', *Historical Research*, 81, (May, 2008), pp. 189–210.
21 Alister McGrath, *Heresy: A History of Defending the Truth*, San Francisco, HarperOne, 2009. McGrath and his predecessors (and colleagues) on this question are quite wrong to argue that heresy is a toxin to the faith and always dangerous.
22 Augustine, *In Johannis evangelium tractatus*, 45.9, in CCL, vol. 36, p. 392.
23 On the principal characters see especially I.S. Robinson, *Henry IV of Germany 1056–1106*, Cambridge, Cambridge University Press, 2003 and H.E.J. Cowdrey, *Pope Gregory VII 1073–1085*, Oxford, Clarendon Press, 1998.
24 Van Engen, 'Multiple Options: The World of the Fifteenth-Century Church', p. 284 but *passim*.

SELECT BIBLIOGRAPHY

The bibliography does not claim to be comprehensive in any of its four parts. It has two basic functions. The first is to assemble the main sources consulted. The second is to offer something of a guide for those wishing to read further. The *Historia et monumenta*, anonymously assembled by Matthias Flacius Illyricus (1520–1575), contains most of the Latin works of Hus along with works which do not belong in the Hus corpus. Some of those texts have been superceded by better editions, others remain accessible only in the 1558/1715 publications or in manuscripts. Not all of the contents of the Flacius edition have been listed. All of Hus' Czech works have been published in the *Magistri Iohannis Hus Opera omnia* series. I have not listed all of them. Neither have I included songs attributed to Hus nor his translations of Wyclif. Generally the list of Hus' works has been limited to those considered important for the arguments of this book. In a good many cases an exact or precise dating of the works of Hus remains either impossible or controversial. I have suggested a general chronology of the corpus of his work only, but point out to the reader that scholarly differences of opinion can be located in the literature. The list of manuscripts and archival sources are restricted to those specifically consulted or referred to in the notes. The same might be said for the listing of those printed primary and secondary sources. The literature on Hus, especially in the Czech language, is somewhat voluminous. Only the most important or those essential for this study are listed.

Works of Jan Hus

University promotional speeches, in Schmidtová, ed. *Positiones, recommendationes, sermones*, pp. 35–96 (1400–1412)

Sermo in cena domini coram populo habitus, in *Opera omnia*, vol. 8, pp. 17–45 (1401–1402)

Sermons for Czech holy days, in *Opera omnia*, vol. 3 (1401–1403)

Synodal sermons, in *Historia et monumenta*, vol. 2, pp. 57–84 (questionable attribution, c.1402–1409)

Leccionarium bipartitum pars hiemalis, in *Opera omnia*, vol. 9 (1403–1404)

Epistolas apostolorum canonicas septem commentarii [Lectures on New Testament Pastoral Epistles of James, I–II Peter, I–III John, Jude], in *Historia et monumenta*, vol. 2, pp. 165–374 (1404–1405)

University sermons, in Schmidtová, ed. *Positiones, recommendationes, sermones*, pp. 99–201 (1404–1411)

Collecta, in *Opera omnia*, vol. 7 (sermons from 30 November 1404 – 22 November 1405)

De omni sanguine Christi glorificato, in *Historia et monumenta*, vol. 1, pp. 191–202 (1405)
Major sermons before the Prague Synod, in *Historia et monumenta*, vol. 2, pp. 39–47 and 47–56 (19 October 1405 and 18 October 1407)
Lectures on the Psalter (109–118), in *Historia et monumenta*, vol. 2, pp. 375–511(1405–1407)
De corpore Christi, in Flajšhans, ed., *Mag. Jo. Hus Opera omnia*, vol. 1, part 2, pp. 3–31 (1406/1408)
De sanguine Christi, in Flajšhans, ed., *Mag. Jo. Hus Opera omnia*, vol. 1, part 3, pp. 3–37 (1406–1407)
Výklad piesniček Šalomúnových [Commentary on the Song of Solomon], in *Opera omnia*, vol. 4, pp. 51–131 (1406–1410)
Orthographia Bohemica, in Schröpfer (1406–1412)
Passio domini nostri Iesu Cristi, *Opera omnia*, vol. 8, pp. 47–249 (1407)
Expositio decalogi, in Flajšhans, ed. *Mag. Jo Hus Opera omnia*, vol. 1, part 1, pp. 1–45 (1407–1408)
Super IV Sententiarum, in Flajšhans, ed. *Mag. Jo Hus Opera omnia*, vol. 2, pp. 3–744 (1407–1409)
De arguendo clero pro concione, in *Historia et monumenta*, vol. 1, pp. 185–191 (1408/1412)
Sermones de sanctis, in Flajšhans, ed. *Spisy M. Jana Husi*, vols. 7–8 (1408)
Response to accusatory articles by Prague priests, in *Documenta*, pp. 155–163 (1408)
Questiones, in *Opera omnia*, vol. 19a (1408–1412)
Quadragesimale, Prague Castle Archive MS E 45.2 (1409)
De libris hereticorum legendis, in *Opera omnia*, vol. 22, pp. 19–37 (June 1410)
Defensio libri de Trinitate, in *Opera omnia*, vol. 22, pp. 39–56 (July 1410)
Sermones in Capella Bethlehem, in Flajšhans, ed. *Mag. Io. Hus Sermones in Capella Bethlehem*, 6 vols (1410–1411)
Quodlibet, in *Opera omnia*, vol. 20 (January 1411)
Devět kusóv zlatých [The Nine Golden Theses], in *Opera omnia*, vol. 4, p. 346 (February 1411)
Contra Iohannem Stokes, in *Opera omnia*, vol. 22, pp. 57–70 (Autumn 1411)
Contra occultum adversarium, in *Opera omnia*, vol. 22, pp. 71–107 (October 1411)
De tribus dubiis, in *Historia et monumenta*, vol. 1, pp. 208–210 (November 1411)
De credere, in *Historia et monumenta*, vol. 1, pp. 210–212 (December 1411)
Explicatio... septem priora capita Primae Epistolae S. Pauli ad Corinthos, in *Historia et monumenta*, vol. 2, pp. 131–165 (1411–1412)
De quinque officiis sacerdotis, in *Historia et monumenta*, vol. 1, p. 191 (1411–1412)
Postilla adumbrata, in *Opera omnia*, vol. 13 (1411–1412)
Adversus indulgentias papales, in *Historia et monumenta*, vol. 1, pp. 215–235 (Spring 1412)
Contra bullam Papae Joannis XXIII, in *Historia et monumenta*, vol. 1, pp. 235–237 (Spring 1412)
Zrcadlo hřiešníka [Mirror of Sinners, two recensions], in *Opera omnia*, vol. 4, pp. 132–146 (1412)
Provázek třípramenný [The Three-Stranded Cord], in *Opera omnia*, vol. 4, pp. 147–162 (1412)
Questio de Indulgentiis, sive de Cruciata Papae Joanne XXIII, in *Historia et monumenta*, vol. 1, pp. 215–235 (17 June 1412)
Contra cruciatam, in *Opera omnia*, vol. 22, pp. 129–39 (summer 1412)
Defensio articulorum Wyclif, in *Opera omnia*, vol. 22, pp. 141–232 (July/August 1412)
De decimis in *Historia et monumenta*, vol. 1, pp. 156–167 (1412)
De ablatione temporalium a clericis in *Historia et monumenta*, vol. 1, pp. 146–155 (1412)
Appellatio M. Joannis Hus a sententiis pontificis Romani ad Jesum Christum supremum judicem, in *Documenta*, pp. 464–466 (18 October 1412)

SELECT BIBLIOGRAPHY 325

Tractatus responsivus, in Thomson, *Mag. Johannis Hus Tractatus Responsivus* (erroneous attribution, 1412)

Výklad víry [Exposition of the Faith, Apostles' Creed], in *Opera omnia*, vol. 1, pp. 63–105 (1412)

Výklad na Páteř [Exposition of the Lord's Prayer], in *Opera omnia*, vol. 1, pp. 330–391 (1412)

Menší výklad na páteř [Smaller commentary on the Lord's Prayer], in *Opera omnia*, vol. 1, pp. 391–392 (1412)

Výklad desatera [Exposition of the Decalogue], in *Opera omnia*, vol. 1, pp. 113–329 (1412)

Výklad kratší na desatera [Shorter commentary on the Ten Commandments], in *Opera omnia*, vol. 1, pp. 327–329 (1412)

Menší výklad na vieru [Smaller commentary on the faith], in *Opera omnia*, vol. 1, pp. 105–112 (1412–1413)

Contra predicatorem Plznensem, in *Opera omnia*, vol. 22, pp. 109–128 (1412–1414)

Katechismus [Catechism], in *Opera omnia*, vol. 4, pp. 325–329 (1412–1414)

O hřieše [On sin], in *Opera omnia*, vol. 4, pp. 334–337 (1412–1414)

O víře [On faith], in *Opera omnia*, vol. 4, pp. 338–345 (1412–1414)

O svatokupectví [On Simony], in *Opera omnia*, vol. 4, pp. 187–270 (December 1412 – February 1413)

De ecclesia, in Thomson, ed. *Magistri Johannis Hus Tractatus De Ecclesia* (end of 1412 – 8 June 1413)

Conditiones concordiae, in *Documenta*, pp. 491–492 (January 1413)

Contra falsa concilia doctorum, in *Documenta*, pp. 499–501 (February 1413)

De sex erroribus, in Ryba, *Betlemské texty*, pp. 41–63 (February/March 1413)

Contra Palecz, in *Opera omnia*, vol. 22, pp. 233–269 (Spring 1413)

Contra octo doctores, in *Opera omnia*, vol. 22, pp. 369–488 (late spring 1413)

O šesti bludiech [On the six errors of the Mass], in *Opera omnia*, vol. 4, pp. 271–296. (June 1413)

Contra Stanislaum, in *Opera omnia*, vol. 22, pp. 271–367 (Summer 1413)

Dcerka: O poznání cěsty pravé k spasení [The Daughter, or how to know the correct way to salvation], in *Opera omnia*, vol. 4, pp. 163–86 (1413/1414)

Revision of the Czech Bible, (late 1413, early 1414)

Česká nedělní postila [Czech Postil], in *Opera omnia*, vol. 2 (completed 27 October 1413)

Jádro učení křesťanského [Kernel of Christian Doctrine], in *Opera omnia*, vol. 4, pp. 330–333 (June 1414)

Knížky proti knězi kuchmistrovi [Books against the Priest-Cookmaster], in *Opera omnia*, vol. 4, pp. 312–323 (Summer 1414)

O manželství [On Marriage], in *Opera omnia*, vol. 4, pp. 297–311 (July–December 1414)

De sufficientia legis Christi, in *Historia et monumenta*, vol. 1, pp. 55–60 (Fall 1414)

De fidei suae elucidatione, in *Historia et monumenta*, vol. 1, pp. 60–64 (Fall 1414)

De pace, in *Historia et monumenta*, vol. 1, pp. 65–71 (Fall 1414)

Utrum expediat laicis fidelibus sumere sanguinem Christi sub specie vini?, in *Historia et monumenta*, vol. 1, pp. 52–54 (November 1414)

Response to the 42 Articles, in *Documenta*, pp. 204–224 (2–3 January 1415)

De mandatis domini, in *Historia et monumenta*, vol. 1, pp. 38–41 (January 1415)

De peccato morali, in *Historia et monumenta*, vol. 1, p. 41 (January 1415)

De cognicione et dilectione dei, in *Historia et monumenta*, vol. 1, pp. 43–44 (January/February 1415)

De tribus hostibus hominis, in *Historia et monumenta*, vol. 1, p. 45 (February 1415)

De penitentia, in *Historia et monumenta*, vol. 1, pp. 46–47 (12 February 1415)
De matrimonio, in *Historia et monumenta*, vol. 1, fols. 41–43 (4 March 1415)
De sacramento corporis et sanguinis domini, in *Historia et monumenta*, vol. 1, pp. 47–52 (5 March 1415)
Response to articles extracted from *De ecclesia* and other works, in *Documenta*, pp. 225–234 (18–20 June 1415)
Correspondence, in Novotný, ed. *M. Jana Husi Korespondence a dokumenty* (between *c.* 1402 – 5 July 1415)

Manuscripts and Archival Sources

Amsterdam, Rijksmuseum
    RP-POB-78.421

Basel, Universitätsbibliothek
    A 1 29, fols. 1^r–24^v
    A 1 29, fols. 143^r–174^v
    A X 66
    E 1 9, fols. 386^r–453^v

Berlin, Staatliche Museen Preussischer Kulturbesitz Kupferstichkabinett
    37–1889

Berlin, Staatsbibliothek, Handschriftenabteilung
    YA 91a
    YA 283
    YA 408
    YA 872

Berne, Zentralbibliothek
    Hist. Helv. I1
    Hist. Helv. 1.16

Cambridge, Corpus Christi Library
    512
    523
    534

Cambridge, Emmanuel College Library
    I.1.9.
    I.4.6.

Cambridge, University Library
    Add. 6981, fols. 2^r–75^r
    Dd. 15.29, fols. 211^v–223^r

Coburg, Kunstsammlungen der Landesstiftung
    Inv. Nr. XIII, 402

Coburg, Kunstsammlungen der Veste Coburg
    XIII. 40.1

Constance, Rosgartenmuseum
    Inv. Hs. 1

Copenhagen, Det Kongelige Bibliothek [Royal Library]
    1551

Edinburgh, University Library
    P.C. 73

Esztergom, Főszékesegyházi könyvtär [Metropolitan Library]
    I. 313

Gotha, Museen der Stadt Gotha Schloßmuseum
    Inv. No. 38.6
    Inv. No. 38.8

Jičín, Státní okresní archiv [Regional Archives]
    book 9, inv. no. 20, olim Sobotka 3

Karlsruhe, Badische Landesbibliothek
    E.M. 11
    St. Georgen 63 (=Codex Pap. Germ. LXIII)

Kraków, Biblioteka Jagiellońska [Jagiellonian University Library]
    385
    1628, fols. 2^r–10^v, 39^r–40^v, 61^r–70^v
    2148, fols. 34^v–39^v

Leipzig, Universitätsbibliothek
    766

London, British Museum, Department of Prints and Drawings
    Satires 1075

Lovosice, Státní okresní archiv Litoměřice [Regional State Archives]
    IV C 1

Melbourne, National Gallery of Victoria
    E2 – 1976

Mladá Boleslav, Okresní museum [Regional Museum]
    II A 1

New York Public Library
    Spencer Collection, 32

New York, St. Mark's Library, General Theological Seminary
    BX 2043. A3 H8

Nürnberg, Germanisches Nationalmuseum
    HB 60
    HB 24592

Olomouc, Knihovna Univerzity Palackého [Palacký University Library]
    M 1 34
    M 1 239, fols. 205^r–251^v
    M 1 288
    M 3 3

Oxford, Bodleian Library
    Sutherland Collection, 169

Paris, Bibliothèque Nationale
    franç. 1278

Prague, Archiv Pražského hradu [Prague Castle Archive = Cathedral Chapter Library]
    A 37, fols. 1^r–470^v
    B 22.2, fols. 89^r–93^v
    B 48.2, fols. 255^v–257^v
    B 61, fols. 192^r–207^v
    C 39.4, fols. 109^v–116^v
    C 63, fols. 2^r–20^v
    C 66.1, fols. 11^r–168^v
    C 66.2, fols. 1^r–125^v
    C 106, fols. 156^r–160^v
    C 114
    C 116, fols. 227^r–306^r
    D 12, fols. 116^v–132^v
    D 48, pp. 378–422
    D 51, fols. 56^r–106^r
    D 53, pp. 188–213

D 54, fols. 60ʳ–63ʳ
D 88, fols. 223ʳ–233ʳ
D 106, fols. 1ʳ–285ʳ
D 109.2, fols. 1ʳ–23ᵛ
D 112, fols. 1ʳ–177ʳ
D 123, fols. 1ʳ–23ʳ
E 37, fols.178ᵛ–183ᵛ
E 45.2
F 29
F 30
K 7
K 13, fols. 266ᵛ–268ᵛ
O 7, fols. 115ᵛ–138ᵛ
O 13
O 27, fols. 282ᵛ–286ʳ
O 50, fols. 133ʳ–137ᵛ

Prague, Archiv Hlavního města Prahy [City Archives]
997
2073
2077
2078

Prague, Národní Knihovna [National Library]
I D 10, fols. 260ʳ–346ʳ
III A 16
III B 20
III F 16
III G 28, fols. 165ʳ–179ᵛ
IV B 2
IV E 13
IV F 25, fols. 171ʳ–173ᵛ
IV G 15, fols. 142ʳ–157ᵛ
IV H 12
V G 3
V G 9, fols. 1ʳ–53ᵛ; 53ᵛ–115ʳ
V G 11, fols. 128ʳ–137ᵛ
V H 27, fols. 1ʳ–56ʳ
VI C 20a
VII A 18
VIII D 15
VIII E 3
VIII F 22, fols. 384ʳ–399ᵛ
VIII G 13

X H 13
XI B 1a–d
XIII E 5, fols. 60^v–79^r
XIII E 7
XVI A 17
XVII A 3
XVII B 21
XX B 1
XXIII F 204
osek 71

Prague, Knihovna Národního Muzea [National Museum Library]
I A 15
I A c 109
I B a 8
I B a 10
II C 7
II D
II H 21, fols. 1^r–157^v
III B 11, fol. 3^r–155^v
III B 12
IV B 9
IV B 24
IV H 30, fols. 54^r–75^r
V C 42
V E 89
XII F 1, fols. 1^r–132^v
XII F 2
XII F 14
XIII D 1
XIII F 20
XV E 15
XVI F 4
54 C 25
TR 1 27

Prague, Strahovský Klášter Knihovna [Strahov Monastery Library]
I d 5, fols. 445^r–516^v
DF IV 48
DR V 12

Rome, Vatican Library
Vat Lat 7307

Tábor, Státní okresní archiv [Regional Archives]
195
sig. A – 1809

Utrecht, Museum Catharijneconvent [St. Catherine's Convent Museum]
Inv. No. RMCC s00057

Vienna, Österreichische Nationalbibliothek
3062
3044
3914, fols. 134ᵛ–138ʳ
4131, fols. 122ʳ–180ᵛ
4384
4488
4491, fols. 1ʳ–28ʳ
4524, fols. 104ᵛ–106ᵛ
4550, fols. 307ᵛ–311ʳ
4673, fols. 17ʳ–38ᵛ; 46ʳ–53ʳ; 59ᵛ–87ʳ
4704, fols. 20ᵛ–147ᵛ
4890
4902, fols. 326ʳ–335ᵛ
4941
5113
13.975
suppl. mus. sam 15492

Zürich, Zentralbibliothek
Wickiana PAS II 13/20
Wickiana PAS II 13/24

Printed Primary Sources

Bartoš, František M. ed. 'Hus a jeho strana v osvětlení nepřátelského pamfletu'. *Reformační sborník*, 4, (1931), pp. 3–8.
_____. *Listy Bratra Jana a Kronika velmi pěckná a Janu Žižovi*. Prague, Blahoslav, 1949.
Borový, Klement and Antonín Podlaha, eds. *Libri erectionum Archidioecesis Pragensis saeculo XIV. et XV.*, 6 vols. Prague, Calve, 1875–1927.
Boubín, Jaroslav, ed. *Jan z Příbramě: Život kněží Táborských*. Příbram, Státní okresní archiv Příbram a Okresní muzeum Příbram, 2000.
Cerretano, Jacob. *Liber gestorum*. In Loomis, pp. 466–531.
Chelčický, Petr. *Síť víry*. Emil Smetánka, ed. Prague, Melantrich, 1929.
Císařová-Kolářová, Anna, ed. *M. Jan Hus Betlemské Poselství*, 2 vols. Prague, Laichter, 1947.
Cochlaeus, Johannes. *Historia Hussitarum libri duodecim*. Mainz, Behem, 1549.
Daňhelka, Jiří, ed. *Husitské písně*. Prague, Československý Spisovatel, 1952.
_____, ed., *Husitské skladby budyšínského rukopisu*, Prague, Orbis, 1952.

De Vooght, Paul. 'Un classique de la littérature spirituelle: La "Dcerka" de Jean Huss'. *Revue d'histoire de la spiritualité*, 48, (1972), pp. 275–314.

Emler, Josef and František Tingl, eds. *Libri confirmationum ad beneficia ecclesiastica Pragensem per archidioecesim (1354–1436)*, 10 vols. Prague, Grégerianis, 1865–1889.

Erben, Karel J., ed. *Tomáše ze Štítného: Knížky šestery o obecných věcech křesťanských*. Prague, Pražská universita, 1852.

_____, ed. *Mistra Jana Husi: Sebrané spisy české*. 3 vols. Prague, Tempský, 1865–1868.

Eršil, Jaroslav, ed. *Acta summorum pontificum res gestas Bohemicas aevi praehussitici et hussitici illustrantia*, 2 vols. Prague, ČSAV, 1980.

Fillastre, Guillaume. *Gesta concilii Constanciensis*. In Loomis, pp. 200–465.

Flajšhans, Václav. *Literární činnost mistra Jana Husi*. Prague, ČAVU, 1900.

_____, ed. *Spisy M. Jana Husi*, 3 vols. Prague, Vilímek, 1904–1908.

_____, ed. *Mag. Io. Hus Sermones in Capella Bethlehem, 1410–1411*, 6 vols. Prague, České společnosti nauk, 1938–1945.

_____, ed. *M. Io. Hus Quodlibet 1411*. Prague, Nákladem Vlastním, 1938.

_____, ed. *Mag. Jo. Hus Opera omnia: Nach neuentdeckten Handschriften*, 3 vols. Osnabrück, Biblio-Verlag, 1966. Orig. 1903–1908

Friedberg, Emil, ed. *Corpus iuris canonici*, 2 vols. Leipzig, Tauchnitz, 1879–1881.

Fudge, Thomas A. *The Crusade against Heretics in Bohemia, 1418–1437: Sources and Documents for the Hussite Crusades*. Aldershot, Ashgate, 2002

_____. 'Jan Hus at "Calvary": The Text of an Early Fifteenth-Century Passio'. forthcoming.

Glorieux, Palémon, ed. *Jean Gerson Oeuvres Complètes*. 10 vols. Tournai, Desclée, 1960–1973.

Goll, Jaroslav, et al., eds. *Fontes rerum bohemicarum*. 8 vols. Prague, Nákladem nadání Františka Palackého, 1873–1932.

_____. *Vypsání o Mistru Jeronymovi z Prahy*. Prague, J. Otto, 1878.

Graham, Barry F.H., ed. *The Litoměřice Gradual of 1517*. Prague, L. Marek, 1999.

Hardt, Hermann von der, ed. *Magnum oecumenicum constantiense concilium*, 7 vols. Frankfurt and Leipzig, C. Genschii, Helmestadi, 1699–1742.

Havránek, Bohuslav, ed. *Výbor z české literatury doby husitské*, 2 vols. Prague, ČSAV, 1963–1964.

Herold, Vilém and Milan Mráz, eds. *Iohannis Milicii de Cremsir: Tres Sermones Synodales*. Prague, Academia, 1974.

Hlaváček Ivan and Zdeňka Hledíková, eds. *Protocollum visitationis archidiaconatus Pragensis annis 1379–1382 per Paulum de Janowicz archidiaconum Pragensem, factae*. Prague, Akademia, 1973.

Höfler, Konstantin von, ed. *Geschichtschreiber der Husitischen Bewegung in Böhmen*, 3 vols. Vienna, Aus der Kaiserlich-Königlichen Hof- und Staatsdruckerei, 1856–1866. [= Fontes rerum austriacarum, vols. 2, 6, 7]

_____, ed. *Concilia Pragensia 1353–1413*. Vienna, Geyer, 1972. [reprint]

Holeton, David R. 'The Office of Jan Hus: An Unrecorded Antiphonary in the Metropolitical Library of Estergom'. In J. Neil Alexander, ed. *Time and Community* [Festschrift for Thomas J. Talley]. Washington DC, The Pastoral Press, 1990, pp. 137–152.

Hus, Jan. *Super IV Sententiarum*, in Václav Flajšhans, ed. *Spisy M. Jana Husi*, 3 vols. Prague, Bursík and Vilímek, 1903–1907.

Illyricus, Matthias Flacius, ed. *Historia et monumenta Ioannis Hus atque Hieronymi Pragensis*, 2 vols. Nürnberg, Montanus and Neuberus, 1558; 1715.

Izbicki, Thomas M., Gerald Christianson and Philip Krey, eds. *Reject Aeneas, Accept Pius: Selected Letters of Aeneas Sylvius Piccolomini (Pope Pius II)*. Washington, Catholic University of America Press, 2006.

Kadlec, Jaroslav, ed. *Traktát Mistra Ondřeje Brodu o původu husitů*. Tábor, Museum of the Hussite Revolutionary Movement, 1980.

———. 'Synods of Prague and their Statutes 1396–1414'. *Apollinaris*, 54, (1991), pp. 227–293.

Kaminsky, Howard, et al., eds. 'Master Nicholas of Dresden: The Old Color and the New'. *Transactions of the American Philosophical Society*, n.s. 55, (Part 1, 1965), pp. 5–88.

Klicman, Ladislav, ed. *Processus iudiciarius contra Jeronimum de Praga habitus Viennae a. 1410–1412*. Prague, Česká akademie císaře Františka Josefa pro vědy, slovesnost a umění, 1898.

Kolár, Jaroslav, Anežka Vidmanová and Hana Vlhová-Wörner, eds. *Jistebnice Kancionál, MS. Prague, National Museum Library II C 7: Critical Edition*. Volume 1, *Graduale*. Brno, L. Marek, 2005.

Krmíčková, Helena. *Studie a texty k počátkům kalicha v Čechách*. Brno, Masarykova Univerzita, 1997.

Kybal, Vlastimil, Otakar Odložilík and Jana Nechutová, eds. Matěj of Janov, *Regulae veteris et novi testamenti*, 6 vols. Prague and Innsbruck, Universitního Knihkupectví Wagnerova, 1908–1926; Munich, Oldenbourg, 1993.

Loomis, Louise R., ed. *The Council of Constance: The Unification of the Church*. New York, Columbia University Press, 1961.

Loserth, Johann. 'Beiträge zur Geschichte der Hussitischen Bewegung'. *Archiv für österreichische Geschichte*, 82, (1895), pp. 327–418 (texts on pp. 348–418).

Ludecus, Matthaeus. *Historia von der erfindung, Wunderwercken und der zerstörung des vermeinten heiligen Bluts zu Wilssnagk*. Wittenberg, Clemens Schleich, 1586.

MacKenzie, Campbell, trans. *Letters of John Huss*. Edinburgh, William Whyte & Co., 1846.

Mansi, Giovanni Domenico, ed. *Sacrorum conciliorum nova, et amplissima collectio . . .*, 53 vols. Graz, Akademische Druck- u. Verlagsanstalt, 1960.

Martínková, Dana, Alena Hadravová and Jiří Matl, eds. *Aeneae Silvii Historia Bohemica* [Fontes rerum Regni Bohemiae, vol. 1]. Prague, Koniasch Latin Press, 1998.

Migne, Jacques Paul, ed. *Patrologia Latina*, 221 vols. Paris, Migne/Garnier, 1844–1865.

Mladoňovice, Petr. *Relatio de Mag. Joannis Hus causa*. In *Fontes rerum bohemicarum*, vol. 8, ed., Václav Novotný. Prague, Nákladem nadání Františka Palackého, 1932.

Molnár, Amedeo, ed. *Dochovaná kázání Jana Želivského z roku 1419*. Prague, ČSAV, 1953.

——— and František M. Dobiáš, eds. *Husova výzbroj do Kostnice*. Prague, Kalich, 1965.

Monumenta historica universitatis Carolo-Ferdinandeae Pragensis, 3 vols. Prague, Spurny, 1830–1848.

Nagy, Balázs and Frank Schaer, eds. *Autobiography of Emperor Charles IV and his Legend of Saint Wenceslas*. Budapest, Central European University Press, 2001.

Nejedlý, Zdeněk. *Prameny k synodám strany pražské a táboré*. Prague, Nákladem Královské České Společnosti Náuk, 1900.

———. *Dějiny husitského zpěvu*, 6 vols. Prague, Československá akademie věd, 1954–1956.

Niem, Dietrich von. *De modis uniendi ac reformandi ecclesiam*. In Hermann Heimpel, ed. *Dialog über Union und Reform der Kirche 1410*, Leipzig, Teubner, 1933.

Novotný, Václav, ed. *M. Jana Husi Korespondence a dokumenty*. Prague, Nákladem komise pro vydávání pramenů náboženského hnutí českého, 1920.

Opočenský, Milan and Jana Opočenská, eds. *Milíč of Kroměříž, The Message for the Last Days: Three Essays from the Year 1367*. Geneva, World Alliance of Reformed Churches, 1998.

Palacký, František, ed. *Staří letopisové čeští od r. 1378 do 1527*. In *Scriptores rerum bohemicarum*, vol. 3. Prague, J.S.P., 1829.

_____, ed. *Archiv český čili staré písemné památky české i moravské*, 6 vols. Prague, Kronberg and Riwnáče, 1840–1872.

_____, ed. *Monumenta conciliorum generalium seculi Decimi Quinti*, 2 vols. Vienna, Typis C.R. Officinae Typographicae Aulae et Status, 1857–1873.

_____, ed. *Documenta Mag. Joannis Hus vitam, doctrinam, causam in constantiensi concilio actam et controversias de religione in Bohemia annis 1403–1418 motas illustrantia*. Prague, Tempsky, 1869.

_____, ed. *Urkundliche Beiträge zur Geschichte des Hussitenkrieges*, 2 vols. Prague, Tempský, 1873.

Palès-Gobillard, Annette, ed. *Le Livre des sentences de l'inquisiteur Bernard Gui (1308–1323)*. 2 vols, Paris, CNRS Éditions, 2003.

Patschovsky, Alexander, *Quellen zur Böhmischen Inquisition im 14. Jahrhundert*. Weimar, Hermann Böhlaus Nachfolger, 1979.

_____ and Kurt-Viktor Selge, eds. *Quellen zur Geschichte der Waldenser*. Gütersloh, Mohn, 1973.

Pez, Bernard, ed. *Thesaurus anecdotorum novissimus seu veterum monumentorum*, 6 vols. Augsburg, Philippi, Martini, & Joannis Veith fratrum, 1721–1729.

Podlaha, Antonín, ed. *Liber ordinationum cleri 1395–1416*. 2 vols. Prague, Pražská kapitula, 1910–1920.

Polc, Jaroslav V. 'Statutes of the Synods of Prague (1386–1395)'. *Apollinaris*, 53, (Nos. 3–4, 1980), pp. 421–457.

Rejchrtová, Noemi, ed. *Jan Hus, Dcerka*. Prague, Kalich, 1995.

Richental, Ulrich. *Chronik des Constanzer Concils*. In Loomis, 1961, pp. 84–199.

_____. *Das Concilium geschehen zu Konstanz*. Augsburg, Anton Sorg, 1483.

_____. *Das Concilium: So zů Constanz gehalten ist worden*. Augsburg, Heinrich Steiner, 1536.

_____. *Costnitzer Concilium*. Frankfurt, Paul Reffler, 1575.

Ryba, Bohumil, ed. *Magistri Iohannis Hus Quodlibet*. Prague, Orbis, 1948; revised ed. Turnhout, Brepols, 2006.

_____, ed. *Betlemské texty*, Prague, Orbis, 1951.

Ryšánek, František, et al., eds. *Magistri Iohannis Hus, Opera omnia*, 25 volumes projected. Prague, Academia and Turnhout, Brepols, 1959–.

Schaff, David S., trans. *The Church by John Huss*. New York, Scribner's, 1915.

Schmidtová, Anežka, ed. *Iohannes Hus, Positiones Recommendationes, Sermones*. Prague, Státní pedagogické nakladatelství, 1958.

_____, ed. *Sermones de tempore qui Collecta dicuntur*. Prague, Academia, 1959.

Schröpfer, Johan. *Hussens traktat 'Orthographia Bohemica' - Die Herkunft des diakritischen Systems in der Schreibung slavischer Sprachen und die Älteste zusammenhängende Beschreibung slavischer Laute*. Wiesbaden, Harrassowitz, 1968.

Sedlák, Jan, ed. 'Počátkové kalicha'. *Časopis katolického duchovenstva*, 52, (1911), pp. 97–105, 244–250, 397–401, 496–501, 583–587, 703–708, 786–791; vol. 54, (1913), pp. 226–232, 275–278, 404–410, 465–470, 708–713, and vol. 55, (1914), pp. 75–84, 113–120, and 315–322.

_____. *Studie a texty k životopisu Husovu*, 3 vols. Olomouc, Matice Cyrilometodějská, 1914–1925.

Šimek, František, ed. *Postilla Jana Rokycany*. 2 vols. Prague, Komise pro vydávání pramenů českého hnutí náboženského, 1928–1929.

_____, ed. *Jakoubek ze Stříbra: Výklad na zjevenie sv. Jana*, 2 vols. Prague, Nákladem Komise vydávání pramenů českého hnutí náboženského, 1932–1933.

_____, ed. *Staré letopisy české z vratislavského rukopisu novočeským pravopisem*. Prague, Historické spolku a společnosti Husova Musea, 1937.

_____. *Mistr Jan Hus: Česká kázání sváteční*. Prague, Blahoslav, 1952.

_____ and Miloslav Kaňak, eds. *Staré letopisy české z rukopisu křižovnického*. Prague, Státní nakladatelství Krásné Literatury, Hudby a Umění, 1939.

Spáčila, Bedřich, ed. *Mistr Jakoubek ze Stříbra: Betlemská kázání z roku 1416*. Prague, Blahoslav, 1951.

Spinka, Matthew, *John Hus at the Council of Constance*. New York, Columbia University Press, 1965.

_____, trans. *The Letters of John Hus*. Manchester, Manchester University Press, 1972.

Strauss, Walter L. *The German Single-Leaf Woodcut*, 3 vols. New York, Abaris, 1975.

Svejkovský, František, ed. *Veršované Skladby doby Husitské*. Prague, ČSAV, 1963.

Tadra, Ferdinand, ed. *Soudní akta konsistoře pražské (Acta judiciaria consistorii Pragensis)*, 7 vols. Prague, Česká akademie císaře Františka Josefa, 1893–1901.

Tanner, Norman P., ed. *Decrees of the Ecumenical Councils*. 2 vols. London, Sheed & Ward, 1990.

Thomson, S. Harrison, ed. *Mag. Johannis Hus Tractatus Responsivus*. Princeton, Princeton University Press, 1927.

_____, ed. 'Four Unpublished *Questiones* of John Hus'. *Medievalia et Humanistica*, 7, (1948), pp. 71–88.

_____, ed. *Magistri Johannis Hus Tractatus De Ecclesia*. Boulder, University of Colorado Press, 1956.

Windecke, Eberhart. *Denkwürdigkeiten zur Geschichte des Zeitalters Kaiser Sigmunds*. Ed. Wilhelm Altmann. Berlin, R. Gaertners Verlagsbuchhandlung, 1893.

Wolkan, Rudolf, ed. *Der Briefwechsel des Eneas Silvius Piccolomini*. In *Fontes rerum austriacarum* II, vol. 68. Vienna, Alfred Hölder, 1918.

Workman, Herbert B. and R. Marvin Pope, eds. *The Letters of John Hus*. London, Hodder and Stoughton, 1904.

Wyclif, John. [*Works*], 33 vols.? London, Trübner/Wyclif Society, 1883–1921. Reprinted, New York, Johnson Reprint Co., 1966.

Žagan, Ludolf von. *Tractatus de longevo schismate*. ed., Johann Loserth. In *Archiv für österreichische Geschichte*, 60, (1880), pp. 343–561.

Secondary Sources

Atwood, Craig. *The Theology of the Czech Brethren from Hus to Comenius*. University Park, Pennsylvania State University Press, 2009.

Bainton, Roland H. 'Dürer and Luther as the Man of Sorrows'. *The Art Bulletin*, 29, (No. 4, 1947), pp. 269–272.

Barford, P.M. *The Early Slavs: Culture and Society in Early Medieval Eastern Europe*. Ithaca, Cornell University Press, 2001.

Bartlová, Milena. 'The Utraquist Church and the Visual Arts Before Luther'. In *The Bohemian Reformation and Religious Practice*, vol. 4. Prague, Academy of Sciences of the Czech Republic, 2002, pp. 215–23.

_____. 'Conflict, Tolerance, Representation, and Competition: A Confessional Profile of Bohemian Late Gothic Art'. In *The Bohemian Reformation and Religious Practice*, vol. 5.2. Prague, Academy of Sciences of the Czech Republic, 2005, pp. 255–265.

_____ and Michal Šroněk, eds. *Public Communication in European Reformation: Artistic and other Media in Central Europe 1380–1620*. Prague, Artefactum, 2007.

Bartoš, František M. 'Zur Geleitsfrage im Mittelalter'. *Zeitschrift für Kirchengeschichte*, 34, (1913), pp. 414–17.

_____. 'M.J. Hussii tractatus responsivus'. *Časopis českého musea*, 101, (1927), pp. 23–35.

_____. 'V předvečer Kutnohorského dekretu'. *Časopis českého musea*, 102, (1928), pp. 92–123.

_____. *Husitství a cizina*, Prague, CIN, 1931.

_____. *Do čtyř pražských articulů*. 2nd edition. Prague, Blahoslavova společnost, 1940.

_____. *Čechy v době Husově 1378–1415*. Prague, Laichter, 1947.

_____. *Literární činnost M. Jana Husi*. Prague, ČSAV, 1948.

_____. 'Sněm husitské revoluce v Betlémské kapli'. *Jihočeský sborník historický*, 18, (1949), pp. 97–102.

_____. 'Husův učitel Dr Jan Štěkna a kaple Betlemská'. *Vestník České Akademie věd a umění*, 58, (1949), pp. 5–13.

_____. 'Milíč a jeho škola v boji proti sociální metle velkoměsta'. *Jihočeský sborník historický*, 21 (1952), pp. 121–132.

_____. 'Hus jako student a profesor Karlovy university'. *Acta universitatis carolinae - philosophica et historica*, 2, (1958), pp. 9–26.

_____. 'Apologie de M. Jean Huss contra son apologiste'. *Communio viatorum*, 8, (1965), pp. 65–74.

_____. *Husitská revoluce*, 2 vols. Prague, ČSAV, 1965–1966.

_____. 'Hus a jeho účast na staročeské bibli'. *Strahovská knihovna*, 3, (1968), pp. 86–112.

_____ and Pavel Spunar, eds. *Soupis pramenů k literární činnosti M. Jana Husa a M. Jeronýma Pražského*. Prague, Historický ústav ČSAV, 1965.

Baum, Wilhelm. *Kaiser Sigismund: Hus, Konstanz und Türkenkriege*. Graz, Styria, 1993.

Benrath, Gustav. 'Wyclif und Hus'. *Zeitschrift für Theologie und Kirche*, 62, (1965), pp. 196–216.

Berger, Wilhelm. *Johannes Hus und König Sigismund*. Augsburg, Verlag von J. Butsch Sohn, 1871.

Betts, R.R. *Essays in Czech History*. London, Athlone Press, 1969.

Bílková, Milena. 'Ikonografie v utrakvistické teologii'. PhD dissertation, Charles University, 2007. (= Kubíková)

Biller, Peter. 'Bernard Gui, Peter Zwicker, and the Geography of Valdesimo or Valdismi'. *Bollettino della Società di Studi Valdesi*, 124, (2007), pp. 31–43.

Boháč, Zdeněk. 'Postup osídlení a demograficky vývoj Českých zemi do 15. století'. *Historická demografie*, 12, (1987), pp. 59–83.

Borovička, Michael. 'Mistr Jan Hus na českém zemském sněmu v roce 1889'. *Husitský tábor*, 9, (1986–7), pp. 249–269.

Brandmüller, Walter. *Das Konzil von Pavia-Siena 1423–1424*, 2 vols. Münster, Verlag Aschendorff, 1974.

Brandmüller, Walter. *Das Konzil von Konstanz 1414–1418*, 2 vols. Paderborn, Ferdinand Schöningh, 1991–1997.
_____. 'Hus vor dem Konzil'. In Seibt, *Jan Hus: Zwischen Zeiten, Völkern, Konfessionen*, 1997, pp. 235–242.
Bredekamp, Horst. *Kunst als Medium sozialer Konflikte: Bilderkämpfe von der Spätantike bis zur Hussitenrevolution.* Frankfurt am Main, Suhrkamp Verlag, 1975.
Brundage, James. *Medieval Canon Law.* London, Longman, 1995.
Čechura, Jaroslav. 'Mor, krize a husitská revoluce'. *Časopis český historický*, 92, (1994), pp. 286–303.
Cegna, Romolo. 'Początki utrakwizmu w Czechach w latach 1412–1415'. *Przegląd Historyczny*, 69, (1978), pp. 103–114.
_____. 'La Scuola della Rosa Nera e Nicolo detto da Dresda (1380?–1417?): Maestro tedesco al Collegio della Rosa Nera in Praga (1412–1415)'. *Mediaevalia philosophica Polonorum*, 30, (1990), pp. 10–67.
Červený, Karel. 'Překlad několika Husových latinských kázání'. In Miloslav Kaňák, ed. *Hus stále živý.* Prague: Blahoslav, 1965, pp. 69–86.
Císařová-Kolářová, Anna. *Žena v hnutí husitském.* Prague, Sokolice, 1915.
_____. *O poznání cěsty pravé k spasení, čili Dcerka.* Prague, Karel Reichel, 1927.
Clifton-Everest, John M. 'The Eucharist in the Czech and German Prayers of Milič z Kroměříž'. *Bohemia*, 23, (No.1, 1982), pp. 1–15.
Comi, Armando. *Verità e Anticristo: L'eresia de Jan Hus.* Bologna, Pendragon, 2007.
Čornej, Petr. *Velké dějiny koruny české*, vol. 5. Prague, Paseka, 2000.
Crespin, Jean. *Le livre des martyrs depuis Jean Hus et Jerome.* Geneva, 1554.
Crews, C. Daniel. 'The Theology of John Hus with Special Reference to His Concepts of Salvation'. PhD dissertation, University of Manchester, 1975.
David, Zdeněk V. 'Utraquists, Lutherans, and the Bohemian Confession of 1575'. *Communio viatorum*, 68, (No. 2, 1999), pp. 294–336.
_____. *Finding the Middle Way: The Utraquists' Liberal Challenge to Rome and Luther.* Washington and Baltimore, Woodrow Wilson Center Press and Johns Hopkins University Press, 2003.
_____. '"The White Mountain, 1620: An Annihilation or Apotheosis of Utraquism"? *Communio viatorum*, 45, (No. 1, 2003), pp. 24–66.
De Vooght, Paul. 'La notion Wiclifienne de l'épiscopat dans l'interprétation de Jean Huss'. *Irénikon*, 28, (1955), pp. 290–300.
_____. *Hussiana.* Louvain, Publications universitaires de Louvain, 1960.
_____. 'Jan Hus beim Symposium Hussianum Pragense (August 1965)'. *Theologisch-praktische Quartalschrift*, 114, (1966), pp. 81–95.
_____. 'Jean Huss. Aujourd'hui'. *Bohemia*, 12, (1971), pp. 34–52.
_____. *Jacobellus de Stříbro (†1429), premier théologien du hussitisme.* Louvain, Publications Universitaires de Louvain, 1972.
_____. *L'Hérésie de Jean Huss.* 2nd edition. Louvain, Publications universitaires de Louvain, 1975.
Didomizio, Daniel. 'Jan Hus's *De ecclesia*, Precursor of Vatican II?' *Theological Studies*, 60, (No. 2, 1999), pp. 247–260.

Dolejšová, Ivana. 'Nominalist and Realist approaches to the problem of Authority: Páleč and Hus'. In *The Bohemian Reformation and Religious Practice*, vol. 2. Prague, Academy of Sciences of the Czech Republic, 1998, pp. 49–55.

Doležalová, Eva, Jan Hrdina, František Šmahel and Zdeněk Uhlíř. 'The Reception and Criticism of Indulgences in the Late Medieval Czech Lands'. In R.N. Swanson, ed. *Promissory Notes on the Treasury of Merits: Indulgences in Late Medieval Europe*. Leiden, Brill, 2006, pp. 101–145.

Drda, Miloš, František Holeček, and Zdeněk Vybíral, eds. *Jan Hus na přelomu tisíciletí*. Tábor, Hussite Museum, 2001. (= *Husitský tábor*, supplement 1)

Drška, Václav. *Zikmund Lucemburský: Liška na trůně*. Prague, Epocha, 1996.

Eberhard, Winfried. *Konfessionsbildung und Stände in Böhmen 1478–1530*. Munich, R. Oldenbourg, 1981.

Escher Felix and Hartmut Kühne, eds. *Die Wilsnackfahrt: Ein Wallfahrts - und Kommunikationszentrum Nord - und Mitteleuropas im Spätmittelalter*. Frankfurt, Peter Lang, 2006.

Evans, G.R. *John Wyclif: Myth and Reality*. Downers Grove, IVP Academic, 2005.

Fajt, Jiří, ed. *Karl IV. Kaiser von Gottes Gnaden: Kunst und Repräsentation des Hauses Luxemburg*. Munich, Hirmer Verlag, 2006.

Flajšhans, Václav. *Mistr Jan řečený Hus z Husince*. Prague, Vílimek, 1901.

_____. 'Husovo odvolání ke Kristu'. *Český časopis historický*, 39, (1933), pp. 237–258.

_____. 'Traktáty Husovy a Kronika Vavřincova'. *Listy filologické*, 61, (1934), pp. 54–66.

Fojtíková, Jana. 'Hudební doklady Husova kultu z 15. a 16. století: Přispěvek ke studiu husitské tradice v době předbělohorské'. *Miscellanea Musicologica*, 29, (1981), pp. 51–142.

Foxe, John. *The Acts and Monuments of John Foxe*, 8 vols. Ed. Stephen Reed Cattley. London, Seeley and Burnside, 1837–1841.

Fudge, Thomas A. '"Ansellus dei"and the Bethlehem Chapel in Prague'. *Communio viatorum*, 35, (No. 2, 1993), pp. 127–161.

_____. 'Art and Propaganda in Hussite Bohemia'. *Religio: Revue pro religionistiku*, 2, (No. 1, 1993), pp. 135–153.

_____. 'The State of Hussite Historiography'. *Mediaevistik: Internationale Zeitschrift für interdisziplinäre Mittelalterforschung*, 7, (1994), pp. 93–117.

_____. 'The Night of Antichrist: Popular Culture, Judgment and Revolution in Fifteenth-Century Bohemia'. *Communio viatorum*, 37, (No.1, 1995), pp. 33–45.

_____. 'Visual Heresy and the Communication of Ideas in the Hussite Reformation'. *Kosmas: Czechoslovak and Central European Journal*, 12, (No. 1, 1996), pp. 120–151.

_____. 'The "Law of God": Reform and Religious Practice in Late Medieval Bohemia". In *The Bohemian Reformation and Religious Practice*, vol. 1. Prague, Academy of Sciences of the Czech Republic, 1996, pp. 49–72.

_____. '"The Shouting Hus": Heresy Appropriated as Propaganda in the Sixteenth Century'. *Communio viatorum*, 38, (No. 3, 1996), pp. 197–231.

_____. 'The "Crown" and the "Red Gown": Hussite Popular Religion'. In Bob Scribner and Trevor Johnson, eds. *Popular Religion in Germany and Central Europe, 1400–1880*. London, MacMillan, 1996, pp. 38–57, 214–220.

_____. 'The Problem of Religious Liberty in Early Modern Bohemia'. *Communio viatorum*, 38, (No.1, 1996), pp. 64–87.

_____. 'Hussite Infant Communion'. *Lutheran Quarterly*, 10, (No. 2, 1996), pp. 179–194.

Fudge, Thomas A. 'Il predicatore di Jan Hus'. In Manlio Sodi and Achille M. Triacca, eds. *Dizionario de Omiletica*. Turin: Editrice Elle Di Ci, 1998, pp. 684–688.

_____. *The Magnificent Ride: The First Reformation in Hussite Bohemia*. Aldershot, Ashgate, 1998.

_____. '"Neither Mine Nor Thine": Communist Experiments in Hussite Bohemia'. *Canadian Journal of History*, 33, (April 1998), pp. 25–47.

_____. '"Infoelix Hus": The Rehabilitation of a Medieval Heretic'. *Fides et Historia*, 30, (No. 1, 1998), pp. 57–73.

_____. 'Image Breakers, Image Makers: The Role of Heresy in Divided Christendom'. In Kras, ed. *Christianity in East Central Europe*, 1999, pp. 205–223.

_____. '"Feel this!": Jan Hus and the Preaching of Reformation'. In *The Bohemian Reformation and Religious Practice*, vol. 4. Prague, Academy of Sciences of the Czech Republic, 2002, pp. 107–126.

_____. 'Concepts of salvation in the western church to the sixteenth century'. *Communio viatorum*, 45, (2003), pp. 217–247.

_____. 'Obrana "Kacířství": Teoretické pojednání'. *Medievalia Historica Bohemica*, 9, (2003), pp. 295–314.

_____. 'Žižka's Drum: The Political Uses of Popular Religion'. *Central European History*, 36, (No. 4, 2003), pp. 546–569.

_____. 'Hussite Theology and the Law of God'. In David Bagchi and David C. Steinmetz, eds. *The Cambridge Companion to Reformation Theology*. Cambridge, Cambridge University Press, 2004, pp. 22–27.

_____. 'An Ass with a Crown: Heresy, Nationalism and Emperor Sigismund'. In Jan P. Skalny and Miloslav Rechcígl, Jr., eds. *The Transformation of Czech and Slovak Societies on the Threshold of the New Millennium and their Role in the Global World*. Plzeň, Aleš Čeněk, 2004, pp. 199–217.

_____. 'Seduced by the Theologians: Aeneas Sylvius and the Hussite Heretics'. In Ian Hunter, John Christian Laursen and Cary J. Nederman, eds. *Heresy in Transition: Transforming Ideas of Heresy in Medieval and Early Modern Europe*. Aldershot, Ashgate, 2005, pp. 89–101.

_____. 'Heresy and the Question of Hussites in the Southern Netherlands (1411–1431)'. In Ludovic Nys and Dominique Vanwijnsberghe, eds. *Campin in Context: Peinture et société dans la vallée de l'Escaut à l'époque de Robert Campin 1375–1445*. Valenciennes-Brussels-Tournai, Presses universitaires de Valenciennes, 2007, pp. 73–88.

_____. 'Želivský's Head: Memory and New Martyrs among the Hussites'. In *The Bohemian Reformation and Religious Practice*, vol. 6. Prague, Academy of Sciences of the Czech Republic, 2007, pp. 111–132.

_____. 'Saints, Sinners and Stupid Asses: The Place of Faith in Luther's Doctrine of Salvation'. *Communio viatorum*, 50, (No. 3, 2008), pp. 231–256.

_____. 'Picturing the Death and Life of Jan Hus in the Iconography of Early Modern Europe'. *Kosmas: Czechoslovak and Central European Journal*, 23, (No. 1, 2009), pp. 1–18.

_____. 'Prokop in the Bath: Some observations on the *Liber diurnus de gestis Bohemorum in Concilio Basileensi*'. In *The Bohemian Reformation and Religious Practice*, vol. 7 [= *Filosofický časopis, Supplementum 1*], (2009), pp. 139–155.

_____. 'The One-Eyed Heretic? An Introduction to the Ethics of Jan Hus.' Paper delivered at the 25th SVU World Congress in Tábor, Czech Republic, 1 July 2010, forthcoming.

Fudge, Thomas A. 'The Medieval "Lives" of Jan Hus in History and Hagiography.' Paper delivered at the ninth 'Bohemian Reformation and Religious Practice' conference in Prague, June 2010, forthcoming.

Gaybba, B. 'John Huss' views on the nature of theology in the introduction to his commentary on the Sentences'. *Studia historiae ecclesiasticae*, 20, (No. 2, 1994), pp. 79–94.

Gladstein, Ruth. 'Eschatological Trends in Bohemian Jewry during the Hussite Period'. In Ann Williams, ed. *Prophecy and Millenarianism.* London, Longman,1980, pp. 241–256.

Graf, Gerhard. 'Albert Hauck über Jan Hus: Zur Selbskritik der Reformationshistoriographie'. *Zeitschrift für Kirchengeschichte*, 83, (1972), pp. 34–51.

Graham, Barry Frederic Hunter. *Bohemian and Moravian Graduals 1420–1620.* Turnhout, Brepols, 2006.

_____. 'The Evolution of the Utraquist Mass, 1420–1620'. *The Catholic Historical Review*, 92, (No. 4, 2006), pp. 553–573.

Grant, Jeanne E. 'The Political Side of Hussitism: Late Medieval Law in Bohemia and the Holy Roman Empire'. PhD dissertation, University of California, Berkeley, 2005.

_____. 'Rejecting an Emperor: Hussites and Sigismund'. In Christopher Ocker, et al., eds. *Politics and Reformations.* Leiden, Brill, 2007, pp. 459–470.

Graus, František. *Chudina městská v době předhusitské.* Prague, Melantrich, 1949.

_____. *Lebendige Vergangenheit: Überlieferung im Mittelalter und in den. Vorstellungen vom Mittelalter.* Vienna, Böhlau, 1975.

_____. 'Krize středověku a husitství'. *Československý časopis historický*, 17, (1969), pp. 507–526.

_____. 'Prag als Mitte Böhmens 1346–1421'. In Emil Meynen, ed. *Zentralität als Problem der mittelalterlichen Stadtgeschichtsforschung.* Vienna, Böhlau, 1979, pp. 22–47.

Gregory, Brad S. *Salvation at Stake: Christian Martyrdom in Early Modern Europe.* Cambridge, MA, Harvard University Press 1999.

Griffith, Jerry, producer. *Truth Prevails: The Undying Faith of Jan Hus.* Documentary film. Cartesian Coordinates, 2007.

Haberkern, Philip. '"After Me There Will Come Braver Men": Jan Hus and Reformation Polemics in the 1530s'. *German History*, 27, (No. 2, 2009), pp. 177–195.

Halama, Ota and Pavel Soukup, eds. *Jakoubek ze Stříbra: Texty a jejich působení.* Prague, Filosofia, 2006.

Halík, Tomáš. 'Not Just About Hus'. Trans., Morven McLean. *Religion, State and Society*, 21, (Nos. 3–4, 1993), pp. 311–318.

Hauffen, Adolf. 'Husz eine Gans - Luther ein Schwan'. *Prager Deutschen Studien*, 9, (1908), pp. 1–28.

Hefele, Karl Joseph von and Henri Leclercq. *Histoire de Conciles*, 9 vols. Paris, Letouzey and Ané, 1907–1952.

Helan, Pavel. 'Mussolini Looks at Jan Hus and the Bohemian Reformation'. In *The Bohemian Reformation and Religious Practice*, vol. 4. Prague, Academy of Sciences of the Czech Republic, 2002, pp. 309–316.

Herkommer, Hubert. 'Die Geschichte vom Leiden und Sterben des Jan Hus als Ereignis und Erzählung'. In Ludger Grenzmann and Karl Stackmann, eds. *Literatur und Laienbildung im Spätmittelalter und in der Reformationszeit.* Stuttgart, Metzler, 1981, pp. 114–146.

Herold, Vilém. *Pražská Univerzita a Wyclif.* Prague, Univerzita Karlova, 1985.

Herold, Vilém. 'Magister Hieronymus von Prag und die Universität Köln'. In Albert Zimmermann, ed. *Die Kölner Universität im Mittelalter.* Berlin, Walter de Gruyter, 1989, pp. 255–273.

———. 'Der Streit zwischen Hieronymus von Prag und Johann Gerson'. In Sophie Włodek, ed. *Société et Eglise: Texts et discussions dans les universités d'Europe centrale pendant le moyen âge tardif.* Turnhout, Brepols, 1995, pp. 77–89.

———. 'How Wyclifite was the Bohemian Reformation?' In *The Bohemian Reformation and Religious Practice*, vol. 2. Prague, Academy of Sciences of the Czech Republic, 1998, pp. 25–37.

———. 'Jan Hus - A Heretic, a Saint, or a Reformer?' *Kosmas: Czechoslovak and Central European Journal*, 15, (No. 1, 2001), pp. 1–15.

Heymann, Frederick G. *John Žižka and the Hussite Revolution.* New York, Russell & Russell, 1969.

Hilsch, Peter. *Johannes Hus (um 1370–1415): Prediger Gottes und Ketzer.* Regensburg, Verlag Friedrich Pustet, 1999.

Hlaváček, Ivan and Alexander Patschovsky, eds. *Reform vom Kirche und Reich zur Zeit der Konzilien von Konstanz (1414–1418) und Basel (1431–1449).* Konstanz, Universitätsverlag, 1996.

Hoensch, Jörg K. *Itinerar König Kaiser Sigismunds von Luxemburg 1368–1437.* Warendorf, Fahlbusch, 1995.

———. *Kaiser Sigismund: Herrscher an der Schwelle zue Neuzeit, 1368–1437.* Munich, Beck, 1996.

Höfler, Konstantin von. *Magister Johannes Hus und der Abzug der deutschen Professoren und Studenten aus Prag, 1409.* Prague, Tempský, 1864.

Holeček, František J. 'Makkabäische Inspiration des hussitischen Chorals "Ktož jsú boží bojovníci" ("Ihr, die ihr Kämpfer Gottes und seines Gesetzes seid")'. In Miloslav Polívka and František Šmahel, eds. *In memoriam Josefa Macka.* Prague, Historický ústav, 1996, pp. 111–125.

———. 'The Problems of the Person, the Life and the Work of Jan Hus: The Significance and the Task of a Commission of the Czech Bishops' Conference'. In *The Bohemian Reformation and Religious Practice*, vol. 2. Prague, Academy of Sciences of the Czech Republic, 1998, pp. 39–47.

———. '"Ministri dei possunt in dampnacionem perpetuam papam male viventem detrudere . . ." (Hus a problém Antikrista)'. In *Husitský tábor*, supplement 1, (2001), pp. 219–244.

Holeton, David R. 'L'Eschatologie et le mouvement eucharistique en Europe centrale pendant la fin du Moyen-Âge'. In A.M. Triacca and E. Pistoia, eds. *Eschatologie et Liturgie.* Rome, C.L.V. - Edizioni Liturgiche, 1985, pp. 115–123.

———. 'The Communion of Infants: The Basel Years'. *Communio viatorum*, 29, (1986), pp. 15–40.

———. 'Wyclif's Bohemian Fate'. *Communio viatorum*, 32, (Winter 1989), pp. 209–222.

———. *La communion des tout-petits enfants: Étude du mouvement eucharistique en Bohême vers la fin du Moyen-Âge.* Rome, CLV Edizioni Liturgiche, 1989.

———. '"Videtur quod, sicut baptismus, sic et communio sacramentalis infancium fundatur in Ewangelio quod consentire videtur"* [MS Prague, NK VIII.D.15 ff. 130ᵛ–136]: A New Text on the Communion of Infants'. *Studie o rukopisech*, 30, (1993–4), pp. 23–28.

———. 'The Bohemian Eucharistic Movement in its European Context'. In *The Bohemian Reformation and Religious Practice*, vol. 1. Prague, Academy of Sciences of the Czech Republic, 1996, pp. 23–47.

Holeton, David R. '"O felix Bohemia - O felix Constantia"': The Liturgical Celebration of Saint Jan Hus'. In Seibt, ed. *Jan Hus: Zwischen Zeiten, Völkern, Konfessionen*, 1997, pp. 385–403.

———. 'The Bohemian origins of the Reformation understanding of confirmation'. In Kras, ed. *Christianity in East Central Europe*, 1999, pp. 248–261.

———. 'The Celebration of Jan Hus in the Life of the Churches'. *Studia Liturgica*, 35, (2005), pp. 32–59.

Hrubý, Blahoslav. 'Time for another Aggiornamento - Rehabilitation of Jan Hus'. *Religion in Communist Dominated Areas*, 25, (Fall, 1986), pp. 146–147.

Hubková, Jana. 'Events in Bohemia as Pictured in Protestant Illustrated Single- and Multiple-Sheet Broadsheets from 1618–1620'. In Bartlová, ed. *Public Communication in European Reformation*, pp. 247–262.

Hudson, Anne. *The Premature Reformation: Wycliffite Texts and Lollard History*. Oxford, Clarendon Press, 1988.

Itzel, Constanze. 'Der Stein trügt: die Imitation von Skulpturen in der niederländischen Tafelmalerei im Kontext bildtheoretischer Auseinandersetzungen des frühen 15. Jahrhunderts'. PhD dissertation, University of Heidelberg, 2004.

———. 'Peinture et hérérodoxie: La peinture flamande à la lumière du débat sur les images'. In Ludovic Nys and Dominique Vanwijnsberghe, eds. *Campin in Context: Peinture et société dans la vallée de l'Escaut à l'époque de Robert Campin*. Valenciennes-Brussels-Tournai, Presses universitaires de Valenciennes, 2007, pp. 139–154.

Iwańczak, Wojciech. 'Prostytucja w późnośredniowiecznej Pradze'. In *Biedni i Bogaci: studia z dziejów społeczeństwa i Kultury ofiarowane Bronisławowi Geremkowi w sześćdziesiątą rocznicę urodzin*. Maurice Aymand, ed. Warsaw, PWN, 1992, pp. 95–104.

Kadlec, Jaroslav. 'Johannes Hus in neuem Licht?' *Theologisch-praktische Quartalschrift*, 118, (1970), pp. 163–168.

Kalivoda, Robert. *Husitská ideologie*. Prague, ČSAV, 1961.

———. 'Joannes Wyclifs Metaphysik des extremen Realismus und ihre Bedeutung im Endstadium der mittelälterlichen Philosophie'. *Miscellanea Mediaevalis*, 2, (1963), pp. 716–723.

———. *Revolution und Ideologie: Der Hussitismus*. Trans., Heide Thorwart. Cologne, Böhlau Verlag, 1976.

Kalousek, Josef. *O historii kalicha v dobách předhusitských*. Prague, KČSN, 1881.

———. *O potřebě prohloubiti vědomosti o Husovi a jeho době*, 2 vols. Prague, Nákladem a tiskem Českoslovanské akciové tiskárny, 1915.

Kaluza, Zenon. 'Le chancelier Gerson et Jérome de Prague'. *Archives d'histoire doctrinale et littéraire du Moyen Age*, 51, (1984), pp. 81–126.

Kamínková, Eva. 'Husova Betlémská kázání a jejich dvě recense'. *Acta universitatis carolinae - philosophica et historica*. Monographia 2. Prague, Universita Karlova, 1963.

Kaminsky, Howard. 'The Prague Insurrection of 30 July 1419'. *Mediaevalia et Humanistica*, 17, (1966), pp. 106–126.

———. *A History of the Hussite Revolution*. Berkeley, University of California Press, 1967.

———. 'The Problematics of Later-Medieval "Heresy"'. In Jaroslav Pánek, ed. *Husitství, Reformace, Renesance: Sborník k 60. narozeninám Františka Šmahela*, 3 vols. Prague, Historický ústav, 1994, vol. 1, pp. 133–54.

Kaminsky, Howard. 'From Lateness to Waning to Crisis: The Burden of the Later Middle Ages'. *Journal of Early Modern History*, 4, (No. 1, 2000), pp. 85–125.
Kavka, František. 'The Hussite Movement and the Czech Reformation'. *Cahiers d'Histoire Mondiale*, 5, (1960), pp. 830–856.
_____. *Poslední Lucemburk na Českém trůně: Králem uprostřed revoluce*. Prague, Mladá fontes, 2002.
Kejř, Jiří. 'Struktura a průběh disputace de quodlibet na pražské universitě'. *Acta universitatis carolinae, Historia universitatis carolinae Pragensis*, 1, (1960), pp. 17–42.
_____. 'Sporné otázky v bádání o dekretu kutnohorském'. *Acta universitatis carolinae, historia universitatis carolinae pragensis*, 3, (No. 1, 1962), pp. 83–119.
_____. *Husitský pravník: M. Jan z Jesenice*. Prague, ČSAV, 1965.
_____. *Kvodlibetní disputace na Pražské Universitě*. Prague, Universita Karlova, 1971.
_____. '"Auctoritates contra communionem parvulorum" M. Jana z Jesenice'. *Studie o rukopisech*, 19, (1980), pp. 5–15.
_____. *The Hussite Revolution*, trans., Till Gottheinerová. Prague, Orbis, 1988.
_____. *Dějiny pražské právnické university*. Prague, Karolinum, 1995.
_____. 'Johannes Hus als Rechtsdenker'. In Seibt, ed. *Jan Hus: Zwischen Zeiten, Völkern, Konfessionen*, 1997, pp. 213–226.
_____. *Husovo odvolání od soudu papežova k soudu Kristovu*. Prague, Albis International, 1999.
_____. *Husův proces*. Prague, Vyšehrad, 2000.
_____. 'Husův proces z hlediska práva kanonického'. *Husitský tábor*, supplementum 1, (2001), pp. 303–309.
_____. *Z počátků české reformace*, Brno, L. Marek, 2006.
_____. 'Husova Pravda'. *Theologická revue*, 77, (2006), pp. 232–243.
_____. 'The Death Penalty during the Bohemian Wars of Religion'. In *The Bohemian Reformation and Religious Practice*, vol. 6. Prague, Academy of Sciences of the Czech Republic, 2007, pp. 143–163.
_____. 'K Husovu procesu v Kostnici'. *Acta universitatis carolinae - historia universitatis carolinae pragensis*, 48, (No. 1, 2008), pp. 11–18.
_____. *Jan Hus známý a neznámý*. Prague, Karolinum, 2009.
Kelly, Henry Ansgar. *Inquisitions and other Trial Procedures in the Medieval West*. Aldershot, Ashgate, 2001.
Klassen, John. *The Nobility and the Making of the Hussite Revolution*. New York, Columbia University Press, 1978.
_____. 'Women and Religious Reform in Late Medieval Bohemia'. *Renaissance and Reformation*, n.s. 5, (No.4, 1981), pp. 203–221.
_____. 'Hus, the Hussites and Bohemia'. In Christopher Allmand, ed. *The New Cambridge Medieval History*, vol. 7, Cambridge, Cambridge University Press, 1998, pp. 367–391.
_____. *Warring Maidens, Captive Wives, and Hussite Queens: Women and Men at War and Peace in Fifteenth-Century Bohemia*. Boulder, East European Monographs, 1999.
Klener, Pavel, ed. *Miscellanea husitica Ioannis Sedlák*. Prague, Katolická teologická fakulta Univerzity Karlovy, 1996.
Kohak, Erazim. 'John Huss: Why Does it Matter?' Trans., Richard T. Davies. *Religion in Communist Dominated Areas*, 28, (Spring 1989), pp. 56–58.
Kolářová-Císařová, Anna. *Žena v hnutí husitském*. Prague, Sokolice, 1915.

Kopičková, Božena and Anežka Vidmanová, *Listy na Husovu obrana z let 1410–1412: Konec jedné legendy?* Prague, Karolinum, 1999.

Kotyk, Jiří. *Spor o revizi Husova procesu.* Prague, Vyšehrad, 2001.

Kouba, Jan. 'Jan Hus und das geistliche Lied: ein Literaturbericht'. *Jahrbuch für Liturgik und Hymnologie*, 14, (1969), pp. 190–196.

Kras, Paweł and Wojciech Polak, eds. *Christianity in East Central Europe*. Lublin, Instytut Europy Środkowo Wschodniej, 1999.

Krmíčková, Helena. 'Jakoubkova utrakvistická díla z roku 1414'. In Ota Halama and Pavel Soukup, eds. *Jakoubek ze Stříbra: Texty a jejich působení*. Prague, Filosofia, 2006, pp. 173–181.

Krofta, Kamil, ed. *Mistr Jan Hus v životě a památkách českého lidu*. Prague, Žaluda, 1915.

Kubíková, Milena. 'The Heretic's Cap of Hus'. In *The Bohemian Reformation and Religious Practice*, vol. 4. Prague, Academy of Sciences of the Czech Republic, 2002, pp. 143–150. (= Bílková)

Kurze, Dietrich. *Quellen zur Ketzergeschichte Brandenburgs und Pommerns*. Berlin, Walter de Gruyter, 1975.

Kuttner, Stephan. 'Ecclesia de occultis non iudicat: Problemata ex doctrina poenali decretistarum et decretalistarum a Gratiano usque ad Gregorium PP. IX.' In *Acta Congressus iuridici internationalis Romae 1934*. Rome, Pontifical Library, 1936, vol. 3, pp. 225–246.

Kybal, Vlastimil. *M. Matěj z Janova: Jeho život, spisy a učení*. Prague, L. Marek, 2000 (1905).

_____. 'M. Matěj z Janova a M. Jakoubek ze Stříbra'. *Český časopis historický*, 11, (1905), pp. 22–37.

Lahey, Stephen E. *John Wyclif*. Oxford, Oxford University Press, 2009.

Lambert, Malcolm. *Medieval Heresy: Popular Movements from the Gregorian Reform to the Reformation*, 3rd edition. Oxford, Blackwell, 2002.

Lášek, Jan B., ed. *Jan Hus mezi epochami, národy a konfesemi*. Prague, Česká křesťanská akademie: Husitská teologická fakulta Univerzity Karlovy, 1995.

Lechler, Gotthard Viktor. *Johannes Hus: Ein Lebensbild aus der Vorgeschichte der Reformation*. Halle, Niemeyer, 1889.

Leff, Gordon. *Heresy in the Later Middle Ages: The Relation of Heterodoxy to Dissent c. 1250–c.1450*, 2 vols. Manchester, Manchester University Press, 1967.

_____. 'Wyclif and Hus: A Doctrinal Comparison'. *Bulletin of the John Rylands Library*, 50, (1967–8), pp. 387–410.

Lenfant, Jacques. *Histoire du Concile de Constance*, 2 vols. Amsterdam, Pierre Humbert, 1727.

Lohse, Bernhard. 'Luther und Huß'. *Luther*, 36, (1965), pp. 108–122.

Loserth, Johann. *Wiclif and Hus*, trans., M.J. Evans. London, Hodder and Stoughton, 1884.

Louthan, Howard. *Converting Bohemia: Force and Persuasion in the Catholic Reformation*. Cambridge, Cambridge University Press, 2009.

Lützow, Franz. *The Life and Times of Master John Hus*. London, Dent, 1909.

Macek, Josef. 'K počátkům táborství v Písek'. *Jihočeský sborník historický*, 22, (1953), pp. 113–128.

_____. *Tábor v husitském revolučním hnutí*, 2 vols. Prague, ČSAV, 1955–1956.

_____. *Jan Hus*. Prague, Melantrich, 1961.

_____. 'Jean Hus et son époque'. *Historica*, 13, (1966), pp. 51–80.

_____. *Jean Hus et les traditions hussites (XVe - XIXe siècles)*. Paris, Plon, 1973.

Macek, Josef, Ernő Marosi and Ferdinand Seibt, eds. *Sigismund von Luxemburg: Kaiser und König in Mitteleuropa 1387–1437: Beiträge zur Herrschaft Kaiser Sigismunds und der europäischen Geschichte um 1400*. Warendorf, Fahlbusch, 1994.

Machilek, Franz. 'Ergebnisse und Aufgaben moderner Hus-Forschung: Zu einer neuen Biographie des Johannes Hus'. *Zeitschrift für Ostforschung*, 22, (1973), pp. 302–330.

Machovec, Milan. *Husovo učení a význam v tradici českého národa*. Prague, ČSAV, 1953.

———. *Bude katolické církev rehabilitovat Jana Hus?* 2nd edition. Prague, Nakladatelství politické literatury, 1965.

Malý, Karel. 'Mistr Jan Hus a Univerzita Karlova'. *Husitský tábor*, supplement 1, (2001), pp. 395–403.

Mályusz, Elemér. *Kaiser Sigismund in Ungarn, 1387–1437*. Anikó Szmodits, trans. Budapest, Akadémiai Kiadó, 1990.

Marin, Olivier. 'Hus et l'eucharistie: Notes sur la critique hussite de la *Stella clericorum*'. In *The Bohemian Reformation and Religious Practice*, vol. 3. Prague, Academy of Sciences of the Czech Republic, 2000, pp. 49–61.

———. *L'archevêque, le maître et le dévot: Genèses du mouvement réformateur pragois années 1360–1419*. Paris, Honoré Champion Éditeur, 2005.

———. 'Les usages de la liturgie dans le prédication de Jean Hus'. In *The Bohemian Reformation and Religious Practice*, vol. 6. Prague, Academy of Sciences of the Czech Republic, 2007, pp. 45–75.

———. *Jan Hus: Naše obrození a naše reformace*. Prague, Bursík and Kohout, 1923.

Masaryk, Tomáš G. *The Making of a State: Memories and Observations, 1914–1918*. New York, Frederick A. Stokes, 1927.

Matthiessen, Wilhelm. 'Ulrich Richentals Chronik des Konstanzer Konzils: Studien zur Behandlung eines universalen Großereignisses durch die bürgerliche Chronistik'. *Annuarium historiae conciliorum*, 17, (No. 1, 1985), pp. 71–191 and vol. 17, (No. 2, 1985), pp. 323–455.

Mendl, Bedřich. 'Z hospodářských dějin středověké Prahy'. *Sborník příspěvků k dějinám hlavního města Prahy*, 5, (1932), pp. 161–389.

Mengel, David C. 'Bones, Stones, and Brothels: Religion and Topography in Prague under Emperor Charles IV (1346–78)'. PhD dissertation, University of Notre Dame, 2003.

———. 'From Venice to Jerusalem and Beyond: Milíč of Kroměříž and the Topography of Prostitution in Fourteenth-Century Prague'. *Speculum*, 79, (April 2004), pp. 407–442.

———. 'A Monk, a Preacher, and a Jesuit: Making the Life of Milíč'. In *The Bohemian Reformation and Religious Practice*, vol. 5, part 1. Prague, Academy of Sciences of the Czech Republic, 2004, pp. 33–55.

Mezník, Jaroslav. 'Mor z roku 1380 a příčiny husitské'. *Časopis český historický*, 93, (1995), pp. 702–710.

Michelis, Laura Ronchi de. 'Hus et le mouvement hussite de la condamnation de l'hérésie à sa réévaluation slave au milieu du XIXe siècle'. *Cahiers du Monde russe et soviétique*, 29, (Nos. 3–4, 1988), pp. 323–336.

Molnár, Amedeo. 'Eschatologická naděje české reformace'. In J.B. Souček, ed. *Od reformace k zítřku*. Prague, Kalich, 1956, pp. 13–101.

———. 'L'évolution de la théologie hussite'. *Revue d'histoire et de Philosophie Réligieuses*, 43, (1963), pp. 133–171.

Molnár, Amedeo. 'Hus et son appel à Jesus-Christ'. *Communio viatorum*, 8, (1965), pp. 95–104.
_____. *Jan Hus: Testimone della verità*. Turin, Claudiana, 1973.
_____. 'K otázce reformační iniciativy lidu: Svědectví husitského kázání'. In Amedeo Molnár, ed. *Acta reformationem bohemicam illustrantia*, vol. 1. Prague, Kalich, 1978, pp. 5–44.
_____. 'Husovo místo v evropské reformaci'. In *Pohyb teologického myšlení: Přehledné dějiny dogmatu*. Prague, Kalich, 1982, pp. 193–209.
Molnár, Enrico Selly. 'Anglo-Czech Reformation Contacts'. ThD dissertation, Iliff School of Theology, 1953.
_____. 'The liturgical reforms of John Hus'. *Speculum*, 41, (April 1966), pp. 297–303.
_____. 'Viklef, Hus a problém autority'. In Lášek, 1995, pp. 104–117.
Mols, Roger. 'Réhabilitation de Jean Hus?' *Nouvelle revue théologique*, 83, (1961), pp. 960–966.
Morée, Peter, C.A. *Preaching in Fourteenth-Century Bohemia: The Life and Ideas of Milicius de Chremsir (†1374) and his Significance in the Historiography of Bohemia*. Heršpice, EMAN, 1999.
_____. 'Jan Hus as a Threat to the German Future in Central Europe: The Bohemian Reformer in the Controversy Between Constantin Höfler and František Palacký'. In *The Bohemian Reformation and Religious Practice*, vol. 4. Prague, Academy of Sciences of the Czech Republic, 2002, pp. 295–307.
_____. 'Not Preaching from the Pulpit, but Marching in the Streets: The Communist Use of Jan Hus'. In *The Bohemian Reformation and Religious Practice*, vol. 6. Prague, Academy of Sciences of the Czech Republic, 2007, pp. 283–296.
Nechutová, Jana. 'Hus a eschatologie'. *Sborník prací filosofické fakulty brněnské university*, series E, 13 (1968), pp. 179–187.
_____. 'Die charismatische spiritualität Böhmen in der vorreformatorischen Zeit'. *Österreichische Osthefte*, 39, (1997), pp. 411–419.
Nejedlý, Zdeněk. *Hus a naše doba*. Prague, Československý spisovatel, 1952.
Novotný, Václav. *M. Jan Hus*, Prague, Otto, n.d. [*c*.1905].
_____. *Hus v Kostnici a česká šlechta*. Prague, Nákl. společností přátel starožitností českých, 1915.
_____ and Vlastimil Kybal. *M. Jan Hus: Život a učení*, 2 vols in 5 parts. Prague, Laichter, 1919–1931.
Odložilík, Otakar. 'Z počátků husitství na Moravě: Šimon z Tišnova a Jan Vavřincův z Račic'. *Časopis Matice Moravské*, 49, (1925), pp. 3–170.
_____. 'The Bethlehem Chapel in Prague: Remarks on its Foundation Charter'. *Studien zur Älteren Geschichte Osteuropas*, 2, (No.1, 1956), pp. 125–141.
Orme, Nicholas. 'John Wycliffe and the Prebend of Aust.' *Journal of Ecclesiastical History*, 61, (No. 1, 2010), pp. 144–152.
Palacký, František. *Würdigung der Alten böhmischen Geschichtsschreiber*. Prague, Borrosch, 1830.
_____. *Geschichte von Böhmen*, 5 vols. Prague, Kronberger and Weber, 1836–1867.
_____. *Die Geschichte des Hussitenthums und Professor Constantin Höfler*. Prague, Tempský, 1868.
_____. *Zur böhmischen Geschichtsschreibung: Aktenmässige Aufschlüsse und Worte der Abwehr*. Prague, Tempský, 1871.
Palmitessa, James R. 'Overlapping and Intersecting Communication Networks in Prague at the Time of the Passau Invasion of 1611'. In Bartlová, ed. *Public Communication in European Reformation*, pp. 263–277.

Pánek, Jaroslav. 'The Question of Tolerance in Bohemia and Moravia in the Age of the Reformation'. In Ole Peter Grell and Bob Scribner, eds. *Tolerance and Intolerance in the European Reformation*. Cambridge, Cambridge University Press, 1996, pp. 231–248.
_____ and Miloslav Polívka, eds. *Jan Hus ve Vatikánu*. Prague, Historický ústav, 2000.
_____ and Oldřich Tůma, eds. *A History of the Czech Lands*. Prague, Karolinum Press, 2009.
Patapios, Hieromonk. '*Sub utraque specie*: The Arguments of John Hus and Jacoubek of Stříbro in Defense of Giving Communion to the Laity under both kinds'. *Journal of Theological Studies*, n.s. 53, (No. 2, 2002), pp. 503–522.
Patschovsky, Alexander. *Die Anfänge einer Ständigen Inquisition in Böhmen ein Prager Inquisitoren-Handbuch aus der ersten Hälfte des 14. Jahrhunderts*. New York, Walter de Gruyter, 1975.
_____. 'Ekklesiologie bei Johannes Hus'. In *Lebenslehren und Weltentwürfe im Übergang vom Mittelalter zur Neuzeit*, *Abhandlungen der Akademie der Wissenschaften in Göttingen, Phil.-hist. Klasse - 3*, (No. 179, 1989), pp. 370–399.
Pauly, Michel and François Reinert, eds. *Sigismund von Luxemburg: Ein Kaiser in Europa*. Mainz, Philipp von Zabern Verlag, 2006.
Pekař, Josef. *Jan Hus*. Prague, Bursik and Kohout, 1902.
_____. *Žižka a jeho doba*, 4 vols. Prague, Vesmír, 1930–1935.
_____. *Der Sinn der tschechischen Geschichte*. trans., Sofie Pommerrenig. Munich, Verlag Pressverein Volksbote, 1961. (1937)
Pořízka, Aleš. 'Listy na obranu Husova ze 12. září až 2. října 1410: Konec druhé legendy?' *Český časopis historický*, 99, (No. 4, 2001), pp. 701–723.
Ransdorf, Milosla. *Mistr Jan Hus*. Prague, Universe, 1993.
Rechowicz, Marian. 'Jan Hus'. *Tygodnik Powszechny*, 19, (No. 52, 1965), p. 833.
Royko, Kašpar. *Hystorye velikého sněmu kostického*. 2 vols. Prague, Widtmann, 1796.
Royt, Jan. 'Ikonografie Mistra Jana Husa v 15. až 18. století'. *Husitský tábor*, supplementum 1, (2001), pp. 405–451.
_____. 'Utrakvistická ikonographie v Čechách 15. a první poloviny 16. století'. In Dalibor Prix, ed. *Pro Arte: Sborník k poctě Ivo Hlobila*. Prague, Artefactum, 2002, pp. 193–202.
_____. 'The Hussite Revolution and Sacred Art'. In Barbara Drake Boehm and Jiří Fajt, eds. *Prague: The Crown of Bohemia, 1347–1437*. New Haven, Yale University Press, 2005, pp. 112–119.
Schaff, David S. *John Huss: His Life, Teachings and Death after Five Hundred Years*. New York, Scribner's, 1915.
Schofield, A.N.E.D. 'The Case of Jan Hus'. *The Irish Ecclesiastical Record*, 109, 5th series, (June, 1968), pp. 394–406.
Sedlák, Jan. *M. Jan Hus*. Prague, Dědictví sv. Prokopa, 1915.
Segert, Stanislav. 'War Orders and Songs - Essenes and Hussites'. *Erets Israel*, 26, (1999), pp. 176–182.
Seib, Gerhard, ed. *Luther mit dem Schwan*. Wittenberg, Schelzky and Jeep, 1996.
Seibt, Ferdinand. 'Johannes Hus und der Abzug der deutschen Studenten aus Prag 1409'. *Archiv für Kulturgeschichte*, 39, (1957), pp. 63–80.
_____. 'Die Zeit der Luxemburger und der hussitischen Revolution'. In Karl Bosl, ed. *Handbuch der Geschichte der böhmischen Länder*, 4 vols. Stuttgart, Anton Hiersemann, 1966–74, vol. 1, pp. 349–580.

Seibt, Ferdinand. Hussitenstudien: Personen, Ereignisse, Ideen einer frühen Revolution. Munich, R. Oldenbourg Verlag, 1987.

_____. 'Ein neuer Hus'. *Communio viatorum*, 35, (No. 1, 1993), pp. 62–73.

_____. *Jan Hus: Das Konstanzer Gericht im Urteil der Geschichte*. Fürth, Flacius Verlag, 1993.

_____. ed. *Jan Hus: Zwischen Zeiten, Völkern, Konfessionen*. Munich, Oldenbourg, 1997.

Seltzer, Joel. 'Framing Faith, Forging a Nation: Czech Vernacular Historiography and the Bohemian Reformation, 1430–1530'. PhD dissertation, Yale University, 2004.

_____. 'Re-visioning the Saint's Life in Utraquist Historical Writing'. In *The Bohemian Reformation and Religious Practice*, vol. 5.1. Prague, Academy of Sciences of the Czech Republic, 2004, pp. 147–166.

Skalicky, Karel. 'Jan Hus, the Catholic Church and Ecumenism'. Trans., Alexandra Moravec. *Occasional Papers on Religion in Eastern Europe*, 10, (July 1990), pp. 44–49.

Šmahel, František. *Jeroným Pražský*. Prague, Svobodné slovo, 1966.

_____. '"Doctor evangelicus super omnes evangelistas": Wyclif's Fortune in Hussite Bohemia'. *Bulletin of the Institute of Historical Research*, 43, (May 1970), pp. 16–34.

_____. 'Jan Hus a viklefské pojetí univerzálií'. *Acta universitatis carolinae - historia universitatis caroline pragensis*, 21, (No. 2, 1981), pp. 49–67.

_____. 'The Kuttenberg Decree and the Withdrawal of the German Students from Prague in 1409: A Discussion'. *History of Universities*, 4, (1984), pp. 153–166.

_____. *La révolution hussite, une anomalie historique*. Paris, Presses universitaires de France, 1985.

_____. *Dějiny Tábora*, 2 vols. České Budějovice, Jihočeské nakladatelství, 1988–90.

_____. 'The Hussite Critique of the Clergy's Civil Dominion'. In Peter A. Dykema and Heiko A. Oberman, eds. *Anticlericalism in Late Medieval and Early Modern Europe*. Leiden, Brill, 1993, pp. 83–90.

_____. *Husitská revoluce*, 4 vols. Prague, Historický ústav, 1993.

_____. 'Literacy and Heresy in Hussite Bohemia'. In Anne Hudson and Peter Biller, eds. *Heresy and Literacy, 1000–1530*. Cambridge, Cambridge University Press, 1994, pp. 237–254.

_____. 'The Hussite Movement: an anomaly of European history?' In Mikuláš Teich, ed. *Bohemia in History*. Cambridge, Cambridge University Press, 1998, pp. 79–97.

_____, ed. *Häresie und vorzeitige Reformation im Spätmittelalter*. Munich, Oldenbourg, 1998.

_____. '*Causa non grata*: Premature Reformation in Hussite Bohemia'. In Kras, ed. *Christianity in East Central Europe*, 1999, pp. 224–231.

_____. *Idea národa v husitských Čechách*. Prague, Argo, 2000.

_____. *Husitské Čechy: Struktury, Procesy, Ideje*. Prague, Lidové noviny, 2001.

_____. 'Mistr Jeroným Pražský na soudu dějin'. *Husitský tábor*, supplement 1, (2001), pp. 313–323.

_____. *Die Hussitische Revolution*, 3 vols. Hannover, Hahnsche Buchhandlung, 2002.

_____. 'The War of Symbols: The Goose and the Chalice against the Cross'. In *The Bohemian Reformation and Religious Practice*, vol. 4. Prague, Academy of Sciences of the Czech Republic, 2002, pp. 151–159.

_____. 'The *Acta* of the Constance Trial of Master Jerome of Prague'. In Helen Barr and Ann M. Hutchison, eds. *Text and Controversy from Wyclif to Bale: Essays in Honour of Anne Hudson*. Turnhout, Brepols, 2005, pp. 323–334.

_____. *Die Prager Universität im Mittelalter: Gesammelte Aufsätze*. Leiden, Brill, 2007.

Smolík, Josef. 'Truth in History according to Hus' Conception'. *Communio viatorum*, 15, (1972), pp. 97–109.

———. 'Die Wahrheit in der Geschichte: Zur Ekklesiologie von Jan Hus'. *Evangelische Theologie*, 32, (1972), pp. 268–276.

Sousedík, Stanislav. 'Huss et la doctrine eucharistique "remanentiste"'. *Divinitas*, 21, (No. 3, 1977), pp. 383–407.

Spáčil, Bohumil. *Učení M. Jana Husi*. Brno, Občanská tiskárna, 1931.

Spěváček, Jiří. *Václav IV. 1361–1419 k předpokladům husitské revoluce*. Prague, Svoboda, 1986.

Spinka, Matthew. *John Hus and the Czech Reform*. Chicago, University of Chicago Press, 1941.

———. *John Hus' Concept of the Church*. Princeton, Princeton University Press, 1966.

———. *John Hus: A Biography*. Princeton, Princeton University Press, 1968.

Stejskal, Karel and Petr Voit. *Iluminované rukopisy doby husitské*. Prague, Národní Knihovna, 1990.

Svejkovský, František. 'The Conception of the "Vernacular" in Czech Literature and Culture of the Fifteenth Century'. In Riccardo Picchio and Harvey Goldblatt, eds. *Aspects of the Slavic Language Question*. New Haven, Concilium on International and Area Studies, 1984, vol. 1, pp. 321–336.

Świeżawski, Stefan. 'John Huss - Heretic or Precursor of Vatican II?' Trans., Richard T. Davies. *Religion in Communist Dominated Areas*, 25, (Fall, 1986), pp. 148–152, 166.

———. 'Jan Hus - A Heretic or a Saint?'. Trans. Alexandra Moravec. *Religion in Eastern Europe*, 14, (April 1994), pp. 36–42.

Takács, Imre, ed. *Sigismundus Rex et Imperator: Kunst und Kultur zur Zeit Sigismunds von Luxemburg (1387–1437)*. Mainz, Philipp von Zabern, 2006.

Talley, Thomas J. 'A Hussite Latin Gradual of the XV Century'. *Bulletin of the General Theological Seminary*, 48, (1962), pp. 8–13.

Thomas, Alfred. 'Czech-German relations as reflected in old Czech literature'. In Robert Bartlett and Angus MacKay, eds. *Medieval Frontier Societies*. Oxford, Clarendon Press, 1989, pp. 199–215.

———. *Anne's Bohemia: Czech Literature and Society, 1310–1420*. Minneapolis, University of Minnesota Press, 1998.

Tomek, Václav Vladivoj. *Dějepis města Prahy*, 12 vols. 2nd edition. Prague, Řivnáč, 1892–1906.

Trapp, Damascus. 'Clm 27034: Unchristened Nominalism and Wycliffite Realism at Prague in 1381'. *Recherches de théologie ancienne et médiévale*, 24, (1957), pp. 320–360.

Turnau, Jan. 'Jan Hus: An Examination of Conscience': Interview with Prof. Stefan Świeżawski. Trans. Alexandra C. Moravec. *Religion in Communist Dominated Areas*, 31, (No. 4, 1992), pp. 71–73.

Van Engen, John. 'Multiple Options: The World of the Fifteenth-Century Church'. *Church History*, 77, (June 2008), pp. 257–284.

Vaněček, Václav. 'Dekret kutnohorský z hlediska dějin státu a práva'. In František Kavka, ed. *Dekret Kutnohorský a jeho místo v dějinách (Sborník k oslavě 550. výročí Dekretu kutnohorského). Acta universitatis carolinae, philosophica et historia*, (No. 2, 1959), pp. 55–69.

Vidmanová, Anežka. 'Husova tzv. postilla De tempore (1408/9)'. *Listy filologický*, 94, (1971), pp. 7–22.

———. 'Hus als Prediger'. *Communio viatorum*, 19, (1976), pp. 65–81.

———. 'Ke spisku Orthographia bohemica'. *Listy filologické*, 105, (1982), pp. 75–89.

Vidmanová, Anežka. 'Základní vydání spisů Jana Husa'. *Husitský tábor*, supplement 1, (2001), pp. 267–276.

Všetečková, Zuzana. 'The Man of Sorrows and Christ Blessing the Chalice: The Pre-Reformation and the Utraquist Viewpoints'. In *The Bohemian Reformation and Religious Practice*, vol. 4. Prague, Academy of Sciences of the Czech Republic, 2002, pp. 193–214.

Wacker, Gisela. 'Ulrich Richentals Chronik des Konstanzer Konzils und ihre Funktionalisierung im 15. und 16. Jahrhundert'. PhD dissertation, University of Tübingen, 2002.

Wagner, Murray. *Petr Chelčický: A Radical Separatist in Hussite Bohemia*. Scottdale, Herald Press, 1983.

Walker, Caroline Bynum. *Wonderful Blood: Theology and Practice in Late Medieval Northern Germany and Beyond*. Philadelphia, University of Pennsylvania Press, 2007.

Walsh, Katherine. 'Wyclif's Legacy in Central Europe in the Late Fourteenth and Early Fifteenth Centuries'. *Studies in Church History Subsidia*, 5, (1987), pp. 397–417.

Weltsch, Ruben E. *Archbishop John of Jenstein, 1348–1400: Papalism, Humanism and Reform in Pre-Hussite Prague*. The Hague, Mouton, 1968.

Werner, Ernst. 'Wort und Sakrament im Identitätsbewusstsein des tschechischen Frühreformators Jan Hus (um 1370–1415)'. *Sitzungsberichte der Akademie der Wissenschaften der DDR, Gesellschaftwissenschaften*, 13, (1989), pp. 3–26.

_____. *Jan Hus: Welt und Umwelt eines Prager Frühreformators*. Weimar, Böhlaus, 1991.

_____. 'Jan Hus im Spiegel Moderner Historiographie'. *Heresis: Revue d'histoire des dissidences européennes*, 16, (1991), pp. 37–54.

Winter, Zikmund. *Život církevní v Čechách: Kulturně-historický obraz z XV. a XVI. století*, 2 vols. Prague, Česká akademie pro vědy, slovesnost a umění, 1895–1896.

_____. *Zlatá doba měst českých*. Prague, J. Otto, 1913.

Zega, Włodzimierz. *Filozofia w Quaestiones sententiarum Mikołaja Bicepsa*. Warsaw, Homini, 2002.

INDEX

There are no general references to Hus, Bohemia, Prague, the Council of Constance, or the Latin Church, as these are very numerous and appear with some regularity throughout the text. Entries for topics such as heresy, Sigismund, Hussites, the eucharist (within Bohemian religious practice), and the emerging Utraquist Church, are selective given their pervasive presence. The same must be said for the various and diverse categories of Hus' life and thought. Names of medieval people have generally been given under their place of origin. Names of churches, monasteries and convents have been listed alphabetically under the headings of 'churches' and 'religious houses'. Czech proper names have ordinarily been given in their native form. The use of abbreviations has been avoided except in the designation of saints. Given the average reader's assumed lack of acquaintance with Czech geography, the names of Bohemian towns are accompanied with an identifier and Prague churches have been located in the relevant town which made up the late medieval city in the time of Hus.

Abelard, Peter 5, 40, 42, 45, 47, 86, 189, 244
Abraham, Priest, *see* Velešovice, Mikuláš
absentee priests 113
Aeneas Sylvius Piccolomini 57, 162, 179, 191, 211, 213
Historia Bohemia 211–212; *see also* Pius II, Pope
Agricola, Johannes 195, 197
Albert the Great, 155, 189
Alexander V, Pope 96, 115, 120, 121, 122, 140
Alexander the Great 60
Alexandria, Clement of 92
Ambrose 31, 52, 101, 111
Ambrosiaster 155
Andrae, Johannes, canonist 138
Anglican Church of Canada 188
Anhalt, George of 202

Anonymous of Passau 139
Anselm 30, 47, 51, 77
antichrist 15, 16, 24, 37, 41, 54, 64–65, 82, 108, 110, 111, 112, 154, 158, 185, 289
  as propaganda 184
  church as 38, 65
  eschatological dimensions of 24, 154
anticlericalism 21, 102, 107, 113, 149
Antioch, Ignatius of 34, 49, 92
Apollonia, St 187
Aquinas, Thomas 5, 30, 43, 51, 60, 104, 107, 138, 152, 153–154, 189, 234
Aquitaine, Prosper of 182–183
Arc, Joan of 237
Aristotle 11
Arius 151
Armenians 31

Arrigoni, Jacob Balardi 144, 150–151
Assisi, Claire of 76
Assisi, Francis of 191
Athanasius 31, 92
Atwood, Craig 224
Augusta, Jan 199
Augustine, Augustinianism 8, 30, 31, 36, 39, 41, 42, 43, 45, 48, 60, 61, 62, 66, 75, 81, 90, 91, 92, 95, 101, 103, 104, 107, 108, 124, 133, 138, 145, 155, 158, 160, 183, 234, 235, 244, 245
    misquoted by Hus 30, 67
Austria 139, 170, 171, 173
    Duke Albrecht of 241
authority, crisis of 20, 144, 219
authority, religious 29, 30, 242, 244
Auxerre, Remigius 111
Avignon 22, 25

Bainton, Roland H. 191
Balbín, Bohuslav 213–214
Bale, John 244
Baltenhagen, Henning of 99, 100
banners 166, 169, 170, 182, 190, 191, 200, 203
Barbara, St 94
Bartoš, František M. 4, 7, 105, 220
Basel, Council of 10, 161, 162, 172, 173, 211
Bayreuth 171, 224, 230
Beaufort, Henry 170
Bechin, Václav of 106
Bechyně Castle 165
Bede 31, 101, 103, 189
Beghards 153
Beguines 76, 85, 132, 153
    in Bohemia 76–77
bells 190, 208
Benedict XIII, Pope 37, 97, 124, 140
Beran, Josef 227–228, 229, 237
Berengar, *see* Tours
Bethlehem Chapel 3, 12, 15, 58–59, 67, 89, 94, 101, 102, 110, 118, 120, 134, 137, 149, 180, 187, 188, 191, 192, 203, 234, 243
    foundation charter 58
    object of polemics 60, 64, 115, 119
    spies in 64, 110, 278
    texts on walls 52, 53, 57, 66, 83, 107, 115, 133, 160, 189–190, 261
Bethlehem, Důra of 86
Beza, Theodore 199, 202
Bibfeldt, Franz 74, 174, 246
Bible 57, 106, 166, 179, 190, 199, 215
Biceps, Mikuláš of Jevíčko 276
Bílková, Milena 4, 224, 225
Bitterfeldt, Heinrich of 155
Black Death 21
Black Rose (Prague) 157
blood, bleeding hosts 14, 27–28, 179, 185
Boff, Leonardo 236, 319
Bohdal, Kateřina (Ješkova) 86
Bohemian Forest, *see* Šumava
'Bohemian Reformation and Religious Practice' 225, 230
Boissard, Robert 199
Boleslav Brethren 199
Bologna 102, 130
Boniface VIII, Pope 34, 37, 138
    Unam sanctam (1302) 34, 138, 143
Boniface IX, Pope 25, 37
Bonaventura 31, 189
book burning 47, 59, 62, 101, 102–103, 117, 137, 142–143, 187, 206, 276
book decorations 208
Bordeaux, François of 140
Borsnitz, John of 128, 321
Bosnia, vicariate of 137, 183
Bracciolini, Poggio 151
Bradwardine, Thomas 31
Brancacci, Rainald 128, 145
Brandenburg, Friedrich of 171
Brandmüller, Walter 224, 231, 233, 318, 320
Bratislava 170

Breslau, *see* Wrocław
Brod, Ondřej of 99, 106–107, 108, 158, 160
Brodský, Pavel 300
Brosius, Václav 199
Bucer, Martin 202
Buda 148, 177
Bugenhagen, Johannes 197
Bullinger, Heinrich 202
Buřenice, Václav Králík of 22
Byzantine rite 1, 92, 157, 160, 188

Caesarea, Basil of 31
Calvin, John and Calvinism 42, 71, 173, 199, 202, 207, 215
Cambridge University 50
canon law 7, 30, 31, 60, 62, 82, 108, 111, 119–120, 125–126, 127, 130, 138, 141, 143, 153–154, 169, 233, 235
Čapek, Jan 162, 293
    Czech Mass 162, 293
Casas, Bartolomé de Las 231, 237
Čáslav (town) 168, 184
Cassidy, Edward 230
Castiglione, Branda da 169
Cathars 54, 127, 234
Catherine, St 94
Causis, Michael de 6, 10, 15, 38, 50, 102, 119, 121, 123, 129, 130, 133, 135–137, 140, 149, 150, 156, 163–164, 178, 195, 234, 237, 244
    false accusations of 6, 135, 136, 137, 234, 244
Čechy, Petr of 28
Čejkovice, Střezka of 86
Cerretano, Jacob of 118, 128
Cesarini, Guiliano 171
České Budějovice (town) 171
Český Dub (town) 184
Chabařovice (town) 206
chalice 152, 154, 155, 156–157, 158, 159, 182, 242
    banned 52, 156, 157, 159, 161, 177

heresy 52, 156, 242
    symbol 189, 203, 309; *see also* eucharist, utraquism
Chamberlain, Neville 1, 309
charismatic spirituality 12, 26, 105
Charlemagne 58
Charles IV, King of Bohemia 8, 9, 19, 20, 24, 25
    Golden Bull of 20
Charles VI, King of France 98
Chartres, Bernard of 245
Cheb and 'Cheb Judge' 171–172
Chelčice Brethren 242
Chelčický, Petr 79–80, 168, 172, 242
children 40, 152, 159–160
Chlum, Jan of 52, 84, 137
    hangs posters in Constance 126
Chrast, Zdeněk of 102
Chrudim (town) 27, 195, 304
Chrysostom, John 31, 60, 158
Chůdek, Jan 182, 193
churches 21–22, 109, 118
    All Saints' (Litoměřice) 23
    Castle Church (Wittenberg) 197
    Chapel of the Body of God (New Town) 262
    Holy Cross (Chrudim) 195
    Holy Trinity (Kutná Hora) 192, 193
    Our Lady of the Snows (New Town) 177, 184
    St Adalbert's (New Town) 135, 157
    St Apollinaris (Prague) 23
    St Benedict's (Old Town) 118
    St Clement's (New Town) 135
    St Clement's by the Bridge (Old Town) 184
    St Gall's (Old Town) 105
    St George's (Eisenach) 201, 306
    St Giles (Old Town) 103, 143, 302
    St Henry's (New Town) 111
    St John the Baptist (Wrocław) 177
    St Martin-in-the-Wall (Old Town) 157
    St Michael's (Old Town) 12, 50, 59,

churches, continued
    95, 118, 157, 159, 298, 308
    St Michael Opatovice (New Town) 204
    St Romedius (Choltice) 206
    St Sebald's (Nürnberg) 169
    St Stephen's (New Town) 102
    St Stephen's (Vienna) 149
    St Václav's (Písek) 206
    St Václav's (Roudníky) 206
    St Valentine's (Old Town) 23
    St Vitus' Cathedral 58, 63, 102
    St Wenceslas Basilica (Stará Boleslav) 212
    Týn Church (Old Town) 23, 135, 173
    Vyšehrad Chapter 22; *see also* Bethlehem Chapel (Old Town)
Città di Castello, Bernard of 128
Clairvaux, Bernard of 31, 35, 60, 64, 76, 77, 110, 155
Clement VII, Pope 37
Cochlaeus, Johannes 182, 213
coins and medallions 190, 208, 309
Cologne 148
Colonna, Odo 119, 121, 122, 140, 221, 274; *see also* Martin V, Pope
Comenius, *see* Komenský, Jan Amos
communion, frequent 24, 50–51, 262, *passim*
    political implications of 153, 154, 158, 161, 163; *see also* eucharist, Stříbro, Jakoubek of, and utraquism
communism in the Czech Lands 218–220, 222, 223, 227–228
Compactata (of Basel) 162, 173
    repealed (1462) 173
conciliarism 32, 33, 48, 130, 140, 144, 169, 232
concomitance 151, 155; *see also* eucharist
concubinage 23, 113, 235
Consilium 17–18
Constance, city 9, 18, 125, 208
    Gelting Gate 145

Constance, Council of 3, 4, 14, 16, 29, 32, 33, 36, 37, 54, 84, 106, 117–146, 149–150, 159, 164, 176, 179, 190, 222, 232, 234, 239, 245
    Haec sancta (1415) 123, 143, 162
    Inter cunctus (1417) 124, 165–166
    procedures 7, 118, 123–124, 128, 133, 141, 221
    ruling on utraquism (1415) 52, 156, 161, 177
    Sacrosancta 124
Constantinople 19
Constantine, Donation of 163
Constitutio Criminalis Carolina 139
contemptus mundi 77, 79, 86, 87, 89, 90–94
contumacy 39, 48, 84, 108, 138, 140, 143, 145, 146, 150, 151, 233; *see also* heresy and canon law
Corbie, Abbey of 49
corruption, ecclesiastical 12, 14, 17, 24, 28, 35, 37, 38, 42, 52, 59, 61–62, 63, 71, 72, 82, 85, 108–115, 266; *see also* papal schism
Cortona, Margaretha of 76
councils, ecumenical 31, 45, 111, 145
Counter Reformation 176, 182, 190
Crespin, Jean 184–185, 213
Crews, C. Daniel 224
Cracow, Matthew of 155
creeds 31
    Apostles' 31
    Athanasian 31
    Nicene 31, 45
crusades 26, 37, 71, 109, 114, 233
    against the Hussites 123, 165, 166–172, 203
        first 166
        second 168
        third 168
        fourth 170
        fifth 171
        sixth (aborted) 172
Cyprian 31, 35, 92, 155, 158, 160
Cyril 60, 101

Czech and Slovak Society of Arts and
    Sciences 224–225
Czech-German animosity 95–97, 98,
    100, 102, 209, 213, 215–216
Czech nobility 120, 127, 163, 164, 165,
    272, 281
    assembly in Bethlehem Chapel
        163
    protest to Constance 164

d'Ailly, Pierre 104, 128, 138, 140, 145,
    150, 243, 254
Damascus, John of 31, 92
Damian, Peter 77, 111
Daucher, Hans 208
David, Zdeněk V. 225, 297
Decretum, *see* canon law, Gratian
deification, Christian doctrine of 92, 271
Deutz, Rupert, 155
De Vooght, Paul 4, 30, 38, 50, 104, 105,
    107, 140, 220, 222, 223, 227, 233, 274
Devotio moderna 77
Dinkelsbühl, Nicholas of 131, 149, 150
Divoký, Mikeš 125
Dolany, Štěpán of 85, 96, 102, 107, 112,
    122–123, 132, 134, 161, 177–178,
    191, 210, 264
Dolejšová, Ivana 225
Domažlice (town) 171
Donatus and Donatism 72, 108, 199,
    256
Dorothy, St 94
Dorre, Jore 128
Doubravský, Jan 213
Dresden Masters 157
Dresden, Nicholas of 156, 157, 158, 159,
    160, 162
Dresden, Peter of 157
Dubá, Jan Roháč of 168, 172, 173
    execution of 172, 186
Dubá, Václav of 84
Dubrovnik, Jan Stojković of 161, 162
Duns Scotus, John 30, 31
Durandus, William 152, 189

Ebner, Margaret 77
ecclesiology, medieval 34–35, 36, 113
Eliášův, Jan 18, 99
Elton, Geoffrey 6
Erasmus 146, 201
Erben, Karel J. 210
eschatology 36, 62, 167
Esztergom 148, 170
eucharist 14, 24, 49–54, 151–163
    and children 152, 159–160
    eschatological dimensions of 154,
        163, 165
    frequent communion 151–152, 153
    intinction 156
    social benefits and implications of
        49–50, 152, 153, 154, 155, 161,
        163; *see also* chalice, concomitance,
        remanence, transubstantiation
Eugenius IV, Pope 124
Evangelical Lutheran Church of Canada
    188
excommunication 45, 52, 107, 110, 115,
    118–119, 120
Eymeric, Nicholas 138, 139

Farel, William 202
Feast of the Ass 10
Fegler, Otto 228
Fiala, Miloslav 231
fides caritate formata, doctrine of 43, 44, 45,
    72, 81, 88, 107
Fillastre, Guillaume 128, 151
FitzRalph, Richard 38
Flajšhans, Václav 32, 86, 210, 216–217
Florence 22
Florence, Leonard of 128
Foligno, Angela of 76
four articles of Prague, *see* Prague
Foxe, John 184–185, 199, 206, 213, 244
France 139, 151
Frederick II, Emperor 142
Frederick V ('winter king') 186, 199, 200
Frederick the Wise 197–199
    dream of 197–199

Galileo Galilei 237
Gaunt, John of 66
Gebaur, Jan 217
Gelasius I, Pope 52, 101, 111, 155
German Reformation 2, 197; *see also* Luther, Martin, Protestantism
Gerson, Jean 34, 42, 104, 116, 123, 131, 137, 140, 141, 143, 145, 148, 150, 242–243, 254, 255, 304
Gertrud the Great 76
Gehazi 111, 112
Giovanni, Stefano di, *see* Sassetta
Goll, Jaroslav 216, 217, 220
goose and swan, legend of 183, 195–197, 310
Gottlieben Castle 142
Graham, Barry F.H. 224, 300
Gran, *see* Esztergom
Gratian 48, 104, 108
Graus, František 220
Greek Church, *see* Byzantine Rite
Gregory, St ('the Great') 31, 60, 67, 90, 111, 155, 189
Gregory VII, Pope 138, 245
Gregory IX, Pope 138, 139
Gregory X, Pope 76
Gregory XII, Pope 37, 97, 98, 100, 124, 140
Gregory XV, Pope 173
Gregory, prison guard at Constance 80
Grillenperk, Andreas 149
Groote, Gerard 86
Grosseteste, Robert 36, 104
Gui, Bernard 138, 139, 141
Guldenmund, Hans 197

Hackeborn, Mechthild of 76
Hagen, Matthäus 177
hagiography 9, 133–134, 175
Hales, Alexander of 51, 104
Hanseatic League 170
Hanselmann, Johannes 230
Harasser, Walter 106
Hardt, Hermann von der 123, 210

Havel, Václav 232, 320
Havlík (Prague priest) 52, 159
Heidelberg University 100
Helan, Pavel 225
Helgesen, Povl 183–184
Héloïse 40, 42, 244; *see also* Abelard
Henry IV 245
heresy 8, 25–26, 38, 53, 96, 97, 117, 121, 123, 124, 137–138, 144, 145, 158, 164, 169, 210, 229, 233, 237, 240, 244, 320
   and law 126, 133, 138–145, 242
   execution for 123, 143, 149, 229, 242
   heretics 54, 100, 107, 115, 123, 236, 243
   inquisitorial proceedings 125, 133, 141
   nomenclature 7–8, 117, 233, 240, 241–242, 279
   torture, use of 141, 142
   trials, medieval 97, 98, 125, 132, 135, 139, 141, 146, 148–149, 221, 237; *see also* Cathars, Hussites, Lollards, Pikarts, Waldensians
Heymann, Frederick G. 220
Hilsch, Peter 223
Hippolytus 92
historiography 4, 5, 147–148, 209–225, 227–228, 299
Hodíšťkov, Mikuláš Konáč of 193
Höfler, Konstantin von 215–216, 220, 222, 312
Holeček, František 225, 230, 231, 232, 315, 316
Holeton, David R. 4, 104, 154, 178, 181, 182–183, 187, 224, 225, 231, 239, 320
Holinka, Rudolf 217, 220
Holmes, George 218–219
Holy Roman Empire 20, 97, 99, 125, 170
Hostiensis, canonist 138
Hradec, Marek of 100
Hradec Králové (town) 184, 208

Hromádka, Josef 225
Hübner, Johannes 106
Huizinga, Johan 20, 250
Hungary 136, 148, 171, 172
Hus, Jan 26, 149, 150, 161, 166, 214
   accused of Donatism 38, 108, 135
   and Bethlehem Chapel 3, 64
   and Wilsnack 27–28, 59, 263
   and Wyclif 2, 6, 14, 16, 18, 38–39, 46, 49, 59, 62, 66, 90, 103, 104, 105, 115, 137, 142–143, 145, 212, 213, 214, 217, 220–221, 222, 223, 233–234, 259, 271, 275
   appeal to Christ 3, 82, 119, 129–130, 132
   appearance of 191–192
   as Elijah 82, 184
   as Judas Iscariot 9, 245
   as lamb of God 180
   as philosopher 210, 220
   attacks clerical wickedness 3, 12, 14, 17, 24, 28, 35, 37, 38, 42, 52, 59, 61–62, 63, 71, 72, 82, 85, 108–115, 264, 266, 278
   burning of 9, 12, 175, 190–191, 203–206, 245
   commemoration of 175–188, 230, 244
   conscience 29, 32, 33, 37, 54, 88–89, 218, 225
   cure of souls 40–41, 80, 82–83
   Czech Bible 14, 48, 215
   Czech language 162
   defrocked 144
   desire for martyrdom 109, 133–135
   divine office for 176, 179
   excommunications of 107, 118–119, 227
   fear of perjury 84
   goose (moniker) 11, 175, 195, 196–197, 202–203, 208, 309
   heretic 6, 7, 8, 16, 31, 96, 118, 121, 126, 137, 139, 166, 178, 183, 190, 211, 213, 216, 221, 223, 228, 233, 235, 239, 240
   iconography of 189–208, 244, 304, 308, 309
   in exile 15, 18, 65, 68, 130, 222
   liturgical celebration of 176, 178
   misunderstanding of the Council 132–133
   miter 9, 192–193, 194, 195–196, 203–204, 206, 207, 245, 307
   morality of 6, 10, 108–115, 243–244
   naïveté of 132, 156
   nationalism 6, 95–96, 214, 219
   parents of 9, 134
   patriotism of 95
   political involvement 95–101, 108–113
   popular saint 176, 177, 180, 182, 190, 240, 243
   power of the keys 38, 109–110
   preaching and sermons 15, 57–73, 100, 109, 118, 121
   priestly duties 14, 44, 55
   prophesying 195–197
   reformer 6, 33, 55, 64, 104, 175, 213
   refusal to recant 133, 144, 145, 146
   rehabilitation of 227–240
   royal support for 127
   safe conduct of 125–127
   sin 40–41
   songs about 57, 176, 180, 184, 187
   spied upon 64, 278
   synodal preacher 14, 64, 264
   tactical errors of 127, 132
   theology and ideas 27–55, 58, 68, 85
      authority 29, 30, 31, 32, 39, 47, 48, 232, 234
      baptism 34, 38, 40, 60, 61, 260
      Christ 31, 32, 39, 43, 45–47, 57, 263
      church 30, 33–39, 62, 232, 234
      confession 17, 36, 40, 42, 82, 92
      cross 45, 61, 71, 92, 94
      entertainment critique 10, 60–61
      ethics 6, 10, 28, 40, 45, 84, 85,

Hus, Jan, continued
    108–115, 175, 243–244
  eucharist 16, 28, 49–54, 66, 67,
    91–92, 155-156, 234, 259, 260,
    314, 318
  faith and works 43–44, 79, 272
  grace 42–43, 61, 91
  hell 39–40, 42, 62, 93
  human life 89–90
  last judgment 39–40, 62, 87, 93
  love 45, 54
  morality 28, 61
  obedience 32, 36, 70, 115,
    120–122
  papacy 17, 37, 232, 234
  prayer 78–79
  preaching 12, 35, 57–73
  predestination 30, 34–35, 41–42,
    61, 107, 116
  reform 64, 104
  repentance 91, 271
  sacra scriptura 29, 32, 33, 44, 45
  salvation 16, 39–45, 61, 80, 262,
    263
  Satan, Devil, demons 35, 39–40,
    45, 52, 54, 61, 81, 85, 86, 90,
    91, 111, 120
  scripture 28, 29, 30, 37, 47–49, 71,
    143
  simul iustus et peccator 44, 258
  spirituality 16, 32, 75–94
  spiritual warfare 78, 91
  trinity 45–46, 87–88
  truth 28–29, 46, 54, 55, 112, 188,
    240
  virgin Mary 27–28, 53, 60, 62; *see
    also* liturgy
  trial of 16, 33, 82, 117–146, 212, 216,
    217, 221, 237
  university master 12
  writings of 9–10, 12, 80, 185,
    209–210, 243
      Biblical commentaries 12, 41
      Dcerka 85–94

De cognicione et dilectione dei 80
De corpore christi 50, 53
De decimis 256
De ecclesia 3, 16, 30, 34, 35, 39,
  62, 67, 210, 221, 275
De libris hereticorum legendis 101
*De mandatis dei et oracione
  dominica* 80
De matrimonio 80
De orthographia bohemica 14
De pace 132
De peccato mortali 80
De penitencia 80
De quinque officiis sacerdotis 14,
  69
*De sacramento corporis et sanguinis
  domini* 51–52, 54, 80, 117
De sufficientia legis Christi 234
De tribus hostibus hominis 80
De trinitate 29
Dixit Martha ad Iesum 60
Errors of the Mass 16, 53, 193
Exposition of the Faith 16, 39,
  42, 53, 60
Exposition of the Lord's Prayer
  16, 78
Exposition of the Ten
  Commandments 16, 78,
  84–85, 95, 111, 134
Letters 48, 85, 134, 210, 215,
  217, 222, 267
Mirror of a Sinful Person 78
O svatokupectví 16, 111, 210,
  268, 275
Postil (Czech) 17, 50–51, 60,
  61, 65, 67, 69, 80
Postil (Latin) 17, 50–51, 59, 69
Proti knězi kuchmistrovi 17
Quaestio de Indulgentiis 36, 63
*Sermones de tempore qui Collecta
  dicuntur* 59
Super IV Sententiarum 13, 29,
  30, 31, 32, 44, 50, 86–87,
  141, 145, 189

Hus, Kateřina 86
Husinec 9, 57
Hussites 7, 23, 105, 108, 151, 153, 163, 176, 186, 207–208, 211, 215, 229, 240, 241
Hussite Church (modern) 187, 239
Hussite iconography 64, 65, 83, 264; *see also* banners, bells, book decorations, coins, Hus, Jan, iconography of, appearance of, Jena Codex
Hussite Revolution 3, 21, 49, 96, 108, 127, 147–173, 211, 245
    armies 165–172, 203
hymnody 153, 176, 182, 258

Ibrāhīm ibn Ya'qūb 19
iconoclasm 102, 149, 186, 189; *see also* book burning
iconography 83, 84, 154
Illyricus, Matthias Flacius 184–185, 199, 202, 210, 213
indulgences 11, 13, 14, 15, 36–37, 41, 61, 102, 109, 114, 197, 234
Innocent II, Pope 111
Innocent III, Pope 77, 93, 111, 127, 138, 139, 143–144
intention (ethics), *see* Héloïse and Abelard
interdict 15, 17, 35, 65, 100
Irenaeus 92
Izbicki, Thomas 284

Jagiełło, Władysław, King of Poland 169
James of the Marches, *see* Giacomo della Marca
Janov, Matěj of 6, 12, 22, 24, 26, 58, 69, 85, 104, 105, 157, 158, 159, 160, 211
    condemnation of 25, 154
    De corpore christi 152
    frequent communion 152–153
    Regulae veteris et novi testamenti 85, 153, 154, 252
Janovic, Pavel (Archdeacon) 22, 23–24, 111

Jaroslav (titular bishop) 120
Jena Codex 191, 304, 308
Jenštejn, Jan of 10, 20, 22, 104, 121, 154
Jerome, St 60, 101, 108, 155
Jerome, *see* Prague, Jerome of
Jerusalem community, *see* Kroměříž, Jan Milíč of
Jesenice, Jan of 18, 97, 98, 99, 100, 106, 117–118, 119–120, 129, 161, 273, 274, 294
    Defensio mandati 100–101
    Ordo procedendi 129, 130
    view of Hus' appeal 129–130, 282
Jesuits, *see* Society of Jesus
Jews 21, 173, 180–181
Jílové (town) 135
Jičín, Jan of 157, 293
Jindřichův Hradec (town) 199
    Prokop Ryšavý of 163–164
John XXIII, Pope 17, 37, 50, 102, 117, 121, 123, 124, 126, 128, 133, 134, 136, 139, 140, 143, 184, 195, 235
John XXIII, Pope (modern) 235
    Pacem in terris (1963) 235
John of the Cross 76
John Paul II, Pope 224, 228, 232
    Hus case 224, 228, 229, 232, 238
    Lateran speech (1999) 238–239, 320
    Reconciliatio et paenitentia (1984) 238
    Tertio millennio adveniente (1994) 238
Jošt, Margrave of Moravia 21
Junius, Franciscus 202
just war 37

Kabuz, Johannes 27
Kalivoda, Robert 6, 219, 220, 221, 274
Kalousek, Josef 216, 217
Kaminsky, Howard 4, 220, 222–223
Kaplice, Jakub Matějův of 154
Kaspar, bishop of Meißen 162
Kbel, Jan 97, 106
Kejř, Jiří 4, 123, 126, 141, 224, 232, 282, 319
Kempis, Thomas à 77, 86

Kladruby, Prokop of 98
Knín, Matěj 97–98, 100, 273
Kojata, Ludwig, priest, 23–24, 252
Kolín, Štěpán of 22, 58
Komenský, Jan Amos 173, 197
Koněprusy, Petr of 100
Koniáš, Antonín 186
Koranda, Václav the Younger 186
Kostelec (town) 184
Kouřim (town) 182, 193
Kozí, Ctibor and Jan of 68
Kozí Hrádek (castle) 16, 60, 68, 85, 111, 218
Knox, John 202
Krakovec Castle 16
Kraków 164, 228
Kralice, Bible of 173
Krofta, Kamil 218
Kroměříž, Jan Milíč of 6, 10, 12, 22, 24, 25, 26, 58, 69, 85, 104, 105, 108, 111, 152, 153, 154, 155, 161, 187, 211, 229, 241, 262
    postil 152
Kubíková, Milena, *see* Bílková, Milena
Küng, Hans 228–229, 236, 319
Kutná Hora (town) 27, 168, 172, 184
    decree of (1409) 14, 96–103, 148, 216
    mine shafts 181, 182, 193
    Peace of (1485) 173
    synod (1441) 159
Kybal, Vlastimil 34, 105, 133, 217

Laboun, Zdeněk of 100
Lambert, Malcolm 223
Langenstein, Henry of 104
Łaski, Jan 202
Lateran Council, IV, 49, 138, 139, 151
Lateran symposium on Hus (1999) 224, 238–239
Laurence, St 134, 176, 192, 206, 308
law of Christ, law of God 16, 28, 31, 33, 38, 44, 45, 71, 98, 105–106, 114–115, 120, 130, 133, 143, 181, 186, 222, 234, 258

Lechler, Gotthard 216, 217
Leff, Gordon 223
Lefl, Jindřich 125
Leipzig University 100
Lenfant, Jacques 214
Lenz, Antonín 217
Leo I, Pope 111, 158
Leo X, Pope 197–198, 202
Letter of Majesty (1609) 173
Liberatus 101
Libočany, Václav Hájek of 211, 212–213, 214, 215
Lipany (town) 172, 173
Lisbon, John of 119
Lithuania 151
Litoměřice gradual 178, 208
Litoměřice (town) 184
Litomyšl, bishop of, *see* Železný, Jan
Litomyšl (town) 27, 59, 164, 193
Liturgy 152
    Hus and 71–72, 75, 83, 176, 266, 268
    liturgical books 179–180, 181, 298
Lobkovice, Mikuláš Bohaty of 99, 100, 273
Lollards 105
Lombard, Peter 30, 31, 47, 49, 103, 107, 276
Loripes, Nicholas 157
Loserth, Johann 103–105, 107, 216, 217, 220, 221, 222, 312
Lotario de' Conti di Segni, *see* Innocent III, Pope
Lucena, Ferdinand of 165
Lucius III, Pope 138
Lucy, St 94
Ludmila, St 59, 195
Lusatia 171
Luther, Martin 2, 6, 43, 71, 134, 183, 215, 244, 306
    and Hus 72, 183, 184, 195–197, 200, 200–201, 207, 223, 309
    as heretic 184, 234
    in iconography 191, 197–198, 199,

Luther, Martin, continued
    200, 202, 207
    liturgy 183–184
    reformer 234; *see also*
        Protestantism
Lutheran Church in America 188
Lutterworth 66
Luxemburgs 20–21
    Charles IV, *see* Charles IV
    John of 20
    Sigismund, *see* Sigismund
Lyra, Nicholas 155

Macek, Josef 218, 220, 221
Machovec, Milan 218, 219
Magdalene, Mary 59, 86
Magdeburg, Mechthild of 76
Maiselstein, Caspar 149
Malešov (town) of 169
Mani and Manicheans 158, 207
Mansi, Giovanni 123, 210, 280
Margaret, St 94
Marca, Giacomo della 183, 284
Marin, Olivier 4, 224, 225
Marmaggi, Francesco 218
Marnix, Phillips van 202
marriage 15, 23, 76, 80, 94
Martin V, Pope 124, 140, 142, 160, 165, 168–169, 171, 176, 221, 242, 298; *see also* Colonna, Odo
Martinice Bible 204
martyrs and martyrdom 78, 102, 109, 133–135, 147, 151, 175, 179, 184–186, 190, 308
Marxist analysis of Hus 209, 219, 220, 222, 223, 228; *see also* Communism
Masaryk, Tomáš G. 218, 220
Matěj, *see* Janov, Matěj of
Maximilian II 173
Maximus 92
Meißen 95, 169, 171
Meistermann, Ludolf 97
Melanchthon, Philip 197, 200, 201, 202
memory and remembrance 5, 83, 175,
    190, 198
mendicants 21, 22
mercy, gifts of 81
    works of 81, 92
Methodius 92
Michelet, Jules 1
Middle Ages 1, 13
Milíč, *see* Kroměříž, Jan Milíč of
Milton, John 8
Mladoňovice, Petr 6, 128, 145, 178, 185, 187, 203–204, 210, 215, 222, 232, 282
    Relatio de Mag. Joannis Hus causa 6, 187, 210–211, 215, 217, 232
Mochov, Anežka of 86
Molnár, Amedeo 220, 231
Molnar, Enrico C.S. 222
monasticism, monks and nuns 11, 54, 85, 113; *see also* religious orders
Mont Lauzen, William of 155
morality, immorality 6, 10, 12, 14, 17, 23, 24, 28, 35, 37, 38, 42, 52, 59, 61–62, 63, 71, 72, 82, 85, 108–115, 243–244, 266
Moravia, Margraviate of 82, 112, 120–121, 136, 157, 159, 171, 173
Moravian Church 173, 188
Mussolini, Benito 223–224
Muyckens, Jan Barentsz 199
mysticism, 75–77, 81
Mýto, Jan of 11

nationalism 209, 214, 216, 217–218
Náz, Jan 273, 279
Nazareth, Beatrice of 76
Nazianzus, Gregory of 31, 92, 111
Neale, John Mason 8
Neander, Johann August Wilhelm 105, 216
Nejedlý, Zdeněk 219–220
Nelahozeves Castle 193
Německý Brod (town) 135
Nestorius 151
Neuhaus, Eberhard III von 150
Neuhaus, Gallus of 139

Neumann, Augustin 217
Nider, Johannes 211
Niem, Dietrich of 33–34, 36, 112, 123, 136, 165, 234, 235, 284
nomenclature 7, 241–242
    heresy 7, 147, 240, 279
    Hussite 7, 147–148, 211, 241–242
    pre-Hussite 12, 22, 25
    Wyclifite 137, 241–242
nominalism 29–30, 50, 124, 254
Nouvion, Jacob 98
Novák, Karel 217
Novotný, Václav 105, 182, 210, 217, 222
Nürnberg 20, 127, 169, 171, 200
    Reichstag 20, 168, 170, 171
Nyssa, Gregory of 31, 92

Ockham, William 30, 31, 60, 104
Oecolampadius, Johannes 202
Ofka (Prague woman) 86
Okrouhlice (town) 208
Old Catholic Church 187
old Czech annalists, *see* historiography
Olomouc (town) 112, 164
    Bishop Bruno of 76–77
    canons of 176, 179
Ondřej, (Prague priest) 154
Ordo procedendi, *see* Jesenice, Jan of
Orebites (Hussite sect) 242
Origen 48, 92, 93, 146
Orphans (Hussite sect) 172, 241–242
Orsini, Giordano 128, 169
Orthodox Church, *see* Byzantine Rite
Osnabrück 113
Ostředek, Jan Zúl 13
Ostrý, Markéta of 86
Ottersdorf, Sixt of 186
Oxford University 66, 104

Palacký, František 105, 214–216, 217, 218, 220, 222
Páleč, Štěpán 15, 18, 34, 47, 48, 66, 97, 102, 104, 105, 122, 123, 134, 135, 137, 140, 144, 163–164, 183, 244, 254, 320
Palomar, Juan 161
papal schism 3, 13, 14, 22, 59, 97, 102, 124, 232
Paris 19, 148
Paschal I, Pope 111
Pasovaře, Ludmila and Kateřina of 86
Pater, Hus' unknown advocate at Constance, 133, 144, 283
Patschovsky, Alexander 222–223
Paul VI, Pope 228
Pavia-Siena, Council of 169, 207
Payne, Peter 157, 170
Pekař, Josef 217–218, 220
Peklo, John 103, 143
Pelagius 61
Pelcl, František M. 214
Pelhřimov, Mikuláš of 60, 242, 289
penance 60, 91, 263
Pereto, Anthony of 128
Pergoschl, Peter 287
Perkins, Thomas 202
Peruc, Markéta of 86
Peter degli Stephaneschi 119, 120
Peters, Edward 284
Petrarch 253
Pez, Bernard 210
Philibert, Bishop of Coutances 161, 162–163
Philip the Good (of Burgundy) 170
Pikarts 199
pilgrims, pilgrimage 14, 27, 43, 78, 91, 92–93, 100, 154
Pisa, Council of 37, 59, 97, 101, 124, 140
Pius, II, Pope 162, 173; *see also* Aeneas Sylvius
Pius IX, Pope 124
Pius, XI, Pope 229
plague, *see* Black Death
Plato 30
Plzeň, Prokop of 162
Plzeň, Václav Koranda of 160
Podbrdy (town) 23
Poděbrady, Jiří of 173, 187, 200, 211

Poitiers, Hilary of 5, 31, 103
Polák, Michael 182
Poland 35, 136, 148, 149, 172, 183
Poříčí, Marta of 182
poverty 10–11, 21, 58, 95, 112, 234
Prachatice, Křišťan of 118, 129
Prachatice (town) 9, 134, 166
Prague 15, 19, 25, 57, 83, 106, 184, 211
   archiepiscopal vacancy 168
   defenestration of (1419) 167
   four articles of 162, 166, 168
   gradual of the Lesser Town 201–202, 207
   Hradčany 19
   inquisitorial office in 124–125
   Kampen Island 184
   Lesser Town 19, 23, 25
   New Town 11, 19, 23, 25, 111, 135, 157, 165, 177, 184
   Old Town 12, 19, 50, 59, 85, 95, 98, 157, 172, 177, 186, 298, 302
   Petřin Hill 184
   population 20
   wages 58; *see also* Vyšehrad
Prague, Jerome of 15, 50, 53, 97, 98, 99, 100, 137, 144, 148–151, 157, 164, 176, 181, 182, 187, 214, 222, 242
     depictions of 190, 200, 202, 207, 208, 212
     heretic 100
     imprisoned in cemetery tower 149
     martyrdom of 151, 175
     safe conduct application denied 149
     saint 176, 177, 182, 190
     trial in Constance 98–99, 148, 150–151
     trial in Vienna (1410) 50, 98, 148–149, 287
     Wyclifite 222
Prague, synods 14, 119, 157, 244
   (1389) 153
   (1392) 154
   (1405) 14, 27, 64, 112, 244, 264

   (1407) 14, 64, 96, 244, 264
   (1418 St Wenceslas Day) 160
   (1421 St Prokop) 160
Prague, university in 10, 19, 33, 39, 72, 96–103, 107, 157, 159, 166, 212
preaching, vernacular 58, 60, 67
Příbram, Jan 190
Prokop Holý 169, 170–172, 208
Prokop, St 195
Prokůpek 171, 172
prostitution 23–24, 85
   and priests 23–24
   Constance 129, 282
   Prague 23–24
   reform of 24, 85
Protestantism 38, 72, 173, 209, 214, 218, 221, 229; *see also* Calvin, Luther
Protiva, Jan 58
Pseudo-Bernard 86
Pseudo-Dionysius 160
Pulka, Peter 149, 282
purgatory, 40, 93

Quodlibet (Prague) 97–98, 132
   (1404) 106
   (1409) 97, 98, 99, 148
   (1411) 33, 98
   (1416) 98
   (1417) 98
Qu'ran 34, 234

Rabus, Ludwig 184–185, 199, 213
Rachowicz, Marian 227
Radbertus, Paschasius 49
Radkovský, František 316
Ragusa, *see* Dubrovnik
Rankův, Vojtěch 22, 155
Ratramnus 49
realism 29–30, 50, 105, 124
Regensburg 208
Regulae veteris et novi testamenti, *see* Janov, Matěj of
Relatio de Mag. Joannis Hus causa, *see* Mladoňovice, Petr

relics 19, 27, 183, 187, 191
religious houses 22, 170
    Břevnov 22
    Erfurt 72
    Melk 210
    Mělník 13
    St James (Lesser Town) 183
    St Mary's on the Sand (Silesia) 171
    Strahov 59
    Vyšši Brod 15
    Waldhausen 22
    Zbraslav 22
religious orders
    Augustinians 113, 183, 241
    Benedictines 22, 210
    Carmelites 183
    Carthusians 96, 122, 132
    Celestines 139
    Cistercians 11, 15, 22, 76, 262
    Dominicans 77, 135, 136, 141, 144, 158, 161, 211, 276
    Franciscans 84
    Minorites 184
    Praemonstratensians 59
    Teutonic Knights 118; *see also* monasticism
remanentism 50, 121, 135, 158, 259, 260, 318; *see also* eucharist
Rheims 243
Říčany, Petra 85, 86
Richental, Ulrich 125, 145, 151, 203, 282–283, 304
    chronicle of 125, 203
Robert, prison guard at Constance 54, 80
Robert the Bugger 139
Rokycana, Jan 158, 161–162, 173, 304
Rome 19, 22, 65, 110, 120, 121, 130, 154
Roskopf, Wendel 208
Roudnice (town) 107, 208
Royko, Kašpar 227
Royt, Jan 4, 224
Rudolf II, Emperor 173
Rupescissa, Jean 128
Ruprecht of the Palatinate 97, 100
Ruspe, Fulgentius of 155
Russia 148, 149
Rvačka, Mařik 279

St Victor, Hugh of 31, 77
Sabellius 151
Sachsenspiegel 139
saints, medieval 154, 178
Sangershausen, Jutta of 76
Sassetta 207–208
Savonarola, Girolamo 231, 237
Saxony 171
    George of 183
Sázava River 166, 168
Schaff, David S. 39, 269
scholasticism 29, 33, 123–124, 155, 243
Schorand, Ulrich 145
Schwabenspiegel 139
Scribner, Robert W. xx, 291, 305
Sebastian, St 206
Sedlák, Jan 217, 220
Seibt, Ferdinand 220, 223
sermons, medieval 57–58, 69
Sezimovo Ústí (town) 16, 111
Sigismund 21, 25, 115, 116, 117, 131, 137–138, 144, 148, 173, 184, 203, 222, 235, 241
    blush 127
    Constance 115, 117, 124, 133, 144, 145, 176, 190, 241
    crusades 168, 170, 177
    death of 172
    Holy Roman Emperor, King of Bohemia and Hungary 21, 25, 115, 124–125, 168, 173, 190
    in propaganda 165, 177, 182
    safe conducts 125, 126, 127, 281
Silesia 139, 170, 171, 173, 183, 241
Simon Magus 111, 112, 113, 184
simony 13, 22, 64, 83, 98, 109, 111, 112, 121, 158
Sión Castle 172, 186, 189
sisters, Bětka, Anežka, Zdena and Ofka 86

Skowronek, Alphons 228
Sleidan, Johann 202
Šmahel, František 4, 106, 154, 218,
    222–223, 225, 231, 315, 317, 320
Smetana, Pavel 239
Smíškovsky gradual 192–193, 195, 300
Smradař, Michael, *see* Causis, Michael de
Sobotka gradual 179
Sobotka (town) 199
Society of Jesus 186, 199, 200, 227, 306;
    see also Counter Reformation
Socrates 151
songs, popular 70, 102, 107, 152, 176
Soukup, Pavel 225
Sousedík, Stanislaw 224
Spáčil, Bohumil 217
Špak, Josef 239
Spinka, Matthew 6, 38, 123, 124,
    221–222, 227, 269
Štěkna, Jan 11, 22, 58, 262
Šternberk, Kačka of 153
Štítný, Anežka 85, 86
Štítný, Tomáš 22, 58, 85, 115, 155, 187,
    229
Stokes, John 50, 106, 137, 141
stove tiles 189, 190, 208, 303
Stříbro, Jakoubek of 15, 18, 33, 51, 79,
    82, 98, 104, 156, 157, 158, 159, 163,
    166, 210
    Bethlehem Chapel sermon
        (1417/8) 82–83, 150, 177
    commentary on the Apocalypse
        158
    infant communion 160–161
    Luke 14 parable 158
    papacy 38, 66
    Pius Ihesus 52
    Salvator noster 158–159
    utraquist revelation 52, 157–158
Stupna, Petr of 58, 262
Sudoměř (town) 166
Šumava 170, 171
Švehla, Antonín 218
Świeżawski, Stefan 228, 235

Tábor and Táborites 7, 16, 147, 159,
    163, 167, 168, 172, 178, 182, 189,
    190, 203, 208, 212, 222, 241, 242
Tachov (town) 170
Taylor, A.J.P. 2
Tempelfeld, Nicholas 177–178
Tertullian 92
Themistius 29, 253
Theobald, Zacharias 213, 214
Theodore 101
theology 2, 4–5, 32, 45, 270
Thuringia, Elisabeth of 76
Tišnov, Šimon of 18, 25, 100, 161
Tomariis, Johannes de 122
Tours, Berengar of 49
transubstantiation 49, 50, 51, 53, 54, 66,
    67, 159, 314
Trapp, Damascus 106
Třebotov (town) 24
Truhlář, Josef 217

Ugolini, Zanghino 138
Uničov, Albík of 119
Uničov, Petr of 135, 158, 244
Unitas Fratrum (Unity of Brethren) 172,
    173, 179, 195, 199, 215, 242
Urban V, Pope 289
Ústí on the Labe River (town) 159, 169,
    206
utraquism 51, 117, 147, 165, 242
    as revelation 52, 157–158
    condemned 52, 156, 242
    necessity of 51, 158, 159, 160–161
    practice of 156–157, 165, 211
    social implications of 155, 163
    theological justification for 51
Utraquist Consistory 186

Václav, St (Wenceslas) 59, 195
Václav IV, King 8, 13, 18, 20, 25, 26, 71,
    97, 98, 102, 114, 117, 140, 150, 156,
    161, 164, 165, 218
    deposed 21, 97
Varentrapp, Albrecht 100

Vartemberk, Kunka of 86
Vatican II 227, 235, 236
   Lumen gentium 235
Vechta, Konrad of 17, 96, 112, 116, 128, 131, 156, 160, 164, 168
Veclov (town) 208
Velešovice, Mikuláš of 109
Vermigli, Peter Martyr 202
Vienna, 50, 148, 171, 203, 214
Vienne, Council of (1311-12) 169
violence 11, 15, 20–21, 23, 25, 37, 54, 102, 107, 109, 162–163, 168, 186, 211, 214, 261; *see also* just war
Virgil 60
Vítkov Hill 166; *see also* Žižka, Jan
Vlačić, Matija, *see* Illyricus, Matthias
Vlk, Miloslav 230, 231, 232, 239, 316
Vlněves altarpiece 193–195
Vltava River 11, 19, 23, 112, 184
Vojtěch, St 59, 193–195
Vrie, Dietrich of 111, 113, 151
Všeradice (town) 23
Všeruby, Petr 113
Vyšehrad 11, 19
Vyškov Synod (1413) 22

Waldensians 13, 22, 31, 54, 136, 234
Waldhauser, Konrad 10, 22–23, 24, 25, 26, 58, 69, 241
Wallenrode, Johann von 150
Wenceslas, *see* Václav, St
Werner, Ernst 223
White Mountain, Battle of 173, 186, 187, 200
Wilsnack (Brandenburg) 14, 27–28, 49, 59
Windecke, Eberhart, 171
Winter, Eduard, 220
'winter king', *see* Frederick V
Wittenberg 197
Włodkowicz, Paveł 283
Wolkenstein, Oswald von 129
women in Bohemia 59, 80, 85–94
Wojtyła, Karol, *see* John Paul II, Pope

Wrocław 165, 171, 177
Wyclif, John 2, 6, 13, 16, 17, 30, 31, 38, 46, 47, 49, 53, 54, 59, 66, 86, 90, 96, 98, 100, 102, 103–108, 111, 115, 137, 140, 142, 150, 151, 184, 185, 189, 199, 201, 202, 207, 210, 217, 233–234, 244
   45 articles of 17, 96, 106
   and Bohemia 13, 103, 104, 105, 106–107, 212
   as heretic 103–108, 118
   De eucharistia 66, 97, 107, 276
   Dialogus 107
   dominion doctrine 105–106
   philosophical works 104, 106
   reputation 103
   theological works 106
   Trialogus 31, 107
Wyclifite Mass (parody) 100
Wyclifites 13, 18, 22, 48, 59, 129, 176, 241
   synonym for Hussites 13, 137, 241

Zabarella, Francesco 128, 133, 140, 143, 144, 150, 283; *see also* pater
Żagan, Ludolf of 183
Zanchius, Girolamo 202
Žatec (town) 22, 168
Zbyněk 13, 14, 15, 27–28, 47, 59, 62, 96, 97, 99, 101, 107, 109, 112, 115, 118, 120, 121, 122, 123, 132, 140, 149, 279
Zdislav the Leper 100
Žebrák (town) 109
Zega, Włodzimierz 106
Železný, Jan 17, 52, 63, 101, 112, 119, 129, 150, 163, 164, 170
Želivský, Jan 66, 67, 161, 165, 177, 184, 293
Zeman, Jarold K. 222
Ziegenthal, Joss von 171
Žižka, Jan 58, 165, 166–170, 182, 191, 199, 200, 208
Znojmo, Peter of 18

Znojmo, Stanislav of 12, 15, 16, 17, 18, 27, 66, 97, 100, 105, 122, 140
Žofie, Queen of Bohemia 58, 117, 120, 164, 243

Zwettl (town) 171
Zwicker, Peter 139
Zwingli, Ulrich 202

www.ingramcontent.com/pod-product-compliance
Lightning Source LLC
Chambersburg PA
CBHW061422300426
44114CB00014B/1493